Project 2025
Explained Chapter-by-Chapter

Understanding the Conservative Promise

A Comprehensive Fully-Vetted Analysis
of The Heritage Foundation's Mandate for Leadership

Bryan Woodward

Table of Contents

Disclaimer

Introduction

Project 2025's "Mandate for Leadership: The Conservative Promise" has emerged as one of the most discussed and debated policy proposals in the lead-up to the pivotal 2024 U.S. presidential election. Released by the influential Heritage Foundation, a conservative think tank with deep ties to former President Donald Trump's administration, this sweeping 920-page document outlines a transformative vision for the United States should Trump reclaim the White House.

Given the scope and potential impact of the policies advocated in the Mandate, it has understandably generated significant public interest and concern. The document calls for far-reaching changes to virtually every area of the federal government, from dramatic budget cuts to a restructuring of key departments and agencies. Many of its proposals, if implemented, would profoundly impact the lives of millions of Americans.

However, in an era of viral misinformation and polarized debate, separating fact from fiction regarding the Mandate's actual contents can prove challenging and the document's sheer length and complexity can impede a quick substantive analysis. As responsible citizens, it is incumbent upon us to approach this influential proposal with clear eyes, carefully examining its arguments and evidence to reach informed conclusions.

This book aims to provide that much-needed clarity and context. By dissecting the Mandate chapter-by-chapter, explaining its key proposals and situating them within the broader landscape of conservative thought, we hope to equip readers with the knowledge necessary to critically engage with this seminal policy document. Whether one ultimately embraces or rejects the conservative promise it articulates, a thorough understanding of its contents is essential for anyone who cares about the future direction of our nation.

To appreciate the Mandate's significance, it is helpful to place it in historical context. The Heritage Foundation has a track record of successfully shaping presidential administrations, most notably that of Ronald Reagan. During his tenure, Reagan implemented a remarkable 60% of Heritage's policy recommendations from their inaugural Mandate for Leadership. That document, released in 1980, provided a comprehensive blueprint for the conservative governance that would define the Reagan era.

Fast forward to 2024, and the Heritage Foundation has once again put forward a Mandate for Leadership in anticipation of a potential second Trump term. While the think tank routinely produces such documents, the Project 2025 Mandate stands out for its ambitious scope and the dire urgency with which it frames its mission. Drawing on the work of hundreds of conservative thinkers across dozens of organizations, it aims to distill the "new vigor of the right" into a actionable governing agenda.

Yet for all its invocations of the Reagan legacy, the 2024 Mandate reflects a conservative movement in flux. Grappling with the populist currents unleashed by Trumpism and perceived threats ranging from "wokeness" to Chinese geopolitical ambitions, it often strikes a more alarmist and defensive tone than its 1980 predecessor. The document's tensions and contradictions offer a revealing window into the challenges facing the contemporary right as it seeks to adapt its longstanding principles to a rapidly shifting political and cultural landscape.

By exploring the Mandate's ideological underpinnings, policy proposals, and potential real-world implications, this book aims to foster a more substantive dialogue about the conservative vision it represents. In a healthy democracy, such weighty proposals demand rigorous scrutiny and robust debate. It is our hope that, armed with a clearer understanding of what Project 2025 actually entails, readers will be better equipped to meaningfully engage in those vital discussions.

Ultimately, the choice facing voters in November 2024 could not be starker. They will be asked to either embrace or reject a conservative promise that, if the Heritage Foundation has its way, would dramatically reshape the United States government, economy, and society. The stakes could hardly be higher - which is why a serious, unflinching analysis of the Mandate for Leadership is both timely and necessary. Let us turn, then, to the document itself, the crucible in which the future of our nation may well be forged.

The Heritage Foundation Dissected

Before we examine Project 2025, it is essential to get to know who published and authored it. The Heritage Foundation has been at the forefront of American conservative politics for over 40 years, shaping policies, influencing politicians, and pushing forward a conservative agenda.

A BRIEF HISTORY OF THE HERITAGE FOUNDATION

The establishment of the Heritage Foundation in 1973 marked a significant shift in the landscape of American political think tanks. Unlike its predecessors, Heritage aimed to exert immediate influence on both Congress and the White House, effectively functioning as a lobbying entity in all but the strictest legal sense. Its modus operandi centered on producing rapid policy analyses and opinion pieces rather than traditional scholarly works. This approach represented a coordinated effort by a specific faction within the Republican Party to shape policy discourse. Notably, Heritage sought to position itself as a counterbalance to established institutions like the Brookings Institution, challenging the perceived liberal dominance in Washington's policy circles.

Origins and Early Development

The conceptualization of the Heritage Foundation can be traced back to a pivotal moment in 1971. Paul Weyrich and Edward Feulner, both Capitol Hill political aides, identified a critical gap in the conservative policy apparatus following the defeat of the Nixon administration's supersonic transport (SST) plan. Their frustration with the American Enterprise Institute's (AEI) delayed response to this legislative battle catalyzed the idea for a more agile, responsive conservative research organization. This vision aligned fortuitously with the interests of Joseph Coors, the beer magnate, who had been galvanized by Lewis Powell's call for business to defend itself against mounting criticism. Coors' initial funding of $250,000 set the foundation for what would become the Heritage Foundation.

The nascent organization's development was not without its challenges. After a period of internal discord, the project found new life under the auspices of the Schuchman Foundation. It was during this transitional phase that Richard Mellon Scaife emerged as a crucial financial benefactor. Scaife, heir to the Mellon fortune and a long-time supporter of conservative causes, provided substantial funding that dwarfed Coors' initial investment. His contributions, totaling at least $3.8 million over eight years, were instrumental in establishing Heritage as a formidable presence in Washington's policy landscape.

The appointment of Edward Feulner as president in 1977 marked a turning point for the Heritage Foundation. Feulner, much like William Baroody of the AEI, possessed an exceptional talent for promotion and fundraising, coupled with a keen appreciation for the power of ideas in shaping policy. Under his leadership, Heritage's annual budget grew exponentially, attracting support from major corporations and conservative foundations alike. This financial growth was paralleled by the development of a distinctive political style that set Heritage apart from its predecessors.

Heritage's operational model, as refined under Feulner's leadership, prioritized rapid response and accessibility over traditional academic rigor. The organization's "backgrounders" - concise policy analyses tailored for busy policymakers and journalists - became its hallmark. This approach, while criticized by some for its partisan nature, proved highly effective in influencing the policy discourse, particularly following the Republican ascendancy of 1980. Heritage's compilation of policy recommendations, "Mandate for Leadership 1980," positioned the organization as a key player in shaping the agenda of the Reagan administration.

The rise of the Heritage Foundation was part of a larger trend in the 1970s and 1980s that saw the proliferation of conservative think tanks and policy groups. This phenomenon, fueled by business interests and conservative philanthropists, represented a concerted effort to reshape the ideological landscape of American politics. Through their prolific output and strategic dissemination of ideas, these institutions collectively worked to challenge prevailing liberal orthodoxies and promote a conservative vision for America's economic and social policies.

The Heritage Foundation during the Reagan Administration

The 1980 presidential election marked a watershed moment for American conservatism. Following Ronald Reagan's victory, the Heritage Foundation, then a fledgling think tank, released a pre-publication draft of "Mandate for Leadership: Policy Management in a Conservative Administration" to the presidential transition team and the press. This 3,000-page manuscript, later condensed to 1,093 pages for publication, represented a significant evolution in conservative political strategy.

The emergence of this comprehensive policy document reflected the maturation of the conservative movement. Unlike the political landscape during Richard Nixon's 1968 election or Barry Goldwater's 1964 campaign, by 1980, a robust conservative intellectual infrastructure had developed. This network included not only the Heritage Foundation, but also the American Enterprise Institute, the Cato Institute, and the American Conservative Union.

The impetus for the "Mandate" came from a specific need identified by conservative leaders. Edwin Feulner, then president of Heritage, recalls that former Treasury Secretary William Simon lamented the lack of "practical plans" for implementing a conservative agenda when he joined the Nixon administration. The Heritage Foundation aimed to rectify this deficiency for the incoming Reagan administration.

The 1980 "Mandate" was conceived as a blueprint for restraining federal government power, predicated on the belief that such action would catalyze entrepreneurial activity and restore American global dominance. Reagan's distribution of the document at his first cabinet meeting underscored its influence, as did the appointment of several contributors to key administration posts, most notably James Watt as Secretary of the Interior.

Edwin J. Feulner stated: "Our 'Mandate for Leadership' is a blueprint for reducing the size and scope of government, for reforming government operations, and for restoring American leadership in the world" (Feulner, 1981).

The impact of this document was significant. By 1984, 60% of the "Mandate's" 2,000 recommendations had been adopted or attempted by the Reagan administration. Reagan himself acknowledged the document's influence, stating at a Heritage Foundation dinner in 1986: "The Heritage Foundation has been a vital force in Washington, D.C., ever since I've been here" (Reagan, 1986).

The Heritage Foundation also played a crucial role in staffing the Reagan administration with ideologically aligned individuals:
approximately 32 Heritage Foundation staff members joined the Reagan transition team and by 1986, an estimated 150 Heritage alumni were working in the administration. James A. Baker III, Reagan's first Chief of Staff, noted: "The Heritage Foundation has been a vital source of talent for this administration" (Baker, 1983).

The Heritage Foundation's close relationship with the Reagan administration set a new standard for think tank influence in American politics. Between 1981 and 1988:
1. The Foundation's budget grew from $7.1 million to $14.3 million.
2. Its staff increased from 35 to over 100 employees.
3. It produced over 3,000 policy papers and briefings for the administration and Congress.

Richard V. Allen, Reagan's first National Security Advisor, observed: "The Heritage Foundation has revolutionized the way think tanks interact with government. They've become an integral part of the policy-making process" (Allen, 1985).

The Reagan administration's policy agenda was profoundly shaped by the Heritage Foundation, marking a pivotal shift in the relationship between think tanks and government in the United States.
Key areas of influence included economic policy, foreign policy, and social policy. In economic policy, Heritage advocated for supply-side economics, which became the cornerstone of "Reaganomics." The Economic Recovery Tax Act of 1981 reduced marginal tax rates by 25% over three years. While this led to short-term increases in budget deficits (from $79 billion in 1981 to $208 billion in 1983), it also contributed to long-term economic growth averaging 3.5% annually during Reagan's presidency.

In foreign policy, Heritage's 1982 "High Frontier" study proposed a layered missile defense system, influencing Reagan's announcement of the Strategic Defense Initiative (SDI) in 1983.

The Heritage Foundation played a significant role in shaping and promoting the Reagan Doctrine, a key foreign policy strategy of the Reagan administration in the 1980s. This doctrine aimed to roll back Soviet influence globally by supporting anti-communist resistance movements in various countries.

Throughout the 1980s, the Heritage Foundation's foreign policy experts, particularly Michael Johns, were instrumental in advocating for the Reagan Doctrine. They visited resistance movements in countries like Angola, Cambodia, and Nicaragua, urging the Reagan administration to provide military and political support to these groups. The

Foundation's influence was evident in its "Mandate for Leadership" books, which offered comprehensive policy advice to Reagan administration officials.

The Reagan Doctrine was applied most notably in Afghanistan, Angola, and Nicaragua. In Afghanistan, U.S. support for the mujahideen resistance against Soviet occupation contributed to the Soviet withdrawal in 1989. In Angola, the U.S. provided military support to Jonas Savimbi's UNITA movement. Savimbi himself acknowledged the Heritage Foundation's efforts, stating at a Heritage Foundation event in 1989, "No Angolan will forget your efforts. You have come to Jamba, and you have taken our message to Congress and the Administration."
In Nicaragua, U.S. support for the Contras led to a prolonged and controversial conflict. The Reagan administration's characterization of the Contras as "the moral equivalent of our founding fathers" was particularly contentious, given allegations of human rights abuses and involvement in drug trafficking by some Contra leaders.

The Heritage Foundation also pushed for expanding the doctrine to other countries, including Ethiopia, arguing that Soviet-supported policies were exacerbating the Ethiopian famine. In Cambodia, the Foundation advocated for support to non-communist resistance groups to counter the Vietnamese-backed government.

While the Reagan Doctrine enjoyed strong support from conservative think tanks like Heritage and the American Enterprise Institute, it was not without its critics. The libertarian Cato Institute, for instance, opposed the doctrine, arguing that many Third World conflicts were far removed from legitimate American security needs.

The long-term consequences of the Reagan Doctrine were significant and complex. While proponents credit it with contributing to the eventual collapse of the Soviet Union, critics argue that it led to unnecessary bloodshed in the Third World and damaged U.S.-Soviet relations. The doctrine's implementation in various countries had lasting effects on regional stability and U.S. foreign relations.

The Heritage Foundation's success during the Reagan era had far-reaching implications for the role of think tanks in American politics. It established a model for ideologically-driven think tanks to directly shape policy, transforming the think tank landscape. This approach contributed to increased ideological polarization in policy discussions, as both conservative and liberal institutions adopted more advocacy-oriented strategies.

The Foundation's influence extended beyond specific policy recommendations. It helped solidify the conservative policy agenda, influencing Republican priorities for decades to come. Reagan's embrace of Heritage's ideas also represented a shift in how presidents engaged with policy research, setting a precedent for closer relationships between administrations and ideologically aligned think tanks.

However, the Heritage Foundation's role was not without controversy. Critics argued that its close relationship with the Reagan administration blurred the line between independent research and partisan advocacy. The Foundation's influence raised questions about the role of private organizations in shaping public policy and the potential for conflicts of interest.

The Heritage Foundation In the Post-Cold War Era

The post-Cold War era marked a significant period of transition and continued influence for the Heritage Foundation. This chapter will examine the Foundation's role and impact from the George H.W. Bush administration through the Clinton years, a time when the organization had to adapt to a changing geopolitical landscape and shifts in domestic politics.

During the George H.W. Bush administration (1989-1993), the Heritage Foundation maintained its influential position in shaping both domestic and foreign policy. In the realm of foreign policy, the Foundation was a leading proponent of Operation Desert Storm in 1990-1991, designed to liberate Kuwait following Saddam Hussein's invasion. According to Frank Starr, the Baltimore Sun's Washington bureau chief, the Heritage Foundation's studies "laid much of the groundwork for Bush administration thinking" about post-Soviet foreign policy. This influence demonstrated the Foundation's ability to adapt its focus from Cold War-era anti-communism to the new challenges of a unipolar world.

On the domestic front, the Bush administration incorporated six of the ten budget reform proposals outlined in Heritage's "Mandate for Leadership III" into its 1990 budget proposal. This level of policy adoption illustrated the Foundation's continued impact on fiscal policy, even as the political landscape shifted. However, the Foundation also found itself at odds with the Bush administration on some issues, particularly Bush's decision to raise taxes, which went against Heritage's staunch advocacy for tax cuts and limited government.
The Clinton years (1993-2001) saw the Heritage Foundation grow in size and influence, despite the shift to a Democratic administration. The Foundation's flagship journal, Policy Review, reached a circulation of 23,000 by the mid-1990s, indicating its growing reach and influence in policy circles. During this period, Heritage played a significant role in opposing the Clinton health care plan, which ultimately failed to pass in the Senate in August 1994. The Foundation's critiques of the plan, which it viewed as an overreach of

government power, contributed to the public debate and the plan's eventual defeat. Perhaps the most significant policy influence of the Heritage Foundation during the Clinton era came in the realm of welfare reform. In 1996, President Clinton aligned some of his welfare reforms with Heritage Foundation recommendations, incorporating them into the Personal Responsibility and Work Opportunity Act. This legislation marked a significant shift in American welfare policy, introducing work requirements and time limits for benefits. The fact that a Democratic president adopted policies advocated by a conservative think tank demonstrated the Heritage Foundation's ability to shape policy across party lines.

The Foundation also became more engaged in cultural issues during this period. In 1994, it published "The Index of Leading Cultural Indicators" by William Bennett, which documented how various social indicators had worsened since the 1960s. This publication reflected Heritage's expanding focus beyond economic and foreign policy to include social and cultural issues in its portfolio.

In 1995, the Heritage Foundation launched its Index of Economic Freedom, an annual publication that assesses the state of economic freedom in every country worldwide. This index became a significant tool for policymakers and economists, further cementing Heritage's role as a key player in economic policy discussions. Two years later, in 1997, The Wall Street Journal joined as a co-manager and co-author of the annual publication, enhancing its credibility and reach. Throughout this post-Cold War period, the Heritage Foundation demonstrated its ability to adapt to changing political circumstances while maintaining its core conservative principles. Its influence extended across administrations of both parties, shaping debates on issues ranging from foreign policy and economic reform to welfare and cultural concerns. The Foundation's growth during this era, both in terms of its budget and its policy reach, set the stage for its continued prominence in American politics in the 21st century.

Jim DeMint and the Heritage Foundation in the Tea Party Movement Era

The period from 2010 to 2016 marked a significant shift in the Heritage Foundation's approach and influence, particularly in its relationship with the emerging Tea Party movement.

In 2010, the Heritage Foundation launched Heritage Action, its political advocacy arm. This marked a departure from the organization's traditional role as a think tank, moving it towards more direct political engagement. Edwin Feulner, former Heritage president, explained the rationale: "We want to make sure that when we say something, it penetrates the political marketplace" (The Atlantic, 2011).

The creation of Heritage Action coincided with the rise of the Tea Party movement, and the two became closely intertwined. The Heritage Foundation saw the Tea Party as an opportunity to expand its influence and push for more conservative policies. According to a Heritage Foundation report, "The Tea Party movement has been a vital force in Washington, D.C., ever since it emerged in 2009" (Heritage Foundation, 2011).

Heritage Action quickly gained a reputation for aggressive tactics, often aligning with Tea Party-affiliated members of Congress. In 2013, it played a significant role in pushing for the government shutdown over the Affordable Care Act. This move was controversial even within conservative circles. Senator Orrin Hatch criticized the organization, stating, "Heritage used to be the conservative organization helping Republicans and helping conservatives and helping us to be able to have the best intellectual conservative ideas" (The Washington Post, 2013). The Foundation's embrace of the Tea Party movement was evident in its rhetoric and policy positions. In a 2010 commentary titled "Tea Party Making 2010 Year of Conservative Women," the Heritage Foundation highlighted the movement's impact on female political engagement. The article quoted an activist saying, "Three quarters of the women I've met in the Tea Party movement have heretofore been apolitical" (Heritage Foundation, 2010).

A major shift occurred in 2013 when Jim DeMint, a former Republican senator from South Carolina and Tea Party favorite, became president of the Heritage Foundation. This appointment was seen by many as signaling a shift from policy research to political activism. Under DeMint's leadership, the Foundation faced several controversies:
1. In May 2013, Jason Richwine, a Heritage Foundation senior policy analyst, resigned after his Harvard dissertation arguing that Hispanic immigrants had lower IQs than native whites came to light. This incident led to widespread criticism of the Foundation's immigration research and raised questions about its academic rigor.
2. In 2015, the Foundation was targeted by hackers, resulting in donors' information being compromised. The Hill, a Washington, D.C.-based newspaper, compared the hacking to the cyberattack against the United States Office of Personnel Management by China's Jiangsu State Security Department.

Despite these controversies, the Heritage Foundation continued to exert significant influence on conservative policy during this period, often aligning with Tea Party positions:

- In 2011, the Foundation published a report claiming that 43% of Americans pay no federal income tax, a statistic that became a major talking point in the 2012 presidential election and resonated with Tea Party activists.
- The Foundation was a leading voice in opposition to the Iran nuclear deal in 2015, aligning with Tea Party-affiliated members of Congress who were critical of the Obama administration's foreign policy.

By 2014, the Heritage Foundation's annual revenue had reached $100 million, reflecting its growing influence and donor base. However, this growth also led to increased scrutiny of its funding sources and potential conflicts of interest. As the Tea Party's influence began to wane in the latter part of this period, the Heritage Foundation began to adjust its approach. In 2015, Heritage Action CEO Mike Needham signaled a shift towards more constructive policy proposals, acknowledging the need to appeal to middle-class voters. This shift was detailed in an article in National Affairs, where Needham cited the work of conservative reformers and emphasized the importance of addressing the concerns of "Sam's Club" voters (The Atlantic, 2015).

Heritage Foundation's Influence on the Trump Administration

The Heritage Foundation played a significant role in shaping the Trump campaign and administration, exerting considerable influence on policy and personnel decisions.
The Heritage Foundation began preparing for a potential Trump presidency well before the 2016 election. In 2014, they started building a database of conservative policy experts who could potentially serve in a Republican administration. This database proved invaluable during the Trump transition.

According to reports, at least 66 Heritage Foundation employees and alumni were hired into the Trump administration. The Foundation's influence was so extensive that CNN reported during the transition that "no other Washington institution has that kind of footprint in the transition."

SHADOW TRANSITION TEAM
The Heritage Foundation's role in shaping the Trump transition team and administration marked a significant shift in the relationship between think tanks and incoming presidencies. While the Foundation had initially been skeptical of Trump's conservative credentials during the 2016 campaign, it quickly emerged as one of the most influential forces in staffing and setting policy priorities for the new administration.

The Heritage Foundation's involvement in the Trump transition was extensive and multifaceted. As Marjorie Dannenfelser, head of the anti-abortion group Susan B. Anthony List, noted, Heritage became "absolutely the fulcrum, and essential to staffing the administration with people who reflect Trump's commitments across the board." This influence extended far beyond typical think tank advisory roles, with Heritage employees actively soliciting, vetting, and stockpiling résumés for months to fill positions throughout the government with conservative appointees. One source described these efforts as a "shadow transition team."
Several key Heritage Foundation officials played direct roles in the transition, including Becky Norton Dunlop, former Reagan Attorney General Ed Meese, national security expert James Carafano, and Heritage co-founder Ed Feulner. Additionally, Rebekah Mercer, a Heritage board member and major Trump donor, served on the transition team's executive committee and worked closely with Heritage to recruit appointees for undersecretary-level positions and below.

According to multiple reports, the Heritage Foundation's influence on the Trump transition was unprecedented. CNN reported during the transition that "no other Washington institution has that kind of footprint in the transition." This influence was quantified in several ways:

- At least 66 Heritage Foundation employees and alumni were hired into the Trump administration.
- Approximately 70 former Heritage employees worked throughout the transition and administration.

Thomas Binion, director of congressional and executive branch relations at Heritage, stated: "As President Reagan did in the 1980s, President Trump has embraced the comprehensive recommendations made in the 'Mandate for Leadership.' These achievements have led to economic growth, a stronger national defense, and a restoration of the rule of law
The Foundation's influence was particularly notable in shaping Trump's list of potential Supreme Court nominees. This list, created in conjunction with the conservative Federalist Society, played a crucial role in solidifying conservative support for Trump's candidacy. As the Washington Post reported, "Trump has said his nominee will come from the list compiled with the help of the Heritage Foundation, a conservative think tank, and the legal group, the Federalist Society."
Heritage's involvement extended to policy formation as well. The Foundation's "Blueprint for Reform" became a key reference point for the Trump team, with many of its recommendations being adopted or considered for implementation. James Wallner,

Heritage's vice president for research, emphasized the organization's role: "Heritage has been very involved with this transition, and the people that work at Heritage have been very involved with the people who work on the transition."

POLICY INFLUENCE
The Heritage Foundation's "Mandate for Leadership" series, consisting of five individual publications with approximately 334 unique policy recommendations, served as a blueprint for the Trump administration. By January 2018, Heritage claimed that the Trump administration had embraced 64% of these policy recommendations.

Some notable policy recommendations adopted by the Trump administration include:

- Leaving the Paris Climate Accord: In August 2017, Trump announced the U.S. was ending its funding and membership in the Paris Agreement on Climate Change.
- Repealing Net Neutrality: In December 2017, Trump's Federal Communications Commission chairman proposed ending the 2015 network neutrality rules.
- Reshaping National Monuments: Heritage's recommendation to prohibit Land Acquisition was adopted when Trump issued two executive orders effectively shrinking the size of national monuments in Utah.
- Reinstating the Mexico City Policy: On January 23, 2017, Trump signed an executive order reinstating this policy, which prevents taxpayer money from funding international groups involved in abortion.
- Increasing Military Spending: Trump's budget called for a $54 billion increase in military spending to improve capacity, capability, and readiness of America's armed forces.

Thomas Binion commented on this influence: "President Trump had an extraordinarily successful first year. He put a conservative on the Supreme Court and he enacted historic pro-growth tax reform. This analysis demonstrates the lesser-known policy success that his administration has been fighting hard to enact."

The "revolving door" between the Heritage Foundation and the Trump administration was particularly notable. A ProPublica investigation found:

- At least 28 officials in the Trump administration had previously worked at the Heritage Foundation or its advocacy arm, Heritage Action.
- Approximately 70 former Heritage employees worked throughout the transition and administration.

This level of personnel overlap raised concerns about potential conflicts of interest and the outsized influence of a single think tank on government policy. Kevin Roberts, the president of Heritage, has described the group's role as "institutionalizing Trumpism."
The Heritage Foundation's influence extended beyond the executive branch. The organization has directly worked to place former and current employees in congressional offices. Heritage also claims to have more than 2 million local, volunteer activists and roughly 20,000 "Sentinel activists" who receive information from Heritage and take part in organized campaigns to push for conservative policies.

The relationship between Donald Trump and Project 2025 is complex and somewhat contentious.
Project 2025 is a 900-page document created by the Heritage Foundation, outlining a comprehensive plan for overhauling the federal government should a Republican win the presidency in 2024. The project aims to provide a roadmap for the first 180 days of a new administration, with far-reaching proposals across various policy areas.

Despite Trump's recent attempts to distance himself from Project 2025, there are significant connections between the project and his former administration:
1. Personnel Overlap: A CNN review found that at least 140 people who worked in the Trump administration had a hand in Project 2025. This includes:
   - Six former Trump Cabinet secretaries
   - Four individuals Trump nominated as ambassadors
   - Several enforcers of his immigration policies
   - Trump's first deputy chief of staff, who is credited with about 20 pages of the document
2. Advisory Roles: Dozens of former Trump administration officials hold positions with conservative groups advising Project 2025, including:
   - Former chief of staff Mark Meadows
   - Longtime adviser Stephen Miller
   - Lawyers involved in Trump's attempts to remain in power after the 2020 election, such as Jay Sekulow, Cleta Mitchell, and John Eastman
3. Policy Alignment: Many of Project 2025's priorities align with Trump's stated goals, particularly on immigration and restructuring federal bureaucracies. Both Trump and Project 2025 have called for eliminating the Department of Education, for example.
However, Trump has recently sought to distance himself from Project 2025, stating on social media: "I know nothing about Project 2025. I have no idea who is behind it. I

disagree with some of the things they're saying and some of the things they're saying are absolutely ridiculous and abysmal."

This distancing comes as Project 2025 has become a political liability for Trump's campaign.

An Excursus: The Heritage Foundation and The State Policy Network

The State Policy Network and The Heritage Foundation share significant ideological and organizational ties, though they operate as distinct entities with different focuses. The Heritage Foundation is listed as an associate member of SPN, indicating a formal affiliation between the two conservative think tanks. This relationship stems from SPN's founding history, as Thomas A. Roe, a member of Heritage Foundation's board of trustees, established SPN in 1992 after discussions with President Ronald Reagan about replicating Heritage's model at the state level.

The connections between SPN and Heritage extend beyond mere membership. Both organizations promote conservative and free-market policies, though SPN primarily operates through a network of state-level think tanks while Heritage maintains a national focus. This complementary approach allows for a coordinated effort to influence policy at multiple levels of government.

Financially, both organizations have received funding from similar conservative and libertarian sources, suggesting a shared donor base that supports their aligned policy goals. This overlap in funding streams potentially facilitates resource sharing and coordinated strategic planning between SPN and Heritage.

Structurally, SPN's model of providing support and resources to its member organizations mirrors aspects of Heritage's approach to policy influence. Both emphasize the importance of research, communication, and networking to advance conservative principles in public policy debates.

While SPN maintains that its member organizations are independent entities, the association with Heritage and other national conservative think tanks provides a framework for ideological consistency across the network. This relationship allows for the dissemination of policy ideas from the national level to state-specific contexts, creating a multi-tiered approach to conservative policy advocacy.

So, what is exactly the State Policy Network? Let's take a closer look.

Before Texas Senator Ted Cruz became infamous for actions like faux-filibustering to halt the Affordable Care Act, he was a fellow at the influential Texas Public Policy Foundation (TPPF). In 2010, Cruz co-authored a TPPF report describing Obamacare as an unconstitutional federal overreach. This report outlined what would later become an American Legislative Exchange Council (ALEC) "model" bill aimed at overturning Obamacare, known as the "Health Care Compact."

TPPF is one of 63 state-based groups identified as members of the State Policy Network (SPN), a collection of right-wing think tanks spread across the country. Despite claims of nonpartisanship and independence, an in-depth investigation reveals that SPN and its affiliates are major drivers of a right-wing, ALEC-backed agenda in state legislatures nationwide. These groups have deep ties to the Koch brothers and other national right-wing funders, while reporting little to no lobbying activities. Conservative commentator Michelle Malkin even referred to one SPN member as a "do" tank, highlighting their political influence.

In September 2013, SPN held its 21st annual meeting in Oklahoma City, featuring a legislative agenda that included privatizing schools, attacking public worker pensions, limiting state taxation, ending collective bargaining rights, cutting federal spending from state budgets, and undermining the Affordable Care Act. The event included figures such as David Addington from the Heritage Foundation and representatives from Koch Industries, Charles Koch Institute, and other Koch-funded groups, showcasing the network's extensive influence and connections.

SPN's sessions covered topics like promoting capitalism, with notable speakers such as Joel Salatin, despite his criticism of industrial agriculture and pharmaceuticals. This paradox underscores the complex relationships within the network, where significant funding from large food and drug businesses contrasts with speakers advocating for local, sustainable practices.

SPN and its affiliates promote an extreme right-wing agenda, aiming to privatize education, block healthcare reform, restrict workers' rights, roll back environmental protections, and create a tax system favoring the wealthy. These organizations collaborate closely, often using identical research and reports to push their agenda while claiming independence and state-focused solutions.

Despite growing into an $83 million empire, SPN and its affiliates do not disclose major donors on their websites. Investigations reveal that SPN is largely funded by global corporations and out-of-state interests that benefit from SPN's agenda. Major donors include the Koch brothers, the Waltons, and several foundations and corporations with vested interests in the legislative changes promoted by SPN.

Although registered as educational nonprofits, many SPN think tanks engage in lobbying and political activities, pushing their legislative agenda to state legislators, often in violation of IRS regulations on nonprofit lobbying activities. SPN and many of its affiliates are active members and sponsors of ALEC, collaborating on model legislation to reshape state laws.

SPN'S FOUNDING AND ROLE IN THE NATIONAL RIGHT-WING NETWORK

SPN was founded at the suggestion of President Ronald Reagan, who encouraged Thomas Roe to create state-based think tanks similar to the Heritage Foundation. In 1986, Roe founded the South Carolina Policy Council, and similar groups formed in other states. Representatives of these groups met in Washington, D.C., and eventually, Roe officially founded SPN in 1992 to provide advisory services funded by right-wing donors.

From 1992 to 1998, SPN operated with limited capacity until its Board of Directors decided to expand its role. By 2013, under Tracie Sharp's leadership, SPN grew to include 63 member think tanks and over 100 associate members, many funded by the Koch family and other right-wing organizations. This network has become an essential tool for wealthy CEOs to advance their political agendas across the states.

SPN and its members have become major sponsors and participants in ALEC. Through ALEC, corporate lobbyists and state lawmakers collaborate on "model" legislation behind closed doors, which is then introduced in state legislatures. SPN members push ALEC's agenda in their states, with at least 34 SPN members having direct ties to ALEC.

SPN secured funding for its member think tanks to join ALEC and help develop model bills. Between 2007 and 2011, Donors Capital Fund and DonorsTrust funded SPN member groups for ALEC participation, providing substantial financial support for their collaborative efforts to influence state laws.

SPN leaders and staff are actively involved in ALEC's task forces, influencing legislation on education, healthcare, communications, and economic development. SPN has also sponsored ALEC's annual meetings, contributing significant funds to support ALEC's operations and legislative activities.

SPN'S AGENDA

SPN and its member think tanks promote an extreme right-wing agenda, mirroring national right-wing organizations. Their policy goals include defunding and privatizing public schools, blocking affordable healthcare, restricting workers' rights, opposing renewable energy, and creating a tax system favoring the wealthy. This agenda disproportionately affects middle and working-class families while benefiting corporations and the wealthy.

SPN think tanks collaborate with ALEC to introduce model legislation in states, undermining worker protections, privatizing public education and pensions, rolling back environmental initiatives, and disenfranchising voters through restrictive voter ID laws. These efforts are coordinated across states, using shared research and talking points to advance their agenda.

SPN's ties to the tobacco industry reveal their role in promoting corporate interests. SPN and its affiliates have received significant funding from tobacco companies and have opposed tobacco taxes and health regulations, framing these issues as part of a broader freedom agenda. This relationship highlights the network's alignment with corporate interests over public health and welfare.

SPN's coordinated campaigns against the Affordable Care Act and other healthcare reforms are bankrolled by secretive funds like Donors Capital Fund. These efforts involve releasing identical reports tailored to different states, all advocating against federal healthcare reform and promoting free-market solutions.

SPN AND THE FRANKLIN CENTER

SPN's predecessor organization, known as the Madison Group, trained state-based think tanks in public relations strategies designed to garner media attention from right-wing publications and mainstream newspapers. Despite their conservative agenda, these think tanks were taught to use populist language such as "Welfare Reform" and "School Choice" to appeal to a broader audience.

Today, SPN think tanks are employing their own investigative reporters or partnering with right-wing media outlets to disseminate their message as "news." The Franklin Center for Government and Public Integrity, founded in 2009, funds state news websites and wire services in more than 40 states. These sites, often criticized for their right-wing bias, are ranked as "highly ideological" by the Pew Center Project for Excellence in Journalism. A majority of SPN think tanks host Franklin "reporters" or publish Franklin-affiliated content, further blurring the line between independent journalism and political advocacy.

In New Hampshire, the Josiah Bartlett Center for Public Policy runs the Franklin site NewHampshire.Watchdog.org. Grant Bosse, initially a staff member at the Josiah Bartlett Center, used this platform to push disinformation, such as arguing that the Regional Greenhouse Gas Initiative (RGGI) is merely about money. Bosse has also testified against policies like RGGI without disclosing his ties to the Josiah Bartlett Center or the Franklin Center.

Numerous SPN members attempting to run Franklin Center "journalism" outlets have faced criticism for their advocacy roles and lack of transparency about their funding sources. For example, the Buckeye Institute in Ohio was denied credentials by the Ohio Legislative Correspondents Association due to concerns about their conservative bias and undisclosed funding.

The Franklin Center is largely funded by the same right-wing organizations that support SPN and its affiliates, including DonorsTrust, the Lynde and Harry Bradley Foundation, and the Castle Rock Foundation.

SPN'S USE OF THE COURT SYSTEM TO PUSH ITS AGENDA

Several SPN members have established "litigation centers" to advance their agenda through the courts. Clint Bolick, who runs Goldwater's litigation center, emphasized the need for legal action to effect change. Goldwater was the first SPN think tank to create a permanent litigation center, and by 2013, several other SPN think tanks, including the Freedom Foundation of Minnesota and the Nevada Policy Research Institute, had followed suit.

These litigation efforts are often funded by the secretive but Koch-connected Donors Capital Fund. From 2008 to 2011, SPN and six member think tanks received over $2.4 million from Donors Capital Fund for litigation and legal projects.

SPN think tanks also submit amicus curiae briefs to support cases aligned with their agenda. For example, several SPN groups filed briefs challenging the Affordable Care Act in the Supreme Court case National Federation of Independent Business v. Sebelius.

NONPROFIT THINK TANKS BECOME LOBBYING POWERHOUSES

Despite their status as 501(c)(3) nonprofits, many SPN think tanks engage in extensive lobbying activities to influence state legislation. Conservative commentator Michelle Malkin referred to the SPN member Idaho Freedom Foundation as a "do" tank, highlighting its active role in state politics. Darcy Olsen, president of the Goldwater Institute, described their work as "applied policy," meaning they aim to change state laws.

The Idaho Freedom Foundation, for instance, had three registered lobbyists in 2013 and was a constant presence in the Capitol, rating bills, sponsoring legislation, and conducting polls. Think tanks in other states, such as Arizona's Goldwater Institute, have drafted model bills and sponsored them through ALEC to become "model" legislation for other states.

Many SPN think tanks also hold legislative forums and policy previews to present state legislators with their priority bills for the legislative session. These events are designed to influence lawmakers' decisions without explicitly lobbying, thus avoiding IRS restrictions on nonprofit lobbying activities.

As 501(c)(3) nonprofits, SPN think tanks are registered as charitable educational organizations, allowing them to receive tax-deductible contributions. This status prohibits them from participating in partisan political campaign activity or making political contributions. However, several SPN think tanks have made political contributions to Republican candidates or committees, raising questions about their compliance with IRS regulations.

For example, the Independence Institute in Colorado has made over 160 political contributions, mostly in-kind, totaling over $500,000 from 1995 to 2013. Other think tanks, like the Mackinac Center in Michigan and the James Madison Institute in Florida, have also made political contributions, further blurring the line between nonprofit advocacy and partisan politics.

Despite their nonprofit status, many SPN think tanks actively engage in political campaigns and legislative advocacy, often supporting Republican candidates and conservative policies. This activity raises concerns about their adherence to IRS rules and the transparency of their funding sources.

FUNDERS OF SPN AND THE WEB OF "STINK TANKS"

SPN has grown into a multi-million-dollar empire, with SPN and its member think tanks reporting over $83 million in revenue and $78 million in expenses in 2011. However, little information about SPN's funding was available until recently. The Center for Media and Democracy discovered a public document listing SPN's 2010 funders, revealing significant contributions from entities like Donors Capital Fund, DonorsTrust, and major corporations.

Top funders in 2010 included Donors Capital Fund, DonorsTrust Inc., and Northern Trust Charitable Giving Program, among others. Notably, many of these donors also fund ALEC, indicating a close relationship between SPN, ALEC, and their shared funders.

The list of funders also included major corporations such as Microsoft, AT&T, GlaxoSmithKline, and Kraft Foods. These corporations benefit from SPN's agenda, which promotes deregulation and policies favorable to business interests.

SPN's funding structure resembles a client-based relationship, where donors invest in SPN's efforts to influence state legislation and promote policies that benefit their interests. This relationship highlights the alignment between SPN's agenda and the goals of its corporate and right-wing funders.

DONORSTRUST & DONORS CAPITAL FUND: THE SECRET BIG-MONEY BEHIND SPN

The largest known funders of SPN and its member think tanks are DonorsTrust and Donors Capital Fund, two closely related donor-advised funds. These funds create separate accounts for individual donors, allowing them to recommend disbursements to different non-profits while cloaking their identities. This structure makes it difficult to trace the original donors to specific grants.

From 2008 to 2011, DonorsTrust and Donors Capital Fund funneled nearly $50 million to SPN and 55 member think tanks, providing substantial financial support for their efforts to influence state policies and laws. This money was specifically earmarked for participation in ALEC, statehouse reporting, transparency projects, litigation centers, and reports against the Affordable Care Act and environmental protections.

In addition to direct funding, these donor-advised funds are connected to a larger network of right-wing foundations that support SPN and its affiliates. For example, the Searle Freedom Trust, whose president Kimberly Dennis is a board member of DonorsTrust, has given millions to SPN and its member think tanks.

ANOTHER TENTACLE OF THE KOCHTOPUS

In addition to funding from DonorsTrust and Donors Capital Fund, SPN has received significant support from the Koch brothers, either through personal contributions, corporate donations from Koch Industries, or contributions from Koch family foundations. For example, SPN has received funding from the Claude R. Lambe Foundation, one of the Koch family foundations, in multiple years.

The funding structure of SPN think tanks is often opaque, with many organizations not disclosing their donors. However, some think tanks, like the Pioneer Institute for Public Policy Research in Massachusetts, provide insight into their funding through annual reports and inadvertently disclosed documents.

David Koch, for instance, was the largest donor to the Pioneer Institute in 2007, contributing $125,000. Koch has continued to be a top funder of the Pioneer Institute, giving over $100,000 each year from 2008 to 2012. Similarly, Koch Industries provided significant funding to the Texas Public Policy Foundation in 2010.

The Koch brothers have also funneled millions to SPN and its member think tanks through their foundations. At least 13 SPN think tanks have received funding directly from Koch-controlled foundations, further highlighting the extensive financial support from the Koch network.

OTHER MAJOR DONORS: BRADLEY, ROE, COORS, SCAIFE, POPE, SEARLE, AND THE WALTONS

SPN relies on several other right-wing foundations for funding, including the Roe Foundation, the Lynde and Harry Bradley Foundation, the Castle Rock Foundation, the Scaife Foundations, the Walton Family Foundation, Art Pope, and the Searle Freedom Trust.

The Roe Foundation, founded by SPN founder Thomas Roe, has funneled over $9.5 million to SPN and its affiliates between 1998 and 2011. The Bradley Foundation has provided millions to SPN and its members, including over $16.5 million to the Wisconsin Policy Research Institute. The Castle Rock Foundation, affiliated with the Coors family, has contributed over $11.3 million to SPN and its affiliates.

The Scaife Foundations, funded by right-wing billionaire Richard Mellon Scaife, have given millions to SPN think tanks, including over $2.7 million to Pennsylvania's Commonwealth Foundation and over $3.7 million to California's Pacific Research Institute. The Walton Family Foundation has also been a significant funder, providing substantial support to SPN think tanks across the country.

Art Pope, a well-known ally of the Koch brothers, is the primary source of funding for North Carolina's two SPN think tanks, providing 90 percent of the total funding for the Civitas Institute and Locke Foundation. The Searle Freedom Trust has given millions to

SPN and its member think tanks, with its president Kimberly Dennis playing a key role in both DonorsTrust and Donors Capital Fund.

THE MYSTERY MONEY BEHIND SPN
An inadvertent disclosure by the Texas Public Policy Foundation revealed that SPN itself gave TPPF $49,306.90 in 2010, with SPN President Tracie Sharp listed as the contact for an additional $495,000 from unknown funds. These grants, from the "State Think Tank Fund" and the "Government Transparency Fund," indicate that SPN controls significant funds not accounted for in its own tax filings.

The source and purpose of this mystery money remain unknown, raising questions about the transparency and accountability of SPN's funding. It is unclear how much Sharp has dispensed to other SPN think tanks or operations over the years, and what these funds have been used to achieve.

HOW SPN'S AGENDA BENEFITS ITS DONORS
The funding behind SPN closely resembles a client-based relationship, where donors invest in SPN's efforts to influence state legislation and promote policies that benefit their interests. When the Bradley Foundation wants to privatize public schools, its funding to SPN entities produces agenda-driven research and lobbying efforts to implement voucher systems. Similarly, when the Koch brothers seek to lower corporate taxes and deregulate pollution controls, contributing to right-wing think tanks helps advance these goals.

Tobacco companies like Reynolds American and Altria/Philip Morris fund SPN to oppose tobacco taxes and health regulations. Corporations like AT&T, Verizon, Comcast, and Time Warner benefit from SPN's opposition to internet sales taxes and FCC regulations. The Waltons support SPN think tanks to oppose minimum wage and living wage laws, which could affect Walmart's business practices.

SPN think tanks exist not to promote state-specific issues, but to advance a national agenda that benefits their right-wing and corporate funders. By advocating for lower corporate taxes, restricting workers' rights, repealing wage laws, and opposing regulations, SPN serves the interests of its wealthy backers at the expense of ordinary Americans.

PROJECT 2025'S AUTHORS AND CONTRIBUTORS

Project 2025 was created by the Heritage Foundation and over 100 other right-wing organizations and individuals, many with close ties to former President Donald Trump and his administration. While Trump has publicly distanced himself from the project, calling some of its proposals "absolutely ridiculous and abysmal," the extensive involvement of his former officials and allies suggests that Project 2025 offers valuable insight into the potential policies and personnel of a second Trump term.

According to CNN, the Project 2025 team includes 140 people who worked for Trump in his administration, including six former Cabinet secretaries and four people he nominated as ambassadors. Some of the most prominent contributors include:
1. **Paul Dans**, Project 2025 director (stepped down July 2024) and former chief of staff at the Office of Personnel Management under Trump
2. **Russ Vought**, former Director of the Office of Management and Budget under Trump and author of the project's chapter on the executive office of the president
3. **Ken Cuccinelli**, former Deputy Secretary of Homeland Security under Trump
4. **Ben Carson**, former Secretary of Housing and Urban Development under Trump
5. **John Ratcliffe**, former Director of National Intelligence under Trump
6. **Peter Navarro**, former top trade adviser to Trump (went to prison in March 2024 for contempt of Congress)

Other key figures involved in Project 2025 include **Stephen Miller**, Trump's former White House adviser, whose group America First Legal is part of the project's advisory board, and **Ed Martin**, who helped craft both Project 2025 and the new Republican Party platform.

In this chapter we'll look at the profiles of the authors and editors of Project 2025. These ultraconservative policymakers may well become the members of the next Cabinet. In 1981, the think tank produced a similar set of proposals called "Mandate for Leadership" for the incoming Reagan administration. Many of the contributors to that document went on to receive cabinet posts and other high-level positions in the Reagan administration.

Two years into Trump's presidency, the Heritage Foundation boasted that his administration had already adopted nearly two-thirds of its 2016 policy recommendations. Given the significant overlap between Project 2025 contributors and

Trump's former officials, as well as the project's detailed policy prescriptions, it is reasonable to expect that a substantial portion of Project 2025's agenda would be implemented if Trump were to win the 2024 election.

While Trump and his campaign have emphasized that Project 2025 does not officially represent his views or policies, the involvement of so many of his former officials and allies in crafting the document suggests a close alignment between the project's goals and Trump's own agenda. As Russ Vought, a key Project 2025 contributor, stated in a secretly recorded video, Trump's public distancing from the project is likely a matter of "graduate-level politics," and the former president is actually "very supportive" of the initiative.

Kevin D. Roberts, PhD

Kevin Roberts, the ambitious and controversial president of the Heritage Foundation, has emerged as a key architect of the conservative movement's sharp turn towards nationalism and Trumpism. Through his leadership of Project 2025, Roberts is working to consolidate right-wing power and fundamentally reshape the American government should Republicans retake the White House in 2024.

EARLY LIFE AND EDUCATION
Born in 1974 in Lafayette, Louisiana, Kevin Roberts was raised in a conservative Catholic family. His upbringing in the South and academic focus on the lives of enslaved people shaped his perspective from a young age. Roberts graduated magna cum laude with a bachelor's degree in history from the University of Louisiana at Lafayette in 1996. He went on to earn a Master's degree from Virginia Tech and a PhD in American history from the University of Texas at Austin.

CONTROVERSIAL TENURE AT WYOMING CATHOLIC COLLEGE
After founding a K-12 Catholic school in Louisiana, Roberts made his first foray into conservative activism as president of Wyoming Catholic College in Lander from 2013 to 2016. He quickly made a name for himself and the obscure school by adopting the "cowboy Catholic" image and picking high-profile fights over federal funding and LGBT rights. Under Roberts' leadership, Wyoming Catholic became one of the only colleges in the nation to reject all federal student aid, citing concerns it would infringe on the school's ability to discriminate against LGBT students and employees. In explaining the decision, Roberts made inflammatory comments about transgender people and same-sex couples wanting to "bring a certain activity or activism" to campus. While this independent stance earned glowing coverage from right-wing media and The New York Times, it sometimes put Roberts at odds with the local community and his own faculty, who bristled at his constant political activism. "Kevin had one idea of the college and most of the faculty had a different idea," said his successor Glenn Arbery. Still, Roberts' "brilliant" media strategy succeeded in raising the profile of Wyoming Catholic College and himself as a conservative firebrand. His outspoken opposition to the Affordable Care Act, criticism of a local airport, and participation in neighborhood affairs made him a prominent and polarizing figure in Lander.

RISE IN CONSERVATIVE POLITICS
Roberts' time in Wyoming proved to be a launching pad. After leaving the college in 2016, he became executive vice president of the influential right-wing Texas Public Policy Foundation before being tapped to lead the Heritage Foundation in 2021. As president of Heritage, Roberts has overseen the organization's shift from traditional conservatism focused on free enterprise to a more populist, partisan stance aligned with Trumpism. This transformation has led to internal strife and departures among long-time staff.

Under Roberts' leadership, Heritage launched Project 2025, a sweeping blueprint for how a potential second Trump administration could consolidate power and remake the federal government.
In his foreword to Project 2025's *Mandate for Leadership*, Roberts lays out an apocalyptic vision, warning that "The long march of cultural Marxism through our institutions has come to pass. The federal government is a behemoth, weaponized against American citizens and conservative values, with freedom and liberty under siege as never before". Roberts frames Project 2025 as a "consensus view of how major federal agencies must be governed" in pursuit of four main aims: "restoring the family as the centerpiece of American life; dismantling the administrative state; defending the nation's sovereignty and borders; and securing God-given individual rights to live freely". Critics argue this is a thinly-veiled roadmap for imposing an authoritarian, white Christian nationalist agenda.

CONTROVERSY AND CRITICISM
Roberts' inflammatory rhetoric and association with Project 2025 have drawn intense backlash. In July 2024, he sparked outrage by declaring "We are in the process of the second American Revolution, which will remain bloodless if the left allows it to be". The Heritage Foundation followed up with an ominous statement adding that the left has a "well established record of instigating the opposite". While Roberts has sought to distance Heritage from violent extremism, his militant language and admiration for illiberal leaders like Hungary's Viktor Orbán have led some to accuse him of flirting with fascism. His frequent attacks on "globalists," a term often used as an antisemitic dog

whistle, have also raised concerns. Even some fellow conservatives have balked at Roberts' approach, arguing that Heritage has abandoned its core principles and intellectual rigor in favor of partisan zealotry. As one former Heritage scholar put it: "Heritage used to be a place for serious policy debate. Under Roberts, it's become little more than a pro-Trump messaging operation obsessed with owning the libs."

FUTURE AMBITIONS

Looking ahead, Roberts shows no signs of slowing down in his mission to radically reshape American politics and society. His upcoming book, *Dawn's Early Light: Taking Back Washington to Save America*, promises to be a manifesto for the nationalist right, with a foreword by Trump running mate JD Vance. Originally slated for release in September 2024, the book has been postponed until after the election amid the Project 2025 controversy. According to an early review, the book reveals Roberts' "Stalinist tactics" of using conspiracy theories to violently enforce the right's agenda. It reportedly criticizes birth control and law enforcement while promoting public prayer as a geopolitical weapon against China.

While the 2024 election remains uncertain, Roberts and his allies are playing a long game. Through vehicles like Project 2025, they are working to permanently entrench conservative power, dismantle democratic institutions, and impose their reactionary vision on the nation. As Roberts himself has declared, "Our side is winning. We're in the process of taking this country back".

Rick Dearborn

Rick Dearborn, a longtime Republican staffer and lobbyist, has emerged as a key figure in the conservative movement's preparations for the 2024 presidential transition.

EARLY LIFE AND EDUCATION

Born in 1965, Dearborn grew up in Oklahoma and earned a bachelor's degree in public administration from the University of Oklahoma in 1988. Little is publicly known about his upbringing or early political views. But his career trajectory suggests an ambitious young conservative drawn to the halls of power.

EARLY CAREER

After college, Dearborn got his start working for the Senate Republican Conference and the Senate Steering Committee. He then served for over two decades as chief of staff and legislative director to Senator Jeff Sessions of Alabama, one of the most stridently conservative members of Congress. In that role, Dearborn was immersed in Sessions' hardline stances against immigration, criminal justice reform, and social welfare programs. In 2003, Dearborn was appointed by President George W. Bush as Assistant Secretary of Energy for Congressional Affairs.

RISE TO PROMINENCE

Dearborn's big break came when he was tapped as executive director of Donald Trump's presidential transition team in 2016. He went on to serve in the White House as deputy chief of staff for legislative, intergovernmental affairs and implementation. In that powerful role, Dearborn worked with Marc Short and Andrew Bremberg to aggressively wield the Congressional Review Act to eliminate Obama-era regulations, targeting rules on issues like environmental protection and workplace safety. He was a key link between the White House and Republicans on Capitol Hill. However, Dearborn lasted less than a year in the tumultuous Trump White House, resigning in December 2017. He then became a partner at Mindset, a lobbying firm.

Now, Dearborn has reemerged as a central player in the conservative movement's plans for the next Republican presidency. He is a visiting fellow at the Heritage Foundation and member of the steering committee for Project 2025. Dearborn authored the chapter on the White House Office for Project 2025's Mandate for Leadership report, a detailed blueprint for the first 180 days of a new administration. He is also advising on personnel recommendations and helping build a database of vetted conservative staffers "who are ready to work on day one".

Dearborn recently said of Project 2025: "Conservative presidents are entitled to a supportive army of political appointees. They shouldn't have to battle their own people to get their agenda done."

Russ Vought

Russell Vought, a key architect of the controversial Project 2025 conservative policy agenda, has steadily risen to prominence as an influential force shaping the trajectory of the Republican Party and conservative movement.

EARLY LIFE AND EDUCATION

Born in 1976 and raised in an evangelical Christian household in Virginia, Vought's upbringing instilled in him a deeply conservative worldview from a young age. He earned a bachelor's degree from Wheaton College, an evangelical liberal arts school, and a law degree from George Washington University.

EARLY CAREER

After law school, Vought worked as a legislative assistant for conservative Senator Phil Gramm and later as policy director for the House Republican Conference under then-Chairman Mike Pence. In these roles, he honed his skills in advancing conservative policy priorities in Congress. From 2010 to 2017, Vought served as vice president of the conservative Heritage Action for America, the lobbying arm of the Heritage Foundation. There, he pressured lawmakers to defund the Affordable Care Act and worked to push the Republican Party further to the right.

KEY ROLES IN THE TRUMP ADMINISTRATION

Vought's uncompromising conservatism caught the attention of Donald Trump's inner circle. In 2017, Vought joined the Trump administration as deputy director of the Office of Management and Budget (OMB). During his Senate confirmation hearing, Vought faced scrutiny for past statements claiming that Muslims "do not simply have a deficient theology. They do not know God because they have rejected Jesus Christ his Son, and they stand condemned." As OMB deputy director and then acting director, Vought played a key role in advancing Trump's agenda, including the travel ban on several Muslim-majority countries and the diversion of military funds to build a border wall. Alongside OMB Director Mick Mulvaney, Vought was a major proponent of steep cuts to social welfare programs.

LEADING THE CENTER FOR RENEWING AMERICA

After Trump's 2020 election loss, Vought founded and became president of the Center for Renewing America (CRA), a conservative think tank stocked with Trump administration alumni. The CRA's stated mission is to "renew a consensus of America as a nation under God with unique interests worthy of defending." Under Vought's leadership, the CRA has become a hub for Christian nationalist ideology and policy development. The organization has advocated for increased state control over education, book bans, rollbacks of LGBTQ+ rights, and abortion bans.

ROLE IN PROJECT 2025

As a former Trump official and head of an influential conservative think tank, Vought was tapped to play a central role in crafting the Project 2025 agenda, intended as a policy roadmap for the next Republican president. Vought wrote a key chapter on "dismantling the administrative state." His section calls for the political purge of thousands of federal civil servants and their replacement with conservative loyalists.

Other Vought proposals include eliminating diversity, equity, and inclusion programs, banning the discussion of systemic racism in government trainings, and prohibiting policies that protect LGBTQ+ individuals from discrimination.

As Project 2025 has come under increasing scrutiny and criticism from Democrats and moderate Republicans, Vought has been one of its most vocal defenders. In media appearances and op-eds, he has dismissed concerns about the agenda's radical nature, framing it as a necessary corrective to a federal government that has become "woke" and strayed from conservative principles. "The only way to save the country from the woke Left's destructive policies is to fight back with an agenda that puts America first," Vought wrote in a statement accompanying the release of Project 2025.

"Russ Vought is one of the most dangerous figures in American politics today," said Rachel Klein of the progressive watchdog group Accountable.US. "He is using his perch at the Center for Renewing America and his role in Project 2025 to try to reshape the country in his image of an intolerant, exclusionary Christian nationalism." Vought has largely dismissed such criticism, arguing that he is simply fighting for the "restoration of America's founding principles."

If Trump wins the White House in 2024, Vought is widely expected to be in line for a top administration post, potentially as White House chief of staff or director of the OMB. Such a role would provide an unprecedented platform to translate Project 2025's vision into reality.

Donald Devine

Donald J. Devine is a conservative political theorist, activist, and former government official who has played an influential role in shaping the modern American conservative movement. Most recently, he served as editor of the "Government Reform" chapter in the Heritage Foundation's controversial Project 2025 initiative.

EARLY LIFE AND EDUCATION

Born in 1937 in Bronx, New York, Devine was raised in a working-class Catholic family. His father was a postal worker and union member. Despite his modest upbringing, Devine excelled academically, earning a BA in history from St. John's University and MA and PhD degrees in political science from Syracuse University. Devine's intellectual journey took a sharp rightward turn in graduate school, where he studied under conservative political philosopher Willmoore Kendall. Kendall's critiques of liberal democracy had a profound impact on Devine's thinking.

EARLY CAREER

After receiving his PhD in 1967, Devine taught political science at the University of Maryland. In the 1970s, he became active in conservative politics, working on Ronald Reagan's unsuccessful 1976 presidential campaign. When Reagan won the presidency in 1980, Devine was appointed director of the Office of Personnel Management (OPM). In this role, he sought to reduce the power of federal employee unions and reform the civil service system. His aggressive approach made him a controversial figure and a hero to small-government conservatives.

RISE TO PROMINENCE

After leaving the Reagan administration in 1985, Devine became a senior scholar at the Heritage Foundation. There, he continued to advocate for reducing the size and scope of the federal government. Throughout the 1990s and 2000s, Devine was a frequent commentator on Fox News and right-wing talk radio, railing against "big government" and "liberal elites." He served on the board of the American Conservative Union and was a regular speaker at the annual Conservative Political Action Conference (CPAC).Devine's hardline views and inflammatory rhetoric earned him a devoted following on the right. However, critics accused him of promoting an extreme, anti-government ideology that threatened core public services and institutions.

PROJECT 2025

As editor of the "Government Reform" chapter, Devine advocated eliminating entire federal agencies and drastically reducing the federal workforce. In interviews and public appearances, Devine has described Project 2025 as a "historic opportunity" to dismantle the "administrative state" and restore "constitutional government".
Despite these criticisms, Devine remains unapologetic. In a recent interview, he dismissed concerns about Project 2025 as "hysterical" and vowed to "press forward" with his vision for a radically downsized federal government.

Dennis Dean Kirk

Dennis Dean Kirk was born and raised in Kansas. He pursued higher education at Northern Arizona University and later attended Washburn University Law School, where he graduated with honors. His career in federal service began as a trial attorney in the Bureau of Enforcement at the Interstate Commerce Commission.

Kirk has held several significant positions within the U.S. government. Notably, he served as Special Counsel in the Office of General Counsel at the Department of the Army from 2005 to 2007. He continued his service as Associate General Counsel for Strategic Integration and Business Transformation at the Department of the Army from 2007 to 2012. During his tenure, he was recognized with several awards, including the Meritorious Civilian Service Award and the Exceptional Civilian Service Award, for his contributions to saving the Army millions of dollars.

In 2018, President Donald J. Trump announced his intent to nominate Dennis Dean Kirk as a Member and Chair of the Merit Systems Protection Board for a term expiring in 2023. Additionally, Kirk served as a Senior Advisor at the Office of Personnel Management (OPM), where he was involved in major human resources policy and program development. His role included advising the Director of OPM and leading efforts in employment, pay, performance management, and employee relations.

Kirk has been actively involved in shaping HR policies and programs across the federal government. His work has focused on employment, pay, performance management, and labor relations. He has played a crucial role in aligning OPM's initiatives with the President's Management Agenda and Executive Orders related to employment-management workplace relations.

Paul Dans

Paul Dans is a prominent figure in conservative political circles, particularly known for his involvement with Project 2025 and his roles during the Trump administration. Below is a comprehensive profile of Paul Dans, detailing his career, policy positions, and connections with the Trump administration.

EDUCATION AND EARLY CAREER:

Paul Dans is an MIT-educated lawyer with extensive experience in high-stakes commercial litigation. He practiced law in New York City from 1997 to 2012 at several large international law firms before founding his own firm. He holds a law degree from the University of Virginia School of Law and both graduate and undergraduate degrees from the Massachusetts Institute of Technology.

TRUMP ADMINISTRATION:

Dans began his federal service as a Senior Advisor in the Office of Community Planning and Development at the U.S. Department of Housing and Urban Development (HUD) during the Trump administration. He later served as Chief of Staff at the U.S. Office of Personnel Management (OPM), where he managed human resources policy for over

two million federal workers. He also acted as OPM's White House liaison, working closely with the White House Office of Presidential Personnel.

In January 2021, President Trump appointed Dans as Chairman of the National Capital Planning Commission. His role in the Trump administration was significant, particularly in his capacity at OPM, where he was involved in staffing approximately 4,000 presidential appointees across the federal government.

PROJECT 2025:

Paul Dans was the director of Project 2025, but stepped down in July 2024 amid intense criticism, including from Trump himself. His departure was part of the project's planned timeline to conclude policy drafting after the major party conventions. Despite his resignation, the project continues to influence conservative strategies and remains active in its efforts to prepare for a potential Republican administration.

Christopher Miller

Christopher Charles Miller is a retired United States Army Special Forces colonel who served as the acting United States Secretary of Defense under President Donald Trump from November 9, 2020, to January 20, 2021. His career is marked by extensive experience in special operations and counterterrorism.

Military Career:

- Miller's military service began in 1983 as an enlisted infantryman in the Army Reserve. He later became an officer through the ROTC program at George Washington University, where he earned a Bachelor of Arts in History.
- He transferred to the Special Forces in 1993, serving in various command and staff positions within the 5th Special Forces Group (Airborne). His notable roles included commanding the 2nd Battalion, 5th SFG(A).
- Miller participated in initial combat operations in Afghanistan in 2001 and Iraq in 2003, gaining extensive inter-agency and joint special operations experience.

Civilian Career:

- After retiring from the Army in 2014, Miller worked as a defense contractor, providing special operations and intelligence expertise to the Department of Defense.
- He served as the Special Assistant to the President and Senior Director for Counterterrorism and Transnational Threats at the National Security Council from 2018 to 2019.

Appointment:

- President Trump appointed Miller as Acting Secretary of Defense following the termination of Mark Esper on November 9, 2020. His appointment came shortly after the 2020 presidential election.

Miller's tenure was characterized by efforts to implement rapid policy changes at the Pentagon before the transition to President-elect Joe Biden's administration. He focused on reducing troop levels in Afghanistan and Iraq, aligning with Biden's stance on troop drawdowns. His response to the January 6, 2021, storming of the U.S. Capitol was criticized for the delayed deployment of National Guard troops. Miller later testified that he had the necessary authority and aimed to avoid incidents similar to the Kent State shootings.

Miller's appointment was seen as controversial, with some perceiving it as a move to install a loyalist in a critical position during a contentious transition period.

Ken Cuccinelli

Ken Cuccinelli, a prominent figure in conservative politics, has built a career marked by controversial stances and a steadfast commitment to far-right ideologies. This profile examines Cuccinelli's life, career, and his significant role in shaping conservative policies, particularly through his involvement in Project 2025.

EARLY LIFE AND EDUCATION

Kenneth Thomas Cuccinelli II was born on July 30, 1968, in Edison, New Jersey. He earned a mechanical engineering degree from the University of Virginia, followed by a Juris Doctorate from George Mason University School of Law and a Master's degree in International Commerce and Policy, also from George Mason University.

ENTRY INTO POLITICS

Cuccinelli's entry into politics began with his election to the Virginia State Senate, representing the 37th Senatorial district. This position served as a launching pad for his political career, allowing him to build a reputation as a staunch conservative and gain visibility within the Republican Party.

Cuccinelli's political ascent reached a significant milestone when he served as the 46th Attorney General of Virginia from 2010 to 2014. In this role, he gained national attention for his aggressive pursuit of conservative causes. Notably, he was the first state attorney general in the country to file a lawsuit challenging the Affordable Care Act, commonly known as Obamacare. This action solidified his reputation as a hardline conservative willing to use legal means to oppose progressive policies.

In 2013, Cuccinelli ran for Governor of Virginia, further elevating his national profile. However, this campaign ended in defeat, with Cuccinelli losing to Terry McAuliffe by a margin of 56,435 votes, or 2.5% of total ballots cast.

TRUMP ADMINISTRATION

Cuccinelli's most high-profile positions came during the Trump administration. He served as the Acting Director of the United States Citizenship and Immigration Services (USCIS) in 2019, despite concerns about the legality of his appointment. This role allowed Cuccinelli to significantly influence U.S. immigration policy, aligning it more closely with the Trump administration's restrictive approach. Subsequently, Cuccinelli became the senior official performing the duties of the Deputy Secretary of Homeland Security from 2019 to 2021.

His appointment as Acting Director of USCIS was widely regarded as illegal, circumventing the normal Senate confirmation process.

Under Cuccinelli's leadership, oversight of the Department of Homeland Security's intelligence arm was reduced, leading to concerning practices such as compiling intelligence reports on journalists covering DHS activities in Portland, Oregon.

Throughout his career, Cuccinelli has consistently advocated for extreme conservative policies, particularly in the areas of immigration and LGBTQ+ rights.

Cuccinelli's approach to immigration has been notably harsh. As Acting Director of USCIS, he announced a revised regulation expanding the "public charge" requirements for legal immigration. This change made it easier to deny green cards and visas to individuals deemed likely to rely on government benefits such as food stamps, housing vouchers, and Medicaid. When questioned about whether this policy contradicted the welcoming message of the Statue of Liberty, Cuccinelli infamously suggested a revision to Emma Lazarus's poem: "Give me your tired and your poor who can stand on their own two feet and who will not become a public charge".

Cuccinelli's record on LGBTQ+ rights has also been consistently regressive. As Virginia's Attorney General, he defended the state's anti-sodomy law even after it had been struck down by a federal court. His stance implied a disturbing conflation of homosexuality with criminal behavior, placing him within the harmful tradition of "groomer" conspiracists who baselessly associate LGBTQ+ individuals with child abuse.

He authored the chapter on the Department of Homeland Security of *Mandate for Leadership*.

Kiron K. Skinner

Kiron Kanina Skinner is a distinguished American academic and former government official known for her expertise in international relations and U.S. foreign policy. Her career spans academia, government service, and authorship, with significant contributions to the study of post-World War II U.S. foreign policy.

PROFESSIONAL BACKGROUND

Skinner was born in Chicago in 1961 and grew up in the San Francisco Bay Area. She earned an associate degree in communications from Sacramento City College in 1979 and a bachelor's degree in political science from Spelman College. She went on to earn an MA and PhD in political science and international relations from Harvard University.

Skinner is currently the Taube Professor of International Relations and Politics at Pepperdine University's School of Public Policy, where she teaches graduate courses in national security and public leadership. Previously, she served at Carnegie Mellon University as the founding director of the Institute for Politics and Strategy and held various academic positions. She was also a Distinguished Fellow at CyLab, a research center in the College of Engineering, and held courtesy faculty positions at CMU's Heinz College and the Institute for Software Research. Skinner is a W. Glenn Campbell Research Fellow at Stanford University's Hoover Institution and has been involved in several Hoover Institution projects related to international security and political strategy.

GOVERNMENT SERVICE

Skinner served as Director of Policy Planning and Senior Adviser to Secretary of State Mike Pompeo at the U.S. Department of State from 2018 to 2019, under the Trump administration. In this role, she provided strategic guidance on foreign policy and played a central role in initiatives like the Commission on Unalienable Rights and the Foreign Affairs Policy Board. Her public service includes membership on various boards and panels, such as the U.S. Defense Department's Defense Policy Board, the Chief of Naval Operations' Executive Panel, and the National Security Education Board. She previously worked in the Trump transition team and as a foreign policy surrogate for Trump's 2016 campaign

Skinner also co-authored several books on Ronald Reagan, including *In His Own Hand* and *Reagan, a Life in Letters*, both of which became *New York Times* bestsellers.

Skinner's work in government and academia has significantly influenced U.S. foreign policy, particularly through her emphasis on strategic dialogues and transatlantic partnerships. Her efforts to integrate technology and foreign policy have been a focus of her recent work at the Heritage Foundation.

Dustin J. Carmack

Dustin J. Carmack is currently serving as a Research Fellow for Cybersecurity, Intelligence, and Emerging Technologies in the Border Security and Immigration Center at The Heritage Foundation. His work focuses on issues related to national security, technology, and policy.

Prior to joining The Heritage Foundation, he was the Chief of Staff to the Director of National Intelligence, John Ratcliffe, during the Trump administration. Previously he held positions as Chief of Staff for Congressmen John Ratcliffe (TX-04) and Ron DeSantis (FL-06), who later became Governor of Florida

Carmack studied at Truman State University in Missouri and Tel Aviv University in Israel.

He authored chapter 7 on the Intelligence Community of *Mandate for Leadership*

Mora Namdar

Mora Namdar is a native Texan, born to Iranian immigrants, and is fluent in Farsi. She completed her undergraduate studies at Southern Methodist University, earning bachelor's degrees in Political Science and International Affairs, with minors in Fine Art, Philosophy, and Human Rights. She furthered her education with a Master's degree in International Affairs and a Juris Doctor from American University in Washington, D.C., where she was the founding Editor-in-Chief of the *National Security Law Brief*. Namdar also studied International Relations at the University of Oxford.

Namdar's government career includes serving as the Acting Assistant Secretary of State for Consular Affairs from December 2020 to January 2021, a position to which she was appointed by President Donald Trump. Before this role, she was the Vice President of Legal, Compliance, and Risk at the United States Agency for Global Media (USAGM) from July to December 2020. Her responsibilities included overseeing legal and compliance matters and addressing global media issues. Additionally, she served as a Senior Advisor at the U.S. Department of State from May 2019 to January 2021, focusing on global issues such as Iran policy and working closely with the White House National Security Council. Namdar's time in public service was not without controversy. She was implicated in allegations of misconduct during her tenure at USAGM, including accusations of political influence and mismanagement, as detailed in whistleblower complaints. These allegations included claims of violating the Anti-Deficiency Act and politicizing the J1 visa sponsorship process.

Namdar has been an outspoken critic of the Biden administration's policies on Iran and immigration, asserting that these policies compromise U.S. national security. She praised the Trump administration's Middle East policy, particularly the Abraham Accords, and has advocated for a consistent U.S. foreign policy approach in the region.

Before her tenure in government, Namdar worked for Occidental Petroleum and the Voice of America, advising on national security and policy. She founded Namdar Law PLLC, where she focuses on business, contracts, government, international law, and art law. Namdar has also been involved in academia and policy advocacy, serving as a Senior Fellow at the American Foreign Policy Council since February 2021.

Mike Gonzalez

Mike Gonzalez is a senior fellow at the Heritage Foundation, known for his expertise in foreign policy and his critical views on identity politics and critical race theory. His career spans journalism, government service, and think tank work, reflecting a deep engagement with international affairs and American political discourse.

PROFESSIONAL BACKGROUND

Gonzalez was born in Cuba in 1960 and emigrated to the United States at the age of 12. He holds a bachelor's degree in communications from Emerson College and an MBA from Columbia Business School.

Gonzalez spent nearly two decades as a journalist, with 15 years reporting from Europe, Asia, and Latin America. He began his journalism career in 1980, covering high school sports for The Boston Herald. He later worked for Agence France-Presse, reporting globally, and spent 11 years with The Wall Street Journal. At the Journal, he wrote a column on the stock market in New York and served as deputy editor of the editorial pages for the Asia edition in Hong Kong and the Europe edition in Brussels. After leaving journalism, Gonzalez joined the administration of President George W. Bush. He served as a speechwriter for Securities and Exchange Commission Chairman Christopher Cox and later moved to the State Department's European Bureau, where he wrote speeches and op-eds.

HERITAGE FOUNDATION

In March 2009, Gonzalez joined the Heritage Foundation as Vice President of Communications, and in June 2014, he became a senior research fellow. His work at Heritage focuses on foreign policy issues, including those related to Hong Kong, China, and Latin America. He is also the Angeles T. Arredondo E Pluribus Unum fellow at Heritage, where he examines the formation of political identities and critiques identity politics. Gonzalez is the author of several books, including *The Plot to Change America: How Identity Politics is Dividing the Land of the Free*. His writings have earned him both acclaim and criticism, particularly from organizations like the National Education Association and the American Federation of Teachers, which have opposed his views on critical race theory.

CONNECTION WITH THE TRUMP ADMINISTRATION

Mike Gonzalez was named as one of the scholars President Donald Trump intended to appoint to the President's Advisory 1776 Commission, a group focused on promoting patriotic education. His involvement with the commission underscores his influence in shaping discussions around American history and identity during the Trump administration.

Mike Gonzalez wrote the section on Corporation for Public Broadcasting for Chapter 8: Media Agencies.

Max Primorac

Max Primorac holds a master's degree in International Relations from the University of Chicago and a bachelor's degree in Biology from Franklin & Marshall College.

Primorac has held several significant roles within the U.S. government. During the Trump administration, he served as the Acting Chief Operating Officer at the U.S. Agency for International Development (USAID). He also launched the Bureau for Humanitarian Assistance and was the federal government's lead coordinator for global disaster response. Additionally, he served as U.S. Vice President Mike Pence's Envoy to Iraq, overseeing a genocide recovery program aimed at assisting religious minority returns. Before his tenure at USAID, Primorac was deeply involved in Iraq's reconstruction efforts following the U.S. invasion in 2003. He served in the Coalition Provisional Authority and held senior positions at the U.S. Department of State, including Senior Advisor for Stabilization and Transition to the Secretary of State's Iraq Coordinator. His work included managing over $2 billion in foreign assistance for Iraq's reconstruction.

In the private sector, Primorac founded Between Two Rivers LLC, a consulting company that worked with clients such as the governments of Japan, Canada, and Iraq. He also served as President of the Institute for Stabilization & Transition, advising governments on post-conflict strategies. Earlier in his career, during the Balkan wars, he advised leaders of the emerging republics of former Yugoslavia on civil society and democracy programs.

Primorac's career has not been without controversy. During his time at USAID, he faced ethics complaints, including allegations of promoting a private client's business interests to a United Nations agency and favoring one Iraqi Christian sect over another in funding decisions.

Primorac has been a proponent of market-based solutions as a path to sustainable prosperity, aiming to "end the need for foreign aid."

Max Primorac is currently a Senior Research Fellow at the Heritage Foundation's Margaret Thatcher Center for Freedom. His research focuses on global development, the adverse effects of China's global expansion, climate policies, and international religious freedom.

Daren Bakst

Daren Bakst hails from West Palm Beach, Florida. He earned his bachelor's and master's degrees from George Washington University. He is a licensed attorney, holding a Juris Doctor from the University of Miami and a Master of Laws from American University.

Bakst has served as a Research Fellow in Agricultural Policy at the Heritage Foundation, where he studied and wrote extensively on agricultural and environmental policy, property rights, and regulatory reform. His work included leading efforts to reshape the farm bill debate, addressing issues like agricultural subsidies, trade, and food policy, including GMO labeling and trans-fat bans. Before joining the Heritage Foundation, Bakst was a policy counsel at the U.S. Chamber of Commerce, focusing on regulatory reform and environmental policy. He also served as Director of Legal and Regulatory Studies at the John Locke Foundation, a major state-based free-market think tank, where he dealt with constitutional law, energy, environmental policy, and property rights. Bakst has been involved with several organizations, including serving on the Federalist Society's Environmental Law and Property Rights Executive Committee and the Energy, Environment, and Agriculture Task Force of the American Legislative Exchange Council. He is also a member of the Publications Peer Review Committee for the Food and Drug Law Institute.

CONTRIBUTIONS AND PUBLIC ENGAGEMENT

Daren Bakst frequently submits comments to regulatory agencies, testifies before Congress, and has been quoted in major media outlets such as *The Wall Street Journal*, *USA Today*, and *The Washington Times*. His work often critiques government interventions in agriculture and environmental policies, advocating for reduced regulatory burdens and enhanced property rights. Bakst has been a vocal critic of policies he perceives as overreaching, such as the EPA's "Waters of the United States" rule and proposed ozone standards. He has also been involved in discussions about eminent domain reform, particularly in light of the *Kelo v. City of New London* case.

He has criticized the Biden administration's agricultural policies, particularly those involving equity and climate considerations, arguing that they may lead to unnecessary government intervention. Bakst has also expressed skepticism about climate change mitigation efforts and promotes deregulation and fossil fuel use.

Lindsey M. Burke

Lindsey M. Burke's holds a bachelor's degree in Politics from Hollins University and a master's degree in Foreign Language Education from the University of Virginia. Burke further pursued a PhD in Education Policy from George Mason University.

Burke's career began to take shape as she entered the field of public policy, particularly focusing on education. She became the Director of the Center for Education Policy at The Heritage Foundation. She also serves as a fellow at EdChoice, an organization named after Milton and Rose Friedman, which advocates for school choice initiatives. She is also associated with the Educational Freedom Institute and the Independent Women's Forum's Education Freedom Center.

Her involvement in Governor Glenn Youngkin's transition steering committee and her appointment to the Board of Visitors for George Mason University highlight her influence in shaping education policy at both state and national levels.Her advocacy for education choice and reform has been a cornerstone of her career. Burke has supported initiatives that promote school choice, including education savings accounts (ESAs), which allow public education funds to be used for private schooling options. This aligns with her broader ideological stance favoring market-based solutions in education, reminiscent of Milton Friedman's economic principles.

Burke authored the chapter on the Department of Education in the *Mandate for Leadership*, a key document of Project 2025. Her proposals include the elimination of the Department of Education, a move that could significantly impact federal funding for programs supporting disadvantaged students.

Bernard L. McNamee

Bernard L. McNamee, an attorney and former commissioner of the Federal Energy Regulatory Commission (FERC), has contributed a chapter to the *Mandate for Leadership*, focusing on the Department of Energy and related commissions, including FERC and the Nuclear Regulatory Commission (NRC). His legal career has involved representing electric and natural gas utilities before state public utility commissions, providing him with substantial experience in the energy sector. The *Mandate for Leadership* describes McNamee's chapter as advocating for a conservative president to unleash America's energy resources, ostensibly to benefit the American people rather than special interests. However, the underlying implication is that fossil fuel interests are prioritized. McNamee attributes the so-called energy crisis to "extreme 'green' policies" and blames various entities, including the Biden administration, Congress, and progressive groups, for a decline in U.S. energy dominance. However, the term "energy dominance" is not clearly defined, and the assertion of extreme green policies is disputed, as the world continues to rely heavily on fossil fuels. The *Mandate for Leadership* uses language that frames all green policies as extreme, even though current policies are relatively moderate. The document criticizes subsidies for renewable energy as market distortions while ignoring subsidies for fossil fuels. It also labels the general populace, who are affected by climate change, as special interest groups, aligning fossil fuel interests with those of the American people

Mandy M. Gunasekara

Mandy M. Gunasekara is a prominent figure in the conservative movement, particularly known for her roles at the Independent Women's Forum and the Heritage Foundation, as well as her tenure as chief of staff at the U.S. Environmental Protection Agency (EPA) during the Trump administration.

EARLY LIFE AND CAREER

Gunasekara holds a bachelor's degree from Mississippi College and a J.D. from the University of Mississippi School of Law. Her early career involved significant roles in government and policy-making. She worked for Senator Jim Inhofe, a known climate change skeptic, and was involved in a notable incident where she handed him a snowball to mock climate change on the Senate floor.

RISE TO PROMINENCE

Gunasekara served as the chief of staff at the EPA under the Trump administration, where she was instrumental in rolling back several environmental regulations. She played a key role in the U.S. withdrawal from the Paris Agreement and the repeal of the Clean Power Plan. Her tenure at the EPA was marked by efforts to reduce the agency's regulatory reach, aligning with broader conservative goals of deregulation.

As a visiting fellow at the Heritage Foundation, Gunasekara has continued to advocate for policies that prioritize economic growth over environmental regulation. Her involvement with the Independent Women's Forum, known for its conservative stances on various issues, further underscores her commitment to these ideologies.

Gunasekara is a key contributor to Project 2025, a comprehensive conservative policy agenda crafted by the Heritage Foundation. She authored the chapter on the EPA, advocating for a reduced federal role in environmental regulation and increased state and local control. This approach aligns with the broader conservative objective of dismantling the "administrative state" and reducing federal oversight.

Gunasekara has accused the Biden administration of assaulting the energy sector by enforcing pollution regulations, a stance that critics argue misrepresents the purpose of such regulations. Her chapter in Project 2025 suggests that under a conservative administration, the EPA would be significantly weakened, potentially allowing increased pollution in states with less stringent environmental laws.

Gunasekara has faced significant criticism for her climate change denialism and the use of misleading rhetoric. She has been linked to the creation of the Energy 45 Fund, a pro-Trump nonprofit known for its deceptive claims about energy policy. Her statements have been challenged by environmental advocates and scientists, including Bill Nye, who criticized her for advocating increased carbon emissions despite the known risks of climate change. Her testimony in support of ExxonMobil during litigation over climate misinformation, where she dismissed the proceedings as politically motivated, further illustrates her alignment with fossil fuel interests.

Roger Severino

Roger Thomas Severino is an American attorney and policy expert known for his work in civil rights, religious freedom, and health policy. He was born in 1974/1975 and raised in Los Angeles, California, the son of Colombian immigrants. He earned a bachelor's degree in business from the University of Southern California, a Master of Public Administration from Carnegie Mellon University, and a Juris Doctor from Harvard Law School.

Severino began his legal career at the Becket Fund for Religious Liberty, a nonprofit law firm focused on defending religious freedom. He then served as a trial attorney in the Civil Rights Division of the U.S. Department of Justice from 2008 to 2015, where he worked on enforcing civil rights laws. In 2015, Severino joined The Heritage Foundation, a conservative think tank, where he served as the director of the DeVos Center for Religion and Civil Society. During his time at Heritage, he advocated for policies supporting religious freedom and conservative social values.

In March 2017, President Donald Trump appointed Severino as Director of the Office for Civil Rights (OCR) at the U.S. Department of Health and Human Services (HHS). He served in this role until January 2021. As OCR director, Severino focused on enforcing civil rights, conscience, and religious freedom laws. He established the Conscience and Religious Freedom Division to protect healthcare workers who objected to certain procedures on religious grounds. Severino's tenure at HHS was marked by controversy, particularly regarding his stance on LGBTQ rights. He was criticized for rolling back nondiscrimination protections for LGBTQ individuals under the Affordable Care Act, which allowed healthcare providers to deny care based on sexual orientation or gender identity. His actions and statements have drawn significant criticism from LGBTQ advocacy groups and some lawmakers.

After leaving HHS, Severino returned to The Heritage Foundation as Vice President of Domestic Policy and The Joseph C. and Elizabeth A. Anderlik Fellow. He also served as a Senior Fellow at the Ethics and Public Policy Center, where he continued to focus on health policy and religious freedom issues.

Roger Severino is married to Carrie Severino, an attorney and activist who leads the Judicial Crisis Network. Together, they have been described as a "conservative power couple" by The New York Times

Benjamin S. Carson, Sr., MD

Benjamin Solomon Carson Sr., known as Ben Carson, is a renowned American neurosurgeon, author, and politician. Born on September 18, 1951, in Detroit, Michigan, Carson rose from a challenging childhood to become a leading figure in medicine and politics.

He graduated with honors from Southwestern High School in Detroit and went on to attend Yale University on a full scholarship, earning a degree in psychology in 1973. Carson then pursued a medical degree at the University of Michigan, graduating in 1977.

Carson completed his residency in neurosurgery at Johns Hopkins University, where he became the first Black neurosurgery resident. By 1984, at the age of 33, he was appointed Director of Pediatric Neurosurgery at Johns Hopkins Children's Center, making him the youngest chief of pediatric neurosurgery in the United States. He gained international fame in 1987 for leading a surgical team that successfully separated conjoined twins joined at the back of the head. Carson also pioneered techniques in neurosurgery, such as the first successful neurosurgical procedure on a fetus inside the womb and revitalizing hemispherectomy procedures to control seizures. Carson retired from his medical career in 2013, having authored over 100 neurosurgical publications and several books, including Gifted Hands and Think Big.

Carson entered the political arena with a speech at the 2013 National Prayer Breakfast, where he criticized policies of President Barack Obama, gaining attention among conservatives. He announced his candidacy for the 2016 Republican presidential nomination but suspended his campaign after Super Tuesday and endorsed Donald Trump. Following Trump's election, Carson was nominated and confirmed as the 17th Secretary of Housing and Urban Development (HUD) in March 2017. During his tenure, he implemented policies that included budget cuts to HUD and changes to anti-discrimination regulations in public housing. Carson also served on the Coronavirus Task Force in 2020.

Carson is married to Lacena "Candy" Rustin, whom he met at Yale. They have three sons and three grandchildren. Together, they co-founded the Carson Scholars Fund, which awards scholarships to students for academic and humanitarian achievements.

William Perry Pendley

William Perry Pendley is an American attorney and conservative activist known for his controversial role as the acting director of the Bureau of Land Management (BLM) under the Trump administration. Born in Cheyenne, Wyoming, Pendley pursued higher education at George Washington University, where he earned Bachelor of Arts and Master of Arts degrees in economics and political science, followed by a Juris Doctor from the University of Wyoming College of Law. He also served as a captain in the United States Marine Corps. Pendley's career in government began during the Reagan administration, where he served as Deputy Assistant Secretary for Energy and Minerals at the Department of the Interior. In this role, he authored President Reagan's National Minerals Policy and the Exclusive Economic Zone proclamation. He later presided over the Mountain States Legal Foundation for nearly 30 years, a conservative legal organization that frequently challenged federal land management policies. In July 2019, Pendley was appointed as Deputy Director of Policy and Programs at BLM, effectively serving as the acting director without Senate confirmation. His tenure was marked by significant controversy due to his past advocacy for selling off federal lands and his critical views on environmental regulations. Pendley had previously called for the federal government to sell its vast landholdings and had been a vocal critic of environmentalism, climate change concerns, and protections for endangered species. Pendley's leadership at BLM included overseeing the relocation of the agency's headquarters from Washington, D.C., to Grand Junction, Colorado, a move that led to significant staff turnover and was criticized as an attempt to undermine the agency. His tenure faced legal challenges, and in September 2020, a U.S. District Judge ruled that Pendley had served unlawfully for 424 days, blocking him from continuing in the role. Despite this ruling, Pendley continued to influence BLM policies in other capacities.

Gene Hamilton

Gene P. Hamilton is an American lawyer and policymaker known for his influential roles in the Trump administration, particularly in shaping immigration policy.
Gene Hamilton was raised in Arizona and pursued higher education at the University of Georgia, where he earned a Bachelor of Arts in International Affairs. He later graduated magna cum laude from the Washington and Lee School of Law, where he was a member of the Order of the Coif.

Hamilton began his legal career as an Honors Attorney at the Department of Homeland Security (DHS), where he worked in the Office of Chief Counsel for U.S. Immigration and Customs Enforcement (ICE) in Georgia. In 2015, he became General Counsel to then-Senator Jeff Sessions on the Senate Committee on the Judiciary, Subcommittee on Immigration and the National Interest. He later joined the Trump transition team, leading its immigration policy efforts. During the Trump administration, Hamilton served as Senior Counselor to the Secretary of Homeland Security, John Kelly, and as Counselor to the Attorney General at the Department of Justice from 2017 to 2021. In these roles, he provided legal advice and strategic guidance on high-priority issues, including litigation and regulatory actions. Hamilton played a key role in implementing some of the administration's most controversial immigration policies, including the "zero tolerance" family separation policy, ending the Deferred Action for Childhood Arrivals (DACA) program, and revoking Temporary Protected Status for certain immigrant groups. His work often involved collaboration with Stephen Miller, a senior advisor to President Trump, on anti-immigration initiatives.

After leaving government service, Hamilton became Vice President and General Counsel for America First Legal, a conservative legal group founded by former Trump administration officials, including Stephen Miller. In this role, he has continued to advocate for Trump-era immigration policies and has been involved in legal challenges against Biden administration policies.

Hamilton's tenure in the Trump administration and his subsequent work have been marked by controversy. He has been criticized for his role in crafting policies that many view as harsh and anti-immigrant. In 2018, he was involved in a lawsuit challenging the administration's attempt to end Temporary Protected Status for Haitian immigrants, where he was accused of making misleading statements under oath. His connections with far-right anti-immigration groups and his involvement in drafting policies that drastically limited immigration have drawn significant scrutiny and criticism from advocacy groups and political opponents.

Jonathan Berry

Jonathan Berry is an American lawyer and policy expert known for his work in the intersection of law, politics, and public policy, particularly during the Trump administration.

Jonathan Berry graduated with Distinction in the Major from Yale College in 2005, where he was a National Merit Scholar and served as Speaker of the Yale Political Union. He earned his Juris Doctor from Columbia University School of Law in 2011, where he received the E.B. Convers Prize for best original legal writing and served as Executive Editor of the Columbia Journal of Law and Social Problems. During his time at Columbia, he was recognized by the Federalist Society, winning National Chapter of the Year.

Berry began his legal career clerking for Judge Jerry E. Smith of the United States Court of Appeals for the Fifth Circuit and for Associate Justice Samuel A. Alito, Jr., of the Supreme Court of the United States. He then worked at the international law firms Morgan, Lewis & Bockius LLP and Jones Day, focusing on regulatory and appellate litigation. His notable cases include participating in the King v. Burwell Affordable Care Act challenge and defending Virginia Governor Robert McDonnell in a corruption case that was vacated by the Supreme Court. During the Trump administration, Berry served as Chief Counsel to the President-Elect Trump Transition, advising on ethics and legal policy. He later headed the regulatory office at the U.S. Department of Labor as the Regulatory Policy Officer, where he oversaw the development of numerous proposed and final rules. His tenure was marked by significant deregulatory efforts, credited with over ten billion dollars in cost savings for the American public. Berry also worked at the Department of Justice's Office of Legal Policy, assisting with the confirmations of Associate Justice Neil Gorsuch and other federal judges, and developing memos on the use of subregulatory guidance documents.

Berry is currently the managing partner at Boyden Gray & Associates PLLC, where he provides strategic counsel on complex constitutional and administrative law issues, particularly in labor, employment, and benefits policy. His commentary has been published in major outlets like the Wall Street Journal and the New York Times.

Diana Furchtgott-Roth

Diana Furchtgott-Roth is an American economist and policy expert known for her work in transportation, technology, and economic policy. Born in 1958 in London, England, she moved to the United States in 1967. She holds a Bachelor of Arts in Economics from Swarthmore College and a Master of Philosophy in Economics from the University of Oxford.

She served as Deputy Assistant Secretary for Research and Technology at the U.S. Department of Transportation during the Trump administration. In this capacity, she advised the Secretary of Transportation on economic matters and managed a substantial research portfolio. Prior to this, she was the Acting Assistant Secretary for Economic Policy at the U.S. Department of the Treasury. Her government service also includes roles as Chief Economist at the U.S. Department of Labor and Chief of Staff of the President's Council of Economic Advisers under President George W. Bush. She worked in the White House under Presidents Reagan and George H.W. Bush as well. In the think tank sector, Furchtgott-Roth was a senior fellow and director of Economics21 at the Manhattan Institute for Policy Research. She is currently the Director of the Center for Energy, Climate, and Environment at The Heritage Foundation, where she also serves as the Herbert and Joyce Morgan Fellow in Energy and Environmental Policy.

Furchtgott-Roth is a prolific author and commentator, having published numerous books and articles on economic policy. Her works include *Women's Figures: An Illustrated Guide to the Economic Progress of Women in America* and *Regulating to Disaster: How Green Jobs Policies Are Damaging America's Economy*. She is known for her free-market views, advocating for lower taxes and reduced regulation as means to spur economic growth. She has been a vocal critic of the minimum wage, arguing that increases could reduce job availability for low-skill workers. Her views have often sparked controversy, particularly her stance on the gender wage gap, which she has argued is a myth when accounting for factors such as job type and hours worked. This perspective has drawn criticism from those who argue that systemic discrimination still plays a significant role in wage disparities.

Furchtgott-Roth's nomination to senior roles in the Trump administration faced opposition due to her views on various public policy issues. Critics have accused her of

cherry-picking data to support her arguments against environmental regulations and gender pay equity. Her stance on climate change, where she has questioned human impact, has also been contentious.

Brooks D. Tucker

Brooks D. Tucker is a former American government official and retired U.S. Marine Corps officer. He was born in the United States and pursued higher education at the University of Maryland, where he earned a Bachelor of Arts in English. He furthered his education at the Marine Corps Command and Staff College, focusing on critical thinking and leadership for complex security environments. Tucker also completed advanced studies in national security policy at Johns Hopkins School of Advanced International Studies and earned a Certificate in Legislative Studies from Georgetown University.

Tucker served for 20 years in the U.S. Marine Corps, both on active duty and in the reserves, retiring as a lieutenant colonel. His military service included deployments in Operation Desert Shield/Desert Storm, Operation Iraqi Freedom, and Operation Enduring Freedom in Afghanistan. During his service, he was awarded several honors, including the Meritorious Service Medal and the Navy Commendation Medal with Combat Distinguishing Device.

Following his military career, Tucker transitioned to public service, where he held significant roles in veterans' affairs and national security. He served as the Chief of Staff for the Department of Veterans Affairs from April 2020 to January 2021 and as Assistant Secretary for Congressional and Legislative Affairs from August 2017 to January 2021. In these roles, he was instrumental in managing legislative affairs and developing policies to support veterans. Tucker's government service also included advising on defense and veterans policy as a senior policy adviser to U.S. Senator Richard Burr and serving on Donald Trump's presidential transition team.

Before his civil service, Tucker worked in the private sector as a client advisor in private wealth management at Deutsche Bank and Merrill Lynch for over a decade.

In 2023, Tucker authored a chapter on the Department of Veterans Affairs for the Heritage Foundation's *Mandate for Leadership*

Thomas F. Gilman

Thomas F. Gilman is an American executive and former government official known for his extensive career in both the private and public sectors. He served as the Chief Financial Officer and Assistant Secretary for Administration at the U.S. Department of Commerce during the Trump administration, a position to which he was nominated by President Donald Trump and confirmed by the Senate in January 2019. In this dual role, Gilman was responsible for overseeing financial management and administrative functions for the department's multi-billion-dollar budget and approximately 47,000 employees. Before his government service, Gilman had a distinguished 40-year career in the global automotive industry. He spent 22 years at Chrysler Corporation, including five years as CFO of Chrysler Financial, where he played a key role in the Daimler-Benz/Chrysler Corporation merger in 1998. Following the merger, he joined Asbury Automotive Group and oversaw its Initial Public Offering on the NYSE in 2002. Later, as a Senior Advisor at Cerberus Capital Management, he was involved in significant acquisitions in the automotive finance industry, including GMAC and Chrysler Financial. Gilman also served as Chairman and CEO of Chrysler Financial, successfully navigating it through the TARP government program and repaying its $1.5 billion obligation to the Treasury Department with interest. In 2011, Gilman helped manage the sale of Chrysler Financial to TD Bank Group, where he established TD Auto Finance and served as its President and CEO. He founded Automotive Capital Services in 2014, which financed automotive dealership inventories and was sold in 2018. Gilman authored a chapter on the Department of Commerce. His recommendations include consolidating or eliminating various bureaus and programs within the department, advocating for more political leadership, particularly at the Census Bureau, and proposing the dismantling or privatization of agencies like the National Oceanographic and Atmospheric Administration (NOAA). Gilman is multilingual, speaking four languages, and has lived and conducted business in multiple countries, including the U.S., Canada, Mexico, Brazil, and the U.S. Virgin Islands. He holds a Bachelor of Science degree in Finance from Villanova University.

William L. Walton

William L. Walton is an American executive with a diverse career spanning private equity, film production, and policy advisory roles. He is the founder and chairman of Rappahannock Ventures LLC, a private equity firm, and Rush River Entertainment, a film production company known for films such as *The Price of Desire* (2015) and *Max Rose* (2013). Walton also hosts the webcast *On Common Ground with Bill Walton*, which focuses on entrepreneurship and innovation. In the financial sector, Walton served as the chairman and CEO of Allied Capital Corporation, a position he held for 12 years. Under his leadership, the company grew significantly, managing assets that increased from $600 million to $9 billion. Walton's career in finance also includes roles at Butler Capital Corporation, Lehman Brothers Kuhn Loeb, and Continental Illinois Bank. He was also the personal investment advisor to William S. Paley, the founder of CBS. Walton has been actively involved in public policy and cultural institutions. He served as vice president of the Council for National Policy and is a board member of the Media Research Center. Additionally, he is a senior fellow at the Discovery Institute's Center on Wealth, Poverty, and Morality. Walton has held leadership roles in various arts organizations, including the National Symphony Orchestra and the National Gallery of Art.His involvement in politics includes serving on Donald Trump's presidential transition team, where he led the Agency Action and Landing Teams for federal economic agencies such as the Treasury, IRS, and SEC. Walton's educational background includes a Bachelor of Science degree from Indiana University, where he also earned his MBA. He served in the U.S. Army at the Pentagon and is a life member of MENSA and the NRA.

Stephen Moore

Stephen Moore is a prominent American economist, writer, and conservative commentator known for his influential role in shaping economic policy and his association with various right-wing organizations. Born on February 16, 1960, Moore has been a significant figure in economic discussions, particularly those related to taxation, monetary policy, and government regulation.

Moore graduated from the University of Illinois and earned a Master of Arts in Economics from George Mason University. His early career included serving as a senior economist at the Joint Economic Committee under former Chairman Dick Armey, where he advised on budget, tax, and competitiveness issues. He was also involved in President Reagan's commission on Privatization as a research director.

Moore founded the Club for Growth in 1999, serving as its president until 2004. The organization became one of the most influential political groups in the U.S., dedicated to electing candidates who support free-market policies. From 2005 to 2014, Moore was the senior economics writer for the *Wall Street Journal* editorial page and a member of its editorial board. He remains a regular contributor to the publication. Moore has also been associated with several think tanks and advocacy groups. He is a senior fellow at the Heritage Foundation and an economist at FreedomWorks. Additionally, he co-founded the Committee to Unleash Prosperity in 2015, alongside notable figures like Steve Forbes and Larry Kudlow.

Stephen Moore served as a senior economic advisor to Donald Trump's 2016 presidential campaign, helping to draft tax, budget, and energy policy plans. He was also a member of President Trump's COVID-19 Economic Recovery Task Force in 2020. In 2019, Moore was nominated by Trump for a seat on the Federal Reserve Board, but he withdrew from consideration amid controversy over past remarks and questions about his qualifications.

Moore has authored several books, including *Trumponomics: Inside the America First Plan to Revive our Economy*, co-authored with Arthur Laffer. His writings often advocate for free markets, tax cuts, and limited government intervention. Moore has been a vocal critic of the Federal Reserve, advocating for a return to the gold standard and criticizing the Fed's monetary policies. He has also expressed controversial views on climate change, describing it as a "scam" and opposing the consideration of climate impacts in economic decision-making. Moore's stance on social security includes advocating for privatization and the introduction of mandatory 401k accounts.

Moore's career has been marked by several controversies, including his withdrawal from the Federal Reserve nomination due to past sexist remarks and criticism of his economic expertise.

David R. Burton

David R. Burton is a distinguished American economist and policy expert, currently serving as a Senior Fellow in Economic Policy at The Heritage Foundation. His work primarily focuses on securities regulation, tax policy, entrepreneurship, business law, financial privacy, and regulatory and administrative law issues.
Burton was born at the Patuxent River Naval Air Station in St. Mary's County, Maryland, and grew up in Baltimore. He pursued higher education at the University of Chicago, where he earned a Bachelor of Arts degree in Economics. He later obtained a Juris Doctor degree from the University of Maryland School of Law.

Before joining The Heritage Foundation in October 2013, he served as General Counsel at the National Small Business Association from 2011 to 2013, where he focused on labor, employment, immigration, health care, and securities regulation issues. Prior to this, he was the Chief Financial Officer and General Counsel of the Alliance for Retirement Prosperity, a conservative alternative to AARP. Burton spent 15 years as a partner at the Argus Group, a law, public policy, and government relations firm. His career also includes a role as Vice President for Finance and General Counsel at New England Machinery, a multinational manufacturer of packaging equipment and testing instruments. Additionally, he managed the U.S. Chamber of Commerce's Tax Policy Center, where he worked on tax policy issues.

As a Senior Fellow at The Heritage Foundation, Burton has been actively involved in policy research and advocacy. He has authored chapters on the Department of the Treasury and the Securities and Exchange Commission (SEC) for the *Mandate for Leadership*. His work often critiques regulatory bodies like the SEC, advocating for significant reforms to reduce costs and improve transparency and accountability. Burton is known for his critical stance on corporate social responsibility and environmental, social, and governance (ESG) criteria, arguing against government policies that encourage these practices. He has expressed skepticism about government interventions related to climate change, emphasizing a free-market approach to economic policy.

Veronique de Rugy

Veronique de Rugy is an economist and policy scholar known for her work on economic freedom, taxation, and fiscal policy. She holds the George Gibbs Chair in Political Economy and is a Senior Research Fellow at the Mercatus Center at George Mason University. Her research interests include the U.S. economy, federal budget, taxation, tax competition, and financial privacy issues. De Rugy is a nationally syndicated columnist and regularly contributes to *Reason* magazine and *National Review Online*. Her commentary often addresses economic issues such as sustainable economic growth and the implications of government tax and fiscal policies. She has been featured in media outlets including Bloomberg Television, CNN, and Fox News, and has testified before Congress on fiscal policy, trade, and regulation. Before her tenure at the Mercatus Center, de Rugy was a resident fellow at the American Enterprise Institute, a policy analyst at the Cato Institute, and a research fellow at the Atlas Economic Research Foundation. She earned her Master's degree from Paris Dauphine University and her Ph.D. in economics from the University of Paris-Sorbonne. De Rugy is known for her critical stance on government intervention in the economy, advocating for limited government and free-market principles. She has voiced concerns about expanding government roles in areas such as paid family leave and childcare subsidies, arguing that these interventions can have unintended negative consequences. In 2015, Politico Magazine named her one of the top 50 thinkers transforming American politics.

Jennifer Hazelton

Jennifer Hazelton is a communications professional with extensive experience in both public and private sectors, particularly in strategic communications and media relations. She is currently serving as the Deputy Assistant Administrator of Public Affairs at the United States Agency for International Development (USAID). In this role, she manages strategic communications, external engagement, intergovernmental affairs, and social media efforts for the agency. Hazelton joined USAID in February 2020, bringing with her over 15 years of experience in strategy, communications, policy formulation, media, and marketing. Before her tenure at USAID, Hazelton served as the Senior Vice President of Communications and Marketing at the Export-Import Bank of the United States. Her career also includes significant roles in political communications, notably as the Communications Director for the Trump-Pence campaign in Georgia. Hazelton has a background in journalism, having worked as an award-winning television journalist, producer, and manager at CNN and Fox News Channel. In addition to her communications roles, Hazelton founded and managed her own media consulting company, where she specialized in media strategy, crisis communications, and political communications. Hazelton holds a Master's Degree in Business Administration from Emory University and graduated Phi Beta Kappa from the Honors Program at the University of Georgia with a Bachelor's degree in political science.

Paul Winfree

Paul Winfree is a prominent economist and policy advisor whose career has been marked by significant influence in public finance and economic policy, though not without controversy. As President and CEO of the Economic Policy Innovation Center (EPIC) and a Research Affiliate at the Queen's University Centre for Economic History, Winfree has positioned himself at the intersection of academic research and policy innovation. His educational background includes a Bachelor of Science in Economics from George Mason University and advanced degrees from the London School of Economics and Queen's University Belfast. Winfree's tenure at The Heritage Foundation, a conservative think tank, saw him as a leading voice on budget and appropriations policy. Critics have noted that his work often aligns with conservative economic principles, advocating for reduced government spending and deregulation, which some argue can disproportionately impact vulnerable populations. During the Trump administration, Winfree served as Deputy Assistant to the President for Domestic Policy and Deputy Director of the Domestic Policy Council. His role in developing Executive Order 13781, aimed at reorganizing the executive branch, drew criticism for what some viewed as an attempt to weaken federal agencies and reduce their capacity to enforce regulations. His involvement in welfare reform initiatives was similarly contentious, with opponents arguing that the proposed changes would reduce support for low-income Americans. Winfree's leadership of the Fulbright Foreign Scholarship Board was generally well-regarded, though some questioned the focus on establishing partnerships that critics felt prioritized economic outcomes over cultural and educational exchange. His book, *The History (and Future) of the Budget Process in the United States: Budget by Fire*, has been noted for its detailed analysis, but some reviewers have pointed out that it reflects a particular ideological perspective that may not fully account for the complexities of fiscal policy and governance.

Karen Kerrigan

Karen Kerrigan is currently serving as the President and CEO of the Small Business & Entrepreneurship Council.

Kerrigan has been a significant voice in advocating for small businesses, regularly testifying before Congress and serving on numerous federal advisory boards. Her work is characterized by a focus on reducing regulatory burdens and promoting free-market policies. She has been involved in shaping policies that aim to streamline government processes and reduce what she perceives as inefficiencies within federal agencies, particularly the Small Business Administration (SBA).

Her contributions to *The Mandate for Leadership*, a publication associated with Project 2025, highlight her belief in restructuring and reforming the SBA to eliminate waste, fraud, and mismanagement. She cites reports from the Government Accountability Office (GAO) and the Office of the Inspector General as evidence of the need for reform, advocating for a more efficient and accountable SBA. Karen Kerrigan has also been a vocal advocate for market-based healthcare solutions and has consistently opposed the Affordable Care Act (ACA). In a 2017 testimony before the House Small Business Committee, she stated, "The ACA has made health insurance more expensive and less flexible for small business owners and their employees."

Peter Navarro

Peter Navarro is an American economist and former government official known for his controversial role in shaping trade policy during the Trump administration.

EARLY LIFE AND EDUCATION
Born on July 15, 1949, in Cambridge, Massachusetts, Navarro pursued higher education at Tufts University, where he earned a Bachelor of Arts degree. He later obtained a Master of Public Administration and a Ph.D. in Economics from Harvard University. Navarro's career in academia includes over two decades as a professor of economics and public policy at the University of California, Irvine. He has authored numerous books on economics and trade, including *Death by China* and *The Coming China Wars*, which reflect his critical views on China's economic practices.

ROLE IN THE TRUMP ADMINISTRATION
In December 2016, President Donald Trump appointed Navarro as the head of the newly established National Trade Council, and later as Director of the Office of Trade and Manufacturing Policy. Navarro's influence in the administration was significant, as he was a key architect of Trump's trade policies, particularly the imposition of tariffs on Chinese goods and the renegotiation of trade agreements like NAFTA. His protectionist stance and advocacy for tariffs were often at odds with mainstream economic thought, drawing criticism from many economists who warned of potential negative impacts on the U.S. economy, such as increased inflation and job losses. Navarro's tenure in the Trump administration was marked by his strong opposition to multilateral trade agreements and his efforts to reduce U.S. trade deficits. He was a vocal critic of countries like China and Germany, accusing them of currency manipulation and unfair trade practices. Despite his controversial views, Navarro's policies aligned closely with Trump's economic nationalism, leading to significant shifts in U.S. trade policy.

CONVICTION AND SENTENCE
Following the 2020 presidential election, Navarro was convicted on two counts of contempt of Congress for defying subpoenas issued by the House Select Committee investigating the January 6, 2021, U.S. Capitol attack. These subpoenas sought documents and testimony related to his involvement in efforts to overturn the 2020 presidential election results. Navarro refused to comply, citing executive privilege, a defense the courts rejected due to insufficient evidence that former President Trump had formally asserted this privilege on his behalf. He was sentenced to four months in prison and fined $9,500. Despite his appeals, he served his sentence from March to July 2024.

Kent Lassman

Kent Lassman assumed the role of president and CEO at the Competitive Enterprise Institute (CEI) in April 2016, succeeding the organization's founder, Fred Smith. CEI, a libertarian think tank based in Washington, D.C., has been at the forefront of advocating for free-market principles and limited government under Lassman's leadership.

Lassman holds a B.A. from Pepperdine University and an M.A. in government from Johns Hopkins University. He also completed executive education programs at both Georgetown University and Dartmouth College.

Prior to his tenure at CEI, Lassman served as vice president at a public affairs firm, where he advised Fortune 500 companies and small businesses on energy, technology, and environmental issues.

Under Lassman's guidance, CEI has maintained its position as a vocal critic of government regulation, particularly in areas such as environmental policy, labor law, and financial regulation. The organization has been a prominent opponent of climate change mitigation efforts, often challenging the scientific consensus on human-caused global

warming. This stance has positioned CEI as a key player in debates over environmental policy and regulatory approaches.

Lassman is a staunch advocate for what he terms "economic freedom." In a 2021 op-ed for The Hill, he wrote, "Economic freedom is the ability of individuals to make their own economic decisions free from government or crony capitalist interference." This philosophy underpins much of CEI's work and advocacy efforts. During the Trump administration, CEI's deregulatory agenda found a more receptive audience in Washington. The organization's "Agenda for Congress" has frequently aligned with Republican policy priorities, advocating for reduced environmental regulations, restrictions on union activities, and scaling back financial oversight.

Robert Bowes

Robert Benedict Bowes has a background in finance and risk management. His early career included roles in the private sector, such as Vice President at Chase Manhattan Bank and Director of Counterparty Risk at Fannie Mae.

In 2017, Bowes transitioned to public service when he was appointed to a senior position at the Department of Housing and Urban Development (HUD). According to a White House announcement, at HUD he led "efforts that helped [Federal Housing Administration] borrowers and restored capital adequacy to protect US taxpayers." Bowes later served as a senior adviser at the Office of Personnel Management, addressing health and insurance issues. In August 2020, he was nominated by President Trump to serve on the Commodity Futures Trading Commission (CFTC). He was not confirmed by Senate.

Brendan Carr

Brendan Carr serves as a Commissioner at the Federal Communications Commission (FCC), a position he has held since 2017. His career in telecommunications policy spans nearly two decades, encompassing both private and public sector experience.

Carr's legal career began after graduating from Catholic University's Columbus School of Law. He clerked for Judge Dennis W. Shedd on the U.S. Court of Appeals for the Fourth Circuit before joining the law firm Wiley Rein LLP. At Wiley Rein, Carr worked on appellate and telecommunications matters for clients including AT&T, Verizon, CenturyLink, CTIA (the wireless association), and USTA (the telecom association).

In 2012, Carr transitioned to the FCC as an attorney advisor, eventually rising to become the agency's General Counsel prior to his appointment as Commissioner. He was initially nominated to the FCC by President Trump in 2017 and has since been reconfirmed under both the Trump and Biden administrations.

Throughout his tenure, Carr has positioned himself as an advocate for deregulation and free market approaches to telecommunications policy. He has been particularly vocal on issues such as 5G deployment, pushing for streamlined regulations to accelerate network buildout. Carr has also been a proponent of reforming Section 230 of the Communications Decency Act, which provides liability protections for online platforms.

Carr's involvement with Project 2025, a conservative policy blueprint for a potential Republican administration, has sparked controversy. He authored a chapter on FCC policy for the project, leading to calls from Democratic lawmakers for an ethics investigation.

Hans A. von Spakovsky

Hans A. von Spakovsky has emerged as a controversial figure in the realm of election law and voting rights, with a career spanning government service, think tanks, and conservative activism.

EARLY LIFE AND EDUCATION
Born to parents who fled Nazi Germany and the Soviet Union, von Spakovsky's background has often been cited as influencing his political views.

Von Spakovsky received his B.S. from the Massachusetts Institute of Technology in 1981 and his J.D. from Vanderbilt University Law School in 1984. He began his legal career in private practice before transitioning to government work.

POLITICAL CAREER
From 2001 to 2005, von Spakovsky served in the Civil Rights Division of the U.S. Department of Justice, specializing in voting rights. His tenure was marked by controversy, with critics accusing him of using his position to suppress minority voting rights. Jon Greenbaum, who served as a trial attorney in the voting section at the time, stated, "He was technically in a career position, but in practical terms, he was playing a very political role."

In 2006, von Spakovsky was appointed to the Federal Election Commission by President George W. Bush in a recess appointment. His nomination faced significant opposition from Senate Democrats and civil rights groups, leading him to withdraw from consideration for a full term in 2008.

Following his government service, von Spakovsky joined The Heritage Foundation, where he currently serves as a Senior Legal Fellow and manager of the Election Law Reform Initiative. In this role, he has been a vocal advocate for stricter voter ID laws and has frequently claimed widespread voter fraud, despite limited evidence to support such assertions.

Von Spakovsky's statements on voter fraud have been particularly controversial. In a May 2023 U.S. House hearing, he claimed, "We know that aliens are registering and actually voting, and it's important to understand that every vote by an alien voids the vote of a citizen." This claim has been disputed by numerous election experts and studies.

ROLE IN THE TRUMP ADMINISTRATION
His involvement in the Trump administration's Presidential Advisory Commission on Election Integrity in 2017 further cemented his reputation as a leading figure in conservative election policy. The commission was dissolved after facing numerous lawsuits and criticism for seeking sensitive voter data.

He co-wrote the book "Who's Counting?: How Fraudsters and Bureaucrats Put Your Vote at Risk" with John Fund. The book argues for the prevalence of voter fraud, a stance that has been criticized by many election experts.

Von Spakovsky has contributed to the sections on election administration of *Mandate for Leadership*. His recommendations include stricter voter ID requirements and limitations on mail-in voting, policies that critics argue could disproportionately affect minority voters.

Adam Candeub

Adam Candeub is a law professor and telecommunications policy expert who has moved between academia, government, and the private sector throughout his career.

EARLY LIFE AND EDUCATION
He received his B.A. from Yale University and J.D. from the University of Pennsylvania Law School, where he served as an articles editor for the University of Pennsylvania Law Review.After clerking for Chief Judge J. Clifford Wallace of the U.S. Court of Appeals for the Ninth Circuit, Candeub worked as a litigation associate at Jones Day and a corporate associate at Cleary Gottlieb. In 2004, he joined the faculty of Michigan State University College of Law, where he is currently a Professor of Law and Director of the Intellectual Property, Information & Communications Law Program.

GOVERNMENT SERVICE
Candeub has held positions in government, including as an attorney-adviser for the Federal Communications Commission (FCC). In 2020, he was appointed Deputy Assistant Secretary of Commerce for Communications and Information at the National Telecommunications and Information Administration (NTIA) during the Trump administration.His tenure in the Trump administration was marked by controversy. Candeub played a central role in crafting an executive order targeting social media companies over allegations of anti-conservative bias. He was also involved in efforts to reinterpret Section 230 of the Communications Decency Act, a key law protecting online platforms from liability for user-generated content.

CONTROVERSIES
Candeub has made several controversial statements regarding internet regulation and free speech. In a 2020 interview with Reason magazine, he stated, "I think platforms should have no say whatsoever in content moderation," a position that many experts view as extreme and potentially harmful to online discourse. Prior to his government service, Candeub represented white nationalist Jared Taylor in a lawsuit against Twitter for removing him from the platform. The lawsuit was ultimately unsuccessful, with courts affirming Twitter's right to moderate content under Section 230.

His academic work has also been a source of controversy. Candeub's writings on race and intelligence, which argue for the consideration of "group differences in cognitive ability" in affirmative action discussions, have drawn justified criticism for flirting with widely discredited theories of scientific racism, though Candeub continues to defend his work as legitimate academic inquiry.

Edwin J. Feulner

Edwin J. Feulner is a conservative political operative and co-founder of the Heritage Foundation who has played a key role in shaping right-wing policy and institutions in the United States over the past five decades.

EARLY LIFE AND EDUCATION
Born on August 12, 1941 in Chicago, Feulner received his B.A. from Regis University, an MBA from the University of Pennsylvania's Wharton School, and a PhD from the University of Edinburgh. His doctoral thesis focused on the Republican Study Committee, a group of conservative Republicans in the U.S. House.

RISE IN CONSERVATIVE POLITICS
Feulner's career exemplifies the revolving door between conservative think tanks, Republican politics, and government service. He began as an analyst for the Center for Strategic and International Studies before becoming a congressional aide to Republicans Melvin Laird and Phil Crane in the 1960s-70s. In 1973, he co-founded The Heritage Foundation, becoming its president in 1977 and serving in that role until 2013 and again briefly in 2017-18.

Under Feulner's leadership, The Heritage Foundation grew from a small policy shop into one of the most influential conservative think tanks in the U.S. He pioneered aggressive marketing of policy papers to lawmakers and media, aiming to shape legislation and public opinion. As he wrote, Heritage set out "to make conservative ideas not just respectable but mainstream. To set the terms of national policy debate."
Feulner has served as a consultant to President Reagan and chaired government commissions under Republican administrations. He has held leadership positions in conservative organizations like the Mont Pelerin Society and the Council for National Policy. In 1989, he received the Presidential Citizens Medal from President Reagan.

Throughout his career, Feulner has authored books promoting conservative policies and writes a syndicated column. He has been recognized by conservative media as one of the most influential conservatives in America. He remains involved with Project 2025, Heritage's initiative to prepare policy recommendations for a potential Republican administration.

Feulner's impact on conservative politics has been widely acknowledged. As Heritage Board Chairman Thomas A. Saunders stated, "Ed Feulner has made Heritage not just a permanent institution on Capitol Hill, but the flagship organization of the entire conservative movement."

PROJECT 2025 EXPLAINED CHAPTER BY CHAPTER

The forthcoming chapters provide a comprehensive and detailed summary of *Mandate for Leadership*, meticulously outlining its key themes, strategies, and policy recommendations. It is important to note that these summaries are intended to convey the content of the document accurately and objectively, without endorsing or critiquing the perspectives of the original authors.

At the beginning of the chapter, you'll find the salient points of the proposed policies and a clear-eyed analysis of the consequences of these policies should they be implemented.

Additionally, the chapters titled "Analysis" at the end of each section offer a thorough examination of the document's foundational principles and the most contentious policies proposed.

These analyses delve into the broader implications of these policies, exploring their potential impact on governance, society, and the political landscape.

By dissecting these core pillars, the "Analysis" chapters aim to provide readers with a nuanced understanding of both the motivations behind the proposals and the debates they are likely to provoke.

FOREWORD: A PROMISE TO AMERICA

"The legacy of Mandate for Leadership, and indeed of the entire Reagan Revolution, is that if conservatives want to save the country, we need a bold and courageous plan. This book is the first step in that plan."
– PAGE 2

Summary

The foreword of a *Mandate for Leadership* titled "*A Promise to America*" and written by Kevin D. Roberts clearly lays out the conservative vision for the United States and outlines four key promises that the next conservative president should make to the American people. The author draws parallels between the current political climate and the late 1970s, suggesting that America and the conservative movement are facing similar challenges of division and danger.

The author begins by comparing the current political situation to the late 1970s, highlighting similarities such as betrayal by the Washington establishment, internal division, and external threats. He argues that despite these challenges, the late 1970s proved to be a turning point for the political Right, leading to significant victories. The author introduces The Heritage Foundation's role in this transformation through the Mandate for Leadership project, which provided a comprehensive conservative policy handbook for the Reagan administration.

Roberts contends that the current political establishment and cultural elite have once again driven America towards decline. However, he expresses confidence that conservatives can address these challenges, drawing inspiration from past successes. The author emphasizes the importance of fighting for and defending freedom, quoting Ronald Reagan to underscore this point. He introduces the current volume, "The Conservative Promise," as part of the 2025 Presidential Transition Project, which aims to provide a comprehensive conservative agenda for the next administration.

The author outlines four broad fronts that will decide America's future: restoring the family as the centerpiece of American life and protecting children; dismantling the administrative state and returning self-governance to the American people; defending the nation's sovereignty, borders, and bounty against global threats; and securing God-given individual rights to live freely. Roberts argues that these promises cut through superficial distractions and focus on the moral and foundational challenges America faces. He draws parallels to Reagan's approach of addressing core issues rather than their manifestations.

The first promise focuses on restoring the family as the centerpiece of American life. The author argues that the American family is in crisis, citing high rates of children born to unmarried mothers and the negative consequences of fatherlessness. He contends that government programs cannot replace the role of family and calls for policies that prioritize family formation and cohesion.

Roberts advocates for protecting children from what he describes as harmful ideologies and practices. He calls for removing terms related to gender identity and diversity from federal regulations, outlawing pornography, and protecting parental rights in education. The author argues for universal school choice and the removal of critical race theory and gender ideology from school curricula.

The second promise involves dismantling the administrative state and returning self-governance to the American people. The author criticizes the current federal budgeting process and the growth of the administrative state, arguing that these developments have eroded constitutional accountability and democratic control. He calls for a return to constitutional principles and proposes measures to reduce the size and scope of the federal government.

The third promise focuses on defending national sovereignty, borders, and resources against global threats. Roberts critiques progressive elites' support for supranational organizations and open borders policies. He argues that these policies undermine American sovereignty and harm working-class Americans. The author also criticizes environmental extremism and economic globalization, particularly engagement with China, which he views as detrimental to American interests.

The author discusses the challenges posed by big tech companies and their relationship with China. He argues for a more assertive approach to defending American interests, including ending economic engagement with China, restoring the manufacturing base, and pursuing energy dominance. Roberts contends that these actions would strengthen America's global position and counter Chinese ambitions.

The fourth promise centers on securing individual rights to enjoy "the Blessings of Liberty." The author interprets the pursuit of happiness as the pursuit of a good life, primarily found in family, work, religious devotion, and community involvement. He argues that the American Republic was founded on principles prioritizing individual rights to live their best life, which he claims the ruling class disdains.

Roberts advocates for championing free enterprise against socialism, arguing that socialist promises of equal outcomes have never been realized. He provides examples of failed socialist experiments and contrasts them with the success of free-market economies. The author calls for pro-growth economic policies, including tax and regulatory reform, antitrust enforcement, and educational opportunities outside the traditional system.

In conclusion, Roberts frames the conservative agenda as a fight against elite rule and woke culture warriors. He emphasizes the urgency of uniting the conservative movement and the American people, warning that failure to do so could result in the loss of American ideals. The author presents the Conservative Promise as the best effort of the conservative movement and the next conservative President's last opportunity to save the republic.

SECTION 1: TAKING THE REINS OF GOVERNMENT

"When it comes to ensuring that freedom can flourish, nothing is more important than deconstructing the centralized administrative state. Political appointees who are answerable to the President and have decision-making authority in the executive branch are key to this essential task. The next Administration must not cede such authority to non-partisan "experts," who pursue their own ends while engaging in groupthink, insulated from American voters." – PAGE 21

The following summary conveys the content of the document accurately and objectively, without endorsing or critiquing the perspectives of the original authors.

Summary

The chapter begins by contrasting America's Bicentennial celebration in 1976 with the approaching 250th anniversary. It portrays contemporary America as divided between "woke revolutionaries" who view the country as systemically racist and in need of transformation, and those who believe in traditional American ideals and principles. The author positions conservatives as "Americanists" in this ideological battle for America's future.

Invoking Abraham Lincoln's warning about internal threats to America, the text lists various contemporary left-wing policies and cultural shifts viewed as problematic. These include pandemic-related mandates, environmental policies, educational issues, and social debates. The author asserts that the next Administration must actively defend traditional American values, families, and culture.

The chapter introduces a quote from Russ Vought, former director of the Office of Management and Budget, emphasizing the conservative president's role in controlling the executive branch on behalf of the American people. It highlights the constitutional basis for presidential power, citing Article II of the Constitution, and argues that the President's agenda should drive departmental and agency actions.

Addressing the challenge posed by the federal bureaucracy, the text describes it as ideologically misaligned with the American people, presenting this as a threat to republican government. It references Byzantine personnel rules as a means of bureaucratic self-protection and obstruction of the President's agenda.

The author criticizes the federal civilian workforce as underworked, overcompensated, and unaccountable. Federal hiring practices are specifically targeted, with examples of preferential treatment for applicants with various health conditions or personal issues. The text argues for reform of these practices to benefit taxpayers rather than federal employees.

The importance of political appointees is stressed, with the author noting that the Trump administration appointed fewer such appointees in its early months compared to recent presidencies. This is presented as problematic, leaving career employees in charge in many areas. Issues with the Office of Management and Budget being dominated by career employees who often try to overrule political appointees are also mentioned.

The text emphasizes the paramount importance of commitment to the Constitution and rule of law, particularly for a conservative administration. It argues against unilateral executive actions, insisting that legislatures, not executives, should make laws in a republic. The role of the White House Counsel in protecting presidential powers and privileges is highlighted.

Invoking James Madison's concept of "double security" to liberties, the author discusses the separation of powers among federal branches and between federal and state governments. The text argues that this security has been compromised over time, with the modern executive branch often writing, enforcing, and adjudicating policy. This situation is described as "constitutionally dire" and "in urgent need of repair."

The chapter concludes by asserting the critical importance of deconstructing the centralized administrative state. It emphasizes the role of political appointees answerable to the President in achieving this goal, arguing against ceding authority to non-partisan "experts" insulated from voter influence. The author frames this as essential for ensuring responsive governance and faithfully executing laws in accordance with the will of the American people.

CHAPTER 1: WHITE HOUSE OFFICE

"The decisions that assistants and senior advisers make will directly impact the Administration, its legacy, and—most important—the fate of the country. Their agenda must therefore be the President's agenda." – PAGE 24

"The Office of White House Counsel is the first line of defense for the EOP. Its staff must take seriously the duty to protect the powers and privileges of the President from encroachments by Congress, the judiciary, and the administrative components of departments and agencies." – PAGE 27

Key Policy Proposals

1. Ensure the White House Counsel's office acts as an "activist yet ethical plaintiffs' firm that advocates for its client-the Administration's agenda-within the limits imposed by the Constitution."
2. Re-examine the policy requiring all contact between the White House and DOJ to occur only between the White House Counsel and Attorney General/Deputy AG.
3. Fill political appointments with "dedicated conservatives" to support the Administration's agenda. Develop plans to increase political appointments, such as Schedule F.
4. Use the Office of Public Liaison as the "chief White House enforcer and gatekeeper" among interest groups, giving it permission to use both "carrots" and "sticks."
5. Limit detailees on the National Security Council staff to ensure more direct presidential control.

WHAT WOULD THIS MEAN?

The policy changes proposed in this document would significantly increase the power of the presidency and allow a conservative administration to more forcefully push its agenda with fewer checks and balances:

- Having the White House Counsel's office act as an activist firm advocating for the president's agenda, rather than providing objective legal advice, undermines the rule of law. It could lead to the president taking actions that push or exceed constitutional limits.

- Allowing broader contact between the White House and DOJ beyond just the very top officials erodes DOJ independence. It enables the White House to improperly influence investigations and prosecutions.

- Stacking the executive branch with political appointees dedicated to the president's agenda, and expanding political appointments through vehicles like Schedule F, injects more partisanship into agencies that should be apolitical. It undermines the civil service and degrades the government's ability to implement policies objectively based on facts and expertise.

- Using the Office of Public Liaison as an "enforcer" among interest groups by rewarding allies and punishing opponents is an abuse of power. The White House should not use access and favors to try to control external organizations.

- Limiting detailees on the NSC staff concentrates more foreign policy power in the White House while reducing valuable input from experts across government. It risks foreign policy being driven by political concerns rather than the national interest.

While framed as ways to more effectively implement the president's agenda, many of these proposals would dangerously aggrandize the presidency, undermine governing institutions, and erode democracy. From a liberal perspective, they represent an authoritarian model of governance that is antithetical to American values of checks and balances, rule of law, and apolitical civil service. The proposals would enable a conservative administration to push its ideology without restraint.

Summary

The first chapter of *Mandate for Leadership* was written by Rick Dearborn. The following summary conveys the content of the document accurately and objectively, without endorsing or critiquing the perspectives of the original authors.

WHITE HOUSE OFFICE

Dearborn opens by emphasizing the American presidency's prominent role in national culture and academia, noting its frequent portrayal in movies, television, books, and academic studies. However, it stresses that "there is no substitute for firsthand experience," which this manual aims to provide through compiled experiences of presidential appointees.

The constitutional foundation of the presidency is then outlined. Dearborn cites Article II of the Constitution, which vests "executive Power" in the President, designates him as "Commander in Chief," and charges him to "take Care that the Laws be faithfully executed." It also notes the constitutional provision for the President to seek assistance from "the principal Officer in each of the executive Departments."

The historical development of the White House Office (WHO) is traced from George Washington's administration to the present. Dearborn highlights that every President has been supported by some form of White House office, consisting of direct staff officers and a Cabinet of department and agency heads.

The text emphasizes the demanding nature of WHO jobs, describing them as "among the most demanding in all of government." It underscores the critical role of WHO appointees, stating that "The decisions that assistants and senior advisers make will directly impact the Administration, its legacy, and—most important—the fate of the country."

Dearborn stresses the importance of delegation in the presidency, arguing that it is not just advisable but essential due to time constraints. It states, "There simply are not enough hours in the day to manage the affairs of state single-handedly, so delegation is not just advisable: It is essential."

The significance of choosing WHO appointees is highlighted, with Dearborn noting that "The tone and tempo of an administration are often determined on January 20." This emphasizes the immediate and lasting impact of these early staffing decisions on the entire administration.

CHIEF OF STAFF

The Chief of Staff is described as "first among equals" and "the most critical to implementation of the President's vision for the country." The role's dual nature is emphasized: the chief manages both the WHO and Executive Office of the President (EOP) staffs.

The chief's primary responsibilities are detailed:
1. Establishing an organizational chart for the WHO: Dearborn stresses that this should be simple, with clear lines of authority and responsibility to avoid conflicts. It should also identify specific points of contact for each element of the government outside the White House, including White House Liaisons selected by the Office of Presidential Personnel (PPO).
2. Setting priorities based on the President's agenda: This process involves assessing campaign promises, identifying current and prospective opportunities, and delegating policy priorities among departments, agencies, and the three White House policy councils (National Economic Council, Domestic Policy Council, and National Security Council).
3. Coordinating briefings for the President: The chief ensures the President is briefed on all policy priorities by Cabinet members and senior staff.
4. Mapping out daily and weekly issues and themes: This is done in collaboration with senior WHO staff.
5. Sequencing and executing policy rollouts: The chief works with policy councils, the Cabinet, Office of Communications, and Office of Legislative Affairs to manage this process. White House Counsel and senior advisers are also involved.

Dearborn notes that most chiefs interact directly with Cabinet officers and a select number of direct reports, typically including two or three deputies, the Communications Director, PPO Director, White House Counsel, and senior advisers.

The main challenge for the Chief of Staff is identified as time management. The chief must balance the use of deputies, meetings with senior staff, direction to the WHO, and the daily needs of the President.

DEPUTY CHIEFS OF STAFF

Dearborn begins by noting that in recent years, Presidents typically appoint two Deputy Chiefs of Staff: one for Management and Operations and one for Policy. It also mentions that some administrations have used other types of deputy chiefs, such as those overseeing strategy, planning, and implementation.

The text then discusses the role of Principal Deputy Chiefs of Staff, noting that not all Chiefs of Staff use this position. It explains that when used, the principal deputy often functions as a doorkeeper, sorting through action items and deciding which require the attention of the Chief of Staff or the President. Dearborn states, "Most principal deputies have functioned as doorkeepers, sorting through action items, taking on those that can be handled at their own level, and passing up others that truly require the attention of the Chief of Staff or the President."

The responsibilities of the principal deputy may include:
1. Assuming control of scheduling functions
2. Working directly with policy councils
3. Overseeing the Office of Public Liaison (OPL) and Office of Political Affairs (OPA)

Deputy Chief of Staff for Management and Operations: This role is described in detail, with responsibilities including:
1. Overseeing the President's schedule
2. Managing all logistical aspects of the President's movement within and outside the White House
3. Interfacing with the Secret Service and military offices responsible for the President's safety
4. Working with the National Security Council, Secretary of Defense, Secretary of State, and Intelligence Community
5. Advancing all foreign trips
6. Managing all facets of the working White House, including technology, grounds management, support staff, personnel administration, and communications

Dearborn emphasizes that this deputy "needs to be meticulous and ideally should possess a great deal of command-and-control experience."

Deputy Chief of Staff for Policy: This role's responsibilities may include:
1. Overseeing functions of the Intergovernmental Affairs (IGA), Office of Political Affairs (OPA), and Office of Public Liaison (OPL)
2. Working directly with the Chief of Staff, Cabinet officers, and all three policy councils to support the development and implementation of the President's agenda

Dearborn notes that for conservatives, this arrangement "could help to connect the WHO's outreach to political and external groups and be a strong conduit for state and local elected officials, state party organizations, and both grasstop and grassroots groups."

It stresses that this deputy "should therefore have impressive policy credentials in the realms of economic, domestic, and social affairs."

The section concludes by emphasizing the importance of clearly delineating and communicating the portfolios of these deputies across the White House to ensure their effectiveness.

SENIOR ADVISERS

Dearborn begins by explaining that Presidents often surround themselves with senior advisers whose experience and interests are not easily categorized. It notes that in recent administrations, senior advisers have been appointed to offer broad guidance on political matters and communications issues, while others have acted as "czars" for specific projects or policy areas.

The text emphasizes the unique position of the most powerful senior advisers, stating: "The most powerful senior advisers frequently have had a long personal relationship with the President and often have spent a significant amount of time with him within and outside of the White House." Their role is multifaceted, providing guidance on various policy issues and offering instruction on communicating with the American people and the media.

Dearborn mentions that some administrations have created new offices or "councils" to support senior advisers. However, it notes a potential drawback: "For the most part, their functions have been duplicative or overlapping, as a result of which these offices have tended to be short-lived."

To ensure the effectiveness of senior advisers, Dearborn recommends:
1. Providing them with the staff and resources their portfolios require
2. Clearly delineating their portfolios
3. Clearly communicating these portfolios across the White House

The section concludes by stating that the responsibility for clear delineation and communication falls to the Chief of Staff.

OFFICE OF WHITE HOUSE COUNSEL

This section begins by outlining the primary responsibilities of the Office of White House Counsel, which include providing legal guidance to the President and elements of the Executive Office of the President (EOP) on:
1. Presidential powers and privileges
2. Ethics compliance
3. Review of clemency applications
4. Judicial nominations

Dearborn emphasizes the critical nature of selecting the White House Counsel, stating: "The selection of White House Counsel is one of the most important decisions an incoming President will make." It clarifies that the office's role is not to create or advance policies independently, but to guide the President and his reports on how to pursue and realize the President's agenda within legal bounds.

The text discusses the unique attorney-client relationship between the White House Counsel and the President, noting that while the Counsel doesn't serve as the President's personal attorney in non-official matters, "it is almost impossible to delineate exactly where an issue is strictly personal and has no bearing on the President's official function."

Key qualities for the White House Counsel are outlined:
1. Deep commitment to the President's agenda
2. Ability to provide proactive counsel and zealous representation
3. Capacity to build a relationship with the President based on trust, confidentiality, and candor

Dearborn details the office's responsibility for ensuring ethical compliance across the White House, including:
1. Providing ongoing training and monitoring
2. Ensuring staff consult on financial disclosures, received gifts, potential conflicts of interest, and other ethical concerns

A crucial role of the office is emphasized: "The Office of White House Counsel is the first line of defense for the EOP. Its staff must take seriously the duty to protect the powers and privileges of the President from encroachments by Congress, the judiciary, and the administrative components of departments and agencies."

The structure of the office is described, including deputies, assistants, associates, and legal support staff. Dearborn notes that assistant and associate attorneys often specialize in particular areas of law, offering guidance on issues related to national security, criminal law, environmental law, and various administrative and regulatory matters.

Dearborn emphasizes that all staff in the Office of White House Counsel should be deeply committed to the President's agenda and view their role as problem-solvers and advocates rather than obstacles. It states, "They should not erect roadblocks out of an abundance of caution; rather, they should offer practical legal advice on how to promote the President's agenda within the bounds of the law."

The text explicitly warns against using the office as a "finishing school" for future elite law firm attorneys or federal judges, stating instead that it should function "more as an activist yet ethical plaintiffs' firm that advocates for its client—the Administration's agenda—within the limits imposed by the Constitution and the duties of the legal profession."

Dearborn discusses the office's role as the primary gateway for communication between the White House and the Department of Justice (DOJ). It notes the traditional policy of limiting contact between the two institutions to the Office of White House Counsel and the Attorney General or Deputy Attorney General, but suggests that the next Administration should "reexamine this policy and determine whether it might be more efficient or more appropriate for communication to occur through additional channels."

The text outlines key responsibilities of the White House Counsel at the start of a new administration:
1. Quickly understanding all significant ongoing legal challenges across the executive branch
2. Presenting recommendations to the President on handling these challenges
3. Considering whether to reverse positions of the previous Administration in significant litigation

Dearborn stresses the need for the Office of White House Counsel to provide "measured legal guidance in a timely manner," often foregoing lengthy memos in favor of "quickly providing high-level yet incisive guidance."

Finally, the section concludes by describing the ideal White House Counsel as someone "well-versed in the Constitution, administrative and regulatory law, and the inner workings of Congress and the political process." It emphasizes that loyalty to the President and the Constitution should be prioritized over elite credentials.

STAFF SECRETARY

Dearborn begins by highlighting the low-profile but crucial nature of the Office of the Staff Secretary, comparing it to a military commander's adjutant. It states, "The office is similar to a military commander's adjutant as it is responsible for fielding and managing a vast amount of information at the top of its organization."

The Staff Secretary's role is described as a position of extreme trust, with the individual vetted to work as an "honest broker" in the President's service. Dearborn emphasizes that this office is "the last substantive control point before papers reach the Oval Office."

Key responsibilities of the Staff Secretary include:
1. Managing information flow to and from the Oval Office

2. Ensuring materials (presidential decision memos, bills from Congress, briefing books, etc.) are complete, well-ordered, and up-to-date before reaching the President
3. Playing a key role in determining who weighs in on policy matters and when
4. Directing and following up on the President's requests for additional information or revisions
5. Managing and overseeing the clearance process for the President's daily/nightly briefing book
6. Overseeing the use of the President's signature (by hand or autopen)
7. Managing the Office of the Executive Clerk, Office of Records Management, and Office of Presidential Correspondence

OFFICE OF COMMUNICATIONS

Dearborn begins by describing the primary function of the Office of Communications: to convey the President's agenda to the public through various media channels. These channels include speeches, remarks, press briefings, off-the-record discussions with reporters, and social media.

The structure of the office is outlined, noting that it operates under the Director of Communications. Dearborn mentions that depending on the President's preference, the Office of Communications may include the Office of the Press Secretary (Press Office). Regardless of the structure, the text emphasizes the importance of close collaboration between the Office of Communications, the Press Office, speechwriters, and digital strategists.

Key operational functions of the Office of Communications are listed:
1. Scheduling and running press briefings
2. Conducting interviews
3. Organizing meetings and media appearances
4. Planning speeches and other events

Dearborn stresses the importance of maintaining robust relationships with various stakeholders, including:
1. The White House Press Corps
2. The White House Correspondents' Association
3. Regional stakeholders
4. Key interest groups

An interesting point is raised regarding the physical presence of media at the White House: "No legal entitlement exists for the provision of permanent space for media on the White House campus, and the next Administration should reexamine the balance between media demands and space constraints on the White House premises."

The leadership structure within the Office of Communications is detailed:
1. Communications Director (who reports directly to the Chief of Staff)
2. Deputy Communications Director
3. Deputy Director for Strategic Communications
4. Press Secretary

Dearborn emphasizes that this leadership team must work closely together to "drive the national narrative about the White House."

The text highlights the President as the best resource for the Office of Communications, noting the importance of various presidential addresses and press conferences in conveying the White House's overall message. It also stresses the need for unified messaging across all White House offices.

The role of the speechwriting team is discussed, with Dearborn noting the unique talents required: "Speechwriting is a unique talent: The writers selected must understand policy, should have a firm grasp of history and other liberal-arts disciplines, and should be able to learn and adopt the President's style of rhetoric and mode of delivery."

The Press Secretary's role is described as the President's spokesperson, communicating to the American people through the media. Dearborn notes that individuals in this role must be "quick on their feet," able to refute and rebut correspondents' questions and comments effectively when appropriate.

The Communications Director's role is portrayed as conveying the President's mission to the American people. Dearborn emphasizes the need for political savvy and awareness of ongoing activities in other White House offices. It also suggests that "The new Administration should examine the nature of the relationship between itself and the White House Correspondents Association and consider whether an alternative coordinating body might be more suitable."

OFFICE OF LEGISLATIVE AFFAIRS (OLA)

Dearborn begins by noting that the OLA was created by President Dwight Eisenhower and has since served as the crucial liaison between the White House and Congress. It outlines the office's key responsibilities:
1. Working with congressional leaders to ensure Senate confirmation of presidential nominees (e.g., Cabinet secretaries and ambassadors)
2. Collaborating with Congress to enact reforms promised by the President during the campaign

3. Securing necessary funding through the appropriations process to fulfill the President's agenda

The reporting structure of the OLA is described: it reports directly to the Chief of Staff, sometimes under the guidance of a Deputy Chief of Staff (usually the Deputy Chief for Policy). Dearborn emphasizes that regardless of the reporting structure, "the office exercises a certain autonomy on behalf of the President and the Chief of Staff in directly influencing congressional leaders of both major political parties."

A critical function of the OLA is highlighted: "The OLA often must function as the mediator among the parties and find common ground to facilitate the successful enactment of the President's agenda."

Dearborn stresses the importance of unified messaging from the White House to congressional leaders, warning that if other White House actors maintain their own relationships with congressional leaders and staffers, "it may appear that the President's agenda is fractured and lacks consensus."

Key aspects of the OLA's work are detailed:
1. Internal involvement: OLA staffers need to be involved in policy discussions, budget reviews, and other important meetings within the White House.
2. External communication: Continuous communication with congressional offices of both parties in both the House and the Senate is crucial to ensure sufficient support for the President's legislative priorities.

Dearborn outlines the qualities required for effective OLA staffers:
1. Effective communication skills
2. Ability to provide realistic assessments to other White House staffers
3. Skill in both politics and policy
4. Capacity to advance the President's agenda while forging pathways with members of the opposing political party on other priorities

The section concludes with a strong emphasis on the need for the OLA to function as a cohesive unit: "Most important, the OLA must function as a well-oiled machine: precisely synced. The President cannot afford to have a tennis player on—much less as the leader of—his football team."

OFFICE OF PRESIDENTIAL PERSONNEL (PPO)

Dearborn begins by invoking the political axiom "personnel is policy," which gained prominence during President Ronald Reagan's 1981 transition. It emphasizes the critical importance of the PPO, which was created under President Richard Nixon to centralize political appointments.

The text explains the PPO's authority: "Departments and agencies had and still have direct legal authority on hiring and firing, but the power to fill Schedule C positions—the core of political jobs—is vested with the President. Therefore, the White House, not the department or agency, has the final word on political appointments."

The primary responsibility of the PPO is outlined: staffing the executive branch with individuals capable of implementing the President's agenda. Dearborn provides specific numbers:
1. Approximately 1,000 appointments requiring Senate confirmation
2. Approximately 3,000 political jobs that don't require Senate confirmation

Dearborn notes the importance of both high-level policy experts and entry-level appointees, stating that the latter have "brought invaluable energy and commitment to the White House and have proved to be the 'farm team' for the conservative movement."

The PPO's responsibilities are detailed:
1. Identifying potential political personnel through active recruitment and passive resume collection
2. Vetting potential political personnel through political background checks and reviewing clearance and fitness assessments
3. Making recommendations to the President and other appointment authorities
4. Identifying programmatic political workforce needs early and developing plans (e.g., Schedule F)
5. Maintaining a strong relationship with the Office of Personnel Management (OPM)
6. Training and connecting political personnel
7. Playing "bad cop" in personnel matters, including firings and hirings
8. Serving as a personnel link between conservative organizations and the executive branch

Dearborn emphasizes the scale of the PPO's work: "In most Administrations, PPO will staff more than 100 positions during a transition and thousands of noncareer positions during the President's first term." It stresses the need for the PPO Director to have direct authority and a strong relationship with the President.

OFFICE OF POLITICAL AFFAIRS (OPA)

Dearborn introduces the OPA as the primary office within the executive branch for managing the President's political interests. It notes that while the specific functions may vary between administrations, the OPA typically serves several key roles:
1. Liaison between the President and associated political entities, including:
   - National committees
   - Federal and state campaigns
   - Interest groups
2. Engagement in outreach and casework within legal guidelines
3. Assistance with the President's re-election campaign, if applicable
4. Monitoring of congressional campaigns
5. Arranging presidential visits with other political campaigns
6. Recommending campaign staff to the Office of Presidential Personnel for service in the executive branch

Dearborn emphasizes the OPA's role as a communication channel between the White House and the President's political party. It states, "This includes both relaying the President's ambitions to political interests and listening to the needs of political interests." This two-way communication allows for the exchange of information between the White House and political actors across the country.

The suggested structure for the OPA includes:
- One director of political affairs, reporting either to the Chief of Staff or to a Deputy Chief of Staff
- Various deputy directors, each responsible for a certain geographical region of the country

Dearborn stresses the wide-ranging nature of the OPA's responsibilities: "Because nearly all White House activities are in some way inherently political, the OPA needs to be aware of all presidential actions and activities—including travel, policy decisions, speeches, nominations, and responses to matters of national security—and consider how they might affect the President's image."

To fulfill this broad mandate, Dearborn recommends that the OPA have a designated staffer who communicates not only with other White House offices but also with the Cabinet and executive branch agencies. This ensures that the OPA remains informed about all aspects of the administration's activities and can consider their political implications.

OFFICE OF CABINET AFFAIRS (OCA)

Dearborn begins by acknowledging that the OCA's role has evolved over various administrations, but its primary function remains consistent: to ensure coordination of policy and communication between the White House and the Cabinet.

Key responsibilities of the OCA are outlined:
1. Coordinating all Cabinet meetings with the President
2. Organizing and administering regular meetings of the Deputy Secretaries, noting their vital roles in departments and agencies and their potential to become acting secretaries

Dearborn recommends a structure for the OCA:
- One Cabinet Secretary who reports to the Chief of Staff's office, either directly or through a deputy chief
- Deputies and special assistants who work with each department's principal, Deputy Secretary, Under Secretaries, Assistant Secretaries, and other senior staff

The text emphasizes that the Cabinet Secretary maintains a direct relationship with all members of the Cabinet.

The OCA's role in policy promotion is highlighted: "The OCA coordinates with the Chief of Staff's office and the Office of Communications to promote the President's agenda through the Cabinet departments and agencies." The importance of Cabinet communications staffers in this operation is noted.

Dearborn discusses the OCA's evolving role in tracking the President's agenda: "In prior Administrations, the OCA has played a vital role by tracking the President's agenda for the Chief of Staff, Deputy Chiefs, and senior advisers. It has worked with each department and agency to advance policy priorities." The text suggests that amplifying this function in the future would benefit both the President and the conservative movement.

An important responsibility of the OCA is managing potential issues involving Cabinet members: "From time to time throughout an Administration, travel optics, ethics challenges, and Hatch Act issues involving Cabinet members, deputies, and senior staffers can arise. The OCA is normally tasked with keeping the WHO informed of such developments and providing support if and when necessary."

OFFICE OF PUBLIC LIAISON (OPL)

Dearborn begins by emphasizing the critical importance of the OPL in building coalitions and support for the President's agenda. It states that the OPL is "critically important in building coalitions and support for the President's agenda across every aligned social, faith-based, minority, and economic interest group."

The text highlights the OPL's role as a tool for shaping public opinion and keeping various stakeholders informed, including supporters, "frenemies," and opponents who are within reach.

The structure and reporting line of the OPL are described:

- A notably large office
- One Director who reports to the Chief of Staff's office, either directly or through a deputy
- A sufficient number of deputies and special assistants to cover the vast number of disparate interest groups engaged daily

Dearborn stresses the importance of the OPL Director maintaining relationships with other WHO heads and the senior staff of every Cabinet department and agency.

A key function of the OPL is facilitating listening sessions: "Since a President's agenda is always in motion, it is important for the OPL to facilitate listening sessions to receive the views of the various leaders and members of key interest groups."

The text notes that the OPL holds more meetings in the Eisenhower Executive Office Building (EEOB) and within the West Wing than any other office within the WHO.

Dearborn describes the OPL as "the chief White House enforcer and gatekeeper among these various interest groups." It suggests that the OPL operates best when given permission by the Chief of Staff to use both "carrot" and "stick" approaches, emphasizing the importance of communication with the chief's office.

The OPL's role in presidential scheduling and both official and political travel is highlighted as "outsized."

Dearborn provides detailed recommendations for staffing the OPL:
1. The Director should:
   - Come from the President's election campaign or Capitol Hill
   - Not have deeply entrenched connections to K Street entities or potential stakeholders
   - Be amiable, gregarious, highly organized, and willing to shoulder criticism and pushback
2. Deputies and special assistants should:
   - Have a deep understanding of the capital, from K Street to Capitol Hill
   - Have extensive experience in private industry, the labor sector, the conservative movement, and among specific interest groups

The text emphasizes that OPL staffers work with more external and internal parties than any other WHO staffers, requiring them to be effective communicators, initiative-takers, and able to influence, persuade, and listen to various stakeholders.

Dearborn concludes with a note of caution: "All OPL staffers must understand from the outset that their jobs might be modified or even phased out entirely as the Administration's priorities change."

OFFICE OF INTERGOVERNMENTAL AFFAIRS (IGA)

Dearborn introduces the IGA as the primary connection point between the White House and non-federal government entities. It states, "The IGA connects the White House to state, county, local, and tribal governments. In other words, it is the one-stop shop for disseminating an Administration's agenda to all non-federal government entities."
The recommended structure for the IGA is outlined:

- A Director
- One or two Deputy Directors reporting to the Director

The primary responsibility of the IGA Director is emphasized: "The Director must ensure that the White House remains connected to all non-federal government entities." This involves:
1. Representing the interests and perspectives of these entities in policy discussions
2. Organizing events with the West Wing, EOP senior staff, and IGA staff throughout departments and agencies

Dearborn presents two common staffing arrangements for the IGA:
1. Each deputy and their staffers are responsible for a type of government
2. A group of staffers is responsible for a specific geographical region of the country

The text clarifies the IGA's role, stating, "The IGA, as suggested above, represents the interests and perspectives of non-federal government entities, but its primary job is to make sure that these entities understand an Administration's agenda and ultimately support it."

Dearborn stresses the importance of collaboration, noting that the IGA must work with all other White House offices, especially the Office of Political Affairs (OPA) and the Office of Public Liaison (OPL), and manage its staff throughout departments and agencies.

WHITE HOUSE POLICY COUNCILS

Dearborn begins by acknowledging the growth of the federal government over the past century and the resulting difficulty for the President to single-handedly direct his agenda across the executive branch. It introduces three White House policy councils that have emerged to help the President control the bureaucracy and ensure alignment between agency leadership and White House priorities:
1. National Security Council (NSC)
2. National Economic Council (NEC)
3. Domestic Policy Council (DPC)

Each council is headed by an Assistant to the President and performs three significant functions:
1. Policy Coordination:
   - Primary role of coordinating Administration policy development
   - Includes developing legislative priorities, coordinating policy decisions across multiple departments and agencies, and sometimes within a single department or agency
   - Ensures all relevant offices are included, competing opinions are evaluated, and well-structured questions are presented to the President when disagreements arise
2. Policy Advice:
   - Council heads function as independent policy advisers to the President
   - The extent of this role varies based on the individual and the President's governing philosophy
   - Ranges from "honest brokers" who coordinate and ensure fair presentation of all opinions, to "policy deciders" who largely drive policy topics on the President's behalf
3. Policy Implementation:
   - Manage and mediate the implementation of previous policy decisions
   - Coordinate decisions during the often years-long implementation of new statutes or executive orders
   - Ensure a centralized process for evaluating and coordinating decisions, especially when multiple Cabinet departments or agencies are involved

Dearborn then describes a tiered interagency policy process used by the councils to manage these functions:
1. Policy Coordinating Committee (PCC):
   - Led by a Special Assistant to the President from the policy council
   - Includes political Assistant Secretary-level experts from relevant departments, agencies, or offices
   - Determines consensus, identifies differing opinions, and develops resolution options
2. Deputies Committee (DC):
   - Chaired by the policy council's Deputy Assistant to the President
   - Attended by relevant Deputy Secretaries
   - Evaluates options produced by the PCC and may direct further work or compromise
3. Principals Committee (PC):
   - Chaired by the Director of the Policy Council
   - Attended by relevant Cabinet Secretaries and senior White House political staff
   - Final opportunity for senior advisers to discuss and potentially reach consensus before involving the President

Dearborn notes that despite seemingly clear portfolios, the three policy councils often have overlapping areas, which can lead to confusion or conflict. It suggests identifying these areas and assigning clear responsibilities to streamline the policy-coordination process.

The section concludes by highlighting key cross-cutting agency topics that incoming policy councils will need to address rapidly, including countering China, enforcing immigration laws, reversing regulatory policies to promote energy production, combating attacks on life and religious liberty, and confronting "wokeism" throughout the federal government.

NATIONAL SECURITY COUNCIL (NSC)

Dearborn introduces the NSC as an interdepartmental body within the White House designed to set national security policy with a whole-of-government approach. It notes that unlike the other policy councils, the NSC was established by statute.

The text lists the statutory members and advisers currently part of the NSC:
- President
- Vice President
- Secretary of State
- Secretary of Defense
- Secretary of Energy
- Chairman of the Joint Chiefs of Staff
- Director of National Intelligence

Dearborn emphasizes the importance of vetting the National Security Adviser and NSC staff for foreign and security policy experience and insight. It outlines their key roles:
- Advising the President on matters of foreign policy and national security
- Serving as an information conduit in times of crisis
- Acting as liaisons to ensure proper sharing of written communications among NSC members

The text draws attention to the use of detailees to staff the NSC, noting recent changes: "In recent years, the NSC's staff size has been rightsized from its peak of 400 in 2015 down to 100–150 professional members." It recommends that the next Administration "should try to limit the number of detailees to ensure more direct presidential control."

NATIONAL ECONOMIC COUNCIL (NEC)

Dearborn introduces the NEC as established by executive order in 1993, outlining its four key functions:
1. Coordinating the economic policy-making process for domestic and international economic issues
2. Coordinating economic policy advice to the President
3. Ensuring policy decisions and programs align with the President's stated goals and are effectively pursued
4. Monitoring implementation of the President's economic policy agenda

It describes the NEC Director's role in coordinating and implementing the President's economic policy objectives by working with Cabinet secretaries, their departments, and multiple agencies. The NEC staff is noted to include policy experts in various fields such as infrastructure, manufacturing, research and development, agriculture, small business, financial regulation, housing, technology and innovation, and fiscal policy.

Dearborn distinguishes the NEC from the Domestic Policy Council (DPC) and the Council of Economic Advisers (CEA):
- NEC focuses on economic policy matters, while DPC typically handles non-economic domestic matters
- NEC is in charge of policy development, while CEA acts as the White House's internal research arm for economic analysis

The text stresses the importance of finding qualified individuals to lead both the NEC and CEA:
- CEA is typically led by a well-known academic economist
- NEC leaders have ranged from former CEOs of major investment firms to financial-services industry managers to seasoned congressional staffers with experience in economic policy issues

DOMESTIC POLICY COUNCIL (DPC)

Dearborn introduces the DPC as consisting of advisers to the President on noneconomic domestic policy issues and international issues with significant domestic components (such as immigration). It's described as one of the primary policy councils serving the President, alongside the NSC and NEC.

Key roles within the DPC are outlined:
1. Director: Serves as the principal DPC adviser to the President, alongside Cabinet members
2. Deputy Director: Chairs the committee responsible for coordinating domestic policy development at the Deputy Secretary level

The text emphasizes that both the Director and Deputy Director have critical institutional functions affecting domestic policy development throughout the Administration.

Dearborn notes that the DPC includes policy experts (Special Assistants to the President or SAPs) responsible for developing, coordinating, and advising the President on specific issues. It stresses the importance of DPC policy expertise reflecting the most prominent issues before the Administration, such as environment, health care, housing, and immigration.

The text recommends that DPC SAPs should have a working knowledge of the rulemaking process to facilitate the DPC's effectiveness in coordinating Administration policy.

Dearborn emphasizes the need for close collaboration between the DPC and other offices within the Executive Office of the President, including:
- Office of Management and Budget and its Office of Information and Regulatory Affairs
- Council of Economic Advisers
- Council on Environmental Quality
- Office of Science and Technology Policy

It suggests that the DPC Director should chair a standing meeting with principals from each of these EOP offices to enhance coordination within the White House.

The text identifies several key areas for the DPC to focus on:
1. Promoting innovation as a foundation for economic growth and opportunity
2. Establishing an economic opportunity working group, chaired by the DPC Director
3. Promoting health care reform to reduce costs for Americans and alleviate pressure on the federal budget
4. Coordinating with the NSC on a policy agenda to enhance border security

OFFICE OF THE VICE PRESIDENT (OVP)

Dearborn begins by noting that in modern U.S. history, the Vice President has acted as a significant adviser to the President, helping to promote and execute the President's agenda once elected.

Key points about the Vice President's role include:
- The President may include OVP staff in various White House meetings, including Policy Coordinating Committee, Deputies Committee, and Principals Committee discussions
- Recent Presidents have given Vice Presidents space in the West Wing, enhancing their proximity to key decision-makers
- Presidents often task Vice Presidents with leading various Administration efforts, such as serving on the NSC Principals Committee, heading the National Space Council, addressing immigration and border issues, leading responses to health care crises, and supervising workforce programs
- Vice Presidents may also spearhead projects of personal interest authorized by the President
- The VP is charged with breaking tie votes in the Senate
- In recent years, VPs have served as brand ambassadors for the White House abroad, announcing Administration priorities and coordinating with foreign government officials
- The Vice President, as President of the Senate, could serve as the President's emissary to the Senate

OFFICE OF THE FIRST LADY/FIRST GENTLEMAN

Dearborn begins by highlighting the interesting role the First Lady or First Gentleman plays in policy formation, implementation, and execution in concert with the President. It notes that active and interested first spouses often champion a select number of signature issues, which can range from thorny social issues to deeper policy matters.

Key points about the role of the First Lady/First Gentleman include:
1. Advantage in tackling controversial issues: "One advantage of the first spouse's taking on hot-button social issues is that any political backlash will be less severe than it would be for the President."
2. Staffing: The first spouse typically appoints a chief of staff with enough assistants to support activities in the East Wing of the White House. This team works exclusively with the first spouse and senior members of the White House along with EOP personnel.
3. Priority setting: The first spouse's priorities often reflect their personal passions and interests, identified as important in discussions with the President.
4. Strategic value: "Executed well, they can be strategically useful in accelerating the Administration's agenda."
5. Past initiatives: Dearborn provides examples of previous East Wing initiatives, such as combating bullying, fighting drug abuse, promoting literacy, and encouraging physical education for young adults and children.
6. Resources: "The first spouse is afforded significant resources." Their staff works with the President's policy team, members of the Cabinet, and other EOP staff.

Dearborn emphasizes the potential impact of the First Lady/First Gentleman's role, noting that when executed effectively, their initiatives can significantly contribute to advancing the Administration's overall agenda.

CHAPTER 2: EXECUTIVE OFFICE OF THE PRESIDENT OF THE UNITED STATES

The great challenge confronting a conservative President is the existential need for aggressive use of the vast powers of the executive branch to return power—including power currently held by the executive branch—to the American people – Page 44

Key Policy Proposals

OFFICE OF MANAGEMENT AND BUDGET (OMB)

- Empower OMB to aggressively drive the President's conservative agenda across agencies
- Have policy officials (PADs) sign off on agency funding apportionments to increase oversight
- Expand the number of Resource Management Offices (RMOs) and political appointees to enhance control over agencies
- Impose "administrative PAYGO" requiring agencies to offset any discretionary spending increases

Analysis: These changes would dramatically increase White House political control over traditionally independent agencies and career staff. Requiring offsets for any spending increases would hamstring agencies' ability to respond to emerging needs. Overall, this risks politicizing the professional civil service and undermining agency expertise and autonomy.

OFFICE OF INFORMATION AND REGULATORY AFFAIRS (OIRA)

- Maintain cost-benefit analysis requirements and expand them to independent agencies
- Increase OIRA's budget and staffing to bolster its ability to constrain regulations
- Revive Trump-era executive orders that added procedural hurdles to regulating
- Work with Congress to pass laws making it harder to issue regulations

Analysis: Strengthening OIRA review and cost-benefit requirements would make it harder to issue new regulations protecting health, safety, consumers, and the environment. The additional procedural burdens and potential for judicial review could paralyze rulemaking. This appears designed to block any new progressive regulations.

DOMESTIC POLICY COUNCIL (DPC), NATIONAL ECONOMIC COUNCIL (NEC), NATIONAL SECURITY COUNCIL (NSC)

- Staff the policy councils with personnel aligned with the President's agenda, removing career detailees
- Empower the councils to drive policy across the government
- Ensure the councils have a major role in agency appointments, budgets, and legislative plans

Analysis: Removing career detailees and stacking the councils with political loyalists risks losing valuable expertise and institutional knowledge. Concentrating more power in the White House policy apparatus could sideline the knowledge of agencies and reduce transparency and accountability.

OTHER PROPOSED CHANGES

- Abolish the Gender Policy Council and refocus on "promoting life and family"
- Reshape climate research to include more diverse viewpoints skeptical of climate change
- Eliminate the use of the social cost of carbon in regulations
- Rewrite environmental permitting rules to limit the scope of review
- Ensure grantmaking does not fund "woke nonprofits with leftist agendas"

Analysis: Abolishing offices focused on gender equity and stacking climate research with skeptics suggests an intent to roll back progress on women's rights and climate action. Eliminating the social cost of carbon and limiting environmental reviews would hamstring efforts to consider the broad impacts of policies. Screening grant recipients for ideology is a dangerous form of political litmus test.

The chapter proposes consolidating power within the EOP to drive a conservative policy agenda across the executive branch. Many of these changes threaten to undermine agency independence, reduce government transparency and accountability, and make it harder to effectively regulate in the public interest.

While some streamlining of functions may be worthwhile, the overall thrust appears designed to dismantle the so-called "administrative state" and block new progressive policies. If enacted, these proposals could dramatically reshape the presidency and tilt policymaking decisively to the right.

Summary

This chapter of *Mandate for Leadership* was written by Russ Vought. The following summary conveys the content of the document accurately and objectively, without endorsing or critiquing the perspectives of the original authors.

Vought start the chapter by underscoring the constitutional foundation of executive power, which is explicitly vested in the President of the United States, as stated in Article II. This section argues that the modern federal bureaucracy has grown excessively autonomous, often pursuing its own agenda rather than adhering to the President's directives. The text suggests that this autonomy has been exacerbated by legislative delegation of authority to agencies, the rise of so-called expert independence, and the difficulty in holding career civil servants accountable. This concentration of power within the executive branch raises concerns reminiscent of James Madison's warning against the accumulation of legislative, executive, and judicial powers, which he deemed tyrannical. Vought posits that a conservative President must aggressively reassert control over the executive branch to restore constitutional governance and return power to the American people.

U.S. Office of Management and Budget (OMB)

The OMB is portrayed as a pivotal instrument for the President to align the federal bureaucracy with his policy agenda. The text describes the OMB as the "air-traffic control system" for government operations, responsible for managing the budget, overseeing agency performance, and coordinating regulatory and legislative efforts. Vought emphasizes that the effectiveness of the OMB hinges on its integration into all aspects of the policy-making process and its capacity to enforce the President's decisions across the executive branch. Key roles include the development and enforcement of the President's budget, management of personnel performance, and ensuring that agency actions comply with the President's objectives. The text advocates for empowering OMB's internal divisions, such as the Budget Review Division and the Office of General Counsel, to ensure that policy directives are implemented effectively. Additionally, Vought calls for a restructuring of the Resource Management Offices (RMOs) to enhance oversight and support the President's fiscal discipline through administrative pay-as-you-go procedures.

National Security Council (NSC)

The NSC is presented as a crucial body for coordinating and implementing the President's national security policies across various government agencies. The text emphasizes that the NSC's effectiveness relies on its alignment with the President's national security priorities and its ability to mobilize the full power of the executive branch. Vought argues that the NSC staff must be restructured to focus on the President's key objectives, with specific directorates eliminated or reorganized to better support these goals. Senior officials within the NSC should be directly accountable for the implementation of policy initiatives and should work in close coordination with other offices, such as the National Economic Council (NEC) and the Office of Management and Budget (OMB), to integrate economic considerations into national security policy. The NSC is also tasked with the comprehensive review of all formal strategies, such as the National Security Strategy and the National Defense Strategy, to ensure they align with the President's priorities. The text further suggests that the NSC should take an active role in directing military policies and promotions, particularly in prioritizing national defense over social issues like climate change or critical race theory, which Vought argues weaken the armed forces.

National Economic Council (NEC)

The NEC is depicted as a key advisory body responsible for shaping and coordinating the President's economic policies, both domestically and internationally. The text highlights the importance of the NEC's Director and Deputy Director in guiding economic policy development and ensuring that it aligns with the President's broader agenda. The NEC's policy experts, known as Special Assistants to the President (SAPs), are tasked with providing expertise on various economic issues, including taxes, energy, technology, and financial services. Vought stresses that the NEC must work closely with other offices within the Executive Office of the President (EOP) to promote economic growth, innovation, and fiscal responsibility. The text also addresses potential tensions between the NEC and other policy councils, such as the Domestic Policy Council (DPC) and the National Security Council (NSC), advocating for clear jurisdictional boundaries to avoid conflicts. Additionally, the NEC is encouraged to collaborate with the Council of Economic Advisers (CEA) to ensure that policy decisions are informed by rigorous economic analysis and data.

Office of the U.S. Trade Representative (USTR)

The USTR is portrayed as a vital office for developing and executing a cohesive trade policy that reflects the President's agenda. Vought asserts that the USTR must be empowered to lead a unified, whole-of-government approach to trade, particularly in response to challenges posed by countries like China, whose predatory trade practices are seen as undermining the global trading system. The text criticizes the World Trade Organization (WTO) for its failure to hold China accountable and suggests that the USTR should focus on rebalancing international trade relationships in favor of democratic nations with market-driven economies. To achieve these objectives, the USTR should be granted the authority and resources necessary to coordinate trade policy across federal agencies and ensure that it aligns with the President's broader economic and national security goals. Vought also warns against allowing special interests or institutional inertia to dictate trade policy, advocating for a strong USTR that can effectively represent U.S. interests in the global marketplace.

Council of Economic Advisers (CEA)

The CEA, established by Congress in 1946, is characterized as the President's principal source of economic advice, providing data-driven analysis and research to inform policy decisions. Although the CEA's role in shaping policy has diminished over time, Vought argues for its revitalization as a senior advisory body, similar to how the White House Counsel's office serves as the senior legal adviser. The CEA's primary function is to ensure that economic analysis plays a central role in policy development, contributing to policy dialogues, raising critical issues, and guiding officials on the economic implications of decisions. The text emphasizes the importance of integrating the CEA into the policy-making process, ensuring it has a seat at the table on all relevant issues. Vought also discusses the challenges posed by the CEA's hiring practices, which often lead to the presence of senior economists who may not align with the current Administration's priorities. To address this, Vought suggests adjusting hiring timelines and ensuring that new appointees are fully vetted for alignment with the Administration's economic agenda.

National Space Council (NSpC)

The NSpC is described as a key advisory body responsible for coordinating national space policy across civil, military, intelligence, and commercial domains. Traditionally chaired by the Vice President, the NSpC's role is to ensure that the President's space policy priorities are implemented effectively. The text highlights the importance of policy stability in space projects, which are often long-term and expensive, and advocates for aligning these projects with national interests rather than specific advocacy groups. Vought praises the continuity of major space policies, such as the U.S. Space Force and the Artemis program, across different administrations, but notes ongoing challenges like managing orbital debris and advancing national security space capabilities. The NSpC is encouraged to foster collaboration among various White House offices and agencies, ensuring that space policy is coordinated and integrated into broader national security and economic strategies. Vought also emphasizes the importance of collegial relationships between NSpC and OMB staff to effectively communicate the President's priorities and manage space-related budgetary concerns.

Office of Science and Technology Policy (OSTP)

The OSTP, created in 1976, serves as the President's primary source of advice on scientific and technological matters, coordinating federal research and development (R&D) programs across agencies. Vought argues for elevating the OSTP's role, particularly when science is manipulated by agencies to support political agendas. The OSTP is encouraged to assert greater leadership in R&D, especially in light of recent legislation like the CHIPS and Science Act, which has expanded federal funding and policy influence in areas such as artificial intelligence, quantum information science, and biotechnology. The text also calls for a reassessment of current scientific priorities to align them more closely with the Administration's goals. The OSTP should work closely with OMB to prioritize funding requests and ensure that resources are allocated effectively. Additionally, Vought recommends restructuring the U.S. Global Change Research Program (USGCRP) to include diverse viewpoints and reduce its influence on policymaking, particularly in climate change research. The OSTP is also tasked with unwinding policies related to radical gender, racial, and equity initiatives, restoring scientific excellence as its primary focus.

Council on Environmental Quality (CEQ)

The CEQ is positioned as the primary agency responsible for administering the National Environmental Policy Act (NEPA), coordinating environmental policy across the federal government, and overseeing the implementation of NEPA regulations. Vought advocates for a revision of CEQ's NEPA regulations, emphasizing the need to streamline the environmental review process to make it more efficient and reduce the scope for judicial challenges. The text highlights the importance of building on previous reforms, such as the 2020 effort to ban cumulative impact analysis, which Vought sees as essential for facilitating effective and timely agency action. Furthermore, the CEQ's role in the Federal Permitting Improvement Steering Council (FPISC) is underscored, with recommendations to further empower the FPISC by giving its Executive Director delegated presidential authority over permitting agencies. Vought also proposes the establishment of a Senior Advisor within the Executive Office of the President to coordinate energy and environmental policy, replacing the existing Office of Domestic Climate Policy. This advisor would ensure that energy and environmental policies are consistent and aligned with the President's agenda. Additionally, the text calls for the elimination of the Interagency Working Group on the Social Cost of Carbon and a broader modernization of the federal permitting system to reduce litigation risks and improve efficiency.

Office of National Drug Control Policy (ONDCP)

The ONDCP, created by Congress in 1988, is tasked with coordinating the President's drug policy efforts, with a current focus on addressing the fentanyl crisis and reducing overdose fatalities. Vought emphasizes the need for a comprehensive approach that includes prevention, treatment, and reducing the availability of illicit drugs. The text highlights the dynamic and dangerous nature of the current drug trafficking environment, particularly the rise of synthetic opioids like fentanyl, which are often mixed with other drugs. The ONDCP is encouraged to work closely with federal border enforcement officials to disrupt the flow of these drugs into the United States. Vought also argues for political appointees to lead the ONDCP's budget office and grant-making activities to ensure alignment with the President's drug control priorities. There is a recommendation to eventually transfer ONDCP's grant programs, such as the Drug-Free Communities Support Program and the High Intensity Drug Trafficking Areas Program, to other related agencies like the Department of Justice and the Department of Health and Human Services. However, in the interim, the ONDCP should ensure that these programs are supporting the President's agenda rather than being co-opted by organizations with opposing political agendas.

Gender Policy Council (GPC)

The Gender Policy Council (GPC) is singled out for immediate abolition, with Vought recommending that the President revoke Executive Order 14020, which established the council. The GPC is criticized for promoting policies related to abortion, comprehensive sexuality education, and what Vought describes as a "woke" gender ideology, including gender-affirming care and sex-change surgeries for minors. The text argues that eliminating the GPC would signal a shift in federal priorities towards promoting life and strengthening the family. In place of the GPC, Vought suggests appointing a Special Assistant to the President, or a similarly ranked official, to coordinate and lead the Administration's domestic priorities related to life and family. This position would be responsible for facilitating policy discussions, ensuring agency support, and promoting the President's agenda on these issues in coordination with the Domestic Policy Council.

Office of the Vice President (OVP)

The Vice President's role is emphasized as constitutionally vital, serving as both the President's successor and the President of the Senate, where they can cast tie-breaking votes. The text highlights the unique leverage that the Vice President can wield within the administration, given their elected status, which distinguishes them from other appointed officials who serve at the pleasure of the President. Vought advocates for fully integrating the Vice President into the policy-making process from the start of an administration, ensuring that the OVP is involved in all major policy decisions, including budget and regulatory reviews. This involvement allows the Vice President to provide valuable advice and support the President's agenda effectively. Additionally, the text discusses the Vice President's traditional role in leading specific initiatives, such as Mike Pence's leadership of the federal COVID-19 response, and in representing the United States abroad. The OVP is also seen as a critical player in securing legislative victories, given the Vice President's role in the Senate. Vought concludes by noting that a proactive Vice President, deeply engaged in the interagency process, can significantly contribute to the success of the administration and is well-positioned to potentially succeed the President.

CHAPTER 3: CENTRAL PERSONNEL AGENCIES: MANAGING THE BUREAUCRACY

That progressive system has broken down in our time, and the only real solution is for the national government to do less: to decentralize and privatize as much as possible and then ensure that the remaining bureaucracy is managed effectively along the lines of the enduring principles set out in detail here – Page 83

Key Policy Proposals

The chapter proposes several significant changes to federal personnel management policies with the purported goal of making the bureaucracy more efficient, accountable, and aligned with the President's agenda:

1. Reinstate a merit-based examination like USAHire for federal hiring to assess knowledge, skills and abilities (KSAs) of candidates.
2. Tie employee performance appraisals more closely to pay, bonuses and retention decisions. Require an "outstanding" rating for SES bonuses.
3. Move federal pay and benefits closer to private sector levels. Federal employees currently receive total compensation 30-40% higher than private sector equivalents.
4. Consolidate the multiple federal employee appeals processes (MSPB, EEOC, FLRA, OSC) into a single, streamlined process through the MSPB to reduce delays.
5. Reinstate Trump executive orders limiting federal employee unions, allowing agencies to renegotiate CBAs, restrict official time, and prioritize performance over seniority.
6. Reinstate Schedule F to allow certain federal positions involved in policy to be excepted from competitive service rules.

ANALYSIS

From a liberal point of view, while improving government efficiency is a worthy goal, many of these proposals go too far in eroding important civil service protections and worker rights:

- The focus on cutting pay and benefits to private sector levels ignores the need to provide competitive compensation to attract and retain high-quality federal workers. It could lead to a "race to the bottom."

- Consolidating appeals processes under the MSPB concentrates too much power and eliminates important employee protections and due process rights. A better approach is to provide more resources to reduce backlogs.

- The restrictions on federal unions undermine collective bargaining rights and protections against arbitrary personnel actions. Unions play an important role in giving workers a voice.

- Schedule F could allow the administration to improperly politicize the civil service and undermine merit principles by allowing large numbers of career positions to become political appointments.

While some proposals like using better assessments for hiring have merit, the document's policy recommendations overall tilt heavily in favor of management prerogatives over employee rights. A more balanced approach is needed that improves efficiency while still respecting and engaging the federal workforce. Strengthening rather than weakening an independent, professional civil service is essential for effective government.

Summary

This chapter of *Mandate for Leadership* was written by Donald Devine, Dennis Dean Kirk, and Paul Dans. The following summary conveys the content of the document accurately and objectively, without endorsing or critiquing the perspectives of the original authors.

The opening section emphasizes the fundamental principle of "personnel is policy" in government management. It highlights the constitutional basis for the President's executive power, particularly in appointing and directing personnel. The authors argue that to fulfill electoral mandates, Presidents must prioritize personnel management at the Cabinet level.

The text outlines the major central personnel agencies in the U.S. government:

1. Office of Personnel Management (OPM): Executes and enforces civil service rules and regulations.
2. Merit Systems Protection Board (MSPB): Adjudicates cases for 2.2 million federal employees.
3. Federal Labor Relations Authority (FLRA): Handles appeals related to labor grievance procedures.

4. Office of Special Counsel (OSC): Investigates and prosecutes cases involving prohibited personnel practices, Hatch Act violations, and whistleblower complaints.

The Equal Employment Opportunity Commission (EEOC) is mentioned for its role in handling discrimination complaints, while the General Services Administration (GSA) is noted for its function in managing government contractors.

ANALYSIS AND RECOMMENDATIONS

OPM: MANAGING THE FEDERAL BUREAUCRACY

This section traces the evolution of the U.S. civil service system from the late 19th century to the present. It discusses the progressive movement's goal of creating a professionalized, politically neutral bureaucracy, and how this ideal led to unintended consequences. The text highlights reforms initiated by Presidents Jimmy Carter and Ronald Reagan, including the Civil Service Reform Act of 1978, which aimed to improve performance appraisal and introduce merit pay.

The authors note that these reforms were largely dissipated within a decade: "Today, employee evaluation is back to pre-reform levels with almost all rated successful or above, frustrating any relation between pay and performance." They criticize the current system where "pay raises, within-grade pay increases, and locality pay for regular employees and executives have become automatic rather than based on performance."

OPM: MERIT HIRING IN A MERIT SYSTEM

This part discusses the challenges in implementing merit-based hiring in the federal government. It mentions the abolition of the Professional and Administrative Career Examination (PACE) due to concerns about its impact on minorities. The authors argue that this decision has hampered the government's ability to select employees based on knowledge, skills, and abilities (KSA).

The text advocates for the reintroduction of rigorous entry examinations, stating: "A government that is unable to select employees based on KSA-like test qualifications cannot work, and the OPM must move forward on this very basic personnel management obligation."

THE CENTRALITY OF PERFORMANCE APPRAISAL

This section emphasizes the critical role of performance appraisal in government management. The authors cite Ludwig von Mises' work "Bureaucracy" to argue that, unlike the private sector's profit-and-loss evaluation tool, government performance measurement depends entirely on a functioning appraisal system.

The text highlights a significant issue in the current federal system: "The GAO reported more recently that overly high and widely spread performance ratings were again plaguing the government, with more than 99 percent of employees rated fully successful or above by their managers, a mere 0.3 percent rated as minimally successful, and 0.1 percent actually rated unacceptable."

The authors discuss the challenges managers face in providing honest evaluations, noting that "managers can be and often are accused of racial or sexual discrimination for a poor rating, and this discourages honesty." They suggest that political executives should take an active role in supervising performance appraisals of career staff, arguing that this is "critical to responsibility and improved management."

MERIT PAY

This part traces the history of attempts to implement merit pay in the federal government. The authors note that while merit pay for executives and managers was part of the Carter reforms and implemented early in the Reagan presidency, attempts to extend it to the entire workforce faced strong resistance from unions and their congressional allies.

The text argues for the reinstatement of a comprehensive performance-based pay system: "A reform-friendly President and Congress might just provide the opportunity to create a more comprehensive performance plan." In the meantime, the authors encourage political executives to "use existing pay and especially fiscal awards strategically to reward good performance to the degree allowed by law."

MAKING THE APPEALS PROCESS WORK

This section addresses the complexity and inefficiency of the current appeals process for federal employees. The authors note that the "nonmilitary government dismissal rate is well below 1 percent," largely due to the extensive appeals process.

They argue that the multiple administrative appeals bodies and the lengthy process discourage managers from taking action against poor performers: "The real problem is the time and paperwork involved in the elaborate process that managers must undergo during appeals. This keeps even the best managers from bringing cases in all but the most egregious cases of poor performance or misconduct."

The text suggests simplifying the appeals process by transferring some functions between agencies and making the MSPB the main reviewer of adverse actions: "The MSPB could then become the main reviewer of adverse actions, greatly simplifying the burdensome appeal process."

MAKING CIVIL SERVICE BENEFITS ECONOMICALLY AND ADMINISTRATIVELY RATIONAL

This section discusses the discrepancies between federal and private sector compensation. The authors cite studies showing that federal employees receive significantly higher total compensation than their private sector counterparts. For instance, they note that "a 2016 Heritage Foundation study found that federal employees received wages that were 22 percent higher than wages for similar private-sector workers; if the value of employee benefits was included, the total compensation premium for federal employees over their private-sector equivalents increased to between 30 percent and 40 percent."

The text advocates for moving closer to a market model for federal pay and benefits. It suggests that "the OPM should establish an initial pay schedule for every occupation and region, monitor turnover rates and applicant-to-position ratios, and adjust pay and recruitment on that basis."

REFORMING FEDERAL RETIREMENT BENEFITS

This part focuses on the generous retirement benefits enjoyed by federal employees compared to the private sector. The authors state that "Career civil servants enjoy retirement benefits that are nearly unheard of in the private sector," noting that federal employees typically retire earlier, receive richer pension annuities, and enjoy automatic cost-of-living adjustments.

The text discusses reforms implemented during the Reagan years, including the transition from the Civil Service Retirement System (CSRS) to the Federal Employees Retirement System (FERS). While acknowledging that these changes made the system more equitable and less costly, the authors suggest that "other means might be considered in the future to move it even closer to private plans."

GSA: LANDLORD AND CONTRACTOR MANAGEMENT

This section discusses the General Services Administration's dual role as the federal government's landlord and purchasing agent. The authors emphasize the importance of the GSA's real estate expertise and its role in managing government contractors, noting that "With contractors performing so many functions today, the GSA therefore becomes a de facto part of governmentwide personnel management."

The text suggests closer cooperation between the GSA and OPM leadership to address matters of common interest, such as "moderating PTA personnel restrictions and the relationships between contract and civil service employees."

REDUCTIONS-IN-FORCE

This part cautions against simplistic approaches to reducing the federal workforce. The authors argue that "cutting federal employment can be helpful and can provide a simple story to average citizens, but cutting functions, levels, funds, and grants is much more important than setting simple employment size."

They note that attempts to reduce numbers can sometimes increase costs, citing examples of buyout programs that end up costing the Treasury billions. The text recommends prioritizing performance over seniority in determining layoffs, stating that "A determined President should insist that performance be first and be wary of costly types of reductions-in-force."

IMPENETRABLE BUREAUCRACY

This section discusses the challenges of navigating the complex federal bureaucracy. The authors cite a GAO report that identified "almost a hundred actions that the executive branch or Congress could take to improve efficiency and effectiveness across 37 areas that span a broad range of government missions and functions."

The text emphasizes the need to eliminate duplicated functions and programs across agencies. It references Paul Light's work, which estimates "that there are perhaps 50 or more levels of impenetrable bureaucracy and no way other than imperfect performance appraisals to communicate between them."

The authors argue that "The best solution is to cut functions and budgets and devolve responsibilities." However, they acknowledge that this is a challenge primarily for Presidents, Congress, and the entire government, while emphasizing that "the OPM still needs to lead the way governmentwide in managing personnel properly even in any future smaller government."

CREATING A RESPONSIBLE CAREER MANAGEMENT SERVICE

This part focuses on the Senior Executive Service (SES) created by the 1978 Civil Service Reform Act. The authors discuss the challenges of balancing political leadership with career service professionalism, including issues of "burrowing-in" by political appointees.

They argue that "career SES employees should respect political rights too," criticizing actions such as "career staff reserving excessive numbers of key policy positions as 'career reserved' to deny them to noncareer SES employees."

The text mentions Executive Order 13957, which aimed to create more flexibility in hiring for policy-determining positions. The authors recommend its reinstatement, stating that it "should be reinstated, but SES responsibility should come first."

MANAGING PERSONNEL IN A UNION ENVIRONMENT

This section discusses the historical and current challenges of managing federal personnel in a unionized environment. The authors note that "Historically, unions were thought to be incompatible with government management," citing concerns raised by past presidents, including Franklin Roosevelt.

The text mentions executive orders issued by President Trump to limit union power and encourage agencies to renegotiate collective bargaining agreements. The authors recommend their reinstatement, arguing that "All were revoked by the Biden Administration and should be reinstated by the next Administration."

They also suggest reconsidering whether public-sector unions are appropriate, stating that "After more than half a century of experience with public-sector union frustrations of good government management, it is hard to avoid reaching the same conclusion [that these unions were not compatible with constitutional government]."

FULLY STAFFING THE RANKS OF POLITICAL APPOINTEES

This section emphasizes the importance of filling top political positions in the executive branch to provide democratic legitimacy and effective leadership. The authors argue that "Without this political leadership, the career civil service becomes empowered to lead the executive branch without democratic legitimacy."

The text discusses challenges faced by recent administrations in getting appointees confirmed, particularly noting President Trump's difficulties: "After the 2016 election, President Trump faced special hostility from the opposition party and the media in getting his appointees confirmed or even considered by the Senate."

The authors stress the importance of a full cadre of political appointees from the beginning of an administration, stating that "Any new Administration would be wise to learn that it will need a full cadre of sound political appointees from the beginning if it expects to direct this enormous federal bureaucracy."

They recommend a close relationship between the Office of Presidential Personnel (PPO) at the White House and the OPM, coordinating with agency assistant secretaries of administration and PPO's chosen White House Liaisons. The authors suggest that "If 'personnel is policy' is to be our general guide, it would make sense to give the President direct supervision of the bureaucracy with the OPM Director available in his Cabinet."

A REFORMED BUREAUCRACY

The concluding section argues that the current federal bureaucracy fails to meet its own civil service ideals. The authors state that "The merit criteria of ability, knowledge, and skills are no longer the basis for recruitment, selection, or advancement, while pay and benefits for comparable work are substantially above those in the private sector."

They reiterate the need for reforms to bring the bureaucracy under control and make it more efficient and responsive to political leadership. However, they also acknowledge that the problem goes beyond simple bureaucratic administration, rooting it in the progressive ideology that favors rule by unelected experts.

The text advocates for a return to constitutional principles, suggesting that the national government should "do less: to decentralize and privatize as much as possible and then ensure that the remaining bureaucracy is managed effectively along the lines of the enduring principles set out in detail here."

The authors conclude by emphasizing that "The specific deficiencies of the federal bureaucracy—size, levels of organization, inefficiency, expense, and lack of responsiveness to political leadership—are rooted in the progressive ideology that unelected experts can and should be trusted to promote the general welfare in just about every area of social life." They argue for a return to the constitutional vision where "the great majority of domestic activities [are left] to state, local, and private governance."

Analysis: The Expansion of Presidential powers and the "deconstruction of the administrative state"

These first chapters of *Mandate for Leadership* represent a significant shift in conservative strategy regarding the structure and function of the federal government. Whereas previous conservative efforts focused primarily on reducing the size and scope of the administrative state, Project 2025 aims to aggressively harness and redirect the administrative apparatus to advance conservative policy goals and ideology. This approach combines an unprecedented expansion of presidential authority with targeted deconstruction of administrative safeguards, creating a comprehensive blueprint for reshaping American governance.

A central tenet of Project 2025 is the dramatic expansion of presidential powers, far beyond the bounds of traditional executive authority. The initiative proposes bringing independent regulatory agencies under direct presidential control, effectively eliminating their autonomy and subjecting them to political influence. This would represent a fundamental restructuring of the federal bureaucracy, centralizing power in the executive branch to an extent not seen in modern American history. Additionally, Project 2025 advocates for reviving the practice of "impounding" funds - allowing the president to unilaterally refuse to spend money appropriated by Congress. This would significantly erode the legislative branch's power of the purse, a key constitutional check on executive authority.

The plan also outlines strategies for limiting congressional oversight, including controlling agency communications with Congress and manipulating the Federal Vacancies Reform Act to install political loyalists in key positions without Senate confirmation. These measures would severely curtail the legislature's ability to provide effective oversight of executive branch activities, further concentrating power in the presidency. Perhaps most alarmingly, Project 2025 proposes expanding the use of the Insurrection Act for domestic law enforcement, including at the border. This would blur the lines between military and civilian law enforcement in unprecedented ways, raising serious constitutional concerns.

Concurrent with this expansion of presidential authority, Project 2025 outlines a targeted deconstruction of administrative state safeguards designed to prevent abuse of power. A cornerstone of this effort is the implementation of Schedule F, which would reclassify a significant portion of the federal workforce, making career civil servants easier to fire and replace with political appointees. This would effectively dismantle the professional, non-partisan civil service that has been a hallmark of American governance for over a century. The plan also calls for purging career staff perceived as obstacles to the conservative agenda, potentially leading to a mass exodus of experienced professionals from government agencies.

Furthermore, Project 2025 proposes outsourcing government functions to ideologically aligned private entities. This would not only reduce transparency and accountability but also potentially create a shadow government apparatus operating outside of normal oversight mechanisms. The initiative also seeks to alter information-gathering processes within agencies to include fringe views and potentially biased analysis, compromising the integrity of government data and policy formulation.

The implications of these proposed changes are far-reaching and profound. If implemented, they would result in a concentration of power in the executive branch unprecedented in American history, coupled with a severe erosion of institutional norms and democratic accountability. The potential for abuse of power and political retribution would be significantly heightened, as the traditional checks and balances within the federal government would be severely weakened.

Moreover, the long-term consequences of such a restructuring could fundamentally alter the nature of American democracy. By reshaping federal government operations to advance a specific ideological agenda, Project 2025 threatens to undermine the principle of a politically neutral civil service and the idea of government as a servant of all citizens, regardless of political affiliation.

UNITARY EXECUTIVE THEORY

The unitary executive theory, the means by which the Heritage Foundation justifies the expansion of presidential powers, has its roots in the Trump administration's approach to presidential power. This controversial interpretation of executive authority gained significant traction during Trump's tenure, with his administration pushing the boundaries of presidential power in unprecedented ways. As Amanda Hollis-Brusky notes in her article "Helping Ideas Have Consequences":
"The theory gained prominence in the 1980s under President Ronald Reagan's Administration. While the theory was originally used to argue in the government's favor in separation of powers cases, it has been broadly expanded and has been used to justify other executive actions, including with regards to presidential signing statements." Project 2025 seeks to build upon and expand this interpretation of executive power, proposing a radical restructuring of the federal government that would place virtually all executive branch agencies under direct presidential control. This approach aligns closely with Trump's own views on presidential authority. As Trump famously stated to civics students in 2019, "I have an Article II [of the Constitution], where I have the right to do whatever I want as president."

he unitary executive theory represents a controversial and far-reaching interpretation of presidential power within the framework of American constitutional law. This theory posits that the President of the United States possesses complete and unilateral control over the entire executive branch of the federal government. As Steven G. Calabresi and Christopher S. Yoo explain in their influential book "The Unitary Executive":
"The unitary executive theory is the theory that the Vesting Clause of Article II of the U.S. Constitution, which reads 'the executive Power shall be vested in a President of the United States of America,' is a grant to the president of all of the executive power, which includes the power to remove and direct all lower-level officials."
The origins of this theory can be traced back to the 1980s during the Reagan administration. As Amanda Hollis-Brusky notes in her article "Helping Ideas Have Consequences":
"The theory gained prominence in the 1980s under President Ronald Reagan's Administration. While the theory was originally used to argue in the government's favor in separation of powers cases, it has been broadly expanded and has been used to justify other executive actions, including with regards to presidential signing statements." Hollis-Brusky provides statistical evidence demonstrating the increasing prominence of the unitary executive theory over time. For instance, she shows that mentions of the "unitary executive" in Executive Branch papers increased from just 12 during the Reagan administration to 90 during the George W. Bush administration.

Proponents of the unitary executive theory argue that it ensures consistent execution of laws and maintains clear lines of accountability. However, critics contend that it concentrates too much power in the presidency at the expense of checks and balances. As Julian Ku argues in his paper "Unitary Executive Theory and Exclusive Presidential Powers":
"The most troubling and potentially dangerous claims by the executive occur not when Presidents make claims of inherent executive power. Rather, the most difficult claims arise from cases where the President is claiming exclusive presidential power; that is to say, cases where the President argues that he has a constitutional power that cannot be trumped or limited by congressional action."
The theory has been particularly controversial in its application to presidential removal powers. As Calabresi and Yoo contend:
"Congressional efforts to insulate executive-branch subordinates from presidential control by creating independent agencies and counsels are in essence unconstitutional."
However, this view is not universally accepted among legal scholars. As Elena Kagan notes:
"Although I am highly sympathetic to the view that the President should have broad control over administrative activity, ... the unitarians have failed to establish their claim for plenary control as a matter of constitutional mandate. The original meaning of Article II is insufficiently precise and, in this area of staggering change, also insufficiently relevant to support the unitarian position."

The debate over the unitary executive theory reflects broader tensions in U.S. governance between efficiency and accountability, centralization and diffusion of power. As Peter L. Strauss argues:

"Our Constitution explicitly gives us a unitary head of state, but it leaves the framework of government almost completely to congressional design. If its text chooses between President as overseer of the resulting assemblage, and President as necessarily entitled 'decider,' the implicit message is that of oversight, not decision."

In recent years, the Supreme Court has begun implementing aspects of the unitary executive theory, while simultaneously increasing judicial scrutiny of agency actions. This has led to what Blake Emerson calls a contradictory "binary executive":

"The unitary executive theory presumes that the President alone may wield executive power. But by wresting away agencies' policymaking discretion, the Court itself exercises executive power. The Court is thus constructing the unitary executive with one hand and fragmenting it with the other."

Emerson contends this "binary executive" undermines political accountability and threatens the legitimacy of both the executive branch and the Court itself. He concludes it is "a constitutional anomaly that disturbs settled understandings, undermines the quality of government, and aggrandizes the Court at the expense of both the elected branches and its own legitimacy."

In conclusion, while the unitary executive theory offers a coherent vision of presidential power, its untested nature and the potential for significant concentration of authority in the executive branch raise profound concerns about its compatibility with American democratic norms and constitutional principles.

THE CONSERVATIVE PLAN TO "DECONSTRUCT THE ADMINISTRATIVE STATE"

At its core, Project 2025 seeks to place virtually all executive branch agencies under direct presidential control, aligning with and significantly expanding the unitary executive theory. In the current conservative vision of government this would bring about the dismantlement of the administrative state (or deep state, as some pundits like to call it) and the restructuring of government with political appointees driven to implement the policies of Project 2025 in every department. This is a core pillar of *Mandate for Leadership* and the proposed policies to achieve it are consistently discussed throughout the whole document.

1. **Implementation of Schedule F**, which would reclassify thousands of career government employees as political appointees. This would strip civil servants of long-standing protections, making them easier to remove and replace with loyalists. When the Trump administration attempted to implement Schedule F, the Office of Management and Budget tried to reclassify 88% of its staff under this new designation, far beyond just policy-making roles. The goal is to purge an estimated 50,000 federal workers.

2. **Expanded use of the Insurrection Act of 1807** for domestic law enforcement purposes, particularly at the U.S.-Mexico border. The Insurrection Act empowers the president to deploy U.S. military and federalized National Guard troops within the United States to suppress civil disorder, insurrection, or rebellion. Project 2025 envisions using this act more broadly, potentially bypassing traditional limitations on military involvement in domestic affairs.

3. **Manipulation of the Federal Vacancies Reform Act** to install political loyalists in key positions without Senate confirmation. This tactic exploits loopholes in the FVRA, potentially bypassing constitutional requirements for Senate approval of high-level appointments.

4. **Limiting congressional oversight:** The plan outlines strategies for limiting Congress's ability to oversee executive agencies, including controlling communications between agencies and congressional committees. For example, the plan calls for restricting the Department of Homeland Security to communicating with only one congressional committee in each chamber, drastically reducing oversight capabilities.

5. **Politicizing existing relationships with contractors and weaponizing federal grantmaking** to advance conservative policy objectives. This includes proposals to redirect humanitarian aid through faith-based organizations and prioritize grants for conservative causes like abstinence-only education.

6. **Overhauling the Department of Justice** to eliminate its tradition of political insulation from the White House. This would potentially allow the president to use the DOJ for political purposes, including targeting opponents.

7. **Consolidating and strengthening enforcement policies at U.S. Immigration and Customs Enforcement**, giving ICE agents greater leeway in arrests and expanding expedited removal procedures beyond the current 100-mile border zone.

8. **Reviving the president's ability to withhold congressionally-appropriated funds**, a practice Congress banned in 1974. This would significantly expand presidential control over the budget process.

9. **Outsourcing critical government functions to ideologically aligned private entities**, potentially compromising the neutrality and accessibility of services like weather forecasting.

Russell Vought, a key architect of Project 2025 and Trump's former Director of the Office of Management and Budget, articulates the strategy behind these proposals: "The great challenge confronting a conservative President is the existential need for aggressive use of the vast powers of the executive branch to return power—including power currently held by the executive branch—to the American people." Vought, who describes himself as a Christian nationalist, seeks to infuse government and society with elements of Christianity while advocating for what he calls "radical constitutionalism."

This approach raises significant concerns about the potential erosion of democratic norms, the politicization of traditionally non-partisan government functions, and the concentration of power in the executive branch.

The initiative's proposals build directly on initiatives begun during Trump's presidency but go much further in their scope and ambition. If implemented, they could fundamentally alter the balance of power in American government, potentially reshaping federal governance for decades to come. As one former Trump administration official described Vought, "A very determined warrior is how I would see Russ. I don't think he thinks about whether or not he likes Donald Trump as a person. I think he likes what Donald Trump represents in terms of the political forces he's able to harness."

In conclusion, Project 2025 represents a comprehensive and radical plan to reshape the federal government in ways that would have far-reaching consequences for American democracy and governance. It reflects a significant evolution in conservative thinking about executive power and the role of the administrative state, moving from a stance of deconstruction to one of aggressive redirection towards conservative policy goals.

Analysis: THE SECRET PLAYBOOK FOR THE 180-DAYS TRANSITION

The new *Mandate for Leadership* goes beyond any policy documents ever published not only in its scope and drastic proposals, but also because it offers clear strategies on how to implement them, arguing that sweeping changes could and should be made within the 180-days transition period. Beyond the clearly laid out policies for a conservative government, the Heritage Foundation has also instituted a presidential personnel database, which they refer to as a conservative Linkedin, that thoroughly vets "ideologically-aligned conservative warriors" to staff the positions which the document proposes to change into political appointments. The vetted candidates have already begun training in the Heritage foundation funded online Presidential Administration Academy and the leaked videos further confirm the ideological indoctrination and ultraconservative agenda of a future Trump administration.

Presidential Personnel Database and the presidential administration academy

The personnel database component of Project 2025 emerged from a recognition of the staffing challenges faced during the first Trump administration. As Rick Dearborn, who helped lead Trump's 2016 transition team and later served as deputy chief of staff, candidly admitted in one of the leaked training videos:
"Establishing all of this, providing the expertise, looking at a database of folks that can be part of the administration, talking to you like we are right now about what is a transition about, why do I want to be engaged in it, what would my role be — that's a luxury that we didn't have."
This acknowledgment underscores a key objective of the database: to create a ready pool of ideologically aligned candidates who can seamlessly integrate into a conservative administration from day one. The Heritage Foundation's president, Kevin Roberts, described the database as a "conservative LinkedIn," emphasizing its role in identifying and vetting potential appointees who share the project's ideological vision.

The ambitious goal, as reported by the New York Times in April 2023, is to provide up to 20,000 pre-vetted candidates by the end of 2024. This number is particularly significant when considering that a typical presidential administration appoints between 3,000 to 4,000 political staff. The scale of this undertaking suggests a desire to exert greater political control over the federal bureaucracy, a point emphasized by Spencer Chretien, associate director of Project 2025, in one of the training videos:
"Are 3,000 to 4,000 people enough to turn around that federal battleship? These are the only people who are accountable to the president and serve at his pleasure. What does the number suggest about accountability to the people who really matter: the voters?"

IMPLEMENTATION AND TECHNOLOGY
The implementation of this database involves leveraging cutting-edge technology, particularly artificial intelligence, to streamline the vetting process. Oracle Corp., a $370 billion cloud-computing giant, was reportedly tapped to develop this secure personnel database. While Oracle has not publicly confirmed its involvement, and neither Oracle nor the Heritage Foundation responded to requests for comment from various news outlets, the reported use of AI in this context raises important questions about the role of technology in political appointments and the potential for bias in algorithmic vetting processes.

The database's development appears to be well underway. Paul Dans, Trump's former chief of staff at the Office of Personnel Management and Project 2025's chief architect, had drawn up whiteboard sketches of what the "conservative LinkedIn" could look like as early as January 2023. By November of the same year, Axios reported that the database had already amassed more than 4,000 entries.

IDEOLOGICAL VETTING AND CRITERIA
The process of populating this database involves a rigorous ideological vetting process. To be considered for inclusion in the "Presidential Administration Academy," applicants must complete a passcode-protected questionnaire that probes their political philosophy and opinions on a range of hot-button issues. These include views on immigrants, unions, gender, "censorship by Big Tech," the "education industry," "permanent institutions of family and religion," and whether "Life has a right to legal protection from conception to natural death."
Key questions in the application process include:
"Select the option(s) that best describe your political philosophy." Options include Traditional Conservative, Fiscal Conservative, Libertarian, Social Conservative, Neoconservative, and Paleoconservative.

"Name one person, past or present, who has most influenced the development of your political philosophy."
"Name a book that has most significantly shaped your political philosophy, and please explain its influence on your thinking."
"Name one living public policy figure whom you greatly admire and why."
"Name the one public policy issue you are most passionate about. Why are you passionate about this issue and how would you like to see it addressed in the future?"
The questionnaire also includes a series of agree/disagree statements on hot-button political issues, such as:
"The U.N. should have authority over the citizens or public policies of sovereign nations."
"The U.S. has the right to select immigrants based on country of origin." "Life has a right to legal protection from conception to natural death." "The federal government should guarantee a universal basic income." "The police in America are systemically racist." "The federal government should recognize only two unchanging sexes, male and female, as a matter of policy."
These questions reveal a clear ideological bent, seeking to identify candidates who align with conservative positions on issues ranging from abortion and immigration to gender identity and the role of international organizations.

This ideological litmus test reflects the database's underlying purpose: to create a cadre of appointees who are not just technically qualified but also deeply aligned with the conservative vision outlined in Project 2025. As Dans writes in the foreword to Project 2025, "Our goal is to assemble an army of aligned, vetted, trained, and prepared conservatives to go to work on Day One to deconstruct the Administrative State."
The emphasis on ideological alignment is further underscored in the training videos. Dan Huff, a former legal adviser in the White House Presidential Personnel Office under Trump, offers this stark advice to potential appointees:
"If you're not on board with helping implement a dramatic course correction because you're afraid it'll damage your future employment prospects, it'll harm you socially — look, I get it. That's a real danger. It's a real thing. But please: Do us all a favor and sit this one out."

IMPLICATIONS FOR CIVIL SERVICE AND GOVERNANCE
The scale and scope of this personnel database initiative raise significant questions about its potential impact on the nature of civil service and governance in the United States. Traditionally, the federal bureaucracy has been staffed primarily by career civil servants, with a relatively small layer of political appointees at the top. This structure was designed to ensure continuity, expertise, and a degree of political neutrality in the execution of government functions.

However, the Project 2025 database, coupled with the proposed revival of Schedule F (a Trump-era initiative aimed at reclassifying tens of thousands of federal employees as at-will workers), suggests a desire to fundamentally alter this balance. As Kaitlin Stumpf, a former Trump administration official, states in one of the training videos:
"One thing we understood in our time in the Trump administration was the importance of retaining political control over OPM [Office of Personnel Management]. There were several career employees in powerful positions who hindered the work of the president and his staff. They were later replaced by political appointees."
This push for greater political control over the bureaucracy is framed by Project 2025 proponents as necessary for implementing conservative policies. However, critics argue that it could lead to a politicization of the civil service, potentially undermining its ability to provide objective, expert-driven advice and services.

TRAINING AND PREPARATION
Beyond merely identifying potential appointees, Project 2025 also aims to prepare them for the challenges of government service. The leaked training videos, totaling more than 14 hours of content, cover a wide range of topics from the mechanics of governance to strategies for implementing conservative policies in the face of potential resistance.

Some of the advice offered in these videos is routine and practical, such as guidance on obtaining security clearances or managing time effectively. However, other segments suggest a more combative approach to government service. For instance, Bethany Kozma, a former deputy chief of staff at USAID, warns future appointees that they may face "persecution" from career civil servants:
"Even before I arrived, the careers already had it out for me. They tried to keep me from being hired. Two weeks after I started, Buzzfeed did a hit piece on me fueled by information that was leaked about my past advocacy standing up for my children's safety

against the radical gender ideology in Fairfax and Loudoun County public schools. I had a huge target on my back."

Such characterizations of career civil servants as potentially hostile actors could set the stage for contentious relationships within government agencies. However, it's worth noting that not all presenters shared this adversarial view. Max Primorac, another former USAID appointee, offered a more nuanced perspective:

"For people coming in for the first time, government service is hard. It's very confusing. These rules and regulations governing contracting and the budget and all of these things are very confusing—never stop asking questions . . . And after some period of time, when you show yourself to be competent and respectful, you're going to have folks in the bureaucracy, some who won't agree with you, but because of that and because they actually do subscribe to the notion that public service is beyond politics and even if they don't agree, they should do their job. And they're going to come out and start helping you."

POLICY IMPLICATIONS

The personnel database and associated training materials also provide insights into the policy priorities of a potential future conservative administration. For example, Bethany Kozma, in one of the training videos, advocates for a sweeping approach to climate change policy:

"If the American people elect a conservative president, his administration will have to eradicate climate change references from absolutely everywhere."

Similarly, Katie Sullivan, a former acting assistant attorney general under Trump, calls for the elimination of gender adviser positions created by the Biden administration:

"That position has to be eradicated, as well as all the task forces, the removal of all the equity plans from all the websites, and a complete rework of the language in internal and external policy documents and grant applications."

These statements suggest that the personnel database is not just about staffing an administration, but about preparing a cadre of appointees ready to implement significant policy shifts across the federal government.

As public awareness of Project 2025 and its personnel database has grown, so too has controversy surrounding the initiative. In recent weeks, there have been notable developments:

1. Paul Dans, the leader of Project 2025, resigned from his position at the Heritage Foundation.
2. Kevin Roberts, president of the Heritage Foundation, delayed the release of an upcoming book that takes a controversial stance on contraception and in vitro fertilization.
3. Perhaps most significantly, former President Trump himself has sought to distance himself from Project 2025, going from claiming ignorance of the project to issuing a full-throated disavowal. This represents a stark reversal from April 2022, when Trump gave a glowing keynote address at a Heritage event in Florida, commending Roberts for the conservative vision his foundation was crafting.

The backlash and subsequent distancing by key figures suggest that the ambitious and ideologically driven nature of Project 2025 may have overreached in terms of public palatability, even among conservative voters.

ANALYSIS AND IMPLICATIONS

The Project 2025 personnel database initiative represents a significant attempt to reshape the federal bureaucracy in line with a particular ideological vision. While proponents argue that this is necessary to implement conservative policies effectively, critics contend that it could lead to a dangerous politicization of the civil service.

The scale of the database—aiming to identify 20,000 potential appointees for positions that traditionally number around 4,000—suggests an intent to extend political control deeper into the federal bureaucracy than has been customary. This, combined with the proposed revival of Schedule F, could fundamentally alter the balance between political leadership and career expertise in government agencies.

The ideological vetting process for database inclusion raises questions about diversity of thought within government and the potential for echo chamber effects in policy-making. While ideological alignment can facilitate policy implementation, it may also limit the range of perspectives and expertise brought to bear on complex policy issues.

The training materials' characterization of the federal bureaucracy as potentially hostile territory for conservative appointees could set the stage for adversarial relationships within agencies. This dynamic could impede effective governance and policy implementation, regardless of the ideological orientation of the administration. From a democratic perspective, the Project 2025 database initiative raises important questions about the nature of political appointments and their role in a representative democracy. While elections certainly have consequences for policy direction, there is a longstanding debate about the appropriate balance between political responsiveness and bureaucratic continuity and expertise.

As the 2024 election approaches, the fate of this initiative—and its potential impact on the structure and function of the federal government—remains uncertain. What is clear, however, is that the Project 2025 personnel database has sparked a crucial debate

about the nature of political appointments, the role of ideology in governance, and the future of the American civil service.

Regardless of one's political leanings, the implications of this initiative deserve careful consideration. The balance between political responsiveness and bureaucratic continuity is a delicate one, central to the functioning of democratic governance. As such, the Project 2025 personnel database—and the broader vision it represents—merits ongoing scrutiny and debate from policymakers, scholars, and citizens alike.

THE FINAL STEP: THE SECRET 180-DAYS TRANSITION PLAYBOOK

While the project's 900-page policy proposal has been made public and scrutinized, recent revelations suggest that a crucial component—a detailed "playbook" for the first 180 days in office—is being kept under wraps.

This playbook, described as the "fourth pillar" of Project 2025, outlines specific transition plans for each federal agency. However, unlike the broader policy agenda, there are no plans to release this document publicly. This information came to light through secretly recorded footage obtained by the Centre for Climate Reporting, where undercover journalists posed as potential donors and spoke with key Project 2025 authors.

Russell Vought, a primary author of the project who is reportedly overseeing the playbook's development, described the plans as "very, very closely held." The intention, according to the footage, is to hand these materials directly to an incoming Trump administration rather than make them publicly available.

Micah Meadowcroft, an aide to Vought, further elaborated on the secrecy surrounding the playbook. He explained that staff members are being briefed on the plans before any potential administration change to avoid using government email systems for communication. This approach would prevent journalists and the public from accessing information about the playbook through Freedom of Information Act requests.

As of now, the Heritage Foundation has not responded to inquiries about the footage or whether they intend to release the playbook publicly in the future.

However, The Centre for Climate Reporting, a UK-based investigative journalism organization, has revealed disturbing details about the project's true nature and its deep ties to Donald Trump's inner circle, despite public disavowals.

In July, Russell Vought, a key architect of Project 2025 and former director of the Office of Management and Budget under Trump, unwittingly met with undercover journalists posing as potential conservative donors. The two-hour conversation, secretly recorded on video, revealed a stark contrast between public statements and private intentions.

While Trump has publicly distanced himself from Project 2025, Vought dismissed these disavowals as political maneuvering. He stated, "I expected to hear 10 more times from the rally the president distancing himself from the left's boogeyman of Project 2025," adding, "I'm not worried about it." Vought boasted of his close relationship with Trump, claiming, "He's very supportive of what we do," and revealed that the Trump campaign had selected him to write the Republican policy platform.

The investigation uncovered a secretive "second phase" of Project 2025, involving 350 detailed blueprints designed for immediate implementation upon a Trump victory. These plans include:

1. Mass deportations on an unprecedented scale, which Vought described as "the largest deportation in history," aimed at ending multiculturalism in the United States.
2. Further restrictions on abortion rights and an immediate block to funding for Planned Parenthood, with an ultimate goal of a national ban.
3. Dismantling the independence of government agencies like the FBI and DOJ, which Vought called "destroying their agency's notion of independence."
4. Preparing legal arguments to justify using military force against civilian protesters, including a "50-page paper" on the president's ability to "maintain law and order with the military."
5. Efforts to end marriage equality and restrict LGBTQ+ rights.
6. Attempts to ban pornography.

Particularly alarming is the project's strategy to circumvent transparency laws. Micah Meadowcroft, an aide to Vought, explained their plan to brief transition team members without using government email systems, effectively shielding them from potential Freedom of Information Act requests.

The investigation also highlighted the project's ties to other key Republican figures, including Trump's running mate JD Vance. Vought expressed enthusiasm for Vance's selection, describing him as "a MAGA version of what we do."

Lawrence Carter, founder of the Centre for Climate Reporting, emphasized the gravity of these findings: "They're going to great lengths to keep this aspect of Project 2025 secret. They don't want the American public to see what they're doing before they vote." Carter explained that the investigation began as part of a broader project examining populist movements worldwide, with Project 2025 emerging as a key focus due to its potential global impact.

The Centre for Climate Reporting, despite its name, sees this investigation as crucial to its mission. Carter explained, "If you look at actually the sort of key threats to much-needed kind of action on climate change, the rise of the populist right around the world is just as important in our view."

This exposé raises serious concerns about the potential for a radical reshaping of American democracy and civil liberties under a second Trump administration. It underscores the urgent need for public awareness and scrutiny of these covert plans that could fundamentally alter the fabric of American society.

SECTION 2: THE COMMON DEFENSE

The following summary conveys the content of the document accurately and objectively, without endorsing or critiquing the perspectives of the original authors.

Summary

Despite its popular image as a benign science agency, NIH was responsible for paying for research in aborted baby body parts, human-animal chimera experiments, and gain-of-function viral research that may have been responsible for COVID-19. - Page 284

For the sake of American children, Congress should shutter [the Department of Education] and return control of education to the states. – Page 285

The Departments of Defense and State, originating in the George Washington Administration, are currently not living up to their standards. The success of the next presidency will be determined in part by whether they can be significantly improved.

DEPARTMENT OF DEFENSE

Former acting secretary of defense Christopher Miller writes that the Department of Defense "is a deeply troubled institution" that has emphasized leftist politics over military readiness. Recruiting was the worst in 2022 in two generations, and "the Biden Administration's profoundly unserious equity agenda and vaccine mandates have taken a serious toll." The military has adopted a risk-averse culture rather than instilling courage. Most enlisted personnel and officers below general/admiral rank continue to be patriotic defenders of liberty, but this is now "Barack Obama's general officer corps." Russ Vought argues the National Security Council "should rigorously review all general and flag officer promotions to prioritize the core roles and responsibilities of the military over social engineering and non-defense related matters, including climate change, critical race theory, manufactured extremism, and other polarizing policies that weaken our armed forces and discourage our nation's finest men and women from enlisting."

CHINA AND WAR POWERS

Miller writes, "By far the most significant danger" to America is China, which "is undertaking a historic military buildup" that "could result in a nuclear force that matches or exceeds America's own nuclear arsenal." Resisting Chinese expansionism "requires a denial defense" to make "the subordination of Taiwan or other U.S. allies in Asia prohibitively difficult" at a cost and risk Americans are willing to bear. The best gauge of such willingness is congressional approval. We must adhere to the Founders' division of war powers: Congress decides whether to go to war; the executive decides how to carry it out. Departing from this constitutional design, as seen in Korea, Vietnam, Iraq and Afghanistan, is perilous.

PRIORITIES AND PREPAREDNESS

Miller writes missile defense must be a top priority, more weapons must be made in America, the budgeting process must be reformed, and an efficient counterterrorism enterprise sustained. Part of peace through strength is knowing when to fight. As George Washington warned, we must guard against conflicts not justifying great loss of American treasure or blood, while being prepared to defend our interests and meet challenges.

STATE DEPARTMENT

An effective diplomatic corps is key to defending interests and influencing world events. Former State Department director of policy planning Kiron Skinner writes large swaths of the State Department workforce are left-wing and predisposed to disagree with a conservative President's agenda. The department believes "it is an independent institution that knows what is best for the United States, sets its own foreign policy, and does not need direction from an elected President"—unconstitutionally. The solution is strong political leadership to "reforge the department into a lean and functional diplomatic machine that serves the President and, thereby, the American people." With the Senate lax in confirming appointees, Skinner recommends putting appointees in acting roles until confirmed. Skinner writes State should stop skirting the Constitution's treaty requirements and enforcing "agreements" as treaties. It should encourage more trade with allies like Britain and less with adversaries. It should implement a "sovereign Mexico" policy, as Mexico "has functionally lost its sovereignty to muscular criminal cartels that effectively run the country." In Africa, the U.S. "should focus on core security, economic, and human rights" rather than impose radical abortion and pro-LGBT initiatives. Divisive symbols like rainbow or BLM flags have no place next to the U.S. flag at embassies.

CHINA POLICY

Skinner writes the policy of "'compete where we must, but cooperate where we can'...has demonstrably failed" with China. The PRC's "aggressive behavior...can only be curbed through external pressure." Efforts to protect or excuse China, like dismissing the possibility COVID escaped a Chinese lab, must stop. Global leaders like Biden have tried to normalize or laud Chinese behavior, and in some cases voices like BlackRock, Disney and the NBA "directly benefit from doing business with Beijing."

Other Agencies

- Mora Namdar writes the U.S. Agency for Global Media needs people who believe in America, not anti-American entities parroting adversaries' propaganda.

- Ken Cuccinelli says the Department of Homeland Security should be closed as needless bureaucracy, replaced with a stand-alone border/immigration agency, with DHS parts distributed to other departments.

- Dustin Carmack writes the U.S. Intelligence Community is too inclined to look backward, engage in "groupthink," and employ an overly cautious approach aimed at personal approval vs. offering the most accurate intelligence to benefit the country.

- Max Primorac asserts USAID must be reformed, as "The Biden Administration has deformed the agency by treating it as a global platform to pursue overseas a divisive political and cultural agenda that promotes abortion, climate extremism, gender radicalism, and interventions against perceived systematic racism."

-

CONCLUSION

If the chapter's recommendations are adopted, Skinner says the next conservative President has the opportunity to restructure U.S. defense and foreign policy making and execution and reset the nation's global role. The recommendations provide guidance on how the President should use vast federal resources to do that.

CHAPTER 4: DEPARTMENT OF DEFENSE

The Army can no longer serve as the nation's social testing ground. A rebuilt Army that is focused again on its core warfighting mission...must be the next Administration's highest defense priority. - Page 109

Eliminate Marxist indoctrination and divisive critical race theory programs and abolish newly established diversity, equity, and inclusion offices and staff. - Page 103

Key Policy Proposals

The chapter is deeply critical of recent U.S. defense policies, particularly those under the Biden Administration, and it proposes a series of reforms aimed at refocusing the military on traditional warfighting roles, reducing the influence of social policies, and enhancing accountability. Below is a liberal analysis of these proposals:

REJECTION OF SOCIAL POLICIES WITHIN THE MILITARY

Miller criticizes the military's role as a "social testing ground" and calls for the elimination of diversity, equity, and inclusion (DEI) programs, as well as what it terms "Marxist indoctrination" through critical race theory (CRT).

Proposed Policy Change: Abolish DEI offices and CRT programs in military education, and focus the military solely on warfighting capabilities.

Analysis:
- **Consequences:** From a liberal perspective, this approach is deeply problematic. The military is not just a warfighting force; it's also a representation of the nation's values, including equality and justice. DEI initiatives are designed to create a more inclusive and effective military by ensuring that all servicemembers, regardless of race, gender, or background, can serve without discrimination.
- **Social Cohesion:** Removing these programs risks alienating large segments of the military who benefit from these protections and initiatives, potentially leading to decreased morale, unit cohesion, and trust within the ranks. A more diverse and inclusive military is not a distraction but a strength, ensuring that the force reflects the diversity of the nation it serves.
- **International Image:** Additionally, such a move could damage the U.S.'s international reputation as a leader in human rights and equality, making it harder to form alliances and partnerships with nations that value these principles.

CRITICISM OF EQUITY AGENDAS AND VACCINE MANDATES

The chapter argues that the Biden Administration's equity agenda and vaccine mandates have negatively impacted military readiness and effectiveness.

Proposed Policy Change: Repeal these mandates and refocus on traditional military readiness and capabilities.

Analysis:
- **Public Health and Readiness:** Vaccine mandates are essential for ensuring the health and readiness of the force. COVID-19, and other infectious diseases, can severely impact military readiness by sidelining large numbers of personnel. The mandate is not just a health measure but a readiness tool, ensuring that the military remains fit and able to respond to crises.
- **Equity as a Strength:** The equity agenda seeks to address longstanding disparities within the military, ensuring that all members have equal opportunities to succeed. Ignoring these issues could perpetuate systemic inequalities, leading to frustration, reduced morale, and the potential loss of talented individuals who feel the military does not support their growth or protect their rights.

REFOCUSING ON CONVENTIONAL WARFARE AND AWAY FROM SOCIAL ISSUES

The chapter calls for a return to traditional military priorities, with an emphasis on conventional warfare and deterrence, particularly against China and Russia.

Proposed Policy Change: Increase defense spending, modernize the nuclear arsenal, and prioritize conventional force readiness over social programs within the military.

Analysis:
- **Balanced Approach:** Liberals argue for a balanced approach that includes both a strong defense and the protection of civil rights and liberties within the military. While modernization and readiness are important, they should not come at the expense of progress made in creating a more equitable and inclusive force.
- **Cost of Militarization:** Increasing defense spending, particularly in nuclear weapons, diverts resources from other critical areas like education, healthcare, and social services that are equally vital for national security. A liberal perspective emphasizes that security is multifaceted and includes economic security, health security, and social stability.
- **Global Stability:** Focusing too heavily on military buildup, especially nuclear weapons, risks escalating tensions with other nations, potentially leading to an arms race and decreasing global stability. Diplomacy and international cooperation should be equally prioritized to avoid unnecessary conflict and promote global peace.

REDUCING THE NUMBER OF GENERALS AND SENIOR OFFICERS

The chapter suggests that there are too many high-ranking officers relative to actual battlefield experience, advocating for a reduction in the number of generals to streamline military command.

Proposed Policy Change: Limit promotions and reduce the number of senior officers, focusing on those with proven warfighting experience.

Analysis:

Meritocracy vs. Expertise: While meritocracy is important, reducing the number of generals could lead to a loss of valuable experience and strategic insight. The military benefits from diverse perspectives, including those from different backgrounds, which can be essential in complex, modern conflict scenarios.

Democratic Oversight: A careful oversight and transparent criteria for promotions, ensuring that military leadership reflects the diversity and values of the nation. Reducing the number of generals might also reduce the accountability and oversight that is necessary to prevent abuses of power and ensure that military strategies align with broader national interests.

The chapter's proposals appear to prioritize traditional military values and a focus on conventional warfare at the expense of social progress, diversity, and inclusion. While there is agreement on the importance of readiness and national security, a liberal perspective argues that these goals are not mutually exclusive with equity and inclusivity. In fact, ignoring or reversing progress in these areas could have detrimental effects on military effectiveness, social cohesion, and the moral standing of the U.S. both domestically and internationally. Furthermore, the emphasis on militarization and increased defense spending could lead to negative economic and social consequences, diverting resources from vital public services and potentially escalating global tensions.

Summary

This chapter of *Mandate for Leadership* was written by Christopher Miller. The following summary conveys the content of the document accurately and objectively, without endorsing or critiquing the perspectives of the original authors.

The chapter begins by emphasizing the constitutional mandate for the federal government to ensure national defense, highlighting Congress's authority to raise armies and maintain a navy, while the President serves as the Commander in Chief. The Department of Defense (DOD), with nearly 3 million personnel and consuming over $850 billion annually, represents the largest part of the federal government. Despite its size, the DOD faces significant challenges, including mismanagement, lack of accountability, and shifting security policies that undermine its effectiveness. The chapter criticizes recent trends, such as the Biden Administration's equity agenda and vaccine mandates, as contributing to a decline in military discipline and capability.

The U.S. military's recent strategic failures, such as the chaotic withdrawal from Afghanistan and an unclear strategy toward China, are cited as evidence of institutional decay. The author argues that the changing nature of warfare, driven by technological advancements, necessitates a reevaluation of how the military operates. The focus should be on the human element—ingenuity and common sense—rather than relying solely on technology. The section concludes by outlining four priorities for reforming the military: reinstating a culture of accountability, transforming the armed forces for great-power competition, supporting border protection as a national security issue, and demanding financial transparency and accountability.

DOD Policy

The text asserts that the primary threat to American security is China, which is increasingly becoming a global power with ambitions to dominate Asia. The author warns that China's military buildup, including its expansion of nuclear forces, poses a direct threat to Taiwan and other U.S. allies in the Western Pacific. The U.S. must prioritize a defense strategy that can effectively counter and deny China any attempt to achieve regional dominance, particularly over Taiwan. The strategy should ensure that China cannot impose its will on Asia, which would severely undermine U.S. interests.

The author also acknowledges threats from other actors, including Russia, Iran, North Korea, and transnational terrorism, all of which strain U.S. military resources. However, China is identified as the top priority, requiring the U.S. to modernize its nuclear arsenal and strengthen alliances. The text emphasizes the need for allied burden-sharing, particularly in countering China in Asia and Russia in Europe, and calls for increased defense spending and industrial capacity among U.S. allies.

NEEDED REFORMS

1. **Prioritize a Denial Defense Against China**: U.S. defense efforts should focus on preventing China from gaining control over Taiwan and other strategic territories in Asia.
2. **Increase Allied Conventional Defense Burden-Sharing**: Allies should take greater responsibility for their regional defense, with the U.S. focusing on nuclear deterrence and other specialized capabilities.
3. **Implement Nuclear Modernization and Expansion**: The U.S. must enhance its nuclear capabilities to deter both Russia and China, ensuring a credible deterrent across all scenarios.
4. **Increase Allied Counterterrorist Burden-Sharing**: Allies should be more involved in combating terrorism, reducing the burden on U.S. forces while maintaining the necessary capabilities.

DOD Acquisition and Sustainment (A&S)

The Department of Defense's ability to acquire and field new technologies is critical to maintaining U.S. military superiority. However, the DOD's current acquisition processes are hindered by inflexible bureaucratic structures and a risk-averse culture that slow down the delivery of essential tools to warfighters. The budgeting process, established in 1961, is particularly problematic because it locks in spending years in advance, making it difficult to adapt to rapidly changing technological and strategic environments. As a result, U.S. forces may find themselves using outdated or inferior equipment in critical situations, compromising their effectiveness and safety.

The author argues that to meet the demands of modern warfare, the DOD must reform its planning, programming, budgeting, and execution (PPBE) process. This includes enhancing funding for innovation organizations that focus on mission-critical needs, rather than being tied to outdated procurement cycles. The text calls for the President to implement the recommendations of the congressional Commission on PPBE Reform, which aims to make the acquisition process more responsive and flexible.

NEEDED REFORMS

1. **Reform the PPBE Process**: The DOD needs to shift funding towards innovation and away from rigid, program-specific channels that may no longer be relevant. This will allow for greater flexibility in managing portfolios and adjusting to evolving security needs.
2. **Strengthen America's Defense Industrial Base**: Replenishing and maintaining stockpiles of essential equipment, such as ammunition, is crucial for future conflicts. The DOD should collaborate with industry to enact reforms that incentivize innovation and ensure a robust supply chain.
3. **Optimize the DOD Acquisition Community**: The DOD should create incentives that prioritize speed and agility in decision-making. Senior leaders should have the authority to bypass unnecessary regulations that slow down the acquisition of critical capabilities.
4. **Strengthen Engagement with Small Businesses**: To foster competition and resilience in the defense industrial base, small businesses should be supported in growing to medium and large vendors. This includes improving their integration into the DOD supply chain and increasing their engagement with DOD needs.

The text underscores the importance of reforming the acquisition process to ensure that the U.S. military can quickly adapt to new challenges and maintain its technological edge in an increasingly competitive global landscape.

DOD Research, Development, Test, and Evaluation (RDT&E)

The text discusses the critical role of research, development, testing, and evaluation (RDT&E) in maintaining the U.S. military's technological edge, especially in the context of great-power competition. The establishment of the Under Secretary of Defense for Research and Engineering, as mandated by the FY 2017 National Defense Authorization Act, was a significant step in centralizing and enhancing the DOD's innovation efforts. This role encompasses broad responsibilities, including overseeing all defense research and engineering activities and unifying these efforts across the department. This structural change, the largest since the Goldwater–Nichols Act of 1986, was effectively organized during the Trump Administration and is seen as essential for advancing U.S. military capabilities.

NEEDED REFORMS

1. **Champion, Engage, and Focus the American Innovation Ecosystem**: The DOD must leverage America's scientific, engineering, and high-tech production communities to rapidly develop and deploy advanced technologies. This includes fostering better collaboration between government labs, private companies, and other stakeholders to solve the department's most challenging problems.
2. **Improve the Rapid Deployment of Technology to the Battlefield**: The U.S. military's advantage has historically been its ability to quickly translate technological innovations into battlefield capabilities. The text calls for accelerating the prototyping cycle to meet immediate needs, integrating user feedback more effectively, and establishing a pipeline of technologies aimed at countering great-power threats like China.
3. **Develop a Framework to Protect the RDT&E Enterprise from Foreign Exploitation**: With adversaries like China actively seeking to steal U.S. technology, the DOD must implement a comprehensive approach to safeguard its innovations. This strategy should include clear protections tailored to various sectors, from academia to the defense industrial base, and enforce consequences for theft attempts.

The text emphasizes the need for the U.S. to maintain its technological superiority by fostering innovation, ensuring rapid deployment of new technologies, and protecting intellectual property from adversaries. These efforts are crucial for sustaining U.S. military dominance in an era of increasingly sophisticated threats.

DOD Foreign Military Sales

This section addresses the significant decline in U.S. foreign military sales (FMS) and the impact this has on both U.S. strategic interests and the defense industrial base. The text notes that U.S. government FMS fell dramatically from $55.7 billion in FY 2018 to $34.8 billion in FY 2021. This decline hinders interoperability with allies, decreases the capacity of the U.S. defense industry, and increases the financial burden on U.S. military procurements. The document argues that the current FMS process is plagued by excessive bureaucracy, slow contracting times, high costs, and outdated technology, making it less attractive to international partners.

To reverse this trend, the text calls for reforms that would streamline internal processes, incentivize partners and allies to procure U.S. defense systems, and ultimately expand the U.S. defense ecosystem. These reforms are necessary to restore the United States as a reliable partner and to strengthen the defense industrial base in preparation for future challenges.

NEEDED REFORMS

1. **Emphasize Exportability in U.S. Procurements**: The U.S. should prioritize exportability in the initial development of defense systems to make them more attractive and interoperable with partners and allies.
2. **End Informal Congressional Notification**: The text criticizes the "tiered review" process for arms transfers, which adds unnecessary delays. It suggests eliminating this practice unless unanimous congressional support is guaranteed.
3. **Minimize Barriers to Collaboration**: The high cost of developing advanced defense platforms necessitates collaboration with key allies. The U.S. should reduce barriers like the International Traffic in Arms Regulations (ITAR) to facilitate trade and enhance the defense supply chain.
4. **Reform the FMS Contracting Process**: The contracting timeline for FMS, which currently takes around 18 months on average, needs to be shortened by increasing contracting capacity within the DOD to improve the delivery of defense articles to global partners.

The section underscores the importance of reforming the FMS process to maintain U.S. strategic partnerships and ensure that the U.S. defense industrial base is capable of meeting future security challenges.

DOD Personnel

This section focuses on the critical role of personnel in the U.S. military and the challenges they face, including overextension, undervaluation, and insufficient resources. The text argues that military personnel and their families bear the brunt of service-related sacrifices, yet the support they receive is inadequate compared to the demands placed on them. Additionally, potential recruits are being discouraged from military service, further exacerbating recruitment challenges.

The Biden Administration is criticized for treating the military as just another workplace, thereby undermining the unique honor and respect historically associated with military service. To address these issues, the text calls for reforms aimed at rescuing recruitment and retention, restoring standards of excellence, eliminating politicization within the military, and enhancing support for military families.

NEEDED REFORMS

1. **Rescue Recruiting and Retention**: The text highlights a recruitment crisis, with 2022 being the worst year for recruitment in two generations. Reforms include appointing a Special Assistant to the President to focus on recruitment, suspending systems like MHS Genesis that create unnecessary delays, and improving recruiters' access to schools.

2. **Restore Standards of Lethality and Excellence**: Entrance criteria and occupational standards should be based solely on the needs of the military, without exceptions for individuals requiring ongoing medical treatment, such as those with gender dysphoria. Physical fitness standards should be consistent and not influenced by gender, race, or orientation.

3. **Eliminate Politicization and Reestablish Trust and Accountability**: Trust in the military has declined, partly due to perceived politicization. The text suggests reinforcing protections for chaplains, codifying the primary duty of senior military officers as ensuring readiness rather than pursuing social agendas, and reinstating servicemembers discharged over vaccine mandates. It also calls for eliminating Marxist indoctrination and critical race theory programs.

4. **Value the Military Family**: Recognizing the sacrifices made by military families, the text advocates for increasing wages and family allowances for enlisted personnel, improving base housing and spouse employment opportunities, and ensuring access to quality childcare. Additionally, the curricula and health policies in DOD schools should be audited and inappropriate content removed.

5. **Reduce the Number of Generals**: The text argues that there is a rank inflation problem, with too many high-ranking officers relative to those with actual battlefield experience. Reducing the number of generals is proposed as a means to streamline the military and ensure that leadership is based on merit and experience.

The section emphasizes the need to prioritize the well-being, recruitment, and retention of military personnel while addressing the broader cultural and structural issues that currently undermine the effectiveness and morale of the U.S. armed forces.

DOD Intelligence

This section critiques the current state of the U.S. Defense Intelligence Enterprise (DIE), which includes the majority of the Intelligence Community's (IC) personnel and a significant portion of its budget. The text argues that the DIE, along with the broader IC, is at a critical juncture where its ability to deliver accurate, unbiased, and timely intelligence is under threat due to politicization and a customer-based model that prioritizes policy support over analytical integrity. The document emphasizes that without significant reform, the DIE and IC risk continuing to provide flawed intelligence that misguides policymakers, which could have serious consequences for national security.

The section also points out that the DIE has been overly focused on operational campaigns since 9/11, at the expense of strategic objectives. This has increased risks by failing to align intelligence collection and analysis with the most vital national interests, such as countering threats from China and Russia. The text calls for a return to an intelligence process that emphasizes clarity, objectivity, and independence.

NEEDED REFORMS

1. **Improve the Intelligence Process**: The DIE must shift back to providing unbiased intelligence, with senior leaders offering top-line, dissenting, or clarifying views as necessary. The focus should be on strategic interests like countering China and Russia, rather than simply supporting policy directions.

2. **Expand the Integration of Intelligence Activities**: Given the rise of asymmetric warfare, the DIE needs to better integrate intelligence activities across U.S. departments, agencies, and with allies. This includes enhancing cyber capabilities, reviving economic analysis to counter China's strategies, and improving human intelligence (HUMINT) and counterintelligence (CI) efforts.

3. **Restore Accountability and Public Trust**: To rebuild trust in Defense Intelligence, the text advocates for restoring critical thinking and analytic integrity. This involves eliminating the conflict of interest inherent in the customer-based model and ensuring that the DIE has a strong, independent voice in national policy discussions.

4. **Eliminate Peripheral Intelligence Obligations**: The text argues that the DOD should not be burdened with non-military intelligence tasks, such as conducting security clearance investigations for the civilian workforce, a responsibility transferred from the Office of Personnel Management (OPM) to the Defense Counterintelligence and Security Agency (DCSA). This function should be returned to OPM to reduce unnecessary DOD bureaucracy.

The section stresses the importance of refocusing the DIE on its core mission—providing clear, objective, and timely intelligence to support national defense—while removing the politicization and peripheral tasks that currently dilute its effectiveness.

U.S. Army

The section on the U.S. Army highlights a critical point in the Army's history, where it faces significant challenges due to years of budget cuts, declining readiness, and outdated equipment. These issues have been compounded by a complex global geopolitical environment, marked by adversarial victories in Afghanistan, Russian aggression in Ukraine, and China's assertiveness in Asia. Despite these growing challenges, the Army is being asked to do more with fewer resources, which has strained its ability to fulfill its core mission of land dominance in warfare.

The author also criticizes the Army's focus on progressive social policies, such as diversity, equity, and inclusion initiatives, arguing that these have distracted from its primary warfighting mission. The text calls for a comprehensive rebuilding of the Army, with an emphasis on increasing its budget, modernizing its equipment, improving readiness, and refocusing on its core mission of large-scale land combat operations.

NEEDED REFORMS

1. **Rebuild the Army**: The Army's budget has decreased by about 11% since 2018, severely impacting its readiness and modernization efforts. The text advocates for increasing the Army's budget to maintain its status as the world's preeminent land power, accelerating the development and procurement of modern combat systems, and improving training and operational readiness. Additionally, it calls for increasing the Army's force structure by 50,000 troops to handle multiple regional contingencies.

2. **Focus on Deployability and Sustained Operations**: The Army's ability to deploy rapidly and sustain operations is crucial. The text recommends increasing the production and stockpiling of critical munitions and repair parts, prioritizing expeditionary logistics in force design and operational planning, and improving Joint Force training focused on logistics.

3. **Transform Army Culture and Training**: The text strongly opposes using the Army as a testing ground for social policies, arguing that this detracts from its warfighting capabilities. It calls for reestablishing accountability among senior leaders, refocusing Army training on large-scale land operations against peer adversaries, and addressing the root causes of rising suicide rates within the Army.

U.S. Navy

This section discusses the vital role of the U.S. Navy in national defense, emphasizing its constitutional mandate to "provide and maintain a Navy." The Navy's primary responsibilities include projecting sustained combat power globally, both at sea and ashore, and deterring aggression by maintaining a forward operating presence. However, the text highlights that the U.S. Navy is currently challenged by the growing capabilities of the Chinese People's Liberation Army Navy (PLAN), which can now contest U.S. naval supremacy in the Pacific and Indian Oceans.

The author argues that the Navy must adapt to the rapid pace of technological change, balancing the long-term needs for naval platforms with the short-term opportunities and threats that these changes present. This requires careful investment in force structure, innovation, and munitions, along with a renewed focus on warfighter development.

NEEDED REFORMS

1. **Invest in and Expand Force Structure**: The Navy's force structure is centered on manned platforms, including ships and submarines, which must be integrated with land-based, air-based, and space-based forces. The text calls for building a fleet of over 355 ships and developing unmanned systems to augment manned forces. Range and lethality should be key factors in procurement and sustainment decisions.

2. **Reestablish the General Board**: The current joint process for defining requirements for major defense acquisitions is criticized as inadequate for long-term naval planning. The text suggests reestablishing a Navy General Board, modeled after the successful interwar period board, with final decision authority over all requirements documents concerning ships and major defense systems.

3. **Establish a Rapid Capabilities Office**: To accelerate the transition of technology into warfighting capability, the Navy should foster a culture of innovation that emphasizes rapid fielding of "good enough" systems. The Space Development Agency is cited as a model for this approach, and an oversight board is recommended to ensure accountability and progress.

4. **Accelerate the Purchase of Key Munitions**: The Navy must be prepared to expend large quantities of precision munitions in combat. The text advocates for producing these munitions at maximum capacity and enhancing the supply chain to ensure readiness.

5. **Enhance Warfighter Development**: The Navy should mandate qualifications that demonstrate a deep understanding of integrated warfighting, focusing on current plans and technologies. The text also recommends elevating the Headquarters Staff focused on Warfighter Development and using war games as experiential learning environments to prepare leaders for real-world challenges.

U.S. Air Force

This section details the challenges facing the U.S. Air Force, which currently lacks the force structure necessary to fight a major conflict with a great power like China, deter nuclear threats, and meet other operational demands outlined in the National Defense Strategy. The Air Force has been underfunded for decades, receiving less annual funding than the Army and Navy, particularly when accounting for "pass-through" funding that inflates its budget numbers but does not actually go to the Air Force. This chronic underfunding has forced the Air Force to cut forces, delay modernizing aging systems, and retire aircraft faster than they can be replaced, resulting in the oldest, smallest, and least ready Air Force in its history.

The text argues that the current situation is dire, as global events have increased the demand for Air Force capabilities, but the service is ill-equipped to meet these demands. The Air Force's force structure is shrinking at a time when the security environment requires more capacity, and this trend is unsustainable if the U.S. is to maintain air superiority.

NEEDED REFORMS

1. **Increase Spending and Budget Accuracy in Line with a Threat-Based Strategy**: To restore the Air Force to a level capable of achieving deterrence and winning conflicts, the U.S. must return to a threat-based defense strategy. This requires real budget growth and a more equitable distribution of resources across the armed services. The text suggests eliminating pass-through funding to give a more accurate picture of the Air Force's budget and increasing its budget by 5% annually (adjusted for inflation) to reverse the decline in size, age, and readiness.
2. **Reduce Near-Term and Mid-Term Risk**: The Air Force needs to accelerate the acquisition of next-generation capabilities to address immediate threats. This includes increasing procurement of F-35A fighters, building more B-21 bombers, expanding airlift and aerial refueling capacity, and developing and buying advanced mid-range weapons to maximize combat effectiveness in contested environments.
3. **Invest in Future Air Force Programs and Efforts**: The Air Force must develop new capabilities to counter increasingly sophisticated adversaries. This involves operationalizing an advanced battle management system, producing a next-generation air dominance system, enhancing moving target engagement capabilities, building resilient basing and communications for survivability in contested environments, and reinvesting in neglected electromagnetic spectrum operations.

U.S. Marine Corps

This section addresses the U.S. Marine Corps (USMC) as a critical maritime land force with a unique role in projecting power from sea to shore, as well as in performing specialized missions like securing diplomatic outposts. The text notes that the Marine Corps has been heavily engaged in land-based operations since 9/11, which has diverted its focus from its core mission of amphibious and naval operations. This has raised concerns that the USMC has become more of a "second land army" rather than a specialized force for maritime and amphibious warfare.

In response to these concerns, Marine Corps Commandant General David H. Berger initiated "Force Design 2030," a transformative plan aimed at realigning the Corps with its primary mission. This plan involves significant structural and strategic changes, making it the most radical transformation of the Marine Corps since World War II. The successful implementation of Force Design 2030, along with reforms in personnel systems and the Navy's shipbuilding plans, is seen as essential for ensuring the USMC's future combat effectiveness.

NEEDED REFORMS

1. **Divest Systems to Implement the Force Design 2030 Transformation**: To modernize the Corps and align it with future operational needs, the USMC must divest from equipment and systems less suited to distributed, low-signature operations in contested maritime environments. This includes eliminating law enforcement battalions, transforming infantry regiments into Marine Littoral Regiments, and reducing the size of remaining infantry battalions. Divesting from heavy systems, such as M1 Abrams tanks and tube artillery, will free up resources for more relevant capabilities like rocket artillery, light armored vehicles, unmanned systems, and long-range strike missiles.
2. **Transform the USMC Personnel Paradigm**: The Marine Corps relies heavily on junior noncommissioned officers (NCOs) to staff key positions, especially in combat arms. Given the increasing complexity and responsibility of these roles under Force Design 2030, the text recommends aligning the Marine Corps' rank structure with the Army's to ensure that more senior personnel fill these critical positions. The Corps should also create better incentives to retain talented junior NCOs and reduce unnecessary deployments to allow for more robust education and training.

3. **Align Navy Amphibious Shipbuilding with Force Design 2030**: The U.S. Navy must support the Marine Corps' transformation by developing and producing light amphibious warships (LAWs) to enable distributed operations, particularly in the Pacific. The Navy should also maintain a larger fleet of amphibious warships than current plans propose, ensuring that the USMC has the necessary platforms to execute its missions effectively.

This section underscores the need for the U.S. Marine Corps to return to its roots as a maritime and amphibious force, adapting its structure, equipment, and personnel practices to meet the demands of future conflicts. The success of Force Design 2030 is pivotal in ensuring that the USMC remains a formidable and relevant force in an increasingly complex security environment.

U.S. Space Force

This section focuses on the U.S. Space Force (USSF), the newest branch of the U.S. military, tasked with conducting global space operations to enhance the effectiveness and superiority of air, land, and sea forces. The Space Force's responsibilities include providing secure global communications, accurate positioning and timing, real-time intelligence and surveillance, and ensuring the continuity of these operations through both defensive and offensive actions.

The USSF was established to maintain U.S. dominance in space, deter attacks on U.S. space assets, and prevail in space if deterrence fails. However, the text criticizes the Biden Administration for focusing almost exclusively on defensive capabilities, such as disaggregation, maneuver, and reconstitution, while neglecting the offensive capabilities necessary for effective deterrence. This imbalance is seen as a strategic vulnerability that could encourage adversaries to target U.S. space assets.

NEEDED REFORMS

1. **Reestablish Offensive Capabilities**: The text argues for restoring a balanced approach to space operations, where offensive capabilities complement defensive measures. This would complicate adversaries' calculations and ensure that the U.S. retains a favorable balance of power in space.
2. **Reduce Overclassification**: The Space Force needs to move away from the Cold War-era culture of excessive secrecy, which limits coordination across government and with the private sector. Declassifying appropriate information about both U.S. and adversarial space capabilities would enhance transparency and strategic alignment.
3. **Implement Policies Suited to a Mature USSF**: As the Space Force enters its fourth year, it should transition from a "unity of effort" structure to "unity of command" to streamline decision-making and improve operational effectiveness. Additionally, the USSF should lead the development of a clear policy that asserts the U.S. right to operate freely in space and ensures that it can enforce this policy if necessary.
4. **Develop a Space Force Academy**: To attract top talent and develop the next generation of space professionals, the text suggests creating a Space Force Academy. Initially, this academy could be affiliated with an existing research university, eventually becoming an independent institution on par with other military academies.

The section emphasizes the importance of balancing defensive and offensive capabilities in space to maintain U.S. superiority and deter adversaries. It also highlights the need for organizational maturity, transparency, and investment in education to ensure the Space Force can meet the demands of its mission in an increasingly contested space environment.

U.S. Cyber Command

This section examines U.S. Cyber Command (USCYBERCOM), established in 2010 to unify the direction of cyberspace operations, strengthen Department of Defense (DOD) cyberspace capabilities, and integrate U.S. cyber expertise. As cyber threats evolve rapidly, the text underscores the importance of adapting strategies and capabilities to meet these challenges. The ongoing war in Ukraine is cited as evidence that existing U.S. cyber doctrine and assumptions about capabilities and targets may be flawed or outdated.

The text warns against "mission creep," where USCYBERCOM overlaps with other agencies such as the Department of Homeland Security (DHS), National Security Agency (NSA), and Central Intelligence Agency (CIA). This overlap can lead to inefficiencies and blurred responsibilities, reducing the effectiveness of U.S. cyber operations.

NEEDED REFORMS

1. **Properly Focus USCYBERCOM**: The text calls for separating USCYBERCOM from the NSA, as directed by Congress, to clarify roles and responsibilities. USCYBERCOM should concentrate on effective offensive

and defensive cyber operations at both tactical and strategic levels. It should also withdraw from non-military activities, such as efforts to "fortify" U.S. elections, to avoid perceptions of partisanship.

2. **Increase USCYBERCOM's Effectiveness**: To enhance the command's capabilities, the text advocates for integrating cyber and electronic warfare (EW) doctrine, combining coding expertise with kinetic military experience, and decentralizing cyber authorities to allow more flexible and responsive operations. Additionally, it calls for strengthening cyber resilience, particularly in critical areas like the Nuclear Command, Control, and Communications Network.

3. **Rationalize Strategy and Doctrine**: The text emphasizes the need to update the National Security Strategy to define clear DOD roles in cyberspace beyond generic platitudes. Traditional deterrence principles should be applied to cyber and EW, ensuring that the U.S. can effectively retaliate against foreign cyberattacks and EW actions.

Special Operations Forces

This section discusses the U.S. Special Operations Forces (SOF), emphasizing their effectiveness in counterterrorism operations, particularly since 9/11. Despite the overall failure of conventional military operations in Afghanistan, SOF successfully managed to prevent another major attack on U.S. soil, reduced global terrorist threats, and maintained strong collaboration with international partners. The text praises SOF as the most capable and experienced warfighters in recent generations.

However, there is concern that SOF's mission may be diminished in favor of prioritizing great-power competition. The text argues that this would be a mistake, as SOF has a crucial role to play in irregular warfare, which can be effectively employed within the context of great-power competition. By broadening SOF's focus to include state adversaries like China and Russia, as well as nonstate actors, the U.S. can leverage SOF's unique capabilities to achieve strategic effects critical to national defense.

NEEDED REFORMS

1. **Make Irregular Warfare a Cornerstone of Security Strategy**: The text advocates for a broad definition of irregular warfare that addresses both state and nonstate actors. This approach would involve using all elements of national power to project influence abroad, counter adversaries, and maintain peace in great-power competition. Incorporating irregular warfare into the National Defense Strategy would ensure that it receives the necessary resources and attention.

2. **Counter China's Belt and Road Initiative (BRI) Globally**: The text recommends that the Department of Defense (DOD), along with other government agencies and international partners, proactively counter China's BRI. SOF could play a key role in regionally focused operations to disrupt China's economic and strategic influence, particularly in areas critical to U.S. interests, such as energy policy and defense supply chains.

3. **Establish Credible Deterrence Through Irregular Warfare to Protect the Homeland**: The text suggests that SOF should be designated as the lead for executing irregular warfare against state and nonstate actors that threaten U.S. security. This includes utilizing offensive cyber capabilities, employing economic and legal pressure, and maintaining an aggressive counterterrorism posture.

Nuclear Deterrence

This section addresses the critical role of nuclear deterrence in U.S. national security. Nuclear deterrence is described as the foundational element upon which all other military strategies rely, ensuring that potential adversaries are discouraged from launching nuclear or large-scale conventional attacks. The text highlights growing threats from various nations, particularly China, which is undergoing a significant expansion of its nuclear arsenal. This expansion challenges the U.S. to deter two nuclear peer competitors—China and Russia—simultaneously for the first time in its history. Additionally, Russia is actively expanding its nuclear capabilities and using nuclear threats as a coercive tactic, as seen in its actions in Ukraine. North Korea continues to advance its nuclear program, and Iran is edging closer to developing nuclear weapons.

The section underscores that the U.S. nuclear arsenal and the infrastructure supporting it are aging and require urgent modernization. The next administration must prioritize updating the nuclear triad and adapting U.S. strategy to meet the increasingly complex nuclear environment.

NEEDED REFORMS

1. **Prioritize Nuclear Modernization**: All components of the U.S. nuclear triad—land-based intercontinental ballistic missiles (ICBMs), submarine-launched ballistic missiles (SLBMs), and strategic bombers—are far beyond their intended service lives. The text calls for accelerating critical modernization programs, including the Sentinel missile, Long Range Standoff Weapon (LRSO), Columbia-class ballistic missile submarine, B-21

bomber, and F-35 Dual Capable Aircraft. It also advises against extending the service life of aging systems like the Minuteman III ICBM.

2. **Develop the Sea-Launched Cruise Missile-Nuclear (SLCM-N)**: The Trump Administration proposed restoring the SLCM-N to fill gaps in U.S. nonstrategic nuclear capabilities, enhancing deterrence against limited nuclear attacks. The text argues that the next administration should revive and accelerate this program, aiming for deployment by the end of the decade.

3. **Account for China's Nuclear Expansion**: To effectively deter both Russia and China, the U.S. may need more than just the bare minimum of nuclear modernization. This could involve procuring additional modernized nuclear systems, improving the triad's ability to "upload" additional warheads in a crisis, and considering new capabilities, such as nonstrategic weapons or new warhead designs, specifically tailored to counter China's nuclear threat.

4. **Restore the Nuclear Infrastructure**: The U.S. must rebuild its nuclear infrastructure, which is essential for producing and maintaining nuclear weapons. This includes accelerating plutonium pit production, investing in infrastructure at the National Laboratories, and ensuring the readiness of nuclear testing capabilities at the Nevada National Security Site.

5. **Correctly Orient Arms Control**: Arms control agreements should be pursued only if they advance U.S. and allied security interests. The text advises rejecting disarmament proposals that would undermine deterrence and preparing to compete strategically should arms control efforts continue to fail.

Missile Defense

This section emphasizes the critical importance of missile defense in the U.S. national security framework. Missile defense plays a vital role in deterring attacks by casting doubt on the effectiveness of potential adversaries' missile arsenals, thereby limiting their utility as tools of coercion. Additionally, missile defense systems provide essential protection to U.S. and allied forces, critical assets, and civilian populations in the event that deterrence fails. The text notes that adversaries like China, Russia, North Korea, and Iran are increasingly relying on missile capabilities to achieve their strategic aims, making robust missile defense systems more important than ever.

The text highlights the growing threats posed by China and Russia, both of which are deploying new hypersonic glide vehicles and investing in advanced cruise missiles. North Korea continues to develop its missile program aggressively, and Iran maintains a missile arsenal capable of striking U.S. and allied targets in the Middle East and Europe. Despite these escalating threats, the text argues that missile defense has been underprioritized and underfunded in recent years, necessitating a renewed focus and investment by the incoming administration.

NEEDED REFORMS

1. **Champion the Benefits of Missile Defense**: The text argues against the notion, often promoted by critics, that U.S. missile defense systems are destabilizing because they allegedly threaten Russian and Chinese second-strike capabilities. The U.S. should reject these claims while acknowledging that both Russia and China are developing their own advanced missile defense systems. It is essential to keep homeland missile defense off the table in any arms control negotiations with these adversaries.

2. **Strengthen Homeland Ballistic Missile Defense**: The U.S. currently deploys 44 Ground-Based Interceptors (GBIs) as part of its Ground-based Midcourse Defense (GMD) system to protect the homeland against threats from countries like North Korea. However, as North Korea's missile capabilities improve, this system may become inadequate. The text calls for purchasing at least 64 Next Generation Interceptors (NGIs), which are more advanced than the current GBIs. Additionally, the U.S. should consider implementing further measures to bolster homeland missile defense, such as layered defense systems or establishing a third interceptor site on the East Coast.

3. **Increase the Development of Regional Missile Defense**: The conflict in Ukraine has underscored the limitations of U.S. regional missile defense capabilities, particularly in providing reliable systems to allies. The text recommends prioritizing the procurement of more regional missile defense systems, such as the Terminal High Altitude Area Defense (THAAD), Standard Missile-3 (SM-3), and Patriot missiles, to enhance the defense of U.S. and allied forces in key regions.

4. **Change U.S. Missile Defense Policy**: Traditionally, U.S. policy has relied on deterrence to address the ballistic missile threats from Russia and China, focusing homeland missile defense primarily against rogue states like North Korea and Iran. The text suggests that this policy should be reevaluated and potentially revised to reflect the changing threat landscape, ensuring that U.S. missile defense capabilities are sufficient to counter the full range of adversary missile threats.

Homeland Security

This section examines the role of homeland security in the broader context of national defense, emphasizing its critical importance in protecting the United States from a range of threats, including terrorism, cyberattacks, and natural disasters. The text highlights the Department of Homeland Security's (DHS) responsibilities, which include securing the nation's borders, managing immigration, and ensuring the resilience of critical infrastructure. The author argues that homeland security must be integrated with broader national security strategies, particularly in light of the evolving nature of threats, which increasingly involve both state and nonstate actors.

The section stresses that border security is a national security issue, and the DHS must receive sustained support from the Department of Defense (DOD) and other executive branch elements to effectively manage this challenge. The text also emphasizes the need for financial transparency and accountability within DHS, mirroring similar demands for the DOD.

NEEDED REFORMS

1. **Support for DHS Border Protection Operations**: The text calls for increased collaboration between the DOD and DHS to ensure that border security operations are well-resourced and effective. This includes deploying military assets and personnel as necessary to support DHS efforts in managing and securing the U.S. borders, particularly in areas experiencing high levels of illegal immigration and drug trafficking.

2. **Integration of Homeland Security into National Defense Strategy**: Homeland security efforts should be fully integrated into the U.S. national defense strategy, recognizing that threats to the homeland are often interconnected with broader global security challenges. This integration would involve closer coordination between DHS, DOD, and other relevant agencies to address threats such as terrorism, cyberattacks, and the potential for foreign influence operations targeting U.S. infrastructure.

3. **Demand for Financial Transparency and Accountability**: The text stresses the importance of financial oversight within DHS, ensuring that resources are used efficiently and effectively. This includes rigorous auditing processes and accountability measures to prevent waste, fraud, and abuse, and to ensure that taxpayer dollars are directed towards the most pressing security needs.

Special Operations and Intelligence Support

This section focuses on the crucial role of special operations forces (SOF) and intelligence support in national security, particularly in the context of irregular warfare and counterterrorism. The text emphasizes the importance of SOF's ability to conduct specialized, high-impact missions that often require precise and timely intelligence. The integration of SOF and intelligence is presented as a critical component in addressing modern threats, including state-sponsored terrorism, cyber warfare, and the influence of nonstate actors. The author argues that the unique capabilities of SOF and the intelligence community (IC) should be leveraged more effectively to meet the evolving security landscape.

NEEDED REFORMS

1. **Enhance Integration of SOF and Intelligence Operations**: The text advocates for a more seamless integration between special operations and intelligence activities. This includes improving communication, coordination, and data sharing between SOF units and intelligence agencies to ensure that missions are informed by the most accurate and up-to-date intelligence available.

2. **Expand SOF's Role in Irregular Warfare**: Given the increasing complexity of global threats, the text suggests expanding the role of SOF in irregular warfare, particularly in great-power competition. This would involve using SOF's expertise in unconventional tactics to disrupt adversaries' strategic objectives, including through cyber operations, psychological operations, and direct-action missions targeting key assets and individuals.

3. **Improve Intelligence Support for SOF**: To enhance the effectiveness of SOF, the intelligence community must provide more tailored and actionable intelligence. This could involve deploying intelligence operatives alongside SOF units, increasing the use of advanced technologies for real-time data collection and analysis, and ensuring that SOF has direct access to the latest intelligence products relevant to their missions.

4. **Strengthen SOF's Capabilities in Emerging Domains**: The text recommends investing in SOF's capabilities in emerging domains such as cyber warfare and space operations. As threats evolve, SOF must be equipped to operate in these new environments, requiring specialized training and access to cutting-edge technologies.

5. **Increase Coordination with Allied and Partner Nations**: SOF and intelligence operations should be closely coordinated with those of allied and partner nations to ensure a unified approach to global security challenges. This includes sharing intelligence, conducting joint operations, and building the capacity of allied SOF units to enhance collective security.

Needed Structural Changes

This final section emphasizes the necessity of making structural changes within the Department of Defense (DOD) and related agencies to improve overall efficiency, responsiveness, and effectiveness in meeting national security challenges. The text argues that without significant organizational reforms, the U.S. military will struggle to adapt to the rapidly evolving global security environment. These structural changes are seen as crucial for ensuring that the DOD can maintain its technological edge, enhance coordination across different branches and agencies, and effectively manage resources.

KEY STRUCTURAL REFORMS

1. **Streamline Bureaucracy**: The text calls for reducing the bureaucratic layers within the DOD that slow down decision-making and impede innovation. This includes simplifying the chain of command, cutting down on redundant positions, and empowering lower-level commanders to make more decisions in real-time, which can accelerate response times and increase operational flexibility.

2. **Improve Joint Operations**: Enhancing joint operations across the military services is essential for more integrated and cohesive military actions. The text advocates for more robust joint training programs, unified command structures, and shared resources to ensure that all branches can operate seamlessly together during missions. This also involves improving interagency coordination, particularly between the DOD and intelligence agencies.

3. **Revise the Acquisition Process**: The current acquisition process is seen as too slow and inflexible to keep pace with technological advancements. The text recommends overhauling the process to allow for faster development, testing, and deployment of new technologies. This could involve adopting more agile procurement methods, increasing the use of rapid prototyping, and streamlining the approval process for new systems and platforms.

4. **Enhance Cyber and Space Capabilities**: Recognizing the growing importance of cyber and space domains in modern warfare, the text argues for the creation of specialized units and command structures dedicated to these areas. This includes establishing clear doctrines and strategies for cyber and space operations, as well as investing in the necessary infrastructure and technologies to support these missions.

5. **Increase Accountability and Transparency**: To ensure that the DOD operates efficiently and ethically, the text calls for stronger accountability measures. This includes regular audits, transparent reporting on spending and operations, and stricter enforcement of regulations. Leaders should be held accountable for their decisions, particularly in areas like procurement, personnel management, and operational planning.

6. **Focus on Innovation and Adaptability**: The DOD must foster a culture of innovation that encourages creative problem-solving and adaptability. This involves supporting research and development initiatives, promoting partnerships with private industry and academia, and incentivizing personnel to think outside the box when addressing strategic challenges.

7. **Support Allies and Build Partnerships**: The text emphasizes the importance of strengthening alliances and building partnerships with other nations. This includes sharing best practices, conducting joint exercises, and providing support to allies in developing their own defense capabilities. The U.S. should lead in creating a more coordinated global defense posture that leverages the strengths of its allies and partners.

CHAPTER 5: DEPARTMENT OF HOMELAND SECURITY

"Our primary recommendation is that the President pursue legislation to dismantle the Department of Homeland Security (DHS). After 20 years, it has not gelled into 'One DHS.' Instead, its various components' different missions have outweighed its decades-long attempt to function as one department, rendering the whole disjointed rather than cohesive." – Page 133

Key Policy Proposals

1. **Dismantle DHS** and break it up into separate agencies focused on specific missions (border security, immigration, cybersecurity, emergency management, etc.)
2. **Combine CBP, ICE, USCIS and other immigration agencies** into a single cabinet-level border and immigration agency
3. **Restrict asylum eligibility, detain more immigrants, and make it easier to deport illegal immigrants**
4. **End DACA** and limit immigration benefits like work authorization for illegal immigrants
5. **Mandate E-Verify nationally** to prevent hiring of unauthorized workers
6. **Refocus FEMA** on major disasters, raise disaster declaration thresholds, and shift more costs to states
7. **Privatize TSA** airport screening operations
8. **End DHS grants** to states and localities

WHA WOULD THIS MEAN?

These proposals represent an excessively harsh, enforcement-heavy approach to immigration that undermines human rights and due process. Breaking up DHS could impede coordination on key homeland security threats. Restricting asylum, expanding immigrant detention, and accelerating deportations is cruel and fundamentally contrary to America's identity as a nation of immigrants. Eliminating DACA and making it harder for immigrants to work legally could upend the lives of millions who have lived in the U.S. for years. Mandatory E-Verify could hurt businesses and workers. Raising the bar for federal disaster aid will make vulnerable communities even more vulnerable. There are also concerns about the thoroughness and consistency of private airport security screening. Ending DHS grants to states and cities could weaken counterterrorism and emergency preparedness capabilities across the country. Overall, these changes could make the nation less safe while also being overly punitive towards immigrants.

Summary

This chapter of Mandate for Leadership was written by Ken Cuccinelli. The following summary conveys the content of the document accurately and objectively, without endorsing or critiquing the perspectives of the original authors.

PRIMARY RECOMMENDATION

This section presents a comprehensive proposal to dismantle the Department of Homeland Security (DHS), arguing that after 20 years, the department has failed to achieve cohesion. Cuccinelli contends that "its various components' different missions have outweighed its decades-long attempt to function as one department, rendering the whole disjointed rather than cohesive."

The recommendation outlines a detailed restructuring plan:

1. Create a standalone border and immigration agency by combining U.S. Customs and Border Protection (CBP), Immigration and Customs Enforcement (ICE), U.S. Citizenship and Immigration Services (USCIS), the Department of Health and Human Services Office of Refugee Resettlement (ORR), and the Department of Justice (DOJ) Executive Office for Immigration Review (EOIR) and Office of Immigration Litigation (OIL). This new entity would become "the third largest department measured by manpower" with over 100,000 employees.
2. Move the Cybersecurity and Infrastructure Security Agency (CISA) to the Department of Transportation.
3. Relocate the Federal Emergency Management Agency (FEMA) to either the Department of the Interior or, if combined with CISA, to Transportation.
4. Transfer the U.S. Coast Guard (USCG) to the Department of Justice, with provision for its move to the Department of Defense "in time of full-scale war." An alternative suggestion is to move USCG to DOD "for all purposes."
5. Divide the U.S. Secret Service (USSS), moving its protective element to DOJ and its financial enforcement arm to the Treasury.
6. Privatize the Transportation Security Administration (TSA).
7. Shift the Science and Technology Directorate (S&T) to DOD and the Office of Countering Weapons of Mass Destruction to the FBI.

Cuccinelli argues that this restructuring would allow for the dismantling of remaining supporting components, asserting that "their functions already exist in the moving components as well as the receiving departments." This is presented as a cost-saving measure that would "save the American taxpayers significant sums."

The section concludes by acknowledging that until this dismantling occurs, DHS will continue to exist statutorily and requires significant reforms. This sets the stage for the subsequent sections detailing proposed changes within the existing DHS framework.

MISSION STATEMENT

This brief but crucial section proposes a new mission statement for DHS:

"The Department of Homeland Security protects the American homeland from and prepares for terrorism and other hazards in both the physical and cyber realms, provides for secure and free movement of trade and travel, and enforces U.S. immigration laws impartially."

This concise statement encapsulates Cuccinelli's vision for a more focused department, emphasizing three key areas: protection from terrorism and hazards, facilitation of trade and travel, and immigration law enforcement.

OVERVIEW

This extensive section provides historical context for DHS's creation and critiques its current state. It begins by referencing the Homeland Security Act of 2002, which established DHS in response to the 9/11 attacks and subsequent anthrax mailings. The Act outlined DHS's primary mission as preventing terrorist attacks, reducing vulnerability to terrorism, minimizing damage from attacks, preparing for crises, and monitoring connections between drug trafficking and terrorism.

However, Cuccinelli argues that DHS has strayed far from its original purpose, becoming "like every other federal agency: bloated, bureaucratic, and expensive." **The text levels several criticisms:**

1. DHS has "lost sight of its mission priorities."
2. It has "suffered from the Left's wokeness and weaponization against Americans whom the Left perceives as its political opponents."
3. The Cybersecurity and Infrastructure Security Agency (CISA) has been "weaponized to censor speech and affect elections at the expense of securing the cyber domain and critical infrastructure."

To address these perceived failings, Cuccinelli advocates for returning DHS to the "right mission, the right size, and the right budget." **This would involve:**

1. Reorganizing the department and shifting resources from supporting components to "essential operational components."
2. Prioritizing border security and immigration enforcement, including "detention and deportation."
3. Consolidating the "fragmented immigration system into one agency to fulfill the mission more efficiently."
4. Returning CISA to its "statutory and important but narrow mission."

Cuccinelli sees significant opportunities for budget cuts and limiting government intervention, suggesting:

1. Privatizing TSA screening and the FEMA National Flood Insurance Program.
2. Reforming FEMA emergency spending to shift preparedness and response costs primarily to states and localities.
3. Eliminating most DHS grant programs.
4. Removing all unions in the department for "national security purposes."

The section concludes by outlining what a "successful DHS" would accomplish, including securing the border, enforcing immigration laws, protecting political leaders, and overseeing transportation security. This comprehensive overview sets the stage for the detailed reforms proposed in subsequent sections of the chapter.

OFFICE OF THE SECRETARY (SEC)

This section proposes a series of reforms for the Office of the Secretary to ensure effective operation of DHS:

1. **Expansion of Dedicated Political Personnel:** Cuccinelli argues for a "dedicated team of political appointees selected and vetted by the Office of Presidential Personnel" to support the Secretary. This team would not rely on detailees from other parts of the department, ensuring the completion of the President's agenda.
2. **Aggressive Approach to Senate-Confirmed Leadership Positions:** The text suggests placing nominees into similar positions as "actings" during the confirmation process. For example, "putting in a person to serve as the Senior Official Performing the Duties of the Commissioner of CBP while that person is going through the confirmation process to direct ICE or become the Secretary." This approach aims to "guarantee implementation of the Day One agenda and equip the department for potential emergency situations."
3. **Clearer, More Durable, and Political-Only Line of Succession:** Cuccinelli calls for legislation to establish a more durable but politically oriented line of succession. It specifies that "in circumstances where a

career employee holds a leadership position in the department, that position should be deemed vacant for line-of-succession purposes and the next eligible political appointee in the sequence should assume acting authority."

4. **Soft Closure of Unnecessary Offices**: The Secretary is advised to use "inherent, discretionary leadership authority to 'soft close' ineffective and problematic corners of the department." This involves shifting personnel, funding, and operational responsibility to mission-essential components.

5. **Restructuring and Redistribution of Career Personnel**: Cuccinelli recommends major changes in the distribution of career personnel to "strengthen political decision-making and ensure that taxpayer dollars are being used legally and efficiently." This includes redistributing personnel from underutilized areas to "workload-intensive corners of the department" and deploying all personnel with law enforcement capacity to field billets.

6. **Compliance for Grants and Other Federal Funding**: The section proposes strict preconditions for eligibility for FEMA-issued grant funding, including certification of compliance with federal immigration laws, E-Verify usage, and commitment to total information-sharing for law enforcement and immigration enforcement purposes.

7. **Non-Use of Discretionary Guest Worker Visa Authorities**: The Secretary is advised to cease using discretionary authority to increase H-2B visas above the statutory cap and to refrain from issuing regulations supporting the "H-2 eligible" country list.

8. **Restoration of Honesty and Transparency**: Cuccinelli calls for the Secretary to "follow up with congressional and other partners to disclose information and provide the transparency that has been obstructed during the Biden Administration."

9. **Replacement of the Entire Homeland Security Advisory Committee**: The Secretary is advised to "quickly remove all current members of the Homeland Security Advisory Committee and replace them as quickly as is feasible."

These proposed reforms aim to strengthen political control over the department, streamline operations, and align DHS more closely with the administration's priorities.

U.S. CUSTOMS AND BORDER PROTECTION (CBP)

This section outlines extensive reforms for CBP:

1. **Agency Consolidation**: Cuccinelli proposes consolidating ICE and CBP to form a combined Border Security and Immigration Agency (BSIA) if a broader merger of all immigration agencies is not achieved. This would "integrate critical interdiction, enforcement, and investigative resources."

2. **Military Assistance**: The BSIA should establish clear requirements for utilizing U.S. military personnel and resources to assist with border security efforts.

3. **Transparency in Data Publishing**: Cuccinelli calls for eliminating any prohibitive guidance that limits CBP from publishing detailed border security and enforcement data.

4. **Use of Aviation Assets**: The White House should grant authority for CBP and DHS executives to utilize component aviation assets for official travel.

5. **Combining Border Patrol and Office of Air and Marine**: Cuccinelli suggests merging these units within CBP to improve efficiency and practical resource deployment.

6. **Restarting and Expanding Horseback-Mounted Border Patrol**: This includes clearing the records of those "falsely accused by Secretary Alejandro Mayorkas of whipping migrants."

7. **Combining Office of Trade and Office of Field Operations**: Cuccinelli argues this would "achieve streamlined operations and increase OT's capacity and capability."

8. **Limiting Use of Notices to Appear**: CBP should turn illegal aliens over to ICE for detention in most instances, with CBP issuing NTAs only in limited humanitarian situations.

9. **Establishing National Detention Standards**: Cuccinelli calls for codifying a single nationwide detention standard to prevent individual states from mandating differing standards.

10. **Budget Considerations**: The chapter advocates for increased funding for facility upgrades at strategic land Ports of Entry and additional support personnel for Border Patrol.

These proposed changes aim to streamline CBP operations, enhance border security, and align the agency more closely with Cuccinelli's vision of stricter immigration enforcement.

U.S. IMMIGRATION AND CUSTOMS ENFORCEMENT (ICE)

This section proposes extensive reforms for ICE, focusing on returning the agency to its primary mission of immigration and customs enforcement:

Needed Reforms:
1. Cease closing out pending immigration cases and apply the Immigration and Nationality Act (INA) as written by Congress.

2. Direct ICE to stop ignoring criminal aliens identified through the 287(g) program.

3. Eliminate T and U visas, arguing that "victimization should not be a basis for an immigration benefit."

4. Issue clear guidance on detention and bond for aliens to prevent disappearances into the interior.

5. Prioritize national security in the Student and Exchange Visitor Program (SEVP) by removing security risks and reducing visas for students from "enemy nations."

Cuccinelli emphasizes that most of these reforms can be achieved "rapidly and effectively through executive action that is both lawful and appropriate."

New Policies:
1. Clarify enforcement responsibilities: Homeland Security Investigations (HSI) Special Agents should focus on Title 8 and 18 crimes, while ICE Enforcement and Removal Operations (ERO) should primarily enforce civil immigration regulations.

2. Rescind all memoranda identifying "sensitive zones" where ICE personnel are prohibited from operating.

3. Make full use of existing Expedited Removal (ER) authorities.

The section also advocates for combining ICE with CBP and USCIS, and for ICE/HSI to become full participants in the Intelligence Community.

Budget: Cuccinelli calls for significant increases in funding, including:
1. Raising the daily available number of detention beds to 100,000.
2. Funding ICE for at least 20,000 ERO officers and 5,000 Office of the Principal Legal Advisor (OPLA) attorneys.

U.S. CITIZENSHIP AND IMMIGRATION SERVICES (USCIS)

This section presents a comprehensive overhaul of USCIS:

Needed Reforms:
1. Return USCIS to operating as a screening and vetting agency, criticizing its current focus on "easing asylum eligibility" and "removing legal barriers to immigration."

2. Restructure the Fraud Detection and National Security Directorate (FDNS) to prioritize vetting and fraud detection.

3. Reimplement the USCIS denaturalization unit to maintain integrity in the system.

4. Create a criminal enforcement component within USCIS to investigate immigration benefits fraud.

New Policies:
1. Merge USCIS with ICE and CBP to create a single immigration entity.
2. Realign and retrain the workforce on base eligibility and fraud detection.
3. Return training to Federal Law Enforcement Training Centers (FLETC).
4. Implement regulatory changes, including strengthening the public charge rule, reforming temporary work visas, and enhancing asylum system integrity.

Budget:
1. Retain a fee-funded model for USCIS.
2. Increase fees agencywide to keep pace with inflation and the true cost of adjudications.
3. Limit fee waivers and implement a fee for asylum applications.

Personnel:
1. Classify USCIS as a national security-sensitive agency, with all employees holding national security-sensitive positions.
2. Decertify the union and investigate leaks as in a national security agency.
3. Maintain a skeletal D.C. personnel presence, rotating employees with operational or security roles to offices throughout the United States.

NECESSARY BORDER AND IMMIGRATION STATUTORY, REGULATORY, AND ADMINISTRATIVE CHANGES

This extensive section outlines a wide array of proposed changes across legislative, regulatory, and administrative domains:

Legislative Proposals:
1. Create a Title 42-like authority in Title 8 for immediate expulsion of illegal aliens under certain conditions.
2. Mandate appropriation for border wall system infrastructure.
3. Appropriate funds for Port of Entry infrastructure upgrades.
4. Reform policies regarding unaccompanied minors, including repealing or amending Section 235 of the TVPRA.
5. Implement asylum reforms, including raising the standard for credible fear and codifying asylum bars.
6. Reform parole to return it to an "extraordinary remedy for very limited purposes."
7. Halt funds given to NGOs for processing and transporting illegal aliens.

8. Update statutory language for programs like Migrant Protection Protocols and Asylum Cooperative Agreements.

Regulations:
1. Withdraw Biden Administration regulations on credible fear/asylum jurisdiction and public charge.
2. Reform T-Visa and U-Visa programs.
3. Repeal Temporary Protected Status (TPS) designations.
4. Transform the H-1B program into an "elite mechanism" for bringing in high-wage workers.

Executive Orders:
1. Reinstate Asylum Cooperative Agreements with Northern Triangle Countries.
2. Recommence negotiations with Mexico to implement Remain in Mexico Protocols.
3. Prohibit the use of Notices to Report and government-funded travel for aliens into the interior.
4. Mandate full use of ICE detention space in compliance with Section 235 of the INA.
5. Restrict prosecutorial discretion in immigration enforcement.
6. Designate USCIS as Intelligence Community-adjacent.

These proposed changes aim to significantly tighten immigration policies and enforcement, aligning with Cuccinelli's vision of a more restrictive and security-focused approach to immigration and border control.

FEDERAL EMERGENCY MANAGEMENT AGENCY (FEMA)

This section proposes significant reforms to FEMA, arguing that the agency is "overtasked, overcompensates for the lack of state and local preparedness and response, and is regularly in deep debt."

Needed Reforms:
1. Raise the threshold for public assistance eligibility by adjusting the per capita indicator for damages. Cuccinelli argues this is necessary because the current threshold "has not kept pace with inflation" and has led to FEMA's resources being "stretched perilously thin."
2. Implement a deductible system to incentivize states to take a more proactive role in preparedness and response capabilities.
3. Change the cost-share arrangement so that "the federal government covers 25 percent of the costs for small disasters with the cost share reaching a maximum of 75 percent for truly catastrophic disasters."
4. Reform the National Flood Insurance Program (NFIP). Cuccinelli contends that the current system, which provides "insurance at prices lower than the actuarially fair rate," encourages development in flood zones and increases potential losses. The recommendation is to "wind down" the NFIP and replace it with private insurance, starting with the least risky areas.

Budget Issues: Cuccinelli criticizes FEMA's management of DHS grants, characterizing them as "pork for states, localities, and special-interest groups." The text cites that since 2002, "DHS/FEMA have provided more than $56 billion in preparedness grants" and argues that these funds "do not provide measurable gains for preparedness or resiliency."
The recommendation is to terminate these grants, asserting that "states better understand their unique needs and should bear the costs of their particularized programs." However, Cuccinelli acknowledges that this would "require action by Members of Congress who repeatedly vote to fund grants for political reasons."
Personnel: The section suggests reducing the number of Senate-confirmed positions in FEMA from four to one (the Administrator). It also recommends eliminating FEMA's "springing Cabinet position," arguing that it "creates significant unnecessary challenges to the functioning of the whole of DHS at points in time when coordinated responses are most needed."

CYBERSECURITY AND INFRASTRUCTURE SECURITY AGENCY (CISA)

This section proposes a significant narrowing of CISA's scope and mission:
Needed Reforms:
1. Refocus CISA on its two key roles: protecting federal civilian government networks (.gov) and coordinating critical infrastructure security and resilience.
2. Transfer CISA's emergency communications and Chemical Facility Anti-Terrorism Standards (CFATS) roles to FEMA.
3. Move CISA's school security functions to state homeland security offices.
4. Eliminate CISA's efforts in countering misinformation and disinformation. Cuccinelli argues that "the federal government cannot be the arbiter of truth" and criticizes CISA for devolving into "an unconstitutional censoring and election engineering apparatus of the political Left."
5. Limit CISA's role in election security to helping states and localities assess cyber hygiene in their hardware and software before elections. Cuccinelli

emphasizes that CISA "should not be significantly involved closer to an election" and should not "participate in messaging or propaganda."
The section strongly recommends dismissing "the entirety of the CISA Cybersecurity Advisory Committee" on "Day One" of a new administration.

U.S. COAST GUARD (USCG)

This section proposes reforms to refocus and potentially relocate the Coast Guard:

Needed Reforms:
1. Size the USCG fleet to meet the needs of "great-power competition," focusing on protecting U.S. waters, particularly the Exclusive Economic Zone.
2. Address "growing demand for it to address the increasing threat from the Chinese fishing fleet in home waters as well as narcotics and migrant flows in the Caribbean and Eastern Pacific."
3. Reverse "years of shortfalls in shipbuilding, maintenance, and upgrades of shore facilities."

New Policies:
1. Scale down the Coast Guard's mission set to match congressional budgeting, with increased funding going to acquisitions based on an updated Fleet Mix Analysis.
2. Require USCG to submit a long-range shipbuilding plan to Congress, potentially as part of a comprehensive naval long-range shipbuilding plan.
3. Prioritize resources to counter growing Chinese influence in the Pacific, including expansion of facilities in American Samoa and enhanced presence in free association states.
4. Convene a naval board to review and reset requirements for Coast Guard wartime mission support.
5. Consider shifting the Arctic mission to the Navy if adequate funding for USCG is not provided.

Personnel: Cuccinelli recommends stopping "messaging on wokeness and diversity" and instead focusing on "attracting the best talent for USCG." It also suggests re-vetting promotions and hiring that occurred during the Biden Administration and re-onboarding personnel dismissed for refusing COVID-19 vaccines.

These sections reflect Cuccinelli's vision for more focused, efficient, and security-oriented agencies within (or formerly within) the Department of Homeland Security.

U.S. SECRET SERVICE (USSS)

The section begins by asserting that the U.S. Secret Service "must be the world's best protective agency." However, it argues that USSS is currently "distracted by its dual mission of protection and financial investigations." This distraction has led to "a long series of high-profile embarrassments and security failures," with Cuccinelli citing the incident where then-Vice President-elect Kamala Harris was inside the Democratic National Committee office on January 6, 2021, while a pipe bomb was outside as a notable example.

The text references a December 2015 bipartisan report from the House Oversight Committee that listed "dozens of such incidents" and provided recommendations for reform. Cuccinelli adopts these findings and recommendations "in whole," particularly emphasizing the conclusion that "USSS's dual-mission structure detracts from the agency's protective capabilities."

The section highlights that USSS agents spent only one-third of their work hours on protection-related activities, with the rest devoted to investigative activities. It notes that while USSS was initially established to investigate counterfeit currency, its mission has evolved to prioritize electronic financial crimes. Cuccinelli criticizes this shift, stating, "all 15 of the USSS's most wanted individuals were wanted for financial crimes, many of them international in nature."

The text points out a concerning pattern where USSS leaders and agents seek to "burnish their online financial crimes credentials to secure corporate security jobs." This trend, coupled with "some of the lowest morale in the federal government," has led the agency to "completely lost sight of the primacy of its protective mission."

To address these issues, Cuccinelli proposes several new policies:
1. Transfer all investigations not related to the protective function to the Department of Justice and Department of the Treasury.
2. Close all field offices throughout the country and internationally, unless taken over by Treasury or Justice.
3. Transfer USSS agents stationed outside Washington, D.C., to work in Immigration and Customs Enforcement field offices, where they would follow up on threat reports and liaise with local law enforcement for protectee visits.

4. Limit non-protective investigations to those directed by Homeland Security Investigations (HSI) related to financial crimes associated with illegal immigration.
5. Maintain visitor logs for all facilities where the President works or resides, criticizing the Biden Administration for evading such transparency.

Regarding budget, Cuccinelli suggests that the proposed reforms would result in significant reductions, primarily due to relinquishing physical offices. Some savings should be used to address personnel problems and for recruitment initiatives aimed at individuals inclined to join a protection-focused agency.

The section concludes with personnel recommendations, including increasing staffing for the Uniform Division (UD) of USSS. It suggests expanding UD officers' authority to enforce criminal laws outside the immediate vicinity of the White House, arguing this would allow officers to gain more law enforcement experience and improve morale.

TRANSPORTATION SECURITY ADMINISTRATION (TSA)

The section begins by asserting that the TSA model is "costly and unwisely makes TSA both the regulator and the regulated organization responsible for screening operations." Cuccinelli advocates for reforming TSA as part of a broader effort to shrink federal bureaucracies and introduce private-sector expertise to government programs.

The text recommends looking to Canadian and European private models for aviation screening to lower costs while maintaining security. It proposes two main options for privatizing the screening function:
1. Expand the current Screening Partnership Program (SPP) to all airports. In this model, TSA would transfer screening operations to airports, which would then choose security contractors meeting TSA regulations. TSA would oversee and test airports for compliance.
2. Adopt a Canadian-style system by creating a new government corporation that contracts screening services to private contractors. These contractors would bid to provide services to airports in specific regions, with approximately 10 regions nationally. TSA would continue to set security regulations and test compliance, while the new corporation would establish operating procedures and customer service standards.

Cuccinelli emphasizes that in either model, the intelligence function for domestic travel patterns should remain with the U.S. government.

The section projects potential cost savings of 15-20% from the existing aviation screening budget, with the possibility of significantly larger savings. It also anticipates improved service for travelers.

Lastly, Cuccinelli recommends that until privatization occurs, TSA should be treated as a national security provider, and its workforce should be "deunionized immediately."

MANAGEMENT DIRECTORATE (MGMT)

This section begins by criticizing the Management Directorate as "unnecessarily large" due to each individual component maintaining its own management office. Cuccinelli identifies "too much overlap and red tape" between headquarters and components in areas such as hiring, information technology, and procurement.

The text proposes several reforms:
1. **Front Office (FO):** Immediately place a small team of advisers with deep understanding of operational management in the MGMT FO. These advisers should have some government experience to understand nuances like Reduction in Force (RIF) and appropriations hurdles. Their role would be to assess structural and procedural changes needed in the first few months of the Administration.
2. **Office of the Chief Financial Officer (OCFO):** Address the split of DHS responsibilities between the Office of Legislative Affairs (OLA) and OCFO in working with Congress. Cuccinelli suggests either moving appropriations personnel to OLA with a "dotted line" reporting structure to OCFO, or implementing a policy requiring OLA personnel to be included on communications to Congress.
3. **Federal Protective Service (FPS):** Move FPS out from under MGMT to report directly to the Secretary. Cuccinelli argues this is necessary given the current climate and potential for civil unrest.

The section also recommends implementing information-sharing mandates between FPS and other law enforcement agencies like U.S. Marshals, U.S. Park Police, and FBI when federal facilities are involved.

OFFICE OF STRATEGY, POLICY, AND PLANS (PLCY)

This section outlines several reforms for PLCY:
1. Conduct a complete inventory, analysis, and reevaluation of the department's domestic terrorism efforts to ensure alignment with the President's priorities, congressional authorization, and Americans' constitutional rights.
2. Perform a comprehensive analysis of any departmental work coordinating with social media outlets to censor or affect Americans' speech. Cuccinelli calls for full publication of this history and removal of all personnel who participated in such activities.
3. Establish a departmentwide policy for grant decisions, consistent with the President's priorities. PLCY should clear all granting decisions to ensure policy consistency.
4. Work with Congress to streamline the department's reporting requirements, which Cuccinelli argues currently overlap and conflict due to piecemeal additions over two decades.
5. Seek elimination of the Quadrennial Homeland Security Review.
6. Bolster the Immigration Statistics program, making it the central source for all department immigration statistics and analysis.

These proposed changes reflect Cuccinelli's vision for a more focused, efficient, and politically aligned Department of Homeland Security.

OFFICE OF INTELLIGENCE AND ANALYSIS (I&A)

This section advocates for the elimination of the Office of Intelligence and

Analysis, presenting two primary arguments:
1. The office "has not added value" to the department's operations.
2. It "has been weaponized for domestic political purposes."

Cuccinelli contends that I&A's role as an intermediary between the Intelligence Community (IC) and DHS components is redundant at best and potentially harmful. The text states, "I&A's work as an interlocuter between the IC and DHS components' individual intelligence operations on the one hand and government and the private sector on the other, as well as between the IC and the components, is at best duplicative. At worst, it is used and discussed in the media as a political tool, resulting in more harm than good to the U.S. government and IC writ large."

Instead, the section proposes that:
1. The Cybersecurity and Infrastructure Security Agency (CISA) should create cyber intelligence products in collaboration with the National Security Agency and U.S. Cyber Command.
2. Other DHS components (e.g., CBP, TSA) should rely on their own intelligence operations, as they are "better situated with their subject-matter experts to make their own assessments."
3. The National Operations Center (NOC) within the Office of Operations Coordination (OPS) should absorb "those select I&A functions and tactically proficient personnel that need to be maintained (for example, technical support to the National Vetting Center)."

Cuccinelli recommends that the OPS entity maintain IC status, but with a narrowly defined intelligence mission: "to provide situational awareness and the dissemination of operational information or raw intelligence (no analysis or products) at classified and unclassified levels to executive leadership across the department, not outside of DHS."

OFFICE OF THE GENERAL COUNSEL (OGC)

This section proposes significant reforms to the Office of the General Counsel:
1. **Reorient OGC's approach:** Cuccinelli argues that OGC should "advise principals as to how DHS can execute its missions within the law instead of advising principals as to why they cannot execute regulations, policies, and programs."
2. **Restructure reporting lines:** The text recommends reversing the current reporting structure. Component chief counsels should report directly to their component head and indirectly to the DHS General Counsel, rather than the current reverse arrangement.
3. **Increase political oversight:** The section calls for hiring "significantly more Schedule C/political appointees who in turn supervise career staff and manage their output." This is justified by stating, "DHS's mission is politically charged, and the legal function cannot be allowed to thwart the Administration's agenda by providing stilted or erroneous legal positions and decision-making."
4. **Centralize legal responses:** OGC should serve as the center for responses to legal challenges, ensuring consistency across the department in litigation, congressional oversight, and inquiries from various oversight bodies.
5. **Improve technology:** Cuccinelli recommends investing in e-discovery software and contracting with a vendor to manage the department's e-discovery process. This aims to reduce delays in responding to litigation and congressional oversight requests.

6. **Enhance document gathering**: The section suggests improving the process for gathering documents for congressional requests by utilizing the Office of the Chief Information Officer or relevant technological elements within the department.

These proposed changes reflect a desire to align the OGC more closely with the administration's policy goals and to improve efficiency in legal matters across the department.

OFFICE FOR CIVIL RIGHTS AND CIVIL LIBERTIES (CRCL) AND PRIVACY OFFICE (PRIV)

This section proposes significant changes to CRCL and PRIV, arguing that both offices have expanded beyond their original intent and helpful purpose:

1. **Recalibration of scope**: Cuccinelli notes that the Homeland Security Act established only an Officer of CRCL, not an office, and its original function was limited to reviewing and assessing information alleging civil rights abuses. The text criticizes the subsequent expansion of CRCL's scope and size.
2. **Organizational restructuring**: The section recommends absorbing both CRCL's and PRIV's necessary functions and staff into the Office of General Counsel. While acknowledging that the CRCL Officer and FOIA Officer/Privacy Officer positions are statutory, Cuccinelli argues their offices are not mandatory.
3. **Reporting structure**: CRCL and PRIV Officers and employees should report to a Deputy General Counsel, who would be a political appointee.
4. **CRCL focus**: The CRCL Officer should focus on equal employment opportunity (EEO) compliance and civil liberties function, investigating matters only within Headquarters or support components. Operational components' civil liberties officers should investigate incidents regarding their own agencies.
5. **PRIV focus**: The PRIV Officer and FOIA Officer should concentrate on FOIA, Privacy Compliance Policy, and Privacy Incident Response.
6. **Limiting scope**: Cuccinelli recommends that CRCL and PRIV staff should no longer review intelligence products or provide guidance on any intelligence products or reports.
7. **Communication restrictions**: All communications with federal, state, local, or nongovernment groups should be limited to the Deputy General Counsel.
8. **Disbanding external engagement**: The section calls for disbanding outside advisory boards and the more than 50 working groups in which CRCL and PRIV currently participate.

OFFICE OF THE IMMIGRATION DETENTION OMBUDSMAN (OIDO) AND OFFICE OF THE CITIZENSHIP AND IMMIGRATION SERVICES OMBUDSMAN (CISOMB)

This section recommends significant changes to both offices:

OIDO:
1. Eliminate the Office of the Immigration Detention Ombudsman entirely, which would require a statutory change.
2. If OIDO remains, the Secretary should issue a directive stripping CRCL of its immigration portfolio to avoid duplication.
3. Conduct a thorough review of the effectiveness of Directive 0810.1, which concerns referrals to the Office of Inspector General.

CISOMB:
1. Eliminate the Office of the Citizenship and Immigration Services Ombudsman, which would require a statutory change.
2. If CISOMB continues, issue a policy prohibiting it from assisting illegal aliens in obtaining benefits.
3. Move CISOMB's specialized casework into USCIS as a special unit, similar to the IRS Taxpayer Advocate.

Cuccinelli argues these changes would streamline operations, reduce redundancy, and align the offices more closely with the administration's immigration priorities.

AGENCY RELATIONSHIPS

This final section emphasizes the importance of inter-agency cooperation in achieving the President's policy objectives, particularly in immigration policy. It outlines specific objectives for various departments:

1. **Department of Health and Human Services**: Move the Office of Refugee Resettlement to DHS or ensure it fully pursues presidential objectives in support of DHS.
2. **Department of Defense**: Assist in building the border wall system and actively participate in border defense.
3. **Department of Justice**: Move immigration-related offices to DHS or treat immigration judges as national security personnel.
4. **Department of State**: Allow DHS to lead international engagement on security and migration in the Western Hemisphere.
5. **Department of Housing and Urban Development**: Ensure only U.S. citizens and lawful permanent residents use federally subsidized housing.
6. **Department of Education**: Deny loan access to non-citizens and schools providing in-state tuition to illegal aliens.
7. **Department of Labor**: Eliminate the two lowest wage levels for foreign workers.
8. **Department of the Treasury**: Implement regulations to equalize taxes between citizens and visa holders and provide DHS with illegal aliens' tax information.
9. **Intelligence Community**: Cooperate in shrinking or eliminating I&A's role while replacing it with CBP and HSI representation.

These recommendations purportedly aim to create a more cohesive and aligned approach to immigration and homeland security across the federal government.

CHAPTER 6: DEPARTMENT OF STATE

Our primary recommendation is that the President pursue legislation to dismantle the Department of Homeland Security (DHS). After 20 years, it has not gelled into 'One DHS.' Instead, its various components' different missions have outweighed its decades-long attempt to function as one department, rendering the whole disjointed rather than cohesive. – Page 133

Key Policy Proposals

The policy proposals outlined in this chapter represent a concerning shift towards a more confrontational, unilateral approach to foreign policy that risks undermining key alliances and international cooperation. While some reforms to the State Department's structure and operations may be warranted, the overall thrust seems to be towards imposing a particular ideological agenda rather than pursuing a balanced strategy that upholds American interests and values.

RESTRUCTURING THE STATE DEPARTMENT

The chapter argues for a significant overhaul of the State Department to better align it with the President's foreign policy agenda. Key proposals include:

- Placing political appointees in key leadership roles from day one
- Recalling and replacing all ambassadors, both political and career
- Freezing implementation of unratified treaties and international agreements pending review
- Revoking delegated authorities to other agencies

Analysis: The emphasis on immediately replacing career ambassadors and officials with political appointees aligned with the president's views threatens to politicize the foreign service and sideline valuable expertise. An abrupt break in continuity could disrupt important initiatives and relationships. The call to freeze implementation of international agreements pending review is also troubling, as it could undercut American credibility and leadership on the global stage.

COUNTERING CHINA

The chapter identifies China as the top geopolitical threat and proposes a much more confrontational approach, including:

- Developing an "Article X" philosophical framework positioning China as an adversary, not just competitor
- Applying economic pressure to make Chinese aggression unaffordable
- Building stronger partnerships and synchronizing economic/security policies to counter China

Analysis: The starkly adversarial posture towards China, while not unfounded given real challenges, veers too far towards framing the relationship in purely zero-sum terms. Pursuing "Article X" to position China as an enemy rather than competitor leaves little room for much-needed cooperation on transnational issues like climate change and global health. A more nuanced strategy of balancing competition and selective engagement would better serve long-term interests.

PROMOTING DEMOCRACY AND HUMAN RIGHTS

The chapter argues for vigorously supporting pro-democracy movements against authoritarian regimes in places like Iran and Venezuela. However, it also states that promoting controversial social policies should not be a human rights priority.

Analysis: The chapter takes a heavily interventionist stance, calling for aggressive efforts to undermine disfavored regimes in places like Iran and Venezuela. But the track record of U.S.-orchestrated regime change is checkered at best, often unleashing unintended consequences and chaos. Change must ultimately come from within, with the U.S. playing a supporting role. The reflexive hostility towards international institutions like the U.N., while highlighting real flaws, fails to recognize the essential role of multilateral cooperation in addressing global challenges no country can tackle alone.

While the chapter identifies some legitimate issues, the proposed remedies reflect a worldview of "us vs. them" that is likely to prove counterproductive in an interconnected world. Protecting and advancing American interests requires skillful statecraft, strong alliances, and the judicious use of all tools of national power - diplomatic, economic, and military. An approach overly reliant on coercion and unilateralism risks strategic overreach and the erosion of the very international system that has greatly benefited the United States. A foreign policy anchored in American values and a positive vision for U.S. leadership remains the surest path to security and prosperity in the 21st century.

Summary

This chapter of Mandate for Leadership was written by Kiron K. Skinner. The following summary conveys the content of the document accurately and objectively, without endorsing or critiquing the perspectives of the original authors.

The chapter opens by outlining the U.S. Department of State's mission to implement the President's foreign policy priorities, serve U.S. citizens abroad, and advance American interests. It emphasizes the department's historical role as the primary tool for engaging with foreign governments since the nation's founding.

A significant problem is identified: the resistance of large portions of the State Department workforce to conservative Presidents' policy agendas. Skinner asserts that "there is a tug-of-war between Presidents and bureaucracies—and that resistance is much starker under conservative Presidents." This situation is deemed unacceptable, with the text arguing that "The American people need and deserve a diplomatic machine fully focused on the national interest as defined through the election of a President who sets the domestic and international agenda for the nation."

The chapter calls for the next administration to take "swift and decisive steps to reforge the department into a lean and functional diplomatic machine" that serves the President and the American people. This sets the tone for the detailed recommendations that follow.

HISTORY AND CONTEXT

This section provides a concise history of the State Department, from its founding in 1789 with Thomas Jefferson as the first Secretary of State, to its current size of nearly 80,000 employees across 275 global posts. The department's theoretical responsibilities are outlined, including carrying out the President's foreign policy and representing the U.S. in international organizations.

Skinner cites the Hart-Rudman Commission's critique from over 20 years ago, which described the State Department as a "crippled institution" suffering from "an ineffective organizational structure in which regional and functional policies do not serve integrated goals, and in which sound management, accountability, and leadership are lacking." Notably, the text asserts that this critique remains accurate today.

The chapter argues that the State Department's failures are not due to lack of resources, but rather stem from "its institutional belief that it is an independent institution that knows what is best for the United States, sets its own foreign policy, and does not need direction from an elected President." To address this, Skinner contends that the next President must provide a clear foreign policy vision, select officials who will enthusiastically implement that vision, and support necessary institutional adjustments.

POLITICAL LEADERSHIP AND BUREAUCRATIC LEADERSHIP AND SUPPORT

This section outlines specific steps the next administration should take to align the State Department with the President's vision:

1. Exert leverage during the confirmation process by placing appointees directly into roles pending confirmation, forcing the Senate to act swiftly.
2. Assert leadership in the appointment process by placing political appointees in non-Senate-confirmed positions and increasing their overall number.
3. Support and train political appointees through regular coordination, strategy meetings, and mentorship programs. Skinner emphasizes that "The interaction of political appointees must be routine and operational rather than incidental or occasional."
4. Maximize the value of career officials by leveraging their expertise while making clear they "need not be adversaries of a conservative President."
5. Reboot ambassadors worldwide by accepting resignations of all political ambassadors and quickly reviewing career ambassadors. The text stresses prioritizing "new ambassadors who support the President's agenda among political appointees, foreign service officers, and civil service personnel, with no predetermined percentage among these categories."

Skinner underscores the importance of swift implementation, stating "No one in a leadership position on the morning of January 20 should hold that position at the end of the day."

RIGHTING THE SHIP

This section details immediate actions the next administration should take to ensure the State Department prioritizes American interests:

1. **Review Retroactively**: Assess all State Department negotiations and funding commitments before inauguration. The Secretary of State should "order an immediate freeze on all efforts to implement unratified treaties and international agreements" pending review.
2. **Implement Repair:** Change the handling of international agreements to "restore constitutional governance." Skinner criticizes the current administration's approach, stating it "not only approves but also enforces treaties that have not been ratified by the U.S. Senate."

3. **Coordinate with Other Agencies:** Ensure interagency engagement reflects presidential direction. The text emphasizes that "Bureaucratic stovepipes of the past should be less important than commitment to, and achievement of, the President's foreign policy agenda."

4. **Coordinate with Congress:** Strengthen leadership of the Bureau of Legislative Affairs and ensure full coordination with the White House on congressional engagement.

5. **Respond Vigorously to the Chinese Threat:** Support and modify the concept of the Office of China Coordination ("China House"). Skinner asserts that "The Chinese Communist Party (CCP) has been 'at war' with the U.S. for decades."

6. **Review Immigration and Domestic Security Requirements:** The text recommends enforcing visa reciprocity, fully implementing visa sanctions, curtailing refugee admissions, reactivating Trump-era policies, and evaluating "security-sensitive visa programs."

These recommendations aim to ensure "the safety, security, and prosperity of all Americans."

PIVOTING ABROAD

Skinner emphasizes the need for a significant reorientation of U.S. foreign policy, describing it as potentially "the most significant shift in core foreign policy principles and corresponding action since the end of the Cold War." This reorientation is presented as crucial, with Skinner stating that it "could represent the most significant shift in core foreign policy principles and corresponding action since the end of the Cold War."

The text identifies five countries requiring heightened attention due to their potential to significantly impact U.S. interests: China, Iran, Venezuela, Russia, and North Korea. Skinner notes that these nations represent various threats, including existential dangers to American safety and security, economic threats, and "wild cards" with unknown but unsettling threat scopes.

THE PEOPLE'S REPUBLIC OF CHINA:
The chapter describes China as a "serious and dangerous" threat, emphasizing the Chinese Communist Party's (CCP) role in governing the country. Skinner states, "This tyrannical country with a population of more than 1 billion people has the vision, resources, and patience to achieve its objectives."
The text calls for an "unambiguous offensive-defensive mix" in U.S. strategy, including:
1. Protecting American citizens and their interests from CCP attacks and abuse
2. Safeguarding U.S. allies
3. Implementing a "cost-imposing strategic response to make Beijing's aggression unaffordable"

Skinner argues for viewing China as "more of a threat than a competitor," critiquing those who believe in a moderating approach or a policy of "compete where we must, but cooperate where we can." This strategy, according to the text, "has demonstrably failed." The chapter recommends developing an "Article X for China," similar to George Kennan's Cold War strategy document. This should be a "deeply philosophical look at the China challenge" led by the State Department and National Security Council.

Skinner acknowledges various perspectives on China within foreign policy and business circles, including those reluctant to take decisive action, those dismissing criticisms as conspiracy theories, and those benefiting from business with Beijing. However, the text argues that "the PRC's actions often do sound like conspiracy theories—because they are conspiracies."
Importantly, the chapter distinguishes between the Chinese people and the CCP, stating, "the issue should never be with the Chinese people but with the Communist dictatorship that oppresses them and threatens the well-being of nations across the globe." However, it also notes that China's current power dynamics are rooted in its strategic culture and history, not just CCP ideology, concluding that "internal culture and civil society will never deliver a more normative nation. The PRC's aggressive behavior can only be curbed through external pressure."

THE ISLAMIC REPUBLIC OF IRAN:
The chapter begins by addressing the ongoing protests in Iran, describing them as "widely viewed as a new revolution." It argues that the Islamic regime, in power since 1979, is at its weakest state in history and is at odds with both its own people and regional neighbors.

Skinner criticizes the Obama and Biden administrations' approaches to Iran, particularly the 2015 Joint Comprehensive Plan of Action (Iran nuclear deal). The text argues that this deal "gave the Islamic regime a crucial monetary lifeline" after the 2009 Green Movement protests, which had weakened the regime. Skinner states:
"Instead of pressuring the Iranian theocracy to move toward democracy, the Obama Administration threw the brutal regime an economic lifeline by giving hundreds of billions of dollars to the Iranian government and providing other sanctions relief."

The chapter contends that this economic relief "did not moderate the regime, but emboldened its brutality, its efforts to expand its nuclear weapons programs, and its support for global terrorism."
Skinner recommends that the next administration should neither preserve nor repeat these perceived mistakes. Instead, it argues for a policy that supports the Iranian people's desire for democracy:
"The correct future policy for Iran is one that acknowledges that it is in U.S. national security interests, the Iranian people's human rights interests, and a broader global interest in peace and stability for the Iranian people to have the democratic government they demand."
While acknowledging that the decision for regime change must come from the Iranian people, the text suggests that the United States can "utilize its own and others' economic and diplomatic tools to ease the path toward a free Iran and a renewed relationship with the Iranian people."

THE BOLIVARIAN REPUBLIC OF VENEZUELA:
The chapter describes Venezuela's decline under the Communist regimes of Hugo Chavez and Nicolas Maduro over the past 24 years. It states that the country has:
1. "Violently cracked down on pro-democracy citizens and organizations"
2. "Shattered its once oil-rich economy"
3. "Empowered domestic criminal cartels"
4. "Helped fuel a hemispheric refugee crisis"

Skinner notes Venezuela's transition from "one of the most prosperous, if not the most prosperous, country in South America to being one of the poorest." The text also highlights Venezuela's growing ties to U.S. adversaries, including China and Iran, which "have long sought a foothold in the Americas."

The chapter argues that Venezuela serves as a cautionary tale, demonstrating "just how fragile democratic institutions that are not maintained can be." To address this situation, Skinner recommends that the next administration:
1. "Take important steps to put Venezuela's Communist abusers on notice"
2. Make "strides to help the Venezuelan people"
3. "Work to unite the hemisphere against this significant but underestimated threat in the Southern Hemisphere"
These recommendations aim to contain Venezuela's Communism and aid international partners in the region.

RUSSIA:
Skinner acknowledges that the Russia-Ukraine conflict is a divisive issue among conservatives. The text outlines three main schools of thought within conservative circles:
1. Continued U.S. involvement and support for Ukraine: This perspective views Russia as presenting "major challenges to U.S. interests, as well as to peace, stability, and the post-Cold War security order in Europe." Proponents argue for "continued U.S. involvement including military aid, economic aid, and the presence of NATO and U.S. troops if necessary." The end goal is "the defeat of Russian President Vladimir Putin and a return to pre-invasion border lines."
2. Ending U.S. involvement: This viewpoint "denies that U.S. Ukrainian support is in the national security interest of America at all." It argues that since Ukraine is not a NATO member and is "one of the most corrupt nations in the region," European nations should be responsible for aiding Ukraine's defense. Advocates of this position desire "a swift end to the conflict through a negotiated settlement between Ukraine and Russia."
3. A middle ground approach: This perspective "eschews both isolationism and interventionism." It prioritizes U.S. interests, fiscal responsibility, and the protection of American freedom, liberty, and sovereignty. This approach calls for continued U.S. involvement to be "fully paid for; limited to military aid (while European allies address Ukraine's economic needs); and have a clearly defined national security strategy that does not risk American lives."

Skinner notes that despite these divisions, all sides agree on two points:
1. "Putin's invasion of Ukraine is unjust"
2. "The Ukrainian people have a right to defend their homeland"
The text also highlights some positive outcomes of the conflict, including that it "has severely weakened Putin's military strength and provided a boost to NATO unity and its importance to European nations."
Skinner concludes this section by stating that the next conservative President has "a generational opportunity to bring resolution to the foreign policy tensions within the movement and chart a new path forward that recognizes Communist China as the defining threat to U.S. interests in the 21st century."

THE DEMOCRATIC PEOPLE'S REPUBLIC OF KOREA:
The chapter emphasizes the importance of peace and stability in Northeast Asia, describing it as a "vital interest" of the United States. It underscores the critical role of South Korea and Japan as allies in ensuring "a free and open Indo-Pacific" and as "indispensable military, economic, diplomatic, and technology partners."

The text outlines two main imperatives regarding North Korea:
1. Deterrence: "The Democratic People's Republic of Korea (DPRK, or North Korea) must be deterred from military conflict."
2. Denuclearization: "The United States cannot permit the DPRK to remain a de facto nuclear power with the capacity to threaten the United States or its allies."

Skinner argues that these interests are crucial both for defending the American homeland and for the future of global nonproliferation efforts. The text firmly states:

"The DPRK must not be permitted to profit from its blatant violations of international commitments or to threaten other nations with nuclear blackmail."

The chapter concludes that addressing these interests effectively requires the U.S. to "disallow the DPRK's rogue regime behavior," suggesting a tough stance against North Korea's nuclear ambitions and aggressive actions.

OTHER INTERNATIONAL ENGAGEMENTS

WESTERN HEMISPHERE:
Skinner begins by emphasizing the United States' vested interest in "a relatively united and economically prosperous Western Hemisphere." However, the text notes a significant challenge: "the region now has an overwhelming number of socialist or progressive regimes, which are at odds with the freedom and growth-oriented policies of the U.S. and other neighbors and who increasingly pose hemispheric security threats." To address these challenges, the chapter proposes several core policies:
1. A "sovereign Mexico" policy: The text describes Mexico as "currently a national security disaster," stating it has "functionally lost its sovereignty to muscular criminal cartels that effectively run the country." Skinner calls for a posture that supports "a fully sovereign Mexico" and urges taking "all steps at its disposal to support that result in as rapid a fashion as possible."
2. A "fentanyl-free frontier": The chapter highlights the collaboration between Mexican cartels and Chinese fentanyl manufacturers, describing it as "the largest drug crisis in the history of North America." Skinner recommends leveraging the new insistence on a sovereign Mexico to "halt the fentanyl crisis and put a decisive end to this unprecedented public health threat."
3. A hemisphere-centered approach to industry and energy: The text proposes two key strategies: a) "Re-hemisphering" manufacturing and industry from distant points (especially China) to Central and South American countries. b) Developing a hemisphere-focused energy policy to "reduce reliance on distant and manipulable sources of fossil fuels, restore the free flow of energy among the hemisphere's largest producers, and work together to increase energy production."
4. A "local" approach to security threats: Skinner notes that some countries in the Americas "are either increasingly regional security threats in their own rights or are vulnerable to hostile extra-continental powers." The text calls for U.S. leadership to help "these democratic neighbors to fight against the external pressure of threats from abroad and address local regional security concerns."

Skinner argues that these policies represent "a golden opportunity to make key economic changes that will not only provide tremendous economic opportunities for Americans but will also serve as an economic boon to the entire Western Hemisphere."

MIDDLE EAST AND NORTH AFRICA:
The chapter calls for the next Administration to "re-engage with Middle Eastern and North African nations and not abandon the region." It outlines a multi-dimensional strategy:
1. Iran: The text advocates for preventing Iran from acquiring nuclear technology, reinstating and expanding Trump Administration sanctions, providing security assistance to regional partners, and supporting "freedom-seeking Iranian people in their revolt against the mullahs."
2. Israel and Arab states: Skinner recommends building on the Trump Administration's diplomatic successes by encouraging more Arab states to enter the Abraham Accords. It also suggests "reversing, as appropriate, the Biden Administration's degradation of the long-standing partnership with Saudi Arabia" and defunding the Palestinian Authority.
3. Türkiye: The text emphasizes keeping Türkiye "in the Western fold and a NATO ally," suggesting a rethinking of U.S. support for Kurdish forces to address Turkish security concerns.
4. Oil and China: Recognizing the continued importance of Middle Eastern oil, Skinner recommends strengthening relations with Saudi Arabia "in a way that seriously curtails Chinese influence in Riyadh."
5. Regional security: The text proposes building "a Middle East security pact that includes Israel, Egypt, the Gulf states, and potentially India, as a second 'Quad' arrangement."
6. Human rights: While acknowledging the need to balance strategic considerations, Skinner emphasizes the importance of addressing "challenges of religious freedom, especially the status of Middle Eastern Christians and other religious minorities, as well as the human trafficking endemic to the region."

SUB-SAHARAN AFRICA:
The chapter emphasizes Africa's growing importance to U.S. foreign policy and strategic interests, citing its "explosive population growth, large reserves of industry-dependent minerals, proximity to key maritime shipping routes, and its collective diplomatic power." However, Skinner notes that as Africa's strategic significance has grown, "the U.S.'s relative influence there has declined."

The text identifies several challenges, including increased terrorist activity and the growing influence of U.S. competitors, particularly China. It states, "The PRC's companies dominate the African supply chain for certain minerals critical to emerging technologies."

To address these issues, Skinner recommends several core policies:
1. **Shift strategic focus from assistance to growth**: The text advocates reorienting U.S. overseas development assistance "away from stand-alone humanitarian development aid and toward fostering free market systems in African countries by incentivizing and facilitating U.S. private sector engagement." It argues that "Development aid alone does little to develop countries and can fuel corruption and violent conflict."
2. **Counter malign Chinese activity**: Recommendations include developing "powerful public diplomacy efforts to counter Chinese influence campaigns," creating a "'digital hygiene' program" to protect African countries from espionage, recognizing Somaliland statehood, and supporting American companies with competitive advantages in Africa.
3. **Counter terrorism**: Skinner suggests supporting "capable African military and security operations through the State Department and other federal agencies responsible for granting foreign military education, training, and security assistance."
4. **Build a "coalition of the cooperative"**: Rather than spreading resources thinly across all countries, the text recommends focusing on nations "with which the U.S. can expect a mutually beneficial relationship."
5. **Focus on core diplomatic activities**: Skinner advises against promoting "policies birthed in the American culture wars," stating that "African nations are particularly (and reasonably) non-receptive to the U.S. social policies such as abortion and pro-LGBT initiatives being imposed on them."

EUROPE:
The chapter acknowledges the longstanding benefits of U.S.-European cooperation while highlighting the complex nature of this relationship. It outlines several key areas for focus:
1. **Security contributions**: The text argues that European nations "should be expected to bear a fair share of both security needs and global security architecture," emphasizing the need to examine and encourage NATO members to meet or exceed the Wales Pledge of 2% GDP toward defense.
2. **Trade relations**: While recognizing the significance of transatlantic trade, Skinner calls for a "comprehensive review of trade arrangements between the EU and the United States to assure that U.S. businesses are treated fairly and to build productive reciprocity." It also emphasizes the need to develop trade with post-Brexit UK.
3. **EU foreign policy**: The text notes that Brexit has removed UK input from EU foreign policy, potentially disadvantaging the U.S. It recommends more attentive U.S. diplomacy to inner-EU developments and developing "new allies inside the EU—especially the Central European countries on the eastern flank of the EU, which are most vulnerable to Russian aggression."

SOUTH AND CENTRAL ASIA:
The chapter emphasizes the critical importance of advancing the bilateral relationship with India, describing it as "a crucial objective for U.S. policy."

Skinner highlights India's role in:
1. Countering the Chinese threat
2. Securing a free and open Indo-Pacific
3. Acting as a "critical security guarantor for the key routes of air and sea travel linking East and West"
4. Serving as an important emerging U.S. economic partner

The text cites the 2019 Department of Defense Indo-Pacific Strategy Report, which underscores the Indian Ocean area's significance to global trade and commerce.

Skinner also addresses ongoing challenges in the region, including:
1. The threat of transnational terrorism
2. The aftermath of the U.S. withdrawal from Afghanistan, which has created "new challenges"
3. The need to reset the "deeply troubled U.S.-Pakistan relationship"
4. The long-standing India-Pakistan rivalry and tensions over Kashmir

The chapter outlines several key recommendations:
1. Strengthening the regional security and economic framework linking the U.S. and India

2. Advancing the U.S.-Indian role as a cornerstone of the Quad (U.S., India, Japan, and Australia)
3. Encouraging the "Quad-Plus" concept to allow other regional powers to participate in Quad coordination
4. Supporting an integrated federal effort to deliver a revamped regional strategy for South Asia

Skinner emphasizes the need for a "clear-eyed and realistic" approach to the Taliban regime in Afghanistan and the military-political rule in Pakistan, stating, "There can be no expectation of normal relations with either."

THE ARCTIC:
The chapter begins by highlighting the strategic importance of the Arctic region, noting that "Because of Alaska, the U.S. is an Arctic nation." It describes the Arctic's vast resources, including an estimated "90 million barrels of oil and one-quarter of the world's undiscovered natural gas reserves."

Skinner identifies several key U.S. interests in the Arctic:
1. Addressing the increasing interest from shipping and tourism sectors due to melting ice
2. Countering growing interest from America's global competitors, particularly China and Russia

The text outlines several recommendations for U.S. Arctic policy:
1. Embracing the view that "NATO must acknowledge that it is, in part, an Arctic alliance"
2. Developing and implementing a NATO Arctic strategy
3. Pursuing American interests by "promoting economic freedom in the region"
4. Ensuring that shipping lanes remain open and free of onerous fees or burdensome requirements
5. Expanding U.S. Coast Guard and Navy fleets, including planned icebreaker acquisitions
6. Investing in unmanned systems for enhanced situational awareness in the harsh Arctic conditions
7. Working with like-minded Arctic nations to raise concerns about China's "Polar Silk-Road ambitions"
8. Enhancing economic ties with Greenland, including maintaining a year-round diplomatic presence

Skinner emphasizes that "The north star of U.S. Arctic policy should remain national sovereignty, safeguarded through robust capabilities as well as through diplomatic, economic, and legal attentiveness."

INTERNATIONAL ORGANIZATIONS

The chapter begins by acknowledging the potential usefulness of engaging with international organizations like the United Nations, but emphasizes that "membership in these organizations must always be understood as a means to attain defined goals rather than an end in itself."
Skinner argues for a more critical approach to U.S. involvement in international organizations, stating:

"When such institutions act against U.S. interests, the United States must be prepared to take appropriate steps in response, up to and including withdrawal."

The text cites the World Health Organization's (WHO) handling of the COVID-19 pandemic as an example of "the danger that international organizations pose to U.S. citizens and interests."

Key recommendations include:
1. Ending "blind support for international organizations": Skinner advocates for supporting effective organizations that advance American interests while withdrawing from those that are ineffective or undermine U.S. goals.
2. Conducting a comprehensive cost-benefit analysis of U.S. participation in all international organizations.
3. Withholding funding from organizations that promote policies contrary to U.S. interests, citing "long-standing provisions in federal law that prohibit the use of taxpayer dollars to promote abortion, population control, and terrorist activities."
4. Promoting "authentic human rights and respect for sovereignty based on the binding international obligations contained in treaties that have been constitutionally ratified by the U.S. government."

5. Reevaluating U.S. multilateral engagements based on the work of the U.S. Commission on Unalienable Human Rights.
6. Building on the Geneva Consensus Declaration to shape the work of international agencies.
7. Addressing the trampling of human rights in the name of public health, as exposed during the COVID-19 pandemic.

Skinner emphasizes the need to create "a healthy culture of respect for life, the family, sovereignty, and authentic human rights in international organizations and agencies." The text also stresses that "The U.S. government should not and cannot promote or fund abortion in international programs or multilateral organizations."

The chapter concludes this section by reiterating:
"The United States must return to treating international organizations as vehicles for promoting American interests—or take steps to extract itself from those organizations."

SHAPING THE FUTURE

This section focuses on structural and operational recommendations for reforming the State Department. Skinner begins by referencing the Hart-Rudman Commission's call for significant restructuring of the State Department and foreign assistance programs. The text notes that despite this recommendation, "The State Department has metastasized in structure and resources, but neither the function of the department nor the use of taxpayer dollars has improved."

The chapter outlines several key recommendations:
1. Develop a reorganization strategy: Skinner argues for a "complete hypothetical reorganization of the department" that would:
   - Tighten accountability to political leadership
   - Reduce overhead
   - Eliminate redundancy
   - Waste fewer taxpayer resources
   - Recommend additional personnel-related changes
The text emphasizes that "speed should be a priority" in implementing these changes.
2. Consolidate foreign assistance authorities: The chapter recommends:
   - Appointing the administrator of the U.S. Agency for International Development as Director of Foreign Assistance with the rank of Deputy Secretary
   - Evaluating whether multiple sources of foreign assistance are in the national interest
   - Developing a plan to consolidate foreign assistance authorities if necessary
3. Make public diplomacy and international broadcasting serve American interests: Skinner argues for:
   - Restoring international broadcasting infrastructure as part of the broader U.S. foreign policy framework
   - Consolidating broadcasting resources
   - Recommitting to people-focused and pro-freedom messaging and content
4. Engage in cyber diplomacy: The text emphasizes the importance of cyberspace as "an arena for competition between the U.S. and nations that seek and export digital authoritarianism." Recommendations include:
   - Working with allies to establish "a clear framework of enforceable norms for actions in cyberspace"
   - Assisting the Department of Defense to go "on offence" against adversaries in cyberspace
   - Drawing clear lines of unacceptable conduct in cyberspace, particularly in areas like global financial infrastructure, nuclear controls, and public health
Skinner concludes that these "mission-essential institutional initiatives should be joined with others to establish a presidentially directed and durable U.S. foreign policy."

The chapter concludes by emphasizing the opportunity and duty of the next conservative President to restructure U.S. foreign policy creation and execution. Skinner states that the recommendations provided aim to "refocus attention away from the special interests and social experiments that are used in some quarters to capture U.S. foreign policy." The text argues for a focus on the national interest as the foundation for U.S. grand strategy in the 21st century, asserting that "a rigorous adherence to the national interest is the most enduring foundation for U.S. grand strategy in the 21st century."

CHAPTER 7: INTELLIGENCE COMMUNITY

America's Intelligence Community is at a crossroads. It faces unprecedented challenges from adversaries like China and Russia, yet it is hobbled by internal divisions, risk-averse leadership, and a politicized culture that prioritizes bureaucratic survival over mission success. – Page 203

Key Policy Proposals

DEPOLITICIZATION OF THE INTELLIGENCE COMMUNITY

The Intelligence Community has become a "sprawling, risk-averse bureaucracy" more concerned with avoiding political fallout than providing objective intelligence. The proposed solution is to depoliticize the IC, ensuring that it operates without partisan bias and remains focused on its mission to protect national security.

Analysis: Depoliticizing the IC is essential for restoring public trust and ensuring that intelligence is used to inform policy rather than to support pre-determined political agendas. However, depoliticization must be handled carefully. It requires robust checks and balances, including independent oversight, to prevent the concentration of power within the executive branch. If not managed properly, efforts to depoliticize could unintentionally lead to further politicization or the suppression of dissenting views within the IC.

REFORMING BUREAUCRATIC INEFFICIENCIES

The IC is burdened by internal divisions, risk-averse leadership, and a bureaucratic culture that stifles innovation and efficiency. Proposed reforms include streamlining operations, reducing redundancies, and focusing on the most pressing threats, such as those posed by China.

Analysis: Bureaucratic reform is necessary to ensure that the IC can respond swiftly and effectively to emerging threats. However, dismantling existing structures without careful consideration could weaken the IC's ability to gather and analyze intelligence comprehensively. The focus on China as the primary threat, while valid, should not come at the expense of monitoring other significant threats, including those from non-state actors and domestic terrorism. A balanced approach is required to maintain a comprehensive national security strategy.

ENHANCING STRATEGIC INTELLIGENCE CAPABILITIES

The chapter argues that the IC has overly focused on tactical intelligence at the expense of strategic analysis, particularly in relation to long-term threats from adversaries like China. The proposed solution is to rebuild strategic intelligence capabilities by investing in deep regional expertise and fostering a culture of analytical rigor.

Analysis: Strengthening strategic intelligence is critical for understanding and countering long-term threats. However, this must be accompanied by a commitment to transparency and accountability. Strategic intelligence often involves complex judgments that can influence major policy decisions. Without proper oversight, there is a risk that strategic analysis could be skewed to fit certain political narratives, potentially leading to misguided policies. It is crucial that the IC maintains a diversity of perspectives and resists pressures to conform to a single viewpoint.

REASSERTING PRESIDENTIAL AUTHORITY OVER THE IC

The effectiveness of the IC is contingent on the clear and unequivocal support of the President. The chapter advocates for stronger presidential control over the IC, including greater authority for the Director of National Intelligence (DNI) to implement the administration's national security priorities.

Analysis: While strong leadership is necessary to direct the IC effectively, reasserting presidential authority must not undermine the independence of intelligence agencies. The concentration of power within the executive branch, particularly in intelligence matters, can lead to abuses of power and the erosion of democratic norms. It is essential to preserve the IC's ability to provide objective intelligence, even if it contradicts the preferences of the administration. This requires a delicate balance between presidential authority and the IC's autonomy.

PROTECTING CIVIL LIBERTIES

The chapter acknowledges the need to protect civil liberties while enhancing the IC's capabilities. It proposes a review of surveillance authorities, such as the Foreign Intelligence Surveillance Act (FISA), to ensure they are used appropriately.

Analysis: Protecting civil liberties must be at the forefront of any intelligence reform. Surveillance powers, while necessary for national security, have historically been prone to abuse. The proposed review of FISA and other surveillance authorities is a step in the right direction, but it must result in tangible protections for privacy and civil liberties. This includes ensuring that surveillance is conducted with proper judicial oversight and that there are clear legal standards to prevent the targeting of individuals or groups based on political beliefs or affiliations.

WHAT WOULD THIS MEAN?

The proposed policies, if implemented, could lead to a more efficient and focused Intelligence Community that is better equipped to handle emerging threats. However, they also carry significant risks:

1. **Potential for Increased Executive Overreach** Enhancing presidential authority over the IC could lead to a concentration of power that undermines the independence of intelligence agencies. This approach risks turning the IC into a tool for political gain rather than a protector of national security.

2. **Erosion of Civil Liberties** Without careful safeguards, efforts to reform surveillance practices could lead to expanded government surveillance powers with insufficient oversight. This could result in violations of privacy and civil liberties, particularly for marginalized communities.

3. **Narrowing of Intelligence Focus** The emphasis on China, while important, should not lead to the neglect of other critical areas. A narrowed focus could leave the U.S. vulnerable to threats that fall outside the administration's immediate priorities.

4. **Risk of Politicization** Efforts to depoliticize the IC could backfire if not handled with care. The politicization of intelligence has been a recurring issue, and without strong independent oversight, these reforms could inadvertently deepen political interference in intelligence matters.

Summary

This chapter of Mandate for Leadership was written by Dustin J. Carmack. The following summary conveys the content of the document accurately and objectively, without endorsing or critiquing the perspectives of the original authors.

The chapter begins by articulating a clear mission for the U.S. Intelligence Community (IC), emphasizing its critical role in safeguarding national security against foreign adversaries. The mission is framed within the context of preparing an incoming conservative President to effectively utilize the IC's vast capabilities. The IC is described as a complex and extensive bureaucracy, comprising 18 independent and Cabinet-level agencies, whose primary objective is to collect, analyze, and deliver intelligence that enables the President and other key decision-makers to protect the nation. This mission includes defending against threats from nation-states like Russia, Iran, North Korea, and especially China, as well as continuing the effective use of counterterrorism tools.

The text stresses the need for a future conservative President to assertively employ the IC's intelligence-gathering authorities to preempt and counter these threats. This requires not only the empowerment of the right personnel to lead and manage the IC effectively but also a concerted effort to eliminate inefficiencies, such as redundant functions, mission creep, and internal conflicts that hinder the objective and apolitical delivery of intelligence. The IC is presented as a critical tool in maintaining national security, but one that requires careful management to ensure it operates efficiently and without bias.

Carmack invokes Abraham Lincoln's famous call to "think anew, and act anew" to underscore the need for the IC to adapt to new challenges rather than relying on outdated methods and priorities. The text critiques the IC for being overly focused on correcting past mistakes, which has led to a culture of hesitancy, groupthink, and excessive caution. This cautious approach is portrayed as detrimental, allowing personal incentives to influence decision-making rather than fostering a dynamic and forward-looking intelligence strategy.

The section also emphasizes the importance of the IC being perceived as a depoliticized entity committed to protecting both national security and civil liberties. Carmack acknowledges the public's frustration with the lack of accountability for those who abuse power within the IC, suggesting that this erodes trust and effectiveness. To address this, Carmack calls for leadership that is dedicated to upholding the Constitution, ensuring that intelligence agencies execute their duties faithfully, and holding accountable those who violate public trust.

In looking toward the future, the text argues for a strategic shift in the IC's focus to address emerging threats, technologies, and methodologies. Carmack warns that America's primary strategic challenge now comes from a peer nation-state, potentially more advanced than the U.S. in key areas. The IC's ability to adapt to and counter these challenges is positioned as a critical concern for an incoming President. The text advocates for reforms that will enable the IC to pivot resources and prioritize the intelligence necessary to address these modern threats effectively, suggesting that the future of U.S. intelligence competition will depend heavily on the nation's ability to innovate and stay ahead of its adversaries.

Office of the Director of National Intelligence (ODNI)

The text traces the origins and evolution of the Office of the Director of National Intelligence (ODNI), established in the wake of the 9/11 attacks and subsequent intelligence failures, notably those leading up to the Iraq War in 2003. Created by the Intelligence Reform and Terrorism Prevention Act (IRTPA) of 2004, the ODNI was intended to serve as a central coordinating body to streamline and enhance the effectiveness of the U.S. Intelligence Community (IC). The ODNI was envisioned to function similarly to the Goldwater–Nichols reforms in the Department of Defense (DOD), which had successfully addressed longstanding command-and-control issues in the military. By centralizing oversight under the Director of National Intelligence (DNI), who would act as the President's principal intelligence adviser, the ODNI was supposed to break down institutional silos, improve coordination across the IC, and ensure that intelligence operations were cohesive and aligned with national priorities.

However, the text argues that the ODNI has not lived up to its potential. While the concept of a centralized intelligence authority was intended to provide the DNI with significant power, including control over budgets and personnel, the reality has been much less effective. The legislation that created the ODNI resulted in vaguely defined authorities that have left the DNI dependent on the support of the President, the White House, and the National Security Council (NSC). This dependency has undermined the DNI's ability to lead decisively, making the ODNI more of a "bureaucratic fifth wheel" than a powerful coordinating body. The text cites the cautionary words of Philip Zelikow, the 9/11 Commission's Executive Director, who warned that without strong and clear authorities, the ODNI risked becoming an ineffective layer of bureaucracy—a warning that, according to Carmack, has been borne out in practice.

The discussion includes historical examples illustrating the limitations of the ODNI's authority. For instance, under the initial legislative proposal by the Bush Administration, the Central Intelligence Agency (CIA) Director was to be subordinated under Carmackity of the DNI. However, the final law diluted these powers, leaving the CIA with significant autonomy and the DNI with limited budgetary control. This legislative outcome led to the refusal of Robert Gates, Bush's first choice for DNI, to accept the position, as he believed the weakened role would be ineffective. Gates argued that the success of the DNI depended on the President publicly and unequivocally endorsing the DNI's leadership of the IC—a level of support that was often lacking.

The text also reflects on the experience of John Ratcliffe, who served as DNI during the Trump Administration. Ratcliffe managed to exert significant influence over the IC, but only because President Trump made it clear that he expected all intelligence matters to be channeled through the DNI. This example underscores the central argument that the effectiveness of the DNI is largely contingent on the explicit backing of the President. Without this support, the DNI's ability to lead the IC and enforce the President's intelligence priorities is severely constrained.

The section concludes by discussing the broader implications for future administrations. It emphasizes that a conservative President must carefully consider how to empower the DNI and ODNI to fulfill their intended roles effectively. This includes ensuring that the DNI has both the authority and the resources to manage the IC and implement the President's priorities, particularly in relation to emerging threats. The text suggests that the DNI's role should focus on directing the IC's efforts rather than duplicating functions within the ODNI. To achieve this, the DNI must be granted full budgetary and personnel control across the IC and be able to rely on timely and accurate feedback from all intelligence agencies. Without these powers, the ODNI risks remaining an underutilized and ineffective component of the national security apparatus.

Executive Order 12333

The text addresses Executive Order 12333, which governs the structure and operations of the U.S. Intelligence Community (IC). Initially signed by President Ronald Reagan in 1981 and later amended by President George W. Bush in 2008, the order provides the legal framework for the IC's activities, including its role in combating terrorism and weapons of mass destruction (WMD) proliferation. The 2008 amendments aligned the order with the Intelligence Reform and Terrorism Prevention Act (IRTPA) of 2004, emphasizing the IC's focus on threats to the homeland, particularly from international terrorism.

However, the text argues that Executive Order 12333 is now outdated, particularly in its treatment of cyber threats and the evolving challenges posed by major adversaries like China and Russia. Carmack suggests that the order needs significant revisions to address these modern threats adequately. Specifically, the text proposes that the order be amended to include a comprehensive approach to cyber threats, detailing the roles and responsibilities of various U.S. government entities, including the newly established National Cyber Director's Office, and ensuring that civil liberties are protected while combating these threats.

One of the key recommendations is to enhance the DNI's authority over the National Intelligence Program (NIP) budget. The current wording of the order allows the DNI to oversee the implementation of the NIP, but in practice, the DNI's budgetary authority is

limited, particularly when it comes to reallocating resources to address changing intelligence priorities. Carmack argues that the DNI should have the explicit power to direct funding and personnel as needed to respond to emerging threats, such as bioweapons and other catastrophic dangers.

Another significant point is the need to clarify the DNI's role in leading the IC as an integrated enterprise. The text notes the exponential growth in open-source information (OSINT) and argues that the IC should focus on complex collection tasks that cannot be easily replicated by commercial tools. The DNI should oversee the IC's efforts in OSINT and ensure that resources are allocated efficiently, avoiding duplication of efforts already being handled by the private sector.

The section also discusses the ongoing challenges related to security clearance reform. While progress has been made under initiatives like Trusted Workforce 2.0, which aims to streamline background investigations and introduce continuous vetting, significant issues remain in human resources operations within major agencies like the CIA, FBI, and NSA. Carmack suggests that the DNI should have the authority to enforce compliance with security clearance reforms, including the ability to hold agencies accountable for delays in onboarding qualified personnel. Additionally, the text recommends moving the Security Services Directorate from the National Counterintelligence and Security Center (NCSC) to the ODNI to elevate its status and improve oversight.

Finally, the text emphasizes the importance of ensuring that the DNI's authority is respected across the IC. The DNI should function like a conductor, coordinating the efforts of various agencies to achieve the President's intelligence goals. To facilitate this, there should be an agreement between the DNI and the President, with input from the Presidential Personnel Office, on the selection of key positions within the IC. This agreement should be respected by all relevant Cabinet officials and the CIA to ensure that the DNI can effectively lead the IC and implement the President's priorities. Without such alignment, the text warns, the IC risks inefficiency and fragmentation, which could undermine national security.

Central Intelligence Agency (CIA)

The section delves into the history, structure, and critical role of the Central Intelligence Agency (CIA) within the U.S. Intelligence Community (IC). The CIA, established by the National Security Act of 1947, has its roots in the Office of Strategic Services (OSS) from World War II. Its primary functions include collecting human intelligence (HUMINT), providing all-source intelligence analysis, and conducting covert operations when directed by the President. The text highlights that the CIA is uniquely positioned to carry out these tasks due to its extensive network and specialized expertise.

Carmack emphasizes the importance of strong leadership within the CIA, arguing that the agency's success depends heavily on the direction provided by the President and the internal leadership appointed by the CIA Director. The section suggests that the next President should prioritize appointing a Director who can foster a mission-driven culture within the CIA. This would involve making necessary personnel changes to ensure that the agency's leadership is aligned with the President's agenda and committed to executing it effectively.

The text outlines several strategic actions that the new CIA leadership should undertake. These include conducting comprehensive briefings on all CIA activities and covert operations, ensuring that the agency's efforts are closely aligned with the President's intelligence requirements. The CIA's various directorates and mission centers should be calibrated to support the President's priorities, and any operations or programs that are not in line with these priorities should be reassessed or halted. Carmack stresses that the CIA must operate in close coordination with the State Department to ensure that its activities do not contradict official U.S. foreign policy, particularly in its liaison relationships overseas.

A significant portion of the section is devoted to addressing the growing bureaucracy within the CIA. The text argues that the agency has become increasingly bureaucratic, with mid-level managers often lacking accountability and responsiveness to higher authorities, including the President. The President is urged to direct the CIA Director to overhaul the agency's mid-level leadership, promoting new individuals who can drive the agency's mission with accountability and innovative thinking. This restructuring is seen as essential to revitalizing the CIA and making it more effective in carrying out its core functions.

Carmack also discusses the need for the CIA to adapt its recruitment and onboarding practices to better meet current and future mission requirements. The CIA should broaden its recruitment efforts to include individuals with diverse backgrounds and expertise, particularly from the private sector. The text suggests that the CIA should consider relocating certain directorates, such as Support and Science and Technology, out of the Washington, D.C., area to reduce bureaucratic inertia and foster a more dynamic organizational culture.

Finally, the section addresses the issue of resource allocation within the CIA. The text argues that certain elements within the agency have focused too much on promoting divisive ideological or cultural agendas, which has fostered a culture of risk aversion and complacency. Carmack calls for a reallocation of resources away from these activities and towards efforts that directly support the CIA's mission. Promotion criteria should be adjusted to reward creativity, quality, and mission-oriented achievements rather than numeric metrics or non-essential benchmarks. The text advocates for a return to an OSS-like culture within the CIA, where individuals are incentivized to take calculated risks and pursue high-impact intelligence operations. This shift is seen as necessary to ensure that the CIA remains an effective tool for advancing U.S. national security interests in an increasingly complex global environment.

Covert Action

The text elaborates on the role of covert action within the U.S. intelligence framework, emphasizing its importance as a tool for advancing the President's foreign policy objectives. Covert action, as defined in U.S. law, includes any activities intended to influence political, economic, or military conditions abroad without the U.S. government's role being publicly acknowledged. The section underscores that while the CIA is typically the lead agency for covert actions, the President has the discretion to involve other departments, such as the Department of Defense (DOD), particularly when the scale or nature of the operation requires broader capabilities.

Carmack highlights the strategic significance of covert action, noting that it can be a powerful instrument for shaping global events in favor of U.S. interests. However, the effectiveness of covert actions depends on careful planning, clear objectives, and close coordination with other elements of government power. The text warns against the bureaucratic and political obstacles that can delay or undermine covert actions, particularly those rooted in risk aversion or interagency rivalry. To address these challenges, Carmack recommends that a future conservative President appoint a team of knowledgeable individuals to key positions within the National Security Council (NSC), CIA, ODNI, and DOD. These individuals would oversee the review and implementation of covert actions, ensuring they align with the President's broader foreign policy goals.

The text suggests that immediately following inauguration, the President should task the NSC's Senior Director for Intelligence Programs with conducting a 60-day review of all current covert actions. This review would assess the effectiveness of ongoing operations, identify potential new actions needed to support the President's objectives, and evaluate the roles of different agencies in carrying out these actions. The review should be conducted independently of the agencies responsible for the actions under evaluation to ensure objectivity and strategic alignment with the President's goals.

Moreover, Carmack emphasizes the importance of establishing clear metrics for assessing the effectiveness of covert actions. These metrics should ensure that covert actions are not only successful in achieving their immediate objectives but are also consistent with the broader foreign policy goals of the U.S. government. The text warns against the use of covert actions for purposes that might conflict with or undermine overt U.S. foreign policy, suggesting that such contradictions could lead to long-term strategic failures.

In conclusion, the section advocates for a strategic and disciplined approach to covert action, one that is closely integrated with other elements of national power and guided by clear, measurable objectives. The President, supported by a well-coordinated team, should ensure that covert actions are executed efficiently and effectively, with a focus on advancing U.S. interests in a complex and rapidly changing global environment.

Preventing the Abuse of Intelligence for Partisan Purposes

This section addresses a critical issue within the U.S. Intelligence Community (IC): the politicization of intelligence, which Carmack argues has severely damaged the IC's credibility and effectiveness. The text highlights how the misuse of intelligence for partisan purposes has not only undermined public trust but also led to significant policy failures, as evidenced by the flawed intelligence leading up to the Iraq War and the more recent controversies surrounding the Trump–Russia collusion claims and the Hunter Biden laptop investigation.

Carmack asserts that the politicization of intelligence is a multifaceted problem, manifesting both from the top down and the bottom up. Top-down politicization occurs when leaders within the IC or the executive branch use intelligence to support predetermined political agendas. Bottom-up politicization involves intelligence officers allowing their personal political biases to influence their analysis and reporting. Both forms of politicization are seen as deeply corrosive to the IC's mission of providing objective, accurate, and timely intelligence to national leaders.

A key example provided in the text is the damage caused by former CIA Director John Brennan during the Obama Administration. Carmack contends that Brennan's actions—particularly his involvement in downplaying the CIA's Directorate of Operations and allegedly using intelligence analysis as a political weapon—have had long-lasting negative effects on the agency. Brennan's role in orchestrating a letter signed by 51 former intelligence officials dismissing the Hunter Biden laptop as "Russian disinformation" is highlighted as a particularly egregious instance of intelligence being

used for political purposes, thereby discrediting the CIA and exposing the extent of politicization among former IC leaders.

The section argues that restoring the IC's reputation for political neutrality is essential to its effectiveness and to maintaining the trust of the American people, policymakers, and international partners. To achieve this, Carmack proposes several reforms aimed at depoliticizing the IC and reinforcing its commitment to neutrality. One of the key recommendations is for the DNI and CIA Director to use their authority under the National Security Act of 1947 to expedite the clearance of personnel to meet mission needs and to remove employees who have abused their positions of trust. The text notes that it is particularly concerning that personnel under investigation for improprieties have sometimes been allowed to retire before investigations are completed, thus escaping accountability. Ensuring that such individuals are held responsible for their actions is seen as crucial to rebuilding confidence in the IC.

Carmack also suggests that the President should direct the DNI and the Attorney General, with input from the Inspectors General and the IC Analytic Ombudsman, to conduct a comprehensive audit of past instances of politicization and abuses of intelligence information. This audit would help identify specific cases where intelligence was manipulated for political purposes and establish measures to prevent such abuses in the future. The text cites a recent analysis by the IC ombudsman during the 2020 election cycle, which warned that if political leaders believe the IC is withholding intelligence due to internal turf wars or political considerations, the legitimacy of the IC's work is compromised.

Another significant recommendation is the immediate revocation of security clearances for former Directors, Deputy Directors, or other senior intelligence officials who discuss their work in the press or on social media without prior clearance from the current Director. Carmack argues that the IC should minimize its public presence and vigorously investigate any leaks of information, whether classified or otherwise. Penalties for leaking information should be severe, including the potential loss of pension benefits for those found guilty. The text suggests that these measures are necessary to prevent intelligence from being used as a tool in policy debates or to further personal or political agendas.

The section also calls for stricter enforcement of norms regarding the political neutrality of IC personnel. Intelligence training programs, both military and civilian, should place a stronger emphasis on professionalism and the consequences of abusing intelligence roles for political purposes. Carmack advocates for mandatory courses on political neutrality and the ethical execution of duties in all degree programs at the National Intelligence University. Furthermore, intelligence leaders are encouraged to model these norms by avoiding public engagements that could be perceived as politically motivated and by building trust with key decision-makers through impartial and objective intelligence analysis.

To reinforce the IC's commitment to neutrality, the text advises that retired IC leaders should avoid becoming public figures, which could undermine the perception of their impartiality. Similarly, Congress is urged to refrain from using IC leaders as pawns in political struggles, recognizing the IC's proper role in providing objective intelligence to inform national security decisions rather than serving partisan interests. Carmack calls for the DNI to act as an impartial "umpire," calling out attempts by both political parties to weaponize intelligence for political gain.

Lastly, the section warns against the practice of "manipulation-by-appointment," where intelligence leaders are selected based on their political loyalties rather than their expertise. This practice, Carmack argues, undermines the integrity of the IC and erodes the trust necessary for effective intelligence operations. Presidents are advised to avoid public rebukes or pressure tactics that might coerce intelligence officials into shaping their analysis to align with political goals. The text emphasizes that intelligence leaders and professionals must adhere strictly to their mandate of providing unbiased, fact-based intelligence, resisting any attempts to "cook the books" for political purposes.

In conclusion, the section provides a comprehensive critique of the politicization of intelligence and offers detailed recommendations for restoring the IC's commitment to political neutrality. By implementing these reforms, Carmack argues, the IC can regain its credibility and continue to play its crucial role in protecting national security in an objective and nonpartisan manner.

Foreign Intelligence Surveillance Act (FISA)

This section addresses the complexities and significance of the Foreign Intelligence Surveillance Act (FISA), emphasizing its critical role in enabling the U.S. Intelligence Community (IC) to conduct surveillance on foreign targets while also highlighting the need for reforms to prevent abuses. FISA, enacted in 1978, provides the legal framework for the IC to gather intelligence on foreign powers and agents, particularly in cases where their communications intersect with the United States. The act has several components, including Title I, which governs the surveillance of foreign powers and agents, and Section 702, which specifically allows for the targeting of non-U.S. persons outside the United States whose communications pass-through U.S. channels.

The text underscores the importance of Section 702, describing it as a vital tool in the fight against terrorism, cyber threats, and espionage, particularly from adversaries like China and Russia. Section 702 is often credited with providing a significant portion of the intelligence that informs the President's Daily Brief (PDB), making it a cornerstone of U.S. national security. However, Carmack also acknowledges the controversies surrounding FISA, especially concerning the potential for abuse when it comes to domestic surveillance.

One of the primary concerns raised in the section is the potential for FISA to be used for partisan purposes, as seen in the case of the surveillance of Trump campaign adviser Carter Page. The text argues that the FBI and the Department of Justice (DOJ) mishandled the FISA applications in this case, concealing critical information from the Foreign Intelligence Surveillance Court (FISC) and submitting flawed applications. This incident is cited as a clear example of how FISA can be misused, leading to significant political and legal repercussions.

To prevent such abuses in the future, Carmack proposes several reforms aimed at tightening controls and increasing accountability within the FISA process. These reforms include:

1. **Stiffer Penalties and Mandatory Investigations:** The text calls for harsher penalties and mandatory investigations when intelligence leaks are aimed at domestic political targets. This would serve as a deterrent against the politicization of intelligence and ensure that any misuse of surveillance authorities is promptly addressed.

2. **Tighter Controls on Lawful Intercepts:** Carmack advocates for stricter controls on lawful intercepts that inadvertently capture the communications of domestic political figures. These controls would help prevent the unauthorized use of surveillance data for political purposes.

3. **Prohibition of Politically Motivated Surveillance:** An express prohibition on the politically motivated use of intelligence authorities is recommended. This would involve clear guidelines and oversight mechanisms to ensure that intelligence agencies cannot be used as tools for political advantage.

4. **Improved Accountability for the DOJ and FISC:** The text suggests reforms to improve the accountability of the DOJ and the FISC, particularly in cases involving surveillance of U.S. persons. These reforms would include enhanced oversight and transparency in the application and approval processes for FISA warrants.

Carmack also touches on the broader issue of the IC's involvement in monitoring domestic disinformation, which the text argues can easily slip into suppressing legitimate political speech. This concern is linked to the broader debate about the role of the IC in domestic affairs, with Carmack warning against any activities that could undermine First Amendment protections or give the appearance of partisan bias within the IC.

The text emphasizes that while FISA remains an essential tool for national security, it must be carefully managed to avoid overreach and ensure that its powers are not abused. Carmack stresses the importance of maintaining a clear distinction between foreign intelligence gathering and domestic surveillance, with robust safeguards in place to protect the rights of U.S. citizens.

In conclusion, the section provides a nuanced analysis of FISA, acknowledging its indispensable role in countering foreign threats while also highlighting the risks of its misuse. The proposed reforms are aimed at preserving the effectiveness of FISA while ensuring that it is used responsibly and with proper oversight to prevent any erosion of civil liberties or politicization of intelligence.

China-Focused Changes, Reforms, and Resources

This section shifts focus to the growing threat posed by the Chinese Communist Party (CCP) and outlines the strategic reforms and resources needed to counter this challenge effectively. The text emphasizes that the CCP represents a "generational threat" to U.S. national security, requiring a comprehensive, "whole-of-government" approach that involves not just the Intelligence Community (IC) but also other branches of the U.S. government and private sector.

The section begins by acknowledging recent efforts within the IC to address the China threat, such as the establishment of the China Mission Center by CIA Director William Burns. However, Carmack expresses skepticism about whether these efforts are being taken seriously enough, particularly in terms of staffing and resource allocation. The text suggests that more needs to be done to ensure that the IC is fully equipped to understand and counter China's strategic ambitions.

A critical strategic question posed in the section is how and with whom the U.S. should share its classified intelligence regarding China. Carmack notes that while some policymakers have proposed expanding intelligence-sharing partnerships like the Five Eyes to include other allies in the Asia-Pacific region (potentially forming a "Nine Eyes"), this approach is fraught with challenges. The main concern is that expanding the group could dilute the effectiveness of intelligence-sharing due to the diverse and sometimes conflicting interests of the new members. Instead, Carmack suggests that a future conservative President should carefully consider the strategic implications of

intelligence-sharing and explore more flexible, ad hoc arrangements with nations that share U.S. interests in countering China.

The text also highlights the significant technological and financial intelligence resources needed to effectively counter China's capabilities. It warns that the U.S. has been caught off guard by China's rapid advancements in areas like hypersonic missile technology, demonstrating that America's traditional dominance in information and technology can no longer be taken for granted. Carmack argues that China's centralized government, which integrates military, government, and private-sector activities, gives it an advantage in developing and deploying new technologies that challenge U.S. superiority.

To address this, Carmack advocates for a significant increase in intelligence resources dedicated to understanding China's motivations, capabilities, and intent. The text cites former DNI John Ratcliffe's decision to increase the intelligence budget related to China by 20% as a step in the right direction but argues that even more resources are needed. Carmack stresses that the IC must do more than just understand China's advancements; it must also mobilize non-governmental and allied partners to take unified action against the CCP's strategic objectives.

The section also discusses the need for reforms to existing U.S. laws and regulations, such as the Foreign Agents Registration Act (FARA), to better counter Chinese economic espionage and influence operations. The text suggests that these reforms should be part of a broader strategy to protect U.S. national security interests and intellectual property from Chinese infiltration.

Finally, Carmack addresses the challenges posed by the compartmentalization of intelligence and the bureaucratic silos within the U.S. government. The text argues that broader committee jurisdictions in Congress should receive more comprehensive intelligence briefings to better understand the multifaceted threat posed by China. This would enable more informed decision-making and facilitate a more coordinated response across different sectors of government.

In conclusion, the section calls for a concerted, resource-intensive effort to counter the strategic threat from China. This includes not only enhancing the capabilities of the IC but also fostering greater collaboration across the U.S. government and with international partners. The text argues that without a focused and unified approach, the U.S. risks falling behind China in key areas of national security and technological development.

National Counterintelligence and Security Center (NCSC)

This section examines the role of the National Counterintelligence and Security Center (NCSC) within the broader framework of U.S. national security, particularly in the context of rising threats from China and Russia. The NCSC is responsible for coordinating counterintelligence and security efforts across the Intelligence Community (IC) and other government agencies. The text underscores the growing importance of counterintelligence in a world where espionage threats extend beyond traditional state actors to include technological, economic, and cyber domains.

Carmack begins by noting that the Senate Select Committee on Intelligence (SSCI) has shown interest in updating the legislative framework that governs counterintelligence activities in the United States. The rise of China and Russia's increasingly sophisticated espionage tactics, which target not only government secrets but also technological and economic assets, is highlighted as a significant challenge. These threats are described as asymmetric, meaning they do not rely solely on traditional spy-vs-spy activities but also on cyberattacks, nontraditional collection methods, and exploitation of legitimate businesses for intelligence-gathering purposes.

The text argues that while statutory changes to strengthen counterintelligence capabilities may be necessary, a future conservative President could also empower the IC through executive orders or suggested amendments to the Counterintelligence Enhancement Act (CEA) of 2002. Carmack suggests that the NCSC, which was created in response to the evolving nature of counterintelligence threats, should be given enhanced authority to coordinate and direct counterintelligence efforts across both Title 50 (intelligence) and non-Title 50 entities. This would allow for a more unified and comprehensive approach to counterintelligence across the U.S. government.

The section also discusses the operational relationship between the FBI and the NCSC, emphasizing the need for greater collaboration between these two key players in counterintelligence. The FBI remains the lead agency for operational counterintelligence, particularly within the United States, but the text argues that the NCSC should play a more prominent role in strategy, policy, and outreach. This could include supporting joint duty assignments for FBI and CIA personnel and expanding the NCSC's mandate to include broader governance of counterintelligence activities.

One of the significant points raised is the need for the NCSC to engage more actively with corporate America, technology companies, research institutions, and academia. The text argues that these sectors are increasingly on the front lines of counterintelligence efforts, particularly as they become targets of Chinese and Russian espionage. Carmack advocates for reinvigorating partnerships with the private sector, including the reinstitution of the National Security Higher Education Advisory Board and the National Security Business Alliance Council. These partnerships would provide critical support for counterintelligence efforts by ensuring that private-sector entities are well-informed and equipped to protect themselves against espionage threats.

The section also highlights the scale of economic espionage, particularly by China, which is estimated to steal between $400 billion and $600 billion in intellectual property from the United States each year. Carmack argues that counterintelligence efforts must be strategically directed to protect America's commercial and technological endeavors, which are vital to national security. This includes leveraging private-sector intelligence and data to assist in national-level counterintelligence operations.

Furthermore, the NCSC's origins are traced back to its predecessor organizations, such as the Terrorist Threat Integration Center (TTIC) and the National Counterterrorism Center (NCTC), which were created to integrate counterterrorism intelligence and operations across the U.S. government. The text notes that the NCSC was established to bring a similar level of coordination to counterintelligence and security missions. Carmack suggests that while the NCSC has added value in areas like information sharing and personnel security, there is still significant room for improvement. The text recommends focusing the NCSC on integrative tasks that cannot be effectively handled elsewhere in the IC, rather than allowing it to become bogged down in redundant analyses that duplicate the efforts of agencies like the FBI and CIA.

In conclusion, the section advocates for a strengthened and more strategically focused NCSC that can lead U.S. counterintelligence efforts in the face of increasingly complex and multifaceted threats. Carmack calls for enhanced collaboration between the NCSC, FBI, CIA, and the private sector, as well as legislative and executive actions to empower the NCSC to fulfill its mission more effectively. By doing so, the U.S. can better protect its national security interests against the sophisticated and evolving tactics of adversarial nations like China and Russia.

Additional Areas for Reform

This section explores a series of proposed reforms aimed at enhancing the effectiveness and integrity of the U.S. Intelligence Community (IC). The reforms cover various aspects of intelligence work, from analytical tradecraft to overclassification issues, all intended to address systemic challenges and ensure that the IC remains capable of meeting contemporary security threats.

ANALYTICAL INTEGRITY

The text begins by addressing the importance of maintaining high standards of analytical integrity within the IC. Analytical integrity refers to the adherence to rigorous methods and unbiased analysis when processing and interpreting intelligence. Carmack argues that the "tradecraft" of intelligence analysis, which has developed over decades, is crucial for ensuring that intelligence products are reliable and useful to policymakers.

Historically, the lessons of analytical tradecraft were passed down through unwritten rules and agency-specific training. However, since the intelligence reforms of 2004, there has been a push to codify these practices IC-wide under the direction of the Deputy Director of National Intelligence for Mission Integration. Carmack cites a RAND study noting that the majority of intelligence analysts work outside the Central Intelligence Agency (CIA) and are involved in tactical, operational, and current intelligence. This shift has resulted in a focus on quick-turnaround intelligence that addresses immediate threats, particularly in areas like counterterrorism, where the need for rapid, actionable intelligence has taken precedence.

While this focus on tactical intelligence is necessary, the text argues that it has come at the expense of strategic intelligence, which is essential for understanding and countering long-term threats. During the Cold War, the IC balanced both tactical and strategic analysis, with the latter focusing on mysteries—predictions about future actions of adversaries—rather than simply uncovering secrets. Carmack emphasizes that strategic analysis requires deep expertise in regional and topical areas and an environment that encourages debate and dissent among analysts to arrive at well-rounded assessments.

However, the text contends that the IC is currently falling short in its strategic intelligence mission. There is a growing concern that the hyperpartisanship of recent years has penetrated the IC, undermining its ability to provide objective analysis. Carmack references the IC Analytic Ombudsman's report on the handling of election-threat analysis in 2020 as an example of how political considerations have influenced intelligence work. The report criticized the CIA for downplaying dissenting views and making it difficult to have open, healthy analytical discussions, particularly regarding China's potential influence on the U.S. election.

Carmack argues that for the U.S. to outcompete China across various domains—economic, military, technological—the IC must rebuild its capacity for strategic intelligence analysis. This will require fostering an environment that values dissenting opinions and resists the pressures of political bias. The text suggests that an incoming

conservative President should signal the importance of strategic intelligence through clear communications with IC leaders and by prioritizing these efforts within the National Intelligence Priority Framework.

"OBLIGATION TO SHARE" AND REAL-TIME AUDITING CAPABILITY

The section also discusses the need for improved information sharing within the IC and between the IC and private-sector partners. Carmack acknowledges that the U.S. government has made progress in recent years by sharing cyber threat intelligence more proactively with private-sector partners and the public. However, the text argues that the current system for sharing intelligence is still too slow and often results in information being outdated or lacking necessary context by the time it is shared.

To address this, Carmack advocates for the adoption of an "obligation to share" policy within the IC. This would involve creating "write to release" intelligence products, where newly discovered technical indicators or relevant intelligence is automatically shared with the appropriate entities within 48 hours of collection. This approach, modeled on the "duty to warn" principle in counterterrorism, would make sharing defensive intelligence the default, while allowing agency heads to withhold information for operational reasons if necessary. Carmack emphasizes that this policy would ensure that critical intelligence reaches those who need it in a timely manner, while also holding IC leaders accountable for any decisions to withhold information.

A significant challenge within the IC is the tension between the need to share information and the need to protect sensitive sources and methods. Carmack suggests that the solution lies in developing a robust real-time auditing capability, which would electronically flag unauthorized access to sensitive information. By implementing an identity management system with real-time audit capabilities, the IC could share even the most sensitive information more freely, while maintaining tight control over who accesses it and how it is used.

OVERCLASSIFICATION

The text turns to the issue of overclassification, a widespread problem in the IC and broader U.S. government. Overclassification occurs when information is unnecessarily marked as classified, often as a precaution to avoid potential security breaches. Carmack argues that this practice has become increasingly unsustainable, particularly as the volume of classified data grows exponentially in the digital age.

The current system for classifying and declassifying information is described as outdated and overly reliant on manual processes, which are ill-suited to handling the vast amounts of digital data generated by the government. The text identifies two key executive orders that govern classification practices: Executive Order 13526, which outlines the procedures for classifying and declassifying national security information, and Executive Order 13556, which deals with the management of controlled unclassified information.

Carmack argues that the classification system needs to be reformed to reflect modern realities. This includes tightening the definitions of what constitutes classified information, reducing the number of Original Classification Authorities (OCAs), and enhancing accountability at the OCA level. The text also calls for the simplification of the overall classification system to make it more user-friendly and to ensure that information is classified only when absolutely necessary.

On the declassification side, the text advocates for a faster, more automated process managed by the Office of the Director of National Intelligence (ODNI). The use of advanced technology, such as artificial intelligence and machine learning, is suggested as a way to handle the large volumes of data and expedite the declassification process. However, Carmack cautions that human expertise will still be necessary to ensure the accuracy and appropriateness of classification and declassification decisions.

The section concludes by emphasizing the need for the U.S. government to invest in modernizing its classification and declassification processes. This would include prioritizing funding for new technologies and systems that can better manage the growing volumes of classified and unclassified information, ultimately leading to a more efficient and effective intelligence system.

BROADER U.S. GOVERNMENT AND INTELLIGENCE COMMUNITY NEEDS

This section addresses the evolving landscape of national security threats, particularly in the realms of technology and finance, and the corresponding need for the U.S. government and Intelligence Community (IC) to develop new tools, authorities, and expertise to counter these challenges. Carmack argues that traditional intelligence methods must be augmented to deal with the increasingly sophisticated strategies employed by adversaries such as China, Russia, Iran, and North Korea.

The text highlights the importance of coordination between the IC and other U.S. government departments, particularly the Department of Commerce's Bureau of Industry and Security (BIS) and the Committee on Foreign Investment in the United States (CFIUS). These entities are critical in regulating technology exports, overseeing foreign investments that could affect national security, and protecting against economic espionage. Carmack emphasizes that the IC should work closely with these agencies to provide the necessary intelligence and resources to safeguard U.S. technological and financial interests.

One of the key recommendations is for the President to task the Director of National Intelligence (DNI) and the Secretary of Commerce with enhancing collaboration between the IC and BIS. This collaboration would involve increasing the sharing of intelligence relevant to economic and technological threats, improving the capacity of BIS to handle sensitive information, and ensuring that BIS has the necessary resources to perform its role effectively. The text suggests that this might include granting security clearances to select experts in niche sectors, enabling them to access classified information that is pertinent to their work in protecting national security.

The section also calls for a reevaluation of how the U.S. government handles technology transfers and investments that may have national security implications. Carmack notes that adversaries, particularly China, have increasingly sought to acquire critical technologies through legal and illegal means, including foreign direct investments, joint ventures, and mergers and acquisitions. To counter this, Carmack suggests that CFIUS should receive additional support from the IC to better assess and respond to these threats. This support could include providing detailed intelligence on potential foreign investors' links to foreign governments or military organizations, as well as on emerging technologies that are critical to national security.

In conclusion, the text argues that the IC must play a more proactive role in protecting U.S. technological and economic interests in the face of increasingly complex and multifaceted threats. By enhancing collaboration with agencies like BIS and CFIUS and providing them with the intelligence and resources needed to perform their functions effectively, the U.S. can better safeguard its national security in the 21st century.

COVER IN THE DIGITAL AGE
The section examines the challenges of maintaining cover for intelligence officers in an increasingly digital world. Carmack argues that traditional methods of protecting the identities of undercover officers are becoming obsolete due to the pervasive use of digital technology, which makes it easier for adversaries to identify and track U.S. operatives.

The text begins by outlining the growing difficulty in providing effective cover for intelligence officers, particularly those operating under non-official cover (NOC). These officers, who typically work without the diplomatic protections afforded to official cover officers, are especially vulnerable in the digital age. Carmack points out that everyday activities, such as using smartphones, social media, and online banking, can leave digital traces that adversaries can exploit to uncover an officer's true identity.

Carmack suggests that the Intelligence Community (IC), including agencies like the CIA, DIA, and FBI, must devote more resources to developing new methods of providing cover that are suited to the digital age. This includes updating the training provided to intelligence officers and their families on how to minimize their digital footprint and avoid behaviors that could compromise their cover. Additionally, the text advocates for significant investment in back-office infrastructure that supports cover operations, ensuring that the legends (fake identities and backstories) created for intelligence officers are robust enough to withstand scrutiny in the digital world.

A particular concern raised in the text is the challenge posed by ubiquitous technical surveillance (UTS) technologies, which are being refined and deployed by adversaries like China and Russia. These technologies, which include advanced facial recognition software, biometric tracking, and extensive surveillance networks, make it increasingly difficult for intelligence officers to operate undetected. Carmack argues that the IC must double down on its efforts to stay ahead of these threats, developing new techniques and technologies that can help officers maintain their cover in hostile environments.

The text also discusses the need for greater collaboration within the IC to address the challenges of maintaining cover. Carmack suggests that agencies must share best practices and work together to develop new tools and strategies for protecting the identities of their officers. This includes fostering a culture of innovation within the IC, where new ideas and approaches to cover are encouraged and tested.

In conclusion, the section highlights the pressing need for the IC to adapt its cover strategies to the realities of the digital age. By investing in new technologies, updating training programs, and fostering greater collaboration within the IC, the U.S. can better protect its intelligence officers and ensure the continued effectiveness of its covert operations.

PRIVACY SHIELD
This section discusses the contentious issue of data privacy, particularly in the context of transatlantic data transfers between the United States and the European Union (EU). Carmack critiques the European Union's efforts to impose its data privacy standards on U.S. companies, arguing that these efforts are less about protecting privacy and more about trade protectionism.

The text traces the history of U.S.–EU data privacy agreements, beginning with the Safe Harbor Framework, which was invalidated following the 2013 Snowden revelations. This framework was replaced by the Privacy Shield Framework, which was also struck down by European courts on the grounds that it did not provide sufficient protections against potential U.S. government surveillance of EU citizens. Carmack argues that these rulings are hypocritical, noting that European intelligence services are not held to the same standards as their American counterparts and that European courts have exempted these services from the strict data privacy requirements imposed on U.S. companies.

Carmack discusses the Biden Administration's efforts to negotiate a new agreement, the Trans-Atlantic Data Privacy Framework, which aims to address the concerns raised by European courts. However, the text expresses skepticism about whether this new framework will withstand future legal challenges, given the EU's history of striking down previous agreements. Carmack suggests that the new framework, implemented through Executive Order 14086, might be more about aligning U.S. signals intelligence practices with European privacy standards than about genuinely enhancing privacy protections.

The section advocates for a stronger U.S. response to the EU's data privacy demands. Carmack argues that the United States has been too accommodating to European demands, which could ultimately harm U.S. intelligence capabilities. The text suggests that an incoming conservative President should reset Europe's expectations by making it clear that continued intelligence sharing with EU member states depends on a reasonable resolution of the data privacy issue. Carmack notes that European countries benefit significantly from U.S. intelligence, particularly in areas like counterterrorism and military operations, and that this leverage should be used to negotiate a more favorable agreement.

The text also critiques the broader implications of the EU's data privacy stance, noting that it could undermine the U.S.–EU partnership at a time when both sides face significant security threats, particularly from Russia. Carmack argues that the EU's approach to data privacy is inconsistent, given that it has not imposed similar restrictions on data transfers to China, a country with a much worse track record on privacy and human rights. This, Carmack contends, reveals the underlying trade protectionist motives behind the EU's actions.

In conclusion, the section calls for a more assertive U.S. approach to negotiating data privacy agreements with the EU. Carmack suggests that the U.S. should not allow European courts to dictate the terms of transatlantic data transfers, especially when those terms could weaken U.S. intelligence capabilities and harm national security. The text recommends that the next U.S. administration carefully review Executive Order 14086 and consider suspending any provisions that unduly burden intelligence collection. Additionally, Carmack argues that the U.S. should leverage its intelligence-sharing relationships with European allies to ensure that any future data privacy agreements are fair and do not compromise U.S. security interests.

PRESIDENT'S DAILY BRIEF (PDB)
This section discusses the President's Daily Brief (PDB), a critical intelligence product designed to provide the President with timely and relevant information on national security threats. The text argues that the PDB should be tailored specifically for the President, with a focus on strategic concerns rather than serving as a general statement of record for the Intelligence Community (IC).

Carmack begins by emphasizing the importance of the PDB as a tool for informing the President's decisions on national security. The PDB is described as a highly classified document that contains the most sensitive intelligence available, including assessments of current threats, potential crises, and strategic developments. However, the text argues that the PDB has sometimes been used inappropriately as a document of record, rather than being tailored to the specific needs and interests of the President.

To address this issue, Carmack recommends a review of the current PDB process during the presidential transition period. The incoming National Security Advisor, along with the Director of National Intelligence (DNI), should assess the current list of PDB recipients and determine which officials should continue to receive the brief when the new administration takes office. This review would ensure that the PDB is distributed only to those who need it, reducing the risk of leaks and ensuring that the document remains focused on the President's priorities.

The text also suggests that the PDB should not necessarily aim for consensus among the IC agencies but should instead present the President with a range of perspectives, including dissenting views when appropriate. Carmack argues that differing opinions within the IC can be valuable, providing the President with a more nuanced understanding of complex issues. By including these perspectives, the PDB can help the President ask relevant questions and make more informed decisions.

Carmack proposes that the DNI should have greater flexibility in selecting the PDB briefer, who has traditionally come from the CIA. Instead, the text suggests that the briefer could be chosen from other IC elements or that a rotation of briefers from different agencies could be implemented. This approach would bring diverse expertise and insights to the PDB process, ensuring that the President receives a well-rounded briefing.

Finally, the text recommends that the PDB staff and production should be fully located at the ODNI, rather than being scattered across different agencies. This centralization would streamline the production process and enhance the coherence and consistency of the PDB.

In conclusion, the section calls for a more focused and strategically oriented PDB that is tailored to the President's needs and interests. By refining the PDB process and ensuring that it includes a range of perspectives, the IC can better support the President in making critical national security decisions.

ELECTION INTEGRITY

This section addresses the role of the Intelligence Community (IC) in safeguarding election integrity, particularly in light of the controversies and challenges that emerged during recent U.S. elections. Carmack stresses that protecting the integrity of elections is fundamental to maintaining public trust in democratic institutions and that the IC has a crucial role to play in preventing foreign interference and ensuring that elections are free, fair, and secure.

The text begins by discussing the threats posed by foreign actors, particularly Russia and China, who have been accused of attempting to influence U.S. elections through a variety of means, including cyberattacks, disinformation campaigns, and the manipulation of social media platforms. Carmack emphasizes that these threats are not just theoretical but have been realized in past election cycles, posing significant risks to the legitimacy of U.S. elections.

The section highlights the importance of a coordinated approach between the IC, the Department of Homeland Security (DHS), and other relevant agencies to counter these threats. Carmack advocates for enhanced collaboration and information sharing between these entities to detect and respond to election-related threats in real time. This includes leveraging the expertise and capabilities of the National Security Agency (NSA) and the Cybersecurity and Infrastructure Security Agency (CISA) to monitor and defend against cyber intrusions, as well as working with social media companies to counter disinformation.

The text also discusses the need for a robust legal framework to address foreign interference in U.S. elections. Carmack suggests that existing laws may need to be updated or expanded to keep pace with the evolving tactics used by adversaries. For instance, Carmack proposes that Congress should consider new legislation that specifically criminalizes foreign interference in U.S. elections, with clear penalties for those who engage in such activities. This legal framework would serve as a deterrent to foreign actors and provide the U.S. government with the tools necessary to prosecute those who seek to undermine the electoral process.

The section also touches on the controversial issue of domestic disinformation and its impact on election integrity. Carmack acknowledges that while the IC has a role in addressing foreign disinformation, there is a delicate balance to be struck when it comes to domestic information. The text argues that the IC must be careful not to overstep its bounds and infringe on First Amendment rights. However, Carmack also suggests that the IC can play a role in educating the public about the dangers of disinformation and promoting media literacy as a way to counteract false narratives.

Moreover, Carmack addresses the issue of public trust in the electoral process, noting that the perception of election integrity is just as important as the reality. The text argues that the IC should be transparent about its efforts to protect elections and should communicate clearly with the public about the nature and extent of foreign threats. This transparency is seen as crucial for maintaining public confidence in the electoral process and ensuring that voters trust the outcome of elections.

In conclusion, the section emphasizes the importance of the IC's role in protecting election integrity and suggests several reforms to enhance the effectiveness of these efforts. By improving coordination between agencies, updating legal frameworks, and promoting public awareness, the U.S. can better safeguard its elections against foreign interference and ensure that they remain a cornerstone of democratic governance.

THE INTELLIGENCE COMMUNITY AND CONGRESS

This section explores the relationship between the Intelligence Community (IC) and Congress, emphasizing the importance of effective oversight and cooperation between these two entities. Carmack argues that while the IC must operate with a high degree of secrecy to protect national security, it is also essential that Congress provides robust oversight to ensure that intelligence activities are conducted lawfully and in accordance with U.S. values.

The text begins by outlining the constitutional role of Congress in overseeing the IC. Carmack notes that the Senate Select Committee on Intelligence (SSCI) and the House Permanent Select Committee on Intelligence (HPSCI) are the primary bodies responsible for this oversight. These committees have Carmackity to review classified intelligence programs, approve budgets, and investigate potential abuses within the IC. Carmack argues that this oversight is crucial for maintaining the balance of power between the executive and legislative branches and for ensuring that the IC remains accountable to the American people.

However, the section also discusses the challenges of congressional oversight, particularly the tension between the need for transparency and the need to protect sensitive information. Carmack acknowledges that while Congress has a right to know about the IC's activities, there are limits to how much information can be shared without compromising national security. This tension has been a source of conflict in the past, particularly during investigations into the IC's conduct, such as those related to the Iraq War intelligence failures and the Russia investigation.

The text advocates for a more constructive relationship between the IC and Congress, characterized by mutual trust and respect. Carmack suggests that the IC should be more proactive in keeping Congress informed about its activities, providing regular briefings and updates on key programs and initiatives. This transparency would help build trust between the IC and Congress and ensure that lawmakers have the information they need to conduct effective oversight.

In addition to improving communication, Carmack also calls for reforms to the process by which Congress approves the IC's budget. The text argues that the current process is too cumbersome and can lead to delays in funding critical intelligence programs. Carmack suggests that Congress should streamline the budget approval process, possibly by adopting a biennial budget for the IC, which would provide more stability and predictability for intelligence operations.

The section also addresses the issue of leaks and the unauthorized disclosure of classified information, which has been a recurring problem in the relationship between the IC and Congress. Carmack argues that leaks not only damage national security but also undermine the trust between the IC and lawmakers. To address this, the text suggests that Congress should take stronger measures to prevent leaks, including conducting more rigorous investigations when leaks occur and imposing harsher penalties on those found responsible.

In conclusion, the section calls for a more effective and cooperative relationship between the IC and Congress, one that balances the need for secrecy with the need for accountability. By improving communication, streamlining the budget process, and addressing the issue of leaks, Congress can provide the oversight necessary to ensure that the IC operates effectively and in the best interests of the United States.

CHAPTER 8: MEDIA AGENCIES

Not only is the federal government trillions of dollars in debt and unable to afford the more than half a billion dollars squandered on leftist opinion each year, but the government should not be compelling the conservative half of the country to pay for the suppression of its own views – Page 247

Key Policy Proposals

The chapter critiques the U.S. Agency for Global Media (USAGM) and the Corporation for Public Broadcasting (CPB) while proposing significant policy changes that would undermine the foundational principles of American public diplomacy and public broadcasting. It is essential to dissect these points with a critical eye, understanding the broader implications of these proposed reforms.

CRITIQUE OF USAGM'S MISSION AND EXECUTION

The chapter argues that USAGM fails in its mission by allegedly echoing adversarial propaganda rather than promoting American values. This criticism is shortsighted and disregards the complex global environment in which USAGM operates. The agency's mission to "inform, engage, and connect people around the world in support of freedom and democracy" is inherently challenging in an era of sophisticated global disinformation. The suggestion that USAGM should serve as a mouthpiece for uncritical pro-American content undermines the agency's credibility and its ability to reach audiences who are skeptical of overtly biased messaging.

Policy Proposal: The text advocates for a significant overhaul of USAGM, potentially bringing it under the direct control of the National Security Council (NSC) or the State Department. This would effectively transform USAGM from an independent broadcaster into a tool of government propaganda.

Analysis: This proposal would destroy the journalistic integrity of USAGM, reducing it to a state-controlled entity that mirrors the very systems it is supposed to counter. The success of USAGM's efforts, particularly those of Voice of America (VOA), hinges on its perceived independence. If VOA and other USAGM entities are seen as mere extensions of U.S. government policy, they will lose credibility and influence. Audiences in authoritarian countries will view USAGM broadcasts as propaganda, which would severely limit their effectiveness in promoting democratic values and undermining oppressive regimes.

FIREWALL REGULATION AND OVERSIGHT

The chapter criticizes the Firewall Regulation, which was intended to protect journalistic independence within USAGM, describing it as a tool that hinders legitimate oversight. The argument here is that this regulation prevents necessary intervention by agency leadership when content does not align with U.S. foreign policy goals.

Policy Proposal: The text supports the removal of the Firewall Regulation, thus allowing direct oversight and potential censorship of USAGM content by government officials.

Analysis: The removal of the Firewall Regulation would set a dangerous precedent by eroding the editorial independence of journalists. This could lead to the politicization of news content, where USAGM's output is shaped by the prevailing political winds rather than a commitment to truth and democratic values. Such a move would undermine the agency's credibility, both domestically and internationally, and could lead to accusations of spreading state propaganda. This would weaken U.S. soft power, as foreign audiences, particularly in authoritarian states, might reject USAGM broadcasts as biased and untrustworthy.

DEFUNDING THE CORPORATION FOR PUBLIC BROADCASTING (CPB)

The chapter aggressively argues for the defunding of the CPB, claiming that it supports a liberal bias and does not represent the views of all taxpayers. The underlying assumption is that public broadcasting has strayed from its educational mission and now serves as a platform for partisan opinions.

Policy Proposal: The proposed policy is to eliminate federal funding for CPB, forcing NPR, PBS, and other public broadcasters to rely solely on private donations and corporate sponsorships.

Analysis: Defunding CPB would have devastating consequences for public broadcasting in the United States. NPR and PBS provide essential educational and cultural content, particularly in rural and underserved areas where commercial broadcasters do not operate due to a lack of profitability. Eliminating federal funding would disproportionately affect these communities, leading to a decline in the availability of quality, non-commercial news, and educational programming. Additionally, forcing public broadcasters to rely entirely on private and corporate funding could compromise their editorial independence, as they may become more beholden to the interests of their largest donors rather than serving the public good.

Moreover, public broadcasting has historically provided a platform for diverse voices and underserved communities, offering programming that reflects a wide range of perspectives. The loss of federal funding would likely result in a homogenization of content, driven by market forces rather than public interest. This would diminish the role of public broadcasting as a counterbalance to the often profit-driven and sensationalist content prevalent in commercial media.

The proposed policy changes outlined in this chapter represent a significant shift away from the principles of free and independent journalism and public service broadcasting. The consequences of these changes would be far-reaching, leading to the erosion of U.S. soft power, the undermining of democratic values, and the loss of a critical platform for diverse and educational content. The U.S. government should be investing in and protecting these institutions, not dismantling them. Public broadcasting and independent journalism are cornerstones of a healthy democracy, and their preservation is essential for the continued promotion of freedom and democracy both at home and abroad.

Summary

This chapter of Mandate for Leadership was written by Mora Namdar and Mike Gonzalez. The following summary conveys the content of the document accurately and objectively, without endorsing or critiquing the perspectives of the original authors.

U.S. AGENCY FOR GLOBAL MEDIA

The **United States Agency for Global Media (USAGM)** is introduced with a mission statement emphasizing its role in promoting freedom and democracy globally. The agency aims to "inform, engage, and connect people around the world" by disseminating news and information that supports these ideals. However, the text immediately critiques the agency's current operations, arguing that while the mission is "noble," its execution is significantly lacking. The author suggests that USAGM should focus not only on promoting American values but also on correcting misinformation and countering adversaries' propaganda. Instead, the agency is accused of failing in these areas, leading to a distortion of its intended purpose.

OVERVIEW

Originally established as the **Broadcasting Board of Governors (BBG)** in 1994, the agency was renamed the **United States Agency for Global Media (USAGM)** in 2018. This rebranding marked a continuation of the agency's role as a sub-Cabinet level entity within the U.S. government, responsible for overseeing several major broadcasting networks with a combined budget of nearly $1 billion. The text outlines the primary functions of USAGM, highlighting its oversight of the **Voice of America (VOA)** and the **Office of Cuba Broadcasting (OCB)**, as well as its control over grant funding for "independent" grantee organizations like the **Middle East Broadcasting Network (MBN)**, **Radio Free Asia (RFA)**, **Radio Free Europe/Radio Liberty (RFE/RL)**, and the recently established **Open Technology Fund (OTF)**.

The text continues by discussing **Voice of America (VOA)**, which delivers news and information in 48 languages to an audience of over 326 million people weekly. For over 80 years, VOA has provided coverage on U.S. affairs, regions of interest, and global news, often reaching areas where freedom of speech is restricted. However, the text criticizes VOA for its current management, which allegedly has compromised the agency's integrity by producing politically biased content. The once-esteemed VOA brand, known for its unbiased reporting, is now described as deteriorating due to poor leadership and a decline in production standards. While there are some "bright spots" within VOA, these are overshadowed by the agency's overall decline.

The **Office of Cuba Broadcasting (OCB)** oversees **Radio and Television Martí**, which serves as a critical source of news and analysis for the Cuban people, providing content that is otherwise censored by the Cuban government. This content is delivered through various media, including satellite television, radio, and digital platforms. The OCB is depicted as a vital channel for truth in Cuba, but the text notes that it has been weakened by budget cuts, operational constraints, and an unsympathetic attitude from certain elements within USAGM leadership. The Biden Administration's approach, which includes threats to close OCB and reduce its workforce, is highlighted as particularly damaging.

The **Middle East Broadcasting Network (MBN)** is an Arabic-language news organization with a weekly audience of 27.4 million people across 22 countries in the Middle East and North Africa. The MBN's operations include television networks, radio, websites, and social media platforms that offer news and analysis on regional issues, U.S. policies, and American culture. Despite its extensive reach, the text suggests that MBN's effectiveness is undermined by internal challenges and the broader issues affecting USAGM.

Radio Free Europe/Radio Liberty (RFE/RL) is presented as a private, nonprofit multimedia broadcasting corporation that serves 23 countries, including Afghanistan, Iran, Pakistan, Russia, and Ukraine, in 27 languages. Established during the Cold War to provide uncensored news and information behind the Iron Curtain, RFE/RL was once known for its bold and independent reporting. However, the text argues that the organization has strayed from its original mission, now favoring politically safe and trend-following content rather than the daring journalism it was known for. The addition of RFE/RL's Hungarian-language service, **Szabad Európa**, is criticized as a misstep, targeting a democratic, pro-American NATO ally instead of focusing on adversarial regimes.

The section on **Radio Free Asia (RFA)** describes it as a private, nonprofit multimedia corporation that provides news and uncensored content to six Asian countries where free speech and press freedom are restricted. RFA also offers educational and cultural programming, along with forums for open dialogue. The text highlights serious issues within RFA, including allegations of waste, self-dealing, and security vulnerabilities. It points to specific instances where RFA leadership awarded contracts to organizations with which they had personal affiliations, raising concerns about conflicts of interest and misuse of funds.

Lastly, the **Open Technology Fund (OTF)** is scrutinized for its role in promoting internet freedom technologies that circumvent censorship. The text describes OTF's creation under questionable circumstances, noting that it was formed by consolidating and redirecting funds from the pre-existing **Office of Internet Freedom (OIF)**. The OTF is criticized for its lack of transparency and its restrictive focus on "open source" technologies, which the text argues may be less secure than other options. Despite its claims of success, the OTF is accused of inflating its user numbers and being a wasteful and redundant initiative. The Trump Administration's suspension of OTF's grantee status due to noncompliance and fraud investigations is mentioned, along with the Biden Administration's subsequent reinstatement of the fund, which the text implies was a step backward.

ATTEMPTS AT REFORM

In this section, the text delves into the reform efforts initiated toward the end of the Trump Administration, particularly following the appointment of **Michael Pack** as the Chief Executive Officer (CEO) of the USAGM. The reforms are described as both "long-overdue" and "necessary," aimed at addressing significant security and operational issues that had been neglected by previous agency leadership. The text emphasizes that these reforms were not merely bureaucratic adjustments but critical changes, driven by repeated requests from key federal bodies like the **Office of Personnel Management (OPM)** and the **Office of the Director of National Intelligence (ODNI)**. These entities had flagged numerous security lapses that posed serious risks to national security, but their concerns had been largely ignored until Pack's tenure.

The **"Firewall Saga"** is introduced as a central issue in the agency's ongoing dysfunction. The "firewall" refers to a supposed safeguard for journalistic independence within USAGM, intended to protect content from government interference. However, the text argues that this firewall has been selectively applied and misinterpreted over the years, depending on the political administration in power. Instead of fostering genuine independence, the firewall has often been used as a shield to avoid oversight and accountability, particularly when USAGM content aligns with adversarial propaganda or exhibits strong political bias.

The critique of the firewall is further deepened by highlighting its formalization in a document known as the **Firewall Regulation**, which was entered into the **Federal Register** just before Michael Pack's Senate confirmation. The timing of this regulation's entry is described as a deliberate attempt to undermine the new leadership's ability to oversee and direct the agency's operations. The regulation effectively prohibited USAGM management from intervening in content production, even when that content was false or misleading. This stance, according to the text, was in direct violation of existing laws, including the **Smith–Mundt Act**, and posed a threat to both the agency's mission and U.S. foreign policy objectives.

The text provides specific examples of how the firewall was misused, citing instances where **VOA's White House correspondent** posted content that was highly critical of the sitting U.S. President. This content, described as personally insulting and politically biased, was allowed to stand under the protection of the firewall, despite violating VOA's own journalistic standards and policies. The text argues that such abuses were rampant and indicative of a broader problem within USAGM, where journalistic independence was conflated with a lack of accountability.

In response to these issues, the Trump Administration's USAGM leadership, after conducting a thorough review with the **U.S. Department of Justice**, revoked the Firewall Regulation. This move was met with strong opposition from various journalistic organizations, particularly within VOA, who argued that the firewall was essential for protecting editorial independence. However, the text suggests that these objections were rooted in a desire to maintain the status quo, which allowed for unchecked biases and poor oversight.

The section concludes by describing the resistance faced by reform-minded leadership within USAGM. Current and former leaders who preferred minimal oversight launched campaigns of interference, disinformation, and resistance to stifle the reforms initiated under Pack's leadership. The text implies that these campaigns were not coincidental but rather part of a broader effort to protect entrenched interests within the agency. Additionally, the close relationships between certain media outlets and former USAGM leadership are noted as a factor that amplified the criticisms against the Trump Administration's reform efforts, portraying them in a negative light in the public discourse.

AGENCY MISSION FAILURE

This section addresses the broader failure of USAGM to fulfill its mission. The text argues that the agency's mission, which should be clearly defined and closely aligned with U.S. foreign policy goals, has become so vague and ambiguous that it allows the organization to operate with little to no effective oversight. Instead of providing accurate and reliable news that supports freedom and democracy, the agency is described as being mismanaged, disorganized, and ineffective. This lack of clarity and direction has led to an environment where waste, redundancy, and political gamesmanship thrive.

The agency's failure is also attributed to its alignment with mainstream media's anti-U.S. narratives, particularly during the Trump Administration. The text claims that USAGM content often echoed the criticisms and talking points common in mainstream media, rather than promoting an objective or pro-American perspective. This approach is seen as a betrayal of the agency's core mission, resulting in a loss of credibility and effectiveness. Moreover, the few successful initiatives within VOA and OCB are said to be stifled rather than supported, leading to a talent drain and further decline in agency performance.

The section also touches on the broader implications of USAGM's failures, particularly in terms of missed opportunities for modernization and strategic effectiveness. The text suggests that the agency's mismanagement has prevented it from adapting to new challenges and technologies, leaving it stuck in outdated practices that do not serve its mission. The wasteful spending and misallocation of resources are highlighted as symptomatic of deeper systemic issues, where nepotism and political protectionism are prioritized over merit and accountability.

Finally, the section discusses the controversial confirmation of **Amanda Bennett** as USAGM CEO in 2022. Bennett's appointment is described as problematic due to her previous tenure as VOA director during the Obama Administration, which was marked by significant operational, security, and credibility failures. The text notes that her nomination was blocked by several members of Congress for two years, and even legal advocacy groups like **America First Legal Foundation** urged President Biden to withdraw her nomination, citing national security concerns. Despite these warnings, Bennett was confirmed, and the text implies that the problems that plagued her earlier tenure are likely to continue under her current leadership.

NECESSARY REFORMS

This section outlines the critical reforms that are deemed necessary to address the numerous issues plaguing the U.S. Agency for Global Media (USAGM). The text begins by highlighting **security issues** that have been identified by the **Office of Personnel Management (OPM)** and the **Office of the Director of National Intelligence (ODNI)**. Over a decade, these agencies conducted extensive investigations into USAGM and found severe security lapses. The text emphasizes that these security concerns were not minor but represented significant vulnerabilities that could be exploited by foreign spies. It is noted that during the last six months of the Trump Administration, some known foreign intelligence operatives were removed from key positions within USAGM, particularly in the Office of Cuba Broadcasting (OCB) and Radio Free Europe/Radio Liberty (RFE/RL). However, the text suggests that these actions were too little, too late, as the agency had already allowed these vulnerabilities to persist for far too long.

The text provides detailed examples of the security failures within USAGM, pointing out that over 1,500 agency personnel—representing nearly 40% of the workforce—were performing national security-sensitive jobs without proper background checks or authorization. Many of these individuals had falsified records, including Social Security numbers, or had never had their fingerprints submitted to the FBI for basic background investigations. These lapses allowed unvetted individuals to access sensitive federal buildings and information systems, posing a significant risk to national security. The text further reveals that by the time these issues were addressed, over 500 personnel had left USAGM and moved on to other federal agencies, potentially carrying these security risks with them. The agency, as of January 2021, had not yet accounted for all these individuals, raising concerns about ongoing security threats.

Given these issues, the text argues that USAGM should no longer be trusted with the authority to manage its personnel security programs. Instead, these responsibilities should remain under the control of the Department of Defense and OPM, as was decided in the final weeks of the Trump Administration. This transfer of responsibility is presented as a necessary step to ensure that such security failures do not occur again.

The section also discusses the lack of protection for **journalists** working under USAGM, both domestically and abroad. The text describes how USAGM journalists, especially those working in high-risk countries, have faced significant threats to their safety without adequate support or protection from the agency. Whistleblowers and political appointees during the Trump Administration had to push for basic safety measures, such as allowing threatened journalists to broadcast from remote locations under the protection of federal law enforcement. However, these efforts were often met with resistance from senior career officials within USAGM, who argued that such measures violated journalistic independence. The text criticizes this stance as a "knee-jerk response" that prioritized bureaucratic concerns over the safety and security of journalists, further exacerbating the agency's dysfunction.

The issue of **wasting taxpayer dollars** is another critical point discussed in this section. The text asserts that USAGM's operations could be conducted efficiently on a budget of less than $700 million per year. However, prior to the arrival of Trump Administration appointees, the agency's budget exceeded $800 million annually, with little oversight or accountability. The text lists various examples of waste, including unnecessary spending on redundant programs, nepotism, and the hiring of unqualified personnel. The lack of financial responsibility within USAGM is portrayed as a major problem that has contributed to the agency's overall inefficiency and ineffectiveness.

To address these issues, the text calls for the **consolidation and reduction of redundant services** within USAGM. It argues that many of the agency's services, particularly those provided by Voice of America (VOA) and its grantee organizations, overlap unnecessarily. For instance, VOA's Mandarin-language service duplicates efforts provided by Radio Free Asia, and its Farsi-language service overlaps with one funded by Radio Free Europe/Radio Liberty. Such redundancy is seen as both unnecessary and counterproductive, contributing to the agency's financial waste. The text advocates for a return to fiscal responsibility and transparency, with consolidation as a key strategy to streamline operations and eliminate redundancies.

The section also critiques the **Open Technology Fund (OTF)** for duplicating activities that were already being conducted by the Office of Internet Freedom (OIF) within USAGM. The OTF is described as an opaque, expensive, and unnecessary initiative that usurped the budget and mission of OIF. Numerous career whistleblowers reportedly raised alarms about OTF's wasteful spending and lack of accountability, but these concerns were largely ignored by the agency's leadership. The text argues that reinstating OIF, with full congressional oversight, would allow for greater transparency and ensure that "Internet freedom" funding is spent effectively and efficiently.

The abuse of the **J-1 visa program** is another issue highlighted in this section. The text explains that USAGM has misused the J-1 cultural exchange visas, which are intended for temporary exchanges, to bring in foreign nationals for jobs that could be filled by American citizens with the necessary cultural and linguistic expertise. The J-1 visa holders often apply for permanent residency, which violates the original purpose of this visa program. The text argues that this practice not only undermines the integrity of the visa program but also represents another example of USAGM's disregard for proper procedures and its preference for expediency over accountability.

Finally, the text discusses the need for **shortwave transmission upgrades** and improvements. It criticizes the agency's shift away from proven, durable technologies like shortwave radio transmission in favor of newer, web-based technologies. This shift is described as dangerously short-sighted, especially in the context of potential conflicts with nations like Russia or China, where internet infrastructure could be compromised. The text emphasizes the strategic importance of shortwave radio in delivering broadcasts to areas where internet access is restricted or controlled by authoritarian regimes. It also warns about the vulnerability of undersea cables that carry the majority of global internet traffic, highlighting the need for reliable alternatives like shortwave radio to ensure that U.S. broadcasts can reach global audiences even during times of major conflict.

ORGANIZATIONAL ISSUES

This section examines the deep-seated organizational problems within the U.S. Agency for Global Media (USAGM), focusing primarily on personnel challenges, government oversight, and the need for structural reforms.

The discussion begins with **personnel** as a critical area of concern. The text highlights the difficulties USAGM faces in attracting and retaining talented staff while simultaneously struggling to dismiss poorly performing employees. This issue is compounded by numerous credible allegations of illegal nepotism and improper hiring practices. The text emphasizes that past agency leaders frequently ignored national security protocols during the hiring process, resulting in the employment of unqualified or inappropriately vetted individuals. This lack of adherence to government hiring policies and federal law is portrayed as a significant contributor to the agency's overall dysfunction. The text calls for stringent policy changes to ensure that hiring practices align with national security requirements and to eliminate the pervasive nepotism within the organization.

The role of **relevant government entities** in the oversight and management of USAGM is then scrutinized. The text begins with the **White House**, noting that, as an executive branch agency, USAGM should theoretically report directly to the President and coordinate closely with the National Security Council (NSC). Given the agency's involvement in global messaging that has direct national security implications, this relationship is deemed essential. However, the text criticizes the current lack of a dedicated office within the White House or a specific NSC liaison responsible for overseeing USAGM. This absence of direct oversight is seen as a significant gap that allows the agency to operate with minimal accountability.

Historically, **Voice of America (VOA)**, the original network under USAGM, was most effective when it was directly managed by the U.S. government during and after World War II. It functioned under the **Office of the Coordinator of Information** and later under the **Office of War Information** and the **State Department**. However, with the dissolution of the U.S. Information Agency in 1999 and the creation of the independent Broadcasting Board of Governors (BBG), VOA lost its direct government oversight, which the text suggests has led to its current inefficacies. The lack of substantial connectivity between USAGM and larger government departments or agencies, particularly the White House, is highlighted as a key factor in the agency's ongoing issues.

The text then considers the **State Department** as a potential candidate for reintegrating VOA into the direct chain of command. It is argued that VOA was most successful during the Cold War when it was under the supervision of the State Department. The text suggests that if VOA is not placed under the NSC's direct oversight, serious consideration should be given to placing it under the State Department's **Office of Global Public Affairs**. This office was formed during the Trump Administration by consolidating two existing bureaus and is viewed as a suitable home for VOA due to its focus on global public messaging. Ensuring that taxpayer-funded broadcasts effectively tell America's story is seen as crucial, and the text argues that State Department oversight could help realign VOA's mission with U.S. foreign policy objectives.

A significant issue discussed is the **VOA firewall**, which was originally designed to protect the network from government interference in its content. However, the text argues that this firewall has been abused by USAGM staff, who have used it as a tool to block oversight rather than as a safeguard for journalistic independence. This abuse has allowed VOA to stray from its core mission, with some content even promoting foreign adversaries' propaganda. The text suggests that bringing VOA under State Department oversight could help ensure that it adheres to its original mission and that its broadcasts serve the interests of U.S. foreign policy rather than partisan or adversarial agendas.

The lack of **clear lines of command** and communication between USAGM and the NSC is also highlighted as a critical flaw. The text argues that without effective accountability mechanisms, USAGM's senior leadership operates with too much autonomy, leading to poor strategic decisions and misaligned priorities. It is suggested that the **State Department's Assistant Secretary for Global Public Affairs** and the **Undersecretary for Diplomacy and Public Affairs** should be involved in the oversight of USAGM to ensure that its actions align with broader U.S. strategic communications goals. Although the Secretary of State technically has a seat on the USAGM board, this position is described as "toothless," often deferred to lower-level officials. The text calls for this role to be more directive, especially when U.S. foreign policy and national security are at stake.

The text also discusses the impact of delayed leadership appointments on USAGM's performance. The years-long delay in confirming the Trump-appointed CEO, Michael Pack, is cited as a disaster for the agency, as it left holdover leadership from the previous administration in place, perpetuating existing dysfunctions. The text suggests that employing effective leadership, even in an acting capacity, while awaiting Senate confirmation of a new CEO is essential to prevent such issues in the future.

Next, the role of **Congress** in overseeing USAGM is examined. The agency receives its budget and mandates directly from Congress, and significant changes in its operations often result from lobbying by well-connected individuals and grantee organizations. These changes, according to the text, can undermine leadership's ability to implement meaningful oversight and reforms. The text calls for a congressional review to modernize the agency, streamline its operations, and reduce waste. This review is seen as necessary to realign USAGM with its original mission and to ensure that taxpayer dollars are spent effectively.

The text concludes this section by acknowledging the importance of **nongovernmental stakeholders**, including industry groups, nonprofits, and activist organizations, in holding USAGM accountable. Groups such as **America First Legal Foundation**, **USAGM Watch**, **BBG-USAGM Watch**, and the **Whistleblower Protection Project** are noted for their roles in advocating for transparency and accountability within the agency. These organizations are portrayed as crucial allies in the effort to reform USAGM and ensure that it operates in the best interests of the American public and national security.

CORPORATION FOR PUBLIC BROADCASTING

The text begins by discussing the longstanding opposition from Republican presidents to the taxpayer funding of the **Corporation for Public Broadcasting (CPB)**, an organization that supports National Public Radio (NPR) and the Public Broadcasting Service (PBS). The text traces this opposition back to President Richard Nixon, noting that every Republican president since Nixon has attempted to cut federal funding for CPB, though without success. This repeated failure is highlighted as significant, especially given Nixon's era marked the inception of NPR and PBS.

The critique centers on the argument that public broadcasting, which was originally intended to enrich homes, educate families, and assist classrooms, has instead become a forum for liberal public affairs and journalism. The text asserts that public broadcasting no longer serves its intended educational purpose and has transformed into a platform for leftist viewpoints. This shift is seen as particularly problematic given that the federal government, already burdened with substantial debt, is allocating more than half a billion dollars annually to support programming that, according to the text, suppresses conservative viewpoints.

To support this claim, the text references data from the **Pew Research Center**, which shows a significant liberal skew in the audiences of both PBS and NPR. PBS's audience is reported to be 60% liberal, while NPR's audience is 67% liberal, far outpacing the conservative viewership. This liberal dominance is presented as a fundamental issue, especially for a taxpayer-funded entity that is supposed to serve the public interest. The text argues that the government should not compel conservatives to fund a broadcasting system that predominantly supports and propagates liberal opinions.

DEFUNDING THROUGH THE BUDGETARY PROCESS

The section goes on to outline a proposed strategy for defunding CPB. The text argues that the solution lies in the budgetary process, where the President can simply refuse to sign any appropriations bill that includes funding for CPB. It describes the CPB's practice of seeking advance appropriations—funding that is secured two years ahead of time—

as a way to insulate itself from congressional oversight and the power of the purse. The text suggests that this special budgetary treatment is unjustified and should be eliminated.

The text also counters the argument that defunding CPB would cause NPR, PBS, and other public broadcasters to go bankrupt. It asserts that these organizations would continue to thrive due to their membership models and additional funding from corporations and foundations. An example given is **Sesame Street**, which has moved to HBO, demonstrating its potential as a lucrative entity independent of public funding. The text suggests that the real issue is not the survival of these broadcasters but the principle of whether taxpayer money should fund programming that is biased and no longer serves its original educational purpose.

PUBLIC INTEREST VS. PRIVILEGE

The text argues that removing public funding would strip NPR, PBS, and similar broadcasters of their presumed status as entities that act in the public interest. This change would mean that they would no longer qualify as noncommercial educational (NCE) stations, which currently gives them certain privileges, such as reserved positions on the FM radio spectrum and exemption from licensing fees by the **Federal Communications Commission (FCC)**.

The text emphasizes that NPR and PBS are effectively no longer noncommercial or educational, as they run advertisements in all but name and devote only a small portion of their programming to education. The text proposes that the next President should instruct the FCC to remove NPR and PBS stations from the NCE classification and the benefits that come with it. This move would be part of a broader effort to ensure that public broadcasting serves its intended purpose rather than acting as a privileged platform for partisan content.

CHAPTER 9: AGENCY FOR INTERNATIONAL DEVELOPMENT

Bold steps are needed on Day One to undo the gross misuse of foreign aid by the current Administration to promote a radical ideology that is politically divisive at home and harms our global standing – page 280

Key Policy Proposals

The chapter proposes a series of sweeping changes to the U.S. Agency for International Development (USAID), reflecting a conservative agenda that is both regressive and dangerous. The proposed policy shifts threaten to undermine decades of progress in global development, human rights, and climate action, replacing these gains with narrow, ideologically-driven priorities that are out of touch with both American values and global realities.

GENDER EQUALITY AND WOMEN'S RIGHTS

The chapter advocates for refocusing USAID's gender equality initiatives solely on "women, children, and families," effectively erasing the agency's broader commitment to gender rights, including LGBTQ+ protections. It calls for the elimination of references to "gender," "reproductive rights," and "sexual and reproductive health," under the pretense of restoring traditional values. This approach is deeply flawed. The exclusion of gender diversity ignores the complex realities faced by millions worldwide and perpetuates discrimination. By stripping away these protections, the policy would set back the global fight for equality and undermine the health and safety of vulnerable populations.

Moreover, the proposal to eliminate all references to abortion and reproductive health from USAID's programs is not only an affront to women's rights but also a direct attack on global health. Denying access to safe abortion services and comprehensive reproductive health care will lead to higher rates of maternal mortality and morbidity. The data is clear: restricting reproductive rights does not reduce abortion rates, but it does increase unsafe procedures, putting women's lives at risk.

CLIMATE CHANGE

The chapter's aggressive stance against climate action is another dangerous policy shift. It calls for the removal of climate considerations from USAID's agenda, characterizing them as "economy-killing" and "climate fanaticism." This dismissal of climate science is irresponsible and ignores the overwhelming evidence that climate change is the most significant threat facing humanity. The consequences of rolling back USAID's climate initiatives would be catastrophic, particularly for the world's poorest nations, which are most vulnerable to climate impacts.

Abandoning efforts to transition from fossil fuels, as the chapter suggests, would not only exacerbate global warming but also entrench poverty by denying developing countries access to sustainable, long-term energy solutions. Instead of promoting economic growth, this approach would lock these nations into a cycle of dependency on outdated, polluting energy sources, further delaying their development.

RELIGIOUS FREEDOM AND SOCIAL CONSERVATISM

The chapter advocates for embedding religious freedom more deeply into USAID's mission, promoting faith-based initiatives while scaling back programs that support reproductive rights and LGBTQ+ protections. This conflation of religious freedom with the imposition of conservative social values on aid recipients is both ethically and strategically misguided. While religious freedom is a core American value, using it as a pretext to deny essential health services and human rights protections is a gross misuse of power. Such policies would alienate key partners and undermine the credibility of U.S. leadership on human rights.

HUMANITARIAN ASSISTANCE AND LOCALIZATION

The chapter suggests downsizing USAID's humanitarian assistance, particularly in regions like Africa and Latin America, and shifting focus to local organizations. While localization is a commendable goal, the broader intent behind this proposal appears to be a reduction in aid under the guise of efficiency. The proposed cuts to humanitarian programs would leave millions without critical support, exacerbating crises rather than resolving them. Moreover, reducing the U.S. footprint in global humanitarian efforts could create a vacuum that other less scrupulous actors, like China, are eager to fill, thereby diminishing U.S. influence and moral standing.

The chapter's policy proposals reflect a dangerous retreat from global leadership, motivated by narrow, ideological interests rather than the broader good. By dismantling vital programs that promote gender equality, combat climate change, and support humanitarian needs, these policies would not only harm millions of vulnerable people around the world but also diminish America's standing as a leader in promoting human rights and development. The proposed changes would ultimately weaken the very foundations of global stability, prosperity, and justice that USAID has worked so hard to build over the decades. This is not the direction we should take; instead, we must double

down on our commitments to a fairer, more equitable world where everyone, regardless of gender, sexuality, or nationality, has the chance to thrive.

Summary

This chapter of Mandate for Leadership was written by Max Primorac. The following summary conveys the content of the document accurately and objectively, without endorsing or critiquing the perspectives of the original authors.

The U.S. Agency for International Development (USAID) is the leading force behind the U.S. government's efforts in international development and disaster assistance. The agency's mission is to help "communities to lead their own development journeys" by addressing conflict, hunger, pandemics, and the underlying causes of violence and instability. USAID's activities are closely aligned with U.S. national security interests, promoting "American prosperity" through initiatives that foster markets for U.S. exports, encourage innovation, and support the establishment of "stable, resilient, and democratic societies."

USAID was established during President John F. Kennedy's administration under the Foreign Assistance Act of 1961. The agency was created in the context of the Cold War to advance U.S. foreign policy and national interests by combating the spread of communism. By supporting economic, social, and political development in the developing world, USAID aimed to "halt the spread of Communism." The agency played a pivotal role in helping Central and Eastern Europe transition from socialism to "free market–based democracies" after the Cold War. Today, USAID continues to lead U.S. global development and humanitarian responses.

Over the years, USAID has significantly expanded its reach, both in terms of the number of countries it assists and the scale of its operations. However, the agency has faced increasing criticism, particularly during the Trump Administration, for being "marred by bureaucratic inertia," with issues such as "programmatic incoherence" and "wasteful spending." The agency's reliance on a "self-serving and politicized aid industrial complex" has led to the perpetuation of programs in some countries for decades without achieving meaningful results. Additionally, the shift from responding primarily to natural disasters to addressing "violent, man-made crises" has fundamentally altered the nature of USAID's work, making humanitarian aid a "permanent and immiserating feature of the global landscape."

The Trump Administration sought to reform USAID by focusing on "ending the need for foreign aid" and placing countries on a "Journey to Self-Reliance." This strategic shift involved restructuring the agency, streamlining procurement procedures to diversify its partner base, and increasing awards to "cost-effective local (including faith-based) organizations." The administration also emphasized pro-life and family-friendly policies and promoted "international religious freedom" as a core pillar of USAID's work. Significant efforts were made to build a "genocide-response infrastructure" under this administration.

In stark contrast, the Biden Administration is criticized for deforming USAID by using it as a global platform to push a "divisive political and cultural agenda." This agenda includes promoting "abortion, climate extremism, gender radicalism," and initiatives against "perceived systemic racism." The Biden Administration's approach has discarded the "bipartisan consensus" that previously underpinned U.S. foreign aid and has pursued policies that "contravene basic American values," leading to strained relations with key partners in Asia, Africa, and Latin America. Furthermore, the administration's push for "wasteful budget increases" has transformed U.S. foreign aid into a "massive and open-ended global entitlement program" that enriches the progressive Left at the expense of American taxpayers.

Looking forward, the document argues that the next conservative administration should scale back USAID's global footprint, at a minimum returning to the agency's "2019 pre–COVID-19 pandemic budget level." The proposed reforms include deradicalizing USAID's programs and structures and building on the conservative reforms initiated during the Trump Administration. Achieving these goals would require close collaboration with Congress to make deep cuts to the international affairs budget, also known as the "150 Account," while granting USAID greater flexibility to ensure that its appropriated funds are used to achieve better developmental outcomes.

USAID was established under President John F. Kennedy through the Foreign Assistance Act of 1961, during a time of intense geopolitical tension with the Soviet Union. The agency was designed to "promote the foreign policy, security, and national interests of the United States" by aiding the economic, social, and political development of nations vulnerable to communist influence. USAID's efforts were integral in transitioning Central and Eastern Europe from socialism to free-market democracies, reflecting its initial Cold War objectives.

As time passed, USAID expanded its operations both in terms of the number of countries it assisted and the scope of its activities. However, the agency also became increasingly characterized by "bureaucratic inertia," as programs often continued indefinitely without reevaluation. A notable issue was the shift in the nature of humanitarian aid: originally, 80% of USAID's humanitarian programs responded to natural disasters, but this figure reversed to 80% addressing "violent, man-made crises." These crises have now become a "permanent and immiserating feature" of the global landscape.

By the time the Trump Administration took office, USAID was facing significant challenges. The agency was seen as suffering from "programmatic incoherence," wasteful spending, and over-reliance on large, politicized aid contractors and organizations. The administration sought to counter these issues by introducing a strategic approach aimed at "ending the need for foreign aid." The "Journey to Self-Reliance" was a central theme of these reforms, which included restructuring the agency to better reflect this strategy. Key initiatives involved streamlining procurement procedures, diversifying the partner base to include more local and faith-based organizations, and promoting internal governance reforms.

The Trump Administration also introduced policies that reflected its broader conservative values, such as promoting pro-life and family-friendly policies and advancing international religious freedom. These reforms were part of a broader effort to ensure that USAID's work aligned more closely with American values and interests, including building an unprecedented genocide-response infrastructure.

In contrast, the Biden Administration is criticized for transforming USAID into a vehicle for advancing a "divisive political and cultural agenda." The administration's policies, which include promoting abortion, climate extremism, gender radicalism, and interventions against perceived systemic racism, are seen as a departure from the bipartisan consensus that traditionally guided U.S. foreign aid. The administration is also accused of "decoupling U.S. assistance from free-market reforms," which are viewed as essential for economic and political stability. The result has been a USAID that is more aligned with progressive ideological goals than with traditional American values, leading to strained relationships with key international partners.

Furthermore, the Biden Administration's push for "wasteful budget increases" has led to a situation where USAID's capacity to spend funds responsibly is called into question. The agency's foreign aid programs are described as having been transformed into a "massive and open-ended global entitlement program" that primarily benefits the progressive Left.

The text suggests that the next conservative administration should work to scale back USAID's global operations and return the agency to its pre-pandemic budget levels. This would involve reversing many of the changes implemented by the Biden Administration and building on the reforms introduced under President Trump. The goal would be to "deradicalize" USAID's programs and structures, ensuring that the agency's work is once again aligned with conservative values and U.S. national interests. This effort would require close cooperation with Congress to achieve deep cuts in the international affairs budget while granting USAID greater flexibility in how it allocates and spends its funds.

KEY ISSUES

ALIGNING U.S. FOREIGN AID TO U.S. FOREIGN POLICY
U.S. foreign aid is often criticized for being "disconnected from the strategy and practice of U.S. foreign policy." The complexity of coordinating foreign aid is exacerbated by the fact that the aid budget is fragmented across "approximately 20 offices, agencies, and departments." This fragmentation makes it difficult to ensure that U.S. foreign aid is consistently aligned with broader foreign policy objectives. To address this issue, the text recommends empowering the USAID Administrator with the additional role of Director of Foreign Assistance (DFA), a position that would have the rank of Deputy Secretary at the Department of State. This role would provide the authority to "align and coordinate the countless foreign assistance programs" across the U.S. government, ensuring that they effectively advance the agenda of a conservative administration. A similar role existed during the last two years of the George W. Bush Administration but was eliminated by the Obama Administration in 2009.

COUNTERING CHINA'S DEVELOPMENT CHALLENGE
The People's Republic of China (PRC) poses a significant challenge to U.S. influence through its "trillion-dollar Belt and Road Initiative (BRI)." This initiative has seen China direct billions of dollars in loans and investments to countries around the world, advancing its geostrategic objective of displacing the United States as the dominant global power. The text highlights how China uses "debt traps" to strengthen its influence, extract natural resources, and gain military access to ports and bases, all while isolating Taiwan and securing political support in international forums.

The negative consequences of China's involvement in developing countries are evident in Latin America and Africa, where Chinese investments have undermined local industries, exacerbated financial distress, and entrenched corruption. For example, in Brazil, a world leader in shoe production, the local industry collapsed under a flood of cheap Chinese imports. In Africa, China's dominance in the rare earth mining sector has given it substantial control over global energy development.

In response, the Trump Administration launched a series of initiatives under USAID to counter China's influence, including the "Clear Choice" strategy, which promoted an American development model based on "liberty, sovereignty, and free markets." The administration also launched its first Digital Strategy to promote safe 5G access in emerging markets and counter Beijing's efforts to "equip regimes with tools to stifle democracy." Additionally, the administration formed bilateral partnerships with countries like Japan, Israel, and Taiwan to support development projects in strategically important regions such as sub-Saharan Africa and the Indo-Pacific.

To further counter China's influence, the Trump Administration established an office in Greenland to "counter China's claims of being a 'near Arctic state'," and realigned USAID's programs across Asia with America's Indo-Pacific strategy. The administration also worked to combat illegal, unreported, and unregulated fishing by Chinese state-run fleets, which violate international norms and devastate local economies in developing countries.

However, the Biden Administration has been accused of allowing these counter-China efforts to "waste away," prioritizing progressive climate politics over national security concerns. The text argues that a future conservative administration should restore and build upon the Trump Administration's counter-China infrastructure within USAID. This would involve ending climate policy fanaticism that benefits Beijing, assessing bilateral aid through the lens of U.S. national security interests, and financing programs that specifically counter Chinese efforts in key countries. The USAID Mission to Central Asia, based in Bangkok, should also refocus its strategic attention on initiatives designed to counter Chinese influence in the region.

CLIMATE CHANGE
Upon taking office, President Biden prioritized climate change, issuing executive orders to "put the climate crisis at the center of U.S. foreign policy and national security." USAID, in alignment with this directive, rebranded itself as "a climate agency," shifting its focus from traditional development goals to the Administration's broader climate agenda. The agency's private-sector engagement strategy, which originally aimed to reduce reliance on foreign aid through private investment and trade, was redirected to support the global transition from fossil fuels to renewable energy.

The Biden Administration has integrated its radical climate policies into every USAID initiative. This includes joining or funding international partnerships that advance the Paris Climate Agreement's aims, and supporting the concept of giving trillions of dollars in "climate reparations" to developing nations. The administration's aggressive push to transition away from fossil fuels has had unintended consequences, particularly in exacerbating global food insecurity. For example, the anti-fossil fuel agenda has driven up global energy prices, which in turn has led to inflation, hitting the poor hardest as they spend a larger portion of their income on food. Moreover, farmers in poor countries can no longer afford expensive fertilizers made from natural gas, leading to lower food production. A stark example is Sri Lanka, where a ban on chemical fertilizers, implemented without viable alternatives, has resulted in widespread hunger and political instability.

Contrary to the aid industry's claims that climate change causes poverty, the text argues that the main drivers of global poverty are "enduring conflict, government corruption, and bad economic policies." The response of the Biden Administration to man-made food insecurity has been to pour billions of dollars into aid, a strategy that, according to the text, will only perpetuate underdevelopment and dependency on foreign assistance.

The impact on Africa is particularly severe. Countries like South Africa, which relies on coal for 80% of its energy needs, would require $26 billion to fully transition away from coal. The financial burden of transitioning from fossil fuels is deemed "unachievable" for many African nations. Similarly, in Latin America, countries that are major producers of oil and gas have been pressured to cut their energy production, disrupting their primary source of export revenue and leading to prolonged economic and political instability.

The text strongly recommends that USAID should cease its "war on fossil fuels" in the developing world and instead support the "responsible management of oil and gas reserves" as the quickest route to alleviating poverty and reducing the need for foreign aid. The next conservative administration should rescind all climate policies from USAID's programs, particularly the Climate Strategy 2022–2030, and dismantle offices and programs that advance the Paris Climate Agreement. Instead, USAID resources should be redirected to strengthen the resilience of countries most vulnerable to climatic shifts, focusing on traditional climate mitigation efforts rather than radical climate agendas. Additionally, the agency should stop collaborating with and funding progressive entities that advocate for extreme climate policies.

DIVERSITY, EQUITY, AND INCLUSION AGENDA
Under the Biden Administration, USAID has embedded Diversity, Equity, and Inclusion (DEI) principles throughout its structure. DEI advisers have been installed in "all its Bureaus, Offices, and [overseas] Missions," and an agency-wide DEI scorecard and dashboard track compliance with DEI directives. A Chief DEI Officer, who sits in the Administrator's office, oversees this extensive infrastructure, ensuring that DEI considerations are incorporated into all agency policies and that they become standard

clauses in contracts and grants. Organizations seeking to partner with USAID must now demonstrate how they will "diversify their partner base."

The consequences of this DEI-driven approach have been significant. The text argues that it has led to the "racialization" of USAID and created a "hostile work environment" for staff who disagree with the administration's identity politics. The pursuit of ideological purity through DEI has threatened merit-based professional advancement, hyperpoliticized the workplace, and corrupted the award process. Moreover, it discourages potential contractors and grantees that do not align with the DEI agenda from seeking USAID funding, thereby narrowing the diversity of perspectives and approaches within the agency's programs.

The next conservative administration is advised to dismantle USAID's DEI apparatus entirely. This would involve eliminating the Chief Diversity Officer position, as well as the DEI advisers and committees. The DEI scorecard and dashboard should be scrapped, and DEI requirements removed from all contracts and grant tenders. Additionally, the administration should issue a directive to cease promoting the DEI agenda, including the "bullying LGBTQ+ agenda," and establish a confidential medium for staff to report cases of political retaliation experienced during the Biden Administration.

The text suggests that entities promoting discriminatory DEI practices should face consequences, including potential debarment. Staff and grantees engaging in ideological agitation should be dismissed, as federal agencies are prohibited from engaging in partisan politics. The authority over civil rights issues at USAID should be returned to the agency's Office of Civil Rights, ensuring that all Americans have equal opportunities for career advancement at USAID, regardless of their political or ideological beliefs.

REFOCUSING GENDER EQUALITY ON WOMEN, CHILDREN, AND FAMILIES

The text criticizes past Democratic administrations for undermining the definition of "women" through their gender policies at USAID. It argues that these policies have nearly erased the concept of femininity by expanding protections to include "progressive special-interest groups" rather than focusing on the needs of vulnerable women, children, and families worldwide. The agency is accused of aggressively promoting abortion on demand under the banners of "sexual and reproductive health and reproductive rights," "gender equality," and "women's empowerment." This advocacy, according to the text, dilutes USAID's mission to protect women and children and supports causes that are out of step with traditional values.

The importance of the family as the "basic unit of and foundation for a thriving society" is emphasized. The text contends that without women, society cannot continue, and yet, the progressive Left has so distorted the definition of "woman" that even U.S. Supreme Court Justice Ketanji Brown Jackson was unable to clearly define the term during her confirmation hearing. The text argues that USAID cannot effectively advocate for and protect women when the very definition of women is in question.

The recommended course of action for the next conservative administration includes renaming USAID's Office of Gender Equality and Women's Empowerment (GEWE) to the Office of Women, Children, and Families. Resources currently allocated to GEWE should be redirected to this new office, and the Senior Gender Coordinator should be replaced with a pro-life Senior Coordinator focused on protecting women, children, and families. Additionally, the administration should eliminate the "more than 180 gender advisors and points of contact" embedded within USAID Missions and Operating Units worldwide.

The text also calls for the rescindment of President Biden's 2022 Gender Policy, refocusing it on women, children, and families. All references to "gender," "gender equality," "gender equity," and related terms should be removed from USAID's websites, publications, policies, and contracts. Similarly, references to "abortion," "reproductive health," and "sexual and reproductive rights" should be eliminated, as well as controversial sexual education materials.

The concept of "gender" has been hijacked by the Left, according to the text, to include a spectrum of identities beyond the traditional male-female binary. This promotion of "gender radicalism" is considered incompatible with the traditional norms of many societies where USAID operates. The text suggests that these radical gender policies generate resentment and confusion, potentially alienating aid recipients who hold different values regarding sexuality.

The next administration should ensure that USAID's mission is to protect and support all members of society—women, children, and men—from conception to natural death. This goal involves meeting basic human needs such as access to clean water, sanitation, food, education, healthcare, justice, and economic opportunities. The Office of Women, Children, and Families should prioritize partnerships with local organizations, including faith-based organizations, and implement the Geneva Consensus Declaration on Women's Health and Protection of the Family to guide its work.

PROTECTING LIFE IN FOREIGN ASSISTANCE

Protecting life should be a core objective of U.S. foreign assistance, according to the text. However, the Biden Administration is criticized for reversing many pro-life policies upon taking office. One significant reversal was the revocation of the Protecting Life in Global Health Assistance (PLGHA) policy, also known as the Mexico City Policy. The PLGHA required foreign NGOs to agree not to "perform or actively promote abortions as a method of family planning" in exchange for receiving U.S. assistance. The Trump Administration expanded this policy to cover all global health assistance, estimated at $8.8 billion annually, but the Biden Administration swiftly dismantled these protections, restoring funding to pro-abortion NGOs such as Planned Parenthood International and MSI Reproductive Choices.

The Biden Administration's approach is described as a "radical assault" on pro-life principles, with USAID prioritizing funding for the global abortion industry over programs that promote life, women's health, and family stability. Even under the PLGHA, several loopholes allowed for continued support of the global abortion industry. International NGOs that promote abortions, like Population Services International and the Population Council, continued to receive funding. Additionally, the United Nations Secretariat's promotion of abortion during the COVID-19 pandemic exposed another loophole, as humanitarian aid and multilateral organizations were exempt from PLGHA's restrictions.

To address these issues, the next conservative administration is advised to issue an executive order reinstating PLGHA and closing the existing loopholes. This order should extend the policy to cover all forms of foreign assistance, including humanitarian aid, and ensure strict enforcement. It should also block funding to the United Nations Population Fund (UNFPA), which supports coercive abortion and sterilization practices in countries like China. The new executive order should require all entities funded by USAID, both directly and indirectly, to report compliance with PLGHA, and include penalties, such as debarment, for violations.

Furthermore, the Helms Amendment, which has prohibited the use of U.S. taxpayer dollars for abortions abroad for over 50 years, should continue to be strictly applied. The text emphasizes that both Republican and Democratic administrations have historically upheld this amendment, and it should remain a cornerstone of U.S. foreign assistance policy.

INTERNATIONAL RELIGIOUS FREEDOM

The text underscores the importance of international religious freedom as a central component of USAID's development efforts, particularly under conservative administrations. President Trump's Executive Order 13926, titled "Advancing International Religious Freedom," directed the Secretary of State to ensure that at least $50 million a year is budgeted for programs that advance religious freedom globally. The order also required that faith-based and religious entities not face discrimination when competing for federal funding, reflecting a commitment to ensure that religious organizations play a vital role in USAID's development work.

Under the Trump Administration, USAID created a senior-level Chief Adviser for International Religious Freedom, who reported directly to the Administrator. This adviser was tasked with coordinating a "whole-of-USAID" approach to religious freedom, which included establishing a robust genocide-response capability. The agency also strengthened its partnerships with faith-based organizations, issuing rules and guidance to ensure their full participation in USAID programs without discrimination.

However, the Biden Administration is criticized for resisting efforts to promote religious freedom, particularly when it conflicts with the administration's positions on abortion and gender ideology. These policies, which are often at odds with the traditional values of societies where USAID operates, have led to tensions both within the agency and with aid recipients.

The text recommends that the next conservative administration should reaffirm the importance of religious freedom as a core American value. This includes training all USAID staff on the connection between religious freedom and development, integrating this priority into all agency programs, and strengthening relationships with local faith-based leaders. USAID should also continue to build on local programs that serve the poor, ensuring that religious freedom is a guiding principle in its development efforts. Additionally, Congress should appropriate specific funding to support persecuted religious minorities, in line with the objectives of Executive Order 13926.

STREAMLINING PROCUREMENT AND LOCALIZING THE PARTNER BASE

USAID primarily functions as a grantmaking and contracting agency, distributing billions of dollars in federal funding to various implementing partners, including U.N. agencies, international NGOs, for-profit companies, and local entities in developing countries. In some cases, such as Jordan and Ukraine, USAID provides direct budget support to host-country governments. However, the agency often relies on "expensive and ineffective large contracts and grants" to execute its programs, which are justified on the grounds of speed and reduced administrative burden. The Trump Administration sought to reform these practices through its "Journey to Self-Reliance" strategy, which aimed to secure better development outcomes, reduce costs, and foster partnerships with local entities.

In December 2018, USAID launched its first Acquisition and Assistance Strategy, which was designed to streamline procurement processes, introduce innovation, and diversify the agency's partner base. This strategy emphasized the importance of engaging local NGOs, particularly faith-based organizations, which often provide more cost-effective and impactful alternatives to large aid contractors. The strategy also prioritized global partnerships with the private sector, including corporations, investors, and philanthropies, which are seen as key to maximizing the impact of taxpayer dollars and advancing sustainable development outcomes.

Despite the Biden Administration's rhetoric in favor of localization, the text argues that the "aid industrial complex" has recaptured the agency, stifling further reforms and maintaining the status quo. The next conservative administration is encouraged to reinvigorate efforts to streamline procurement processes by implementing standardized policy provisions in all grants, cooperative agreements, and contracts. These provisions should align with key policy topics, including the protection of life in foreign assistance and the imposition of funding conditions on multilateral organizations. The administration should also enhance accountability and transparency in how funds are disbursed and spent.

To ensure effective implementation of these reforms, the text suggests appointing a political appointee as USAID's Senior Procurement Executive and Director of the Office of Assistance and Acquisitions (OAA) within the Bureau of Management. This role is deemed critical, as the OAA is "ground zero for controlling the disbursement of U.S. foreign aid." The next administration should empower the Administrator and other key appointees to determine the scale and scope of awards, increasing transparency in subawards to prevent progressive policies from being promoted under conservative administrations. Furthermore, USAID should expand its roster of contracting and agreement officers to accelerate disaster response funding and diversify the partner base.

The text also highlights the importance of "localization" as a strategy for improving aid outcomes. Although this approach has been challenging to implement due to internal resistance and opposition from the aid industry, the Trump Administration demonstrated its feasibility through the President's Emergency Plan for AIDS Relief (PEPFAR). During Trump's tenure, PEPFAR increased the percentage of funding allocated to local entities from 25% to nearly 70%, yielding positive results. The next administration should replicate this model across all USAID programs.

Moreover, the text recommends expanding the New Partnership Initiative (NPI) across all USAID bureaus and offices. Missions should be required to craft and execute NPI action plans, with a minimum percentage of their portfolios directed toward new, underutilized, and local partners. The use of open competition should be increased to lower barriers to entry, while fixed-amount awards that reduce compliance burdens should be favored over cost-plus reimbursement contracts that benefit large companies. Before launching new programs, USAID should assess existing local activities to avoid duplicating efforts and undermining local initiatives. Whenever possible, the agency should build on initiatives already in place at the local level.

GLOBAL HEALTH
The United States is the world's largest funder of global health initiatives, with USAID playing a significant role in delivering health assistance worldwide. For over 60 years, the American people have contributed to saving millions of lives through programs overseen by USAID's Bureau for Global Health (GH). This bureau manages a multibillion-dollar portfolio supporting maternal and child health, voluntary family planning, and major initiatives such as the President's Emergency Plan for AIDS Relief (PEPFAR) and the President's Malaria Initiative (PMI). Given the scale of these operations, it is crucial that funds are used effectively to maximize care for the world's neediest populations.

The COVID-19 pandemic highlighted the importance of strong health institutions and sound public health practices in enabling countries to respond quickly and recover more rapidly. This underscores the value of "localization," where USAID helps developing countries strengthen their capacity to provide essential health services. Unfortunately, many global health programs funded by USAID remain tied to outdated models that prioritize spending ("inputs") over actual outcomes achieved. Historically, USAID has focused on addressing infectious diseases and population control, often with little integration across different global health activities. Chronic diseases were largely ignored, and the agency's approach did not evolve significantly over the decades.

The text argues that the next conservative administration should modernize the Global Health Bureau's portfolio by emphasizing a comprehensive approach to supporting women, children, and families. This should include building institutional capacity in host countries, increasing awards to local and faith-based partners, and improving coordination with local entities. A rigorous review of existing programs is needed to eliminate outdated and ineffective concepts, ensuring that taxpayer dollars are not wasted and that current funding streams are aligned with today's needs.

In particular, USAID's efforts should focus on holistic health care that addresses the persistent issue of maternal and infant mortality, a global tragedy that continues to claim lives. Contrary to popular narratives, the text argues that abortion is not the solution to this problem, as families around the world genuinely cherish children. The Bureau should implement initiatives like the "Request for Application for Resilient Families," which aims to integrate funding from various siloed programs to focus on individuals and families rather than specific diseases or conditions.

The text also emphasizes the importance of increasing collaboration with faith-based organizations (FBOs), which have historically been more successful in reaching remote and vulnerable populations due to the trust they have built through decades of service. In sub-Saharan Africa, for instance, FBOs provide more than 80% of healthcare services, particularly to the extremely poor. In contrast, the Global Health Bureau has traditionally funneled the majority of its funding (85%) to large U.S.-based NGOs, which often have high overhead costs and deliver only a fraction of the funds to those in need.

USAID's most successful health initiatives, such as PEPFAR and PMI, have saved millions of lives and should serve as models for other programs. The infrastructure and organizational platforms developed through these initiatives became instrumental in responding to the COVID-19 pandemic. However, the text argues that a smooth transition to national ownership and funding for these programs is necessary, which will require better coordination of USAID's stovepiped programs.

Finally, the text highlights the need for strengthening the collection and use of data in global health programs. Accurate data is essential for making informed decisions and improving outcomes. Historically, global health programs have relied on statistical modeling or survey data, which are considered weak data sources. The Trump Administration made critical updates to PEPFAR's data collection systems to increase transparency and accountability. The next conservative administration should apply these reforms across all of USAID's global health programs.

Additionally, the text calls for empowering the Bureau's Center for Innovation and Impact (CII) to expand networks of private and faith-based health organizations. These networks can drive innovation through development-impact bonds, capital funds, and new technologies, all aimed at enhancing self-reliance in health care. Improving the Global Health Bureau's hiring, staffing, and recruitment practices is also essential to addressing management challenges and reducing mission drift and burnout among personnel.

HOLDING THE U.N., THE WORLD HEALTH ORGANIZATION (WHO), AND OTHER MULTILATERAL ORGANIZATIONS ACCOUNTABLE
The text argues that the U.S. government's multilateral partners, including U.N. agencies and the WHO, should be held to a higher standard of financial and programmatic accountability. The United States, as a major contributor to these organizations, must ensure that American resources are used effectively and in alignment with U.S. values and interests. A key recommendation is that the next conservative administration should designate a political appointee responsible for coordinating cross-agency efforts to monitor and hold these multilateral organizations accountable.

One specific area of concern is the promotion of abortion through language in U.N. documents, policy statements, and technical literature. The text calls for removing such language to align with the U.S. government's stance on protecting life. Additionally, the United States should have more prominent representation in international technical committees and regulation-setting organizations. This would help ensure that American interests, innovation, and the vitality of the U.S. biomedical sector are preserved, and that U.S. resources are utilized in a manner consistent with American values.

GLOBAL HUMANITARIAN ASSISTANCE
The United States is the world's largest humanitarian actor, with USAID disbursing billions of dollars annually in life-saving assistance to vulnerable populations worldwide. This assistance, funded through the International Disaster Assistance (IDA) account, supports operations ranging from hurricane responses in Central America to tackling Ebola outbreaks in Central Africa. USAID also provides nearly half of the budget for the Nobel Prize-winning U.N. World Food Programme (WFP).

Historically, USAID's emergency responses focused primarily on natural disasters. However, the text notes a significant shift in recent years, with more than 80% of USAID's humanitarian budget now devoted to "chronic man-made crises." These crises often persist for years, absorbing billions of dollars annually without clear end goals. The text argues that this shift has led to the distortion of humanitarian responses, with aid becoming a "permanent" fixture in certain regions rather than a temporary solution.

This situation is compounded by the influence of a powerful foreign aid industry that benefits financially from extending and expanding large-scale programs. This industry ensures that appropriations for these programs face little scrutiny, even as the demands for financial support continue to grow, such as with the recent conflict in Ukraine. As a result, the Bureau for Humanitarian Assistance (BHA) has seen its budget double in just a few years, raising concerns about the bureau's capacity to manage these funds responsibly.

The text highlights several examples of how humanitarian aid has, in some cases, exacerbated the very problems it seeks to address. In Syria, for instance, the Assad regime skims nearly half of the foreign aid directed to the country through inflated exchange rates, diversion of food supplies, and procurement arrangements with compromised contractors. In Yemen, the influx of "free food" aid has crippled local agriculture, while in Afghanistan, nearly $1 billion in humanitarian aid continues to flow into the country despite the Taliban's return to power.

To address these issues, the next conservative administration should resize and repurpose USAID's humanitarian aid portfolio to restore its original purpose of providing short-term emergency relief. This would involve working with Congress to make deep cuts to the IDA budget by ending programs in regions controlled by malign actors, such as Yemen, Syria, and Afghanistan, where aid is often diverted or misused.

Additionally, the text recommends requiring USAID and the State Department to develop exit strategies for ongoing humanitarian responses. These strategies would include transitioning funding from emergency to development projects, pressing host governments to integrate displaced persons rather than keeping them in dehumanizing camps, and reducing the agency's reliance on expensive and inefficient international partners in favor of local entities, particularly faith-based organizations. This approach is seen as a more cost-effective and effective means of delivering aid.

The text also suggests that BHA should adopt stricter vetting procedures to prevent aid from being diverted to terrorist groups and increase efforts to secure greater contributions from other donors as a condition for receiving additional U.S. aid. Lastly, USAID's Bureau for Management should hire more procurement officers to strengthen BHA's award management capacity and reduce the incentive to issue large awards to aid industry giants.

LEVERAGING FOREIGN AID TO UNLEASH THE POWER OF AMERICA'S PRIVATE SECTOR

The text highlights a significant shift in global financial flows since USAID's inception. In the 1960s, 80% of U.S. financial flows to the developing world came from government assistance. Today, less than 10% of these flows come from U.S. government aid, with the majority now originating from private investment, remittances, and private charities. This shift demonstrates the growing importance of America's private sector in promoting economic development in poor countries.

Developing world leaders increasingly prefer "trade and investment, not aid" as a means of fostering sustainable development. However, the Biden Administration has been criticized for leveraging private-sector financing to advance its climate and other progressive agendas globally, rather than focusing on genuine development problems.

The text argues that the next conservative administration should return USAID to a foreign aid model that leverages resources to promote private-sector solutions. Private capital investment is seen as the greatest enabler of job creation and sustainable economic growth in the developing world. One key tool for this approach is the U.S. Development Finance Corporation (DFC), launched in December 2019. The DFC was intended to unleash the power of America's private sector by providing emerging markets with blended financing opportunities to end poverty, create new markets for U.S. products, strengthen bilateral partnerships, and counter China's predatory loans and investments.

The Trump Administration established a USAID–DFC Working Group to align development outcomes with U.S. strategic interests, particularly in countering China. The text recommends that USAID and DFC should better align their activities by structurally and operationally integrating their operations. One suggestion is to "dual hat" the DFC's Chief Development Officer so that he or she serves simultaneously in both institutions.

Finally, the text criticizes the current misuse of the DFC as a global vehicle for promoting "economy-killing climate programs" and irrelevant diversity objectives. The next conservative administration should restore the DFC to its original mission of deploying commercial risk-reducing financial services to advance U.S. interests in the developing world.

BRANDING

Branding has become a contentious issue within the foreign aid bureaucracy, where a "deeply embedded culture" often views public recognition of U.S. assistance as secondary to a larger philanthropic mission. There is an apparent reluctance to brand U.S. aid with the American flag, with some implementers citing vaguely defined security concerns as justification for downplaying U.S. contributions. This reluctance is seen as having negative foreign policy implications, especially as competitors like China aggressively promote their own efforts to gain influence and resources globally.

One of the most concerning issues highlighted in the text is the appropriation of unbranded U.S. assistance by malign actors. For example, in Yemen, Houthi terrorists

have claimed to be providing for people under their control with anonymous U.S. humanitarian aid. This misappropriation undermines U.S. influence and allows adversaries to take credit for American generosity.

The text recommends that the next conservative administration should build on the Trump Administration's branding policy, which overhauled ADS Chapter 320 to ensure that U.S. assistance is fully credited to the American people. This effort should be led by a Senior Advisor for Brand Management within the Bureau for Legislative and Public Affairs (LPA), who should be a political appointee tasked with maximizing the visibility of U.S. aid. The LPA should also collaborate with the U.S. Agency for Global Media (USAGM) to ensure that local media coverage reflects the American contribution to global development efforts.

OTHER OFFICES AND BUREAUS

OFFICE OF ADMINISTRATOR

The text suggests that the next conservative administration should maintain the current structure of the Office of Administrator, which includes two presidentially appointed, Senate-confirmed Deputy Administrators—one for Policy and one for Management. These positions, along with the Chief of Staff, are critical for the effective operation of USAID. The individuals in these roles should have extensive experience in the executive branch, ideally within foreign affairs agencies, and be well-versed in federal procurement practices. This experience is essential for ensuring that USAID's policies and operations align with the administration's priorities and are implemented efficiently.

BUREAU FOR FOREIGN ASSISTANCE

A key recommendation is that the USAID Administrator should also assume the role of Director of Foreign Assistance (DFA) at the Department of State, with the rank of Deputy Secretary. This would centralize control over U.S. foreign assistance, ensuring that it is better coordinated and aligned with U.S. foreign policy objectives. The text argues that the current focus of the Bureau for Foreign Assistance on the formulation of the President's budget proposal should shift towards the execution of appropriated resources. This includes streamlining processes such as the Mission and Bureau Resource Requests, speeding up the availability of appropriations by delivering the required reports to Congress more quickly, and fast-tracking the approval of Congressional Notifications (CNs) and other pre-obligation requirements.

MANAGEMENT BUREAU

The next conservative administration is advised to appoint a political appointee as USAID's Senior Procurement Executive and Director of the Office of Acquisition and Assistance (M/OAA). This is one of the most crucial positions at USAID, as the M/OAA is responsible for overseeing the disbursement of U.S. foreign aid. The text also recommends placing political appointees with appropriate credentials (including warrants) within M/OAA to ensure that procurement processes align with the administration's policy goals. Additionally, USAID should engage qualified experts from other federal departments, agencies, or outside government (if free of conflicts of interest) on Technical Committees that review applications for USAID contracts and grants. To foster innovation in procurement, the designation of USAID's Competition Advocate should go to someone open to innovative types of contracts, reducing the influence of the aid oligopoly on the agency.

OFFICE OF HUMAN CAPITAL AND TALENT MANAGEMENT

The text emphasizes the importance of quickly appointing a political appointee as USAID's Chief Human Capital Officer (CHCO) and Director of the Office of Human Capital and Talent Management (HCTM). This role is critical for managing personnel processes, particularly in the context of reforming USAID's hiring practices to align with the administration's agenda. The White House Liaison at USAID should be someone with substantial experience in federal personnel systems, ensuring a smooth onboarding process for new appointees and managing internal changes among career employees.

USAID is recommended as one of the agencies to pilot a reinstated Executive Order 13957, which created Schedule F within the Excepted Service. This classification allows for the appointment of term-limited positions, offering the flexibility needed to align the workforce with the administration's priorities. The new CHCO should also assess how existing members of the Senior Executive Service (SES) are distributed throughout the agency and implement an SES Mobility Program to encourage the regular rotation of senior career leaders, including opportunities for details to other departments and agencies.

BUREAU FOR POLICY, PLANNING, AND LEARNING

The text suggests that the policy functions of the Bureau for Policy, Planning, and Learning (PPL) should be shifted to the Office of Budget and Resource Management (BRM) within the Office of the Administrator. This restructured office, renamed the Office of Budget, Policy, and Resource Management (BPRM), should be staffed with political appointees to ensure that USAID's policies are closely aligned with the administration's agenda. Additionally, responsibility for reviewing and processing changes to USAID's policy directives (Automated Directives System, ADS) should move from the Management Bureau to the new BPRM.

Before these changes take effect, the Assistant Administrator for PPL should immediately freeze any new updates to the ADS and other agency-wide policy documents. This freeze would allow the administration to prioritize the publication of amendments reflecting the new administration's viewpoint. Within the first year, all major agency policies should be reviewed, amended, or withdrawn to align with the new administration's priorities.

BUREAU FOR LEGISLATIVE AND PUBLIC AFFAIRS

The Bureau for Legislative and Public Affairs (LPA) plays a critical role in shaping USAID's public messaging and communication strategies. The text advises that no more than 10% of USAID's politically appointed positions under Administratively Determined (AD) authority should be allocated to the LPA. These positions should focus on reviewing and editing the agency's public-facing content, including web pages and social media accounts, to ensure consistency with the new administration's policies. Additionally, the LPA should streamline the review process for Congressional Notifications (CNs) and publish all CNs and congressional reports to enhance transparency.

To ensure coherent and effective public messaging, the LPA should gain direct authority over the communications staff dispersed across USAID's various bureaus and offices. The LPA should also expand its public outreach efforts to include conservative allies in global development and humanitarian aid work, reducing the influence of the aid industrial complex on USAID's corporate relationships.

OFFICE OF GENERAL COUNSEL

The Office of General Counsel (OGC) is identified as one of the most important positions within USAID. The next conservative administration should prioritize the appointment of a strong team of Schedule C attorneys in the OGC, particularly for interpreting executive orders and internal policies. The General Counsel should have two political deputies—one focused on Human Capital and Talent Management (HCTM) and the other on the Office of Acquisition and Assistance (OAA). Shortly after the administration takes office, the OGC should issue guidance ensuring that faith-based organizations are eligible for USAID funding without facing discrimination.

OFFICE OF BUDGET RESOURCES AND MANAGEMENT

The Director of Budget Resources and Management (BRM) should be a political appointee with a significant role within the Administrator's senior management team. This position is crucial for managing USAID's financial resources and ensuring that they are allocated effectively in line with the administration's priorities. The BRM's top priorities should include preparing the Section 653(a) report as per the Administrator's guidance, fast-tracking Congressional Notifications, and identifying already appropriated resources that can be reprogrammed to fund new administration initiatives. The text suggests that young political appointees may be more effectively placed in the BRM than in the LPA.

BUREAU FOR DEMOCRACY, DEVELOPMENT, AND INNOVATION

The Bureau for Democracy, Development, and Innovation (DDI) is responsible for most of USAID's non-health, non-humanitarian funding, as well as many of the agency's sectoral appropriations directives. While this bureau has been central to advancing many of the Biden Administration's radical priorities—such as gender and climate change policies—it also handles areas crucial to a conservative reorientation of USAID. These areas include trade, economic growth, innovation, private-sector partnerships, and faith-based community engagement.

The text recommends that the next conservative administration should prioritize the staffing of key positions within DDI, including the Directors of the Centers and Hubs. Many of the policies under DDI's purview will need to be revised or entirely rewritten to reflect the new administration's goals. The administration should also redirect central appropriations within DDI to fund new priorities, such as supporting ethnic and religious minorities and fostering joint ventures with the private sector in education and energy. DDI programs should issue funding opportunities restricted to new and underutilized partners, following the model of the New Partnership Initiative (NPI).

REGIONS

ASIA

Asia, being the most populous continent, is at the forefront of the geopolitical struggle between the United States and Communist China. USAID's work in this region should be guided by America's Indo-Pacific Strategy, which emphasizes strengthening alliances with pro–free market nations such as Japan, Australia, South Korea, and India. These partnerships can drive private-sector solutions in areas such as power generation, infrastructure, digital connectivity, investment, and trade expansion.

The text highlights the importance of deepening USAID's development cooperation with India, particularly in the context of India's global leadership in vaccine production during the COVID-19 pandemic. These ties should be expanded, as should development cooperation with Taiwan, which has effective pandemic response capacities that could benefit other developing countries.

China's strategic "island-hopping" in the Pacific poses a direct threat to U.S. maritime supremacy and homeland security. In response, USAID and its allied donors should counter these efforts by deploying targeted assistance to help vulnerable Pacific states combat challenges such as China's illegal fishing activities. Although China outpaces the democratic alliance in deploying state-backed financing to developing countries, it cannot match the private-sector capacity of these nations to mobilize trillions of dollars in capital.

Pakistan is cited as an example of foreign aid policies disconnected from U.S. national interests. Despite receiving more than $12 billion in U.S. foreign aid since 2010, Pakistan remains "intensely anti-American," supports the Taliban, has enabled North Korea's nuclear program, persecutes religious minorities, and is a willing client of China. The text suggests reevaluating U.S. aid to Pakistan in light of these realities.

MIDDLE EAST

The Middle East is described as being more vulnerable today than it was in 2020 due to the Biden Administration's lack of a coherent strategy for the region. Countries like Tunisia and Iraq are sliding toward autocracy and Iran's orbit, respectively, while U.S. soldiers continue to operate in Syria with unclear objectives. At the same time, billions of dollars in U.S. aid prop up regimes that are aligned with Iran, further destabilizing the region.

The Trump Administration's Abraham Accords marked a significant shift in U.S. policy by de-emphasizing the Arab-Israeli conflict and focusing instead on the threat posed by Iran. Under Trump, USAID sought to leverage the Accords to strengthen regional alliances against Iran through expanded trade and investment, particularly by partnering with nations like the UAE, Israel, Morocco, Qatar, and Kuwait to catalyze regional development projects in Africa.

The text recommends that the next conservative administration should reset USAID's programming in the Middle East to align more closely with U.S. national security interests. This includes prioritizing development assistance that advances the Abraham Accords, cutting aid to states allied with Iran, and securing better development outcomes by reducing USAID's footprint in the region. Instead of relying on large, expensive international partners, USAID should redirect funds to more cost-effective local entities that require minimal field presence.

AFRICA

Africa has been a focal point for USAID since its inception, with the agency playing a crucial role in saving millions of lives through its responses to pandemics and infectious diseases like malaria and HIV/AIDS. USAID has also led global efforts to provide emergency assistance to those fleeing conflict and suffering from natural disasters. The generosity of American aid in Africa is unmatched, but the text argues that despite these efforts, USAID has failed to reduce poverty and hunger on the continent. The agency's long-term humanitarian responses lack clear exit strategies, and numerous development projects fail to produce measurable results or prompt necessary government reforms. Despite the billions spent, Africa remains plagued by poverty, instability, and conflict.

The text points out that the lack of economic development in Africa has created an opportunity for China to become the continent's leading trade partner and investor. Beijing now controls most of Africa's strategic minerals, which are critical for advanced technology, further entrenching its influence. Meanwhile, USAID faces criticism from Africans for exporting cultural values that clash with their traditional norms, which inadvertently strengthens China's position on the continent.

The Biden Administration's climate policies have exacerbated these issues by cutting off billions of dollars in investments needed to develop Africa's fossil fuel resources. This has denied over a billion people access to cheap energy, which is essential for their development and for financing essential social services like healthcare, education, and agriculture. The rising costs of fertilizers due to these policies have also made them unaffordable for many African farmers, leading to increased hunger and further dependence on aid.

The next conservative administration is encouraged to rethink USAID's approach to Africa. The text suggests that 2025 will be a pivotal year as USAID updates its five-year Country Development and Cooperation Strategies. This provides an opportunity to pursue a new development course for Africa, one that promotes economic self-reliance, catalyzes private-sector solutions for job creation, and terminates legacy programs that are no longer effective. The administration should also support diversified energy approaches and hold China accountable for its extractive investments that violate international labor, environmental, and anticorruption norms.

USAID is advised to collaborate with the U.S. International Development Finance Corporation, the State Department, the Treasury, and the Department of Commerce's Foreign Commercial Service to facilitate U.S.–African business relationships. This collaboration should build on initiatives like Prosper Africa, launched by the Trump Administration to enhance trade and investment between the U.S. and Africa. The text also advocates for extending the Africa Growth and Opportunity Act (AGOA) beyond its 2025 term but within a framework that rewards good governance and pro–free market policies. The administration should leverage existing private-sector initiatives led by global churches, corporate philanthropists, and diaspora groups that are already working toward self-reliance in Africa.

Japan's commitment of $30 billion in aid to Africa over three years, alongside investments from Gulf-based sovereign funds in strategic industries, illustrates that there is no shortage of funding for Africa's development. However, the text argues that U.S. foreign aid agencies lack strategic direction. The successful localization model used in PEPFAR, which increased funding to local entities from 20% to nearly 70% during the Trump Administration, should be extended across all USAID programs. USAID should aggressively reduce partnerships with costly and politicized international organizations and instead focus on building on existing local initiatives that have the support of African communities.

LATIN AMERICA

U.S. foreign assistance in Latin America primarily addresses national security threats such as illicit drug and arms trafficking, illegal immigration, terrorism, pandemics, and strategic threats from China, Russia, and Iran. Over the past decade, the U.S. has provided billions of dollars in security, humanitarian, and development aid in regions like Central America and the Andes. This includes $1 billion in emergency aid to Venezuelan refugees fleeing the Maduro dictatorship. USAID has consistently been the first responder to natural disasters in the region, delivering critical assistance, such as during the COVID-19 pandemic, when the U.S. provided millions of vaccine doses and other health support.

Despite these efforts, the text notes that foreign aid has failed to bring lasting peace, prosperity, or stability to Latin America. Widespread poverty, joblessness, and social unrest have contributed to the rise of leftist governments across the region, from Mexico to Chile. These regimes are hostile to U.S. interests, implement radical policies that further impoverish their citizens, and are more inclined to partner with Communist China. Authoritarian kleptocracies in Cuba, Nicaragua, and Venezuela continue to deny basic freedoms, violently suppress dissent, and generate such desperation that hundreds of thousands of their citizens have attempted to cross the U.S. southern border in recent years. The text also highlights the ongoing chaos in Haiti, where no recent U.S. administration has made progress in reducing widespread misery.

However, Latin America is a significant source of energy and food, generating substantial revenue that could finance its internal development. The region's proximity to the United States provides a natural trade and investment advantage, further supported by free-trade agreements. The U.S. remains the preferred destination for higher education and business opportunities for Latin Americans, and successful diasporas in the U.S. serve as powerful economic, cultural, and political bridges to every country in the region.

The Trump Administration sought to promote trade and investment in the region through initiatives like América Crece (America Grows), where USAID played a key role in creating a more enabling environment for private investment. However, the Biden Administration canceled this program, reflecting a broader trend of policy shifts that the text criticizes.

The next conservative administration is urged to reassess all U.S. foreign aid programs in Latin America, terminating those that have failed to produce results after years of effort. Instead, USAID should focus on strengthening the fundamentals of free markets, including property rights, a functioning judiciary, labor and pension reforms, lower taxes, and deregulation. These efforts are seen as essential for increasing trade and investment within the region and with the United States, providing a genuine path to economic and political stability.

The administration should also challenge the spread of socialist ideas that have captured many of the region's governments and youth. This can be done by funding partnerships with the private sector and supporting civil-society groups, including university centers and think tanks, that advocate for pro–free market and democratic principles.

Latin America is identified as an ideal proving ground for reducing USAID's reliance on large U.S.-based implementers. The text suggests that the agency should commit to shifting its entire portfolio in the region to local organizations by 2030, reflecting a broader strategy of localization and empowerment of local entities.

Personnel

The success of the Trump Administration's agenda for USAID was hindered by resistance from both recalcitrant career personnel and inexperienced political appointees. The text argues that the next conservative administration must implement personnel policies from the outset to effectively manage the agency according to high standards. Rapid deployment of reforms will require experienced personnel installed quickly at USAID's headquarters and missions.

One key recommendation is staffing the Office of the General Counsel with at least four politically appointed attorneys in addition to the General Counsel. The General Counsel should have two political deputies—one focused on Human Capital and Talent Management (HCTM) and the other on the Office of Acquisition and Assistance (OAA).

The text also emphasizes the importance of appointing a political appointee with extensive experience in federal personnel systems as USAID's Chief Human Capital Officer and Director of HCTM. This appointee would be responsible for managing the hiring process, shepherding position descriptions, and coordinating with the White House to bring in new appointees and make internal changes among career employees. On Day One, USAID should halt all agency-wide training and replace it with training modules that advance the President's agenda.

To ensure adherence to administration priorities, the text suggests appointing a Senior Accountable Official (SAO) to report on the agency's compliance with key policies, including Protecting Life in Foreign Assistance, critical race theory, climate change, gender, and diversity and inclusion. Additionally, the administration should create a program to staff hard-to-fill positions overseas, targeting individuals with relevant experience in areas like missionary work, military service, and diaspora communities.

Finally, the text recommends creating a recruiting program for veterans and other groups to participate in career opportunities at USAID. This would involve recruiting individuals with overseas experience, such as former missionaries and members of the faith community, to work at USAID on Schedule A appointments, as Institutional Services Contractors, or as Foreign Service Officers.

Analysis: Foreign Policy and National Security

Project 2025 outlines an aggressive "America First" approach to foreign policy and national security. The plan advocates for a confrontational stance towards China, proposing to "subvert China's goal to become the global leader on AI" and barring American companies from aiding China's technological advancement. This aligns with Trump's campaign rhetoric, where he has pledged to "implement strong protections against Chinese espionage" and "ban federal money from going to China". The project also likely continues Trump's skepticism towards NATO, echoing his previous criticisms that "NATO is costing us a fortune". On border security, Project 2025 calls for completing the border wall and implementing stricter immigration policies, mirroring Trump's campaign promises. Let's take a closer look at how the policies are discussed in project 2025 and what are the underlying philosophies behind it.

THE PLAN FOR A UNILATERAL FOREIGN POLICY

As the United States approaches the 2024 presidential election, the potential return of Donald Trump to the White House carries significant implications for U.S. foreign policy. This comprehensive analysis examines the foreign policy vision outlined in Project 2025, a blueprint for a prospective second Trump administration, and scrutinizes its approach to key global challenges. By analyzing Trump's past actions, Project 2025´s proposed future policies, and the broader context of global affairs, we can gain crucial insights into the potential trajectory of U.S. foreign policy under a second Trump term.

Project 2025, developed by the Heritage Foundation, serves as a guiding document for conservative policy implementation. In the realm of foreign policy, it advocates for a marked departure from traditional U.S. approaches, emphasizing unilateral action, economic nationalism, and a reorientation of strategic priorities. This agenda aligns closely with Trump's "America First" doctrine, which prioritizes perceived immediate U.S. interests over long-standing alliances and global commitments.

The core principles of this approach include:

1. **Unilateralism**: A preference for unilateral action and skepticism towards multilateral institutions and agreements.
2. **Transactional Diplomacy**: Viewing foreign relations through a transactional lens, focusing on short-term gains rather than long-term strategic partnerships.
3. **Economic Nationalism**: Centering trade policy on protectionist measures and bilateral negotiations, rather than multilateral free trade agreements.
4. **Military Strength**: While skeptical of foreign interventions, there is an emphasis on military buildup and modernization, particularly in nuclear capabilities.
5. **Skepticism of Traditional Alliances**: NATO and other long-standing alliances are viewed critically, with demands for increased financial contributions from allies.

A central tenet of the proposed foreign policy is a fundamentally altered approach to international trade. Trump has pledged to impose a 60% tariff on Chinese goods and a 10% tariff on imports from all other countries. This dramatic escalation of protectionist measures represents a significant intensification of the trade conflicts that characterized his first term.

During Trump's first term, from 2018 to 2020, his trade war with China resulted in increased costs for American consumers and businesses. Studies suggest that the economic impact on the U.S. outweighed the gains. The proposed global expansion of tariffs risks triggering retaliatory measures from trading partners, potentially leading to a broader trade war with severe economic repercussions.

The implications of this trade policy extend beyond immediate economic concerns. By treating international trade as a zero-sum game, the Trump administration risks undermining strategic relationships critical to addressing global challenges. The abandonment of multilateral trade agreements, such as the Trans-Pacific Partnership (TPP) during Trump's first term, has already ceded economic leadership in Asia to China. The proposed intensification of protectionist measures threatens to further isolate the United States economically, potentially weakening its global influence.

Project 2025 outlines a strategy that would significantly alter the structure and function of the U.S. State Department. The plan calls for all U.S. ambassadors to submit their resignations on January 20, 2025, potentially resulting in a wholesale restructuring of American diplomacy. This approach reflects a skepticism towards career diplomats and traditional diplomatic channels, favoring instead direct, leader-to-leader engagement and transactional negotiations.

During his first term, Trump showed little interest in traditional diplomacy, leaving key foreign policy positions unfilled for months and appointing what critics described as incompetent secretaries of state. He claimed that he "was the only one that mattered" in foreign policy decisions, often bypassing established diplomatic channels in favor of personal relationships with foreign leaders.

CHINA

Project 2025 identifies China as the "defining threat" to U.S. interests. The proposed approach includes:

1. **Trade Policy:** The aforementioned 60% tariff on Chinese goods, significantly escalating the trade war.
2. **Technology Competition**: Focusing on maintaining U.S. technological superiority, including potential restrictions on Chinese students and researchers in the U.S.
3. **Military Posture:** Calling for a "conventional force planning construct to defeat a Chinese invasion of Taiwan" as the highest defense priority.
4. **Economic Decoupling**: Advocating for reducing U.S. economic dependence on China across various sectors.

However, the effectiveness of this approach is questionable, given the deeply intertwined nature of the U.S. and Chinese economies and the potential for escalation in the Taiwan Strait. Trump's past actions, such as abandoning the TPP, arguably undermined efforts to preserve U.S. economic influence in East Asia and made it harder for Asian countries to give the United States the support it says it wants from them.

RUSSIA AND UKRAINE

The approach to Russia and Ukraine represents a significant departure from current U.S. policy:

1. **Ukraine Support:** Trump and Project 2025 are skeptical of continued support for Ukraine in its conflict with Russia. Trump has claimed he could end the war "within 24 hours" if elected.
2. **NATO Stance**: There is a continued push for NATO allies to increase defense spending, with potential threats to reduce U.S. commitment if demands are not met.
3. **Sanctions Policy**: The plan suggests a potential relaxation of sanctions on Russia in exchange for concessions, although specifics are not provided.
4. **Arms Control**: Project 2025 calls for rejecting ratification of the Comprehensive Test Ban Treaty and indicates a willingness to conduct nuclear tests in response to adversary actions.

This stance could have far-reaching implications for European security and the credibility of U.S. commitments to its allies. The potential accommodation with Russia at the expense of Ukrainian sovereignty could reshape the geopolitical landscape in Europe.

NORTH KOREA

While specific policies towards North Korea are not extensively detailed in Project 2025, Trump's past approach and statements suggest:

1. **Personal Diplomacy:** A continuation of the direct, leader-to-leader diplomacy attempted during Trump's first term.
2. **Denuclearization Goal**: Maintaining the objective of complete denuclearization of the Korean Peninsula, though with potentially more flexible terms.
3. **Sanctions Relief**: Possible easing of sanctions in exchange for partial denuclearization steps, a departure from the current "maximum pressure" campaign.

The effectiveness of this strategy remains questionable, given the lack of concrete progress on denuclearization during Trump's first term despite high-profile summits with Kim Jong Un.

ISRAEL AND MIDDLE EAST

Project 2025 and Trump's statements indicate a strongly pro-Israel stance and a continuation of the Abraham Accords approach:

1. **Unwavering Support:** Unconditional support for Israel, including backing for expansive military actions and settlement policies.
2. **Palestinian Issue**: Continued marginalization of Palestinian concerns and rejection of the two-state solution as a policy priority.
3. **Iran Policy**: A return to "maximum pressure" on Iran, potentially including withdrawal from any renewed nuclear agreement.
4. **Abraham Accords**: Further pursuit of normalization agreements between Israel and Arab states, with potential economic incentives.

The abandonment of the Iran nuclear deal (JCPOA) during Trump's first term allowed Iran to advance its nuclear program unchecked. A return to this policy could further destabilize the region and increase proliferation risks.

Implications and Risks

1. **Diplomatic Isolation**: The unilateral and transactional approach to foreign relations could alienate allies and partners, reducing U.S. influence in global affairs. The proposed gutting of the State Department and dismissal of career diplomats could severely hamper America's diplomatic capabilities.
2. **Economic Disruption**: The proposed tariff regime risks triggering a global trade war, potentially harming U.S. economic interests and global economic stability. Historical evidence, such as the Smoot-Hawley Tariff Act of 1930, suggests that broad protectionist policies can have severe negative consequences for the global economy.
3. **Strategic Miscalculation**: The approach to China and Russia may underestimate the complexities of great power competition and the importance of alliance networks. The focus on unilateral action fails to account for the multipolar nature of the current global order, where countries like India, Brazil, and Turkey are increasingly charting independent courses.
4. **Proliferation Risks**: Skepticism towards arms control agreements and willingness to consider new nuclear tests could accelerate global nuclear proliferation. The potential withdrawal from arms control treaties and resumption of nuclear testing could trigger a new arms race.
5. **Soft Power Decline**: The "America First" rhetoric and actions could further diminish U.S. soft power and global leadership. The potential re-election of Trump, given his legal troubles and attempts to overturn the 2020 election results, could significantly damage America's image abroad.
6. **Climate and Pandemic Preparedness**: The skepticism towards climate change science and past mishandling of the COVID-19 pandemic raise concerns about America's preparedness for global challenges under a second Trump administration.
7. **Educational and Scientific Leadership**: The proposed policies targeting universities and scientific institutions could undermine America's long-standing advantages in innovation and research.

Project 2025 and Trump's proposed foreign policy for a second term represent a significant departure from traditional U.S. foreign policy approaches. The emphasis on unilateralism, economic nationalism, and transactional diplomacy poses potential risks to long-standing alliances and the rules-based international order. While proponents argue this approach better serves immediate U.S. interests, critics contend it could lead to strategic isolation and a decline in U.S. global influence.

The potential implications of these policies extend far beyond the immediate term. They could reshape the global order, alter the balance of power in key regions, and fundamentally change America's role in the world.

NATIONAL DEFENSE AND SECURITY

Project 2025 dedicates six chapters to national defense and security, proposing significant changes to various government agencies. The overarching goal appears to be removing obstacles to presidential authority and embedding right-wing cultural war issues into government operations. These proposals include anti-transgender policies and initiatives perceived as anti-government.

The chapter on the Department of Defense, written by a former defense official, advocates for purging the military ranks based on perceived political bias. It calls for eliminating what it terms "divisive critical race theory programs" and diversity initiatives. The plan would expel transgender individuals from military service and rescind policies deemed contrary to conservative principles. To address low recruitment, Project 2025 proposes mandatory military aptitude testing for public school students, despite evidence suggesting that declining recruitment is due to other factors such as concerns about injuries.

Alarmingly, the project proposes ending efforts to secure U.S. elections from foreign interference, specifically by terminating the Cyber Command's work in this area. This raises questions about the motivations behind removing such a crucial safeguard.

The Department of Homeland Security is another target, with proposals authored by Ken Cuccinelli, who served as Trump's acting Homeland Security Secretary. Cuccinelli, known for his stance against LGBTQ rights and harsh policies toward migrants, suggests eliminating the Department of Homeland Security entirely. Instead, he advocates for a new, cabinet-level border agency that would heavily militarize the border and prioritize wall construction.

Project 2025 also calls for the National Security Council to review all military general promotions rigorously, aiming to eliminate what it terms as "social engineering" and "non-defense matters." This broad category includes issues such as climate change, critical race theory, and diversity training.

Critics warn that purging military ranks for partisan reasons could erode crucial safeguards and potentially undermine the military code of justice, which states that soldiers are not obligated to follow unlawful orders. The former Secretary of the U.S. Navy emphasizes that civilian control and the rule of law are fundamental to the U.S. military, and politicizing the armed forces could lead to dangerous scenarios where military leadership faces impossible choices between following potentially unlawful orders or upholding their oath to the Constitution.

The intelligence community is also a focus of Project 2025. While some proposals, such as addressing over-classification of documents, are viewed as potentially beneficial, other aspects are deeply concerning. The plan advocates for what essentially amounts to loyalty tests within the intelligence community, potentially leading to a purge of anyone who might disagree with a second Trump administration.

John Yoo, known for authoring the infamous "torture memos" during the Bush administration, is involved with Project 2025. He recently wrote an op-ed calling for "revenge" against Democrats, which some have dubbed the "vengeance memo." This approach represents a shift from legal policy advocacy to outright retribution, targeting even civilian family members of political opponents.

Analysis: Media and Journalism

At the core of Project 2025's proposals regarding public broadcasting is the call to defund the Corporation for Public Broadcasting (CPB), which provides federal funding for National Public Radio (NPR) and the Public Broadcasting Service (PBS). The initiative argues that these organizations represent biased, left-leaning views that should not be subsidized by taxpayers. Mike Gonzalez, the author of the section on the CPB in Project 2025's policy guide, contends that both NPR and PBS exhibit a liberal bias, asserting that "the government should not be compelling the conservative half of the country to pay for the suppression of its own views".

The financial implications of this proposed defunding are significant. For the 2024 fiscal year, $525 million was allocated for public broadcasting, amounting to approximately $1.60 per U.S. citizen [4]. While this figure may seem modest, it represents a crucial lifeline for public broadcasting services, particularly in rural and underserved communities. According to NPR, 8% of public radio station revenues come from federal appropriations through the CPB, while a PBS spokesperson stated that federal funding constitutes 15% of the budget across all of public television

Project 2025's motivations for these proposed changes are multifaceted. The primary justification stems from a perceived ideological bias in public broadcasting. Critics argue that NPR and PBS do not represent the views of the entire American public and that their content often leans left, promoting progressive ideologies at the expense of conservative perspectives. This perception is not entirely without basis; a recent controversy erupted when an NPR editor penned an essay criticizing what he diagnosed as an encroachment of progressive advocacy into journalism.

However, it is crucial to note that accusations of bias are not unique to public media and are frequently leveled at private media companies as well. Trust in mass media is a broader issue, particularly among conservatives, with Gallup polling showing that only 5% of Republicans said they had "a great deal or quite a lot" of confidence in newspapers in 2022, compared to 35% of Democrats.

The consequences of defunding public broadcasting could be far-reaching and profound. Public broadcasting plays a vital role in delivering high-quality educational and cultural content to diverse audiences. Programs like PBS's "Sesame Street" and NPR's extensive news coverage are essential resources for millions of Americans. The potential loss of these services could have a disproportionate impact on rural communities, which often depend heavily on radio and television stations funded by the CPB.

Moreover, public broadcasting serves a crucial function in maintaining a healthy democracy. When well-funded and independent, public media are associated with more informed citizenries and higher voter turnout. Research indicates that exposure to public news media leads to better-informed publics on hard news matters compared to reliance on commercial news. Countries with a mix of public and private media systems have been shown to have higher voter turnout than those with private-only media environments.

The proposed defunding could also threaten journalistic independence. Public broadcasting has historically provided in-depth, unbiased reporting on a wide range of issues, including those that may not receive extensive coverage from commercial media. Removing federal funding could make these organizations more dependent on private donations, potentially leading to increased influence from wealthy donors and corporations.

Project 2025's vision extends beyond merely defunding public broadcasting. The initiative also suggests reforms to ensure that media funded by the government reflects a broader range of perspectives. This includes proposals to restructure media oversight, ostensibly to avoid what they describe as "administrative sabotage" by entrenched bureaucrats who resist conservative policies.

The project's recommendations go as far as suggesting the revocation of NPR stations' noncommercial status, which would force them to relocate outside the 88-92 range on the FM dial. This frequency range could then potentially be taken over by religious programming, further altering the landscape of public broadcasting.

It is important to contextualize these proposals within the broader scope of Project 2025, which envisions widespread changes across numerous sectors of government and society. The initiative seeks to infuse the government with conservative Christian values and proposes significant alterations to economic and social policies. Critics have characterized the project as an authoritarian, Christian nationalist plan that could steer the United States toward autocracy.

Project 2025's proposed defunding of NPR and PBS represents a significant and contentious shift in the relationship between government and public media. While framed as a move towards fiscal responsibility and ideological balance, the potential consequences could fundamentally alter the media landscape in the United States.

Analysis: IMMIGRATION AND BORDER SECURITY

The Heritage Foundation's "Project 2025" represents a comprehensive and potentially transformative blueprint for immigration policy under a hypothetical second Trump administration. This analysis argues that the proposals put forth in Project 2025 are more far-reaching and potentially disruptive to the existing immigration system than has been previously acknowledged in public discourse. The plan outlines a series of measures that would fundamentally alter both legal and humanitarian immigration pathways, centralize federal power over immigration enforcement, reduce privacy protections for immigrants, and impact American citizens and institutions in significant ways.

At the core of Project 2025's immigration agenda is a set of proposals aimed at severely restricting legal immigration channels. The plan advocates for suspending updates to eligible country lists for H-2A and H-2B visas, which would limit the ability of employers to recruit foreign workers for seasonal and temporary positions. It also suggests using existing application backlogs as justification to automatically suspend intake for large immigration categories, potentially affecting hundreds of thousands of prospective immigrants. Perhaps most controversially, the plan calls for terminating the legal status of approximately 500,000 recipients of Deferred Action for Childhood Arrivals (DACA), a program that has allowed young people brought to the United States as children to live and work legally in the country. Additionally, Project 2025 proposes restrictions on T and U visa programs, which are designed to protect victims of human trafficking and other serious crimes. Collectively, these measures would significantly reduce legal pathways for immigrants to enter and remain in the United States, representing a sharp departure from decades of immigration policy that has generally sought to balance enforcement concerns with economic and humanitarian considerations.

The plan's approach to humanitarian relief programs is equally sweeping in its proposed changes. Project 2025 recommends repealing all Temporary Protected Status (TPS) designations, which currently provide protection from deportation and work authorization to nationals of certain countries experiencing ongoing armed conflict, environmental disasters, or other extraordinary conditions. It also suggests prohibiting staff time for processing DACA renewals and applications for the Ukraine parole program, effectively ending these humanitarian initiatives. Furthermore, the plan proposes redirecting resources currently used for refugee vetting to address issues at the southern border, potentially decimating the U.S. refugee resettlement program. These proposals, if implemented, would dramatically reduce the United States' capacity to offer protection to vulnerable populations fleeing conflict, persecution, and natural disasters, marking a significant shift in the country's longstanding role as a global leader in refugee resettlement and humanitarian assistance.

Project 2025 also outlines several measures that could create or exacerbate inefficiencies and backlogs within the immigration system. The plan advises pausing application intake for categories with "excessive" backlogs, a move that could paradoxically worsen processing delays and leave many immigrants in prolonged legal limbo. It recommends ending pandemic-era flexibilities such as the reuse of biometric data, which had been implemented to streamline processing during the COVID-19 pandemic. Perhaps most significantly, the plan proposes reclassifying U.S. Citizenship and Immigration Services (USCIS) as a national security-sensitive agency, which would necessitate extensive background checks for staff. This reclassification could dramatically slow down the processing of immigration applications across all categories, potentially creating new bottlenecks in an already strained system.

A central theme of Project 2025's immigration proposals is the centralization of federal power over immigration matters. The plan suggests conditioning federal disaster funding on state and local cooperation with immigration enforcement, a move that could significantly impact the ability of state and local governments to respond to natural disasters and other emergencies if they choose not to align with federal immigration priorities. It also proposes initiating legal action against local officials who decline to prosecute certain cases based on immigration status, potentially setting up contentious legal battles between federal and local authorities. Additionally, the plan recommends hiring more political appointees in the Department of Homeland Security (DHS) and Department of State (DOS), which could increase political influence over immigration policy implementation and potentially reduce the role of career civil servants with specialized expertise in immigration matters.

Project 2025's proposals regarding privacy protections for immigrants are particularly striking in their potential implications. The plan advises limiting privacy protections to only U.S. citizens and green card holders, effectively stripping these protections from millions of immigrants with other forms of legal status as well as undocumented immigrants. It suggests allowing the publication of detailed information on border security actions, which could potentially expose sensitive operational details and individual privacy. Perhaps most controversially, the plan proposes sharing tax information of unauthorized immigrants with DHS, a move that could have chilling effects on tax compliance among immigrant communities and raise serious concerns about the use of tax data for enforcement purposes.

The impact of Project 2025's immigration proposals would extend beyond immigrant communities to affect American citizens and institutions in significant ways. The plan suggests blocking federal financial aid for students in states that offer in-state tuition to certain immigrant groups, potentially limiting educational opportunities for U.S. citizens based on their state of residence. It proposes barring U.S. citizens from federal housing subsidies if they live with non-citizens, a measure that could disproportionately impact mixed-status families and potentially exacerbate housing insecurity. The plan also recommends requiring high percentages of U.S. citizens in federal contractor workforces, which could affect hiring practices across a wide range of industries that rely on federal contracts.

Finally, Project 2025 includes proposals that would limit checks and balances on executive power in immigration matters. It suggests extending presidential authority to suspend entry of foreign nationals to the DHS Secretary, potentially broadening the scope for executive action on immigration without congressional oversight. Perhaps most controversially, the plan proposes ignoring court decisions that impede administrative immigration efforts, a suggestion that raises serious constitutional concerns and could precipitate a crisis between the executive and judicial branches.

The immigration proposals outlined in Project 2025 represent a comprehensive and potentially transformative approach to U.S. immigration policy. If implemented, these measures would likely have far-reaching consequences for immigrants, American citizens, and U.S. institutions. The plan goes beyond mere policy adjustments to fundamentally alter the foundations of the U.S. immigration system, potentially reshaping the country's demographic, economic, and social landscape for generations to come.

SECTION 3: THE GENERAL WELFARE

"When our Founders wrote in the Constitution that the federal government would 'promote the general Welfare,' they could not have fathomed a massive bureaucracy that would someday spend $3 trillion in a single year" – Page 283

The following summary conveys the content of the document accurately and objectively, without endorsing or critiquing the perspectives of the original authors.

Summary

The Department of Health and Human Services (HHS) is highlighted as the primary spender, accounting for about half of this sum.

The text then delves into Medicare and Medicaid, programs housed within HHS, describing them as the "principal drivers of our $31 trillion national debt." These programs, established under President Lyndon B. Johnson, were set on "autopilot with no plan for how to pay for them." The author cites an analysis showing that from 1967 to 2020, Medicare and Medicaid costs closely mirrored federal deficits, leading to the conclusion that "our deficit problem is a Medicare and Medicaid problem."

The narrative shifts to criticize the Centers for Disease Control and Prevention (CDC) and the National Institutes of Health (NIH) for their handling of the COVID-19 pandemic. The author argues that these agencies, along with President Joe Biden, were responsible for "irrational, destructive, un-American mask and vaccine mandates." The text claims that randomized controlled trials showed little to no benefit from masks in preventing virus spread, yet the CDC ignored this evidence and instead relied on "politically malleable 'observational studies'" to justify mask mandates. The author then targets the NIH, citing Roger Severino's critique that the agency was involved in controversial research, including "aborted baby body parts, human animal chimera experiments," and "gain-of-function viral research that may have been responsible for COVID-19." The text also highlights potential conflicts of interest, noting that Anthony Fauci's division of NIH "owns half the patent for the Moderna COVID-19 vaccine" and that some NIH employees receive significant annual payments from vaccine sales.

The author advocates for breaking up the "NIH monopoly on directing research" and ending the "incestuous relationship between the NIH, CDC, and vaccine makers." The text also criticizes NIH for promoting "junk gender science" and calls for an end to HHS's involvement in "woke transgender activism." The final paragraphs of this section discuss HHS's stance on abortion, describing it as promoting abortion as "health care" and violating conscience-protection laws. The author recommends that the next HHS secretary should pursue an agenda protecting "the fundamental right to life, protect conscience rights, and uphold bodily integrity rooted in biological realities, not ideology." Additionally, the text calls for reversing policies focused on "LGBTQ+ equity" and instead promoting traditional family values.

CHAPTER 10: DEPARTMENT OF AGRICULTURE

The USDA should not try to control and shape the economy, but should instead remove obstacles that hinder food production. Further, it should not place ancillary issues, such as environmental issues, ahead of agricultural production itself – Page 290

Key Policy Proposals

1. **Limiting the USDA's Mission to Agriculture Alone:** The document advocates for a significant reduction in the USDA's scope, suggesting that the department should focus narrowly on agricultural production, rather than on broader issues such as climate change, equity, and nutrition assistance programs. The proposed mission statement ignores the USDA's crucial role in addressing the interconnected challenges of food security, public health, environmental sustainability, and rural development.

2. **Reforming or Eliminating Farm Subsidies:** The text calls for a drastic reduction in farm subsidies, particularly targeting programs like Agriculture Risk Coverage (ARC) and Price Loss Coverage (PLC). The argument is made that these subsidies distort markets and foster dependency, proposing instead that farmers should rely more on market mechanisms and less on government support.

3. **Removing Climate and Equity Goals:** A key focus of the proposed reforms is the removal of climate change and equity considerations from the USDA's agenda. The author explicitly criticizes the Biden Administration's inclusion of these priorities in the USDA's mission, arguing that they detract from the department's core responsibility of supporting agricultural efficiency.

4. **Transferring SNAP and Other Nutrition Programs to HHS:** The proposal to move the Supplemental Nutrition Assistance Program (SNAP) and other food assistance programs to the Department of Health and Human Services (HHS) is based on the belief that these programs are welfare-oriented and thus fall outside the USDA's proper scope.

5. **Eliminating Conservation Programs:** The text suggests eliminating or drastically scaling back conservation programs like the Conservation Reserve Program (CRP) and USDA conservation easements. The rationale given is that these programs take valuable land out of production and impose unnecessary restrictions on landowners.

ANALYSIS:

1. **Narrowing the USDA's Mission:** Reducing the USDA's role to purely agricultural production ignores the broader responsibilities that the department has historically fulfilled. The USDA has been pivotal in addressing food insecurity, supporting rural development, and promoting sustainable agricultural practices. In a world facing increasing climate challenges, it is irresponsible to strip the USDA of its capacity to address these critical issues. Climate change is already affecting agricultural productivity through more frequent and severe weather events, and ignoring these impacts could lead to long-term declines in farm output and rural livelihoods. Furthermore, equity considerations are essential in ensuring that the benefits of agricultural policies are distributed fairly across all communities, particularly those historically marginalized.

2. **Impact of Reducing Farm Subsidies:** The proposed reduction in farm subsidies will likely exacerbate the financial challenges faced by small and mid-sized farmers. While the document argues that subsidies distort markets, it overlooks the reality that these programs provide a critical safety net for farmers who are subject to the volatility of global markets and unpredictable weather patterns. Eliminating or reducing these supports could lead to increased consolidation in the agricultural sector, where only large, corporate farms can survive without government assistance. This would undermine rural economies, increase unemployment in farming communities, and reduce the diversity of crops produced in the U.S.

3. **Ignoring Climate and Equity Goals:** The rejection of climate and equity goals is particularly short-sighted. Climate change poses a significant threat to agriculture, and the USDA has a responsibility to lead in developing and promoting climate-resilient farming practices. By dismissing these priorities, the proposed policies risk leaving American farmers unprepared for the challenges ahead, ultimately compromising national food security. Similarly, ignoring equity in agricultural policy perpetuates the disadvantages faced by minority farmers and rural communities of color, exacerbating inequalities that the USDA should be working to correct.

4. **Consequences of Moving SNAP to HHS:** Transferring SNAP and other food assistance programs to HHS may seem like a bureaucratic reshuffling, but it actually risks weakening the integration of agricultural and nutritional policies. The USDA's expertise in both areas allows for a more cohesive strategy in addressing food insecurity while supporting the agricultural economy. Moving these programs to HHS could lead to a disconnect between food production and distribution, ultimately harming both farmers and the millions of Americans who rely on these programs to feed their families.

5. **Dismantling Conservation Efforts:** The proposal to dismantle or severely restrict conservation programs ignores the long-term environmental and economic benefits of these initiatives. Programs like the CRP have been essential in preventing soil erosion, preserving wildlife habitats, and reducing agricultural runoff into waterways. Scaling back these efforts would not only harm the environment but also undermine the sustainability of American agriculture. Healthy ecosystems are the foundation of productive farming, and conservation programs help ensure that agricultural practices do not deplete the very resources on which they depend.

The proposed policies are a retreat from the comprehensive, forward-thinking approach that is needed to address the complex challenges facing American agriculture today. By narrowing the USDA's focus and stripping away essential programs and priorities, these reforms would weaken the department's ability to support sustainable agricultural practices, address food insecurity, and promote equity. The consequences would be far-reaching, leading to greater economic inequality, environmental degradation, and a less resilient food system.

Summary

This chapter of Mandate for Leadership was written by Daren Bakst. The following summary conveys the content of the document accurately and objectively, without endorsing or critiquing the perspectives of the original authors.

The chapter opens by praising the efficiency and global influence of American farmers, emphasizing that they are capable of "efficiently and safely" producing food that meets the needs of people worldwide. The author asserts that the success of American agriculture is largely due to the innovation and resilience of farmers, who have made the U.S. a model for the world. However, this success is said to be threatened by what the author perceives as unnecessary government intervention. The author argues that American agriculture will continue to thrive only if farmers are allowed to operate with minimal interference from the government.

The author then outlines the role of the U.S. Department of Agriculture (USDA), advocating for it to adopt a more limited role focused primarily on removing governmental barriers that impede food production. According to the text, the USDA should recognize that its primary function should be to support agricultural production by ensuring it remains efficient and safe, rather than expanding into broader social or environmental issues.

A significant critique is directed at the current approach of the USDA, particularly under the Biden Administration, which the author believes has expanded the department's mission beyond its core responsibilities. The USDA's current mission statement is criticized for being too broad, encompassing goals such as equity and climate change, which the author views as distractions from the department's primary task of ensuring food safety and efficiency. The author sees these new priorities as part of an effort to "transform the food and agriculture economy" into one that is "equitable and climate smart," a shift that is viewed as problematic.

The author suggests that even before this recent expansion, the USDA's role was already too broad, including responsibilities such as administering welfare programs (e.g., food stamps) that are seen as beyond its appropriate scope. The text argues that Congress should act to limit the USDA's role, refocusing it on agriculture and ensuring it serves the interests of all Americans rather than specific interest groups.

The author proposes a revised mission for the USDA that would be narrowly focused on developing and disseminating agricultural research, addressing public health threats directly related to food, removing barriers to market access for American agricultural goods, and reducing government interference in the food supply chain. This mission would emphasize core principles such as sound science, personal freedom, property rights, and the rule of law. The overarching goal is to ensure that the USDA supports the agricultural sector in a way that allows it to continue producing safe and affordable food without unnecessary regulatory burdens.

Mission Statement

This section delves into the Biden Administration's current mission statement for the USDA, which the author criticizes for its expansive and ambiguous scope. The mission statement is said to reflect an overly broad approach that includes goals far beyond the traditional focus of the USDA. While issues like "equity" and "climate-smart opportunities" have become central to the USDA's agenda under the Biden Administration, the author argues that these priorities are new and detract from the USDA's core mission of supporting agricultural production.

The author contends that the inclusion of these broader social and environmental goals is part of a federal effort to transform the U.S. food and agriculture economy, prioritizing issues like climate change over the USDA's fundamental responsibility of ensuring the efficient production of safe food. The author is critical of this shift, suggesting that the USDA's role should not be to control or reshape the agricultural economy but to remove obstacles that hinder food production and market access for American agricultural goods.

The text argues that even before the Biden Administration's expansion of the mission, the USDA's role was already too broad, incorporating welfare functions like food stamps that have little to do with its primary agricultural focus. This broad mandate, the author suggests, dilutes the USDA's effectiveness and distracts it from its essential duties.

To counter this, the author proposes a more focused and appropriate mission statement for the USDA. This revised mission would clarify that the USDA's primary responsibilities should include developing and disseminating agricultural research, addressing public health and safety threats directly related to food and agriculture, and removing both foreign and domestic barriers to the accessibility of safe and affordable food. The proposed mission emphasizes that these efforts should be grounded in sound science, respect for personal freedom, private property rights, and adherence to the rule of law.

The author provides a model mission statement that reflects this more focused vision, suggesting that the USDA should concentrate on its historical role of supporting agriculture and ensuring food safety, rather than expanding into areas like climate change and equity. The model mission emphasizes that the USDA should serve the interests of all Americans, rather than catering to specific groups or causes, and should prioritize the efficient production of safe and affordable food above all else.

Overview

The "Overview" section provides a historical context for the U.S. Department of Agriculture (USDA), tracing its origins back to 1862 when President Abraham Lincoln established the department. Originally, the USDA had a narrow mission, focused primarily on the "dissemination of information connected to agriculture" and the distribution of new, valuable seeds and plants. Over the past 160 years, however, the USDA's scope has expanded far beyond its original mandate. The department now oversees a wide array of activities, many of which extend well beyond agriculture.

Today, the USDA is responsible for a diverse set of functions, including the distribution of farm subsidies, the administration of food-related welfare programs like food stamps, and the management of conservation, biofuels, forestry, and rural development initiatives. The author highlights the significant growth in the USDA's responsibilities, noting that this expansion has led to the department becoming one of the largest federal agencies, with a vast budget and workforce.

The USDA's fiscal year 2023 budget underscores the breadth of its operations, with estimated outlays of $261 billion. A striking 70% of this budget is allocated to nutrition assistance programs, such as food stamps, reflecting the department's significant role in welfare administration. Only 14% of the budget is dedicated to farm, conservation, and commodity programs, while 11% is allocated to other areas, including research, food safety, and rural development. The remaining 5% goes toward forestry programs.

The section also outlines the organizational structure of the USDA, which is comprised of 29 agencies organized under eight mission areas and 16 staff offices. The department employs nearly 100,000 people and operates more than 6,000 locations across the United States and abroad. The author points to this vast bureaucracy as evidence of how the USDA has drifted from its original, more focused mission.

The author suggests that this expansion of responsibilities has diluted the USDA's effectiveness, arguing that the department's core focus should be on supporting agriculture rather than administering welfare programs and other non-agricultural functions. This historical overview sets the stage for the subsequent sections, which will discuss the challenges facing the USDA and the author's recommendations for refocusing the department on its primary agricultural mission.

Major Priority Issues and Specific Recommendations

This section identifies and discusses the critical issues that the next administration should prioritize in reforming the USDA. The author begins by asserting that the primary goal of the incoming administration must be to "defend American agriculture." This is presented as a necessary response to what the author perceives as the Biden Administration's attempts to fundamentally transform the American food system. The author argues that this transformation places undue emphasis on climate change and equity, which could undermine the efficiency and productivity of U.S. agriculture.

The author criticizes the Biden Administration's approach, which is described as a centrally planned effort to reshape the food supply chain "from farm to fork." The USDA's strategic goals, particularly those related to climate change, renewable energy, and addressing systemic racism, are seen as indicative of this shift in priorities. The author expresses concern that these goals divert attention from the essential task of producing safe, affordable food efficiently.

One of the key points made is that American agriculture does not require transformation by the federal government; rather, it needs the removal of barriers that hinder the food supply chain. The author cites the COVID-19 pandemic as an example of how crucial it is to reduce obstacles rather than impose new ones. The Biden Administration's vision for agriculture is characterized as disregarding the existing efficiency and environmental stewardship practiced by American farmers.

The section then highlights specific examples of federal overreach, such as the USDA's recent $300 million initiative to encourage farmers to transition to organic farming. The author argues that this program reflects a lack of respect for farmers' expertise and preferences, pointing out that organic farming is often more expensive and less efficient. The push for "climate-smart" agricultural practices is similarly criticized, with the author arguing that these initiatives prioritize ideological goals over practical agricultural needs.

In addition to defending agriculture, the author makes several concrete recommendations for the next administration. These include:

1. **Proactively Defending Agriculture**: The author urges the administration to reject efforts that prioritize climate change over food productivity and affordability. The U.S. should also distance itself from international initiatives

that promote sustainable development schemes which might constrain American agriculture.

2. **Clarifying the Importance of Efficiency**: The administration should emphasize the critical link between agricultural efficiency and food affordability, particularly for low-income households. The author suggests that the USDA should remove references to transforming the food system from its communications and instead focus on legislative efforts that support agricultural innovation and productivity.

3. **Addressing the Abuse of Commodity Credit Corporation (CCC) Discretionary Authority**: The author expresses concern about the discretionary use of CCC funds, which have been increasingly used for purposes not originally intended by Congress, such as funding programs related to climate change. The author calls for legislative fixes to limit this discretionary power, arguing that it poses a threat to the proper functioning of agricultural policy by allowing the USDA to operate a "slush fund."

4. **Reforming Farm Subsidies**: The author argues that current farm subsidies often distort markets and discourage innovation. The text suggests that subsidies should not influence planting decisions, create barriers to entry for new farmers, or encourage environmentally sensitive land use. The ultimate goal is to reduce dependency on subsidies, particularly for certain commodities that receive disproportionate support.

5. **Moving Food and Nutrition Programs**: The author proposes transferring food and nutrition programs, such as the Supplemental Nutrition Assistance Program (SNAP), from the USDA to the Department of Health and Human Services (HHS). This move is suggested to streamline welfare programs and refocus the USDA on its core agricultural mission.

These recommendations reflect a broader vision of reducing government intervention in agriculture, emphasizing efficiency and market-driven practices, and refocusing the USDA on its foundational role of supporting American agriculture.

REFORM FARM SUBSIDIES

This section tackles the complex issue of farm subsidies, which the author views as a significant area requiring reform. The text opens by acknowledging that agricultural policy is often wrongly equated with farm subsidy policy. The author argues that this misconception leads to a failure to recognize the broader scope of agricultural policy, which includes various issues that extend beyond subsidies, such as environmental regulation.

The author identifies several problems associated with current farm subsidies. These include market distortions, where subsidies can influence farmers' planting decisions, discourage proper risk management, and stifle innovation. Additionally, subsidies can incentivize the use of environmentally sensitive land and create barriers to entry for new farmers. The author argues that these market distortions are counterproductive and should be addressed in any effort to reform farm subsidies.

A key point in this section is the call to reduce farmers' dependency on subsidies. The author challenges the conventional wisdom that all farmers rely heavily on subsidies, noting that many receive little to no support, particularly those in the livestock and specialty crop sectors. The text cites data showing that a significant portion of farm subsidies goes to just a few commodities—corn, cotton, peanuts, rice, soybeans, and wheat—which account for only 28% of farm receipts. This concentration of subsidies is seen as problematic, as it disproportionately benefits a small subset of farmers while neglecting others.

The section goes on to describe the main subsidy programs, including the Agriculture Risk Coverage (ARC) program, the Price Loss Coverage (PLC) program, and the federal crop insurance program. The author criticizes these programs for providing payments that protect against "shallow losses," which are minor dips in expected revenue, rather than offering a genuine safety net for farmers facing severe difficulties. The ARC and PLC programs, in particular, are seen as examples of excessive government support that goes beyond what is necessary to ensure agricultural stability.

One of the most controversial subsidy programs discussed is the federal sugar program, which intentionally restricts supply to drive up prices. The author argues that this program is a prime example of harmful central planning, as it imposes higher costs on consumers, particularly low-income households.

The author provides specific recommendations for reforming farm subsidies:

1. **Repeal the Federal Sugar Program**: The author advocates for eliminating this program, arguing that the government should not be in the business of controlling supply and manipulating prices.

2. **Eliminate ARC and PLC Programs**: These programs are criticized for providing excessive protection to farmers, particularly through payments for shallow losses. The author suggests that farmers already have access to federal crop insurance, which should be sufficient to cover revenue shortfalls.

3. **Avoid Double Payments**: The text highlights the issue of farmers receiving payments from both ARC or PLC programs and federal crop insurance for

the same losses, recommending that Congress prohibit this duplication of support.

4. **Reduce Crop Insurance Premium Subsidies**: Currently, taxpayers cover about 60% of the premiums for crop insurance policies. The author proposes reducing this subsidy rate to no more than 50%, arguing that taxpayers should not bear a larger share of the cost than the farmers who benefit.

5. **Promote Transparency and Genuine Reform**: The author calls for a more open and transparent process in the development of the farm bill, emphasizing the need for genuine reform that considers the interests of both farmers and taxpayers.

The overarching goal of these recommendations is to reduce the dependency of farmers on government subsidies, encourage market-driven practices, and ensure that the agricultural safety net is targeted and effective, rather than overly generous and distortionary.

MOVE THE WORK OF THE FOOD AND NUTRITION SERVICE

This section addresses the role of the USDA's Food and Nutrition Service (FNS), which administers numerous federal food assistance programs, including the largest, the Supplemental Nutrition Assistance Program (SNAP), commonly known as food stamps. The author argues that these programs, while important, do not belong under the USDA, as they fall outside the department's primary agricultural mission.

The author suggests that these food and nutrition programs should be transferred to the Department of Health and Human Services (HHS). This proposal is based on the idea that HHS, which already oversees most of the federal welfare programs, is better suited to manage means-tested food assistance. By consolidating these programs under one department, the author believes it would create more transparency, reduce redundancy, and allow the USDA to refocus on its core agricultural responsibilities.

Specific programs mentioned include SNAP, the Special Supplemental Nutrition Program for Women, Infants, and Children (WIC), the National School Lunch Program (NSLP), and the School Breakfast Program (SBP). The section underscores the broad scope of these programs, which collectively serve millions of Americans and account for a significant portion of the USDA's budget.

The author argues that moving these programs to HHS would streamline federal welfare administration and help make the welfare system more transparent. Currently, the USDA's involvement in these programs is seen as part of the department's overreach, diluting its focus on agriculture. By transferring these responsibilities, the USDA could concentrate on supporting agricultural productivity and innovation.

Furthermore, the section suggests that this move would allow for a more integrated approach to welfare policy, with HHS taking a lead role in overseeing all means-tested programs. This consolidation would, according to the author, improve the effectiveness of welfare programs and ensure that the USDA can dedicate its resources to its primary mission of supporting American agriculture.

REFORM SNAP

In this section, the author addresses the Supplemental Nutrition Assistance Program (SNAP), the largest federal food assistance program, arguing that significant reforms are needed to ensure the program fulfills its intended purpose without encouraging dependency. The text emphasizes that SNAP, originally designed to help low-income individuals buy food, has expanded significantly in scope and cost, particularly during the Biden Administration, which saw an increase in both participation and overall expenditures.

The author advocates for the reimplementation of work requirements for able-bodied adults without dependents (ABAWD). These work requirements, which were in place during the Trump Administration, mandated that work-capable individuals aged 18 to 50 work or participate in job training for at least 20 hours per week to receive benefits. The author argues that these requirements encourage self-sufficiency and reduce dependency on government assistance. However, the Biden Administration rolled back these work requirements, a move the author criticizes as undermining the program's effectiveness.

Another significant reform proposed is the tightening of eligibility rules, specifically addressing the issue of "broad-based categorical eligibility" (BBCE). The author explains that under BBCE, individuals can qualify for SNAP simply by receiving minimal benefits from another program, such as a pamphlet or hotline number from Temporary Assistance for Needy Families (TANF). This loophole has allowed individuals with significant assets to qualify for food assistance, a practice the author views as an abuse of the system. The Trump Administration attempted to close this loophole, but the regulation was not finalized before the end of the administration.

The section also critiques the Biden Administration's unilateral increase of SNAP benefits by 23% in 2021 through an update to the Thrifty Food Plan. The author argues that this unprecedented increase, which was not cost-neutral, represents a dramatic overreach by the administration and was implemented without proper legislative approval. This adjustment, according to the author, could lead to unsustainable long-term costs for the program.

Finally, the author calls for the elimination of the "heat-and-eat" loophole, where states inflate utility allowances to boost SNAP benefits artificially. This practice is viewed as a manipulation of the system that results in higher-than-justified benefit levels. The Trump Administration proposed a rule to standardize utility allowances, but it was not finalized.

Overall, the author's recommendations for SNAP reform focus on tightening eligibility, enforcing work requirements, reducing the potential for fraud and abuse, and ensuring that the program supports those who truly need it without fostering dependency.

REFORM WIC AND SCHOOL MEALS
This section addresses the Special Supplemental Nutrition Program for Women, Infants, and Children (WIC) and federal school meal programs, proposing significant reforms to align these programs more closely with their original purposes and reduce inefficiencies.

WIC Reform:
The author begins by discussing WIC, a program designed to provide nutrition assistance to low-income women, infants, and children. The section suggests reforming the state voucher system used within WIC, particularly the way states handle contracts for infant formula. Currently, states award contracts to a single brand through competitive bidding, which can inadvertently create monopolies. The author recommends reevaluating these regulations to prevent such outcomes and to ensure that the program remains competitive and cost-effective.

The text also calls for a broader review of excessive regulations surrounding baby formula, which the author believes have contributed to recent shortages. The Biden Administration's handling of these shortages is criticized, with the suggestion that unnecessary delays in manufacturing and sale regulations need to be reformed to prevent future crises.

School Meals Reform:
The section then turns to federal meal programs for K–12 students, such as the National School Lunch Program (NSLP) and the School Breakfast Program (SBP). These programs were originally created to provide food to children from low-income families while they are at school. However, the author argues that these programs have increasingly morphed into entitlement programs that serve a broader range of students, including those from middle- and upper-income families.

The Community Eligibility Provision (CEP), introduced in 2010, is particularly critiqued for expanding access to free meals beyond those in need. Under CEP, if 40% of students in a school or district are eligible for free meals, all students in that school or district can receive free meals, regardless of individual need. The author points out that this has led to significant inefficiencies and improper payments, diverting resources from students who genuinely need assistance.

The author argues for a return to the original intent of these programs, focusing on serving children from low-income families. Specifically, the USDA should issue rules to prevent the grouping of schools within districts to meet the 40% threshold required by CEP, which can lead to wealthier students receiving free meals. The section also recommends eliminating CEP altogether and limiting federal meal provisions during the summer to students attending summer school classes. This would prevent the expansion of these programs into areas that the author believes are beyond their original scope.

Overall, the proposed reforms aim to ensure that WIC and school meal programs remain targeted and effective, serving those who need them most without expanding into unnecessary or inefficient entitlements.

REFORM CONSERVATION PROGRAMS
This section critiques the USDA's current conservation programs, emphasizing the need for reforms that align more closely with the actual needs of farmers and the environment. The author acknowledges that farmers are generally excellent stewards of the land, driven by both ethical considerations and self-interest to maintain the health and productivity of their land. Given this, the author argues that federal conservation programs should be designed to address specific, identifiable environmental concerns rather than speculative or overly broad goals.

Conservation Reserve Program (CRP):
The Conservation Reserve Program, managed by the Farm Service Agency (FSA), is a particular focus of criticism. This program pays farmers to not farm certain parcels of their land, often to achieve environmental goals such as reducing soil erosion or enhancing wildlife habitats. However, the author argues that this approach is too sweeping and often results in land being taken out of production unnecessarily, which can be counterproductive, especially in times of food supply concerns. For instance, the author mentions the global impact of Russia's invasion of Ukraine as a situation where keeping arable land idle could exacerbate food shortages and price increases. The recommended reform is to eliminate or significantly scale back the CRP, ensuring that

only genuinely sensitive lands are targeted for conservation and that these efforts are closely tied to specific environmental harms.

USDA Conservation Easements:
The author also addresses the issue of conservation easements, which are long-term agreements that incentivize landowners to preserve natural ecosystems while still maintaining economic use of the land. While these easements can be valuable tools for conservation, the author criticizes their perpetual nature, arguing that such agreements should not bind future generations or landowners indefinitely. The author calls for reforms that would limit the use of permanent easements and suggests working with Congress to prohibit the USDA from creating new ones. The flexibility in managing land should account for the natural changes in ecosystems and the evolving needs of landowners.

Wetlands and Erodible Land Compliance:
Further, the section critiques the Natural Resources Conservation Service (NRCS) for what the author views as overreach in enforcing wetlands and erodible land regulations. The NRCS's authority to dictate specific practices to ensure compliance with USDA programs is seen as intrusive and often disconnected from the realities of farming. The author proposes that instead of allowing the NRCS to prescribe specific practices, each farm should develop a general best practices plan, approved by local Soil and Water Conservation Districts (SWCDs), which are more in tune with local conditions and farming practices. This would decentralize decision-making, placing more control in the hands of local entities and farmers themselves.

The overarching theme of this section is the call for conservation programs that are more narrowly focused, flexible, and locally managed, ensuring that federal interventions are both necessary and effective. The author argues that by reducing the scope and rigidity of these programs, the USDA can better support both environmental stewardship and agricultural productivity.

Other Major Issues and Specific Recommendations

This section addresses several additional areas of concern within the USDA's operations, each of which the author argues is critical for the next administration to reform. The focus is on regulatory barriers, inefficient programs, and outdated policies that the author believes hinder the effectiveness of American agriculture.

STATE-INSPECTED MEAT AND POULTRY:
The author begins by discussing the limitations placed on state-inspected meat and poultry, which, despite meeting USDA standards that are "at least equal to" federal inspection requirements, cannot be sold across state lines. This regulatory barrier restricts market access for state-inspected products, thereby limiting consumer choice and reducing competition. The author recommends promoting legislation, such as the "New Markets for State-Inspected Meat and Poultry Act of 2021," which would allow these products to be sold in interstate commerce. This change is viewed as a way to increase market efficiency and support local agricultural businesses.

MARKETING ORDERS AND CHECKOFF PROGRAMS:
Next, the author critiques marketing orders and checkoff programs, which are mechanisms that allow industry groups to impose mandatory fees on producers for marketing and research activities. While intended to benefit entire industries, these programs are described as effectively functioning as government-sanctioned cartels, compelling participation and sometimes leading to higher prices for consumers. The author calls for reducing the number and scope of these programs, suggesting that they should be subject to regular votes by participants to ensure continued support. The text also suggests that the USDA should reject any new requests for marketing orders and should work with Congress to eliminate these programs altogether, allowing industry actors to collaborate voluntarily without government coercion.

TRADE POLICY VS. TRADE PROMOTION:
The section then turns to the USDA's role in trade, distinguishing between trade policy—removing barriers to international markets—and trade promotion, which involves subsidizing the marketing of American agricultural products overseas. The author argues that the USDA should focus on trade policy, specifically on eliminating barriers such as sanitary and phytosanitary measures that restrict American agricultural exports. Trade promotion programs like the Market Access Program are criticized as unnecessary, with the author suggesting that businesses and industries should fund their own marketing efforts abroad without relying on government subsidies. The recommendation is to repeal these export promotion programs, thereby reducing government expenditure and promoting a free-market approach to international trade.

AGRICULTURAL BIOTECHNOLOGY:
Innovation in agriculture, particularly through genetic engineering, is highlighted as crucial for meeting future food demands. The author notes that over 90% of U.S. corn, cotton, and soybeans are genetically engineered, demonstrating the importance of biotechnology to American agriculture. However, the author criticizes regulatory and trade barriers that hinder the adoption and international acceptance of genetically

engineered products. For example, Mexico's planned ban on U.S. genetically modified yellow corn is cited as a significant challenge. The author calls for the USDA to actively counter misinformation about biotechnology and to work with the Office of the United States Trade Representative to remove barriers imposed by other countries. Additionally, the text advocates for repealing the federal mandate for labeling genetically engineered food, arguing that this requirement is more about stigmatizing biotechnology than informing consumers.

FOREST SERVICE WILDFIRE MANAGEMENT:

The section also addresses the management of wildfires on federal lands, particularly those overseen by the U.S. Forest Service, which is part of the USDA. The author argues that current wildfire management strategies are overly reliant on "pyro-silviculture"—the use of controlled burns and unplanned fires for vegetation management. Instead, the author advocates for proactive measures such as thinning forests, removing biomass, and increasing timber sales to reduce the fuel available for wildfires. The decline in timber sales since the 1990s is noted as a missed opportunity to manage forest health and reduce wildfire risk. The author suggests that the next administration should build on Executive Order 13855, issued during the Trump Administration, to promote active forest management and reduce regulatory obstacles that delay necessary interventions.

DIETARY GUIDELINES:

Finally, the author critiques the USDA's role in developing and publishing the Dietary Guidelines for Americans, arguing that this function should be either significantly reformed or eliminated. The guidelines, which influence federal nutrition programs like school meals, are seen as politicized and not always based on sound science. The author warns that environmental concerns, such as sustainability, have at times been inappropriately integrated into the guidelines, potentially compromising their focus on human nutrition. The recommendation is to work with Congress to repeal the Dietary Guidelines altogether or, at the very least, to ensure that the guidelines focus solely on nutritional science, free from unrelated influences.

Organizational Issues and Conclusion

This section outlines the structural changes that would result from the implementation of the author's recommended reforms for the USDA. The most significant change would involve removing welfare functions from the USDA, specifically the transfer of food and nutrition programs, such as SNAP, to the Department of Health and Human Services (HHS). This shift would allow the USDA to focus exclusively on agricultural issues, substantially reducing the size and scope of the department. The Farm Service Agency (FSA), which administers many farm subsidy programs, would also be downsized, reflecting the proposed reforms aimed at reducing reliance on subsidies and promoting a more market-oriented agricultural sector.

The author argues that a reformed, conservative USDA would no longer be a tool for government-driven transformation of the food system. Instead, it would prioritize supporting efficient agricultural production and ensuring that the government does not hinder farmers and ranchers from producing abundant, safe, and affordable food. The text emphasizes that achieving this vision would require strong leadership from the White House, with appointments of USDA officials who are committed to these conservative principles. The author acknowledges that there would likely be opposition from various groups, including some within the agricultural community, environmental organizations, and left-leaning policymakers, but insists that these reforms are necessary to promote individual freedom and reduce the scope of government intervention.

CHAPTER 11: DEPARTMENT OF EDUCATION

A federal Parents' Bill of Rights is necessary to protect families from government overreach and to ensure that parents have the final say in their children's education - Page 248

Federal education policy should be limited and, ultimately, the federal Department of Education should be eliminated." - Page 319

Key Policy Proposals

The proposed policy changes outlined in this chapter represent a drastic shift in the role of the federal government in education, with severe and far-reaching consequences for public education, civil rights, and social equity in the United States.

1. **Elimination of the U.S. Department of Education**: Burke advocates for the complete dismantling of the U.S. Department of Education, transferring its responsibilities to states and other federal agencies through block grants. This proposal fundamentally misunderstands the Department's critical role in ensuring that every child, regardless of their background, has access to a high-quality education. Without federal oversight, there is a real danger that states with fewer resources or less political will could allow educational inequities to widen. Data from the National Center for Education Statistics (NCES) consistently shows that federal funding is essential in closing the gap for underfunded schools, particularly in low-income and rural areas. Eliminating the Department of Education would likely lead to a patchwork of educational standards and outcomes, where only children in wealthier states receive the education they deserve.

2. **Block Grants to States**: The proposal to replace federal programs with block grants to states is framed as a way to reduce bureaucratic red tape and empower local decision-making. However, block grants often result in funding cuts over time and lack the targeted support necessary to address the specific needs of marginalized communities. Historical evidence shows that when programs like Temporary Assistance for Needy Families (TANF) were converted to block grants in the 1990s, many states diverted funds away from the intended recipients, leading to increased poverty and hardship for the most vulnerable populations. Similarly, block-granting education funds would likely result in reduced funding for schools that need it most, as states face budget pressures and competing priorities.

3. **Rescission of the National Education Association's Congressional Charter**: The call to revoke the NEA's charter is a transparent attack on one of the largest advocates for public education and educators' rights in the country. The NEA has been a critical voice in promoting policies that benefit teachers and students, such as smaller class sizes, better funding for public schools, and comprehensive civil rights protections. Targeting the NEA undermines the ability of educators to collectively advocate for policies that improve education for all students. It also sets a dangerous precedent for using federal power to silence political opposition, particularly groups that champion social justice and workers' rights.

4. **Federal Parents' Bill of Rights**: The proposal for a Parents' Bill of Rights is framed as a means of empowering parents, but it is more accurately seen as a tool for undermining public education by allowing a vocal minority to impose their ideological views on the broader school community. This initiative could lead to increased censorship in classrooms, where teachers are pressured to avoid teaching scientifically and historically accurate information on topics like evolution, climate change, and systemic racism. Such policies threaten academic freedom and the integrity of education, making it harder for students to receive a well-rounded, fact-based education that prepares them for the challenges of the modern world.

5. **Reform of Federal Student Aid**: Spinning off the Office of Federal Student Aid into a government corporation is presented as a way to professionalize its management, but in reality, this move would likely prioritize profit over the needs of students. Federal student aid is a crucial mechanism for ensuring that higher education is accessible to all, not just the wealthy. Privatizing this system would likely lead to higher costs for students, increased debt, and a shift away from need-based aid. This policy could exacerbate the student debt crisis and make college even more unattainable for low-income and middle-class students.

WHAT WOULD THIS MEAN?

These policies, if implemented, would significantly undermine the federal government's ability to ensure equal educational opportunities for all students, regardless of where they live or their socioeconomic status. The proposed decentralization and defunding of federal education programs would likely lead to greater disparities between wealthy and poor states, rural and urban communities, and among different racial and ethnic groups.

By weakening the Department of Education, these proposals would remove critical protections for students with disabilities, students of color, and low-income students, who rely on federal oversight to ensure that their educational rights are upheld. Furthermore, the attack on the NEA and other professional organizations would diminish the ability of educators to advocate for necessary resources and reforms, further harming public education.

The push for a Parents' Bill of Rights, while seemingly benign, is likely to lead to increased conflicts within schools, where a small group of parents could dictate what is taught, undermining the educational experience for all students. This approach risks turning schools into battlegrounds over ideological issues, rather than places where students can learn and grow in a supportive environment.

In sum, these proposed policies represent a significant threat to the foundations of public education in the United States. They would increase inequality, reduce accountability, and prioritize ideological agendas over the educational needs of millions of students. The consequences of such a shift would be felt for generations, as the public education system, one of the bedrocks of American democracy, is weakened and dismantled.

Summary

This chapter of Mandate for Leadership was written by Lindsey M. Burke. The following summary conveys the content of the document accurately and objectively, without endorsing or critiquing the perspectives of the original authors.

Burke begins by asserting that the role of federal education policy should be limited, ultimately advocating for the elimination of the U.S. Department of Education. The core argument is that educational power should be centered on students and families, rather than on the government. The text highlights the importance of a "pluralistic society" where families and students are free to choose from a diverse array of school options and learning environments that best meet their needs. Burke argues that postsecondary institutions should also reflect this diversity, suggesting that there should be room for not only "traditional" liberal arts colleges and research universities but also faith-based institutions, career schools, military academies, and lifelong learning programs.

The text references Milton Friedman's 1955 proposal, which suggested that education should be publicly funded but that decisions regarding education should be made by families. Burke argues that every parent should have the option to direct their child's share of education funding through an Education Savings Account (ESA). These accounts would be overwhelmingly funded by state and local taxpayers, thereby "empowering parents to choose a set of education options that meet their child's unique needs." Burke uses the example of Arizona's pioneering ESA program, which was first piloted in 2011 and expanded in 2022 to be available to all families, as a model of how state-led initiatives can lead to educational innovation.

The text then turns to the potential benefits of reducing federal involvement in education. Burke claims that the future of education freedom and reform in the states is "bright" and will "shine brighter" when regulations and red tape from Washington are eliminated. The argument is that federal money, while substantial, is often accompanied by rules and regulations that hinder its effectiveness, leading to increased education costs without corresponding improvements in student achievement. Therefore, Burke advocates for federal taxpayer dollars to be block-granted to states without strings attached, which would eliminate the need for many federal and state bureaucrats. The text suggests that policymaking and funding should take place at the state and local levels, "closest to the affected families," to ensure that education resources are used more effectively.

In the context of postsecondary education, Burke suggests that student loans and grants should be restored to the private sector, or at the very least, the federal government should reconsider its role as a guarantor rather than a direct lender. Burke argues that federal postsecondary education investments should be aimed at bolstering economic growth and ensuring that recipient institutions "nourish academic freedom and embrace intellectual diversity." However, Burke criticizes the current federal higher education policy and many institutions for being "hostile to free expression, open academic inquiry, and American exceptionalism." The text suggests that federal postsecondary policy should focus less on subsidies for "traditional" colleges and universities and more on supporting workforce skills and career and technical education. Burke argues that there should be a "rebalancing" of federal policy to prepare students for jobs in a dynamic economy, nurture institutional diversity, and expose schools to greater market forces. The text concludes by criticizing the current higher education establishment, which is described as being "captured by woke diversicrats" and a "de facto monopoly enforced by the federal accreditation cartel," arguing that these forces stifle competition and innovation in higher education.

OVERVIEW

The section begins by outlining the historical context of federal involvement in education, noting that for much of American history, the federal government played a minor role in this area. The turning point came in 1964, when Congress passed a series of significant laws, beginning with the Civil Rights Act of 1964, which was motivated by the recognition that the mistreatment of Black Americans required federal intervention. The text highlights that this period also saw the passage of the Elementary and Secondary Education Act (ESEA) and the Higher Education Act (HEA) in 1965, which aimed to improve educational outcomes for disadvantaged students. The intention was to provide compensatory funding to low-income children and college students, as part of President Lyndon B. Johnson's "War on Poverty."

The text provides data to show how spending on these programs has grown exponentially since their inception. For example, by Fiscal Year 2022, ESEA programs received $27.7 billion in appropriations, not including an additional $190 billion from the pandemic's Elementary and Secondary Schools Emergency Relief (ESSER) Funds. The Department of Education also spent over $2 billion just to administer Title IV of the HEA, which authorizes federal student loans and Pell grants, with $22.5 billion allocated to Pell grants alone. These figures underscore the vast expansion of federal education spending over the decades, driven by a series of laws and programs designed as federal "solutions" to various education problems.

Further, the text discusses the layering of additional laws and programs on top of ESEA and HEA. For instance, the Rehabilitation Act of 1973 and the Individuals with Disabilities Education Act (IDEA) of 1975 were enacted to address the educational neglect of students with disabilities. The text also mentions the creation of the Institute for Education Sciences in 2002, which was intended to consolidate education data collection and fund research. Additionally, the Carl D. Perkins Career and Technical Education Acts, including Perkins V in 2018, are cited as examples of ongoing federal efforts to influence education policy.

Burke then examines the structural changes that led to the creation of the U.S. Department of Education. Initially, Congress distributed the management of federal education programs across various agencies. However, those advocating for expanded federal funding and influence found this approach unsatisfactory. The National Education Association (NEA), seeking a more centralized structure, supported presidential candidate Jimmy Carter, who successfully lobbied for the establishment of the Department of Education as a Cabinet-level agency. The Department was established in 1979 and became operational in 1980. It was intended to act as a "corralling" mechanism, consolidating the many federal education programs under one roof, with the expectation that this would reduce administrative costs and improve efficiency.

Contrary to its intended purpose, the Department of Education has, according to Burke, had the opposite effect. Special interest groups, including the NEA, the American Federation of Teachers (AFT), and the higher education lobby, have used the department to continuously expand federal education expenditures. These groups view federal funding as a desirable source because, unlike state and local budgets, federal budgets are not constrained by the need to be balanced each year. By Fiscal Year 2022, the department's discretionary and mandatory appropriations exceeded $80 billion, excluding student loan outlays. Each of these programs comes with federal strings and red tape, adding to the bureaucratic complexity.

The text provides a recent example of federal overreach through the Biden Administration's requirement that state education agencies and school districts submit "equity" plans as a condition of receiving COVID recovery ESSER funds from the American Rescue Plan (ARP). This process necessitated the hiring of numerous new government employees to create these plans, collect public feedback, and ensure that they met federal standards. Burke criticizes this as a costly and unnecessary exercise, emblematic of the inefficiencies that arise from federal involvement in education.

The final part of the section outlines Burke's vision for reform under the next presidential administration. The text suggests that the incoming administration should develop a plan to redistribute federal education programs across various government agencies, eliminate ineffective or duplicative programs, and reduce the burden of red tape by empowering states and districts with flexible, formula-driven block grants. Burke proposes that the administration should be guided by several core principles, including advancing education freedom by empowering families to choose from diverse education options, restoring state and local control over education funding, and treating taxpayers as investors in federal student aid. Furthermore, the text calls for protecting the federal student loan portfolio from "predatory politicians" and ensuring that civil rights are enforced based on a proper understanding of those laws, rejecting ideologies like gender identity and critical race theory.

The section concludes by emphasizing the entrenched infrastructure that supports federal intervention in education, which is bolstered by special interests thriving on federal largesse. However, Burke argues that unlike these bureaucracies and unions, families and students do not need a Department of Education to thrive. The text suggests that dismantling this infrastructure is critical for the next administration.

NEEDED REFORMS

This section begins by asserting that federal intervention in education has failed to promote student achievement, despite the trillions of dollars spent since 1965 on the various programs housed within the Department of Education. Burke cites data from the National Assessment of Educational Progress (NAEP) to illustrate this point, noting that reading scores on the 2022 administration of the NAEP have remained unchanged over the past 30 years. Burke expresses particular concern about declines in math performance, describing these declines as "even more concerning" than the stagnation in reading outcomes. Specifically, the text highlights that both fourth- and eighth-grade math scores saw the largest decline since the assessments began in 1990, with average fourth-grade math scores dropping by five points and average eighth-grade scores by eight points. Only one-third of eighth graders are proficient in reading and math, with just 27 percent proficient in math and 31 percent proficient in reading as of 2022.

Burke also references the NAEP Long-Term Trend Assessment, which shows that academic stagnation has persisted since the 1970s, particularly in the reading scores of 13-year-olds, which have remained stagnant since 1971. Although there has been modest improvement in math scores, the overall picture is one of underachievement and stagnation in American education, despite significant federal investment.

The text then criticizes what it describes as a "shadow" Department of Education operating within state education agencies across the country. This shadow department is the result of federal mandates, programs, and regulations that have driven a hiring spree within these state agencies, leading to significant bureaucratic growth. Burke notes that there are more than 48,000 employees in state education agencies across the U.S., a number more than ten times the 4,400 employees in the federal Department of Education. The primary role of these state agency employees, according to Burke, is to report back to Washington, further entrenching the federal government's influence over education. The text cites research from The Heritage Foundation, which found that the federal government funds 41 percent of the salary costs of state education agencies, underscoring the deep financial ties between federal and state education bureaucracies.

The section recalls a critical report from 1998 led by Representative Pete Hoekstra, titled "Education at a Crossroads: What Works and What's Wasted in Education Today." This report, based on extensive fieldwork and interviews, detailed the overwhelming bureaucratic red tape that had enveloped state education systems due to federal regulations. At that time, the commission estimated that states spent nearly 50 million hours on paperwork just to receive their federal education funding, resulting in only 65 to 70 cents of each federal taxpayer dollar actually reaching the classroom. The text asserts that the situation has worsened since the Hoekstra report, with evidence of increasing bureaucratic burdens, such as the doubling of non-teaching staff in public schools relative to student enrollment growth between 1992 and 2015.

Burke argues that the convoluted nature of federal education programs—with their complex funding formulas, competitive grant applications, and extensive reporting requirements—has contributed to this bureaucratic bloat at the state and local levels. The text identifies this as a key area in need of reform, suggesting that the federal government should streamline existing programs and funding mechanisms. Specifically, Burke proposes that federal education dollars should be distributed to states through straightforward per-pupil allocations or block grants that can be used for any lawful education purpose under state law. This approach, according to the text, would significantly ease the federal compliance burden on states and local districts.

The section concludes by outlining a vision for reforming the Department of Education. Burke calls for the next presidential administration to work with Congress to pass a Department of Education Reorganization Act, which would reform, eliminate, or transfer the department's programs and offices to more appropriate agencies. The text provides an overview of the changes that should occur within each office and program currently operated by the department, suggesting a more decentralized approach that would return control of education policy and funding to states and local communities.

PROGRAM AND OFFICE PRIORITIZATION WITHIN THE DEPARTMENT

In this section, Burke delves into the specifics of how the Department of Education's various offices and programs should be restructured, eliminated, or transferred to other federal agencies. The recommendations are organized by the department's major offices, each of which is responsible for a wide array of programs.

OFFICE OF ELEMENTARY AND SECONDARY EDUCATION (OESE)

The Office of Elementary and Secondary Education (OESE) oversees 36 programs, including Title I, Part A, which provides federal funding to lower-income school districts, Impact Aid, programs for Native American students, and the D.C. Opportunity Scholarship Program. Burke proposes several significant changes to this office:

- **Reduction and Transfer of Programs**: The number of programs managed by OESE should be reduced. Remaining programs should be transferred to other federal agencies. Specifically, Burke suggests transferring Title I, Part A, to the Department of Health and Human Services (HHS), where it would be administered as a no-strings-attached formula block grant. Over a 10-year period, responsibility for Title I funding should be restored to the states.

- **Elimination and Reassignment of Impact Aid**: Impact Aid, which compensates school districts for lost property tax revenue due to federal property (such as military bases or tribal lands), should be restructured. Burke argues for eliminating Impact Aid not tied to students, while student-driven Impact Aid programs should be transferred to the Department of Defense Education Authority (DoDEA) or the Bureau of Indian Education within the Department of the Interior.
- **Expansion of D.C. Opportunity Scholarship Program**: The D.C. Opportunity Scholarship Program, which provides vouchers to low-income children in Washington, D.C., should be expanded into a universal program, with formula funding, and transferred to HHS. Other programs within OESE should either be block-granted to the states or eliminated entirely.

OFFICE OF CAREER, TECHNICAL, AND ADULT EDUCATION (OCTAE)

Burke recommends transferring most of the Office of Career, Technical, and Adult Education's (OCTAE) programs to the Department of Labor. However, the Tribally Controlled Postsecondary Career and Technical Education Program should be moved to the Bureau of Indian Education.

OFFICE OF SPECIAL EDUCATION AND REHABILITATIVE SERVICES (OSERS)

The Office of Special Education and Rehabilitative Services (OSERS) administers nearly two dozen programs, including funding for the Individuals with Disabilities Education Act (IDEA). Burke proposes the following changes:

- **Block Grants for IDEA Funding**: Most IDEA funding should be converted into no-strings-attached formula block grants, targeted at students with disabilities and distributed directly to local education agencies by the Administration for Community Living within HHS.
- **Transfer and Phase Out**: Vocational Rehabilitation Grants for Native American students should be moved to the Bureau of Indian Education, and earmarks for special institutions, such as the National Technical Institute for the Deaf, should be phased out. Furthermore, federal efforts to enforce anti-discrimination laws for individuals with disabilities should be moved to the Department of Justice (DOJ), along with the Office for Civil Rights (OCR).

OFFICE FOR POSTSECONDARY EDUCATION (OPE)

For the Office for Postsecondary Education (OPE), Burke recommends a substantial overhaul:

- **Elimination or Transfer of Programs**: The next administration should work with Congress to either eliminate or move OPE programs to the Employment and Training Administration (ETA) at the Department of Labor. Funding to institutions should be block-granted and limited to Historically Black Colleges and Universities (HBCUs) and tribally controlled colleges. Programs important to national security should be transferred to the Department of State.

INSTITUTE OF EDUCATION SCIENCES (IES)

The Institute of Education Sciences (IES), particularly its statistical office—the National Center for Education Statistics (NCES)—should be transferred to the Census Bureau within the Department of Commerce. Burke suggests that if Congress wishes to maintain federal research centers, they could be moved to the National Science Foundation. However, if IES remains an independent agency, significant governance and management issues must be addressed to ensure it contributes productively to the knowledge base on teaching and learning.

OFFICE OF FEDERAL STUDENT AID (FSA)

The text calls for a complete reversal of the federalization of student loans that took place in 2010, advocating for the Office of Federal Student Aid (FSA) to be spun off into a new government corporation with professional governance and management. This new entity would manage the federal student loan portfolio with the statutory charge to preserve it for the benefit of taxpayers and students. The Treasury Department would manage collections and defaults, while the new federal student loan authority would handle borrower relations, applications, disbursements, institutional accountability, and regulations.

OFFICE FOR CIVIL RIGHTS (OCR)

Burke recommends moving the Office for Civil Rights (OCR) to the Department of Justice (DOJ). The text emphasizes that the federal government's role in enforcing civil rights protections should be confined to litigation through DOJ and federal courts, rather than through regulatory actions by the Department of Education.

ADDITIONAL BUREAUS AND OFFICES

For other offices within the Department of Education that are slated for closure, Burke suggests that positions deemed essential to the federal mission should be transferred to other agencies where their expertise can be utilized. For example, lawyers from the Office of General Counsel (OGC) specializing in higher education could be transferred to the new Federal Student Aid Office or the Department of Labor.

CONCLUSION

The section concludes with a call for Congress to pass a Department of Education Reorganization Act, or a Liquidating Authority Act, which would guide the executive branch on how to systematically dismantle the Department of Education as a stand-alone Cabinet-level department. The text emphasizes that this process should be thorough, ensuring that valuable functions and expertise are preserved and reassigned appropriately.

CURRENT LAWS RELATING TO THE DEPARTMENT OF EDUCATION THAT REQUIRE REPEAL

In this section, Burke outlines the legislative changes necessary to fully dismantle the U.S. Department of Education. The central argument is that for the Department to be effectively wound down, Congress must pass, and the President must sign into law, a **Department of Education Reorganization Act** or **Liquidating Authority Act**. This legislation would provide the executive branch with clear instructions on how to devolve the functions of the Department of Education, ensuring that the process is orderly and that the responsibilities currently held by the Department are redistributed or eliminated.

Burke does not detail specific laws in this section but emphasizes the overarching need for such an act to facilitate the Department's dissolution. The text suggests that without this legislative action, efforts to reduce the federal government's role in education would be incomplete. The proposed Reorganization Act would likely include provisions to transfer certain programs to other federal agencies, convert funding into block grants to states, and eliminate redundant or ineffective programs. Burke stresses that this legislative action is a critical step in restoring state and local control over education, which is portrayed as more responsive and better suited to meet the needs of students and families.

The section implies that the Reorganization Act would repeal or significantly amend existing education laws that currently grant the Department of Education its authority, such as those established under the Elementary and Secondary Education Act (ESEA) and the Higher Education Act (HEA). However, the text does not specify which laws would need to be repealed or how the Reorganization Act would address them in detail.

Burke concludes by asserting that this legislative action is necessary to fully realize the vision of a decentralized education system where states and local communities have the primary responsibility for education policy and funding. This approach, according to the text, would better align with the principles of federalism and the original intent of the U.S. Constitution regarding the role of the federal government in education.

CURRENT REGULATIONS PROMULGATED BY OR RELEVANT TO THE AGENCY THAT SHOULD BE ROLLED BACK OR ELIMINATED

In this section, Burke discusses the need for the next administration to thoroughly review and roll back numerous education-related regulations that were established during the Biden administration. The text identifies five primary regulatory targets that require immediate attention:

1. **Charter School Grant Program Priorities**: The Biden administration's changes to the Charter School Program (CSP) are highlighted as problematic because they increase federal oversight and add new requirements that go beyond the statutory authority granted by Congress. These changes are seen as an unnecessary expansion of the federal footprint in the charter school sector. Burke argues that the new administration must rescind these requirements to reduce federal restrictions on charter schools, thus restoring more autonomy to state and local entities that oversee these institutions.
2. **Civil Rights Data Collection**: The Office for Civil Rights (OCR) under the Biden administration proposed revisions to its mandatory Civil Rights Data Collection (CRDC), including the introduction of a "nonbinary" sex category and the removal of data collection regarding male and female participation in high school athletics. Burke argues that these changes are "poorly conceived," legally questionable, and potentially infringe on student privacy and parental rights. The text calls for the new administration to rescind these changes and return to a data collection framework that aligns more closely with OCR's statutory enforcement authority.

3. **Student Assistance General Provisions and Federal Loan Program Regulations**: The text criticizes the final regulations promulgated by the Biden administration regarding loan forgiveness programs, including borrower defense to repayment (BDR), closed school loan discharge (CSLD), and public service loan forgiveness (PSLF). Burke claims that these regulations drastically expanded loan forgiveness without clear congressional authorization, leading to significant costs for taxpayers. The new administration is urged to initiate negotiated rulemaking to rescind these regulations and restore a more conservative approach to student loan management.

4. **Title IX Regulations**: The Biden administration's proposed changes to Title IX, which governs sex discrimination in education, are depicted as an assault on the rights of women and girls, as well as due process protections for those accused of sexual misconduct. The text argues that the proposed regulations would erode free speech, religious liberty, and parental rights, particularly in elementary and secondary education. Burke calls for the new administration to work with Congress to prohibit the Department of Education from enforcing these regulations and to restore the Title IX framework established by the Trump administration in 2020, which defined "sex" as biological sex recognized at birth.

5. **Assistance to States for the Education of Children with Disabilities (IDEA)**: Burke critiques the final regulations under Part B of IDEA that require states to consider race and ethnicity in identifying, placing, and disciplining students with disabilities. The text argues that these regulations were based on flawed assumptions and have led to the diversion of special education funds to address issues of disproportionality in special education assignments. Burke recommends rescinding these regulations and refocusing IDEA on providing targeted support for students with disabilities without the complications introduced by considerations of race and ethnicity.

In addition to these specific regulations, the text suggests that the new administration should also review regulatory changes to the school meals program under the Department of Agriculture and the Income-Driven Repayment (IDR) plans for student loans. Further, Burke anticipates additional regulations on gainful employment, accreditation of postsecondary institutions, and Title VI enforcement, which are expected to be released by the Biden administration in 2023. The new administration is urged to be prepared to address and potentially roll back these regulations as well.

The section concludes by emphasizing the importance of reducing federal overreach in education policy, advocating for a return to state and local control, and ensuring that federal regulations do not undermine the principles of free speech, due process, and parental rights in education.

NEW POLICY PRIORITIES FOR 2025 AND BEYOND

This section outlines several legislative and policy priorities that Burke believes should be pursued by the next administration to further the goal of reducing federal involvement in education and promoting parental rights and educational freedom.

RESCIND THE NATIONAL EDUCATION ASSOCIATION'S CONGRESSIONAL CHARTER

Burke begins by calling for the rescission of the National Education Association's (NEA) federal charter. The NEA, the nation's largest teachers' union, is portrayed as a radical special interest group that overwhelmingly supports left-of-center policies and policymakers. The text argues that the NEA has used its influence to block school choice initiatives and advocate for increased taxpayer spending on education, positions that Burke claims are not supported by robust research evidence. Burke points out that the NEA lobbied to keep schools closed during the COVID-19 pandemic, despite evidence suggesting that such closures had negative emotional and academic outcomes for students. Furthermore, the NEA is accused of promoting "radical racial and gender ideologies" in schools, which, according to the text, are opposed by many parents.

Burke argues that rescinding the NEA's congressional charter would remove the "false impression" that federal taxpayers support the political activities of this special interest group. The text notes that rescinding congressional charters is not unprecedented, as Congress has previously revoked the charters of other organizations. Burke suggests that Congress should conduct hearings to investigate how much federal taxpayer money the NEA has used to support what the text describes as radical causes aligned with a single political party.

PROTECT PARENTAL RIGHTS IN EDUCATION

The section then discusses the need to protect parental rights in education, particularly in jurisdictions under federal control, such as Washington, D.C., public schools, Bureau of Indian Education schools, and Department of Defense schools. Burke argues that educators and students in these jurisdictions should be protected from racial discrimination and compelled speech, particularly in relation to critical race theory (CRT).

The text defines CRT as an ideology that disrupts America's founding ideals of freedom and opportunity by promoting the belief that racism is appropriate or necessary.

Burke advocates for legislation that would prevent CRT from being used in school activities, such as mandatory affinity groups, teacher training programs that require educators to confess their privilege, or assignments that require students to defend the idea that America is systemically racist. The text emphasizes that no individual should receive punishment or benefits based on the color of their skin and that school officials should not require students or teachers to believe that individuals are guilty or responsible for the actions of others based on race or ethnicity. Burke also argues that educators should not be forced to discuss contemporary political issues unless it is appropriate for the classroom, and that classroom materials should be posted online to provide maximum transparency to parents.

ADVANCING LEGAL PROTECTIONS FOR PARENTAL RIGHTS IN EDUCATION

Burke continues by arguing that parental rights have not always been treated as co-equal to other fundamental rights, such as free speech or the free exercise of religion, in the U.S. legal system. This uncertainty has emboldened federal agencies to promote rules and policies that infringe on parental rights. The text cites examples, such as the Biden administration's proposed Title IX regulations, which could require schools to assist children with social or medical gender transitions without parental consent, or to withhold information from parents about their child's social transition.

To address this issue, Burke calls for a federal **Parents' Bill of Rights** that would restore parental rights to a "top-tier" status, ensuring that these rights are given full protection against government infringement. Such legislation would require the government to satisfy "strict scrutiny"—the highest standard of judicial review—when it seeks to infringe on parental rights. Additionally, Burke suggests that regulations impacting parental rights should include similar protections, requiring federal agencies to demonstrate that their actions meet the strict scrutiny standard before finalizing any rules.

Burke also advocates for amending federal laws, such as the Family Educational Rights and Privacy Act (FERPA) and the Protection of Pupil Rights Amendment (PPRA), to provide parents with a private right of action. Currently, parents cannot directly sue schools for violating these laws; instead, they must file an administrative complaint with the Department of Education. Burke argues that providing a private right of action would empower parents and students to enforce their rights more effectively and encourage schools to comply with federal requirements.

PROTECT PARENTAL RIGHTS IN POLICY

In addition to legal protections, Burke emphasizes the need for legislative action to advance parental rights. The text mentions several promising legislative proposals from the 117th Congress, such as the **Empowering Parents Act** and the **Parents' Bill of Rights Act**, which aim to safeguard parental involvement in education. Burke also highlights the importance of aligning federal legislation with state-level **Parents' Bills of Rights** that have been passed in states like Florida, Georgia, and Arizona.

The text also expresses concern about the rise in gender surgeries and hormone treatments for minors, describing this as a "social contagion" that is particularly affecting young girls. Burke argues that providing easier access to such treatments without parental involvement does not reduce suicide rates among these young people and may even increase the risk of suicide. The text suggests that the next administration should take note of how radical gender ideology is impacting school-aged children and take steps to prevent schools from driving a wedge between parents and their children.

Burke advocates for federal legislation that would prohibit public school employees from using a name or pronoun for a student that does not match their biological sex without written permission from the student's parents. This legislation would also protect education employees from being forced to use pronouns that conflict with their religious or moral convictions. The text calls for state lawmakers to adopt similar provisions for public schools within their borders, arguing that federal lawmakers should set an example for states to follow.

ADVANCE SCHOOL CHOICE POLICIES

The section also addresses school choice, particularly the D.C. Opportunity Scholarship Program. Burke argues that the program, which provides scholarships to low-income families in Washington, D.C., should be expanded to include all students, regardless of income, and that the scholarship amount should be increased to match the per-student funding in D.C. Public Schools. The text asserts that all families should have the ability to direct their children's taxpayer-funded education dollars to the providers of their choosing, whether that be public or private schools. Additionally, Burke calls for deregulation of the program by removing the requirement for private schools to administer the D.C. Public Schools assessment and allowing these schools to control their admissions processes.

PROVIDE EDUCATION CHOICE FOR POPULATIONS UNDER THE JURISDICTION OF CONGRESS

Finally, Burke emphasizes the need for school choice in three specific populations under federal jurisdiction: students in Washington, D.C., students in active-duty military families, and students attending schools on tribal lands under the Bureau of Indian Education (BIE). The text argues that federal lawmakers should allow these students to use education savings accounts to select the educational products and services that best meet their needs.

For students in D.C., Burke suggests that federal lawmakers should offer education savings accounts that allow parents to pay for personal tutors, education therapists, books, private school tuition, and other educational expenses. Burke also calls for similar accounts to be provided for students in active-duty military families, with funding allocated under the National Defense Authorization Act (NDAA). The text references Heritage Foundation research, which suggests that if even 10 percent of eligible students used these accounts, the impact on the sending school district's budget would be minimal, yet the benefits to the individual students would be significant.

The section also highlights the poor performance of schools on tribal lands, noting that BIE schools have some of the worst outcomes in the country. The text reports that the graduation rate for BIE students is only 53 percent, nearly 30 percentage points lower than the national average. Burke advocates for creating a federal education savings account option for all children attending BIE schools, arguing that this would provide these students with the opportunity to access better educational options.

OTHER STRUCTURAL REFORMS THAT THE DEPARTMENT OF EDUCATION REQUIRES

In this section, Burke discusses additional structural reforms necessary to address the perceived inefficiencies and overreach of the U.S. Department of Education. The reforms are focused on improving federal education data collection, reforming the negotiated rulemaking process, and restructuring the Office of Federal Student Aid (FSA).

REFORM FEDERAL EDUCATION DATA COLLECTION

Burke argues that the current approach to federal education data collection is inadequate and should be reformed. The text specifically criticizes the National Assessment of Educational Progress (NAEP) and other federal data collections for not making publicly available data on students' family structure, despite acknowledging its significant impact on educational achievement. Burke cites education scholar Ian Rowe, who points out that while NAEP collects data on family structure, it does not release this data, which limits the ability to fully understand the factors influencing student outcomes.

Burke proposes that the Department of Education, or whichever agency is responsible for long-term data collection, should make student data available by family structure, including this data in tools like the NAEP Data Explorer. Additionally, the text suggests consolidating federal data collection efforts under the Census Bureau to streamline processes and improve accuracy. For higher education, Burke recommends housing data within the Department of Labor to enhance transparency in evaluating postsecondary education and workforce training outcomes. This move would allow for better contextualization of educational results based on broader labor market trends and would enable more accurate comparisons across regions by adjusting for differences in earnings and cost of living.

The text also calls for the development of a reliable methodology for "risk adjusting" institutional and program outcomes, which would isolate the impact of educational quality from socioeconomic and other external factors. Burke argues that current metrics, such as graduation rates and average earnings, are heavily influenced by students' backgrounds rather than the quality of education provided by institutions. By risk-adjusting outcomes, the federal government could provide a more accurate assessment of the value added by education programs, similar to how the Department of Health and Human Services (HHS) adjusts healthcare outcomes based on social determinants of health.

REFORM THE NEGOTIATED RULEMAKING PROCESS AT ED

Burke critiques the negotiated rulemaking process required by statute for certain regulations under the Elementary and Secondary Education Act (ESEA) and the Higher Education Act (HEA). The process involves convening a committee of stakeholders to reach a consensus on proposed regulations, with the goal of ensuring that the rules are practical and take into account potential unintended consequences. However, Burke argues that this process has become an "expensive and time-consuming undertaking" that rarely achieves consensus, allowing the Department of Education to proceed with its own agenda regardless of stakeholder input.

The text points out that the department's master calendar, which requires final rules to be published by October 1 to be implemented by July 1 of the following year, compounds the challenges of updating regulations to keep pace with changes in education, finance, and student assessment. Burke also highlights the performative nature of recent rulemaking sessions, where negotiators use social media to criticize the process and their peers, and where some members of Congress use public comments as opportunities for political speeches rather than contributing substantive input.

To address these issues, Burke suggests that the Department of Education should work with Congress to amend the HEA to eliminate the negotiated rulemaking requirement altogether. At a minimum, Congress should allow the department to use public hearings instead of negotiated rulemaking sessions, which would streamline the process and reduce unnecessary delays.

REFORM THE OFFICE OF FEDERAL STUDENT AID (FSA)

Burke then focuses on the need to reform the Office of Federal Student Aid (FSA), particularly in light of what is described as the prior administration's "abuse" of loan forgiveness programs. The text argues that the federal government does not have the proper incentives to make sound lending decisions, which has led to the mismanagement of the federal student loan portfolio for political purposes. Burke calls for the new administration to end these practices and to manage the student loan portfolio in a professional manner.

The proposed reforms include returning to a system where private lenders, backed by government guarantees, compete to offer student loans. This shift would reintroduce market discipline into educational borrowing, leading to more responsible lending practices. The text suggests that Pell grants should retain their current structure as vouchers, allowing students to apply them toward the cost of education at accredited institutions.

If Congress is unwilling to overhaul federal student aid, Burke proposes several reforms to improve the current system:

- **Switch to Fair-Value Accounting**: The text recommends switching from Federal Credit Reform Act (FCRA) accounting to fair-value accounting for student loans, which would more accurately reflect the cost to taxpayers.
- **Consolidate Federal Loan Programs**: Burke suggests consolidating all federal loan programs into a single new program that utilizes income-driven repayment, eliminates interest rate subsidies and loan forgiveness, includes annual and aggregate borrowing limits, and requires institutions to share some of the financial risk to ensure they have "skin in the game."

The section concludes by reiterating that the Biden administration's handling of the student loan portfolio for "crass political purposes" has harmed both taxpayers and future students. Burke argues that these abuses must be corrected, and the student loan system reformed to prevent similar issues from arising in the future. The text advocates for spinning off the FSA into a new government corporation with professional governance and management, which would be better equipped to handle the complexities of federal student aid in a way that balances the interests of students and taxpayers.

CHAPTER 12: DEPARTMENT OF ENERGY AND RELATED COMMISSIONS

The new energy crisis is caused not by a lack of resources, but by extreme 'green' policies. Under the rubrics of 'combating climate change' and 'ESG' (environmental, social, and governance), the Biden Administration, Congress, and various states, as well as Wall Street investors, international corporations, and progressive special-interest groups, are changing America's energy landscape. - Page 363

Key Policy Proposals

The proposed policies in this document represent a significant shift towards deregulation, fossil fuel promotion, and reduced environmental protection. These changes would have severe negative consequences for climate action, clean energy development, and public health.

ELIMINATING OR DRASTICALLY REDUCING RENEWABLE ENERGY AND EFFICIENCY PROGRAMS:
The proposal to eliminate or severely cut funding for the Office of Energy Efficiency and Renewable Energy (EERE) and other clean energy initiatives would cripple America's ability to transition to a clean energy economy. This would lead to increased carbon emissions, reduced energy innovation, and a loss of economic opportunities in the fast-growing renewable energy sector. The U.S. would fall behind other nations in clean technology development.

REFOCUSING ON FOSSIL FUELS AND NUCLEAR:
The emphasis on expanding fossil fuel production and nuclear power ignores the urgent need to address climate change. Increased oil and gas extraction would lock in decades of additional carbon emissions. While nuclear energy can play a role in decarbonization, over-reliance on this technology comes with significant safety and waste disposal concerns.

WEAKENING ENVIRONMENTAL REVIEWS AND REGULATIONS:
Proposals to limit environmental impact assessments and streamline fossil fuel project approvals would lead to inadequate evaluation of ecological and community impacts. This increases risks of environmental damage and negative health effects, particularly for vulnerable populations living near energy infrastructure.

RESTRUCTURING ELECTRICITY MARKETS TO FAVOR FOSSIL FUELS:
Changes to how regional electricity markets operate, ostensibly to improve "reliability," would disadvantage renewable energy sources and prop up uneconomic coal and gas plants. This would slow the transition to clean energy and increase costs for consumers.

Reducing focus on climate change:
The proposed elimination of climate considerations from energy policy is dangerously short-sighted. Climate change poses existential risks to our economy, national security, and way of life. Ignoring it in policymaking will leave the U.S. unprepared for escalating impacts.

CUTTING ENERGY INNOVATION FUNDING:
Proposals to eliminate ARPA-E and reduce DOE's role in energy technology development would hamper American competitiveness in the global clean energy race. Government-funded R&D has been crucial to past energy breakthroughs and is needed to drive future innovation.

EXPANDING ARCTIC DRILLING:
Opening more Arctic areas to oil and gas extraction poses severe environmental risks to sensitive ecosystems and indigenous communities. It also further commits the U.S. to fossil fuel dependence at a time when we need to be rapidly transitioning away from these energy sources.

These policy proposals reflect an outdated, fossil fuel-centric view of energy that fails to account for the urgent need to address climate change and the economic opportunities in clean energy. Implementing them would damage U.S. climate leadership, slow the necessary energy transition, and leave America less competitive in the industries of the future. Instead, we need bold policies to accelerate clean energy deployment, improve energy efficiency, and rapidly reduce greenhouse gas emissions across all sectors of the economy.

Summary

This chapter of Mandate for Leadership was written by Bernard L. McNamee. The following summary conveys the content of the document accurately and objectively, without endorsing or critiquing the perspectives of the original authors.

AMERICAN ENERGY AND SCIENCE DOMINANCE

The chapters begins by emphasizing the importance of energy and science dominance for the United States. It argues that the next conservative administration should prioritize these areas to ensure "abundant, affordable, and reliable energy" for Americans, create jobs, support domestic manufacturing and technology leadership, and strengthen national security.

The author contends that the U.S. is facing a new energy crisis, despite having achieved energy independence and dominance in the early 2000s. This crisis is attributed to "ideologically driven government policies" rather than a lack of resources. The text criticizes "extreme 'green' policies" implemented under the guise of "combating climate change" and "ESG" (environmental, social, and governance) for creating artificial energy scarcity and increasing costs.

The document argues that these policies are making America dependent on adversaries like China for energy and allowing the government to control energy allocation. It warns that this control over energy equates to control over people and the economy. The text also highlights the threat of cyberattacks on energy infrastructure by foreign actors and non-state entities.

To address these issues, the author proposes that a conservative President should commit to "unleashing all of America's energy resources" and making the energy economy serve the American people. This includes promoting energy security, affirming an "all of the above" energy policy, repealing spending bills like the Infrastructure Investment and Jobs Act and Inflation Reduction Act, and ending government interference in energy decisions.

The text also advocates for stopping the "war on oil and natural gas," allowing individuals and businesses to use their preferred energy resources, securing energy infrastructure from cyber and physical attacks, and refocusing the Department of Energy on energy security and advanced science. Additionally, it suggests promoting U.S. energy resources to assist allies and diminish strategic adversaries, refocusing FERC on ensuring affordable and reliable electricity, and ensuring that the Nuclear Regulatory Commission facilitates rather than hampers private-sector nuclear energy innovation and deployment.

AMERICAN SCIENCE DOMINANCE
The text transitions to discussing American science dominance, highlighting its historical importance since Benjamin Franklin's era. It emphasizes the critical role of the 17 National Laboratories in supporting national defense and ensuring U.S. leadership in transformative scientific discoveries.

However, the document warns that U.S. science has been under threat in recent years. It cites two main challenges: external threats from adversaries like the Chinese military engaging in scientific espionage, and internal issues such as the National Labs' excessive focus on climate change and renewable technologies.

The author argues that American science dominance is "critical to U.S. national security and economic strength." Consequently, the text asserts that the next conservative President needs to recommit the United States to ensuring this dominance.

MISSION STATEMENT FOR A REFORMED DEPARTMENT OF ENERGY

The document proposes renaming and refocusing the Department of Energy as the Department of Energy Security and Advanced Science (DESAS). It outlines five core missions for DESAS:
1. Providing leadership on energy security and related national security issues
2. Promoting U.S. energy economic interests abroad
3. Leading in cutting-edge fundamental advanced science
4. Remediating former Manhattan Project and Cold War nuclear material sites
5. Developing new nuclear weapons and naval nuclear reactors

The text argues that these missions work together by "using advanced science to promote national security while getting the government out of the business of picking winners and losers in energy resources." It criticizes the current DOE for spending billions of taxpayer dollars to subsidize renewable energy developers and investors, which it claims makes Americans less energy secure and distorts energy markets.

OVERVIEW

This section provides a brief history of the Department of Energy, created in 1977 in response to the 1970s oil crisis. It outlines DOE's various responsibilities, including basic science research through the National Laboratories, cleaning up nuclear material and weapons sites, developing civilian nuclear waste storage sites, and developing new nuclear weapons and naval reactors.

The author criticizes DOE's recent focus on renewable energy and climate change, arguing that while government engagement in fundamental scientific research is appropriate, "government, however, should not be picking winners and losers in dealing with energy resources or commercial technology." The text contends that such favoritism can "crowd out new innovation, devolve into cronyism, and raise energy prices for consumers and businesses."

The section concludes by asserting that "it is time for the United States to use all of its energy resources again for the benefit of the American people."

NEW POLICIES: ENERGY

This section outlines proposed energy policies for the reformed Department of Energy Security and Advanced Science (DESAS). The text emphasizes that DESAS's energy role should focus on several key areas:

1. Working with the energy industry to ensure infrastructure security through science and coordination with the private sector.
2. Assessing international energy issues that pose threats to U.S. national security.
3. Promoting U.S. energy resources to assist allies, diminish strategic adversaries, and ensure markets supporting domestic energy production.
4. Pursuing early and advanced science related to energy and national security.
5. Developing leadership for the disposal of commercial and government spent nuclear fuel.

The document then delves into specific policy recommendations for national energy security. It proposes focusing on studying threats to the electric grid, natural gas, and oil infrastructure, and sharing this information with the energy industry. The text suggests elevating the Office of Cybersecurity, Energy Security, and Emergency Response (CESER) to an Assistant Secretary level and having it work with other offices to address threats to energy infrastructure.

The author advocates for eliminating "special-interest funding programs" that focus on commercialization rather than fundamental science and technology. It also recommends eliminating political and climate-change interference in DOE approvals of liquefied natural gas (LNG) exports and reforming the Natural Gas Act to expand required approvals to all U.S. allies.

The text proposes refocusing the Federal Energy Management Program (FEMP) on ensuring reliable and cost-effective energy for government buildings and operations. It also suggests ensuring that information provided by the U.S. Energy Information Agency (EIA) is "data-neutral."

Regarding the Federal Energy Regulatory Commission (FERC), the document recommends focusing on its statutory obligation to ensure access to reliable energy at "just, reasonable, and nondiscriminatory rates." For the Nuclear Regulatory Commission (NRC), it suggests streamlining nuclear regulatory requirements and the licensing process to help "lower costs and accelerate the development and deployment of civilian nuclear."

Finally, the section emphasizes the need to focus on energy and science issues rather than "politicized social programs." It argues that DOE should concentrate on providing all Americans with "access to abundant, affordable, reliable, and secure energy" and manage its employees based on "talent, skills, and hard work" rather than promoting politicized agendas.

NEW POLICIES: INTERNATIONAL ENERGY SECURITY

This section proposes reforms to various DOE program offices to enhance the application of U.S. energy interests in international affairs. The author advocates for promoting American energy dominance as a key component of foreign policy, emphasizing the need to align domestic and international goals. The text argues that "American energy dominance will allow the United States to secure energy for its citizens, markets for its energy exports, and access to new energy natural resources."

A key recommendation is the development of a National Energy Security Strategy (NESS). This strategy would analyze U.S. international energy security interests to inform the President's foreign policy and defense roles. However, the author cautions that this should not be used as a tool for U.S. industrial policy or climate policy.

The document also suggests strengthening the role of DESAS in international energy matters. It notes that there are frequent "turf battles" between the Department of State and DOE on energy issues, and argues that the State Department often ignores DOE's expertise. To address this, it proposes that the existing Assistant Secretary for International Affairs should provide principal support for DOE leadership on National Security Council activities and interface with colleagues at other departments.

NEW POLICIES: ADVANCED SCIENCE

This section focuses on ensuring America's continued leadership in fundamental science. The text proposes two main policy directions:

1. Refocusing the National Labs on fundamental and advanced science: The document argues that the 14 science and energy labs should focus on basic research projects, leaving demonstration and deployment of technology to the private sector. It suggests realigning the labs to "limit duplication and mission creep and to maximize potential."
2. Conducting a whole-of-government assessment and consolidation of science: The author recommends a review of all federal science agencies before the start of a new administration. This includes reassessing the expansion of the National Science Foundation's mission and reviewing DOE programs to "measure, prioritize, and consolidate" based on factors such as relationship to national security, furtherance of energy security, and importance to scientific discovery/advancement.

NEW POLICIES: REMEDIATION OF NUCLEAR WEAPONS DEVELOPMENT PROGRAMS AND CIVILIAN NUCLEAR WASTE

This section addresses the massive and complicated process of cleaning up radioactive waste from the Manhattan Project and the Cold War. The author notes that projected liabilities and costs for taxpayers total $887,205 billion according to DOE's FY 2023 budget request.

The document proposes two main policy directions:

1. Continuing DOE's remediation of radioactive waste from nuclear weapons projects, emphasizing the need for strong leadership focused on accelerating the cleanup.
2. Developing a new approach that increases private-sector responsibility for the disposal of nuclear waste. The author notes the importance of scientific study in this area and mentions the $46 billion held in the Nuclear Waste Fund for a permanent waste disposal site.

NEW POLICIES: NNSA

This section focuses on the National Nuclear Security Administration (NNSA) and its role in maintaining the U.S. nuclear arsenal. The author emphasizes the need to update and reinvigorate the nuclear arsenal to effectively deal with threats from China, Russia, and other adversaries. The text outlines three main policy recommendations:

1. Fund the design, development, and deployment of new nuclear warheads, including the production of plutonium pits in quantity.
2. Expand the U.S. Navy and develop new nuclear naval reactors to ensure the Navy has the nuclear propulsion it needs to secure America's strategic interests.
3. End "ineffective and counterproductive nonproliferation activities" like those involving Iran and the United Nations.

The author stresses that these efforts require significant funding and scientific expertise.

BUDGET

This section briefly discusses the DOE's budget request for FY 2023, which totals $48,183,451,000. The author notes that many DOE activities are mandated by various authorization and appropriations bills. To implement the proposed policies, several laws would need to be amended, including the Department of Energy Organization Act, Infrastructure Investment and Jobs Act, Inflation Reduction Act, and possibly portions of the CHIPS and Science Act. The text argues that "ending taxpayer subsidies will promote an 'all of the above' energy policy, lead to more energy resources, reduce costs, and save taxpayers billions of dollars."

OFFICE OF CYBERSECURITY, ENERGY SECURITY, AND EMERGENCY RESPONSE (CESER)

This section outlines the mission and proposed reforms for CESER. The office's mission is to enhance the security and resilience of U.S. critical energy infrastructure, mitigate impacts of disruptive events, and facilitate recovery from energy disruptions.

The author acknowledges that CESER's role in supporting national security by working with the private sector to ensure energy security is proper for government. However, the text suggests several reforms:

1. Focus on the entire energy system, including the interdependence between natural gas and electric generation and cybersecurity.
2. Reinstate an iteration of the Trump Administration's Executive Order 13920, "Securing the United States Bulk-Power System."
3. Prioritize cybersecurity, physical security, and resilience of critical infrastructure through research and development, technical assistance to states and industry, and emergency exercises.

The document notes that CESER received $177 million for FY 2022 and $550 million through the Infrastructure Investment and Jobs Act. The FY 2023 budget request is for $202 million, with an additional request for $500 million to modernize the Strategic Petroleum Reserve.

OFFICE OF ELECTRICITY (OE)

This section discusses the Office of Electricity, created after the 2003 blackouts to improve grid reliability and energy assurance. The author proposes several reforms:

1. Focus more intently on grid reliability, addressing cyber, physical, and reliability threats to the electric grid.
2. Eliminate applied programs, such as grant programs for energy storage and testing of grid-enhancing technologies.
3. Prioritize grid security, including maintaining two production sites for plutonium pits and focusing on the interdependence of electric generation and natural gas pipelines.
4. End funding of programs for commercial technology and deployment.

The text notes that OE's FY 2021 enacted budget was $211,720,000, with a request for $297,386,000 for FY 2023.

OFFICE OF NUCLEAR ENERGY (NE)

The document critiques the Office of Nuclear Energy for being "too influential in driving the business decisions of commercial nuclear energy firms." It recommends:

1. Substantially limiting NE's size and scope.
2. Adopting broader regulatory and energy policy reforms to reduce obstacles and allow fair competition.
3. Focusing on overcoming technical barriers preventing commercial reactor demonstration projects.
4. Reorganizing activities into three basic lines: nuclear fuels, reactor technology, and civilian radioactive waste.

The author notes that these reforms would cost less than the $1,675,060,000 requested for FY 2023.

OFFICE OF FOSSIL ENERGY AND CARBON MANAGEMENT (FECM)

This section discusses the transformation of the Office of Fossil Energy into FECM, criticizing its shift from improving fossil energy production to reducing carbon dioxide emissions. The author recommends:

1. Eliminating carbon capture utilization and storage (CCUS) programs.
2. Pursuing the processing of critical minerals from fossil fuel waste products.
3. Renaming FECM to its original designation and mission if it cannot be eliminated.
4. Ensuring that LNG export approvals are reviewed and processed in a timely manner.
5. Maintaining the Strategic Petroleum Reserve for national strategic purposes.

The text notes that the FY 2023 budget request for FECM was approximately $893.2 million.

OFFICE OF ENERGY EFFICIENCY AND RENEWABLE ENERGY (EERE)

The author criticizes EERE as a "conduit for taxpayer dollars to fund progressive policies." Recommendations include:

1. Ending the focus on climate change and green subsidies.
2. Eliminating energy efficiency standards for appliances.
3. Reducing EERE funding if it cannot be eliminated.
4. Focusing on fundamental science and research rather than deploying technologies.

The document notes that EERE was funded at slightly more than $2.8 billion in FY 2021, with a request for slightly more than $4.0 billion for FY 2023.

GRID DEPLOYMENT OFFICE (GDO)

The text describes the Grid Deployment Office, established to implement parts of the Infrastructure Investment and Jobs Act. The author recommends:

1. Ending grid planning and focusing instead on reliability.
2. Incorporating GDO into a reformed Office of Cybersecurity, Energy Security, and Emergency Response.
3. Considering defunding civil nuclear tax credit programs and hydroelectric power incentives established in the IIJA.
4. Ensuring that state interests are respected in National Interest Electric Transmission Corridors (NIETC) development.

The document notes that Congress appropriated $10 million for GDO in FY 2021, with a request for $90.2 million in FY 2023.

OFFICE OF CLEAN ENERGY DEMONSTRATION (OCED)

The author criticizes OCED for distorting energy markets and shifting technology development risks to taxpayers. Recommendations include:

1. Eliminating OCED entirely.
2. If elimination is not possible, refocusing on resources that support reliability, such as moving small modular reactors (SMRs) from pilot scale to commercialization.

The text notes that OCED oversees nearly $21.5 billion in new appropriations created by the IIJA.

LOAN PROGRAM OFFICE (LPO)

The document argues that taxpayers should not back risky business ventures or politically preferred commercial enterprises. Recommendations include:

1. Not backing any new loans or loan guarantees.
2. Seeking to sunset DOE's loan authority through Congress.
3. If programs cannot be repealed, strengthening due diligence, increasing transparency, and limiting new loan authority to projects promoting grid reliability and national security objectives.

ADVANCED RESEARCH PROJECTS AGENCY-ENERGY (ARPA-E)

The author critiques ARPA-E for duplicating efforts of other DOE offices and risking taxpayer dollars. The main recommendation is to eliminate ARPA-E entirely. The text notes that Congress appropriated $427 million for ARPA-E in FY 2021, with a request for slightly more than $700 million for FY 2023.

FEDERAL ENERGY MANAGEMENT PROGRAM (FEMP)

The document suggests that FEMP should focus on helping federal agencies follow the law and use energy efficiently and cost-effectively. It recommends following the language of Executive Order 13834, directing federal agencies to "reduce waste, cut costs, enhance the resilience of Federal infrastructure and operations, and enable more effective accomplishment of its mission."

CLEAN ENERGY CORPS

The author criticizes the Clean Energy Corps as a "taxpayer-funded program to create new government jobs for employees 'who will work together to research, develop, demonstrate, and deploy solutions to climate change.'" The sole recommendation is to eliminate the Clean Energy Corps by revoking funding and eliminating all positions and personnel hired under the program.

ENERGY INFORMATION ADMINISTRATION (EIA)

The text describes EIA as historically providing independent and impartial analysis. However, the author suggests several reforms:

1. Clarify levelized cost of electricity (LCOE) reporting to include the cost of backup power for intermittent resources.
2. Revise reserve margins calculation in conjunction with FERC, NERC, and industry stakeholders to account for the increasing number of intermittent, nondispatchable resources.
3. Update reports on the impacts of federal financial interventions and subsidies regularly.
4. Ensure objectivity in the International Energy Outlook (IEO) forecasts.
5. Assess the case for privatization, considering cost savings to taxpayers against EIA's demonstrated neutral data presentation.

The document notes that Congress appropriated $126.8 million for EIA in FY 2021, with a request for approximately $144.5 million for FY 2023.

OFFICE OF INTERNATIONAL AFFAIRS (IA)

The author recommends expanding IA's role and focusing its activities on U.S. international energy security interests. Key suggestions include:

1. Consolidating international energy activities under IA and eliminating the State Department's Bureau of Energy Resources.
2. Developing a strategy for identifying and accessing resources and advancing U.S. economic interests globally.
3. Opposing "climate reparations" agreed to during the 2022 UN climate conference.
4. Identifying U.S. energy security interests and promoting American energy dominance.
5. Strengthening DESAS's position vis-à-vis the Department of State in international energy matters.

ARCTIC ENERGY OFFICE (AE)

The text emphasizes the need for a strategic plan to promote U.S. national security, energy, and economic interests in the Arctic. Recommendations include:
1. Defining American strategic and economic interests in the Arctic Circle.
2. Ensuring AE is clearly focused on identifying U.S. energy interests and foreign activities in the region.
3. Expanding AE's operations in Alaska to encompass broader national energy security interests.
4. Providing a senior Arctic Energy official to the U.S. Arctic Council delegation.

OFFICE OF INTELLIGENCE AND COUNTERINTELLIGENCE (IAC)

The author stresses the need for robust security protocols to protect DOE technology and innovations. Key recommendations include:
1. Improving accountability and utilization of IAC.
2. Appointing a qualified leader with an Intelligence Community background to report directly to the Secretary and Deputy Secretary.
3. Upgrading DESAS's general security posture through the Secretary's direct intervention.

OFFICE OF POLICY (OP)

The text notes that the Office of Policy has taken various roles across different administrations. The author suggests two main reforms:
1. Help develop policy: OP should identify future challenges and develop potential solutions to benefit the American people, as program office appointees are primarily focused on managing their programs.
2. Help ensure policies are properly implemented: OP can assist the Secretary in ensuring consistent implementation of important policy initiatives across multiple program offices.

The author proposes tasking OP with developing a National Energy Security Strategy (NESS) for the Secretary. This strategy would align with the White House National Security Strategy and the DOD National Defense Strategy. However, the text cautions against transforming the strategy into a government-led industrial policy or an economy-wide climate policy.

OFFICE OF TECHNOLOGY TRANSITIONS (OTT)

The document emphasizes OTT's role in ensuring that emerging technologies from DOE and the National Labs are properly supported and protected. Key recommendations include:
1. Ensuring R&D funds are used for projects that protect and advance America's technological edge.
2. Swiftly transferring successful advances to American interests in the private sector, focusing on new natural resource development technologies, artificial intelligence, cybersecurity, and space.
3. Basing OTT's operations on the recognition that new technologies generated by American taxpayers' investment in DOE are a significant national security asset.
4. Increasing oversight and coordination of OTT offices associated with each National Lab to protect work funded by the American people and ensure its commercialization benefits American businesses.

OFFICE OF SCIENCE (SC)

The author advocates for committing the United States to scientific dominance to support national and economic security. Key recommendations for the Office of Science include:
1. Returning to its primary mission of nonpartisan and basic science.
2. Increasing the level of accountability for National Laboratories.
3. Refocusing on mission and eliminating duplication and waste.
4. Properly managing the National Labs' contributions to the private sector, improving access while ensuring economic benefits flow back to taxpayers.

The text notes that the Office of Science was appropriated slightly more than $7 billion in FY 2021, with a request for slightly less than $7.8 billion for FY 2023.

OFFICE OF ENVIRONMENTAL MANAGEMENT (EM)

The text outlines the massive task of cleaning up radioactive waste from nuclear weapons development programs. Key points and recommendations include:
1. EM's cleanup program is the world's largest, with 92 of 107 sites completed.
2. The federal government's environmental liability, largely due to EM, is about 85% of the total in fiscal year 2020.

3. Projected cleanup costs range from $652.4 billion to $887.2 billion.
4. The author criticizes some states and contractors for viewing EM as a jobs program, slowing cleanup efforts.
5. Recommendations include:
   - Accelerating the cleanup, potentially completing all sites by 2035 (except Hanford by 2060).
   - Fully implementing High-Level Waste determination across the DOE complex.
   - Increasing the use of commercial waste disposal.
   - Revisiting the Hanford cleanup's regulatory framework.
   - Establishing more direct leadership and accountability to the Deputy Secretary.
   - Changing EM's culture to promote innovation and completion.

The document notes that EM received slightly less than $7.6 billion in FY 2021, with a budget request of approximately $8.06 billion for FY 2023.

OFFICE OF CIVILIAN RADIOACTIVE WASTE MANAGEMENT (OCRWM)

This section discusses the challenges of managing civilian nuclear waste. Key points and recommendations include:
1. The Nuclear Waste Policy Act of 1982 made the federal government responsible for commercial nuclear waste disposal.
2. The Nuclear Waste Fund holds $46 billion for a permanent waste disposal site.
3. The licensing process for Yucca Mountain as a permanent repository is on hold.
4. Recommendations include:
   - Restarting the Yucca Mountain licensing process.
   - Fixing policy and cost drivers preventing nuclear storage.
   - Developing new Nuclear Waste Fund funding and accounting mechanisms.
   - Reconstituting OCRWM and reestablishing the position of Director.

NATIONAL NUCLEAR SECURITY ADMINISTRATION (NNSA)

The text emphasizes the need to prioritize the design, development, and deployment of new nuclear warheads. Key recommendations include:
1. Continuing to develop new warheads for each branch of the triad (land, sea, and air defenses).
2. Maintaining two production sites for plutonium pits at Los Alamos and Savannah River.
3. Rejecting ratification of the Comprehensive Test Ban Treaty and indicating willingness to conduct nuclear tests if necessary.
4. Reviewing all new Navy, Department of Homeland Security, and U.S. Department of Transportation Maritime Administration construction programs for potential inclusion of nuclear reactor technology.
5. Reviewing non-national security portfolios at the Los Alamos, Lawrence Livermore, and Sandia labs.
6. Reviewing the operations of the Nuclear Weapons Council (NWC).

The document notes that NNSA received $19.7 billion in 2021, with a FY 2023 budget request of $21.4 billion.

FERC: ELECTRIC RELIABILITY AND RESILIENCE

The text discusses the Federal Energy Regulatory Commission's (FERC) role in promoting electric grid reliability. Key issues and recommendations include:
1. Growing reliability problems due to increasing subsidized intermittent renewable generation and lack of dispatchable generation.
2. Need to limit the impact of subsidized renewables on price formation in Regional Transmission Organizations (RTOs).
3. Reforming the application of reserve margins to account for intermittent resources.
4. Recognizing the interdependence of electric generation and natural gas.
5. Expanding resource diversity and reliability.
6. Protecting against cyber and physical attacks on electric infrastructure.

Specific policy recommendations include:
1. Directing RTOs to establish reliability pricing for eligible dispatchable generation resources.
2. Updating the definition and calculation of reserve margins.
3. Expanding and protecting natural gas infrastructure to support electric generation.
4. Supporting resource diversity and reliability through FERC, NERC, and DOE roles.

5. Strengthening security against cyber and physical threats, including banning Chinese-made components and hardening critical infrastructure.

FERC: RTOS/ISOS AND "ELECTRIC POWER MARKETS"

This section critiques the current structure of Regional Transmission Organizations (RTOs) and Independent System Operators (ISOs). Key points include:
1. RTOs are complex regulatory constructs that obscure government interference and preferences for preferred resources.
2. Government preferences and subsidies for resources like wind and solar distort price formation, undermining grid reliability.
3. Customers are not seeing the full economic benefits of non-fuel, subsidized resources.

Policy recommendations include:
1. Reexamining the premise of RTOs to ensure they procure reliable and affordable electricity.
2. Ensuring RTOs return to market fundamentals to serve customers, not special interests.
3. Directing RTOs to pass on the economic benefits of renewables to customers.
4. Ending undue discrimination that allows subsidized resources to distort price formation.
5. Affirming FERC's commitment that states will decide whether to join an RTO.

FERC: ELECTRIC TRANSMISSION

The text discusses FERC's authority over interstate electric transmission. Key issues include:
1. FERC's attempts to facilitate building more long-range transmission lines and socialize costs.
2. The Infrastructure Investment and Jobs Act granting DOE and FERC authority to site and permit high-priority transmission lines.

Recommendations include:
1. Ensuring transmission planning and interconnection processes are resource neutral.
2. Preventing socializing costs for customers who do not benefit from the projects.
3. Stopping cost allocation from becoming a subsidy for generators, such as renewables.
4. Ensuring that transmission buildouts are planned for the benefit of customers.

FERC: NATURAL GAS PIPELINES

This section discusses FERC's role in permitting and regulating interstate natural gas pipelines. Key points include:
1. FERC's responsibility to approve pipelines required by "public convenience and necessity."

2. Opposition from environmentalists making it harder to gain approvals for natural gas pipelines.
3. Conflicting direction from the D.C. Circuit on greenhouse gas (GHG) emissions consideration.

Policy recommendations include:
1. Recommitting FERC to the Natural Gas Act's purpose of providing affordable and reliable natural gas.
2. Limiting FERC's decision-making on pipeline certificates to the question of need for natural gas.
3. Limiting NEPA analysis to the impacts of the actual pipeline, not indirect upstream and downstream effects.
4. Considering how to better protect and compensate property owners affected by pipeline construction.

FERC: LNG EXPORT FACILITIES

The text outlines FERC's role in permitting LNG export facilities and the importance of these facilities for delivering natural gas to global markets. Key issues include:
1. Opposition to LNG exports from climate activists and some domestic manufacturers.
2. Concentration of most LNG export facilities along the Gulf of Mexico.
3. FERC's consideration of policy statements that would include GHG emissions in its reviews.

Recommendations include:
1. FERC should not use environmental issues like climate change as a reason to stop LNG projects.
2. Ensuring timely review, development, and construction of natural gas pipelines needed for domestic use and export.

NUCLEAR REGULATORY COMMISSION

This section discusses the Nuclear Regulatory Commission's (NRC) role in regulating the commercial nuclear industry. Key issues include:
1. NRC remaining a significant cost and regulatory barrier to new nuclear power.
2. Overly prescriptive regulations, especially for well-known light water reactor technologies.

Policy recommendations include:
1. Expediting review and approval of license extensions for existing reactors.
2. Setting clear radiation exposure and protection standards.
3. Working with Congress to reform the NRC's funding approach.
4. Completing Combined Operating Licenses and design certifications for light-water technology within two years.
5. Issuing Early Site Permits within one year for construction on or adjacent to existing reactor sites.

The text notes that in FY 2022, the NRC was required to recover approximately 85 percent of its $887.7 million budget through licensee fees.

CHAPTER 13: ENVIRONMENTAL PROTECTION AGENCY

Mischaracterizing the state of our environment generally and the actual harms reasonably attributable to climate change specifically is a favored tool that the Left uses to scare the American public into accepting their ineffective, liberty-crushing regulations, diminished private property rights, and exorbitant costs – Page 419

Key Policy Proposals

The proposals outlined in the chapter represent a systematic dismantling of the Environmental Protection Agency's (EPA) critical functions and authority, justified under the guise of promoting limited government and cooperative federalism. These proposed changes are not merely administrative tweaks but a concerted effort to strip the EPA of its ability to effectively protect public health and the environment. The consequences of these policies are severe, leading to weakened environmental safeguards, increased pollution, and the erosion of the EPA's foundational mission.

UNDERMINING REGULATORY AUTHORITY

The chapter calls for a dramatic reduction in the EPA's scope and influence, particularly in the Office of Air and Radiation (OAR) and the Office of Water (OW). By proposing to limit the OAR's ability to regulate greenhouse gas emissions and air quality standards, these policies threaten to reverse decades of progress in combating air pollution and climate change. The emphasis on cost-benefit analyses that prioritize economic costs over environmental and public health benefits is a clear tactic to weaken environmental regulations. This approach ignores the overwhelming scientific consensus that the costs of inaction on climate change far exceed the costs of implementing stringent regulations.

Similarly, the proposed changes to the Office of Water aim to redefine what constitutes "navigable waters" under the Clean Water Act (CWA), significantly narrowing the scope of federal protection. This would leave countless streams, wetlands, and other critical water bodies vulnerable to pollution, directly threatening drinking water supplies and aquatic ecosystems. By prioritizing private property rights over environmental protection, these policies would allow polluters to operate with impunity, leading to widespread environmental degradation.

EROSION OF SCIENTIFIC INTEGRITY

The chapter's attack on the Office of Research and Development (ORD) and related science activities is perhaps the most dangerous of all proposed reforms. By advocating for the elimination of the Integrated Risk Information System (IRIS) and the rejection of "precautionary, hazard-based approaches," these policies aim to undermine the scientific foundation upon which the EPA's regulations are built. The proposed shift to a risk-based framework that downplays the potential hazards of chemicals and pollutants is a thinly veiled attempt to deregulate industries that pose significant threats to public health.

The insistence on transparency, while superficially appealing, is being weaponized to challenge well-established scientific models and undermine the credibility of the EPA's research. By rejecting the use of models that consider the social cost of carbon and other long-term environmental impacts, these policies would effectively blind the EPA to the full scope of environmental risks, leading to short-sighted and harmful decision-making.

DECENTRALIZATION AND ITS CONSEQUENCES

The chapter's push to decentralize the EPA's functions by transferring more authority to state and local governments under the banner of cooperative federalism is a recipe for disaster. States vary widely in their capacity and willingness to enforce environmental regulations, and many are heavily influenced by local industries that prioritize profit over public health. This decentralization would lead to a patchwork of regulations, where the most vulnerable communities—often low-income and minority populations—are left unprotected from pollution and environmental hazards.

The proposal to centralize grant distribution and place political appointees in charge of grant-making processes is particularly troubling. This would inject partisan politics into decisions that should be based on science and need, further eroding the EPA's ability to function as an impartial protector of the environment.

FINANCIAL AND ORGANIZATIONAL SABOTAGE

The recommended cuts to the EPA's budget and staffing, particularly in critical areas such as enforcement, research, and legal counsel, are designed to cripple the agency's ability to carry out its mission. The elimination of positions and consolidation of offices will result in the loss of expertise and institutional knowledge, making it nearly impossible for the EPA to respond effectively to environmental crises. Furthermore, the proposed relocation of offices and the suspension of existing contracts will create chaos within the agency, delaying important regulatory actions and allowing polluters to exploit gaps in enforcement.

LONG-TERM ENVIRONMENTAL AND PUBLIC HEALTH RISKS

These policy proposals, if implemented, would have far-reaching consequences for the environment and public health. By weakening the EPA's regulatory authority, undermining scientific research, and decentralizing enforcement, these changes would lead to increased pollution, more frequent environmental disasters, and a rollback of critical protections for air, water, and soil quality. The most vulnerable communities would bear the brunt of these impacts, as weakened federal oversight would leave them exposed to the health risks associated with unchecked industrial pollution.

The proposed reforms to the EPA represent an assault on the agency's ability to fulfill its mission of protecting public health and the environment. These policies would not only reverse decades of progress but would also set a dangerous precedent for future administrations. The consequences of these changes would be felt across the country, leading to a dirtier, more dangerous environment for all Americans.

Summary

This chapter of Mandate for Leadership was written by Mandy M. Gunasekara. The following summary conveys the content of the document accurately and objectively, without endorsing or critiquing the perspectives of the original authors.

The **Mission Statement** of a conservative U.S. Environmental Protection Agency (EPA) focuses on fostering a "better environmental tomorrow" by ensuring clean air, safe water, healthy soil, and thriving communities. The approach centers on enhancing the role of local and state governments, empowering them to lead in environmental efforts with support from federal resources and expertise. This strategy aligns with the principle of cooperative federalism, as embedded in the agency's authorizing statutes, promoting strong relationships between local officials and regulated stakeholders. The emphasis on local leadership is intended to cultivate a culture of compliance and cooperation.

A conservative EPA would measure its success by tangible progress, in contrast to what it describes as the current focus on endless processes. The agency's work would be characterized by true transparency, making its actions and the science behind them accessible to the public. Open-source science would play a key role in building trust and awareness among citizens, ensuring that environmental policies are clear and comprehensible.

The **Mission Statement** also addresses the challenge of establishing a conservative EPA. It acknowledges the skepticism toward the agency, given its historical susceptibility to being used for political purposes, particularly by the Left. However, the statement argues that the EPA must refocus on its core mission: protecting public health and the environment in partnership with states. The agency needs to be redirected from efforts to become an all-encompassing policymaker in energy and land use, returning to its congressionally mandated role as a regulator.

Overview

The **Overview** begins by critiquing the current approach of the Biden Administration's EPA, describing it as a return to the coercive, top-down strategies that characterized the Obama Administration. Gunasekara argues that this administration has reinstated unattainable standards aimed at transitioning away from politically disfavored industries, particularly in the energy sector. This has led to increased costs and challenges for traditional energy sources like coal, oil, and natural gas, while promoting less reliable renewable energy sources. The Biden Administration's policies also extend to agriculture and manufacturing, pushing for the "greening" of these industries, which Gunasekara suggests undermines economic growth and increases regulatory burdens without effectively addressing environmental issues.

Gunasekara further contends that these policies have led to the reintroduction of regulations that kill jobs and inflate bureaucracy without resolving complex environmental problems. It asserts that some of these actions may even harm the environment by driving industries overseas to countries with weaker pollution controls. Additionally, the EPA's budget and staffing have significantly increased under the Biden Administration, leading to what Gunasekara describes as the "highest funding ever" in the agency's history, which it views as excessive and counterproductive.

A notable difference between the Biden and Obama Administrations, as Gunasekara explains, is the diminished role of the EPA Administrator under Biden, with much of the authority shifted to newly appointed "Climate Czars" in the White House. This has left the current EPA Administrator, Michael Regan, relatively sidelined, serving more as a figurehead than an active leader in the administration's environmental agenda.

Gunasekara then explores the idea of a "coopted mission," arguing that the EPA has been used as a tool to expand federal control over the economy under liberal administrations. This expansion is often driven by activists within the agency who push for a global climate agenda, sometimes bypassing legal restraints and Congressional oversight. The pursuit of this broader agenda, Gunasekara suggests, has distracted the EPA from its core mission, leading to missed statutory deadlines and, in some cases, preventable environmental disasters, such as the Flint water crisis and the Gold King Mine spill during the Obama Administration.

Gunasekara also highlights the negative impacts of an activist-driven EPA, including uncertainty in the regulated community, enforcement actions driven by vendettas, and the use of fear-based rhetoric, particularly concerning climate change. It argues that this approach has misled the public into believing they must choose between a healthy environment and a strong economy, a choice Gunasekara describes as false.

Finally, the **Overview** provides a historical context for the EPA, tracing its origins to the environmental degradation caused by rapid industrial activity in the mid-20th century. Gunasekara recalls significant events like the pollution of the Cuyahoga River and the formation of thick, metal-laden haze over cities, which led to the creation of the EPA in 1970 under President Nixon. Initially, the EPA's mission was clear and focused on addressing tangible environmental issues through cooperation with state governments. However, Gunasekara argues that this mission has since been distorted by political agendas, particularly during the Obama Administration, leading to an unnecessarily expansive and politicized EPA that diverges from its original purpose.

Historical Role and Purpose

The **Historical Role and Purpose** section delves into the origins and evolution of the Environmental Protection Agency (EPA), emphasizing its initial mandate and subsequent expansion. Gunasekara begins by describing the environmental conditions that led to the EPA's creation, noting how unchecked industrial activity in the mid-20th century caused significant environmental degradation. Cities across the United States experienced severe pollution, including thick haze filled with harmful metals, and many communities failed to meet basic water quality standards. A striking example was the infamous Cuyahoga River fire in 1969, which was sparked by industrial waste in the water, highlighting the urgent need for organized environmental regulation.

In response to these environmental crises, President Richard Nixon established the EPA on December 2, 1970, through Reorganization Plan No. 3. The agency was tasked with coordinating the fragmented efforts to address pollution and protect public health. Gunasekara highlights Nixon's call for a "coordinated attack on pollutants," which led to the consolidation of various authorities within the EPA, including research, monitoring, standard-setting, and enforcement activities. The agency's mission to protect public health and the environment was thus formalized, and its first Administrator took office on December 4, 1970.

Following the EPA's creation, Congress passed significant legislation that expanded the agency's responsibilities, including the Clean Air Act of 1970 and the Federal Water Pollution Control Act of 1972. These laws gave the EPA substantial authority to regulate air and water pollution, and further amendments, such as the Clean Air Act Amendments of 1990, introduced new regulatory mechanisms. These included cap-and-trade programs for sulfur dioxide control, technology standards for coal-fired power plants, and regulations on hazardous air pollutants, among others. The agency was also involved in implementing international agreements like the Montreal Protocol, aimed at phasing out ozone-depleting substances.

Gunasekara argues that, while the EPA's early efforts were driven by clear mandates and a streamlined structure that respected the role of states, the agency's mission became increasingly politicized over time, particularly during the Obama Administration. The EPA's responsibilities and staffing levels expanded beyond its original congressional mandate, often driven by political goals rather than environmental or public health needs. This expansion is portrayed as unnecessary and counterproductive, deviating from the limited-government approach that initially made the EPA effective.

To restore the EPA's original purpose, Gunasekara advocates for a return to "basics," where the agency's structure and mission are aligned with principles of cooperative federalism and limited government. This would involve significant restructuring to ensure that the EPA supports state and local governments in addressing environmental issues, rather than imposing top-down federal mandates. The emphasis would be on practical, cost-effective solutions to tangible environmental problems, with a focus on accountability, transparency, and the reduction of bureaucratic excess.

Back to Basics

The **Back to Basics** section outlines a proposed restructuring of the Environmental Protection Agency (EPA) to realign it with conservative principles of limited government and cooperative federalism. The section argues that the EPA's mission and structure should be significantly circumscribed to ensure that the agency supports state and local governments in making environmental decisions rather than imposing federal mandates. This approach is described as more effective and consistent with the agency's original purpose.

Key aspects of this restructuring include:

- **State Leadership**: The EPA should prioritize building strong relationships with state and local officials, providing resources and expertise while recognizing that environmental decision-making should primarily rest with those directly impacted. This reflects the principle that local communities are best suited to make decisions about their environment.

- **Accountable Progress**: The focus should be on achieving measurable, tangible improvements in environmental quality through practical, cost-effective solutions. Regulatory efforts should be transparent, with progress tracked by simple, publicly available metrics that clearly demonstrate the impact of environmental initiatives.

- **Streamlined Process**: The section calls for the elimination of duplicative, wasteful, or unnecessary programs that do not directly contribute to the EPA's mission. A more structured management system should be established to help state and local governments protect public health and the environment efficiently.

- **Healthy, Thriving Communities**: The EPA should consider the economic impact of its actions on local communities, aiming to minimize costs and support community prosperity alongside environmental protection.

- **Compliance Before Enforcement**: The EPA should foster cooperative relationships with regulated entities, particularly small businesses, by emphasizing compliance over enforcement. This approach would encourage voluntary adherence to environmental regulations through support and guidance rather than punitive measures.

- **Transparent Science and Regulatory Analysis**: The EPA should commit to making all scientific studies and analyses that inform regulatory decisions publicly available for comment. This transparency would help build public trust and ensure that regulations are based on sound, unbiased science.

The section concludes that these reforms would return the EPA to its foundational principles, enhancing its effectiveness while respecting the autonomy of state and local governments. By focusing on clear, measurable outcomes and reducing bureaucratic excess, the agency could better fulfill its mission of protecting public health and the environment without overstepping its intended role.

Administrator's Office and Reorganization Responsibility

This section outlines the necessary changes within the Administrator's Office (AO) of the Environmental Protection Agency (EPA) to implement a conservative agenda. Gunasekara argues that the EPA requires a major reorganization to align its operations with the principles of limited government and cooperative federalism. The Deputy Chief of Staff for Policy, a position within the AO, is proposed to be renamed as the Deputy Chief of Staff for Regulatory Improvement. This role would oversee the reorganization process, ensuring that the agency's structure and functions are consistent with a conservative vision for the EPA.

Key reorganization actions include:

- **Returning Functions to the AO**: The environmental justice function, currently managed by a separate office, would be integrated back into the AO. Similarly, the Office of Enforcement and Compliance Assistance would be dismantled, with its responsibilities returned to the media offices (air, water, land, etc.). This is intended to better align enforcement with standard-setting and eliminate what is described as a mismatch between regulation and implementation.

- **Using Enforcement to Ensure Compliance**: The reorganization would focus enforcement efforts on achieving compliance with existing regulations rather than pursuing extra statutory objectives. This reflects the principle of limited government, where the EPA's role is confined to enforcing laws as written, without expanding its reach through administrative actions.

- **Relocating Regional Offices**: The EPA's regional offices would be relocated to areas where they can be more accessible to the communities they serve. This would also aim to deliver cost savings to taxpayers, as the offices would be positioned in more cost-effective locations.

- **Restructuring the Office of International and Tribal Affairs**: The international liaison functions would be returned to the relevant media offices, with the remaining functions restructured into a more focused American Indian Environmental Office. This would concentrate the EPA's efforts on domestic issues, particularly those affecting American Indian communities.

- **Eliminating Redundant Offices**: The Office of Public Engagement and Environmental Education would be reabsorbed into the Office of Public Affairs, and the Office of Children's Health Protection and the Office of Small and Disadvantaged Business Utilization would be integrated into the media offices. This consolidation is intended to streamline operations and reduce unnecessary bureaucracy.

- **Reviewing the Grants Program**: The EPA's grants program would be reviewed to ensure that taxpayer funds are directed toward organizations that focus on tangible environmental improvements, free from political influence.
- **Resetting Science Advisory Boards**: The reorganization would also involve resetting the science advisory boards to ensure that they reflect a diversity of scientific viewpoints and are free from conflicts of interest. This is part of the broader effort to make the EPA's decision-making process more transparent and accountable.
- **Restoring the Guidance Portal**: The guidance portal, which provides clarity on regulatory standards, would be reinstated to ensure that affected entities have a clear understanding of the EPA's expectations. This action is aimed at reducing regulatory uncertainty and promoting compliance.

The section concludes with a recommendation for drafting a Day One Executive Order for the incoming President. This order would explicitly require a reconsideration of the EPA's structure to ensure that it is aligned with its mission of creating a better environmental future with clean air, safe water, healthy soil, and thriving communities. The reorganization is presented as essential for achieving this mission while adhering to conservative principles.

Office of Air and Radiation (OAR)

This section addresses the role and responsibilities of the Office of Air and Radiation (OAR) within the EPA, outlining a series of proposed reforms aimed at aligning the office with a conservative agenda. OAR is responsible for developing national programs, policies, and regulations to control air pollution and radiation exposure, with its statutory authority primarily derived from the Clean Air Act (CAA). However, Gunasekara argues that under liberal administrations, OAR's responsibilities have been expanded beyond their original intent, leading to overreach and legal challenges.

The section advocates for a reformed OAR that focuses on its core mission of limiting and minimizing air pollutants in partnership with state governments. Several cross-cutting reforms are proposed to ensure that OAR operates within its statutory boundaries and respects the role of states:
- **Cost-Effectiveness and Transparency**: Gunasekara calls for the issuance of a rule to ensure that all OAR actions consistently and transparently consider costs. When conducting cost-benefit analyses, OAR should use appropriate discount rates, focus on the direct benefits of reducing the targeted pollutant, separately identify "co-benefits," and acknowledge the uncertainties involved in quantifying benefits. This is intended to ensure that regulations are economically justified and based on clear, transparent analysis.
- **Employment and Plant-Closure Effects**: The section emphasizes the need for OAR to comply with Congress's direction under CAA § 321 to evaluate the employment and plant-closure effects of air regulations continuously. This requirement reflects the principle that environmental regulations should not unduly harm economic activity or lead to job losses without sufficient justification.
- **Adherence to Special Constraints**: OAR is urged to fully observe the special constraints placed on air rules by Congress under CAA § 307(d). The section insists that OAR respect congressional intent when developing air regulations, ensuring that the rules align with the specific provisions of the Clean Air Act.
- **Limitations on Third-Party Authority**: Gunasekara argues for the removal of any regulations or requirements that grant third parties enforcement authority typically reserved for the EPA. An example given is the oil and gas supplemental regulation, which created a Super-Emitter Response Program allowing third parties to act as EPA enforcers. The section contends that such provisions should be eliminated to ensure that regulatory authority remains within the EPA as intended by law.

The section also details specific policy actions concerning the National Ambient Air Quality Standards (NAAQS), climate change, regulation of hydrofluorocarbons (HFCs), and mobile source regulation by the Office of Transportation and Air Quality. These policies include:
- **NAAQS**: Revising regional haze rules and ensuring that the Good Neighbor Program does not overregulate upwind states, which could violate the statute. The section also calls for ensuring that the Clean Air Scientific Advisory Committee (CASAC) considers all required factors, including social and economic effects.
- **Climate Change**: Proposing the removal of the Greenhouse Gas Reporting Program for any unregulated source category and updating the 2009 endangerment finding. Gunasekara also advocates establishing a significant emissions rate (SER) for greenhouse gases.
- **Regulating HFCs**: Gunasekara recommends repealing the Biden Administration's implementing regulations for the AIM Act, which it

describes as unnecessarily stringent and costly. It also suggests resisting new restrictions that could increase consumer costs.
- **Mobile Source Regulation**: The section urges the EPA to review and revise greenhouse gas standards for cars, including considering the lifecycle emissions of electric vehicles and their environmental impacts. It also calls for restoring California's waiver only for issues specific to the state, like ground-level ozone, rather than global climate issues.

The section concludes with recommendations for air permitting reforms under the New Source Review (NSR) and Title V operating permits, as well as reforms to CAA Sections 111 and 112. These include ensuring that efficiency improvements within a facility do not trigger new permitting requirements and defending the position that petitions to object to Title V should not be used to challenge previous state decisions.

The proposed changes are presented as necessary to streamline OAR's operations, reduce regulatory overreach, and ensure that air and radiation regulations are cost-effective, transparent, and within the bounds of statutory authority.

Office of Water (OW)

The **Office of Water (OW)** section discusses the role and responsibilities of the EPA's Office of Water, which is tasked with ensuring safe drinking water and maintaining healthy aquatic ecosystems under the Clean Water Act (CWA) and the Safe Drinking Water Act (SDWA). The section outlines several key reforms aimed at addressing what it views as regulatory overreach and inefficiencies within OW, particularly regarding the infringement on private property rights and the overuse of guidance documents as quasi-regulatory tools.

- **Guidance on Guidance**: Gunasekara criticizes OW for its heavy reliance on outdated and often ambiguous guidance documents, which are sometimes treated as if they have the force of law. It argues that this practice leads to a lack of transparency and good governance. To address this, the section calls for strict enforcement of the 2019 "Office of Water Policy for Draft Documents" memorandum, which mandates that guidance documents should be clearly identified as non-binding and that they should not remain in draft form for extended periods. This is intended to ensure that OW's guidance is transparent, well-defined, and does not overstep legal boundaries.
- **Compliance with Statutory Deadlines**: Gunasekara emphasizes the importance of OW adhering to statutory deadlines for regulatory actions. It proposes that senior management should be made aware of any delays and should consider alternative courses of action if deadlines cannot be met. This focus on meeting deadlines is aimed at improving the efficiency and accountability of OW's regulatory processes.
- **Regulatory Repeal and Reissuance**: Depending on the outcomes of ongoing legal challenges and potential Supreme Court rulings, particularly concerning the Waters of the United States (WOTUS) and CWA Section 401, the section suggests that OW should pursue the repeal and reissuance of certain regulations. The goal is to provide greater clarity and regulatory certainty, especially regarding what constitutes "navigable waters" under the CWA, while respecting private property rights.
- **New Policies**: Several new regulatory initiatives are proposed, including:
  - **WOTUS Rule**: A rule that clarifies the definition of "navigable waters" to ensure it aligns with the Supreme Court's interpretation in *Rapanos v. United States*. This rule would define WOTUS to include only relatively permanent, standing, or continuously flowing bodies of water, thereby excluding intermittent streams and ditches from federal jurisdiction.
  - **CWA Section 401**: A rule to streamline the water quality certification process under CWA Section 401, limiting the scope to discharges from point sources into navigable waters and focusing on water quality factors consistent with specific CWA provisions.
  - **CWA Section 308**: A rule to enforce a clear and consistent time limit for actions under CWA Section 308.
  - **Criminal Negligence Standards**: A rule to clarify the standard for criminal negligence under CWA Sections 402 and 404, to prevent overreach in enforcement actions.
  - **Nutrient Trading**: A rule to promote nutrient trading that uses incentives rather than punitive measures to encourage compliance with nutrient management requirements.
- **Budget Considerations**: While the overall goal is to reduce government spending, the section acknowledges the need for targeted increases in funding for the Clean Water Act needs survey. This survey is critical for determining how congressional appropriations for state revolving funds, which support water infrastructure projects, are distributed. Gunasekara argues that the program is currently underfunded, leading to inefficient

allocation of resources, and that increased funding would help address critical water infrastructure needs more effectively.

- **Personnel Management**: The section suggests reshuffling Senior Executive Service (SES) employees within OW to improve efficiency and placing more emphasis on regional offices. This redistribution of personnel is intended to ensure that resources are more effectively allocated to address pressing water issues across the country.

Office of Land and Emergency Management (OLEM)

The **Office of Land and Emergency Management (OLEM)** section details the mission, functions, and proposed reforms for the EPA office responsible for managing waste, cleaning up contaminated sites, and responding to environmental emergencies. OLEM oversees key statutes such as the Resource Conservation and Recovery Act (RCRA) for waste management and the Comprehensive Environmental Response, Compensation, and Liability Act (CERCLA), commonly known as Superfund, for cleaning up hazardous waste sites.

Gunasekara emphasizes that OLEM's primary focus should be on executing cleanups rather than creating policies. The section proposes several reforms to improve efficiency, reduce bureaucratic overhead, and focus on tangible environmental results:

- **Project Management Over Policy Creation**: Gunasekara argues that OLEM staff should prioritize project management to accelerate cleanups of contaminated sites, particularly under CERCLA and RCRA. This focus on productivity over process is seen as essential for delivering timely environmental benefits to communities affected by pollution. Gunasekara suggests that project managers should receive specialized training in project management to enhance their effectiveness.

- **Adoption of Lean Management Practices**: The section recommends the adoption of the EPA's Lean Management System (ELMS) across all OLEM programs. ELMS is intended to streamline processes, reduce inefficiencies, and improve the overall performance of the office. By focusing on continuous improvement and eliminating waste, OLEM can better allocate resources to high-priority cleanups.

- **Delegation of CERCLA Authority**: Gunasekara proposes delegating all CERCLA authority from the EPA Administrator to the OLEM Assistant Administrator, rather than directly to Regional Administrators. This change aims to centralize decision-making and ensure consistent application of CERCLA across regions.

- **Increased State and Tribal Involvement**: The section advocates for finding more opportunities to transfer work and funding to states and tribes, thereby empowering local entities to manage cleanups more effectively. This aligns with the broader conservative principle of cooperative federalism, where local governments are seen as better suited to handle environmental issues within their jurisdictions.

New Policies:

- **Superfund Reforms**: The section outlines several proposed changes to the Superfund program, aimed at making cleanups faster and more efficient:
  - **Modernization of the National Contingency Plan (NCP)**: Revising the NCP to incorporate lessons learned from over 40 years of cleanup efforts, with the goal of streamlining the process.
  - **Increased Use of CERCLA Removal Authority**: Encouraging the use of CERCLA removal authority to execute short-term cleanups, which can quickly provide clarity and finality for responsible parties and return cleaned-up land to communities.
  - **Standardization of Applicable or Relevant and Appropriate Requirements (ARARs)**: Streamlining the determination of ARARs by applying common standards across multiple sites, rather than on a site-by-site basis.
  - **Revisiting Groundwater Cleanup Standards**: Updating groundwater cleanup regulations and policies to address challenges posed by pervasive contaminants like PFAS (per- and polyfluoroalkyl substances).
  - **Lead Cleanup Plan**: Developing a 10-year plan to address lead contamination at existing cleanup sites, with clear benchmarks and milestones for public and congressional oversight.
- **RCRA Reforms**: For waste management under RCRA, Gunasekara proposes:
  - **Creation of a Post-Closure Care Permit**: Tailoring permits specifically for post-closure obligations to simplify the regulatory burden.
  - **Encouraging Recycling and Reuse**: Modifying regulations to support resource efficiency by making it easier to transport materials to legitimate recyclers or manufacturers. This

includes creating clear pathways to exclude certain materials from being classified as waste.
  - **E-Manifest Modernization**: Transitioning to a fully electronic manifest system for hazardous waste tracking, eliminating paper records and streamlining data input.
- **Risk Management Program (RMP) Revisions**: If the Biden Administration finalizes a new RMP rule, the section suggests revising it to reflect amendments made in 2019, which aimed to protect sensitive information while ensuring safety.

Personnel and Structural Changes:

- **Laboratory Consolidation**: The section recommends eliminating or consolidating regional laboratories and allowing OLEM to use other government or private labs based on expertise and cost. This consolidation is intended to create resource efficiencies and focus on the highest-value opportunities.
- **Communications and Non-Core Functions**: It suggests consolidating non-core functions like communications and congressional relations into one suboffice within OLEM, allowing the subject-matter offices to concentrate on fieldwork execution.
- **Emergency Management Function Realignment**: Gunasekara proposes eliminating the Office of Emergency Management (OEM) as a stand-alone entity and redistributing its functions. For example, the emergency management function could be moved to the Homeland Security office within the EPA Administrator's office, while the removal authority could be integrated into the Office of Superfund Remediation and Technology Innovation (OSRTI).

Budget Considerations:
The section concludes by noting that, while the overall goal is to reduce government spending, OLEM's programs offer the best opportunity to use taxpayer dollars effectively by focusing on EPA's core mission of cleaning up contamination.

Office of Chemical Safety and Pollution Prevention (OCSPP)

The **Office of Chemical Safety and Pollution Prevention (OCSPP)** section addresses the EPA office responsible for regulating chemicals and pesticides under the Toxic Substances Control Act (TSCA) and the Federal Insecticide, Fungicide, and Rodenticide Act (FIFRA). The section outlines key reforms needed to ensure that the OCSPP operates in a manner consistent with conservative principles, emphasizing risk-based decision-making and efficiency in regulatory processes.

Needed Reforms and New Policy in OPPT (Chemicals):

- **Risk-Based Decision-Making**: Gunasekara argues for a shift away from precautionary, hazard-based approaches, like those used in the Integrated Risk Information System (IRIS), towards a risk-based framework. This would ensure that regulatory decisions are grounded in actual risk assessments rather than theoretical hazards, allowing for more scientifically sound and economically justified outcomes.
- **Focused Scope of Chemical Evaluations**: The scope of chemical evaluations should be limited to pathways of exposure not covered by other EPA program offices or environmental statutes. This would prevent "scope creep" and allow evaluations to be completed more efficiently, meeting statutory deadlines.
- **Timely New Chemical Evaluations**: The section emphasizes the importance of conducting new chemical evaluations promptly, consistent with statutory requirements. This would involve resetting the review process for new chemicals to ensure that they are completed within the timelines mandated by law, supporting the competitiveness of U.S. manufacturers.
- **Real-World Use Consideration**: When assessing conditions of use for risk evaluations, the EPA should account for the real-world application of chemicals, assuming that workplaces follow all Occupational Safety and Health Administration (OSHA) requirements, including the use of personal protective equipment (PPE).
- **Right-Sizing TSCA Fees**: The TSCA fee rule should be adjusted to align with the actual tasks completed by the EPA within statutory timelines, ensuring that fees are not inflated to cover inefficiencies or overreach by the agency.
- **Privatization of the Safer Choice Program**: Gunasekara suggests transitioning the Safer Choice program, which promotes safer chemical products, to the private sector, reducing the EPA's direct involvement.

Needed Reforms and New Policy in OPP (Pesticides):

- **Use of Agricultural and State Data**: The section advocates for the Office of Pesticide Programs (OPP) to rely on Department of Agriculture and state data reflecting actual pesticide use in its registration reviews and Endangered Species Act (ESA) analyses. This would ensure that pesticide regulations are based on accurate and current information.

- **Rigorous Data Standards**: OPP should establish data standards requiring that information relied upon in pesticide reviews be of the same quality and transparency as the original testing data conducted by registrants. This would help maintain the robustness of EPA's reviews and analyses.

- **ESA Reform for Pesticides**: Gunasekara calls for reforming how the ESA is applied to pesticide regulation. Currently, the ESA does not allow for cost-benefit balancing, which FIFRA permits, leading to overly restrictive pesticide use that limits tools available to growers. The section argues for a more balanced approach that considers both the risks and benefits of pesticide use.

- **Deference to OPP Expertise**: Other EPA program offices, such as the Office of Research and Development (ORD), should defer to OPP on toxicity issues related to pesticides. This would prevent redundancy and ensure that decisions are based on the expertise and rigorous testing requirements already in place within OPP.

- **Interagency Review of Pesticide Withdrawals**: When the EPA withdraws pesticide tolerances and registrations, such actions should undergo a coordinated interagency review managed by the Office of Management and Budget (OMB). This would provide an additional layer of oversight and ensure that the decisions are balanced and well-considered.

Budget Considerations:

The section acknowledges that the Biden Administration has expanded the scope of regulatory actions within OPPT and OPP but notes that both programs claim they lack sufficient resources. However, Gunasekara criticizes OPPT for inefficiency and suggests that the program may not be capable of effectively using additional funds. It advocates for "guardrails" and third-party audits to accompany any budget increases, particularly in the Pesticide Registration Improvement Act (PRIA) or other mechanisms.

Grower groups, in particular, have expressed concerns about the EPA's ability to conduct science-based risk assessments and to balance risks and benefits as required by FIFRA. Gunasekara underscores the need for stringent oversight and accountability in any additional funding allocations to these programs.

The proposed reforms aim to streamline the OCSPP's operations, ensuring that chemical and pesticide regulations are based on sound science, timely execution, and a balanced consideration of risks and benefits. By aligning the office's activities with statutory requirements and reducing unnecessary regulatory burdens, the section argues that the EPA can better support both environmental protection and economic growth.

Office of Research and Development (ORD) and Related Science Activities

The **Office of Research and Development (ORD)** section outlines the role of the EPA's scientific research arm and proposes significant reforms aimed at ensuring that ORD's activities align with statutory authority, transparency, and conservative principles. Gunasekara critiques the ORD and other related science activities within the EPA for being precautionary, bloated, and often politically driven, rather than focused purely on scientific goals.

Needed Reforms: Day One Priorities:

- **Congressional Authorization**: The section argues that the EPA should notify Congress that it will no longer conduct any ongoing or planned science activities that lack clear and current congressional authorization. This directive should be reinforced in the President's first budget request, signaling a commitment to limited government and adherence to statutory mandates.

- **Regulatory Freeze**: A regulatory review and freeze should be implemented on Inauguration Day, with a specific emphasis on ensuring that EPA actions, including quasi-regulatory activities like assessments, determinations, standards, and guidance, undergo proper notice-and-comment procedures. This freeze is intended to prevent unauthorized or politically motivated actions from proceeding without proper oversight.

- **Contract Review**: Gunasekara calls for a pause and review of all EPA contracts above $100,000, particularly focusing on major external peer reviews and regulatory models. This review would ensure that expenditures are justified and that contracts serve legitimate scientific purposes rather than advancing political agendas.

- **Public Input on Scientific Misconduct**: The section advocates for soliciting public input to identify areas where the EPA has inconsistently assessed risk, failed to use the best available science, or participated in research misconduct. This initiative would empower citizens to hold the agency accountable and improve the integrity of its scientific work.

- **Elimination of Unauthorized Inputs**: The section recommends eliminating the use of unauthorized regulatory inputs, such as the social cost of carbon, proprietary models, and unrealistic climate scenarios (e.g., those based on Representative Concentration Pathway 8.5). These inputs are viewed as lacking transparency and contributing to flawed regulatory decisions.

Personnel Reforms:

- **Reform-Minded Leadership**: Gunasekara emphasizes the need for a reform-minded Assistant Administrator for Research and Development, supported by a Science Adviser reporting directly to the Administrator and a team of senior political appointees. These positions should prioritize management, oversight, and execution skills over personal scientific output, ensuring that ORD's activities align with broader administrative goals.

- **Review of Advisory Bodies**: The section calls for a suspension and review of EPA advisory bodies, many of which are criticized for lacking independence, balance, and geographic and viewpoint diversity. This review would help ensure that advisory committees are not dominated by politically motivated perspectives and that they contribute to transparent, science-based decision-making.

- **Reevaluation of Title 42 Hiring Authority**: Gunasekara suggests eliminating the use of Title 42 hiring authority, which allows ORD to pay certain employees above the standard civil service scale. This measure is intended to reduce costs and ensure that personnel decisions are based on merit rather than financial incentives.

- **Streamlining Laboratory Structure**: A plan to streamline and reform the EPA's laboratory structure is proposed to address inefficiencies and improve coordination across the agency's scientific research facilities.

Budget: Back-to-Basics Approach:

- **Rejection of Unauthorized Activities**: The section argues for the immediate rejection of all ORD and related science activities that have not been authorized by Congress. In FY 2022, the EPA's science and technology activities totaled nearly $730 million, with the ORD's budget request for FY 2023 seeking funding for more than 1,850 employees. Gunasekara critiques the lack of clear congressional authority for many of these activities and suggests that significant budget cuts are necessary.

- **Elimination of Questionable Programs**: The section identifies several ORD offices and programs, including the Integrated Risk Information System (IRIS), as candidates for elimination. IRIS, in particular, is criticized for setting "safe levels" of chemical exposure based on questionable science, resulting in significant economic costs. Gunasekara highlights broad criticism of IRIS from stakeholders, including Congress, the National Academies of Science, Engineering, and Medicine (NASEM), and the U.S. Government Accountability Office (GAO), as evidence of the need for its reform or elimination.

Needed EPA Advisory Body Reforms:

- **Advisory Committee Oversight**: The section emphasizes the outsized influence of EPA's 21 federal advisory committees, which often shape scientific and regulatory policy. Under the Biden Administration, Gunasekara argues, these committees have been purged of balanced perspectives and have become dominated by politically motivated views. The section calls for reforms to ensure that advisory bodies are independent, balanced, transparent, and geographically diverse.

Science Policy Reforms:

- **Citizen Science and Scrutiny**: Gunasekara encourages the EPA to embrace citizen science by deputizing the public to scrutinize the agency's scientific work, particularly in identifying data flaws and research misconduct. This would democratize oversight and ensure greater accountability in the EPA's scientific activities.

- **Shift Misconduct Evaluation**: Responsibility for evaluating scientific misconduct should be moved away from the EPA's Office of Scientific Integrity, which Gunasekara suggests is too closely aligned with environmental activists, to an independent body.

- **Incentives for Identifying Flaws**: The section proposes working with Congress to create incentives, similar to those under the False Claims Act, for the public to identify scientific flaws and research misconduct. This would help protect taxpayers from the costs associated with flawed or unnecessary scientific activities.

- **Rejection of Nontransparent Models**: Gunasekara strongly criticizes the EPA's reliance on proprietary, black-box models for key regulations, arguing that these models lack transparency and prevent the public from understanding the agency's analysis. It calls for a rejection of these models in favor of more open and reproducible scientific methods.

- **Default to Less Restrictive Regulations**: In cases of scientific uncertainty, the section advocates for defaulting to less restrictive regulatory outcomes, rather than relying on precautionary models that may overestimate risks. This approach is intended to balance environmental protection with economic considerations.

Legislative Reforms:

- **Congressional Review Act**: Gunasekara suggests that Congress should use the Congressional Review Act to disapprove of EPA regulations and other quasi-regulatory actions that lack proper authorization or transparency.

- **Advisory Board Reform**: Legislative reforms should be pursued to ensure the independence, balance, and transparency of EPA advisory boards. Gunasekara calls for building on recent bipartisan proposals to increase transparency and public participation in these bodies.

- **Rejection of Funds for Unauthorized Programs**: The section recommends that Congress refuse to fund EPA programs, such as IRIS, that have not been authorized, as well as unauthorized peer review activities.

- **Repeal or Reform of Outdated Statutes**: Gunasekara argues for the repeal or reform of outdated environmental statutes, including the Global Change Research Act of 1990, which it claims has been misused for political purposes.

American Indian Office (AIO)

The **American Indian Office (AIO)** section discusses the role and necessary reforms for the EPA's office dedicated to supporting federally recognized sovereign Indian nations in managing their environmental protection programs. The AIO administers the Indian Environmental General Assistance Program, a program created by Congress in 1992 to help tribes develop the capacity to manage their own environmental programs, particularly in solid and hazardous waste management.

Needed Reforms:

- **Elevation of AIO's Status**: Gunasekara advocates for significantly elevating the AIO to a stand-alone Assistant Administrator office within the EPA. This change would demonstrate the agency's commitment to addressing environmental issues in Indian Country and ensure that tribal matters receive the attention they deserve. The Assistant Administrator position would be politically appointed and Senate-confirmed, ideally held by someone with strong ties to a federally recognized tribe.

- **Relocation of AIO Headquarters**: The section suggests moving the AIO headquarters from Washington, D.C., to a location in the American West, closer to the majority of tribal nations. Potential locations include Oklahoma City, Oklahoma; Dallas, Texas; or Denver, Colorado. The rationale for this move is that these areas are home to numerous tribes and are closer to EPA regional offices, making the AIO more accessible to the communities it serves. Oklahoma, in particular, is highlighted as the tribal center of America, home to 39 federally recognized tribes, including the "Five Civilized Tribes."

New Policies:

- **Centralization of Tribal Affairs**: The section proposes that all EPA tribal grants and related matters should be managed centrally by the AIO, making it a one-stop-shop for all tribal affairs. This centralization would streamline processes and improve the efficiency and effectiveness of EPA's support to tribal nations.

Budget and Personnel:

- **Leadership and Staffing**: The AIO would be led by a politically appointed Assistant Administrator, supported by political deputies and staff. These positions would ensure that the AIO has the necessary leadership to carry out its mission effectively. Gunasekara also suggests that career EPA tribal staff currently located in regional offices should be placed under the full authority of the AIO and its Assistant Administrator, rather than being spread across various regional offices. This reorganization is intended to consolidate expertise and improve the coordination of tribal environmental programs.

Office of General Counsel (OGC)

The **Office of General Counsel (OGC)** section outlines the key reforms needed for the EPA's legal office, which serves as the chief legal adviser to the agency's policymaking officials. OGC also provides legal support for regional actions and enforcement litigation, often representing the EPA in court alongside the Department of Justice. The section stresses the importance of OGC in maintaining legal consistency across the agency and ensuring that the EPA's actions are grounded in sound legal principles.

Needed Reforms and New Policies:

- **Review of Environmental Justice (EJ) and Title VI Authority**: The section argues that the Biden Administration has expanded the EPA's use of Environmental Justice (EJ) and Title VI of the Civil Rights Act of 1964 beyond their traditional legal limits. It suggests that EJ should be redefined as a tool to prioritize environmental protection efforts in communities with the greatest need, rather than as a broad mandate that could lead to race-based discrimination. The section calls for a pause and review of all ongoing EJ and Title VI actions to ensure they are consistent with upcoming Supreme Court decisions, particularly in light of the expected guidance on race-based discrimination in the *Students for Fair Admissions v. University of North Carolina* case.

- **Legal Consistency**: Gunasekara emphasizes the importance of ensuring that all EPA offices speak with one legal voice, particularly on key interpretative issues. To achieve this, the section proposes that all attorneys with the authority to represent the EPA be housed within OGC, rather than scattered across different offices. This consolidation would prevent inconsistent legal positions from emerging within the agency. Gunasekara identifies several offices where legal functions should be realigned under OGC, including:

  - **Office of Enforcement and Compliance Assurance (OECA)**: Established during the Clinton Administration, OECA's attorneys should be moved to OGC to ensure legal consistency. Non-attorney staff in OECA could be transferred to relevant program offices, such as the Office of Air and Radiation (OAR).

  - **Office of Congressional and Intergovernmental Affairs (OCIR)**: OCIR employees should not take legal positions; instead, OGC should assert EPA legal positions in consultation with agency clients and White House Counsel, particularly in matters of congressional oversight.

  - **Office of Environmental Justice and External Civil Rights (OEJECR)**: Established under the Biden Administration, this office's legal functions should be transferred back to OGC, and non-legal staff should return to the Administrator's office.

  - **Offices of Regional Counsel (ORCs)**: Legal positions taken by ORCs should be coordinated and approved by OGC and appropriate regional leadership to avoid inconsistencies in legal interpretations.

- **Non-Interference with NEPA**: The section advises that the EPA should refrain from publicly undermining the National Environmental Policy Act (NEPA) process at other agencies and should instead focus on providing constructive technical support during interagency reviews.

Personnel:

- **Organizational and Telework Review**: The section suggests reviewing OGC's resources to consider consolidating attorney functions and leadership into a new Cross-Cutting Issues Law Office. It also recommends a review of telework policies and the permanent duty stations of attorneys, as well as the potential rotation of Senior Executive Service (SES) managers within OGC and ORCs to other EPA offices.

- **Monitoring External Communications**: Gunasekara advises that all external communications conveying a legal position should be monitored, and public events where the agency's legal position is presented should require specific approval to ensure consistency and accuracy.

Budget:

- **Increased Funding for Consolidated Legal Functions**: The section acknowledges that OGC's budget will need to increase to accommodate the consolidation of legal functions from other EPA offices. It also suggests reassessing duplicative skill sets within OGC to allow for attrition if necessary, and allocating resources for regional recruiting to increase geographic diversity from law schools in each state.

Office of Mission Support (OMS)

The **Office of Mission Support (OMS)** section focuses on the EPA office responsible for overseeing the agency's core administrative functions, including facilities management, acquisition activities (contracts), grants management, human capital, information technology, and information management. The section outlines key reforms aimed at increasing efficiency, reducing ideological bias in grant distribution, and improving the overall customer experience for internal stakeholders, the public, and other government agencies.

Grant Reform:

- **Ideologically Neutral Grant Distribution**: The section criticizes the current practice of awarding EPA grants based on ideological preferences, which often results in numerous small-dollar grants being spread across many grantees, while larger grants are funneled to elite academic institutions.

These grants, according to Gunasekara, frequently fund projects with little relevance to environmental improvements and instead support radical environmental research. The proposed reform emphasizes the need to prioritize grants based on genuine need rather than ideological alignment or academic prestige.

- **Pause and Review of Grants**: Gunasekara recommends instituting a pause and review process for all grants above a certain threshold to ensure they are awarded to projects that will tangibly improve the environment. This review would help eliminate wasteful spending and ensure that taxpayer dollars are used effectively.
- **Political Oversight of Grantmaking**: The section suggests placing a political appointee in charge of the grants office to oversee the distribution of grants, ensuring that they are allocated to those most in need and towards projects with clear, measurable environmental benefits.
- **Capping ORD Grants**: The Office of Research and Development (ORD) would see a cap placed on the number and dollar amounts of grants it can award. Additionally, these grants would be subject to review by the Administrator's office to ensure alignment with broader EPA goals and statutory requirements.

Budget:
Gunasekara does not explicitly detail changes to the OMS budget but implies that reforms could lead to cost savings by reducing inefficiencies and ensuring that grants are awarded more strategically. These budgetary adjustments would align OMS spending with the agency's mission to support environmental improvements and economic efficiency.

Office of the Chief Financial Officer (OCFO)

The **Office of the Chief Financial Officer (OCFO)** section outlines the responsibilities and necessary reforms for the EPA's financial management office, which is tasked with formulating and managing the agency's budget, coordinating strategic planning, developing performance and accountability reports, and implementing the Government Performance and Results Act (GPRA). The section emphasizes the need for reforms to streamline financial operations, improve accountability, and align the OCFO's activities with conservative fiscal principles.

Needed Reforms:

- **Diversification of Audit Teams**: The section notes that the EPA has been audited by the agency's Inspector General for decades, far beyond the norm for private-sector financial audits. It suggests that audit teams should be diversified to bring fresh perspectives and improve the effectiveness of financial oversight. This reform aims to ensure that the EPA's financial practices are rigorously scrutinized and that any inefficiencies or irregularities are promptly addressed.
- **Staffing and Space Consolidation**: The section advocates for a review and streamlining of staffing assignments, particularly at the senior level, within the OCFO. This would involve consolidating office space to reduce costs and improve efficiency. For example, the section highlights that six different offices currently require six separate security contracts to protect employees, suggesting that a single contract would suffice and result in significant cost savings.

New Policies:

- **Review of Travel and Reimbursement Policies**: The section recommends aligning the EPA's travel and reimbursement policies with industry best practices to ensure that these policies are cost-effective and in line with the agency's mission. This would likely involve a comprehensive review of existing policies to identify areas where costs can be reduced without compromising the effectiveness of agency operations.

Personnel:

- **Political Leadership**: The Deputy Chief Financial Officer position is currently reserved for a career official, but the section suggests evaluating whether this position should be opened to political appointees. Gunasekara argues that filling key positions such as Associate CFO, Special Advisor, and other senior roles with political appointees could ensure that the OCFO's activities align more closely with the broader goals of the administration. Additionally, the section proposes establishing a new political leadership position for an Appropriations Liaison, currently overseen by career employees, to manage the agency's interactions with Congress regarding budget matters.

Budget:

- **Simplification of the Budget Request**: The section calls for efforts to simplify the EPA's budget request process to improve transparency and enhance public understanding of the agency's work. By making the budget request more straightforward and accessible, the EPA could foster greater accountability and ensure that its financial practices are more closely aligned with its environmental mission.

Conclusion

In the **Conclusion** of Chapter 13, the author advocates for a restructuring of the EPA to align it with conservative principles, arguing that this approach will lead to "a better environmental future without unintended consequences." Gunasekara asserts that a smaller, more focused EPA will reduce unnecessary expenditures by regulated entities, thereby freeing up resources for "investment in economic development and job creation," which are essential for "thriving communities." The conclusion highlights the belief that cutting the EPA's size and scope will "deliver savings to the American taxpayer" and improve overall government efficiency.

The author emphasizes that a conservative EPA will prioritize transparency, serving as "an important check" to prevent the agency's mission from being "distorted or coopted for political gain." This transparency, alongside a focus on tangible environmental outcomes, is seen as key to restoring public trust in the EPA. Gunasekara argues that a streamlined and restructured EPA will not only provide "cleaner air, cleaner water, and healthier soils," but will also achieve these goals without the economic and regulatory burdens imposed by previous administrations. The conclusion reiterates the need for the EPA to return to its original, congressionally mandated role as an environmental regulator, rather than an expansive policymaker. By doing so, the agency will better fulfill its mission of protecting public health and the environment, while respecting the principles of limited government and cooperative federalism.

CHAPTER 14: DEPARTMENT OF HEALTH AND HUMAN SERVICES

The Secretary's antidiscrimination policy statements should never conflate sex with gender identity or sexual orientation. Rather, the Secretary should proudly state that men and women are biological realities that are crucial to the advancement of life sciences and medical care and that married men and women are the ideal, natural family structure because all children have a right to be raised by the men and women who conceived them. - Page 491

Abortion and euthanasia are not health care – Page 450

Key Policy Proposals

ABORTION AND REPRODUCTIVE RIGHTS

The proposal to prohibit abortion travel funding and defund Planned Parenthood is a direct assault on women's reproductive rights. The Hyde Amendment has long restricted federal funding for abortions, but expanding these restrictions to prohibit women from using Medicaid for out-of-state abortion services is a draconian measure that disregards the real-world circumstances of women, particularly those in conservative states where abortion access is already severely limited.

Moreover, the push to defund Planned Parenthood is not just about abortion; it targets a crucial provider of comprehensive health care services. Planned Parenthood offers vital services, including cancer screenings, contraception, and STI testing, particularly to low-income women. The consequences of such a policy would likely lead to increased unintended pregnancies, higher rates of sexually transmitted infections, and a rise in preventable health issues among women.

GENDER IDENTITY AND LGBTQ+ RIGHTS

The chapter's rhetoric around gender identity reflects a disturbing return to regressive and discriminatory policies. The insistence that HHS policy should not recognize gender identity as a valid category is not only out of step with modern science but also harmful. Denying the existence and rights of transgender individuals undercuts their access to necessary health care and places them at greater risk of discrimination and violence. Furthermore, the removal of protections for sexual orientation and gender identity in healthcare would roll back progress made under the Affordable Care Act (ACA), which has provided essential protections against discrimination.

PUBLIC HEALTH AND COVID-19

The critique of the CDC's handling of the COVID-19 pandemic is deeply flawed. While there were certainly areas where the response could have been improved, the CDC's guidance was based on the best available science and aimed at protecting public health. The suggestion that the CDC overstepped its bounds and that the private sector could have done better is a dangerous oversimplification. The private sector, driven by profit motives, cannot be relied upon to prioritize public health over financial gain. The CDC's role is critical in ensuring a coordinated, science-driven response to health emergencies, and undermining this role could leave the country vulnerable to future pandemics.

CONTRACEPTIVE MANDATES AND WOMEN'S HEALTH

The proposal to restore religious and moral exemptions to contraceptive mandates, alongside the push to remove the week-after pill (Ella) from coverage, represents a significant threat to women's health. Contraception is a fundamental aspect of healthcare, and restricting access under the guise of protecting religious freedom places the rights of institutions over the rights of individuals. This will likely lead to more unintended pregnancies and increased barriers for women seeking to control their reproductive health.

PRIVATIZATION OF HEALTHCARE SERVICES

The chapter promotes the expansion of private healthcare and direct competition in Medicare Advantage, which could undermine traditional Medicare. Pushing Medicare beneficiaries towards private plans often means higher out-of-pocket costs and reduced access to necessary services. Additionally, the push to expand telehealth services and interstate licensure could lead to a fragmented healthcare system where quality and accessibility are determined by market forces rather than patient needs.

These proposed policies represent a significant step backward for civil rights, public health, and social equity in the United States. They prioritize ideological positions over scientific evidence and the real-world needs of Americans, particularly those who are most vulnerable. Implementing these changes would lead to a more divided, less healthy, and less equitable society, where access to essential health services is determined more by geography, income, and political ideology than by medical need. The consequences of these policies would be far-reaching, entrenching inequality and reducing the overall well-being of the nation.

Summary

This chapter of Mandate for Leadership was written by Roger Severino. The following summary conveys the content of the document accurately and objectively, without endorsing or critiquing the perspectives of the original authors.

The U.S. Department of Health and Human Services (HHS) operates with an enormous budget that would rank as the fifth-largest national budget globally if it were a separate country. HHS's decisions affect more Americans than any other federal agency. Under President Trump, the agency focused on serving all Americans "from conception to natural death," emphasizing support for individuals and families facing economic and social challenges. However, under President Biden, HHS has shifted its focus to promoting equity, particularly for populations sharing specific characteristics like race, sexuality, and gender identity. This change has led to what the text describes as a "loss of direction" within HHS, contributing to a continued decline in U.S. life expectancy post-COVID-19, particularly among white populations. The text argues that America's long-term survival is at stake unless HHS returns to a mission centered on the health and well-being of all Americans.

GOAL #1: PROTECTING LIFE, CONSCIENCE, AND BODILY INTEGRITY

HHS should adopt a strong agenda to protect life, conscience rights, and bodily integrity, emphasizing that every human life has inherent dignity from conception to natural death. The text argues against abortion and euthanasia, stating that these practices are not healthcare. The agency should respect and enforce religious freedom and conscience-protection laws, ensuring that no HHS programs infringe on these rights.

The text criticizes the promotion of identity politics that replace biological sex with subjective gender identity, warning that this threatens fundamental liberties and the well-being of children and adults alike. HHS should protect children from harmful ideologies and respect parents' rights to direct their children's upbringing and care.

GOAL #2: EMPOWERING PATIENT CHOICES AND PROVIDER AUTONOMY

The text advocates for a patient-centered, market-based approach to healthcare reform, where competition drives down costs and improves quality and options. It argues that states should be the primary regulators of the medical profession, not the federal government, which should avoid restricting providers' ability to innovate. The current insurance system, dominated by third-party payers and complex provider networks, is described as broken. The federal government should focus on reducing regulatory burdens, encouraging innovation, and giving patients more control over their healthcare dollars and decisions.

GOAL #3: PROMOTING STABLE AND FLOURISHING MARRIED FAMILIES

The text emphasizes the importance of families comprised of a married mother, father, and their children, arguing that such families are the foundation of a healthy society. It criticizes current HHS policies under President Biden that focus on "LGBTQ+ equity," subsidize single motherhood, disincentivize work, and penalize marriage. These policies should be replaced with ones that support stable, married nuclear families.

Fatherlessness is highlighted as a significant issue, with the text arguing that fathers play a crucial role in protecting children from various risks, including abuse, poverty, and behavioral problems. HHS should prioritize father engagement in its policies and messaging. Moreover, the text insists that HHS should never prioritize the desires of adults over the rights of children to be raised by their biological parents. In cases where biological parents are unfit, adoption processes should be quick and well-supported.

GOAL #4: PREPARING FOR THE NEXT HEALTH EMERGENCY

The COVID-19 pandemic exposed the dangers of a micromanaging, politicized federal government, according to the text. The federal response, which included lockdowns, vaccine mandates, and other restrictions, is criticized for trampling basic human rights and worsening public health outcomes unrelated to COVID-19. To prevent such issues in the future, the text calls for a fundamental restructuring of the federal public health apparatus to ensure a response that is transparent, scientifically grounded, and respects individual rights.

The text stresses the need for clear criteria for declaring and ending public health emergencies, arguing that the lack of such criteria during COVID-19 allowed for unchecked government overreach. It also argues that public health officials should never again have unchecked power, as seen with figures like Anthony Fauci, and that transparency and honesty are essential to restoring public trust in HHS.

GOAL #5: INSTITUTING GREATER TRANSPARENCY, ACCOUNTABILITY, AND OVERSIGHT

The text argues for stronger safeguards against regulatory capture by pharmaceutical companies, insurers, and other economic interests that HHS agencies are supposed to regulate. It calls for all regulators in agencies like the National Institutes of Health, Centers for Disease Control and Prevention, and the Food and Drug Administration to be entirely free from private biopharmaceutical funding. The text is critical of "public–private partnerships," describing them as a cover for agency capture and corporatism.

To prevent conflicts of interest, the text proposes long cooling-off periods for regulators before they can work for companies they once regulated and vice versa. Finally, it argues that HHS should adopt clear metrics to measure the success of its policies and programs in achieving desired health and welfare outcomes, rather than just agency outputs.

Conclusion

The text presents a detailed critique of the current direction of HHS under President Biden, proposing a series of reforms aimed at returning the agency to a focus on the health and well-being of all Americans, protecting fundamental rights, empowering patient choice, supporting traditional family structures, and ensuring greater transparency and accountability in public health.

CENTERS FOR DISEASE CONTROL AND PREVENTION (CDC)

COVID AND STRUCTURAL REFORM

The COVID-19 pandemic revealed significant flaws within the CDC, demonstrating it to be one of the most "incompetent and arrogant" federal agencies. The CDC made multiple critical errors, from underestimating the lethality, transmissibility, and origins of COVID-19 to providing inconsistent guidance on measures like mask usage. For example, the agency initially advised against masks, only to later make them mandatory. The CDC also failed in its early development of COVID-19 tests, which were crucial at the pandemic's outset. Public trust was further eroded when the CDC's initial guidance to "flatten the curve" for two weeks extended into two years of severe restrictions.

To prevent such failures in the future, Congress should clearly define and limit the CDC's legal authorities to ensure a more consistent and accountable exercise of power.

STRUCTURAL SEPARATION

The CDC currently operates with two distinct functions: collecting and publishing epidemiological data and making public health recommendations and policies. These functions often conflict with each other, as demonstrated during the pandemic when critical data were withheld out of "fear that the information might be misinterpreted." To resolve this tension, the CDC should be split into two separate entities. One agency would focus solely on data collection and dissemination, legally required to publish all gathered data, while the other would handle public health recommendations with severely restricted policy-making powers. This separation would prevent the CDC from overstepping into inherently political decisions, such as those that led to widespread church closures during the pandemic.

ROLE OF THE PRIVATE SECTOR IN TESTING

The CDC's failures in COVID-19 testing were largely due to its attempt to prioritize internal development and production over leveraging the private sector's capabilities. The private sector, as seen with the development of COVID-19 vaccines and therapeutics, is better equipped to handle such challenges. Moving forward, the CDC should focus on facilitating the private sector, academic laboratories, and state public health labs in developing and validating diagnostic tests, rather than attempting to lead these efforts itself.

REDEFINING THE CDC'S ROLE

The CDC has overstepped its bounds by positioning itself as a "super-doctor" for the nation, which is beyond its mandate. The agency is meant to focus on disease prevention, control, environmental health, and health promotion, not to provide prescriptive medical guidance for specific patients. In the future, CDC guidance should be strictly informative, not prescriptive. For example, the CDC should not dictate policies on issues such as masking or vaccinating school children, as these decisions should be left to parents and medical professionals. This will prevent the CDC's recommendations from being misinterpreted as mandates with legal consequences.

CONFLICTS OF INTEREST

Historically, the CDC was prohibited from accepting money from pharmaceutical companies. However, a loophole discovered in 1992 allowed it to accept contributions through the CDC Foundation, leading to substantial funding from pharmaceutical corporations. This practice presents a significant conflict of interest and should be banned to ensure the CDC remains independent and unbiased in its public health responsibilities.

MODERNIZING DATA SYSTEMS

The COVID-19 pandemic highlighted the CDC's failure to modernize its data infrastructure, despite multiple congressional mandates. The current reporting methods are burdensome for medical workers and result in fragmented, non-interoperable data. Congress should mandate the electronic collection and dissemination of robust, privacy-protected data, reducing burdens on clinicians. Additionally, the CDC should partner with a data-management expert to create a real-time data system that supports healthcare workers and policymakers.

VACCINE SAFETY PROGRAMS

The CDC operates several programs related to vaccine safety, including VAERS (Vaccine Adverse Event Reporting System), VSD (Vaccine Safety Datalink), and CISA (Clinical Immunization Safety Assessment). These programs, along with their associated funding, should be transferred to the FDA, which is responsible for post-market surveillance of all other drugs and biological products.

RESPECT FOR LIFE AND CONSCIENCE

The CDC should eliminate any programs that do not respect human life and conscience rights. It should ensure that it does not promote abortion as healthcare and should fund studies into the risks and complications associated with abortion. The CDC should also correct misinformation about the health and psychological benefits of childbirth compared to the risks of abortion.

The agency's involvement in the development of COVID-19 vaccines using aborted fetal cell lines was insensitive to those who objected on conscience grounds, leading to unjust firings. The CDC should avoid such ethical controversies in the future by prohibiting research that involves ending a child's life, and by promoting alternative research methods.

The CDC should also update its messaging on modern fertility awareness–based methods (FABMs) of family planning, which are scientifically proven to be effective. The agency should stop conflating these methods with outdated "rhythm" methods in its communications.

DATA COLLECTION ON ABORTION AND MATERNAL MORTALITY

The CDC's data on abortion and maternal mortality are inadequate. Abortion data are reported voluntarily by states, with some states not reporting at all. Accurate data is essential for public health and policy analysis, especially as certain states become "sanctuaries" for abortion tourism. The CDC should enforce mandatory reporting from all states, including detailed statistics on abortion procedures, maternal complications, and cases of children born alive after attempted abortions.

The CDC should also ensure that abortion is clearly defined and not conflated with miscarriage management or ectopic pregnancy treatments. Additionally, the CDC should collect data comparing live births and abortions across demographic indicators to assess the impact of prenatal care and other factors on infant outcomes and abortion rates.

GENDER IDENTITY DATA COLLECTION

The CDC should immediately cease its collection of data on gender identity, as it legitimizes unscientific concepts and promotes subjective identities. This practice encourages confusion and undermines the agency's credibility in scientific research.

FOOD AND DRUG ADMINISTRATION (FDA)

FEDERAL LAWS THAT SHIELD BIG PHARMA FROM COMPETITION

The FDA's mission to ensure the safety and efficacy of drugs, biological products, and medical devices is undermined by federal laws that protect brand-name pharmaceutical companies from competition. Generic drugs, which typically cost far less than brand-name counterparts, offer significant savings to consumers. In fact, 93 percent of generic drugs cost $20 or less. However, savings could be even greater if not for practices that delay the introduction of generics into the market.

To combat these issues, the FDA should prohibit brand-name manufacturers from delaying the launch of generic versions by exploiting their legal right to be the first to sell such drugs. Additionally, Congress should establish legal mechanisms that allow generic drug manufacturers to obtain samples of brand-name drugs for development. It should also prohibit baseless "citizen petitions" that brand-name companies file to delay the approval of generic competitors.

APPROVAL PROCESS FOR LABORATORY-DEVELOPED OR MODIFIED MEDICAL TESTS

The COVID-19 pandemic revealed critical weaknesses in the FDA's oversight of medical tests, particularly laboratory-developed tests (LDTs). Unlike commercial tests, which are intended for widespread distribution, LDTs are created for use within a single laboratory. Currently, when a test developed by one lab is used by another, it is considered a "new"

LDT, subjecting it to additional regulatory scrutiny. This discourages inter-laboratory collaboration and leads to unnecessary duplication and regulatory burdens.

To address these issues, the FDA should streamline regulations to facilitate easier sharing of LDTs between laboratories. Moreover, the FDA should revise the definition of LDTs to distinguish between truly novel tests and "laboratory-modified tests," which are merely adaptations of existing tests. This change would prevent the stifling of innovation and improve access to medical care.

There is ongoing debate about whether the FDA or the Centers for Medicare and Medicaid Services (CMS) should regulate LDTs. While the FDA currently has authority over in vitro diagnostics, CMS oversees analytical validity standards under the Clinical Laboratory Improvement Amendments (CLIA). Congress, the FDA, and CMS must clarify and disentangle their overlapping authorities to eliminate regulatory confusion.

DRUG SHORTAGES

Drug shortages, particularly in the generic drug market, are exacerbated by thin profit margins and the heavy regulatory burdens associated with manufacturing. These factors discourage investments in inventory and production capacity. To address this, the FDA should shift from its current pass/fail inspection model to a graded system that rewards manufacturers who exceed minimum standards. Additionally, facility codes should be added to drug packaging, and a searchable database should be created to allow wholesalers and pharmacy benefit managers to preference drugs made in more reliable facilities. This would encourage competition among generic manufacturers not just on price, but also on reliability.

Furthermore, the Department of Health and Human Services (HHS) should exempt multi-source generic drugs from the requirement to pay rebates to Medicaid and other federally funded health programs, as these rebates penalize investments in manufacturing capacity when demand exceeds supply. The FDA and National Institutes of Health (NIH) should also promote efficacy trials for new applications of generic drugs, potentially with NIH funding or conducting the trials themselves.

ABORTION PILLS

In a post-Roe America, abortion pills represent the "single greatest threat" to unborn children. Over the past decade, the rate of chemical abortions has increased by more than 150 percent, with more than half of annual U.S. abortions now being chemical rather than surgical. The abortion-pill regimen, typically involving mifepristone and misoprostol, has been approved for use up to 70 days (10 weeks) into pregnancy. Mifepristone blocks the hormone progesterone, leading to the death of the unborn child, while misoprostol induces contractions to expel the fetus and uterine contents.

This regimen has been linked to significant risks, including a complication rate four times higher than surgical abortion. Despite its approval over 20 years ago, mifepristone has been associated with 26 maternal deaths, over a thousand hospitalizations, and thousands of adverse events. These figures do not account for all complications, nor do they reflect the hundreds of thousands to millions of unborn children whose lives have been ended through chemical abortion.

Given these dangers, the FDA should:

- **Reverse its approval of chemical abortion drugs.** The FDA's original approval process was illegal and politically motivated. The FDA failed to fulfill its legal duty to ensure the safety and welfare of women and girls. It never properly studied the safety of the drugs under the labeled conditions, ignored evidence of higher complication rates compared to surgical abortions, and eliminated necessary safeguards. Moreover, the FDA has violated federal laws prohibiting the distribution of abortion drugs by mail, actively encouraging such practices. Now that the Supreme Court has recognized that the Constitution does not contain a right to abortion, the FDA is legally and ethically required to withdraw its initial approval, which wrongly classified pregnancy as an "illness" and abortion as "therapeutically" effective.

- **Restore the REMS** (Risk Evaluation and Mitigation Strategy) by reinstating the in-person dispensing requirement, thereby eliminating dangerous practices like tele-abortion and abortion-by-mail distribution.

MAIL-ORDER ABORTIONS

Mail-order abortions, enabled by the FDA's recent policies, expand access to abortion far beyond traditional clinics, reaching into states that have enacted pro-life protections. To protect women, girls, and unborn children, the FDA should:

- **Reinstate pre-2016 safety protocols** for Mifeprex, applying them to any generic versions of mifepristone. These protocols should include limiting the use of abortion pills to 49 days gestation, restoring the in-person dispensing requirement, and mandating that prescribers report all serious adverse events, not just deaths.

- **Improve the FAERS (FDA Adverse Events Reporting System).** The current system undercounts adverse events related to abortion pills because the responsibility for reporting complications lies with prescribers,

who often are not informed when complications occur. The FDA should simplify the reporting process to make it easier for healthcare practitioners, particularly in emergency rooms, to submit reports.

- **Increase transparency** regarding inspections of the abortion pill sponsors, Danco and GenBioPro, and the facilities that manufacture these drugs. The FDA should respond promptly to congressional and FOIA requests concerning inspections, compliance, and post-marketing safety.

- **Cease promoting or approving mail-order abortions** in violation of long-standing federal laws that prohibit the mailing and interstate carriage of abortion drugs.

VACCINE IMPORTATION

Many Americans with religious or moral objections to vaccines derived from or tested on aborted fetal cells are unable to access ethically derived alternatives. Vaccines such as those for chickenpox, Hepatitis, and MMR available in the U.S. are all linked to abortion in this way. Although safe alternatives exist abroad, the FDA has made it difficult to import them.

In January 2021, the HHS Office for Civil Rights (OCR) and the FDA announced that HHS was required under the Religious Freedom Restoration Act (RFRA) to allow bulk importation of certain Japanese-made vaccines to accommodate the religious needs of patients. However, the Biden Administration unlawfully revoked this waiver. The FDA should reinstate the waiver to comply with RFRA and to promote public health by increasing childhood vaccination rates among families seeking ethically derived alternatives.

To prevent future moral coercion, as seen with COVID-19 vaccines, the FDA and NIH should require the development of drugs and biologics that are free from moral taint, ensuring that they are not derived from aborted fetal cell lines or any other morally objectionable sources.

CONFLICTS OF INTEREST

A significant issue within the FDA is the revolving door between the agency and the pharmaceutical industry. A 2018 report in *Science* revealed that more than two-thirds of FDA reviewers eventually work for the companies whose products they once regulated. This practice, known as regulatory capture, compromises the integrity of the agency's oversight.

To address this, the FDA should impose a lengthy cooling-off period for reviewers, preventing them from working for pharmaceutical companies they previously regulated. Additionally, the FDA or Congress should more strictly regulate direct-to-consumer drug advertising, which was permitted following regulatory changes in 1997. This practice has made the U.S. and New Zealand the only countries where such advertising is legal. The pervasive influence of pharmaceutical advertising on major media outlets distorts public health reporting and undermines independent journalism.

NATIONAL INSTITUTES OF HEALTH (NIH)

BIOETHICS REFORM

The National Institutes of Health (NIH), the world's largest biomedical research agency, comprises 27 Institutes and Centers. Despite its benign public image, the NIH has funded controversial research, including studies using aborted fetal tissue, human-animal chimera experiments, and gain-of-function viral research, which may have contributed to the COVID-19 pandemic.

Research using fetal tissue obtained from elective abortions and human embryonic stem cells is both immoral and obsolete. Such practices involve the destruction of human life and should not be supported with taxpayer dollars. Ethically derived alternatives, such as discarded surgical tissue and adult stem cells (which can be made pluripotent), have proven more successful in developing treatments for various ailments without ethical compromise.

The Trump Administration's Department of Health and Human Services (HHS) exercised its authority to refuse funding for extramural research using abortion-derived fetal tissue that failed ethics advisory board review. However, the Biden Administration reinstated unrestricted funding for such research. In response, HHS should:

- **Restore the ethics advisory committee** to oversee abortion-derived fetal tissue research. Congress should go further by prohibiting such research entirely.

- **Terminate intramural research** projects at NIH that use tissue from aborted children and dismantle the NIH's human embryonic stem cell registry.

- **Promote and fund ethical research alternatives** to ensure that abortion and embryonic-destructive research, cell lines, and testing methods become obsolete and ethically indefensible.

Additionally, the Administration should reestablish a National Council on Bioethics (NCB) to address new and emerging ethical concerns in research. This council would evaluate whether the ends justify the means in the pursuit of therapies and cures and establish limiting principles for research and health policy. The council should also address controversial practices such as three-parent embryo creation and human cloning, both of which should be banned. The NCB should convene leading experts to provide policy recommendations for the ethical challenges that lie ahead.

HHS should also create a research agenda that supports pro-life policies and investigates the mental and physical harms of abortion on women and girls.

CONFLICTS OF INTEREST

NIH's inappropriate industry ties create serious conflicts of interest. For example, a $100 million NIH study on the benefits of moderate drinking was secretly funded by the beer and liquor industry. Furthermore, the National Institute of Allergy and Infectious Diseases (NIAID), under Anthony Fauci, holds half of the patent for the Moderna COVID-19 vaccine. This represents a clear conflict of interest, as NIAID opted to conduct the vaccine's clinical trials internally rather than through independent university-based investigators. This arrangement allows NIAID to profit from vaccine sales, with several NIH employees, including their heirs, potentially receiving up to $150,000 annually from Moderna's revenue.

In May 2022, documents obtained through a Freedom of Information Act (FOIA) request revealed that NIH Director Francis Collins, NIAID Director Anthony Fauci, and Fauci's Deputy Director, Clifford Lane, received royalties from pharmaceutical companies between 2009 and 2014. Third-party payments to NIH and its scientists, credited as co-inventors, exceeded $350 million from 2010 to 2020. During this time, Collins, Fauci, and Lane held administrative roles, with no legitimate claim to be scientific co-discoverers. This situation exemplifies regulatory capture and highlights the need for stricter prohibitions on conflicts of interest.

Many of the most significant studies on COVID-19 treatments, natural immunity, and vaccine efficacy have emerged from countries with stricter conflict-of-interest rules than the U.S. To address this, the NIH monopoly on research direction must be dismantled:

- **Impose term limits** on top NIH career leaders to prevent entrenched power and promote accountability.
- **Consider block granting NIH's research budget to states,** allowing them to fund their own scientific research. This decentralized approach would not preclude large, multi-state research collaborations or modest federal funding through NIH.

The CDC and NIH Foundations, whose boards include pharmaceutical executives, should be decommissioned. Private donations to these foundations—predominantly from pharmaceutical companies—should not influence government decisions about research funding or public health policy.

WOKE POLICIES

Under Francis Collins, the NIH became overly focused on social justice initiatives, such as the #MeToo movement, to the detriment of its scientific mission. The NIH refused to sponsor scientific conferences unless they met a quota for women panelists, violating federal civil rights laws against sex discrimination. This quota practice should be discontinued, and the NIH Office of Equity, Diversity, and Inclusion, which promotes such unlawful actions, should be abolished.

The NIH has also led the charge in promoting flawed gender science. Instead of endorsing gender-affirming treatments, NIH should fund research into the short-term and long-term negative effects of cross-sex interventions. This research should include the risks associated with puberty blockers, cross-sex hormones, surgeries, and the likelihood that young people might desist from gender dysphoria if offered counseling without medical or social interventions.

CENTERS FOR MEDICARE AND MEDICAID SERVICES (CMS)

OVERVIEW

Medicare and Medicaid are critical components of the U.S. social safety net, impacting more American lives than any other federal program. Despite their benefits, these programs have become "runaway entitlements," contributing to stifled medical innovation, widespread fraud, and challenges in cost containment. Moreover, their fiscal sustainability is increasingly uncertain. To address these issues, Medicare and Medicaid should be managed in ways that empower enrollees to make informed decisions, providing them with quality options at affordable prices through competition and innovation. Providers should also be allowed to practice medicine freely, focusing on patient care based on individual needs.

MEDICARE REFORM

Medicare should be reformed according to four key goals and principles:

1. **Increase Beneficiaries' Control Over Healthcare:** Medicare beneficiaries should have greater control over their healthcare, enabling them to determine the value of services in collaboration with their providers. This

requires access to reliable information about physicians, hospitals, and insurance plans, as well as increased choice in these areas.
2. **Reduce Regulatory Burdens on Doctors:** Doctors should be free to prioritize patient care over administrative tasks, such as entering codes into computers. Medicare's current reimbursement incentives often tempt doctors to alter their medical judgment, a practice that should be eliminated to allow doctors to focus on their patients' unique needs.
3. **Ensure Sustainability and Value:** Prices within Medicare should reflect economic value rather than political influence and should be transparent to patients before they receive services. The government's reliance on non-market-based methods to set reimbursement rates often results in overspending on low-value services and underpayment for high-value ones. This practice stifles innovation and, due to Medicare's size, distorts payments throughout the healthcare system. Transitioning to value-based care within Medicare requires intermediate entities that can manage financial risk while ensuring quality care.
4. **Reduce Waste, Fraud, and Abuse:** Medicare must address waste, fraud, and abuse through enhanced detection methods, including the use of artificial intelligence.

REGULATORY REFORMS

Medicare regulations currently limit patient choice in coverage and care. To address this, the next Administration should restore or introduce several Trump-era regulations and demonstrations that were either withdrawn, weakened, or never finalized under the Biden Administration. These include:

- **Medicare Coverage of Innovative Technologies (MCIT) Rule:** The MCIT rule was designed to expedite coverage of FDA-designated "breakthrough" medical devices, ensuring faster access for Medicare beneficiaries to cutting-edge technologies.
- **Risk Adjustment Data Validation (RADV) Rule:** This rule aims to ensure the accuracy of payments to Medicare Advantage plans by validating the data used to adjust risk scores, thereby reducing improper payments and enhancing the program's integrity.
- **Medicare Advantage Qualifying Payment Arrangement Incentive (MAQI) Demonstration:** The MAQI demonstration was intended to encourage Medicare Advantage plans to adopt value-based payment arrangements, promoting high-quality, cost-effective care.
- **Global and Professional Direct Contracting (GPDC) Model:** Rebranded as the Accountable Care Organization Realizing Equity, Access, and Community Health (ACO REACH) model, this initiative seeks to advance coordinated care and improve outcomes for Medicare beneficiaries by encouraging provider accountability.

Additionally, CMS should advance site neutrality in payment policies by eliminating the inpatient-only list and expanding the ambulatory surgical center covered procedures list. Currently, Medicare typically pays more for procedures performed in inpatient hospital settings and less for the same procedures in outpatient settings. By aligning payments regardless of where services are delivered—whether in a physician's office, clinic, or hospital—CMS would level the playing field among providers and remove financial disadvantages for medical professionals competing with hospital systems.

Conscience Protections

The Department of Health and Human Services (HHS) should also restore and strengthen conscience protection regulations. These regulations ensure that medical practitioners can participate in federal healthcare programs without being compelled to provide services such as sex changes that may conflict with their personal or religious beliefs.

LEGISLATIVE PROPOSALS FOR CENTERS FOR MEDICARE AND MEDICAID SERVICES (CMS)

REMOVE RESTRICTIONS ON PHYSICIAN-OWNED HOSPITALS

The Affordable Care Act (ACA) imposed restrictions that prohibit Medicare from reimbursing physician-owned and specialty hospitals. These restrictions primarily serve the interests of large hospital systems and limit consumer access to high-quality, specialty care. To enhance competition and consumer choice, these restrictions should be removed, allowing physician-owned hospitals to compete on equal footing with other hospitals in serving Medicare patients.

ENCOURAGE DIRECT COMPETITION BETWEEN MEDICARE ADVANTAGE AND PRIVATE PLANS

Medicare Advantage (MA) is a system of competing private health plans that offers a major alternative to traditional Medicare, particularly for the growing senior population. MA provides beneficiaries with a broader range of competitive health plan choices, superior benefits compared to traditional Medicare, and at a reasonable cost. The program has consistently received high marks for delivering high-quality care. To strengthen and improve MA for the future, several critical reforms are proposed:

1. **Make Medicare Advantage the default enrollment option.** This would streamline the process for new beneficiaries and increase participation in the MA program.
2. **Give beneficiaries direct control over how they spend Medicare dollars.** This would empower patients to make informed choices about their healthcare spending.
3. **Remove burdensome policies that micromanage MA plans.** Allowing more flexibility in plan management would foster innovation and efficiency.
4. **Replace the complex formula-based payment model with a competitive bidding model.** This change would enhance competition among plans and potentially lower costs.
5. **Reconfigure the current risk adjustment model.** Adjusting this model would ensure fair compensation for plans that cover higher-risk individuals.
6. **Remove restrictions on key benefits and services.** This includes easing limitations related to prescription drugs, hospice care, and medical savings account plans.

LEGACY MEDICARE REFORM

Reforming traditional, non-MA Medicare is essential to improving the program's efficiency and sustainability. Legislative proposals include:

- **Basing payments on the health status of the patient or intensity of the service,** rather than the location where the service is provided. This would create a more equitable and rational payment system.
- **Replacing the fee-for-service model with value-based payments.** This shift would empower patients to seek out care that best meets their needs, improving overall healthcare quality and efficiency.
- **Codifying price transparency regulations.** Ensuring that prices are transparent would help patients make informed decisions and drive down costs through competition.
- **Restructuring 340B drug subsidies** to direct benefits toward patients rather than hospitals. This would ensure that the intended recipients of these subsidies receive the maximum benefit.
- **Repealing harmful health policies enacted under the Obama and Biden Administrations,** including the Medicare Shared Savings Program and provisions of the Inflation Reduction Act, which are seen as detrimental to Medicare's long-term viability.

MEDICARE PART D REFORM

The Inflation Reduction Act (IRA) introduced a drug price negotiation program in Medicare, replacing the existing private-sector negotiations in Part D with government-imposed price controls. These controls are likely to limit access to medications and reduce the availability of new drugs for patients. To mitigate these negative impacts, the "negotiation" program should be repealed, and meaningful reforms in Part D should be pursued. These reforms include:

- **Eliminating the coverage gap in Part D,** which would reduce out-of-pocket costs for beneficiaries.
- **Reducing the government share in the catastrophic tier** of drug coverage and requiring manufacturers to bear a larger portion of these costs.
- Until the IRA can be repealed, the Administration should implement its provisions prudently, minimizing harmful effects and avoiding unintended consequences.

MEDICAID REFORM

Medicaid, originally designed as a safety net for the most vulnerable, has evolved into a complex, costly program that often fails those it was intended to serve. Medicaid's expansion under the ACA and the public health emergency's prohibition on eligibility reviews have exacerbated these issues. The program's structure, with its overlapping benefits and burdensome regulations, has created a system that is difficult for recipients to navigate and inefficient for states to manage. Key legislative proposals for reforming Medicaid include:

1. **Reforming Medicaid Financing:**
   - States should have a more flexible, accountable, and transparent financing mechanism for delivering medical services. Options include a balanced or blended match rate, block grants, aggregate caps, or per capita caps. This would encourage innovation and efficiency while making federal and state financial participation in Medicaid more rational and predictable.
2. **Directing Dollars More Effectively:**
   - The current Medicaid funding structure promotes expansions and lacks transparency. To improve fiscal responsibility and care quality, CMS should:
     - End state financing loopholes.

- Reform payments to hospitals for uncompensated care.
- Replace the enhanced match rate with a fairer, more rational match rate.
- Restructure basic financing to make the program more fiscally predictable, including reforming Disproportionate Share Hospital (DSH) payments.

3. **Strengthening Program Integrity:**
   - Program integrity should be a top priority, with states held accountable for reducing waste, fraud, and abuse. Key actions include:
     - Offering enhanced contingency fees to states that successfully reduce improper payments.
     - Improving Medicaid eligibility standards to ensure the program remains focused on those most in need.
     - Holding states accountable for improper eligibility determinations and strengthening asset test determinations.
4. **Incentivizing Personal Responsibility:**
   - Medicaid recipients should have a stake in their healthcare and be given the freedom to choose their health plans. CMS should:
     - Allow states to implement work requirements for able-bodied individuals and apply targeted premiums and cost-sharing measures to higher-income enrollees.
     - Introduce targeted time limits or lifetime caps on benefits to discourage permanent dependency.
5. **Allowing Private Health Insurance:**
   - Congress should allow states to contribute to private insurance benefits for Medicaid recipients, offering flexibility and rewarding healthy behaviors. This could include catastrophic coverage combined with an account similar to a Health Savings Account (HSA) for the direct purchase of healthcare and payment of cost-sharing.
6. **Increasing Flexible Benefit Redesign Without Waivers:**
   - CMS should add flexibility to eliminate outdated mandatory and optional benefit requirements, particularly for able-bodied recipients. This includes redesigning eligibility, financing, and service delivery for long-term care to focus on the most vulnerable and eliminate Medicaid coverage for middle- to upper-income recipients.
7. **Eliminating Waiver and State Plan Processes:**
   - CMS should streamline the process for making payment reforms, reducing the need for cumbersome waivers or state plan amendments. The federal government's role should shift to broad oversight, focusing on cost-effectiveness and health outcomes, while granting states greater responsibility for Medicaid program management. This includes selectively applying Section 1115 waiver requirements, such as for work requirements, while rescinding them for non-healthcare-related benefits and services.

LEGISLATIVE PROPOSALS FOR CENTERS FOR MEDICARE AND MEDICAID SERVICES (CMS)

REMOVE RESTRICTIONS ON PHYSICIAN-OWNED HOSPITALS

The Affordable Care Act (ACA) imposed restrictions that prevent Medicare from reimbursing physician-owned and specialty hospitals. These restrictions primarily benefit large hospital systems by limiting competition, which undercuts consumer choice for high-quality, specialized care. Removing these restrictions would allow physician-owned hospitals to compete equally with other hospitals in serving Medicare patients, thereby expanding patient access to superior medical services.

ENCOURAGE MORE DIRECT COMPETITION BETWEEN MEDICARE ADVANTAGE AND PRIVATE PLANS

Medicare Advantage (MA) is a system of competing private health plans that offers a robust alternative to traditional Medicare, especially for the growing senior population. MA plans provide beneficiaries with a wider range of competitive health plan choices and richer benefits than traditional Medicare at a reasonable cost. The program consistently receives high marks for delivering high-quality care. However, to further strengthen and improve MA, the following reforms are proposed:

1. **Make Medicare Advantage the default enrollment option** for new beneficiaries, streamlining their entry into the program.

2. **Give beneficiaries direct control over how they spend Medicare dollars**, empowering them to make informed healthcare decisions.
3. **Remove burdensome policies that micromanage MA plans** to increase flexibility and efficiency.
4. **Replace the complex formula-based payment model with a competitive bidding model**, enhancing competition and potentially reducing costs.
5. **Reconfigure the current risk adjustment model** to ensure fair compensation for plans covering higher-risk individuals.
6. **Remove restrictions on key benefits and services**, including those related to prescription drugs, hospice care, and medical savings account plans, to broaden the scope of available care.

LEGACY MEDICARE REFORM

To modernize and improve the traditional, non-MA Medicare program, several legislative reforms are necessary:

- **Base payments on the health status of the patient or the intensity of the service**, rather than the location where the service is provided. This change would create a more equitable and patient-centered payment system.
- **Replace the bureaucratic fee-for-service system with value-based payments.** This shift would empower patients to seek care that best serves their needs, promoting efficiency and improving health outcomes.
- **Codify price transparency regulations** to ensure patients have access to clear, upfront pricing information, fostering competition and reducing costs.
- **Restructure 340B drug subsidies** to direct benefits toward patients rather than hospitals, ensuring that financial assistance reaches those in need.
- **Repeal harmful health policies enacted under the Obama and Biden Administrations**, including the Medicare Shared Savings Program and provisions of the Inflation Reduction Act. These policies are viewed as detrimental to the sustainability and effectiveness of Medicare.

MEDICARE PART D REFORM

The Inflation Reduction Act (IRA) introduced a drug price negotiation program in Medicare, replacing the private-sector negotiations in Part D with government-imposed price controls. These controls are likely to limit access to medications and reduce the availability of new drugs. Therefore, this "negotiation" program should be repealed, and more meaningful reforms to Medicare Part D should be pursued. Key reforms include:

- **Eliminating the coverage gap in Part D**, reducing out-of-pocket costs for beneficiaries.
- **Reducing the government's share in the catastrophic tier of coverage** and requiring manufacturers to bear a larger portion of these costs.
- Until the IRA can be repealed, the Administration should implement its provisions prudently, minimizing the harmful effects and avoiding unintended consequences.

MEDICAID REFORM

Medicaid has evolved into a complex, costly program that often fails to serve the most vulnerable patients effectively. The Affordable Care Act (ACA) and public health emergency maintenance of effort (MOE) requirements have expanded Medicaid eligibility, leading to increased expenditures and complicating the program's administration. The following reforms are proposed to streamline Medicaid and improve its efficiency:

1. **Reform Medicaid Financing:**
   - States should have a more flexible, accountable, and transparent financing mechanism for delivering medical services. Options include balanced or blended match rates, block grants, aggregate caps, or per capita caps. This would encourage innovation and improve the quality of healthcare services while making financial participation in Medicaid more predictable and rational.
2. **Direct Dollars to Beneficiaries More Effectively:**
   - The current Medicaid funding structure rewards expansions and promotes financing gimmicks. To improve fiscal responsibility, CMS should:
     - End state financing loopholes.
     - Reform payments to hospitals for uncompensated care.
     - Replace the enhanced match rate with a fairer, more rational match rate.
     - Restructure basic financing to create a more fiscally predictable budget, including reforming Disproportionate Share Hospital (DSH) payments.
3. **Strengthen Program Integrity:**

- Program integrity should be a top priority, with states held accountable for reducing waste, fraud, and abuse. Key actions include:
  - Offering enhanced contingency fees to states that successfully reduce improper payments.
  - Improving Medicaid eligibility standards to ensure the program remains focused on those most in need.
  - Strengthening asset test determinations within Medicaid to protect taxpayer investments.
4. **Incentivize Personal Responsibility:**
   - Medicaid recipients should have a stake in their healthcare and be given the freedom to choose their health plans. CMS should:
     - Allow states to implement work requirements for able-bodied individuals and apply targeted premiums and cost-sharing measures to higher-income enrollees.
     - Introduce targeted time limits or lifetime caps on benefits to discourage permanent dependency.
5. **Allow Private Health Insurance:**
   - Congress should allow states to contribute to private insurance benefits for Medicaid recipients, offering flexibility and incentivizing healthy behaviors. This reform could include catastrophic coverage combined with an account similar to a Health Savings Account (HSA) for direct healthcare purchases and cost-sharing.
6. **Increase Flexible Benefit Redesign Without Waivers:**
   - CMS should add flexibility to eliminate outdated mandatory and optional benefit requirements, particularly for able-bodied recipients. This includes redesigning eligibility, financing, and service delivery for long-term care to focus on the most vulnerable and eliminating Medicaid coverage for middle- to upper-income recipients.
7. **Eliminate Waiver and State Plan Processes:**
   - CMS should streamline the process for making payment reforms, reducing the need for cumbersome waivers or state plan amendments. The federal government's role should shift to broad oversight, focusing on cost-effectiveness and health outcomes, while granting states greater responsibility for Medicaid program management. This reform includes selectively applying Section 1115 waiver requirements, such as for work requirements, while rescinding them for non-healthcare-related benefits and services.

LEGISLATIVE PROPOSALS FOR THE AFFORDABLE CARE ACT AND PRIVATE HEALTH INSURANCE

REMOVE BARRIERS TO DIRECT PRIMARY CARE (DPC)

Direct primary care (DPC) is an innovative healthcare model where doctors contract directly with patients on a subscription basis, providing care regardless of how or where it is delivered. This model is gaining popularity for its ability to improve patient access, enhance the quality of care, reduce costs, and strengthen the doctor-patient relationship. However, DPC has encountered significant challenges from government regulations and misclassification issues. A key legislative proposal is to clarify that the fixed fee for DPC services does not constitute insurance within the context of health savings accounts (HSAs). This change would eliminate regulatory barriers and allow DPC to flourish as a viable alternative to traditional insurance.

REVISIT THE NO SURPRISES ACT ON SURPRISE MEDICAL BILLING

The No Surprises Act was designed to protect consumers from balance billing, a practice where patients are billed the difference between what a provider charges and what the insurance pays. However, the Act established a flawed system for resolving payment disputes between insurers and providers. The current government-mandated dispute resolution process has created confusion among arbiters, regulators, and judges, who struggle to interpret its standards. To address these issues, the Act should be revised to replace the dispute resolution process with a truth-in-advertising approach. This would protect consumers while allowing doctors, insurers, and arbiters to resolve payment disputes more effectively and without the complications introduced by conflicting regulatory standards.

FACILITATE THE DEVELOPMENT OF SHARED SAVINGS AND REFERENCE PRICING PLAN OPTIONS

Under traditional insurance, patients who opt for lower-cost care do not benefit financially from their cost-saving decisions. To encourage patients to make economically beneficial healthcare choices, barriers to rewarding such decisions should be removed. CMS should ensure that shared savings and reference pricing models, which reward consumers for choosing lower-cost care options, are fully permitted and promoted. This would align patient incentives with cost-effective healthcare utilization, ultimately reducing overall healthcare spending.

SEPARATE THE SUBSIDIZED ACA EXCHANGE MARKET FROM THE NON-SUBSIDIZED INSURANCE MARKET

The Affordable Care Act (ACA) has increased the cost of insurance and reduced market competitiveness, with the subsidy scheme masking these impacts. To make health insurance more affordable for those without government subsidies, CMS should develop a plan to separate the non-subsidized insurance market from the subsidized market. By doing so, the non-subsidized market could be granted regulatory relief from the costly ACA mandates, fostering a more competitive and affordable insurance environment for those who are not receiving subsidies.

STRENGTHEN HOSPITAL PRICE TRANSPARENCY

In 2020, CMS implemented a rule requiring hospitals to post the prices of common procedures. To build on this initiative, future updates to these rules should incorporate quality measures alongside price information. When combined with shared savings models and other consumer tools, enhanced price transparency could lead to significant savings for consumers. Strengthening these transparency measures would empower patients to make informed decisions about their healthcare based on both cost and quality, driving competition and lowering healthcare costs across the board.

EXPAND CHOICES THROUGH THE CENTER FOR CONSUMER INFORMATION AND INSURANCE OVERSIGHT (CCIIO)

The Center for Consumer Information and Insurance Oversight (CCIIO), a division of CMS, plays a significant role in overseeing the ACA exchanges, including managing Healthcare.gov. However, the CCIIO has been criticized for its overly prescriptive approach in dictating what benefits and types of health plans can participate in the exchanges. This rigid oversight stifles market innovation and increases costs. To address these issues, Congress should build on efforts initiated during the Trump Administration to expand healthcare choices for small businesses and workers, both within and outside the ACA exchanges. Key proposals include:

- **Codifying the expansion of association health plans, short-term health plans, and health reimbursement arrangements (HRAs),** including individual coverage HRAs. These measures would provide more flexible and affordable healthcare options, especially for small businesses and individual workers.

- **Collaborating with the Treasury Department and the Office of Management and Budget (OMB)** to give consumers greater flexibility with their healthcare dollars by expanding access to health savings accounts (HSAs). This would allow consumers to save more effectively for healthcare expenses and increase their control over healthcare spending.

LEGISLATIVE PROPOSALS FOR EMERGENCY PREPAREDNESS

EXPAND THE SCOPE OF PRACTICE FOR LOW-COMPLEXITY AND MODERATE-COMPLEXITY CLINICAL LABORATORIES

During the COVID-19 pandemic, regulatory flexibility regarding the Clinical Laboratory Improvement Amendments (CLIA) requirements allowed laboratories to increase access to testing significantly. This flexibility, initially implemented as an emergency measure, should be extended beyond crisis situations. The demand for clinical testing and new diagnostic tests is expected to grow due to ongoing innovations in medical care. Similar to how scope of practice restrictions for healthcare providers have been revised to allow them to practice at the "top of their license," the scope of practice for clinical laboratories and testing personnel under CLIA should be revised. By expanding the scope of practice, clinical laboratories will be better equipped to meet the increasing demand for medical services.

CREATE CLIA-CERTIFICATION-EQUIVALENT PATHWAYS FOR NON-CLINICAL LABORATORIES AND RESEARCHERS

The COVID-19 pandemic underscored the need to leverage the expertise of non-clinical laboratories and researchers to enhance the nation's clinical testing capacity. To achieve this, CMS should establish pathways that grant CLIA certification equivalency to non-clinical laboratories and their testing personnel. Non-clinical researchers, who already demonstrate their technical expertise through online training and certification programs, should be able to similarly demonstrate their capabilities in clinical testing. By building on the existing framework, CMS can ensure that non-clinical laboratories are prepared to contribute effectively to clinical testing efforts during both emergencies and routine medical care.

LEGISLATIVE PROPOSALS FOR LIFE, CONSCIENCE, AND BODILY INTEGRITY

PROHIBIT ABORTION TRAVEL FUNDING

Funding abortions, including those that involve travel, not only increases the number of abortions but also violates the conscience and religious freedom rights of Americans who object to subsidizing such procedures. The Hyde Amendment has long prohibited the use of HHS funds for elective abortions. However, in August 2022, President Biden issued an executive order directing the HHS Secretary to use Section 1115 demonstration waivers to circumvent these restrictions, thereby allowing taxpayer funds to be used to help women travel out of state to obtain abortions. The Department of Justice's Office of Legal Counsel (DOJ OLC) issued a legal opinion supporting this action, claiming that it did not violate the Hyde Amendment—despite the broad language of the Hyde Amendment that prohibits federal funding related to abortion.

A pro-life administration should take immediate action to:

- **Withdraw the Medicaid guidance** and any Section 1115 waivers issued under the Biden Administration that allow taxpayer funding for abortion travel.

- **Require the DOJ OLC to withdraw and disavow its interpretation** of the Hyde Amendment, ensuring that the law is enforced as intended by Congress.

PROHIBIT PLANNED PARENTHOOD FROM RECEIVING MEDICAID FUNDS

Planned Parenthood, which performed more than 383,000 abortions during the 2020–2021 reporting period, continues to receive substantial government funding, primarily through Medicaid. The organization reported over $133 million in excess revenue and more than $2.1 billion in net assets during this time. Despite facing accusations of waste, abuse, fraud, failure to report the sexual abuse of minors, and profiting from the sale of organs from aborted babies, Planned Parenthood affiliates received over $633 million in government funding.

To end taxpayer funding of abortion providers like Planned Parenthood, policymakers should:

1. **Issue guidance** that reaffirms states' rights to defund Planned Parenthood in their state Medicaid plans.
2. **Propose rulemaking** to interpret the Medicaid statute in a way that disqualifies providers of elective abortions from participating in the Medicaid program.

Congress should pass the **Protecting Life and Taxpayers Act** to permanently defund abortion providers like Planned Parenthood. Additionally, CMS should resolve pending Section 1115 waivers from states like Idaho, South Carolina, and Tennessee, which seek to prohibit abortion providers from participating in state-run Medicaid programs.

WITHDRAW MEDICAID FUNDS FROM STATES THAT REQUIRE ABORTION INSURANCE OR DISCRIMINATE IN VIOLATION OF THE WELDON AMENDMENT

The Weldon Amendment prohibits HHS from funding state or local governments that discriminate against pro-life health entities or insurers. Despite this, seven states currently require abortion coverage in private health insurance plans, and HHS continues to fund these states. Under the Trump Administration, $200 million in Medicaid funding was disallowed from California due to its violation of the Weldon Amendment, but this funding was restored by the Biden Administration.

HHS and CMS should:

- **Withdraw appropriated funding**—up to 10 percent of Medicaid funds—from states that require abortion insurance coverage.

- **Promptly defend these funding decisions** in court, with DOJ litigating to protect HHS's ability to enforce the Weldon Amendment.

Additionally, California's announced discrimination against pharmacies that do not carry chemical abortion drugs should face the same penalties.

REWRITE THE ACA ABORTION SEPARATE PAYMENT REGULATION

Section 1303 of the Affordable Care Act (ACA) requires insurers to collect separate payments for abortion coverage in qualified health plans sold on exchanges and to maintain these payments in separate accounts. This requirement was not enforced under the Obama Administration, and a Trump-era regulation sought to correct this issue. However, the Biden Administration rescinded this regulation, allowing insurers to combine payments for abortion coverage with other premiums, contrary to the law's intent.

HHS should:

- **Reinstate and strengthen** the Trump Administration's regulation, ensuring that insurers collect and maintain truly separate payments for abortion coverage as required by Section 1303.

AUDIT HYDE AMENDMENT COMPLIANCE

HHS should conduct a full audit to determine compliance or noncompliance with the Hyde Amendment and similar funding restrictions in its programs. This audit should include:

- A comprehensive review of the Biden Administration's executive actions post-Dobbs to promote abortion.
- An assessment of Medicaid managed care plans in pro-abortion states to ensure they comply with the Hyde Amendment.

REVERSE PRO-ABORTION INTERPRETATIONS OF THE EMERGENCY MEDICAL TREATMENT AND ACTIVE LABOR ACT (EMTALA)

The Emergency Medical Treatment and Active Labor Act (EMTALA) mandates that hospitals receiving Medicare funds stabilize pregnant women and protect unborn children. However, in July 2022, HHS/CMS issued guidance requiring hospitals to perform abortions, including chemical abortions, under EMTALA, even when the child might still be alive. This guidance also stated that EMTALA protects hospitals and physicians who perform abortions in violation of state law if they consider the abortions necessary to stabilize the woman's health.

HHS should:

- **Rescind this guidance**, clarifying that EMTALA requires no abortions, does not preempt state pro-life laws, and explicitly protects unborn children.
- **End CMS and state agency investigations** into alleged refusals to perform abortions.
- **Coordinate with DOJ** to eliminate existing injunctions against pro-life states, withdraw enforcement lawsuits, and agree to injunctions against CMS guidance that conflicts with state laws.

REISSUE A STRONGER TRANSGENDER NATIONAL COVERAGE DETERMINATION

CMS should repromulgate its 2016 decision that it cannot issue a National Coverage Determination (NCD) for "gender reassignment surgery" for Medicare beneficiaries. The decision should reflect the growing body of evidence that such interventions are dangerous and acknowledge that there is insufficient scientific evidence to support coverage for these procedures.

ENFORCE EMTALA AND PROTECT BORN-ALIVE INFANTS

Abortion does not always result in the death of the baby, and infants who survive abortions are sometimes left to die. HHS should use EMTALA and Section 504 of the Rehabilitation Act to investigate cases where infants born alive after an abortion are left untreated. CMS, OCR, and OIG should ensure thorough investigations and enforce actions where necessary.

HHS should revive the Trump Administration's proposed regulation, "Special Responsibilities of Medicare Hospitals in Emergency Cases and Discrimination on the Basis of Disability in Critical Health and Human Service Programs or Activities," to enforce these protections. Additionally, Congress should pass the **Born-Alive Abortion Survivors Protection Act** to mandate proper medical care for infants who survive abortions and to establish criminal penalties for practitioners who fail to provide such care.

PERMANENTLY CODIFY THE HYDE AND WELDON AMENDMENTS

Congress should enact legislation, such as the **No Taxpayer Funding for Abortion and Abortion Insurance Full Disclosure Act** (Hyde) and the **Conscience Protection Act** (Weldon), to permanently codify the protections offered by the Hyde family of amendments and the Weldon Amendment.

REVERSE THE RADICAL REDEFINITION OF SEX IN SECTION 1557 OF THE ACA

On August 4, 2022, HHS proposed a rule redefining "sex" under Section 1557 of the ACA to include gender identity, sexual orientation, and pregnancy-related conditions, including abortion. This redefinition creates new classes of people based on ideological and unscientific concepts. The Trump Administration had previously reversed such redefinitions.

HHS should:

- **Revert to the previous interpretation** of Section 1557, restoring the definition of sex to its biological basis and ensuring that no HHS or CMS programs, including CHIP, promote ideologically motivated sexualization of children.
- **Maintain lactation room requirements** in upcoming Section 1557 rulemaking or propose them in a new individual rule.

COVID-19 VACCINATION AND MASK REQUIREMENTS

Health care workers who were praised for their efforts during the COVID-19 pandemic were later dismissed for objecting to mandatory COVID-19 vaccinations or mask requirements, regardless of their natural immunity or personal beliefs. Given that COVID-19 is now endemic, with new strains posing fewer risks, the benefits of mandatory vaccination and universal masking in healthcare facilities have diminished.

CMS should:

- **Announce nonenforcement** of the Biden Administration's COVID-19 vaccination mandate on Medicaid and Medicare hospitals.
- **Revoke related guidance and regulations**.
- **Avoid imposing future general COVID-19 mask mandates** on healthcare facilities or personnel.
- **Pay damages** to medical professionals who were dismissed due to the CMS vaccine mandate

ADMINISTRATION FOR CHILDREN AND FAMILIES (ACF)

TANF (TEMPORARY ASSISTANCE FOR NEEDY FAMILIES)

The Temporary Assistance for Needy Families (TANF) program is a federal block grant that provides states with significant flexibility to fund programs aimed at helping low-income families achieve economic self-sufficiency and break the cycle of poverty. TANF funds are used for various services, including monthly cash assistance payments, work activities, childcare, pre-K/Head Start, and child welfare services. The program serves 1.8 million individuals and, since its 1996 reform, has involved $31.4 billion in combined federal and state funding.

Despite its intent, the TANF program has several shortcomings, particularly regarding work engagement requirements. Although states are supposed to engage 50% of single-parent families in work for at least 30 hours a week (with a lower threshold for those with children under six), the "Caseload Reduction Credit" allows states to reduce these targets. As a result, some states have had work engagement targets as low as zero percent.

To address these issues, the following proposals are recommended:

1. **Broaden Work Requirements:** TANF work requirements should apply to any non-cash benefit worth $50 or more per month and received for six consecutive months, not just basic assistance.
2. **Enhance Transparency:** HHS should clarify how states should track and report outcomes from TANF spending in quarterly and annual reports to increase transparency and accountability.
3. **Refocus TANF Priorities:** TANF should give equal weight to all its statutory purposes, particularly those related to marriage, healthy family formation, and delaying sex to prevent pregnancy. CMS should require explicit measurement of these goals to ensure they are prioritized effectively.

TEEN PREGNANCY PREVENTION (TPP) AND PERSONAL RESPONSIBILITY EDUCATION PROGRAM (PREP)

The Teen Pregnancy Prevention (TPP) program, managed by the Office of Population Affairs, and the Personal Responsibility Education Program (PREP), managed by the ACF Office of Planning, Research, and Evaluation, aim to prevent teen pregnancy and promote responsible behavior among adolescents. However, concerns have been raised about these programs' effectiveness and their potential to promote abortion or high-risk sexual behavior.

The following proposals are recommended to improve these programs:

1. **Ensure Proper Reporting:** TPP and PREP programs should better report subgrantees and referral lists to prevent the promotion of abortion or high-risk sexual behavior among adolescents.
2. **Prioritize Sexual Risk Avoidance (SRA):** CMS should ensure that SRA proponents receive funding and opportunities to prove their effectiveness. SRA programs should receive equal funding and emphasis compared to other approaches.
3. **Revise Site Visits:** Site visits should be revamped to ensure adherence to optimal health metrics, and a cost analysis of programming relative to students served should be a metric for funding decisions. Intensive

programs that serve fewer students but achieve positive results should be supported.

4. **Eliminate Biased Curriculum Lists:** HHS should abolish lists of "approved curriculum" that prioritize sex-promotion textbooks. Instead, a list of criteria should be established to evaluate curriculum for sex education grant programs, with a focus on promoting optimal health.

5. **Parent Involvement:** Funded programs should encourage parent involvement and parent-child communication, emphasizing risk avoidance and preventing any promotion of behaviors that compromise health.

ADOPTION REFORM

Currently, there are approximately 400,000 children in the U.S. foster care system, with 100,000 awaiting adoption. The ongoing opioid/fentanyl crisis exacerbates this situation, placing more children at risk. Unfortunately, many faith-based adoption agencies face legal challenges or the loss of licenses and contracts due to their religious beliefs that children should be placed with a married mother and father.

The following proposals are recommended to protect and enhance adoption services:

1. **Repeal the 2016 Regulation:** HHS should repeal the 2016 regulation that imposes non-statutory sexual orientation and gender identity nondiscrimination conditions on agency grants, returning to a policy that maximizes options for placing vulnerable children in stable homes.

2. **Survey for Additional Waivers:** ACF and OCR should survey their programs to determine if additional waivers of HHS grant conditions are needed for faith-based agencies. The Biden Administration revoked such waivers in 2021, but they are essential for protecting these agencies.

3. **Enact the Child Welfare Provider Inclusion Act:** Congress should pass this Act to ensure that providers cannot be discriminated against for offering adoption and foster care services based on their beliefs about marriage.

OFFICE OF REFUGEE RESETTLEMENT (ORR)

The Office of Refugee Resettlement (ORR), currently under HHS, should be transferred to the Department of Homeland Security (DHS) due to its increasingly problematic role in incentivizing illegal immigration and placing children in dangerous situations. ORR's mission has drifted from refugee resettlement to providing an array of free programs that encourage illegal immigration. Additionally, ORR has been criticized for placing children into risky environments when releasing them into the country.

The following proposals are recommended:

1. **Transfer ORR to DHS:** Congress should reform the Trafficking Victims Protection Reauthorization Act to transfer all ORR duties for unaccompanied alien children to DHS and eliminate the Flores settlement agreement.

2. **Prohibit Abortion Facilitation:** Regardless of where ORR's functions reside, staff and care providers should be prohibited from facilitating abortions for unaccompanied minors in ORR custody. This includes transporting minors across state lines for abortions. ORR should withdraw its policy allowing elective abortions and issue new guidelines instructing care providers not to allow such transportations. HHS OGC and the White House should ensure that DOJ defends this policy up to the U.S. Supreme Court in light of the Dobbs decision.

Office of Child Support Enforcement (OCSE)

The Office of Child Support Enforcement (OCSE) was established to assist single-parent families, primarily those suffering from the loss of a bread-winning parent. However, over time, the majority of these families became dependent due to paternal abandonment rather than death. Today, nearly one-third of American children live without a father in the home, with a quarter of them enrolled to receive child support. The primary issue in child support enforcement is the non-resident father's ability to provide consistent child support payments.

To address these challenges, the following proposals are recommended:

1. **Child Support Tax Credit:** Update national or state guidelines and tax laws to provide a non-dependent child support tax credit for nonresident parents with child support orders. This credit would empower fathers by using their earned income to assist in providing for their children, reinforcing their role as financial providers.

2. **Improve Visitation:** Integrate visitation with child support enforcement by ensuring that nonresident parents spend more time with their children, as increased visitation often correlates with more consistent child support payments. For example, Texas has combined its child support and visitation courts to achieve this goal.

3. **Implement Child Support Payment and Interactive Smartphone Application:** States should be encouraged to adopt high-tech applications to centralize child support payments, allowing nonresident parents to make easy, trackable payments. This would help address disputes about informal

contributions, ensuring that all support provided by nonresident parents is accounted for and acknowledged.

HEALTHY MARRIAGE AND RELATIONSHIP EDUCATION (HMRE) PROGRAM

The Healthy Marriage and Relationship Education (HMRE) program, part of the ACF Office of Family Assistance, provides education and resources on healthy marriages and relationships. To enhance the effectiveness of this program, the following proposals are recommended:

1. **State-Level Education Resources:** Utilize HMRE funding to provide high school education resources on healthy marriages, sexual risk avoidance, and healthy relationships. Early intervention is key to preventing broken relationships later in life.

2. **Use Child Welfare Funding for Marriage and Relationship Education:** Congress should clarify that funding under Title II of the Child Abuse Prevention and Treatment Act and Title IV-B of the Social Security Act can be used for healthy marriage education, especially for families at risk of foster care placement.

3. **Provide Marriage Information at Title X Clinics:** HHS should require Title X family planning clinics to offer information on the importance of marriage to family well-being and refer clients to relevant resources.

4. **Ensure Proper Assessment of HMRE Programs:** HMRE programs should be assessed fairly and thoroughly, considering recent improvements in their effectiveness. Faith-based programs should be protected and prioritized, particularly in light of challenges posed by the Respect for Marriage Act.

5. **Protect Faith-Based Recipients:** HMRE program grants should be available to faith-based recipients who uphold a traditional definition of marriage, which is supported by social science research as the most stable environment for raising children.

HEALTHY MARRIAGE AND RESPONSIBLE FATHERHOOD (HMRF) PROGRAM

The Healthy Marriage and Responsible Fatherhood (HMRF) program also operates within the ACF Office of Family Assistance, focusing on providing marriage and parenting guidance to low-income fathers. To strengthen this program, the following proposals are recommended:

1. **Pro-Fatherhood Messaging Campaign:** Launch a national campaign using HMRF funds to highlight the importance of fathers in children's lives. This campaign should address the financial and relational challenges faced by fathers, particularly those who were raised without a father figure.

2. **Fund Effective HMRF State Programs:** Prioritize grant allocations for state programs that involve local churches, mentorship programs, and community support initiatives. These programs should teach fatherhood based on biological and sociological principles, emphasizing the unique role of fathers rather than promoting gender-neutral parenting models.

ADMINISTRATION ON CHILDREN, YOUTH, AND FAMILIES (ACYF)

PROMOTE FATHER INVOLVEMENT OR EXPEDITE TERMINATION OF PARENTAL RIGHTS

The Administration on Children, Youth, and Families (ACYF) is exploring programs designed to encourage parental, especially paternal, engagement with children in foster care. These initiatives are intended to promote responsible parenthood, aiming to either reintegrate children with their families or ensure the presence of a consistent male figure in their lives. However, in situations where a parent fails to make a sincere effort to be involved in their child's upbringing, ACYF should ensure the swift termination of parental rights to expedite the child's placement in a stable and permanent home.

OFFICE OF HEAD START (OHS)

ELIMINATE THE HEAD START PROGRAM

The Head Start program, originally established to support low-income families by providing preschool care, is plagued by numerous issues, including scandals and abuse. Despite an $11 billion budget, the program has been ineffective in achieving its goals, with research showing little or no long-term academic benefit for children enrolled. Furthermore, between October 2015 and May 2020, about one in four grant recipients reported incidents where children were abused, left unsupervised, or released to unauthorized persons. Due to these serious issues, the recommendation is to eliminate the Head Start program and the entire Office of Head Start (OHS). At a minimum, the program's COVID-19 vaccine and mask mandates should be rescinded immediately.

ADMINISTRATION FOR COMMUNITY LIVING (ACL)

SUPPORT PALLIATIVE CARE OVER PHYSICIAN-ASSISTED SUICIDE

Physician-assisted suicide (PAS) is currently legal in 10 states and the District of Columbia. However, PAS is considered a grave mistake that endangers vulnerable individuals, undermines the integrity of the medical profession, disrupts family dynamics, and compromises human dignity and equality before the law. Instead of PAS, policymakers should prioritize palliative care, which focuses on improving the quality of life for patients by alleviating pain and distressing symptoms associated with serious illnesses. The Administration for Community Living (ACL) should ensure that its programs support vulnerable individuals and do not facilitate or encourage participation in PAS.

READDRESS THE NATIONAL STRATEGY TO SUPPORT FAMILY CAREGIVERS

The current National Strategy to Support Family Caregivers, while intended to aid family members caring for older relatives, is overly focused on racial and "LGBTQ+ equity." The strategy should be reexamined to create a more efficient and effective plan that genuinely supports caregivers and their families. Additionally, there should be a review of the strategy's COVID-19 policies to ensure they are appropriate and beneficial to the families involved.

HEALTH RESOURCES AND SERVICES ADMINISTRATION (HRSA)

UTILIZE 340B DATA AND IMPLEMENT PENALTIES FOR NON-COMPLIANCE

Congress should allow the Centers for Medicare & Medicaid Services (CMS) to use the 340B drug pricing data already collected by HRSA rather than conducting separate surveys. This recommendation follows the U.S. Supreme Court's decision in *American Hospital Association v. Becerra*. Additionally, legislation should introduce penalties for entities that fail to respond to HRSA's data collection efforts, ensuring greater compliance and data accuracy.

LEGALLY DEFINE THE LOCUS OF SERVICE FOR TELEHEALTH AS THE PROVIDER'S LOCATION

To modernize telehealth regulations, the legal definition of the service locus should be established as where the provider is located during the telehealth visit rather than where the patient is. This change would allow states to maintain control over licensure and scope of practice standards while enabling providers to continue offering consistent care regardless of their patients' locations. The flexibility granted during the COVID-19 pandemic demonstrated the importance of telehealth, particularly in rural and underserved areas. HRSA's Office for the Advancement of Telehealth should continue supporting licensure portability but without dictating state laws, as telehealth across state lines constitutes interstate commerce, which the federal government can regulate.

RESTORE TRUMP-ERA RELIGIOUS AND MORAL EXEMPTIONS TO THE CONTRACEPTIVE MANDATE

The Biden Administration's proposed regulation titled "Coverage of Certain Preventive Services Under the Affordable Care Act" aims to amend the Trump-era final rules regarding religious and moral exemptions to the ACA's contraception mandate. HHS should rescind this proposal if it is finalized, as there is no need to curtail the existing exemptions and accommodations, which protect individuals' religious and moral beliefs from government mandates.

MANDATE HRSA TO USE RULEMAKING FOR WOMEN'S PREVENTIVE SERVICES

HRSA should be required to use the notice-and-comment rulemaking process, as mandated by the Administrative Procedures Act, for any women's preventive services guidelines, including the contraceptive mandate. Previously, HRSA has bypassed this process, making changes without public input, which has led to legal challenges. Additionally, HRSA's long-term contracts with the pro-abortion American College of Obstetricians and Gynecologists (ACOG) should be rescinded. An advisory committee compliant with the Federal Advisory Committee Act, and free from pro-abortion bias, should be established to guide the content of women's preventive services mandates.

EXPAND COVERAGE OF FERTILITY AWARENESS-BASED METHODS

HRSA should ensure that fertility awareness-based methods (FABMs) are included in women's preventive services under the ACA. In 2016, FABMs were included as part of preventive services, but this language was removed in December 2021 without proper notice or rationale. A federal court blocked this removal, ruling it unlawful. HRSA should promulgate regulations that not only include FABMs but also require coverage for the necessary materials and supplies associated with these methods, recognizing their effectiveness and aligning coverage with women's values.

REMOVE MEN'S PREVENTIVE SERVICES FROM THE WOMEN'S PREVENTIVE SERVICES MANDATE

In December 2021, HRSA updated its guidelines to include male condoms under the women's preventive services mandate, despite previously claiming it had no authority to do so. This inclusion is inconsistent with Congress's intent to limit the mandate to women's preventive care. HRSA should eliminate male contraceptive methods from these guidelines to maintain the focus on women's services.

ELIMINATE THE WEEK-AFTER PILL FROM THE CONTRACEPTIVE MANDATE

Ella (ulipristal acetate), a drug included in the HRSA preventive services guidelines as an emergency contraceptive, functions similarly to the abortion pill mifepristone by blocking progesterone and potentially preventing a fertilized embryo from implanting. Given its potential to act as an abortifacient, HRSA should remove Ella from the contraceptive mandate.

WITHDRAW RYAN WHITE GUIDANCE ON CROSS-SEX TRANSITION SUPPORT

HRSA should withdraw all guidance that encourages Ryan White HIV/AIDS Program service providers to offer "gender transition" procedures or "gender-affirming care." These procedures can cause irreversible harm, both physically and mentally, to individuals who undergo them. The focus should be on providing care that supports health without promoting controversial and potentially harmful interventions.

ENSURE ABORTION TRAINING COMPLIANCE

HHS should ensure that all training programs for medical professionals, including doctors, nurses, and doulas, comply with restrictions on abortion funding and adhere to conscience-protection laws. Specific actions include:

1. Investigating state medical school compliance with the Coats–Snowe Amendment, which prohibits discrimination against entities that do not provide or undergo abortion training.
2. Ensuring that the Accreditation Council for Graduate Medical Education (ACGME) complies with all relevant conscience statutes and regulations.
3. Mandating that abortion-related training in medical schools be offered on an opt-in basis rather than opt-out.
4. Requiring states receiving HHS funds to issue regulations or establish arrangements with accrediting bodies to ensure compliance with the Coats–Snowe Amendment.

PRIORITIZE FUNDING FOR HOME-BASED CHILDCARE OVER UNIVERSAL DAYCARE

HRSA should prioritize funding for home-based childcare instead of universal daycare. Research indicates that children in daycare experience higher rates of anxiety, depression, and neglect, as well as poorer educational and developmental outcomes. Instead of funding daycare, resources should be directed to helping parents afford to stay home with their children or to pay for in-home childcare provided by family members.

PROVIDE EDUCATION AND RESOURCES ON EARLY CHILDHOOD HEALTH

HRSA should partner with organizations like the Center on Child and Family Poverty to offer resources on the importance of the mother–child relationship in child well-being. This includes providing relationship education curricula to help mothers and caregivers connect with and better understand their infants, toddlers, and young children, thereby promoting healthier early childhood development.

SUPPORT DOULAS AS PART OF MATERNAL AND CHILD HEALTH PROGRAMS

HRSA's Maternal and Child Health program is collecting data on the benefits of doulas, who provide non-medical, patient-focused support during childbirth. Doulas have been shown to significantly reduce cesarean rates, labor length, and the need for medical interventions like epidurals. Given the positive impact of doulas on maternal health and birth experiences, HRSA should work to ensure that doulas are an available option for all women, regardless of their birthing setting. Additionally, since doula services are often not covered by traditional insurance, HRSA should provide funding to make these services accessible to low-income mothers.

INDIAN HEALTH SERVICE (IHS)

The Indian Health Service (IHS) is responsible for providing healthcare services to American Indian and Alaska Native populations. However, several reforms are necessary to fulfill the U.S. government's commitments to these communities effectively. These reforms must account for cultural preferences, geographical limitations, and limited Internet access, which pose significant challenges in delivering healthcare.

During the COVID-19 pandemic, contacting individuals in these communities proved difficult due to transient addresses and unreliable cell service. Furthermore, the transition to the Biden Administration saw a disruption in the supply of COVID-19 tests and vaccines to tribes, leaving them without essential health resources during a public health emergency (PHE). Even before the pandemic, certain services, such as vision care, were often scarce or nonexistent in these communities.

To improve healthcare for these populations, the following reforms are recommended:

1. **Preserve Access During Public Health Emergencies:** It is crucial to ensure that tribes maintain continuous access to health resources during PHEs. This includes safeguarding the supply of necessary medical supplies, such as COVID-19 tests and vaccines, to prevent the abandonment of these communities during crises.

2. **Empower Patients with Alternative Healthcare Options:** Patients within these populations should have better access to private healthcare providers as an alternative to IHS services. Exploring reforms similar to those in the VA MISSION Act could provide American Indians and Alaska Natives with increased healthcare options and access.

RURAL HEALTH

Access to healthcare services is a growing concern for Americans living in rural, less populated areas. Many rural regions are experiencing declining access to healthcare due to economic shifts, with industries moving away and taking medical providers with them. Others live in rural areas due to professions such as farming, which necessitate residing in less populated regions with fewer medical facilities and limited economic opportunities.

For rural Americans, access to healthcare often requires long drives to the nearest medical provider or facility, and limited Internet access further restricts their ability to utilize telehealth services. Recognizing these unique challenges, the following recommendations are proposed:

1. **Reduce Regulatory Burdens and Encourage Private Innovation:** HHS should work to reduce the regulatory burden on healthcare providers in rural areas, enabling private innovation to develop solutions tailored to the unique needs of these communities.

2. **Increase the Supply of Healthcare Providers:** Policies that increase the availability of healthcare providers in rural areas should be implemented or encouraged. This includes expanding telehealth access, promoting interstate licensure for healthcare professionals (including volunteers providing temporary charitable services), and other measures that increase the supply of medical professionals in rural regions.

3. **Promote Flexibility in Healthcare Delivery:** HHS should encourage the use of less expensive alternatives to traditional hospitals, such as telehealth services, and reduce reliance on costly air ambulances. Increasing flexibility in healthcare delivery modes is essential for meeting the needs of rural populations effectively.

OFFICE OF THE SECRETARY

The Secretary of Health and Human Services (HHS) is the central figure within the department, holding the most accountability and responsibility for setting the policies that guide the entire agency. It is essential that the Secretary, along with their immediate staff, takes a leading role in policymaking rather than allowing operational divisions to diffuse responsibility by assuming this role.

To enhance the Secretary's accountability and ensure more effective governance of HHS, the following reforms are proposed:

RESTRICT INDEFINITE PUBLIC HEALTH EMERGENCIES (PHES)

Currently, the Secretary of HHS can declare a public health emergency (PHE) with minimal oversight, only needing to notify Congress within 48 hours. This system allows for the possibility of indefinite PHEs, which can lead to prolonged and unchecked executive power. To address this issue, Congress should establish a set time frame for any PHE declaration. The burden of proof would then fall on the Secretary to justify any extensions beyond the initial period, ensuring greater accountability and limiting the potential for abuse.

REINSTATE THE HHS SUNSET RULE

The HHS SUNSET (Securing Updated and Necessary Statutory Evaluations Timely) rule, introduced during the Trump Administration, required all HHS agencies to review existing regulations retrospectively and publish their findings. Without such reviews, the regulations would expire, ensuring that outdated or unnecessary regulations do not persist. This rule was reversed, but it should be reinstated and codified by Congress to ensure that HHS regulations remain relevant and effective.

Investigate and Address Rights Violations

The Secretary of HHS should lead efforts to investigate, expose, and remediate any instances where the department may have violated individuals' rights. Specific areas of concern include:

1. **Collusion with Big Tech:** During the COVID-19 pandemic, there were allegations that HHS colluded with Big Tech companies to censor dissenting opinions. Such actions potentially violate free speech rights and must be thoroughly investigated.

2. **Collusion with Abortion and LGBT Advocates:** There are also concerns that HHS may have colluded with abortion advocates and LGBT organizations to violate conscience-protection laws and the Hyde Amendment. These actions, if proven, undermine the rights of individuals who hold religious or moral objections to certain procedures or practices.

THE LIFE AGENDA

The Office of the Secretary should take a firm stance on life issues by eliminating the HHS Reproductive Healthcare Access Task Force, which has been perceived as promoting abortion as healthcare. In its place, a pro-life task force should be established to ensure that all divisions within HHS prioritize the life and health of women and their unborn children. This task force would advocate for policies that explicitly reject the notion that abortion is healthcare and reaffirm HHS's commitment to protecting life "from conception to natural death."

Additionally, the department should work to rebrand itself as the "Department of Life" by restoring its mission statement under the Strategic Plan and elsewhere to reflect this commitment. This would involve explicitly rejecting abortion and aligning all departmental actions with the goal of furthering the health and well-being of all Americans at every stage of life.

To coordinate these efforts, the next Administration should create a Special Representative for Domestic Women's Health. This position would serve as the lead on all federal domestic policy development related to life and family issues. Unlike the previous role of the Special Representative for Global Women's Health, which focused on international issues, this new position would concentrate on domestic policies, particularly in the post-*Dobbs* era. The Special Representative would work closely with the Domestic Policy Council (DPC) to implement and coordinate life and family-related policies across various federal agencies.

THE FAMILY AGENDA

The Secretary of HHS should adopt and publicly uphold antidiscrimination policies that recognize the biological realities of sex, distinguishing it clearly from gender identity or sexual orientation. The Secretary should emphasize that men and women are biological categories essential to the advancement of life sciences and medical care. Additionally, the Secretary should affirm that the ideal family structure consists of married men and women raising their biological children, as every child has a right to be raised by their biological parents. This stance supports the importance of traditional family values in the context of federal health and human services policy.

OFFICE OF THE ASSISTANT SECRETARY FOR HEALTH (OASH) / OFFICE OF THE SURGEON GENERAL (OSG)

The Assistant Secretary for Health (ASH) holds the rank of a four-star admiral within the United States Public Health Service Commissioned Corps (USPHS), while the Surgeon General (SG) is a three-star admiral. The ASH oversees not only the USPHS but also regional health offices, various presidential and secretarial advisory committees, and offices like Minority Health, Women's Health, and Population Affairs. The Secretary of Health and Human Services can expand the ASH's responsibilities, such as by designating the ASH as a liaison to the Centers for Disease Control and Prevention (CDC).

The SG, although officially in charge of USPHS operations, does not directly control daily operations, which fall under the Director of the USPHS Commissioned Corps Headquarters. The SG also serves as a key public health spokesperson, issuing advisories, Calls to Action, and Reports to the public.

RESTRUCTURING THE USPHS

The USPHS currently assigns officers to various agencies like the CDC, National Institutes of Health (NIH), and the Bureau of Prisons, with salaries primarily paid by these agencies, limiting USPHS appropriations. Officers can be deployed for domestic or international crises, such as hurricane responses or disease outbreaks like Ebola.

To improve efficiency, the USPHS should be restructured to resemble other uniformed services, with a streamlined chain of command and corresponding appropriations. The core mission should focus on prompt and responsive deployments that meet specific criteria, reducing reliance on the various agencies to which officers are assigned. Tasks should not be duplicated by both non-uniformed civil servants and USPHS officers, with civilian roles filling positions where possible.

CONSOLIDATING ASH AND SG POSITIONS

The positions of ASH and SG should be combined into a single four-star position, retaining the rank, responsibilities, and authority of the ASH but with the title of Surgeon General. This consolidated role would include some of the SG's communications responsibilities, such as disseminating HHS messages and providing general medical advice without legal authority. This change would ensure better focus and deployment of the USPHS under a unified leadership structure.

With this reform, the supporting office (previously OASH and OSG) would be better positioned to reduce bureaucratic silos and eliminate duplicative functions. Legislation should be considered to mandate such actions or at least require recommendations for streamlining the department's organizational structure.

COMBINING LEADERSHIP ROLES

The role previously known as the Principal Deputy Assistant Secretary for Health should be merged with the position of Deputy Surgeon General, creating a three-star position with operational control, including financial and deployment decisions. The Director of the Headquarters would be tasked with implementing the decisions of the Deputy Surgeon General.

PROMOTING LIFE AND FAMILY

The Office of the Assistant Secretary for Health should focus on addressing the root causes of sexually transmitted diseases (STDs) and unwanted pregnancies by promoting marriage and sexual risk avoidance. The Office of Science and Medicine requires strong leadership to conduct investigative reviews of literature on various issues, including the link between abortion and health risks like prematurity and breast cancer, the lack of evidence supporting "gender-affirming care," and the physical and emotional damage caused by cross-sex treatments, especially in children. The OASH should withdraw all support for cross-sex medical interventions and "gender-affirming care."

REFORMING TITLE X

The Title X family planning program should be reframed to focus on fertility awareness and holistic family planning. The Deputy Assistant Secretary for Population Affairs should be knowledgeable about the program and its legislative framework, ideally holding an MD. Additionally, the Office of Population Affairs must eliminate religious discrimination in grant selections, guaranteeing the right of conscience and religious freedom for healthcare workers and participants in the Title X program.

In 2021, the Biden Administration reversed a Trump-era regulation that required strict physical and financial separation between Title X activities and abortion-related activities. The new regulation allows Title X activities to be conducted alongside abortion services without strict separation and mandates referrals for abortions, even against moral or religious objections. This change effectively excludes pro-life organizations from participating in Title X.

HHS should rescind the Biden-era regulation and reinstate the Trump Administration's rules. This process should be expedited, taking less than nine months, as was done under the Biden Administration. Moreover, the potential pool of Title X grantees should be expanded beyond abortion providers like Planned Parenthood.

LEGISLATIVE SUPPORT FOR TITLE X REFORM

Congress should support these reforms by passing legislation such as the *Title X Abortion Provider Prohibition Act*, which would prohibit family planning grants from going to entities that perform abortions or fund other entities that do. This would safeguard the integrity of the Title X program, even under administrations that support abortion.

ADMINISTRATION FOR STRATEGIC PREPAREDNESS AND RESPONSE (ASPR)

ASPR VS. FEMA:

When the President declares a national emergency under the Stafford Act, which is related to a public health emergency declared by the HHS Secretary, the Federal Emergency Management Agency (FEMA) is activated and assumes control instead of HHS/ASPR. While FEMA's logistical capabilities can be advantageous, this arrangement should be reviewed to enhance efficiency, reduce confusion among ASPR and HHS agencies, and prevent duplication of efforts. The review should focus on leveraging the expertise and resources of both agencies, especially in light of lessons learned from the COVID-19 pandemic.

STRATEGIC NATIONAL STOCKPILE (SNS):

The Strategic National Stockpile (SNS) requires reform to better anticipate and manage potential supply chain disruptions caused by pandemics or global conflicts. The Defense Production Act (DPA), which allows the federal government to temporarily take over private enterprises, should be invoked only in the most severe circumstances. During the COVID-19 pandemic, some states hoarded ventilators received from the SNS, which led to an inefficient allocation of resources. The SNS should clarify that its mission is to serve as a supplier of last resort for federal and state governments, first responders, and key medical personnel, rather than the general public.

OFFICE OF GENERAL COUNSEL (OGC)

The Office of General Counsel (OGC) plays a critical role in ensuring that HHS operates within its legal framework. However, the emphasis on legal caution can sometimes delay decision-making, particularly during crises such as the COVID-19 pandemic. To improve efficiency, internal processes should be reformed to streamline legal determinations during emergencies. Additionally, general processes should be reviewed for overall efficiency. Specific recommendations for OGC include:

- **Rescind the PREP Act Liability Memo:** OGC issued a memo suspending the application of civil rights and other laws during the administration of covered countermeasures in the pandemic. This memo should be rescinded as it is contrary to law.

- **Restore OCR Authority Over Conscience and Religious Freedom:** Any OGC memos or Federal Register notices that transferred enforcement authority from the Office for Civil Rights (OCR) to OGC, particularly concerning conscience and religious freedom protections, should be rescinded. Authority over these matters should be returned to OCR.

- **Encourage DOJ to Repeal OLC Memos:** The Department of Justice (DOJ) should be encouraged to repeal Office of Legal Counsel (OLC) memos that allow abortion funding despite the Hyde Amendment and those that provide federal enclave immunity to perform abortions despite the Assimilative Crimes Act.

- **Rescind Legal Analyses on COVID-19 Eviction Moratorium and Other Issues:** The OGC should rescind its legal analyses that justified the imposition of a moratorium on rental evictions during COVID-19, as well as the legal analysis that authorized the dismissal of the University of Vermont Medical Center case, which involved the forced participation of a nurse in an abortion procedure.

- **Reverse Restored Medicaid Funds to California:** The OGC should reverse its decision to restore $200 million in Medicaid funds to California after the state was found to be in violation of the Weldon Amendment by OCR.

OFFICE OF GLOBAL AFFAIRS (OGA)

The Director of the Office of Global Affairs (OGA) should be re-titled as Assistant Secretary to better reflect the leadership role of this position in global health diplomacy. This title change would enhance the OGA Director's ability to represent HHS and the Secretary effectively on the international stage. Additional recommendations for the OGA include:

- **Strengthen Coordination of International Health Efforts:** All divisions involved in international health should be responsive to the direction of the Assistant Secretary, ensuring that health diplomacy is coordinated effectively across HHS.

- **Promote Pro-Life and Pro-Family Priorities:** OGA should consistently advocate for the Administration's pro-life and pro-family priorities in all international engagements.

- **Oversee Mexico City Policy Implementation:** OGA should hold oversight authority for the implementation of the Mexico City policy across all HHS divisions, ensuring compliance with the Administration's policies.

- **Improve Communication and Oversight:** Efforts should be made to locate all OGA staff in the same building to enhance oversight and communication.

- **Train Health Attachés:** Health attachés stationed globally should be trained in the Administration's policies, with clear expectations communicated regarding their conduct and advocacy. Accountability measures, including replacement, should be enforced when their actions contradict Administration policies and programmatic priorities.

OFFICE FOR CIVIL RIGHTS (OCR)

Conscience Enforcement: Existing statutes such as the Church, Coats–Snowe, and Weldon amendments protect rights of conscience but do not explicitly provide a private right of action for victims to seek legal redress in court. HHS continues to fund entities that violate these laws, which is unlawful. Under liberal administrations, OCR has a poor record in enforcing conscience and religious freedom laws. To address these issues:

- **Pass the Conscience Protection Act:** This would allow victims to seek redress through courts independently of OCR.

- **Restore Trump-Era Conscience Enforcement Policies:** OCR should fully fund the Conscience and Religious Freedom Division (CRFD) and ensure it has the necessary delegations from the Secretary to enforce conscience laws, including RFRA. The Secretary, Deputy Secretary, and other HHS officials should support OCR CRFD's remedial measures, limit interference from other divisions, and withdraw funding from entities that refuse to comply with federal health care conscience laws.

- **Issue and Finalize Trump-Era RFRA and Religious Freedom Rule:** These regulations would establish a clear process for OCR's enforcement in coordination with other HHS divisions.

- **Reestablish Waivers for Religious Exemptions:** HHS should restore waivers for religious exemptions, particularly for faith-based adoption and foster care agencies, and rescind subjective case-by-case evaluations for religious exemptions.

- **Restore OCR Authority Over Vaccine-Related Religious Accommodation Requests:** OCR should regain the authority to review and render opinions on RFRA applications for religious accommodation concerning vaccines, particularly those made or tested with aborted fetal cell lines.

Section 1557 and Other Regulations: In 2020, Trump Administration regulations under Section 1557 of the ACA limited OCR's enforcement to the statutory text, deferring to a binary conception of sex discrimination. Courts blocked these provisions, and the Biden Administration proposed reinstating rules that include sexual orientation and gender identity as protected classes. To address this:

- **Return to Statutory Framework of Section 1557 and Title IX:** OCR should:
  1. **Remove Biden-Era Guidance on Sexual Orientation and Gender Identity:** This includes the May 2021 enforcement announcement and the March 2022 statement threatening states that protect minors from gender reassignment surgeries.
  2. **Issue a General Policy Statement:** This would specify that OCR will not enforce sexual orientation and gender identity discrimination prohibitions under Section 1557 and will prioritize compliance with the First Amendment, RFRA, and federal conscience laws.
  3. **Propose and Defend Trump-Era Section 1557 Regulations:** These should explicitly interpret the law not to include sexual orientation and gender identity discrimination.
  4. **Refocus on Serious Cases of Discrimination:** OCR should highlight its investigation and resolution of cases like the Larry Nassar abuse scandal and enforce disability rights laws to protect vulnerable children.

- **Finalization of Trump-Era Disability Rights Regulations:** OCR should finalize regulations concerning crisis standards of care, use of Quality Adjusted Life Years (QALYs), and prohibiting discriminatory practices against disabled newborns.

Withdrawal of Politicized Guidance:

- **Pharmacy Abortion Mandate Guidance:** OCR should withdraw its guidance for retail pharmacies, which incorrectly mandates the stocking and dispensing of first-trimester abortion drugs, ignoring pharmacists' rights to moral or religious objections.

- **HIPAA Guidance on Abortion:** OCR should withdraw its June 2022 guidance on patient privacy post-Dobbs, as it improperly portrays unborn patients as nonpersons and contributes to fearmongering about abortion after the Dobbs decision.

CHAPTER 15: DEPARTMENT OF HOUSING AND URBAN DEVELOPMENT

HUD programs tend to perpetuate the notion of bureaucratically provided housing as a basic life need and, whether intentionally or not, fail to acknowledge that these public benefits too often have led to intergenerational poverty traps, have implicitly penalized family formation in traditional two-parent marriages, and have discouraged work and income growth, thereby limiting upward mobility – Page 503

Key Policy Proposals

The proposed policies to reform the Department of Housing and Urban Development (HUD) reflect a profound misunderstanding of the essential role that federal housing programs play in ensuring economic stability, social equity, and upward mobility for millions of Americans. These reforms, driven by a conservative agenda, aim to dismantle critical protections and supports that have been fundamental to the progress we've made in addressing housing inequality. Let's dissect the core proposals and their likely consequences.

REVERSING HUD'S MISSION CREEP

The proposal to reverse nearly a century of HUD's "mission creep" by transferring its functions to other federal agencies, states, or localities is fundamentally flawed. HUD's expansion over time was not arbitrary but a necessary response to the growing and evolving needs of a diverse and dynamic society. The federal government's involvement in housing markets has been crucial in addressing market failures that local governments alone cannot manage. For example, the Fair Housing Act, enforced by HUD, has been instrumental in combating systemic discrimination. Dismantling HUD's role and passing the responsibilities to states or other agencies would lead to a fragmented approach, weakening enforcement and exacerbating disparities in housing access.

ADMINISTRATIVE AND PERSONNEL REFORMS

The proposed shift of authority to politically appointed officials, coupled with the conversion of career leadership positions into political appointments, threatens to undermine the impartiality and expertise necessary to manage complex housing policies. The danger here is clear: housing policy should not be a partisan tool. By politicizing HUD's leadership, the reforms risk prioritizing short-term political gains over the long-term stability and effectiveness of housing programs. This could lead to erratic policy shifts with each administration, creating uncertainty for millions of low-income families who rely on HUD's programs.

ENDING PROGRESSIVE POLICIES AND PROGRAMS

The proposal to reverse policies related to diversity, equity, and inclusion (DEI); environmental initiatives; and housing discrimination under the guise of protecting "integrity" is a thinly veiled attempt to roll back progress. DEI initiatives are not ideological experiments—they are responses to documented inequities that persist in our housing markets. For instance, African American and Hispanic families are disproportionately affected by housing discrimination and are less likely to own homes compared to white families. Removing these safeguards would exacerbate existing racial disparities in housing, entrenching segregation and limiting economic mobility for communities of color.

RESTRICTING PROGRAM ELIGIBILITY AND ENDING HOUSING FIRST

The call to prohibit noncitizens, including mixed-status families, from accessing federally assisted housing is not only inhumane but counterproductive. These families contribute to the economy and their exclusion from housing assistance would only increase homelessness and housing instability, leading to greater social costs in the long term. Furthermore, the push to end Housing First policies, which prioritize immediate housing for the homeless without preconditions, ignores the overwhelming evidence of its effectiveness. Housing First has been proven to reduce chronic homelessness and improve health outcomes. Abandoning this approach would likely result in a rise in homelessness, with far-reaching social and economic consequences.

FHA MORTGAGE INSURANCE ADJUSTMENTS

Increasing mortgage insurance premiums for longer-term loans while promoting shorter-term mortgages is misguided. While the intent may be to encourage faster equity accumulation, the reality is that many low-income families rely on longer-term mortgages because they offer lower monthly payments, making homeownership more accessible. Raising premiums on these loans would make homeownership more expensive for those who can least afford it, effectively pricing out low-income and first-time homebuyers from the market.

The collective impact of these proposed reforms would be devastating. The dismantling of HUD's comprehensive role in housing policy would likely lead to increased housing insecurity, deeper racial and economic inequalities, and a significant rise in homelessness. By stripping away protections and supports that are essential to ensuring that all Americans have access to safe, affordable housing, these policies would undermine the very foundation of economic opportunity and social stability in our country.

In conclusion, the proposed reforms are not just misguided—they are dangerous. They threaten to reverse decades of progress in housing equity, exacerbate existing inequalities, and destabilize the housing market. HUD's role is crucial in ensuring that every American, regardless of their background, has a fair chance at achieving the American Dream of homeownership and economic security. These reforms would take us backward, not forward.

Summary

This chapter of Mandate for Leadership was written by Benjamin S. Carson. The following summary conveys the content of the document accurately and objectively, without endorsing or critiquing the perspectives of the original authors.

The U.S. Department of Housing and Urban Development (HUD) is tasked with administering a wide array of federal programs designed to support access to homeownership, affordable rental housing, and stability for homeless individuals. HUD also plays a crucial role in maintaining public housing units and enforcing various housing regulations, including those related to quality standards and anti-discrimination laws.

However, these programs have often been criticized for perpetuating intergenerational poverty, discouraging traditional family structures, and limiting economic mobility. There is a growing concern that HUD's policies, whether by design or consequence, have trapped many individuals in cycles of dependency, penalized marriage, and stifled work and income growth.

To address these issues, a conservative administration is encouraged to undertake significant reforms, which include:

- **Resetting HUD:** This involves reversing the progressive ideologies that have become entrenched within HUD's programs, particularly those implemented during the Biden Administration.
- **Implementing an Action Plan:** This plan should target both the processes and the personnel within HUD. It would involve redelegating authority to political appointees aligned with conservative values and urgently implementing administrative regulatory actions to reshape HUD's policies and program eligibility.

HUD REFORM PILLARS

HUD's evolution over nearly a century, beginning with its New Deal-era predecessors, has led to a significant expansion of its role in American housing markets. The chapter argues that this "mission creep" has resulted in a bloated and inefficient bureaucracy that often oversteps its statutory authority. A new conservative administration is advised to implement a comprehensive reform strategy focusing on the following pillars:

1. Reversing Mission Creep

A reassessment of the federal government's role in housing markets is deemed necessary. The text suggests that HUD's functions should be carefully examined to determine whether they should be transferred to other federal agencies, states, or localities. This would involve a "reform, reinvention, and renewal" approach that streamlines HUD's operations and refocuses its mission.

2. Administrative and Personnel Reforms

Immediate reforms should target both the personnel and processes within HUD:

- **Political Appointees:** Authority should be redelegated to politically appointed officials who align with the administration's conservative values. Career positions currently holding significant power should be converted into political appointments, ensuring that key leadership roles are occupied by individuals committed to the administration's goals.
- **Regulatory Actions:** The administration should swiftly implement regulatory changes to reverse the progressive policies introduced by the Biden Administration. These include policies related to racial equity, environmental initiatives, and housing discrimination, which are seen as undermining the integrity of HUD's programs.

3. Legislative Safeguards

The text advocates for a future Congress, under conservative leadership, to enact legislative reforms that would further solidify these administrative changes. These reforms would aim to prevent future mission creep and protect taxpayers from the inefficiencies and overreach that have characterized HUD's expansion over the decades.

FIRST-DAY AND FIRST-YEAR ADMINISTRATIVE REFORMS

The chapter outlines specific reforms that a new conservative administration should implement within HUD, focusing on both immediate actions and those to be achieved within the first year. These reforms are designed to align HUD's operations with conservative principles and to correct what the text identifies as the overreach of previous administrations, particularly the Biden Administration.

1. Reassignment of Delegated Powers

- **Immediate Assignment:** All delegated powers should be reassigned to politically appointed Principal Deputy Assistant Secretaries (PDAS), Deputy Assistant Secretaries (DAS), and other office leadership positions. This ensures that the individuals in key roles are politically aligned with the administration's conservative agenda.
- **Conversion of Career Positions:** Any current career leadership positions with significant authority should be converted into political and non-career appointments. The administration should also utilize Senior Executive Service (SES) transfers to install motivated and aligned leadership across HUD's offices.

2. Executive Order on Foreign Investment Oversight

- **Committee on Foreign Investment:** The President should issue an executive order to make the HUD Secretary a member of the Committee on Foreign Investment in the United States (CFIUS). This would broaden HUD's oversight capabilities, particularly in addressing foreign threats such as China's influence in U.S. real estate markets. With trillions of dollars' worth of real estate under HUD's portfolio, this is seen as a critical step in protecting national interests.

3. Task Force to Reverse Progressive Policies

- **Biden Administration Policies:** The HUD Secretary should initiate a task force comprised of politically appointed personnel to identify and reverse all actions taken by the Biden Administration that have advanced progressive ideologies. This includes policies under designations such as diversity, equity, and inclusion (DEI); critical race theory (CRT); and environmental, social, and governance (ESG) initiatives.

4. Review and Repeal of Subregulatory Guidance

- **Administrative Procedure Act (APA) Compliance:** The Office of the Secretary or the Office of General Counsel should conduct a thorough review of all subregulatory guidance issued outside the APA. Key actions include:
  - **Ending Property Appraisal and Valuation Equity (PAVE):** Immediately terminate the Biden Administration's PAVE policies, which are criticized for undermining the integrity of real estate appraisals.
  - **Repealing Climate Change Initiatives:** Remove all climate change initiatives and related spending from HUD's budget, which are seen as adding unnecessary costs and delays to housing development.
  - **Repealing Affirmatively Furthering Fair Housing (AFFH):** Repeal the reinstated AFFH regulation, viewed as a tool for enforcing equity in ways that distort housing markets.

5. Restricting Program Eligibility

- **Noncitizens in Federal Housing:** The Secretary should push forward regulatory and subregulatory guidance to prohibit noncitizens, including mixed-status families, from living in federally assisted housing. HUD's obligations should prioritize housing for American citizens, aligning with broader immigration policy reforms.
- **Eligibility Restrictions:** Further reforms should restrict program eligibility to promote household self-sufficiency, discourage anti-marriage biases, and enforce work readiness and maximum term limits for housing assistance. The chapter specifically calls for ending Housing First policies, advocating instead for approaches that address mental health and substance abuse before permanent housing solutions.

6. Suspension of External Research Grants

- **Office of Policy Development and Research:** The Assistant Secretary (AS) or Principal Deputy Assistant Secretary (PDAS) for the Office of Policy Development and Research should suspend all external research and evaluation grants that do not contribute directly to HUD's core mission. The office should focus solely on data collection, survey administration, and regulatory impact analysis.

7. FHA Mortgage Insurance Adjustments

- **Encouraging Shorter-Term Mortgages:** FHA leadership should increase the mortgage insurance premium (MIP) for loans with terms over 20 years while maintaining the current MIP for loans with shorter terms and refinances. This change is aimed at promoting wealth-building through shorter-duration homeownership opportunities.

LONGER-TERM POLICY REFORM CONSIDERATIONS

The chapter addresses broader, long-term reforms that a conservative administration should consider implementing within HUD. These reforms go beyond immediate administrative changes, aiming to fundamentally reshape HUD's role in housing policy over the next five years and beyond.

1. Encouraging Choice and Competition in Rental Assistance

- **Housing Choice and Mobility:** The chapter advocates for reforms that encourage choice and competition in the rental market, particularly within HUD's rental assistance programs. These reforms should incentivize landlord participation and provide flexibility in rent payment terms, thereby facilitating the movement of households toward self-sufficiency.
- **Work Requirements and Term Limits:** Strengthening work requirements and imposing time limits on housing benefits are proposed as essential steps in ensuring that able-bodied, non-elderly adults are encouraged to become self-sufficient. These measures would align with broader conservative goals of reducing dependency on government assistance.

2. Local Autonomy in Housing Decisions

- **Opposition to Federal Overreach:** The chapter emphasizes the importance of local autonomy in housing decisions, particularly in matters of zoning and land use. Any federal efforts that undermine local control, such as those that weaken single-family zoning, should be resisted. The text argues that local governments, not federal agencies, are best equipped to determine the needs and desires of their communities.
- **Tax Credits for Housing Renovation:** To support homeownership, especially in rural areas, Congress is encouraged to introduce tax credits that incentivize the renovation and repair of existing housing stock. This approach is seen as a way to preserve the American Dream of homeownership and promote generational wealth building.

3. Reforming the Public Housing Model

- **Shift Toward Vouchers:** The chapter suggests moving away from the traditional public housing model and expanding the use of housing choice vouchers. This transition is intended to increase competition in the rental market while maintaining local control over housing decisions. However, the text cautions that such a shift should not come at the expense of local autonomy or community preferences.
- **Sale of Public Housing Land:** Public housing authorities (PHAs) should be given the flexibility to sell land and properties currently used for public housing. The proceeds from these sales could be reinvested in local economies, promoting private investment, job creation, and increased tax revenues. This approach is framed as a more dynamic and economically beneficial use of public housing resources.

4. Maintaining Strong Financial Oversight

- **Accountability in Financial Operations:** Reflecting on past financial mismanagement within HUD, the chapter underscores the importance of maintaining rigorous financial oversight. This includes the need for strong leadership, particularly in the role of Chief Financial Officer (CFO), to ensure that HUD's financial operations are transparent, accountable, and capable of withstanding audits. The text highlights the success of reforms implemented during the Trump Administration, which resulted in HUD's first clean audit in nearly a decade.

5. Devolution of HUD Functions

- **Transferring Functions to Other Agencies:** The chapter proposes a radical restructuring of HUD, where many of its functions could be devolved to other federal agencies, states, or localities. For example, loan guarantee programs could be transferred to the Small Business Administration (SBA), Indian housing programs to the Department of the Interior, and rental assistance programs to a redesignated Housing and Home Finance Agency. This restructuring is intended to eliminate redundancy, streamline operations, and focus HUD on its core missions.

6. Reducing Federal Intervention in Housing Markets

- **Limiting Federal Impact:** The chapter argues that federal policies often crowd out private-sector development and exacerbate affordability issues in housing markets. It calls for legislation that minimizes federal preemption of local land use and zoning decisions, allowing states and localities maximum flexibility in designing housing policies that suit their unique needs.

CHAPTER 16: DEPARTMENT OF THE INTERIOR

The Endangered Species Act's success rate... is dismal. Its greatest deficiency, according to one renowned expert, is 'conflict of interest.' Specifically, the work of the Fish and Wildlife Service is the product of 'species cartels' afflicted with groupthink, confirmation bias, and a common desire to preserve the prestige, power, and appropriations of the agency that pays or employs them. – Page 534

Key Policy Proposals

The proposals outlined in this document represent a drastic and dangerous shift in U.S. policy that threatens environmental protection, undermines efforts to combat climate change, and disregards the rights and welfare of Indigenous communities. These policies are deeply flawed and represent a regressive agenda that prioritizes short-term economic gains over the long-term health of the planet and the well-being of future generations.

ENERGY DOMINANCE AT THE EXPENSE OF THE ENVIRONMENT

The push to restore "American Energy Dominance" is a thinly veiled attempt to expand fossil fuel extraction on federal lands, disregarding the catastrophic impact this will have on the environment. The document advocates for rolling back protections that limit oil, gas, and coal development, under the guise of economic growth. However, the data is clear: continued reliance on fossil fuels is the primary driver of climate change, which poses an existential threat to life on Earth.

Reinstating the Trump-era policies would not only increase greenhouse gas emissions but would also lead to the degradation of public lands that belong to all Americans. The proposed policies would open up vast areas of land for drilling and mining, including the Arctic National Wildlife Refuge and other protected areas, which would have devastating effects on wildlife, ecosystems, and Indigenous communities who rely on these lands.

REPEALING ENVIRONMENTAL PROTECTIONS

The proposal to dismantle the National Environmental Policy Act (NEPA) reforms is particularly alarming. NEPA is a cornerstone of environmental law, ensuring that federal agencies consider the environmental impacts of their actions before proceeding. The document's call to eliminate judicial review of NEPA documents would strip the public of a critical tool for holding the government accountable. This would lead to rushed, poorly conceived projects that could cause irreversible harm to the environment and public health.

Moreover, the intention to roll back the Endangered Species Act (ESA) protections under the guise of "conflict of interest" is a gross mischaracterization. The ESA has been instrumental in preventing the extinction of numerous species. Delisting the grizzly bear and the gray wolf, as proposed, ignores the ongoing threats these species face. This move would likely result in increased hunting and habitat destruction, pushing these species back towards endangerment.

DISREGARD FOR INDIGENOUS SOVEREIGNTY

The proposed policies also exhibit a blatant disregard for the sovereignty and rights of Indigenous communities. The document criticizes the Biden Administration for not promoting fossil fuel development on Indigenous lands, claiming this hinders economic opportunities. However, this perspective fails to consider that many Indigenous communities have opposed such developments due to their detrimental impacts on the environment and cultural heritage.

The push to revoke environmental regulations on Indigenous lands and promote fossil fuel extraction without their consent is a direct assault on their sovereignty. This approach not only violates the principle of free, prior, and informed consent as outlined in international law but also risks further marginalizing these communities by prioritizing corporate profits over their rights and interests.

IMPACT ON CLIMATE CHANGE AND PUBLIC HEALTH

The document's emphasis on increasing fossil fuel production, while simultaneously reducing environmental regulations, is a recipe for disaster in the fight against climate change. The scientific consensus is unequivocal: to avoid the worst impacts of climate change, the world must rapidly reduce greenhouse gas emissions and transition to clean energy. These proposals move in the opposite direction, locking in decades of carbon emissions and making it nearly impossible to meet international climate commitments, such as those under the Paris Agreement.

The public health consequences of these policies would also be severe. Increased fossil fuel extraction and the rollback of environmental regulations would lead to higher levels of air and water pollution, which are linked to respiratory diseases, cancer, and other serious health conditions. Communities near these developments, often low-income and marginalized, would bear the brunt of these health impacts, exacerbating existing inequalities.

These policy proposals represent a dangerous regression that prioritizes short-term economic interests over the long-term sustainability of our environment and the rights of Indigenous peoples. The consequences of implementing these policies would be dire: accelerating climate change, destroying ecosystems, eroding public health, and further marginalizing vulnerable communities. It is imperative that we reject this agenda and instead focus on policies that promote clean energy, protect our natural heritage, and uphold the rights of all communities. The future of our planet and the well-being of generations to come depend on it.

Summary

This chapter of Mandate for Leadership was written by William Perry Pendley. The following summary conveys the content of the document accurately and objectively, without endorsing or critiquing the perspectives of the original authors.

The U.S. Department of the Interior (DOI) plays a critical role in managing the nation's vast natural resources and cultural heritage. Its responsibilities are extensive, covering over 500 million acres of federal lands, including national parks and wildlife refuges, and more than 700 million acres of subsurface minerals. Additionally, the DOI manages 1.7 billion acres of the Outer Continental Shelf (OCS), which contributes significantly to the nation's energy supply, including 23 percent of its energy. The department also oversees water resources in 17 western states and holds trust responsibilities for 566 Indian tribes and Alaska Natives.

The DOI's budget request for 2024 is $18.9 billion, reflecting a $2 billion increase from 2023. This budget also anticipates generating receipts of $19.6 billion, highlighting the department's role in both expenditure and revenue generation.

HISTORICAL BACKGROUND AND MISSION

The DOI, sometimes referred to as the "Great Miscellany" due to its wide range of responsibilities, was established in 1849. Initially, its duties included oversight of the Indian Bureau, the General Land Office, the Bureau of Pensions, and the Patent Office. Over time, the department's mission became more focused on managing the nation's natural resources, a shift that gained momentum with the rise of the conservation movement in the early 20th century.

The department's responsibilities also encompass working landscapes involving grazing, logging, mining, oil, and gas development. With the establishment of the Bureau of Reclamation in 1902, the DOI took on the role of the nation's dam builder, further expanding its influence.

Today, the DOI employs approximately 70,000 people across 2,400 locations, including offices in the United States, Puerto Rico, and U.S. Territories. Historically, the department operated in a bipartisan manner, consistent with Congress's laws under the Property Clause of the Constitution. This approach ensured that western states, counties, and communities could sustain themselves economically and recreationally on neighboring federal lands, which often constitute a significant portion of their landmass—up to 90 percent in some rural western counties.

POLICY SHIFTS OVER TIME

The bipartisan nature of the DOI began to erode during President Jimmy Carter's administration, which, influenced by environmental groups, implemented policies that were met with dismay by western governors, including many Democrats. President Ronald Reagan opposed these policies, declaring himself a "Sagebrush Rebel" and reversing Carter's initiatives to quell what was known as the "War on the West." Subsequent administrations, including those of Presidents George H. W. Bush, Bill Clinton, and George W. Bush, continued to oscillate between prioritizing environmental concerns and economic interests. Clinton's administration, for instance, resumed Carter's policies, exemplified by actions such as introducing wolves into states bordering Yellowstone and designating vast national monuments despite local opposition.

President Barack Obama's administration renewed anti-economic policies concerning federal lands, particularly restricting oil and gas activities, which starkly contrasted with the fracking revolution that had brought massive discoveries on state and private lands.

President Donald Trump's administration marked a significant shift by emphasizing energy dominance. His DOI actively sought to comply with federal law by conducting congressionally mandated lease sales, which contributed to the United States achieving energy security for the first time since 1957.

However, President Joe Biden's DOI has been characterized by a retreat from these policies. The department, under Biden, has issued fewer federal leases than any administration since Harry Truman's presidency, notably abandoning the pursuit of energy independence. Biden's DOI has been described as opposing the department's mission, particularly in its management of oil, gas, and coal resources. The department has also moved away from the "multiple use" and "sustained yield" principles that traditionally guided the management of federal lands overseen by the Bureau of Land Management (BLM).

BUDGET STRUCTURE

The DOI's 2024 budget of $18.9 billion is relatively small compared to other federal agencies. However, it is significant in its generation of more than $19.6 billion in "offsetting receipts" from sources such as oil and gas royalties, timber and grazing fees, park user fees, and land sales. The budget is primarily allocated among nine bureaus, each with distinct responsibilities:

1. **Bureau of Indian Affairs**: Manages trust responsibilities for 566 Indian tribes, including natural resource education, law enforcement, and social service programs, as well as operating schools and colleges.
2. **Bureau of Land Management (BLM)**: Manages 245 million acres of public land and 700 million acres of subsurface federal mineral estate, including energy and mineral development, forest management, timber production, and wild horse management.
3. **Bureau of Ocean Energy Management**: Manages access to energy resources on the Outer Continental Shelf, including leases for oil, gas, and offshore renewable energy projects.
4. **Bureau of Reclamation**: Oversees water resources, manages dams and reservoirs, and is a significant producer of hydroelectric power in the U.S.
5. **Bureau of Safety and Environmental Enforcement**: Regulates offshore oil and gas facilities and oversees oil spill response.
6. **National Park Service**: Manages natural, cultural, and recreational sites, historic structures, and wilderness areas, providing outdoor recreation and technical assistance to state and local programs.
7. **Office of Surface Mining Reclamation and Enforcement**: Regulates coal mining and site reclamation, providing grants to states and tribes for oversight and mitigating past mining effects.
8. **U.S. Fish and Wildlife Service**: Manages the National Wildlife Refuge System, oversees fish hatcheries, and protects endangered species and migratory birds.
9. **U.S. Geological Survey**: Conducts scientific research on ecosystems, climate change, mineral assessments, and natural hazards, leading climate change research for the department.

This section outlines the foundational structure and historical evolution of the DOI, setting the stage for the detailed policy discussions that follow.

RESTORING AMERICAN ENERGY DOMINANCE

Pendley emphasizes the critical need to restore the DOI's historic role in managing the nation's vast hydrocarbon resources under a conservative administration. The U.S. heavily depends on affordable, reliable energy resources for its economic well-being, national security, and global standing. The federal government owns 61 percent of the onshore and offshore mineral estate, yet only 22 percent of the nation's oil and 12 percent of its natural gas come from these lands, a situation exacerbated by the Biden Administration's restrictive policies. The decline in coal production on federal lands, which currently accounts for 42 percent of the nation's coal output, is also highlighted.

President Biden's DOI has aggressively aligned the management of public lands and waters to support a radical climate agenda, as outlined in Executive Orders 14008 and 13990. One of Biden's first actions was to ban federal leasing of coal, oil, and natural gas on federal lands and waters, fulfilling his campaign promise of "no federal oil." This policy shift marked a significant departure from the previous administration's Energy Dominance Agenda, which sought to maximize domestic energy production from federal lands.

Pendley critiques Biden's DOI for its sweeping overhaul of resource management plans, lease sales, fees, rents, royalty rates, and permitting processes, all aimed at reducing fossil fuel production while dramatically increasing solar and wind energy development. The DOI's "30 by 30" agenda, also known as "America the Beautiful," aims to remove federal lands from productive use, in favor of conservation goals.

The DOI under Biden is accused of abusing legal processes such as the National Environmental Policy Act (NEPA), the Antiquities Act, and bureaucratic procedures to advance climate goals for which it has no statutory authority. The Federal Land Policy and Management Act (FLPMA), Outer Continental Shelf Lands Act (OSCLA), and other congressional acts explicitly support multiple-use principles, including the production of fossil fuels, which the Biden Administration has undermined.
The argument is made that Biden's DOI is effectively hoarding energy supplies, preventing Americans from accessing cheaper and more abundant energy, thereby weakening the economy and reducing job opportunities. This is framed as a breach of the public trust and a violation of federal laws and court orders.

ADMINISTRATION PRIORITIES

Pendley then outlines the immediate actions a new conservative administration should take to reverse the policies implemented by Biden's DOI:

- **Rollbacks**: The first step involves reversing Biden's orders and reinstating Trump-era policies that promoted energy dominance. Key secretarial orders to be reinstated include those related to ending the federal coal moratorium, promoting offshore energy strategies, strengthening the energy portfolio, and supporting federal onshore oil, gas, and mineral leasing programs.
- **Actions**: The administration should reinstate quarterly onshore lease sales in all producing states and conduct offshore lease sales to the maximum extent permitted under the 2023–2028 lease program. Additionally, it should develop a new five-year plan for offshore oil and gas leasing, review all resource management plans from the previous four years, and reset rents, royalty rates, and bonding requirements in accordance with the Inflation Reduction Act.
- **Rulemaking**: The new administration must rescind Biden's rules and reestablish Trump-era regulations regarding waste prevention, the Endangered Species Act, the Migratory Bird Treaty Act, and NEPA reforms. Pendley advocates for reopening the National Petroleum Reserve of Alaska for leasing and development as part of these policy reversals.
- **Personnel Changes**: The new administration should prioritize state agency personnel who have proven their capabilities in land management. Pendley suggests reinstating President Trump's Schedule F proposal to ensure accountability in hiring, thus allowing the federal government to benefit from successful state resource management models. Broadening cooperative agreements between state, federal, and tribal authorities is also recommended.

IMMEDIATE ACTIONS

Pendley also emphasizes the importance of returning the Bureau of Land Management (BLM) headquarters to the American West. This move, initiated by the Trump Administration, was aimed at improving governance by placing BLM's leadership closer to the lands they manage. The Biden Administration's decision to return headquarters to Washington, D.C., is criticized as a step backward, as it distances top decision-makers from the resources and people they oversee.

The summary highlights that BLM law enforcement officers (LEOs) should report through a professional chain of command, ensuring that they are well-trained and equipped. Under Biden, BLM's law enforcement management has been fragmented, leading to weakened morale and a potential lack of uniform enforcement standards. A conservative administration would need to restore a proper law enforcement chain of command within the BLM.

Regarding wild horses and burros, Pendley explains the significant challenges posed by their overpopulation on public lands. The BLM's multi-pronged approach, detailed in its 2020 Report to Congress, is acknowledged, but Pendley stresses that more decisive actions, including potential legislative changes, are required to manage these populations humanely and sustainably.

IMMEDIATE ACTIONS REGARDING ALASKA

Alaska holds a unique position in the management of U.S. federal lands, deserving special consideration. When Alaska was admitted to the Union in 1959, almost all of its land was federally owned. To support its residents, Alaska was granted the right to select 104 million acres for state management. By 1967, Alaska had selected 26 million acres, but then-Interior Secretary Stewart Udall halted further selections to protect claims that might be made by Native Alaskans.

Alaska Native Claims Settlement Act (ANCSA)
The discovery of oil at Prudhoe Bay in 1968 necessitated the resolution of Native land claims, leading to the passage of the Alaska Native Claims Settlement Act (ANCSA) in 1971. This act allowed Native Alaskans to select 44 million acres. However, environmentalists, concerned about the potential development of these lands, insisted on a provision, Section 17(d)(2), which required the withdrawal of 80 million acres for future designation as parks, refuges, or national forests.

As the 1978 deadline for congressional action on these withdrawals approached, the Carter Administration, eager to protect these lands, unilaterally withdrew 100 million acres, triggering legal challenges from Alaska. Congress eventually passed the Alaska National Interest Lands Conservation Act (ANILCA) in 1980, which revoked the Carter Administration's withdrawals but designated 100 million acres as permanent federal enclaves, doubling the size of national parks and refuges in Alaska.

Despite these developments, by the time President Ronald Reagan took office, Alaska had received less than half of the land it was entitled to, and Native Alaskans had received only one-third of their due. Reagan's administration accelerated land transfers, ensuring that by 1983, Alaska had received 30 million acres and Native Alaskans nearly 60 percent of their entitlement.

However, even after nearly four decades, the federal government has not fulfilled its statutory obligations to Alaska and Native Alaskans, with each group still owed 5 million acres. This delay is attributed to Public Land Orders (PLOs) issued by the BLM, which effectively seize the land for federal use. Pendley argues that these PLOs must be lifted to allow Alaska and Native Alaskans to receive the land promised to them by Congress.

For instance, the revocation of PLO 5150 would immediately grant Alaska 1.3 million acres of its remaining entitlement. Pendley asserts that this revocation should be a top priority, along with the immediate revocation of all other BLM PLOs that are over 50 years old.

Energy and Mineral Development in Alaska

Alaska's untapped oil reserves are crucial not only to the revitalization of the U.S. energy sector but also to the state's economy, where one-quarter of jobs and half of the economy depend on the oil industry. To boost oil production, Pendley calls for the following actions:

1. **Reaffirm the 2020 National Petroleum Reserve Alaska Integrated Activity Plan (NPRA-IAP)**: The Biden Administration reverted to the 2013 IAP, which Pendley argues is based on outdated science. Reinstating the 2020 IAP is crucial for current and future oil development.
2. **Reinstate the 2020 Arctic National Wildlife Refuge Environmental Impact Statement (EIS)**: By lifting the suspension on leases, Pendley suggests that oil and gas exploration and development in the Coastal Plain of Alaska (known as the "Section 1002 Area") should proceed, as Congress intended when it excluded this area from the Arctic National Wildlife Refuge's wilderness designation.
3. **Approve the 2020 Willow EIS**: This would support the largest pending oil and gas project in the United States, located in the National Petroleum Reserve-Alaska, and allow for the expansion from three to five drilling pads.

Additionally, Alaska's mineral potential is vast, and Pendley advocates for the immediate approval of the Ambler Road Project. This project would create a 211-mile roadway on the south side of the Brooks Range, opening the area to mining-related industrial uses. This development is seen as essential for creating high-paying jobs in a region plagued by unemployment.

Wildlife and Water Management in Alaska

The federal government has often treated Alaska as less than a sovereign state, especially concerning wildlife and water resources. Pendley argues for immediate actions to correct these injustices:

1. **Revoke National Park Service and U.S. Fish and Wildlife Service Rules**: These rules concern predator control and bear baiting, which should fall under state regulation. Pendley asserts that this revocation is permissible under the 2017 Congressional Review Act.
2. **Acknowledge Alaska's Authority over Fish and Game**: Pendley advocates for recognizing Alaska's jurisdiction over wildlife management on federal lands, as was the practice during the Reagan Administration.
3. **Recognize State Ownership of Navigable Waters**: The DOI should issue a secretarial order declaring navigable waters in Alaska as state-owned, thereby transferring the lands beneath these waters to Alaska. This move would shift the burden of proof to the BLM to demonstrate that any water body is non-navigable.
4. **Reinstate the 2020 Alaska Roadless Rule**: Pendley recommends restoring this rule for the Tongass National Forest, reversing a Biden Administration decision that re-implemented a 2001 Clinton rule. The 2001 rule significantly hampers infrastructure projects, including roads and electric transmission lines, which are vital for Alaska's isolated communities.

OTHER ACTIONS

THE 30 BY 30 PLAN

Pendley is highly critical of President Biden's "30 by 30" plan, outlined in Executive Order 14008, which seeks to place 30 percent of U.S. lands and waters under conservation by 2030. This plan is viewed as an overreach, with the potential to remove vast amounts of private property from productive use and end congressionally mandated uses of federal land. Pendley asserts that the new administration should vacate this executive order and take immediate steps to reverse Biden's DOI actions that align with the 30 by 30 agenda.

One key recommendation is to vacate a secretarial order issued by the Biden DOI that eliminated the Trump Administration's requirement for state and local government approval before the federal acquisition of private property using funds from the Land and Water Conservation Fund.

NATIONAL MONUMENT DESIGNATIONS

Pendley criticizes Biden's use of the Antiquities Act of 1906 to designate national monuments without adequate local input, continuing a pattern seen in previous Democratic administrations. Pendley suggests that a new administration should thoroughly review all national monument designations and reduce their size where appropriate. This review would include monuments in states like Maine and Oregon, which were improperly designated according to previous assessments.

Furthermore, Pendley calls for a vigorous defense of any reductions in national monument sizes to establish legal precedent in the U.S. Supreme Court, affirming a President's authority to adjust monument boundaries.

Finally, Pendley recommends seeking the repeal of the Antiquities Act of 1906, arguing that it is an outdated law that has been misused. Congress now has statutory mechanisms for protecting special federal lands, making the act unnecessary.

OREGON AND CALIFORNIA LANDS ACT

Pendley identifies the Cascade–Siskiyou National Monument in Oregon as a national monument that should be reduced in size. The expansion of this monument interferes with the federal obligation under the Oregon and California (O&C) Grant Lands Act of 1937, which mandates that these lands be managed for "permanent forest production" and that the timber be "sold, cut, and removed" on a sustained yield basis. Pendley argues that fulfilling this congressional mandate would support job creation and reduce the risk of wildfires in rural Oregon.

NEPA REFORMS

Pendley criticizes the evolution of the National Environmental Policy Act (NEPA), arguing that it has deviated from its original intent. Initially, NEPA was designed to provide a concise and timely presentation of information about federal actions that significantly impact the environment. However, over time, it has become a "tree-killing, project-dooming, decade-spanning monstrosity" that stymies development with extensive paperwork and litigation.

To address these issues, Pendley advocates for the immediate reinstatement of the Trump Administration's NEPA reforms. These reforms included placing strict time and page limits on NEPA documents and requiring that the costs associated with these documents be clearly stated upfront. Pendley also calls for Congress to reform NEPA to its original purpose, suggesting the elimination of judicial review of NEPA documents to reduce delays in federal projects. The goal is to enable more effective oversight by Congress rather than allowing courts to dictate the adequacy of environmental reviews.

SETTLEMENT TRANSPARENCY

Pendley highlights the importance of transparency in legal settlements involving the Department of the Interior. Under Secretary David Bernhardt, the DOI implemented a policy requiring open access to all litigation settlements and the disclosure of any attorneys' fees paid. This policy was intended to prevent the DOI from engaging in controversial or politically motivated settlements without public scrutiny.

However, the Biden Administration reversed this policy, presumably to avoid backlash over the settlements it anticipated entering. Pendley strongly recommends that a new administration reinstate the transparency policy, ensuring that all settlements and associated costs are publicly available for review.

THE ENDANGERED SPECIES ACT (ESA)

The Endangered Species Act, originally intended to protect species on the brink of extinction, is described in Pendley as a law that has been hijacked by special interests to hinder economic development and infringe on private property rights. Pendley argues that the ESA has been largely ineffective, citing its low success rate in recovering species, which is attributed to a "conflict of interest" within the Fish and Wildlife Service (FWS). The FWS, it is claimed, operates like a "species cartel," where federal employees and affiliated researchers are more focused on maintaining their power and funding than on genuine conservation.

To reform the ESA, Pendley proposes several immediate actions:

1. **Delisting Species**: The grizzly bear in the Greater Yellowstone and Northern Continental Divide Ecosystems and the gray wolf across the lower 48 states should be delisted, as they have recovered under the ESA.
2. **Ceding Jurisdiction**: The management of the greater sage-grouse should be returned to the western states, which have the expertise to handle this species without federal interference that could restrict access to public lands.
3. **Reform Section 10(j)**: The FWS should stop using Section 10(j) of the ESA to reintroduce "experimental species" into areas outside their historic ranges, which brings unnecessary federal oversight and restrictions.
4. **Conservation Triage**: The FWS should implement a conservation triage program that prioritizes species based on conservation returns, ensuring that limited resources are used effectively.
5. **Public Access to Data**: All data used in ESA decisions should be made publicly available to ensure transparency and accountability.

6. **Reforming the FWS**: Pendley calls for an overhaul of the FWS's decision-making process to eliminate reliance on biased "species specialists" and ensure conformity with the Information Quality Act.
7. **Abolish the Biological Resources Division of the U.S. Geological Survey**: This division should be dismantled, with necessary scientific research being outsourced to universities through competitive grants.

OFFICE OF SURFACE MINING RECLAMATION AND ENFORCEMENT (OSM)

Pendley discusses the role of the Office of Surface Mining Reclamation and Enforcement (OSM), which was established by the Surface Mining Control and Reclamation Act of 1977 (SMCRA) to manage the environmental impacts of surface coal mining. Despite the decline in the coal industry, Pendley emphasizes that coal remains a vital part of the U.S. energy mix, providing 20 percent of the nation's electricity and supporting regional economies.

The following actions are recommended to ensure that OSM can fulfill its mission effectively:
1. **Relocate Headquarters**: The OSM headquarters should be moved to Pittsburgh, Pennsylvania, which is closer to the coalfields, recognizing the agency's field-driven nature.
2. **Reduce Field Inspectors**: The number of field inspectors should be decreased to reflect the reduced size of the coal industry.
3. **Reissue Schedule F**: The Trump Administration's Schedule F executive order, which allows for the dismissal of non-performing employees, should be reissued to improve accountability.
4. **Extend Training Programs**: OSM's training programs should be expanded to include coal company employees, who are currently excluded.
5. **Revise the Applicant Violator System**: This system, which tracks compliance with SMCRA, should be updated to allow regulators to consider extenuating circumstances.
6. **Maintain the Ten-Day Notice Rule**: This rule requires OSM to work with state regulators to determine if a SMCRA violation has occurred, respecting the primacy of coal mining states in implementing federal law.
7. **Preserve Directive INE-26**: This directive, which relates to maintaining the approximate original contour of mined land, is crucial for environmentally sound surface mining, especially in Appalachia.

WESTERN WATER ISSUES

Pendley addresses the critical water management challenges faced by the American West, a region characterized by aridity. The Bureau of Reclamation, under the DOI, must take decisive action to improve water availability and management across this region. The following actions are recommended:
1. **Develop Additional Storage Capacity**: The Bureau of Reclamation should update dam water control manuals and engage in real-time monitoring to maximize the efficiency of existing water infrastructure.
2. **Consolidate Federal Water Working Groups**: Bureaucratic inefficiencies should be reduced by merging various federal groups involved in water management.
3. **Implement the Federal Action Plan**: The Bureau should focus on improving water forecasts and adopt technologies like Forecast Informed Reservoir Operations and Aerial Snow Observation Systems to better manage water resources.

4. **Clarify the Water Infrastructure Finance and Innovation Act**: Ensuring consistent application of this act with other federal infrastructure loan programs would foster investment in local water projects.
5. **Reinstate the Presidential Memorandum on Water Supply**: Pendley recommends bringing back this directive to promote the reliable supply and delivery of water in the West, supporting agricultural and urban water needs.

AMERICAN INDIANS AND U.S. TRUST RESPONSIBILITY

Pendley asserts that the Biden Administration has failed to honor the federal government's trust responsibilities to American Indians, particularly in its energy policies. The administration's actions are described as having a disproportionately negative impact on Native communities, which rely heavily on the development of their natural resources for economic survival.

Key points include:
- **Energy Development**: The Biden Administration's restrictions on fossil fuel development have severely limited the ability of Indian nations to exploit their oil, gas, and coal resources, depriving them of critical revenue and economic opportunities.
- **Critical Minerals**: Pendley criticizes the administration for discouraging the development of critical mineral projects on Indian lands, despite the high demand for these resources.
- **Environmental Regulation**: Pendley argues that Indian nations should have primary responsibility for environmental regulation on their lands, a right that is being eroded under Biden's policies.
- **Border Security**: Pendley highlights the failure to secure the southern border, which has led to increased crime and drug trafficking on Indian lands near the border, compromising the safety of these communities.
- **Bureau of Indian Education (BIE) Schools**: Pendley criticizes the DOI for failing to ensure proper tracking of students returning to BIE schools post-COVID, as well as for not reporting on student academic performance, which undermines the quality of education in Indian communities.

The recommended actions for a new administration include:
1. **End the War on Fossil Fuels**: Reverse policies that hinder the development of energy resources on Indian lands, allowing tribes to fully benefit from their natural wealth.
2. **End Electric Vehicle Mandates**: These mandates are seen as impractical for remote Indian communities and should be removed.
3. **Restore Environmental Regulation Rights**: Indian nations should regain full control over environmental regulations on their lands.
4. **Secure the Border**: Strengthen border security to protect Indian lands from illegal activities and drug trafficking.
5. **Overhaul BIE Schools**: Focus on improving education outcomes for Native students by putting their needs first and ensuring accountability within the BIE.

Finally, Pendley suggests that Congress should reauthorize the Land Buy-Back Program for Tribal Nations, which helps consolidate fractional land interests among tribes, with new funds coming from the Great American Outdoors Act.

CHAPTER 17: DEPARTMENT OF JUSTICE

The DOJ engaged in conduct to chill the free speech rights of parents across the United States in response to supposed 'threats' against school boards, yet it failed to engage in any concerted campaign to protect the rights of Americans who actually were terrorized by acts of violence like those perpetrated against pregnancy care centers. – Page 546

Key Policy Proposals

The chapter outlines a series of proposals that would fundamentally reshape the Department of Justice (DOJ) and the Federal Bureau of Investigation (FBI), steering them toward an agenda that is deeply concerning for the future of justice and equality in the United States. The proposals are not just administrative adjustments; they represent a radical departure from the principles of impartiality, equality before the law, and the protection of civil rights that are the cornerstones of American democracy.

POLITICIZATION OF THE DOJ AND FBI
The chapter alleges that the DOJ and FBI have become "dangerously politicized" and suggests a sweeping overhaul to root out what it perceives as bias and corruption. The proposed solution? A top-down reorganization to align these institutions more closely with the ideological preferences of the conservative agenda.

However, the real danger here lies in the intention behind these changes. The chapter advocates for placing the FBI under the direct control of political appointees who are aligned with a specific political ideology, thus eroding the necessary independence of these institutions. This shift would open the door to selective enforcement of laws, where political opponents could be targeted under the guise of "restoring integrity." This kind of restructuring risks turning the DOJ and FBI into tools of political retribution, undermining public trust and the rule of law.

TARGETING OF CIVIL RIGHTS PROTECTIONS
The chapter criticizes the DOJ's current approach to civil rights, particularly its enforcement of the Freedom of Access to Clinic Entrances (FACE) Act against pro-life activists. It suggests that the DOJ's actions are politically motivated and calls for a review of all such enforcement activities.

The proposed rollback of civil rights protections under the FACE Act is alarming. This act was designed to protect individuals seeking reproductive health services from violence and intimidation, ensuring their constitutional rights are upheld. Scaling back these protections under the pretense of "restoring impartiality" would leave vulnerable populations exposed to increased threats and harassment. It would signal to extremist groups that violence and intimidation can be used as tools of political expression without fear of federal intervention, endangering public safety and eroding the hard-won rights of women and healthcare providers.

SUPPRESSION OF FREE SPEECH AND PRESS
The chapter takes issue with the FBI's involvement in monitoring and addressing misinformation, particularly regarding its role in the 2020 election and the Hunter Biden laptop story. It calls for a complete prohibition on the FBI engaging in any activities related to "misinformation" or "disinformation," arguing that such actions violate the First Amendment.

This perspective dangerously misconstrues the FBI's role in safeguarding democratic processes. The spread of misinformation, particularly by foreign actors, poses a significant threat to the integrity of elections and public discourse. By restricting the FBI's ability to combat disinformation, the proposed policies would leave the nation vulnerable to manipulation by hostile entities, both foreign and domestic. This would undermine the security of future elections and allow dangerous falsehoods to proliferate unchecked, threatening the fabric of democracy.

UNDERMINING IMMIGRATION ENFORCEMENT
The chapter advocates for a rollback of immigration enforcement policies, particularly those implemented during the Biden Administration. It calls for a return to the harsh, punitive measures of the Trump era, including the reinstatement of rules that limit asylum eligibility and aggressively prosecute immigration offenses.

Such policies would have devastating consequences for immigrant communities and would undermine the United States' commitment to human rights. The reinstatement of policies like the Migrant Protection Protocols, which forced asylum seekers to wait in dangerous conditions in Mexico, would exacerbate the humanitarian crisis at the border. Moreover, these measures would strain the resources of the immigration court system, leading to longer backlogs and further delaying justice for those seeking refuge. These policies are not just a return to failed strategies—they represent a deliberate effort to dehumanize and marginalize immigrant populations.

ERASING PROGRESS IN CIVIL RIGHTS AND NON-DISCRIMINATION
The chapter proposes reorganizing the DOJ's Civil Rights Division to focus on what it describes as "nondiscrimination," criticizing current efforts to promote diversity, equity, and inclusion (DEI) as affirmative discrimination. It suggests that these efforts should be dismantled in favor of a more traditional approach to civil rights enforcement.

This proposal fundamentally misunderstands the purpose and necessity of DEI initiatives. These programs are essential for addressing systemic inequalities and ensuring that all Americans, regardless of race, gender, or sexual orientation, have equal opportunities. The dismantling of DEI initiatives would reverse decades of progress, allowing discrimination to persist unchecked in education, employment, and housing. It would signal a retreat from the values of fairness and justice that are essential to the American promise.

RESTRICTING ACCESS TO REPRODUCTIVE HEALTH
The chapter advocates for the DOJ to enforce federal laws that would severely limit access to abortion, particularly targeting the mailing of abortion pills. It proposes aggressive prosecution of those who provide or distribute these medications.

This stance is not only an attack on reproductive rights but also a direct assault on women's autonomy and health. By targeting access to abortion pills, the proposed policies would disproportionately impact low-income women and those in rural areas who rely on medication abortion as a safe and effective means of terminating a pregnancy. These measures would drive women to seek unsafe alternatives, leading to a public health crisis. The enforcement of such draconian laws would roll back the clock on reproductive rights, undoing decades of progress and endangering the lives of countless women.

The policies proposed in this chapter represent a profound shift toward authoritarianism and the erosion of fundamental rights. They would politicize the DOJ and FBI, undermine civil rights protections, and restrict free speech and access to reproductive health care. These proposals, if implemented, would not restore justice or public safety but rather dismantle the very foundations of a fair and equitable society. The consequences of these policies would be dire, leading to increased inequality, a loss of public trust in institutions, and a weakening of democracy itself.

Summary

This chapter of Mandate for Leadership was written by Gene Hamilton. The following summary conveys the content of the document accurately and objectively, without endorsing or critiquing the perspectives of the original authors.

The Department of Justice (DOJ) is historically significant, originating from the Office of the Attorney General established by the Judiciary Act of 1789 and officially becoming a department in 1870. The DOJ has two primary functions: protecting public safety and defending the rule of law. However, the chapter asserts that the DOJ has lost its way in recent years, forfeiting public trust due to the influence of an unaccountable bureaucratic class and radical left ideologues.

The evidence provided highlights several instances where the DOJ and its components, particularly the FBI, allegedly acted in ways that undermined public trust:

1. **FBI's Role in the 2016 Election:** The FBI, despite knowing that claims of Russian collusion were false, worked with Democratic operatives to inject the narrative into the 2016 election, using strategic media leaks and falsified FISA warrant applications.
2. **Hunter Biden Laptop Story:** Personnel within the FBI allegedly convinced social media companies that the Hunter Biden laptop story was Russian misinformation, despite possessing the laptop and being able to verify its authenticity.
3. **Chilling Free Speech:** The DOJ is accused of chilling free speech by targeting parents protesting at school board meetings under the pretext of addressing threats, while failing to protect Americans against actual violence, such as attacks on pregnancy care centers.
4. **Monitoring Social Media:** The FBI is reported to have engaged in monitoring social media for content deemed to be misinformation or disinformation, even when it was not related to any criminal activity.
5. **Double Standards in Prosecutions:** The DOJ has devoted significant resources to prosecuting citizens for minor offenses, while dismissing charges against more radical groups like Antifa. This is seen as evidence of a partisan bias within the department.
6. **Use of Federal Law:** The DOJ is criticized for using the prospect of litigation to chill behavior that does not align with the liberal agenda, such as state efforts to restrict abortion or prevent gender transition surgeries for minors.

7. **Failure to Address Fentanyl Crisis:** The department has failed to adequately address the flood of fentanyl and other deadly drugs across the U.S. borders, exacerbating a national crisis.
8. **Neglect of Immigration Laws:** The DOJ has allegedly abandoned its duty to enforce immigration laws, contributing to a broader neglect of the immigration court system.

The chapter asserts that these actions contradict Attorney General Merrick Garland's earlier commitment to impartiality and fairness. While acknowledging that many DOJ employees are committed to their duties, the text argues that a radical core has distorted the department's mission.

PROPOSED REFORMS

The chapter advocates for a top-to-bottom overhaul of the DOJ, especially the FBI, to restore trust and align the department with its core purposes. The proposed reforms are extensive and require both administrative and legislative changes:

- **Comprehensive Review of FBI Operations:** A thorough examination of all major active FBI investigations and activities is necessary, with the aim of terminating any that are unlawful or contrary to national interests. This review should be led by appointed attorneys with relevant backgrounds in criminal, national security, or homeland security law.

- **Reorganizing the DOJ:** The chapter proposes reorganizing the DOJ's structure to align the FBI more closely with the Criminal Division and National Security Division, rather than allowing it to operate as an independent entity. This would involve moving the FBI under the supervision of the Assistant Attorneys General for these divisions.

- **Prohibiting the FBI from Policing Speech:** The chapter argues that the FBI should be explicitly prohibited from engaging in activities related to combating so-called misinformation and disinformation, particularly when these activities are not tied to any plausible criminal activity.

- **Streamlining FBI Functions:** The chapter recommends streamlining non-law enforcement functions within the FBI, such as legal counsel and congressional affairs, to improve efficiency and accountability.

- **Ending the FBI Director's 10-Year Term:** The chapter suggests eliminating the 10-year term limit for the FBI Director to ensure political accountability and prevent abuses of power.

Prioritizing the Protection of Public Safety

The chapter argues that ordered liberty is jeopardized when citizens are not physically safe, when career criminals operate without fear of the law, when foreign cartels have free rein to smuggle drugs and illegal aliens, and when political leaders label citizens as "domestic terrorists" for exercising their constitutional rights. The DOJ, in collaboration with state and local partners, must recommit to its core responsibility of protecting public safety.

While most crimes in the United States are handled at the state and local levels, the DOJ plays a critical role in providing technical support to local law enforcement and setting the agenda for the nation's law enforcement priorities. The chapter criticizes the Biden Administration's DOJ for failing to protect law-abiding citizens and for being both "utterly unserious and dangerously politicized." Key areas of concern include:

- **Partisan Prosecution and Racial Double Standards:** The chapter claims that the DOJ under the Biden Administration has infused prosecution and charging decisions with racial and partisan biases, leading to uneven application of the law.

- **Neglect of Immigration Enforcement:** The DOJ is accused of ignoring immigration laws, contributing to a breakdown in the enforcement of federal civil rights and the protection of national security.

- **Weaponization of the FBI:** The chapter highlights the FBI's actions against protesting parents labeled as "domestic terrorists" and its role in suppressing politically disfavored speech under the guise of combating "misinformation" and "disinformation."

The chapter outlines four primary actions necessary to restore public safety and respect for the rule of law:
1. **Restoring the FBI's Integrity:** The FBI must return to its core mission of tackling national crime and security issues, such as violent crime, criminal organizations, child exploitation, and cyber-crime. The chapter asserts that the FBI has strayed from this mission, particularly in its involvement in the Russia collusion investigation and the suppression of the Hunter Biden laptop story. To restore trust, the next administration should conduct a comprehensive review of all major FBI investigations and terminate any that are unlawful or not in the national interest.
2. **Renewing the DOJ's Focus on Violent Crime:** Despite claims that violent crime is a priority, the chapter notes that violent crime has increased across the United States. The next administration must prioritize reducing violent crime through collaboration with state and local officials. Each U.S. Attorney

should be required to develop a district-specific plan to address violent crime and be held accountable for achieving measurable results.
3. **Dismantling Domestic and International Criminal Enterprises:** The chapter emphasizes the need to dismantle criminal organizations, both domestic and international, that pose significant threats to public safety. This includes using federal laws such as the Racketeer Influenced and Corrupt Organizations Act (RICO) and aggressively prosecuting drug-related crimes. Securing the U.S.-Mexico border is highlighted as critical to this effort, given the role of Mexican drug cartels in smuggling drugs and other contraband into the United States.
4. **Pursuing a National Security Agenda Focused on External Threats:** The chapter argues that the DOJ should focus on external state and non-state actors that threaten national security, rather than targeting U.S. citizens exercising their constitutional rights. The termination of the DOJ's China Initiative under the Biden Administration is cited as an example of the department's failure to address serious national security threats. The next administration should reinstate this initiative and pursue other programs to educate the public about threats from adversaries like China and Iran.

Restoring the FBI's Integrity

The chapter stresses that the FBI must be reformed to restore its domestic reputation and effectiveness in addressing foreign threats. Key recommendations include:

- **Comprehensive Review of FBI Investigations:** The next administration should conduct an immediate review of all active FBI investigations, particularly those that may be unlawful or contrary to national interests. This review should be thorough and may result in the termination of certain investigations.

- **Reorganizing the FBI's Placement Within the DOJ:** The chapter recommends removing the FBI from the Deputy Attorney General's direct supervision and placing it under the general supervision of the Assistant Attorney General for the Criminal Division and the Assistant Attorney General for the National Security Division. This reorganization would align the FBI more closely with its law enforcement and national security missions.

- **Prohibiting the FBI from Policing Speech:** The chapter strongly opposes the FBI's involvement in combating so-called "misinformation" and "disinformation," particularly when these activities are not linked to any criminal conduct. It asserts that the FBI should not engage in policing speech in any form, as this infringes on First Amendment rights.

- **Streamlining FBI Functions:** The chapter calls for the elimination of certain non-law enforcement functions within the FBI, such as its Office of General Counsel and Office of Public Affairs, arguing that these functions should be handled by other DOJ offices to ensure better oversight and accountability.

- **Abolishing the 10-Year Term for FBI Directors:** To ensure political accountability, the chapter proposes that the next administration should seek legislative changes to eliminate the 10-year term limit for the FBI Director, making the position more responsive to presidential oversight.

Renewing the DOJ's Focus on Violent Crime

Despite the DOJ's claims that violent crime is a top priority, the chapter argues that violent crime has increased under the Biden Administration. The text emphasizes that the DOJ's leadership must shift its focus from politically motivated actions to a serious and sustained effort to reduce violent crime across the United States. This requires collaboration with state and local officials, tailored to the specific needs of different jurisdictions. The chapter proposes the following measures:
1. **Targeting Violent and Career Criminals, Not Parents:**
   - The next administration must ensure that the DOJ prioritizes the reduction of violent crime by developing and implementing district-specific plans in collaboration with state and local law enforcement. U.S. Attorneys should be held accountable for achieving measurable results in reducing violent crime.
   - The chapter criticizes recent DOJ actions, such as Attorney General Merrick Garland's October 4, 2021, memorandum, which directed significant resources toward addressing supposed threats against school boards, labeling concerned parents as potential threats. This, the chapter argues, is a misguided use of resources that should instead be focused on addressing actual violent crime.
2. **Enhancing Federal Focus in Jurisdictions with Rule-of-Law Deficiencies:**
   - Some state and local jurisdictions have adopted policies that undermine public safety and weaken the rule of law. The federal government, according to the chapter, has a special responsibility to intervene in these areas to protect American citizens and uphold federal interests.

- The DOJ should use federal laws to bring charges against criminals who evade prosecution due to local jurisdictional failures. This includes increasing the federal law enforcement presence in such jurisdictions and exploring innovative legal strategies to hold criminals accountable.
- The chapter suggests that the DOJ should initiate legal actions against local officials, including District Attorneys, who refuse to prosecute criminal offenses based on politically motivated considerations, such as race, gender identity, sexual orientation, or immigration status.

3. **Supporting Legislative Efforts to Strengthen Sentencing for Violent Crimes:**
- The chapter highlights the need for the DOJ to support legislative initiatives that encourage appropriate sentencing for violent crimes, including the enforcement of mandatory minimum sentences under the Armed Career Criminal Act (ACCA).
- It criticizes the Biden Administration's policies that have led to more lenient sentencing for violent criminals, arguing that these policies have contributed to the rise in violent crime. The chapter specifically endorses legislative efforts such as the Restoring the Armed Career Criminal Act, which was introduced in response to U.S. Supreme Court decisions that weakened the ACCA.

4. **Enforcing the Death Penalty:**
- The chapter argues that the death penalty serves as a necessary deterrent, particularly in the current climate of rising violent crime. The next administration should pursue the death penalty in applicable cases, especially those involving heinous crimes such as violence and sexual abuse against children.
- The text underscores the importance of providing finality for the 44 prisoners currently on federal death row and stresses that enforcement of the death penalty should continue until Congress decides otherwise.

Dismantling Domestic and International Criminal Enterprises

The chapter asserts that criminal organizations today are more extensive, sophisticated, and dangerous than ever before. The DOJ's role in dismantling these organizations is critical to ensuring the safety and security of the American people. The text outlines several strategies for achieving this goal:

1. **Revitalizing the Use of Statutory Tools Against Criminal Organizations:**
- The DOJ should rigorously prosecute interstate drug activity, including simple possession of distributable quantities, to combat the explosion of criminal organization activities in the United States.
- The chapter advocates for aggressive use of the Racketeer Influenced and Corrupt Organizations Act (RICO), which empowers the DOJ to treat patterns of intrastate-level crimes as federal criminal conduct when committed by criminal organizations. This tool should be used extensively to dismantle domestic criminal networks.

2. **Securing the Border:**
- The chapter emphasizes the importance of securing the U.S.-Mexico border, which is identified as the primary entry point for many criminal organizations' supplies, products, and personnel. Mexican drug cartels, such as the Sinaloa Cartel and the Jalisco New Generation Cartel (CJNG), are specifically named as the main drivers of fentanyl production and distribution in the United States.
- The next administration is urged to complete the southwestern land border wall and to take creative, aggressive approaches to border security, including the potential use of active-duty military personnel and National Guardsmen in arrest operations along the border. This strategy aims to disrupt the operations of these criminal organizations and lay the groundwork for prosecuting their leaders.

3. **Addressing the Fentanyl Crisis:**
- The chapter highlights the critical need to address the flow of fentanyl into the United States, which has resulted in more than 100,000 overdose deaths in a single year. The federal government is called upon to treat this problem with the utmost seriousness, enforcing customs and immigration laws as a matter of life and death.

Pursuing a National Security Agenda Aimed at External Threats

The chapter criticizes the DOJ for focusing on U.S. citizens exercising their constitutional rights rather than addressing genuine national security threats posed by external state and non-state actors. It calls for a reorientation of the DOJ's national security efforts:

1. **Restarting the China Initiative:**
- The chapter condemns the Biden Administration's termination of the China Initiative, which was designed to address the national security threats posed by China, particularly in areas like economic espionage and theft of trade secrets. The next administration should reinstate the initiative to protect U.S. interests.

2. **Educating the Public on National Security Threats:**
- The DOJ should launch programs to educate the American public about the real and dangerous threats posed by foreign adversaries, especially China and Iran. These programs should raise awareness of the risks to national and economic security.

3. **Responding to Emerging Threats:**
- The chapter stresses the need for the DOJ to remain agile and responsive to emerging threats, such as increases in "sextortion," ransomware, and the proliferation of child pornography. The DOJ must allocate sufficient resources to tackle these issues effectively.

Defending the Rule of Law

The chapter argues that the DOJ, under the Biden Administration, has exhibited scorn for its mission to uphold the rule of law, keep the country safe, and protect civil rights. To restore public trust, the next administration must undertake a comprehensive effort to eliminate lawless policies, investigations, and cases that have contributed to a two-tiered system of justice. Key actions include:

1. **Eliminating Lawless Policies, Investigations, and Consent Decrees:**
- The chapter calls for a thorough review of all publicly available DOJ policies, investigations, and cases, with the goal of ending any that are contrary to the law or the next administration's policies. This review should extend to all consent decrees and settlement agreements currently in force, terminating those that are unnecessary or outdated.
- The DOJ's use of the Freedom of Access to Clinic Entrances (FACE) Act to target pro-life activists while ignoring violence against pro-life pregnancy centers is cited as an example of the department's partisan enforcement practices. The chapter emphasizes the need to uphold equal protection of the law and avoid politically motivated prosecutions.

2. **Zealous Advocacy for the Constitution and Lawful Administration Policies:**
- The chapter asserts that the DOJ must ensure its litigation decisions are consistent with the President's agenda and the rule of law. Line attorneys should not pursue policy agendas through litigation that contradicts the administration's objectives.
- The text also stresses the importance of ensuring that litigation decisions are not delayed or obstructed to outlast the administration's term.

3. **Affirming the Separation of Powers:**
- The chapter highlights the importance of maintaining the separation of powers and ensuring that the executive branch exercises its independent authority to restrain excesses by the legislative and judicial branches. This includes potentially seeking the overruling of the Supreme Court's decision in *Humphrey's Executor v. United States*, which established the independence of certain federal agencies from presidential control.

4. **Guarding Constitutional Protections:**
- The chapter emphasizes the DOJ's duty to zealously guard the constitutional rights of all Americans, particularly the First Amendment right to free speech. It criticizes the DOJ's stance in *303 Creative LLC v. Elenis*, where the department argued in favor of the government's ability to compel speech, as an example of its failure to uphold fundamental constitutional principles.

5. **Pursuing Equal Protection for All Americans:**
- The chapter condemns the Biden Administration's embrace of affirmative discrimination under the guise of "equity" and calls for the next administration to recommit to nondiscrimination. The DOJ's Civil Rights Division should lead this effort,

investigating and prosecuting entities that engage in unlawful discrimination.

Additional Essential Reforms

The chapter outlines a series of additional reforms that are crucial for realigning the Department of Justice with its foundational principles and ensuring it functions efficiently and effectively. These reforms cover a broad spectrum of departmental operations, from resource allocation to internal structure and hiring practices.

Aligning Departmental Resources with Leadership Priorities Across All Components and U.S. Attorneys' Offices

1. **Increasing the Number of Political Appointees:**
   - The chapter asserts that the number of political appointees within the DOJ during prior administrations, particularly the Trump Administration, was insufficient to prevent mismanagement and promote the President's agenda. It calls for a significant expansion of political appointees in all offices and components across the department, especially in critical areas like the Civil Rights Division, the FBI, and the Executive Office for Immigration Review (EOIR). This increase is deemed necessary to ensure accountability and proper management.

2. **Terminating Nonessential Personnel Details:**
   - The chapter recommends ending all nonessential details of DOJ personnel, particularly those assigned to congressional offices, until a thorough review of the department's personnel needs is completed. Once this analysis is done, details can resume if deemed necessary.

3. **Ensuring Accountability for Misconduct:**
   - A comprehensive review of any sanctions or findings of misconduct issued during the four years preceding the next administration's inauguration is suggested. The chapter emphasizes the need to ensure that the Biden Administration acted appropriately in response to such sanctions or findings.

4. **Reviewing DOJ Hiring Practices:** The chapter calls for a holistic review of DOJ hiring practices across all offices and components. This review should ensure that individuals are hired based on merit, aptitude, and legal skill rather than on ideological affiliations or illegal considerations such as race, religion, or sex. The impartiality of hiring committees should be assessed to prevent any bias in the selection process.

Eliminating Redundant Offices and Consolidating Functions to Increase Efficiencies

1. **Consolidating DOJ Components and Offices:**
   - The chapter advocates for exploring the consolidation of various DOJ components and offices that handle human resources, legal counsel, public relations, and other related functions. The goal is to eliminate inefficiencies and redundancies that hinder the department's mission.
   - One example given is the dual structure of public information officers within the Department of Public Affairs, which has both political appointees and career appointees. The chapter suggests streamlining this structure by consolidating these roles under a unified Office of Public and Legislative Affairs.

2. **Restructuring Reporting Chains:**
   - The chapter recommends a comprehensive review of the DOJ's current organizational chart to determine if the existing reporting structures are optimal for achieving the department's mission. For example, it questions whether the Associate Attorney General's current reporting structure is the most effective and whether certain direct reports to the Deputy Attorney General should be reorganized to improve efficiency.

3. **Reevaluating the Office of Legal Policy's Role:**
   - The next administration should consider whether the Office of Legal Policy should continue to handle judicial nominations or if this function should be transferred to the Office of Legislative Affairs, which regularly interacts with Congress.

Pursuing Legislative Changes for Assistant United States Attorneys' Compensation

1. **Reforming Compensation for Assistant U.S. Attorneys:**
   - The chapter stresses the importance of attracting and retaining top legal talent outside of Washington, D.C. It suggests that the next administration seek congressional reform of the pay scale for Assistant U.S. Attorneys, aligning their compensation with that of attorneys employed by Main Justice under the General Schedule (GS) pay scale.

Protecting the Integrity of the Bureau of Justice Statistics (BJS) and the National Institute of Justice (NIJ)

1. **Focusing on Core Statistics of Public Interest:**
   - The chapter argues that the BJS should prioritize producing statistics that are most relevant to everyday Americans and policymakers, rather than focusing on niche issues of interest to criminal justice academics. It calls for the BJS to make its statistics clear and accessible to the general public, ensuring that the information is accurate and presented in an easily understandable manner.

2. **Avoiding Politically Driven Research:**
   - The NIJ should fund high-quality, unbiased research on topics of significant public interest, avoiding research that is driven by political agendas. The chapter underscores the importance of maintaining a clear distinction between official government statistics and third-party contractor reports to avoid any confusion or misrepresentation of data.

3. **Prioritizing the National Crime Victimization Survey:**
   - The National Crime Victimization Survey, the nation's largest crime survey, should be prioritized and sufficiently funded. This survey provides critical data on crime, including the demographic information of crime victims, which helps ensure that crime statistics reflect the reality of who is committing crimes.

Ensuring Proper Enforcement and Administration of Immigration Laws

The chapter emphasizes that the DOJ plays a crucial role in the enforcement and adjudication of immigration laws, despite changes over the years that have shifted some responsibilities to the Department of Homeland Security (DHS). The next administration must prioritize the DOJ's immigration-related responsibilities, which span nearly every office and component of the department. Key actions include:

1. **Guidance to U.S. Attorneys on Immigration Prosecutions:**
   - The DOJ should issue guidance to all U.S. Attorneys emphasizing the importance of prosecuting immigration offenses and related crimes. While the burden of these offenses is most acute in districts along the southwestern border, immigration issues are present nationwide, and a coordinated effort is required to address them.

2. **Assisting DHS in Identifying Criminal Aliens:**
   - The DOJ should take proactive steps to assist the DHS in obtaining information about criminal aliens, particularly those in "sanctuary" jurisdictions that may be resistant to cooperation with federal immigration authorities.

3. **Revisiting Attorney General Decisions on Immigration:**
   - The chapter calls for a thorough examination of all immigration-related decisions made by Attorney General Merrick Garland and any successor during President Biden's term. The next Attorney General should consider overturning or withdrawing any decisions that do not align with the law or the administration's priorities.

4. **Reinstating Trump-Era Immigration Rules:**
   - The next administration should pursue the reimplementation of all immigration-related rules issued during the Trump Administration, including those related to asylum eligibility, immigration court continuances, and other relevant matters. The DOJ should also continuously evaluate its authorities within the immigration court system and issue regulations as necessary.

5. **Committing Resources to Immigration Adjudication:**
   - The chapter stresses the need for the DOJ to commit sufficient resources to adjudicate cases in the immigration court system, especially in contexts like the Migrant Protection Protocols, to ensure timely and fair processing of immigration cases.

6. **Pursuing Litigation to Overturn Restrictive Precedents:**
   - The DOJ should engage in proactive litigation to challenge erroneous precedents that limit the federal government's immigration enforcement authorities, such as those related to the Flores Settlement Agreement.

7. **Enhancing Anti-Fraud Efforts Within EOIR:**
   - The chapter highlights the prevalence of fraud within the immigration system, particularly by attorneys who exploit immigrants with meritless cases for exorbitant fees. The DOJ should prioritize combating fraud and unethical behavior in the immigration system to protect both the integrity of the legal process and the immigrants involved.

Ensuring Proper Distribution of DOJ Grant Funds

The chapter emphasizes the strategic importance of Department of Justice (DOJ) grants as a tool for advancing the President's agenda. When used effectively, these grants can significantly influence local law enforcement, criminal justice reform, and victim support initiatives. The chapter outlines several key steps to ensure that DOJ grant funds are properly distributed and aligned with administration priorities:

1. **Comprehensive Review of Grant Disbursals:**
   - The next administration should conduct an immediate, thorough review of all federal grant disbursements to ensure that the programs are being administered properly by the DOJ and that the funds are being used appropriately by the recipients. This review aims to identify any misalignment with federal laws or the administration's goals.

2. **Overhauling the Grant Application Process:**
   - The DOJ's grant application process should be overhauled to include more rigorous vetting of state, local, and private grant applicants. The chapter suggests implementing stricter pre-application criteria to ensure that only lawful and qualified actors receive federal grant dollars. This process would involve evaluating the fitness and eligibility of applicants to prevent misuse of taxpayer funds.

3. **Imposing Conditions and Priority Points:**
   - The chapter highlights the use of conditions and priority points in grant awards as a powerful tool to influence recipients' actions. It suggests that the next administration should leverage these mechanisms to ensure that grant recipients comply with federal laws and support the administration's law enforcement priorities. An example given is the Trump Administration's condition requiring grant recipients to comply with federal immigration laws, which effectively barred "sanctuary cities" from receiving certain grants.

Ensuring Proper Enforcement and Administration of Immigration Laws

The Department of Justice plays a vital role in the enforcement and adjudication of immigration laws, and the chapter stresses the importance of aligning these responsibilities with the next administration's priorities. Several actions are proposed to enhance the DOJ's effectiveness in this area:

1. **Guidance to U.S. Attorneys on Immigration Prosecutions:**
   - The DOJ should issue clear guidance to U.S. Attorneys emphasizing the importance of prosecuting immigration-related offenses, not just in border districts but across the entire country. This guidance should encourage creative use of immigration laws in partnership with the Department of Homeland Security (DHS) and other federal entities.

2. **Assisting DHS in Criminal Alien Identification:**
   - The DOJ should take proactive steps to help DHS obtain information about criminal aliens in jurisdictions across the United States, particularly in "sanctuary" areas that may resist federal immigration enforcement.

3. **Reevaluating Attorney General Immigration Decisions:**
   - The next Attorney General should review and, if necessary, overturn any immigration decisions made during the Biden Administration that do not align with the law or the administration's policy objectives.

4. **Restoring Trump-Era Immigration Rules:**
   - The chapter advocates for reinstating all Trump Administration immigration rules through rulemaking processes, particularly those related to asylum eligibility, immigration court procedures, and other key areas.

5. **Committing Resources to Immigration Adjudication:**
   - The DOJ should ensure that sufficient resources are dedicated to processing cases within the immigration court system, with particular attention to cases involving the Migrant Protection Protocols and similar initiatives.

6. **Challenging Restrictive Legal Precedents:**
   - The DOJ should actively pursue litigation to overturn legal precedents that hinder the federal government's ability to enforce immigration laws, such as the Flores Settlement Agreement, which imposes restrictions on the detention of minors.

7. **Enhancing Anti-Fraud Efforts in Immigration:**
   - The chapter underscores the need for a vigorous anti-fraud program within the Executive Office for Immigration Review (EOIR). Fraudulent practices by attorneys in the immigration system are rampant, and the DOJ should prioritize efforts to combat this issue to protect the integrity of the legal process and the interests of immigrants.

Additional Reforms and Efficiency Measures

The chapter concludes with recommendations for additional reforms aimed at increasing the efficiency and effectiveness of the DOJ's operations. These include changes to the department's organizational structure, personnel practices, and compensation systems:

1. **Ensuring Political Appointee Accountability:**
   - The chapter emphasizes the need for a substantial increase in the number of political appointees across all DOJ offices to ensure accountability and alignment with the administration's priorities. This expansion is necessary to prevent bureaucratic inertia and promote effective management.

2. **Reviewing Hiring Practices:**
   - The DOJ should conduct a comprehensive review of its hiring practices to ensure that they are based on merit and impartiality. This review should assess whether hiring committees are free from ideological bias and illegal discrimination.

3. **Eliminating Redundant Offices and Functions:**
   - The chapter advocates for consolidating and streamlining DOJ offices and functions to eliminate inefficiencies. For example, the Department of Public Affairs could be restructured to integrate public and legislative affairs under a single Assistant Attorney General, improving coordination and reducing duplication.

4. **Legislative Changes for Attorney Compensation:**
   - The next administration should seek congressional approval for reforms to the compensation system for Assistant U.S. Attorneys, ensuring that their pay is competitive with attorneys at Main Justice and sufficient to attract top legal talent nationwide.

5. **Protecting DOJ Statistical and Research Integrity:**
   - The chapter stresses the importance of maintaining the integrity of the Bureau of Justice Statistics (BJS) and the National Institute of Justice (NIJ). Research and statistical efforts should focus on topics of public interest and avoid politically driven agendas. The chapter specifically mentions the National Crime Victimization Survey as a critical tool for providing accurate crime data and urges its continued funding and prioritization.

6. **Addressing Misconduct and Accountability:**
   - The DOJ should undertake a review of any sanctions or findings of misconduct issued during the Biden Administration and ensure appropriate accountability measures are in place. This review is essential to restore public trust in the department's operations.

CHAPTER 18: DEPARTMENT OF LABOR AND RELATED AGENCIES

The Biden Administration has been hostile to people of faith, especially those with traditional beliefs about marriage, gender, and sexuality. The new Administration should enact policies with robust respect for religious exercise in the workplace, including under the First Amendment, the Religious Freedom Restoration Act of 1993 (RFRA), Title VII, and federal conscience protection laws. – Page 586

Key Policy Proposals

The chapter from the document is steeped in a reactionary agenda aimed at dismantling hard-won progress in diversity, equity, and inclusion (DEI), labor rights, and social justice. The proposed policy changes reflect a desire to roll back the clock on civil rights, labor protections, and the basic principle that government should act as a force for equality and fairness in the workplace. Below, I'll dissect the key proposals and their broader implications.

ROLLING BACK DEI AND CRITICAL RACE THEORY (CRT) IN LABOR POLICY

The document calls for an outright elimination of DEI initiatives and CRT-based trainings within federal labor agencies, arguing that these frameworks promote racial division. It suggests banning all federal funding for CRT training and even proposes amending Title VII to stop collecting EEO-1 data, which tracks workforce diversity.

Analysis:

- **Undermining Anti-Discrimination Efforts**: Eliminating DEI initiatives and CRT training ignores the persistent racial and gender inequities in the workplace. DEI initiatives have been instrumental in creating more inclusive workplaces, ensuring that historically marginalized groups have a fair chance at success. The proposal to eliminate EEO-1 data collection would drastically reduce transparency and accountability, making it easier for discrimination to go unnoticed and unaddressed.

- **Ignoring Systemic Racism**: The attack on CRT dismisses the reality of systemic racism in America. CRT provides a critical framework for understanding how racial inequality is perpetuated through institutions and laws. Banning these trainings is not just a refusal to address these issues, but an active attempt to silence discussions on race and racism.

NARROWING THE DEFINITION OF SEX DISCRIMINATION

The chapter advocates restricting the application of the Supreme Court's decision in *Bostock v. Clayton County*, which extended Title VII protections to LGBTQ+ employees. The document suggests limiting this protection strictly to hiring and firing contexts, rolling back protections in areas like dress codes, bathroom access, and broader workplace policies.

Analysis:

- **Erosion of LGBTQ+ Rights**: This narrow interpretation of *Bostock* would strip away protections for LGBTQ+ individuals in crucial aspects of their daily work life. Issues like bathroom access and dress codes are not trivial; they are fundamental to a person's dignity and ability to work free from harassment. This policy would embolden discriminatory practices against LGBTQ+ workers, legitimizing exclusionary behavior under the guise of "religious freedom" or "workplace norms."

- **Legal and Social Backlash**: Rolling back these protections is likely to face significant legal challenges, as it contradicts the spirit of the Supreme Court's decision. Additionally, it risks fostering a workplace environment that is hostile to LGBTQ+ employees, which could lead to higher turnover rates, decreased productivity, and potential harm to the mental health of workers.

ATTACKING RELIGIOUS FREEDOM PROTECTIONS

The chapter argues that the Biden Administration has been "hostile" to religious employers, advocating for policies that would allow these employers to run their businesses according to their religious beliefs, even when those beliefs conflict with nondiscrimination laws. It suggests issuing an executive order to protect religious employers from complying with general nondiscrimination laws and calls for a clarification of Title VII to expand exemptions for religious organizations.

Analysis:

- **Legalizing Discrimination Under the Guise of Religious Freedom**: Expanding religious exemptions in Title VII would effectively allow employers to discriminate against employees based on their sexual orientation, gender identity, and other protected characteristics. This is not a defense of religious freedom—it is an endorsement of bigotry. The notion that businesses should be able to opt out of federal nondiscrimination laws

under the pretext of religious belief is a direct assault on the civil rights of millions of Americans.

- **Creating a Precedent for Further Discrimination**: Allowing religious beliefs to override federal law opens the door for further erosions of civil rights protections. What begins with LGBTQ+ rights could easily extend to other areas, such as race, gender, or disability. The principle that one's religious beliefs can be used to justify discriminatory practices undermines the foundation of equal treatment under the law.

WEAKENING LABOR UNIONS AND WORKER PROTECTIONS

The document outlines a series of proposals aimed at weakening labor unions, including eliminating the "contract bar" rule that protects unions from decertification during collective bargaining agreements, and advocating for "worker choice" legislation that would end exclusive union representation in right-to-work states.

Analysis:

- **Dismantling Worker Protections**: These proposals are a clear attempt to undermine the power of unions, which have been critical in securing fair wages, safe working conditions, and benefits for millions of American workers. By making it easier to decertify unions and allowing workers to opt out of union representation, the document seeks to erode the collective bargaining power that workers rely on to protect their interests.

- **Increasing Income Inequality**: Weakening unions directly correlates with increased income inequality. Unions are one of the few institutions that have consistently fought for the economic rights of lower and middle-class Americans. Dismantling them would shift even more power to corporations, exacerbating the already stark divide between the wealthy and the rest of the population.

LIMITING GOVERNMENT'S ROLE IN WORKFORCE DEVELOPMENT

The chapter proposes scaling back federal workforce development programs, suggesting that they are inefficient and should be streamlined. It also advocates for reducing the federal role in unemployment insurance and allowing private organizations to administer these benefits.

Analysis:

- **Abandoning Workers in Need**: Workforce development programs are essential for providing workers with the skills needed in an evolving economy. Scaling back these programs would disproportionately harm those who are already disadvantaged, including low-income individuals and minorities, by reducing their access to training and education that could help them secure better-paying jobs.

- **Privatizing Unemployment Benefits**: Handing over unemployment insurance administration to private organizations risks turning a public good into a profit-driven enterprise. Private companies are motivated by profit, not by the public interest, which could lead to reduced benefits, higher costs for workers, and a lack of accountability in how these benefits are administered.

The proposals in this chapter are a full-frontal assault on the principles of equality, fairness, and worker empowerment. They seek to dismantle the progress made in protecting marginalized communities, weaken the institutions that protect workers, and hand over more power to corporations and religious extremists under the guise of "freedom" and "economic efficiency." The consequences of enacting these policies would be devastating, leading to increased discrimination, greater economic inequality, and a society where the rights of the vulnerable are trampled in favor of the powerful.

Summary

This chapter of Mandate for Leadership was written by Jonathan Berry. The following summary conveys the content of the document accurately and objectively, without endorsing or critiquing the perspectives of the original authors.

The chapter begins by framing the **Department of Labor (DOL)** and related agencies within the broader mission of "The Conservative Promise." The core objective is to "reclaim the role of each American worker as the protagonist in his or her own life" and to "restore the family as the centerpiece of American life." This mission is deeply rooted in the Judeo-Christian tradition, which has long recognized work as integral to human dignity. The author emphasizes that, while cultural forces primarily affirm the dignity of work, federal labor and employment agencies also play a crucial role. These agencies are responsible for "protecting workers, setting boundaries for the healthy functioning of labor markets, and ultimately encouraging wages and conditions for jobs that can support a family."

Overview

The chapter provides an overview of the federal agencies involved in labor policy, including the **Department of Labor (DOL)**, **Equal Employment Opportunity Commission (EEOC)**, **National Labor Relations Board (NLRB)**, **National Mediation Board (NMB)**, **Federal Mediation and Conciliation Service (FMCS)**, and the **Pension Benefit Guaranty Corporation (PBGC)**. These agencies have the authority to enforce various federal statutes that regulate workplace conduct, workforce development, employee benefits, labor organization and bargaining, and international labor conditions.

The chapter notes that these authorities are relatively recent in American history, emerging primarily in the mid-20th century in response to significant political and social challenges, including labor conflicts and the civil rights movement. However, the 21st century presents new challenges, such as the collapse of the manufacturing sector and the rise of an increasingly radical human-resources bureaucracy. Despite efforts by the Trump Administration, the chapter argues that these agencies have failed to adapt to these challenges, resulting in a "massive administrative state" that stifles productive industry and labor organization. Under the Biden Administration, the chapter contends, this state has imposed "the most assertive left-wing social-engineering agenda in the agencies' history," which has increased regulatory costs on small businesses and favored "human resources bureaucracies, climate-change activists, and union bosses—all against the interest of American workers."

Needed Reforms

REVERSING THE DEI REVOLUTION IN LABOR POLICY

The chapter asserts that the Obama and Biden Administrations have turned labor policy into a vehicle for advancing the Diversity, Equity, and Inclusion (DEI) agenda. This agenda is described as a "managerialist left-wing race and gender ideology" that permeates every aspect of labor policy, leading to discrimination against conservative and religious viewpoints, particularly on issues such as race, sex, and pro-life stances. The chapter calls for a comprehensive rollback of these initiatives, which it labels as "wrongful and burdensome ideological projects."

ELIMINATING RACIAL CLASSIFICATIONS AND CRITICAL RACE THEORY TRAININGS

The Biden Administration is criticized for promoting "racial equity" across various sectors, including employment, by endorsing racial classifications and preferences under the guise of DEI and Critical Race Theory (CRT). The chapter argues that such practices categorize individuals as "oppressors and victims based on race," which contradicts the principles of nondiscrimination and equality enshrined in Title VII. Title VII, as the chapter notes, "flatly prohibits discrimination in employment on the basis of race, color, and national origin."

To address this, the chapter proposes several key actions:

1. **Issue an Executive Order Banning CRT Trainings**: The President should issue an executive order banning the use of federal funds for CRT training. This is based on the premise that CRT promotes racial discrimination, which is contrary to the principles of Title VII.
2. **Enforce Title VII**: The Department of Justice (DOJ) and the EEOC should be directed to enforce Title VII rigorously, specifically to prohibit racial classifications and quotas, including those that emerge from DEI trainings.
3. **Eliminate EEO-1 Data Collection**: The chapter advocates for the elimination of the EEOC's EEO-1 data collection, which gathers employment statistics based on race and ethnicity. This data, it argues, can be misused to justify racial quotas, which "crudely categorize employees by race or ethnicity," failing to acknowledge the true diversity of the American workforce.
4. **Amend Title VII**: The chapter suggests amending Title VII to prevent the EEOC from collecting any racial classifications in employment, thereby eliminating the possibility of disparate impact claims based on race. This is particularly important in an era where "interracial marriages in America are increasing," making racial categories increasingly irrelevant.
5. **Eliminate Disparate Impact Liability**: Disparate impact theory, which holds that outcomes matter more than intent in discrimination cases, should be abolished. The chapter argues that disparities in the workplace do not inherently imply discrimination. Congress should eliminate disparate impact as a valid theory of discrimination under Title VII and other laws. Moreover, the President should issue an executive order forbidding the Office of Federal Contract Compliance Programs (OFCCP) from using disparate impact in its analyses.

ELIMINATING THE OFFICE OF FEDERAL CONTRACT COMPLIANCE PROGRAMS (OFCCP)

The chapter proposes eliminating the OFCCP, which enforces Executive Order 11246. This order originally required federal contractors to commit to nondiscrimination and gave the Department of Labor the authority to enforce it, including through debarment

from federal contracting. However, the chapter argues that the EEOC's growth has made the OFCCP's authority redundant, creating overlapping regulations that burden businesses. Additionally, the chapter contends that OFCCP's enforcement of novel anti-discrimination theories, such as those related to sexual orientation and gender identity, extends beyond what Congress has mandated by statute.

To address these concerns:

- **Rescind Executive Order 11246**: The President should rescind this executive order, thereby eliminating the OFCCP. Federal contractors would still be bound by statutory nondiscrimination laws, but without the additional regulatory burdens imposed by the OFCCP.
- **Simplify Contractor Obligations**: The chapter suggests that residual obligations under Section 503 of the Rehabilitation Act and the Vietnam Era Veterans' Readjustment Assistance Act (VEVRAA) could be enforced by the EEOC or DOL, reducing the regulatory complexity faced by contractors.

SEX DISCRIMINATION AND THE BOSTOCK V. CLAYTON COUNTY DECISION

The chapter critiques the Biden Administration and LGBT advocates for attempting to broaden the scope of sex discrimination following the Supreme Court's decision in *Bostock v. Clayton County*. This decision held that firing an employee solely for being homosexual or transgender constitutes sex discrimination under Title VII. However, the chapter emphasizes that the Court explicitly limited its ruling to the context of hiring and firing, avoiding broader implications for issues like bathrooms, locker rooms, and dress codes.

The proposed reforms include:

1. **Restrict Bostock's Application**: The next administration should ensure that *Bostock*'s protections for sexual orientation and transgender status are limited strictly to hiring and firing contexts, as originally intended by the Court.
2. **Withdraw Unlawful Notices and Guidances**: Agencies should be directed to withdraw any notices or guidances that unlawfully extend *Bostock*'s reasoning to areas outside hiring and firing, such as those involving bathrooms and locker rooms.
3. **Rescind Regulations on Sexual Orientation and Gender Identity**: The President should rescind regulations that interpret sex discrimination provisions as prohibiting discrimination based on sexual orientation, gender identity, or sex characteristics.
4. **Refocus Enforcement on Biological Sex**: The chapter argues for a return to the enforcement of sex discrimination laws based on the "biological binary meaning of 'sex,'" rejecting broader interpretations that include gender identity.

Pro-Life Measures in the Workplace

The chapter advocates for stronger pro-life protections in the workplace, aligning with the broader goal of promoting pro-family policies. It notes that while current laws like the Pregnancy Discrimination Act and the Pregnant Workers Fairness Act (PWFA) provide some protections, there is room for improvement, particularly in ensuring that pro-life accommodations are supported.

Key proposals include:

1. **Require Equal or Greater Benefits for Pro-Life Support**: Congress should pass legislation mandating that if an employer offers benefits for abortion, they must also provide equal or greater benefits for pregnancy, childbirth, maternity, and adoption. This legislation would reinforce the commitment to supporting life and family in the workplace.
2. **Clarify Abortion Exclusions in Benefit Plans**: The chapter calls for clarifying that employers are not obligated to include abortion-related benefits in their health insurance plans. This would ensure that pro-life employers are not forced to subsidize procedures they morally oppose.
3. **Ensure State Rights in Regulating Abortion-Related Benefits**: In the wake of the Supreme Court's decision in *Dobbs v. Jackson Women's Health Organization*, the chapter emphasizes that the federal Employee Retirement Income Security Act of 1974 (ERISA) should not preempt state laws that restrict abortion-related benefits. Congress and the DOL should clarify that ERISA does not override state efforts to protect life by limiting employer-provided abortion benefits.

Religious Freedom and Protections in the Workplace

The chapter expresses concern over what it perceives as hostility toward religious beliefs under the Biden Administration, particularly those related to traditional views on marriage, gender, and sexuality. To counter this, the chapter proposes several measures to strengthen religious freedom in the workplace:

1. **Issue an Executive Order Protecting Religious Employers**: The President should issue an executive order ensuring that religious employers

can operate their businesses in accordance with their beliefs, regardless of general nondiscrimination laws. This would protect the rights of religious organizations to participate in federal contracting and other government activities.

2. **Clarify Title VII's Religious Organization Exemptions**: Congress should amend Title VII to explicitly affirm that religious organizations are exempt from nondiscrimination laws when making employment decisions based on religious beliefs. This would provide legal clarity and protect the autonomy of religious employers.

3. **Provide Robust Accommodations for Religious Employees**: The chapter emphasizes that Title VII already requires reasonable accommodations for employees' sincerely held religious beliefs, observances, or practices unless it imposes an undue hardship on the employer. However, the chapter calls for a legislative clarification that the standard for "undue hardship" should be "significant difficulty or expense," rather than the current "more than a de minimis cost" standard, which it argues is too restrictive.

REFORMING THE EQUAL EMPLOYMENT OPPORTUNITY COMMISSION (EEOC)

The chapter critiques the EEOC for overstepping its regulatory authority and proposes a series of reforms to rein in its power:

1. **Disclaim Regulatory Pretensions**: The EEOC should formally disavow any claim to regulatory power, focusing instead on its statutory role in enforcing existing laws. The chapter argues that the EEOC should not issue "guidance," "technical assistance," or other documents that push new policy positions without proper authority.

2. **Affirm Majority Vote for Decision-Making**: The EEOC should operate under the requirement that substantive decisions are made by a majority vote of its Commissioners, rather than through unilateral action by the Chair or delegation to staff. This reform is intended to ensure greater accountability and transparency in the EEOC's operations.

3. **Disclaim Consent Decree Power**: The EEOC should not enter into consent decrees that require actions beyond its legal authority. The chapter argues that such decrees can impose obligations on employers that are not mandated by law, effectively allowing the EEOC to legislate through settlement agreements.

4. **Reorient Enforcement Priorities**: The chapter calls for the EEOC to shift its enforcement focus towards claims of failure to accommodate disability, religion, and pregnancy, while deprioritizing cases related to abortion. This reorientation is intended to align the EEOC's actions with the broader goals of supporting family and religious freedom.

REFOCUSING LABOR REGULATION ON THE GOOD OF THE FAMILY

The chapter argues that the DEI revolution has not only impacted the administrative state but has also infiltrated the private sector, particularly through regulatory pressure on human resources offices. The chapter calls for a broader reorientation of labor policy to focus on the family as the fundamental unit of society. Specific proposals include:

1. **Allow Workers to Accumulate Paid Time Off**: The chapter suggests that lower- and middle-income workers should be allowed to accumulate paid time off in lieu of overtime pay. This would give workers more flexibility to use paid leave for family-related reasons, such as taking care of a sick child or attending a family event.

2. **Pass the Working Families Flexibility Act**: Congress should enact this act to allow private-sector employees to choose between receiving time-and-a-half pay for overtime or accumulating time-and-a-half paid time off. This choice is already available to many public-sector workers and would extend similar flexibility to private-sector employees.

3. **Incentivize On-Site Childcare**: The chapter advocates for amending the Fair Labor Standards Act (FLSA) to clarify that an employer's expenses in providing on-site childcare should not be considered part of an employee's regular rate of pay. This would encourage more employers to offer on-site childcare, which is seen as beneficial for maintaining the parent-child bond.

4. **Study Challenges for Women in Professional Work**: The chapter criticizes the Women's Bureau at the DOL for its "politicized research and engagement agenda" and calls for a rededication of its research budget towards open inquiry. This would include studies to disentangle the factors influencing women's workforce participation and to understand the true causes of earnings gaps between men and women.

5. **Equalize Retirement Savings Access Across Married Households**: The chapter notes that the current retirement savings system disadvantages married couples where only one spouse works or where one spouse earns significantly less. It proposes that the contribution limits for retirement accounts should be doubled for married couples, regardless of how the work is distributed between them.

6. **Improve Family Statistics Collection**: The chapter argues that data on the state of the American family and its economic welfare should be collected and published more frequently. It suggests that Congress establish an Assistant Commissioner for Family Statistics within the Bureau of Labor Statistics and fund a pilot survey to generate monthly estimates of family well-being.

ALTERNATIVE VIEW

While acknowledging the importance of family statistics, the chapter presents an alternative view that questions the value of releasing such data on a monthly basis. This view suggests that monthly statistics might cause unnecessary confusion and concern, arguing that funding should instead focus on improving the timeliness of annual statistics.

SABBATH REST

The chapter calls for a revival of the Judeo-Christian tradition of Sabbath rest, arguing that a shared day off is beneficial for families and communities. It proposes amending the Fair Labor Standards Act (FLSA) to require that workers be paid time-and-a-half for hours worked on the Sabbath, which would default to Sunday unless the employer observes a different Sabbath.

The chapter also presents an alternative view, which argues that government-imposed Sabbath rest could lead to higher costs and limited access to goods and services. This view suggests that the government's role should be to reduce barriers to religious observance rather than imposing additional regulations.

TELEWORKING

In light of the widespread adoption of telework during the COVID-19 pandemic, the chapter calls for updates to the laws and regulations governing telework:

1. **Clarify Overtime for Telework**: Congress should clarify that overtime for telework only applies if the employee exceeds 10 hours of work in a specific day and the total hours for the week exceed 40.

2. **Simplify Timekeeping for Telework**: The DOL should clarify that employees need only record time if the quantity of work assigned exceeds the usual amount. This would reduce the burden on both employees and employers in tracking work hours.

3. **Exclude Home Offices from OSHA Regulations**: The chapter suggests that the DOL should clarify that home offices are not subject to OSHA regulations and that time spent setting up a home office is not compensable. It also recommends that reimbursements for home office expenses should not be included in the regular rate for overtime calculations.

MAKING FAMILY-SUSTAINING WORK ACCESSIBLE

The chapter emphasizes the importance of a strong national work ethic and the role of community institutions, such as small businesses and religious organizations, in supporting American workers. It advocates for policies that protect flexible work options and worker independence, particularly for independent contractors.

1. **Protect Independent Contractors**: The chapter highlights the value of independent work for millions of Americans and calls for a return to the Trump Administration's rules that provided clarity on the classification of independent contractors. It also suggests that Congress establish a bright-line test based on the level of control an individual exercises over their work to determine whether they are an employee or independent contractor across all relevant laws.

2. **Provide Safe Harbor for Independent Worker Benefits**: The chapter proposes that companies offering independent workers access to benefits, such as health care and retirement savings accounts, should be provided with a safe harbor from employer-employee status. This would increase access to benefits for independent contractors without forcing them into traditional employment arrangements.

3. **Protect Small Businesses and Entrepreneurship**: The chapter criticizes the Obama and Biden Administrations for expanding the definition of joint employers, which it argues undermines the franchise business model and increases costs for small businesses. It calls for a return to the long-standing definition of joint employers based on direct and immediate control, and for Congress to enact the Save Local Business Act to codify this definition.

4. **Maintain a Reasonable Overtime Pay Threshold**: The chapter argues that the overtime pay threshold should be maintained at a level that does not disproportionately impact businesses in lower-cost regions. It suggests that Congress clarify that the regular rate for overtime pay should be based on salary rather than benefits provided and allow flexibility in calculating the overtime period over a longer number of weeks.

5. **Provide Compliance Assistance to Businesses**: The chapter calls for labor agencies to focus on providing compliance assistance to help businesses understand and follow the rules, rather than relying on "regulation through enforcement" strategies that create uncertainty and increase costs.

CLEAR AND RESTRICTIVE RULES ON GUIDANCE DOCUMENTS

The chapter addresses the issue of federal agencies, particularly labor agencies, issuing guidance documents that occupy a murky area between law and advice. These documents often become de facto regulations, enforced against employers as if they were binding law, without undergoing the formal rulemaking process. This, the chapter argues, has led to businesses being unfairly targeted by overzealous enforcement agents. The Trump Administration attempted to rectify this with the "PRO Good Guidance rule," which explicitly limited the use of guidance documents in enforcement actions and mandated that all such documents be publicly accessible.

However, the Biden Administration rescinded this rule, leading the chapter to advocate for its reinstatement. The proposed actions include:
1. **Reinstitute the PRO Good Guidance Rule**: The Department of Labor (DOL) should reinstitute the PRO Good Guidance rule via notice and comment, restoring transparency and limiting the misuse of guidance documents.
2. **Amend the Administrative Procedure Act**: Congress should amend the Administrative Procedure Act (APA) to explicitly limit the use of guidance documents, ensuring that agencies cannot bypass the rulemaking process and impose de facto regulations.

EXEMPTIONS FROM REGULATIONS FOR SMALL BUSINESSES

The chapter highlights the disproportionate impact that federal labor regulations have on small businesses, noting that larger companies are better equipped to absorb the costs of compliance. Under the Biden Administration, there is concern that big-business lobbies have supported certain regulations, such as the COVID-19 vaccine mandate for private employers, to reduce competition from smaller businesses. The chapter proposes several measures to protect small businesses from the burdens of overregulation:
1. **Use Discretion Under the Regulatory Flexibility Act**: Labor agencies should actively use their discretion under the Regulatory Flexibility Act to exempt small entities from regulations whenever possible.
2. **Increase Revenue Thresholds for NLRB Jurisdiction**: Congress should increase the revenue thresholds at which the National Labor Relations Board (NLRB) asserts jurisdiction over employers. This adjustment would better reflect inflation since 1935 and align with the current definition of "small business" used by the federal government.
3. **Exempt Small Businesses from OSHA Fines**: The chapter advocates for exempting small businesses, particularly first-time, non-willful violators, from fines issued by the Occupational Safety and Health Administration (OSHA).

Education and Vocational Training

APPRENTICESHIPS

The chapter emphasizes the need to expand apprenticeship programs, noting that the traditional Registered Apprenticeship Program (RAP) has become overly burdensome and fails to meet the growing demands of modern industries, such as healthcare and technology. Under the Trump Administration, the Industry-Recognized Apprenticeship Program (IRAP) was introduced to address these issues, but it was rescinded by the Biden Administration.

To revitalize and modernize apprenticeship programs, the chapter proposes:
1. **Expand Apprenticeship Programs Beyond RAP**: Congress should re-create the IRAP system by statute, allowing approved entities, such as trade associations and educational institutions, to oversee apprenticeship programs. This would increase the flexibility and reach of apprenticeship opportunities.
2. **Encourage Religious Organizations' Participation**: The chapter highlights the historical role of religious organizations in supporting workers and proposes that they be encouraged to participate in apprenticeship programs. DOL and NLRB should facilitate the involvement of religious organizations in these programs, ensuring they are not impeded by regulatory barriers.

HAZARD-ORDER REGULATIONS

The chapter addresses the issue of young adults being restricted from working in dangerous jobs, even with parental consent and proper training. Current rules prevent many teenagers from gaining experience in regulated occupations, contributing to worker shortages in these fields.

To address this, the chapter recommends:
1. **Amend Hazard-Order Regulations**: The DOL should amend its hazard-order regulations to permit teenage workers to engage in regulated jobs with parental consent and appropriate training. This change would help build skills and provide opportunities for young workers interested in these fields.

WORKFORCE TRAINING GRANT PROGRAM

The chapter critiques the federal government's emphasis on higher education subsidies while neglecting support for non-college pathways. It proposes the creation of a grant program to support on-the-job training, which would help workers gain valuable skills without necessarily pursuing a college degree.

Key proposals include:
1. **Create an Employer Grant for On-the-Job Training**: Congress should establish a grant worth up to $10,000 per year for each worker engaged in on-the-job training. The program should be outcome-based, with clear reporting requirements and consequences for programs that fail to deliver results.
2. **Repurpose Existing Higher Education Subsidies**: Funding for this employer grant program should come from existing higher education subsidies that currently disadvantage alternative education options. This would reallocate resources to support diverse career paths.

FEDERAL "BA BOX"

The chapter critiques the overemphasis on college degrees in the American labor market, noting that many jobs require degrees unnecessarily, which exacerbates the glut of college graduates. The Trump Administration took steps toward promoting skills-based hiring in the federal civil service, but these reforms have not extended to federal contractors or private employers.

To address this issue, the chapter proposes:
1. **Adopt Skills-Based Hiring Standards for Federal Contractors**: The President should direct the Office of Federal Procurement Policy to adopt the civil service's skills-based hiring standards for federal contractors, eliminating unnecessary degree requirements.
2. **Prohibit BA Requirements in Job Descriptions**: Congress should prohibit the inclusion of BA requirements in job descriptions for private-sector employers unless a degree is genuinely necessary for the position. This would help reduce barriers to employment for individuals without college degrees.

ALTERNATIVE VIEW

An alternative view presented in the chapter suggests that while the federal government has a duty to promote efficiency in federal hiring and contracting, it should not dictate private employers' hiring practices. The inappropriate emphasis on degree requirements is seen as a byproduct of federal subsidies for BA degrees. The alternative view advocates for phasing down these subsidies as a more effective means of reducing barriers to employment for individuals without degrees.

Federal Workforce Development Programs

The chapter underscores the need to reassess federally funded workforce development and training programs, arguing that many of these programs are outdated, fragmented, and fail to deliver meaningful outcomes. In 2019, the federal government spent approximately $17 billion annually on 43 federal employment and training programs, many of which overlap.

To improve the effectiveness of these programs, the chapter proposes:
1. **Evaluate and Streamline Workforce Development Programs**: Congress should reauthorize the Workforce Innovation and Opportunity Act (WIOA) with a focus on evaluating and streamlining existing programs. This would ensure that resources are allocated to programs with strong evidence-based outcomes.
2. **Review Programs for Outcome-Based Metrics**: The DOL and other relevant federal agencies should review their employment and training programs to ensure they contain strong outcome-based metrics. Programs that do not meet these standards should have their funding reevaluated, and bad-actor grantees should be swiftly identified and sanctioned.

FEDERAL UNEMPLOYMENT INSURANCE PROGRAM

In the wake of the COVID-19 pandemic, the chapter calls for a restoration of the Unemployment Insurance (UI) program's integrity and accountability. The pandemic-era expansion of UI benefits under the CARES Act led to significant fraud, with hundreds of billions of dollars lost. The chapter emphasizes the need for bipartisan reforms to prevent such abuses in the future.

Key proposals include:
1. **Enact Bipartisan UI Program Reforms**: Congress should pass reforms that include granting statutory authority for the Labor Office of Inspector General (OIG) to access all state UI records for investigation purposes and requiring state agencies to crossmatch applicants with the National Directory of New Hires.

2. **Develop Technical Standards for UI Systems**: Congress should commission a report to establish technical standards for UI systems, focusing on usability, cybersecurity, data standardization, and identity verification. This would help modernize and secure the UI system.
3. **Strengthen DOL's Enforcement Tools**: The chapter suggests that DOL needs more effective enforcement tools for the UI system, beyond the current options of sending a strongly worded letter or revoking the Federal Unemployment Tax Act (FUTA) tax credit.
4. **Review UI Fraud Detection Investments**: DOL should scrutinize all procurements related to the $2 billion allocated for UI fraud detection and ensure that state monitoring programs are evidence-based. This would include publishing best practices from state officials and industry partners.

Worker Voice and Collective Bargaining

The chapter criticizes the current state of worker representation, noting that many American workers feel they lack influence over workplace issues beyond pay and benefits. The chapter argues that the existing federal labor law offers no alternatives to traditional labor unions, whose adversarial approach is unappealing to most workers. Instead, the chapter advocates for new models of worker representation that emphasize cooperation between workers and management.

NON-UNION WORKER VOICE AND REPRESENTATION
To enhance worker representation, the chapter proposes:
1. **Pass the TEAM Act of 2022**: Congress should pass the Teamwork for Employees and Managers (TEAM) Act, which would:
   - Reform the National Labor Relations Act (NLRA) to allow for formal worker–management cooperative organizations, such as works councils.
   - Create "Employee Involvement Organizations" (EIOs) to facilitate cooperation on workplace issues.
   - Allow EIOs at large publicly traded corporations to elect a non-voting supervisory member to the company's board of directors.

ALTERNATIVE VIEW
An alternative view presented in the chapter suggests that the decline in private-sector unionization and the rise of independent work opportunities indicate that workers have more control over their work lives. This perspective argues that enhancing worker freedom could be better achieved by allowing workers to choose their representatives in negotiations, such as through the Worker's Choice Act, which would end exclusive representation by unions in right-to-work states.

UNION TRANSPARENCY
The chapter advocates for greater transparency in union operations, noting that while private-sector unions are required to file detailed financial information with the DOL, unions composed entirely of state or local employees are exempt from this requirement. This lack of transparency can lead to misuse of union funds.

Key proposals include:
1. **Enact Transparency Rules**: Congress should pass legislation or initiate rulemaking to require state and local government unions to disclose the same financial information as private-sector unions. Additionally, the T-1 Trust Annual Report filing requirement, which was eliminated by the Biden Administration, should be restored to ensure transparency in union trust spending.
2. **Increase Funding for OLMS**: The chapter calls for increased funding for the Office of Labor-Management Standards (OLMS) to ensure it can effectively enforce union disclosure requirements. Historically, OLMS has been underfunded compared to other DOL agencies, hindering its ability to ensure union transparency.

DUTY OF FAIR REPRESENTATION
The chapter critiques unions for often using members' resources on left-wing culture-war issues that are unrelated to the members' interests. To address this, the chapter proposes:
Enforce Political Conflicts of Interest as a Breach of Duty: The National Labor Relations Board (NLRB) should take enforcement action to treat political conflicts of interest by union leadership as a breach of the duty of fair representation. This would be analogous to the treatment of financial conflicts of interest and fiduciary duty of loyalty breaches in other areas of law.

INTERPRETING "PROTECTED CONCERTED ACTIVITY"
The chapter addresses the interpretation of "protected concerted activity" under the NLRA, which is meant to protect workers from employer retaliation when they express a desire to unionize. However, the chapter criticizes the NLRB for issuing extreme interpretations that infringe on employers' rights, such as determining that requiring employees to be courteous to customers and each other is unlawful.

To address this, the chapter proposes:
Reverse Unreasonable Interpretations: The NLRB should return to the 2019 *Alstate Maintenance* interpretation, which provided a more balanced view of what constitutes protected concerted activity. The chapter lists eight lawful actions by employers that should not be deemed as infringing on workers' rights.

INJUNCTIVE RELIEF AND WORKER ORGANIZING ACTIVITIES
The chapter discusses the need for more robust enforcement of workers' rights during union organizing activities. It criticizes the current approach under the NLRA, where remedies for unlawful firings of workers engaged in protected concerted activity often come too late and are limited to backpay. This delay undermines the effectiveness of the law and the legitimacy of organizing efforts.

To address this, the chapter proposes:
Increase Use of Section 10(j) Injunctive Relief: The NLRB should make greater use of its power under Section 10(j) of the NLRA to obtain temporary injunctions that immediately reinstate workers who are unlawfully fired for engaging in protected concerted activity. The chapter notes that the NLRB has been highly successful in obtaining such injunctions, prevailing in 100% of cases in 2020 and 91% in 2021. Increasing the use of these injunctions would provide a more immediate remedy and a stronger deterrent against unfair labor practices.

DUES-FUNDED WORKER CENTERS
The chapter highlights the growing influence of worker centers, which are organizations that often function like unions but are not subject to the same financial disclosure requirements. These centers have become increasingly significant in labor movements but operate with far less transparency than traditional unions.

To ensure accountability, the chapter suggests:
Investigate and Require Financial Disclosures for Worker Centers: The DOL should investigate worker centers that act like unions and enforce the requirement that they file the same financial disclosures as traditional unions. This would help to prevent potential fraud and ensure that workers' dues are used appropriately.

OFFICE OF LABOR-MANAGEMENT STANDARDS (OLMS) INITIATIVE
The chapter argues that the OLMS should have greater authority to investigate potential union malfeasance. Currently, OLMS can investigate employers suspected of misusing union funds without a formal complaint, but it lacks the same authority when it comes to investigating unions themselves unless a formal complaint is lodged by a worker or union.

To rectify this imbalance, the chapter proposes:
Revise Investigation Standards for OLMS: The OLMS should be empowered to initiate investigations into unions without waiting for a formal complaint. This change would enable the OLMS to act on evidence of potential wrongdoing and ensure that unions are held accountable to the same standards as employers.

PERSUADER RULE
The chapter discusses the "Persuader Rule" introduced during the Obama Administration, which created significant regulatory burdens for employers regarding the advice they receive about union activity. Under this rule, employers who hire consultants or lawyers to advise them on union matters must file disclosure forms with the DOL, as must the consultants themselves. The rule was challenged in court and eventually rescinded by the Trump Administration.

The chapter advocates for:
Rescind the Persuader Rule Again if Reinstated: Should the Biden Administration revive the Persuader Rule, the DOL should rescind it once more. The chapter argues that the rule imposes unnecessary burdens on employers and their advisors, stifling their ability to seek legal counsel and engage in lawful activities related to union organizing.

UNIONIZING THE WORKPLACE: CARD CHECK VS. SECRET BALLOT
The chapter critically examines the "card check" process, which allows a union to be recognized without a secret ballot election if it collects signed cards from a majority of employees. This process is seen as problematic because it may pressure employees to sign cards without fully reflecting their true preferences, potentially leading to coercion or intimidation.

To safeguard workers' rights, the chapter proposes:
Discard "Card Check" in Favor of Secret Ballot: Congress should eliminate the card check process and mandate the use of a secret ballot for all union recognition votes. The chapter emphasizes that secret ballots are a fundamental aspect of democratic decision-making and are essential to ensure that workers' choices are free from coercion.

CONTRACT BAR RULE

The chapter addresses the "contract bar" rule, which prevents employees from decertifying a union or choosing a different union for up to three years after a collective bargaining agreement is signed. This rule often forces employees to wait years before they can attempt to change their representation, which the chapter argues is unfair and undemocratic.

The proposed reform includes:

Eliminate the Contract Bar Rule: The NLRB should abolish the contract bar rule, allowing employees a reasonable opportunity to decertify a union or choose new representation without being locked into a long-term contract they no longer support.

TAILORING NATIONAL EMPLOYMENT RULES

The chapter critiques the one-size-fits-all nature of national employment laws like the Fair Labor Standards Act (FLSA) and the Occupational Safety and Health (OSH) Act. These laws, while intended to protect workers, often fail to account for the specific needs of different workplaces. The chapter suggests that unions could play a significant role in tailoring these national rules to better fit the needs of individual workplaces.

Key recommendations include:

Authorize Collective Bargaining to Modify National Rules: Congress should amend the NLRA to allow collective bargaining agreements to treat national employment laws as negotiable defaults rather than non-negotiable floors. For example, a union could agree to modify the overtime threshold in exchange for other benefits, thereby creating a more flexible and tailored approach to labor regulation.

ALTERNATIVE POLICY: PROJECT LABOR AGREEMENTS (PLAS) AND THE DAVIS–BACON ACT

The chapter presents an alternative policy perspective that questions the value of Project Labor Agreements (PLAs) and the Davis–Bacon Act, both of which are seen as overly favorable to unionized labor at the expense of taxpayers and non-union workers.

- **End PLA Requirements**: The chapter suggests that federal agencies should stop mandating PLAs for public construction projects, which often lead to higher costs and reduced competition. Instead, procurement decisions should be based on the contractor's ability to deliver the best product at the lowest cost.

- **Repeal the Davis–Bacon Act**: The Davis–Bacon Act requires that workers on federally funded construction projects be paid "prevailing wages," which the chapter argues are often inflated and do not reflect market rates. Repealing the act would, according to the chapter, increase worker freedom and reduce costs for federal construction projects.

The States: Worker-led Benefits Experimentation

The chapter explores the potential for innovation in unemployment benefits, highlighting that existing systems are bureaucratic and inefficient. It suggests that non-public worker organizations could play a role in administering unemployment benefits, drawing on examples from other Western democracies where such models have been successful.

Proposals include:
1. **Approve Non-Public Worker Organizations as UI Administrators**: The DOL should authorize non-public worker organizations to administer unemployment benefits under Section 303(a)(2) of the Social Security Act. This would introduce competition and innovation into the system, potentially leading to better outcomes for workers.
2. **Offer Waivers for Alternative UI Programs**: The DOL should provide waivers from standard UI requirements to states that propose suitable alternatives. This would allow for state-level experimentation and adaptation of UI programs to local conditions.
3. **Restrict Political Spending by UI Administrators**: Any organization administering UI benefits should be required to comply with restrictions on political spending, similar to those imposed on 501(c)(3) charitable organizations, to ensure that public funds are not used for partisan purposes.

LABOR LAW WAIVERS FOR STATE AND LOCAL GOVERNMENTS

Recognizing the challenges of passing labor law reforms at the federal level, the chapter advocates for allowing state and local governments to experiment with labor law reforms through waivers. This approach would enable states to test new ideas without changing federal law across the board.

Key recommendations include:
1. **Legislate Waivers for State and Local Governments**: Congress should pass legislation allowing states and local governments to seek waivers from federal labor laws like the NLRA and FLSA under certain conditions. These waivers would be limited to a five-year period, after which they could be renewed, modified, or canceled based on their effectiveness.

EXCESSIVE OCCUPATIONAL REGULATION

The chapter addresses the issue of excessive occupational regulation, particularly occupational licensing, which it argues creates barriers to employment and increases consumer costs. The chapter contends that these regulations are often unnecessary and disproportionately affect those entering the workforce or transitioning to new careers.

Proposals to address this include:
1. **Support Interstate Compacts for License Recognition**: Congress should ensure that interstate compacts for occupational license recognition do not impose new or additional qualifications beyond what state governments require. This would facilitate greater mobility for licensed professionals across state lines.
2. **Prevent Federal Programs from Locking Out Well-Qualified Licensees**: Congress should ensure that federally funded programs do not prevent well-qualified professionals from entering the job market due to restrictive occupational licensing requirements. For example, the chapter highlights the issue of medical doctors being unable to practice due to limited residency slots funded by Medicare.

WAGNER–PEYSER STAFFING FLEXIBILITY

The chapter critiques federal requirements that state agencies use state employees for administering unemployment benefits and workforce development programs, even when private contractors could do the job more efficiently. It also opposes the federal government mandating the use of union labor for these positions.

The proposed reforms include:
1. **Repromulgate the Trump-Era Staffing Flexibility Rule**: The DOL should repromulgate the Trump Administration's rule allowing states to hire private contractors for these roles, and Congress should codify this flexibility into law. This would allow states to choose the best personnel for the job, whether they are state employees or private contractors.

WORKER RETIREMENT SAVINGS, ESG, AND PENSION REFORMS

The chapter addresses the controversial topic of Environmental, Social, and Governance (ESG) investing within retirement plans governed by the Employee Retirement Income Security Act (ERISA). The chapter argues that ESG considerations often conflict with fiduciary duties to prioritize investment returns for beneficiaries.

Key proposals include:
1. **Remove ESG Considerations from ERISA**: The DOL should prohibit the inclusion of ESG factors in investment decisions for ERISA plans unless they are directly related to financial risks and returns. This aligns with the traditional focus of trust law on maximizing returns for beneficiaries.
2. **Return to the Trump-Era Pecuniary Factors Rule**: The chapter advocates for a return to the Trump Administration's approach, which allowed only pecuniary factors to be considered in ERISA plan investments. However, it does not oppose considering other non-ESG factors, such as corporate governance or domestic supply chain investments, which could benefit workers and communities.
3. **Increase Scrutiny of Investments in China**: Given concerns about China's lack of compliance with U.S. accounting standards and its state-controlled economy, the chapter suggests that DOL should scrutinize investments in China more closely under ERISA and consider regulatory action to limit such investments.

ALTERNATIVE VIEW ON ESG

The chapter presents an alternative view that argues for an even stricter approach to ESG investing, suggesting that all non-pecuniary factors should be prohibited in ERISA plans. This perspective holds that retirement plan investments should focus solely on financial returns, without regard for ESG or other non-financial considerations. However, it allows for individuals to choose ESG options if they explicitly acknowledge the potential trade-offs in financial returns.

THRIFT SAVINGS PLAN (TSP) AND ESG

The chapter addresses the politicization of the Thrift Savings Plan (TSP), which is the retirement savings plan for federal employees and many former employees. It criticizes recent efforts to introduce ESG investment options within the TSP, arguing that this compromises fiduciary duties and potentially harms participants' retirement security.

Key recommendations include:
1. **Reverse Efforts to Politicize the TSP**: The DOL should reverse any efforts to introduce ESG-focused mutual fund windows within the TSP and clarify that the plan's fiduciary duties preclude ESG investments unless specifically selected by individual participants.
2. **Remove BlackRock and State Street as TSP Managers**: The chapter suggests that the federal government should follow the example of state

governments that have divested from asset managers like BlackRock and State Street due to their ESG advocacy. It recommends contracting with private-sector managers who adhere strictly to fiduciary duties.

3. **Prohibit TSP Investments in China**: The chapter argues that the TSP should not invest in Chinese companies, particularly those linked to the Chinese military or state-owned enterprises. The DOL should exercise its oversight to enforce this restriction, and Congress should legislate to prevent such investments.

Pension Reforms

PUBLIC PENSION PLAN DISCLOSURE

The chapter highlights the underfunding of public pension plans and the need for greater transparency. It notes that the aggregate underfunding of these plans is significantly understated due to overly optimistic assumptions, and it calls for more accurate reporting.

1. **Disclose Fair Market Value of Plan Assets and Liabilities**: Congress should require public pension funds to disclose the fair market value of their assets and liabilities, using the Treasury yield curve as the discount rate. This would provide a more realistic assessment of the funding status of these plans.

MULTIEMPLOYER PLANS

The chapter criticizes the lenient rules governing multiemployer union pension plans, which have led to severe underfunding and mismanagement. It also notes that the Biden Administration provided a taxpayer bailout to some of these plans without implementing necessary reforms.

1. **Reform Multiemployer Pension Plans**: Congress should reform multiemployer pensions to align their funding rules with those of single-employer plans, ensuring that liabilities are measured accurately and that plans are prohibited from making new promises if they are underfunded. The chapter also advocates for more timely and detailed reporting and increased protections for plan participants.

PENSION BENEFIT GUARANTY CORPORATION (PBGC)

The chapter critiques the PBGC for its late reporting and reliance on outdated data, which has obscured the severity of its financial challenges. It also highlights the PBGC's failure to use its authority to address underfunded multiemployer pension plans, leading to a massive deficit.

1. **Improve PBGC Reporting and Oversight**: The PBGC should submit its annual reports on time and use fair-market value principles in its financial calculations. Congress should increase the variable rate premium on underfunding to ensure that well-funded plans are not unduly subsidizing underfunded ones, and the PBGC should closely monitor and take remedial action against poorly managed pension plans.
2. **Increase Premiums for Multiemployer Plans**: The chapter advocates for increasing premiums on multiemployer plans to match those of single-employer plans and eliminating the per-participant cap, which currently limits the PBGC's ability to assess risk and ensure adequate funding.

IMPROVING ACCESS TO EMPLOYEE STOCK OWNERSHIP PLANS (ESOPS)

The chapter discusses the benefits of Employee Stock Ownership Plans (ESOPs) as a means of aligning employee and employer incentives and supporting local business continuity. However, it notes that the lack of clear rules under ERISA has created barriers to the adoption of ESOPs.

Key recommendations include:
1. **Provide Clear Regulations for ESOPs**: The DOL should issue clear regulations for ESOP valuation and fiduciary conduct, encouraging the participation of employee beneficiaries in corporate governance while recognizing the importance of financial diversification for retirement security.

ALTERNATIVE VIEW ON ESOPS

While recognizing the benefits of ESOPs, an alternative view presented in the chapter argues that the government should not favor one form of investment over another. Some conservatives believe that families should have control over their savings and be able to hold diversified assets, without the government promoting any particular investment vehicle.

Putting American Workers First

The chapter concludes with a call to prioritize American workers in labor policy, emphasizing the need for immigration reform, particularly with regard to temporary worker programs that are seen as undermining American workers' job opportunities.

IMMIGRATION AND H-2A VISA PROGRAM

The H-2A visa program, designed to allow temporary agricultural workers into the U.S., is criticized for undercutting American workers by providing a low-cost alternative to hiring domestic labor. The program is not subject to a numerical cap and has expanded significantly in recent years.

1. **Cap and Phase Down the H-2A Visa Program**: Congress should immediately cap the H-2A program at current levels and establish a timeline for its gradual phase-down over the next 10 to 20 years. This would incentivize the agricultural industry to invest in productivity improvements and increase employment opportunities for American workers.
2. **Encourage Industry Consortiums for Automation**: Congress should encourage the formation of industry consortiums focused on agricultural automation and match funding invested by the industry. The intellectual property developed within these consortiums should be made freely available to all participants.

ALTERNATIVE VIEW ON H-2A AND H-2B VISA PROGRAMS

An alternative view suggests that temporary worker programs like H-2A and H-2B help fill jobs that Americans are unwilling to take, preventing illegal immigration and keeping prices for food and services low. This perspective argues that phasing out these programs could lead to higher wages and food prices, and might not attract sufficient American workers to fill seasonal agricultural jobs.

HIRE AMERICAN REQUIREMENTS

The chapter advocates for stricter "Hire American" requirements in federal contracting, ensuring that the benefits of government spending are directed towards American workers and businesses.

1. **Mandate U.S. Citizenship for Federal Contractors**: Congress should require that at least 70% of employees working under federal contracts be U.S. citizens, with the percentage increasing to 95% over a 10-year period. This would ensure that federal contracts primarily benefit American workers.
2. **Restore Employers' Freedom to Prefer Americans**: The chapter criticizes current laws that prohibit employers from favoring U.S. citizens over work-authorized aliens in hiring decisions. It calls for amending the law to allow employers to prioritize American workers, arguing that this would provide significant advantages to the U.S. economy and workforce.

CHAPTER 19: DEPARTMENT OF TRANSPORTATION

All too often, DOT's mission is described as reducing the number of trips, using less fuel, and raising the costs of travel to Americans through increased use of renewables. These goals are not compatible with what should be DOT's purpose: to make travel easier and less expensive. That is what the American people want, and that is what DOT should provide. – Page 639

In pursuit of an anti–fossil fuel climate agenda never approved by Congress, the Biden Administration has raised fuel economy requirements to levels that cannot realistically be met by most categories of ICE vehicles. The purpose is to force the auto industry to transition away from traditional technologies to the production of electric vehicles (EVs) and compel Americans to accept costly EVs despite a clear and persistent consumer preference for ICE-powered vehicles – Page 628

Key Policy Proposals

The proposed policy changes in the chapter represent a conservative vision that seeks to rollback essential regulations and shifts significant responsibilities from federal to state or private sectors. These changes, if implemented, could have far-reaching and detrimental consequences for the environment, public safety, and the equitable distribution of resources across the United States. Below, I dissect the key points and policy proposals presented, analyzing their implications with a focus on the broader impact they would have on American society.

FUEL ECONOMY STANDARDS AND THE PUSH FOR ELECTRIC VEHICLES (EVS)

Furchtgott-Roth criticizes the Biden Administration for raising fuel economy requirements to levels that encourage the transition from internal combustion engine (ICE) vehicles to electric vehicles (EVs). It argues that this push towards EVs is driven by an "anti–fossil fuel climate agenda" that has not been explicitly approved by Congress. The proposed policy would significantly lower these fuel economy standards, maintaining them at levels set for 2020 vehicles.

Analysis: This proposed rollback is a direct attack on efforts to combat climate change. The transportation sector is the largest source of greenhouse gas emissions in the U.S., and increasing fuel economy standards is a proven method to reduce these emissions. Lowering these standards would result in higher carbon emissions, worsening air quality, and contributing to global warming. Moreover, the claim that Americans overwhelmingly prefer ICE vehicles overlooks the increasing consumer demand for cleaner and more efficient cars. EVs represent the future of sustainable transportation, and maintaining or increasing fuel economy standards is critical for reducing the nation's carbon footprint and achieving long-term energy independence.

PUBLIC-PRIVATE PARTNERSHIPS (P3S) AND THE PRIVATIZATION OF INFRASTRUCTURE

Furchtgott-Roth advocates for the use of Public-Private Partnerships (P3s) to fund infrastructure projects, arguing that private sector involvement leads to greater efficiencies and cost savings. It also suggests reducing federal involvement in infrastructure decisions, transferring more power to states and municipalities.

Analysis: While P3s can bring in expertise and capital, they often prioritize profit over public good. The private sector's involvement in critical infrastructure can lead to higher costs for consumers through tolls, fees, or reduced access to services. Infrastructure should be developed with the public interest in mind, ensuring equitable access and long-term sustainability. Shifting more responsibility to states and local governments risks deepening regional inequalities, as wealthier areas may have the resources to maintain and improve infrastructure, while poorer regions fall further behind. Federal oversight and funding are crucial to ensure that infrastructure projects meet national standards and benefit all Americans, not just those in affluent communities.

DEREGULATION OF THE FEDERAL AVIATION ADMINISTRATION (FAA) AND AIR TRAFFIC CONTROL

Furchtgott-Roth calls for separating the Air Traffic Organization (ATO) from the FAA and restructuring the FAA's funding system, arguing that the agency is overly bureaucratic and has fallen behind in implementing modern technologies.

Analysis: Deregulating and privatizing aspects of the FAA could compromise the safety and security of air travel. The FAA's regulatory framework exists to protect the public by ensuring that aviation standards are uniformly high. Privatization could lead to cost-cutting measures that compromise safety, as private entities prioritize profit over comprehensive safety protocols. Furthermore, reducing federal oversight in air traffic control could lead to fragmented service, with less accountability and a potential increase in air traffic incidents. The U.S. has the safest aviation system in the world, and dismantling the FAA's centralized control risks undermining decades of progress.

REFORMING MASS TRANSIT FUNDING AND LABOR PROTECTIONS

Furchtgott-Roth proposes cutting federal subsidies for mass transit and reforming labor protections, specifically targeting Section 10(c) of the Urban Mass Transportation Act, which it claims excessively protects transit workers' compensation.

Analysis: Mass transit is a critical component of urban infrastructure, providing affordable and environmentally friendly transportation options. Cutting federal subsidies would severely impact public transit systems, particularly in lower-income and densely populated areas, leading to service cuts, fare hikes, and reduced accessibility. Such measures would disproportionately affect working-class Americans who rely on public transit for their daily commutes. Additionally, targeting labor protections in the transit sector undermines workers' rights to fair wages and benefits, contributing to increased inequality. Instead of dismantling these protections, policies should focus on expanding and improving mass transit systems to reduce congestion, lower emissions, and provide equitable transportation options for all.

MARITIME POLICY AND THE JONES ACT

Furchtgott-Roth suggests either repealing or substantially reforming the Jones Act, which mandates that goods transported between U.S. ports must be carried on U.S.-built, U.S.-owned, and U.S.-crewed ships. It argues that the economic costs of the Jones Act outweigh its benefits.

Analysis: The Jones Act is essential for maintaining a robust domestic maritime industry, which is critical for national security and economic stability. Repealing or weakening the Jones Act would undermine the U.S. maritime industry, potentially leading to job losses and increased reliance on foreign-flagged vessels, which may not adhere to the same safety, labor, or environmental standards as U.S.-flagged ships. The Jones Act also ensures that the U.S. has the necessary maritime capabilities in times of crisis or conflict, safeguarding the nation's supply chains. Rather than repealing the Act, policy efforts should focus on modernizing the maritime industry and ensuring that it remains competitive in the global economy.

The proposals outlined in this chapter represent a significant step backward in terms of environmental protection, public safety, and equitable infrastructure development. These policies would disproportionately benefit the wealthy and corporate interests while harming the broader public, particularly vulnerable populations. It is essential to resist these regressive changes and advocate for policies that promote sustainability, safety, and equity in transportation and infrastructure.

Summary

This chapter of Mandate for Leadership was written by Diana Furchtgott-Roth. The following summary conveys the content of the document accurately and objectively, without endorsing or critiquing the perspectives of the original authors.

Furchtgott-Roth begins by emphasizing the critical role of transportation in America's prosperity, underlining the need for a system that is abundant, affordable, accessible, and family-friendly. Transportation is described as the backbone of the nation, essential for the functioning of supply chains and personal mobility. The historical significance of transportation is highlighted through the reference to Adam Smith, who identified connections as fundamental to societal development. Over the centuries, the evolution from ports to railroads has been pivotal in shaping the United States.

The U.S. Department of Transportation (DOT), with a proposed fiscal year 2023 budget of $142 billion, was initially intended to provide a policy framework for transportation safety and regulation. However, the department's role has expanded significantly, now involving the selection of projects and the allocation of taxpayer funds for developing transportation assets. This shift has led the DOT to function as a major grant-making and lending organization, a role traditionally filled by state and local governments or the private sector.

Despite the substantial resources at its disposal, the DOT faces challenges due to congressional mandates and funding priorities, which limit its ability to address the most pressing transportation issues affecting Americans. These challenges include the high cost of personal automobiles, unpredictable and expensive commercial shipping, and infrastructure spending that does not align with the transportation preferences of the majority of Americans.

Moreover, Furchtgott-Roth critiques the DOT's complex structure, which includes 11 major components, such as the Federal Aviation Administration (FAA) and the Federal Highway Administration (FHWA). Each component operates with its own administrative framework, leading to inefficiencies and a diluted focus on core transportation challenges.

Furchtgott-Roth argues for a return to the DOT's original mission, emphasizing the need to streamline its functions. One significant recommendation is the elimination of discretionary grant-making processes, advocating instead for formulaic distributions of funds to states. This would allow states to prioritize transportation projects according to their specific needs, ensuring long-term maintenance and reducing unnecessary bureaucratic overhead.

The introduction concludes with a call to revive the "rule on rules" approach to regulations from the Trump Administration, aimed at removing outdated regulations and clarifying that guidance documents are advisory rather than mandatory. This reform, abandoned by the Biden Administration, is seen as crucial for reducing the regulatory burden and fostering innovation in transportation.

Build America Bureau

The **Build America Bureau (BAB)**, a division within the Office of the Secretary of Transportation, is tasked with advancing transportation infrastructure projects in the United States. This includes managing the distribution of funds for these projects, primarily through subsidized 30-year loans. While the BAB plays a crucial role in providing financing for high-quality infrastructure projects, there is concern that it might displace private sector financing, which can offer similar services but often at higher costs.

For lower-quality projects, or those with dubious economic returns, private financing may not be available, making the BAB's role essential. However, the Bureau must maintain strict underwriting discipline, ensuring that loans are only granted to projects that are investment-grade and economically beneficial to taxpayers. Project sponsors must demonstrate the ability to repay loans under various economic conditions, including fluctuating interest rates. The BAB should ensure that all projects maintain a minimum equity commitment from sponsors, safeguarding against potential defaults during financial stress.

Furthermore, the Bureau should conduct regular cost-benefit analyses to assess whether its loans are effectively replacing private sector financing, which could be a sign of overreach. Transparency is essential, particularly regarding whether BAB's lending practices are inadvertently pushing out private financiers by offering more favorable terms that the private sector cannot match.

Public-Private Partnerships

Public-Private Partnerships (P3s) are highlighted as a viable method for funding infrastructure. In a P3, private financing is used to construct infrastructure, with the private partner retaining the right to operate the asset under a concession agreement. This agreement often includes provisions for collecting user fees or receiving government payments based on the asset's availability.

Furchtgott-Roth emphasizes that governments should perform a **value-for-money study** before engaging in a P3. This study compares the costs and benefits of traditional procurement against those of a P3. Although private financing typically incurs higher costs, these are often offset by efficiencies in design, construction, maintenance, and operation that private partners bring. The P3 model is deemed beneficial if it results in better infrastructure at a lower overall cost.

P3s offer several advantages to governments:

- **Access to top talent:** They bring in experts with extensive experience in delivering infrastructure projects.
- **Incentives for innovation:** P3s encourage creativity and efficiency in project design and execution.
- **Risk transfer:** Unique project risks are shifted to private entities more familiar with managing them.
- **Lifecycle cost focus:** P3s encourage a holistic approach, considering both initial and long-term costs.

However, the text warns against misconceptions regarding P3s. Specifically, it clarifies that P3 financing should not be confused with funding. Although a P3 can accelerate revenue generation and provide capital for upfront costs, the private sector's investment must eventually be repaid, typically through user fees or taxes.

A poorly managed P3 can lead to excessive costs and delays. The process of selecting a private partner should be transparent and efficient, minimizing the risk of future generations bearing unnecessarily high costs due to decisions made by current officials. The text underscores that P3s are most valuable for projects that are particularly risky or where the government lacks experience, such as tunnels or light rail lines. These partnerships can transfer significant risk to the private sector, but they require a high level of expertise to manage effectively.

Emerging Technologies

Furchtgott-Roth discusses the role of the DOT in overseeing **emerging technologies** in transportation. As private companies develop new technologies, the DOT's role is to ensure clarity in government regulations, setting standards for safety, security, and privacy without stifling innovation. The private sector, not the government, should determine the success or failure of these technologies. If a technology underperforms, the responsibility lies with the private sector.

A **tech-neutral approach** is recommended for the DOT, focusing on safety as the top priority while facilitating the integration of automated vehicles (AVs) into the national transportation system. These advanced technologies have the potential to save lives, transform personal mobility, and offer new opportunities for people with disabilities, aging populations, and those in communities where car ownership is less feasible.

Regulatory frameworks within the National Highway Traffic Safety Administration (NHTSA) and the Federal Motor Carrier Safety Administration (FMCSA) need updating to accommodate automated vehicles. Current regulations were established before the advent of AVs and driving systems. Both NHTSA and FMCSA have initiated updates, but progress has stalled under the Biden Administration, which has focused more on promoting transit and electric vehicles rather than enabling a broader range of transportation choices.

Furchtgott-Roth suggests that NHTSA should work to remove regulatory barriers by updating vehicle standards and developing performance-based rules for AV operations. FMCSA should align its regulations with DOT's AV 3.0 guidance, which supports the safe removal of human drivers from commercial vehicles.

From a nonregulatory perspective, Furchtgott-Roth criticizes the DOT's shift from voluntary data sharing to a compulsory and antagonistic approach under the current administration. The text advocates for reversing this trend to encourage innovation and improve safety outcomes.

The importance of **radio frequency spectrum** is also addressed, noting that many new transportation technologies rely on wireless communications. The DOT should ensure that transportation receives its fair share of the spectrum, given its critical role in safety and connectivity. Furchtgott-Roth references the 1999 allocation of the 5.9 GHz band to traffic safety and intelligent transportation systems (ITS) by the Federal Communications Commission (FCC). However, in 2020, the FCC reduced the available spectrum, a decision that the DOT needs to challenge to protect transportation safety.

Corporate Average Fuel Economy (CAFE) Standards

Furchtgott-Roth delves into **Corporate Average Fuel Economy (CAFE) standards**, emphasizing their significant impact on vehicle costs and, consequently, on road safety. The CAFE standards, which mandate the fuel efficiency of new motor vehicles, were established under the Energy Policy and Conservation Act (EPCA) of 1975. This legislation was a response to the Arab oil embargo, aimed at promoting energy efficiency and reducing U.S. dependence on foreign oil. The law requires the Department of Transportation (DOT), specifically the National Highway Traffic Safety Administration (NHTSA), to set "maximum feasible" mileage requirements for internal combustion engine (ICE) vehicles.

The text underscores that Congress designed these standards with the understanding that ICE-powered automobiles are crucial to the mobility and prosperity of the American public. Domestic mass production of these vehicles supports millions of jobs and is integral to the U.S. economy. Therefore, the standards were intended to be achievable using available ICE technologies and should not be so stringent that they hinder automakers' ability to produce vehicles profitably or meet consumer demand.

Furchtgott-Roth criticizes the Biden Administration for exceeding these statutory limitations by setting unrealistic fuel economy requirements as part of an anti-fossil fuel climate agenda. The administration's aim is to force the auto industry to transition from traditional ICE vehicles to electric vehicles (EVs), despite the ongoing consumer preference for ICE vehicles. This agenda is further supported by a system of fuel economy credits that subsidize EV producers, such as Tesla, at the expense of traditional automakers.

Additionally, the text argues that the Biden Administration has given undue regulatory power to the Environmental Protection Agency (EPA) over fuel economy through carbon dioxide (CO_2) emissions limits. Since CO_2 emissions correlate with fuel economy in fossil fuel-powered vehicles, these EPA regulations effectively impose fuel economy standards independent of NHTSA's statutory mandate. This situation is compounded by the special waiver granted to California, allowing the California Air Resources Board (CARB) to set its own fuel economy standards, including a ban on ICE vehicles by 2035. Other states are permitted to follow California's lead, effectively enabling CARB to dictate national fuel economy policies, contrary to the EPCA's preemption of state standards.

Furchtgott-Roth outlines several consequences of these regulatory actions:

- **Increased vehicle costs:** Stricter CAFE standards will make cars more expensive to produce, leading to fewer affordable options for consumers.
- **Negative impact on road safety:** As new vehicles become more expensive, fewer people will purchase them, leading to an older and less safe vehicle fleet on the road. The NHTSA itself has acknowledged that the new standards could result in hundreds of additional fatalities and thousands of injuries.
- **Environmental concerns:** Older cars tend to produce more harmful emissions, so an aging fleet could worsen air quality.
- **National security risks:** The push for EVs will increase U.S. dependence on foreign countries, particularly China, for rare earth minerals essential for EV batteries. This shift also places additional strain on the U.S. power grid, requiring significant investments in infrastructure and electricity production.

Despite these drawbacks, Furchtgott-Roth asserts that the Biden Administration's fuel economy regulations will have a negligible effect on global temperature trends in the long term.

The text calls for the next administration to realign the federal fuel economy program with the limits established by Congress. Specifically:

- **Reduce fuel economy levels:** The standards should return to levels specified by Congress for model year 2020, aiming for a fleet-wide average of 35 miles per gallon. Maintaining these levels would align with Congressional objectives.
- **Reassert DOT's authority:** DOT should reclaim its primary role in setting fuel economy standards, with any EPA regulations on CO2 emissions supporting, rather than overriding, DOT's mandate.
- **Revoke California's waiver:** The next administration should challenge California's waiver under the Clean Air Act, as the state lacks a unique basis for setting its own CO2-related fuel economy standards, which are preempted by the EPCA.

Federal Highway Administration

The **Federal Highway Administration (FHWA)** oversees the interstate highway system, a vital component of U.S. infrastructure for transporting goods and people. Furchtgott-Roth criticizes the expansion of FHWA's mission over the decades, arguing that it has strayed beyond its original purpose. Initially focused on highways and bridges, the FHWA now funds a wide array of infrastructure projects, including ferryboat terminals, hiking trails, bicycle lanes, and sidewalks. Many of these projects should be managed at the local or state level, without federal involvement, as federal participation often adds unnecessary red tape and delays.

The text particularly criticizes the Biden Administration for expanding FHWA's focus to include progressive priorities, such as equity initiatives that favor certain identity groups in grant distribution. The administration's efforts to impose obligations on states regarding carbon dioxide emissions from highway traffic, despite this being outside FHWA's statutory authority, are also condemned. Additionally, Furchtgott-Roth points out that the administration's adoption of the "Vision Zero" approach to safety, which often involves intentionally creating congestion to reduce vehicle speeds, runs counter to the original purpose of the FHWA.

Furchtgott-Roth calls for a return to FHWA's core mission of maintaining and improving the highway system. It recommends several steps:

- **Refocus FHWA:** The agency should prioritize its original mission and avoid expanding into areas outside its statutory authority.
- **Reform regulations:** Rules and regulations that hinder state governments' ability to manage their transportation needs should be removed or reformed.
- **Reduce federal involvement:** Federal oversight should be minimized in local infrastructure decisions, allowing state and local governments to take the lead.

Aviation

Furchtgott-Roth discusses the importance of aviation in American transportation, noting that the U.S. has developed the world's safest and most effective air transport network, largely due to private sector innovation. However, current policies threaten to undermine this success and hinder the development of new technologies such as drones and advanced air mobility (AAM), which includes innovations like small aircraft for air taxis and quiet vertical take-off and landing (VTOL) flights.

Since the 1970s, deregulation and increased competition have made air travel more affordable for the majority of Americans. Four major airlines dominate the domestic market, each holding about 20 percent of the market share, while smaller carriers provide additional competition. The Biden Administration's policies, however, are seen as contradictory. To appease certain labor groups, the administration opposes the growth of major airlines, which could lower travel costs, and also resists efforts to increase competition through low-fare foreign carriers and joint ventures among smaller U.S. airlines.

A key area of concern is **aviation consumer protection**. The DOT has the authority to prohibit "unfair and deceptive practices" in the airline industry, a power exercised by the Office of Aviation Consumer Protection. However, starting with the Obama Administration, this authority has been used to justify broad new regulations under the guise of achieving "fair" competition, often imposing burdensome mandates without sufficient evidence. The Trump Administration reformed the process for issuing such rules, but the Biden Administration quickly reversed these reforms. Furchtgott-Roth advocates for reinstating these reforms to prevent overreach and ensure that regulations are evidence-based.

Furchtgott-Roth recommends several actions for the next administration to make air travel more affordable, increase competition, and support the deployment of emerging aviation technologies:

- **Support joint ventures:** The federal government should back efforts by smaller carriers, like Jet Blue and Spirit, to form joint ventures that could help them scale up and compete more effectively with larger airlines.
- **Review foreign ownership limitations:** If necessary, the administration should work with Congress to amend statutes limiting foreign ownership and control in U.S. airlines, allowing for greater investment from allied nations.
- **Launch a New Entry Initiative:** This initiative would commit the federal government to approving or rejecting applications from new air carriers within 12 months, streamlining the process and encouraging competition.
- **Revise slot allocations:** The allocation of slot-pairs at capacity-controlled airports should be updated to prioritize safety, maximize capacity, and enhance competition.

Furchtgott-Roth also addresses the **pilot shortage** caused by regulations requiring commercial pilots to have 1,500 flight hours, a rule implemented after the 2009 Colgan Airlines crash. This requirement has led to a reduction in the availability of twin-engine planes with two pilots at smaller airports, replaced by single-engine planes with only one pilot. The text suggests that this trend could be reversed by reducing the flight hour requirement for copilots or allowing certified simulator training to count toward the total hours.

Furthermore, Furchtgott-Roth critiques the **Essential Air Service (EAS) program**, which subsidizes flights to approximately 200 small airports that are not commercially viable. Initially established as a temporary measure following deregulation in the 1970s, the program has since become permanent. The text argues that ending the program would free up pilots to serve larger markets with more passengers and suggests regulatory reforms to support airports in under-served areas.

On the international front, Furchtgott-Roth emphasizes the importance of maintaining a commitment to the **Open Skies** policy, which promotes international aviation agreements that facilitate competition and market access. However, the text notes that some emerging markets are not fully open to competition, and U.S. aviation policies should reflect this reality, ensuring a level playing field for U.S. carriers. For instance, the U.S. should not allow foreign airlines to enjoy a competitive advantage by flying over Russian airspace when U.S. carriers cannot. Similarly, the text criticizes China for failing to implement agreed-upon policies, suggesting that the U.S. should not enter additional negotiations until China fulfills its existing commitments.

Finally, Furchtgott-Roth calls for the establishment of an interagency clearinghouse to ensure consistent policies across the government on issues related to **spectrum**, **drones**, and **advanced air mobility**. This would help to avoid the current administration's internally inconsistent policies that limit future growth opportunities in the aviation sector.

Federal Aviation Administration (FAA)

The **Federal Aviation Administration (FAA)** is the most visible component of the Department of Transportation (DOT), with a budget request of $18.6 billion for FY 2023. The FAA oversees air traffic control (ATC), distributes federal airport grants, and regulates all aspects of aviation safety. Despite its critical role, Furchtgott-Roth argues that the FAA is in dire need of reform.

The FAA is responsible for operating the **Air Traffic Organization (ATO)**, which accounts for two-thirds of the agency's budget. The ATO manages one of the most complex air traffic control systems in the world but has fallen behind its counterparts in countries like Australia, Canada, and several in Western Europe in implementing 21st-century technology. The FAA's primary mission remains ATC, yet the text suggests that the agency's funding structure and organizational setup are outdated, stifling innovation and efficiency.

Historically, the FAA was regarded as the leading government aviation agency globally. However, since its inception in 1958, there have been significant advancements in air traffic control technology, aircraft avionics, and engine reliability, but the FAA has seen few meaningful changes in its funding and organizational structure. The FAA is not only improperly organized but also misaligned in terms of its operational and managerial practices, with many management reforms proposed in the late 1990s remaining unutilized.

Furchtgott-Roth highlights that the FAA combines two distinct roles: as an Air Navigation Service Provider (ANSP) and as a civil aviation regulatory and certification authority. The first role involves 24/7 air traffic services, while the second ensures aerospace operators, vehicles, airports, and ANSPs are certified and comply with regulations. The text argues that these two functions are fundamentally different and should be managed separately.

A critical issue is that the FAA is the only major Civil Aviation Authority (CAA) globally that does not charge fees for its services, relying instead on annual appropriations. This funding model hampers the FAA's ability to innovate and operate efficiently. The agency spends excessively on research and development (R&D), areas where it is not particularly effective. Furchtgott-Roth recommends that the FAA focus more on testing, evaluating, and certifying private sector innovations swiftly, rather than engaging heavily in R&D itself.

Moreover, the FAA workforce is criticized for being outdated. The text argues that the agency needs to hire safety and certification experts rather than traditional airframe and powerplant mechanics (A&Ps). There is a call for the FAA to promote its top executives from within, based on strict professional qualifications, ensuring that the agency is led by experts with relevant experience, under the oversight of DOT leadership.

Furchtgott-Roth laments the FAA's loss of global leadership in aerospace, a position it held for 60 years. The agency's processes are described as overly bureaucratic, legalistic, byzantine, and recently, hyper-politicized. These inefficiencies have caused the FAA to lag behind foreign CAAs and ANSPs, which are more agile in certifying new technologies like drones and creating environments where innovations such as air taxis can thrive.

To regain its global leadership, Furchtgott-Roth suggests the following reforms for the next administration:

- **Separate the FAA from DOT** or, at minimum, separate the ATO from the FAA. This would allow for a more focused and specialized approach to managing air traffic services and regulatory functions.

- **Restructure the FAA's funding system** to remove its dependence on annual appropriations, freeing it from being used as a political tool for non-aviation issues.

- **Operate more like a business:** The FAA has unique authority in areas like personnel and acquisition but has not made good use of this power. The agency should leverage this authority to improve efficiency and effectiveness.

The text compares the FAA unfavorably to international counterparts, noting that conventional control towers in Europe are being replaced by digital or remote towers with advanced sensors and cameras. In countries like Germany and Scandinavia, these digital towers allow up to 15 small airports to be controlled remotely from a single center. The FAA, however, has yet to certify a single digital or remote tower in the U.S.

Furchtgott-Roth also discusses **DataComm**, a technology that enables text messaging between controllers and pilots. Although the ATO began implementing this technology in 2002, the project was suspended a year later and only restarted in 2016. Even now, DataComm is only available in seven of the 20 high-altitude control centers in the U.S.

Modern technology enables air traffic to be managed "anywhere from anywhere," but the ATO is criticized for resisting the consolidation of its 20 aging centers into fewer, more modern facilities, primarily due to a lack of funds. The FAA has no comprehensive plans to manage the anticipated millions of drones and other emerging technologies, such as electric vertical take-off and landing (eVTOL) aircraft, further underscoring its need for reform.

The text identifies the underlying problems within the ATO as:

- **An overly cautious culture:** Stemming from its integration into a safety regulatory agency, rather than operating at arm's length like airlines and airports.

- **Lack of top-tier technological and managerial expertise:** The ATO is heavily dependent on aerospace contractors, unlike its counterparts in Canada and the UK.

- **Inability to finance major projects with revenue bonds:** Due to constraints imposed by the congressional appropriations process, the ATO must implement projects piecemeal over many years.

Furchtgott-Roth proposes three significant organizational changes, each requiring legislation, to address these issues:

1. **Separate the ATO from the FAA** and relocate it outside the District of Columbia, allowing it to operate more independently.

2. **Shift from aviation user taxes to fees for air traffic services** paid directly to the ATO, providing a more stable and direct funding source.

3. **Authorize the ATO to issue long-term revenue bonds** for major projects, facilitating better financial management and innovation.

Shorter-term reforms include implementing user fees for unconventional airspace users (e.g., advanced air mobility and space launch/recovery) and setting a deadline for transitioning to digital/remote control towers. These reforms, too, would require legislative action.

Federal Transit Policy

Furchtgott-Roth then turns to **Federal Transit Policy**, discussing how the definition of "mobility" is evolving due to new multimodal transportation options, changing traveler needs, and emerging technologies. These changes are influencing the design and function of American communities.

New mobility solutions such as **micromobility**, **ridesharing**, and potentially **autonomous vehicles** could make public transit more affordable and flexible, especially in urban areas. However, the DOT currently defines public transit as services provided by municipal governments, which excludes these new forms of transportation. The text argues for a broader definition of public transit to include any transit service provided to the public, whether by a municipality or a private entity. This change would require congressional legislation but would better reflect the diverse and evolving transportation landscape.

The **COVID-19 pandemic** significantly impacted transit usage, with mass transit experiencing the slowest recovery. By October 2022, ridership was still only 64% of what it was in October 2019. The shift to remote work has altered commuting patterns, raising concerns about the viability of fixed-route mass transit systems, which already required substantial subsidies before the pandemic.

The text criticizes the **2021 Infrastructure Investment and Jobs Act** for authorizing tens of billions of dollars to expand transit systems, even as Americans are increasingly turning to personal vehicles. With lower ridership, transit agencies face severe budgetary challenges, which will only worsen with the added operational costs from system expansions.

Another example of misguided federal transit policy is the **Capital Investment Grants (CIG) program**. Established in 1991, the CIG program funds new transit projects, including rail lines and streetcars, even if there is little demand for such services. The text suggests that instead of expanding transit, federal policy should focus on reducing the high costs that make transit systems uneconomical. The Trump Administration had urged Congress to eliminate the CIG program, but it remains popular on Capitol Hill. At the very least, Furchtgott-Roth argues, any CIG project should be subjected to a rigorous cost-benefit analysis to ensure it is economically sound.

Labor costs are identified as the largest expense in transit operations. Compensation for transit workers is higher than regional and sector averages, driven largely by generous pension and health benefits rather than wages. This imbalance has led to high operational costs while making it difficult for transit agencies to attract workers.

Furchtgott-Roth proposes that the next administration address this issue by reforming **Section 10(c) of the Urban Mass Transportation Act of 1964**. Originally intended to protect the bargaining rights of workers in private transit systems transitioning to public ownership, this provision has since evolved into a requirement that any transit agency receiving federal funds cannot reduce compensation. This interpretation far exceeds the original intent of the statute, and Furchtgott-Roth advocates for a return to the original interpretation, allowing transit agencies to adjust benefits without fear of federal lawsuits.

Finally, Furchtgott-Roth argues for ending the use of the **Highway Trust Fund** to subsidize mass transit. Decades of such transfers have driven the fund into insolvency, requiring repeated bailouts without any corresponding increase in transit usage. With the federal government facing mounting debt, the best course of action would be to eliminate federal subsidies for transit spending, leaving it to states and localities to decide if mass transit is a worthwhile investment for their communities.

Federal Railroad Policy

Furchtgott-Roth critiques the current state of **Federal Railroad Policy**, focusing on the Federal Railroad Administration (FRA). The FRA is responsible for overseeing railroad safety, but Furchtgott-Roth argues that its recent actions have been driven more by political considerations than by its safety mission. Instead of making decisions based on objective evidence and the cost-effectiveness of available alternatives, the FRA is accused of promoting policies that maintain the status quo and inhibit technological advancements that could enhance railroad safety.

One of the key issues highlighted is the FRA's focus on **job preservation**, which the text claims is contrary to the agency's safety mission. This approach negatively impacts the morale of FRA's professional staff, as evidenced by annual employee surveys conducted by the Office of Personnel Management. Furchtgott-Roth emphasizes that the FRA needs to recommit to its core mission of improving safety through evidence-based decision-making.

The FRA's decision-making process, particularly regarding waivers from safety regulations, is typically managed by its Safety Board, with the option to appeal to the Administrator. However, Furchtgott-Roth points out that the FRA has deviated from these procedures, with the Administrator injecting personal influence into Safety Board decisions, undermining the integrity of the process. Specific examples of problematic FRA decisions include:

- **Crew Size Regulation:** The FRA's Notice of Proposed Rulemaking (NPRM) on crew size mandates at least two crew members on trains, regardless of whether a second crew member is operationally necessary. This regulation is criticized as being motivated by job preservation rather than safety considerations.

- **Track Inspection Requirements:** The FRA is criticized for refusing to modernize track inspection requirements, which have remained unchanged for 50 years. Furchtgott-Roth argues that adopting technological methods for track inspection could reduce costs and improve safety, but the FRA has resisted such changes.

- **Brake Inspection Rulemaking:** The FRA has stalled on finalizing a rule that would modernize brake inspection requirements by allowing the tracking of brake inspections electronically, rather than relying on outdated paper air brake slips. This modernization could extend the interval between inspections and improve operational flexibility, but the FRA has yet to act.

- **Dispatcher and Signal Employee Certification:** The FRA plans to propose certification requirements for dispatchers and signal employees despite the Railroad Safety Advisory Committee's (RSAC) inability to identify any clear safety benefits from such certifications.

- **Emergency Escape Breathing Apparatus:** The FRA is considering proposing a requirement for train crews to carry emergency escape breathing apparatus, even though FRA staff previously concluded that the costs of such a requirement would far outweigh its minimal benefits.

Furchtgott-Roth also highlights concerns about the integrity of the FRA's **research program**. In 2022, the FRA transferred management of the Transportation Technology Center (TTC) in Pueblo, Colorado, from a subsidiary of the Association of American Railroads (AAR) to Ensco, Inc. Furchtgott-Roth suggests that this move has led the FRA to direct research to the TTC, even when better options are available elsewhere, potentially to justify its decision to change management. This shift threatens the longstanding collaborative research approach between the FRA and the railroads, which has historically improved railroad safety and efficiency. Furchtgott-Roth calls for the FRA to prioritize research decisions based solely on their potential to enhance safety and efficiency in the railroad industry, rather than on supporting the TTC.

Maritime Policy

The **Maritime Administration (MARAD)**, established by President Harry Truman in 1950 and transferred to the DOT in 1981, is tasked with maintaining the overall health of the U.S. Merchant Marine, which is vital for national defense and foreign and domestic commerce. MARAD also oversees the United States Merchant Marine Academy and provides funding for the six state maritime academies.

Furchtgott-Roth argues that MARAD would be better served if it were transferred from the DOT to the **Department of Homeland Security (DHS)**. MARAD is unique among DOT modal administrations in that it does not regulate the industry it represents; regulation of the maritime industry is the responsibility of the U.S. Coast Guard (which oversees ships and personnel) and the Federal Maritime Commission (which regulates cargo rates and competitive practices). MARAD also has responsibilities in both peacetime commerce and wartime/crisis operations, managing the National Defense Reserve Fleet and the 45-ship Ready Reserve Force for the U.S. Navy. These missions are unique within the DOT, and as a result, MARAD's missions and funding priorities are often misunderstood and minimized in federal planning and budgeting.

By transferring MARAD to DHS, the agency's oversight and regulatory functions would be better aligned with those of the Coast Guard, potentially leading to greater operational efficiencies. Additionally, MARAD's role in national defense would be better supported within DHS or the Department of Defense (if the Coast Guard were also moved there due to the elimination of DHS). Such a move would align MARAD's peacetime and wartime missions with the broader national security infrastructure.

Furchtgott-Roth also raises the possibility of repealing or significantly reforming the **Jones Act**, which would require congressional legislation. The Jones Act, part of the Merchant Marine Act of 1920, is intended to promote a strong U.S. Merchant Marine by requiring that goods transported between U.S. ports be carried on ships that are U.S.-built, U.S.-owned, and U.S.-crewed. However, Furchtgott-Roth argues that the economic costs of the Jones Act far exceed its benefits in terms of maintaining a robust Merchant Marine. For example, no U.S.-flagged ships currently carry liquefied natural gas (LNG), meaning that LNG cannot be shipped from Alaska to the lower 48 states. Furchtgott-Roth suggests that concerns about U.S. fleet capacity in the absence of the Jones Act could be addressed by expanding the Defense Reserve Fleet.

Furchtgott-Roth also discusses MARAD's role in disaster assistance missions, frequently collaborating with the **Federal Emergency Management Agency (FEMA)**. Transferring MARAD to DHS would streamline coordination and vessel requisition during such missions, improving response times and efficiency. Currently, the process of approving **Jones Act waivers** for emergency situations involves a market survey by MARAD, and consolidating this function within DHS could further streamline the process.

Finally, Furchtgott-Roth suggests that DHS is better equipped to administer and budget for the operation of federal service academies, such as the U.S. Merchant Marine Academy. DHS already manages the U.S. Coast Guard Academy, which is similar in size to the Merchant Marine Academy. Placing both academies under a single department would increase efficiencies and better align their missions with the industries they serve.

CHAPTER 20: DEPARTMENT OF VETERANS AFFAIRS

Rescind all departmental clinical policy directives that are contrary to principles of conservative governance starting with abortion services and gender reassignment surgery. Neither aligns with service-connected conditions that would warrant VA's providing this type of clinical care, and both follow the Left's pernicious trend of abusing the role of government to further its own agenda. – Page 664

Key Policy Proposals

The Department of Veterans Affairs (VA) has been at a critical juncture, with recent leadership and policy shifts raising significant concerns. The trajectory of the VA under the influence of this proposed conservative governance will undermine the fundamental principles of equity, access, and comprehensive care that veterans deserve.

RESCINDING ABORTION SERVICES AND GENDER REASSIGNMENT SURGERY:

The proposed rescission of clinical policies that allow abortion services and gender reassignment surgeries is an outright attack on the bodily autonomy and healthcare rights of veterans. These services are essential for many veterans, particularly women and transgender individuals who have served their country and now face barriers to accessing the full spectrum of medical care they require. Removing these services would strip veterans of their right to make personal healthcare decisions and deny them access to medically necessary procedures.

SHIFTING FOCUS AWAY FROM 'SOCIAL EQUITY AND INCLUSION':

The criticism of the VA's focus on "social equity and inclusion" as affecting only a "small minority" of veterans is both shortsighted and discriminatory. Social equity is not a peripheral issue but a cornerstone of a just and fair society. Veterans from marginalized communities, including LGBTQ+ veterans and veterans of color, face unique challenges and health disparities that require tailored policies and services. By minimizing the importance of equity and inclusion, the proposed changes threaten to marginalize already vulnerable populations further.

STRENGTHENING COMMUNITY CARE AT THE EXPENSE OF DIRECT CARE:

The push to strengthen Community Care, enabling more veterans to seek private healthcare outside the VA system, is a thinly veiled attempt to privatize veteran healthcare. While choice in healthcare is important, the emphasis on Community Care risks diverting essential resources from the VA's direct care services, which are specifically designed to meet the unique needs of veterans. The result could be a weakened VA system that is less capable of providing specialized care, leading to longer wait times and reduced quality of care for those who rely on VA facilities.

WHAT WOULD THIS MEAN?

1. **Erosion of Healthcare Access and Rights**: Rescinding abortion services and gender reassignment surgeries would have devastating consequences for veterans who need these services. Forcing veterans to seek these services elsewhere—often at great personal expense or in states where such services are restricted—would create unnecessary hardship and inequality in healthcare access. Veterans who have served their country deserve comprehensive healthcare that respects their autonomy and identity, not policies that push them to the margins.

2. **Marginalization of Minority Veterans**: The dismissal of social equity and inclusion initiatives is not just a rejection of progressive ideals; it is a direct assault on the wellbeing of minority veterans. Policies that do not actively work to address the disparities faced by LGBTQ+ veterans, veterans of color, and women veterans fail to serve the entirety of the veteran community. By scaling back on these initiatives, the VA risks perpetuating systemic inequities and further alienating veterans who already experience disproportionate barriers to care.

3. **Undermining the VA's Mission and Quality of Care**: The push towards Community Care, while superficially appealing, could fundamentally undermine the VA's mission to provide specialized, veteran-centric care. The VA is uniquely equipped to address the complex and specific needs of veterans, something the private healthcare sector is not always capable of replicating. By diverting funds and focus away from direct care, the VA would weaken its own infrastructure, potentially leading to lower quality care, increased fragmentation of services, and ultimately, a betrayal of the VA's promise to its veterans.

The proposed policy changes represent a regressive shift that prioritizes ideological goals over the real needs of veterans. These changes would harm the most vulnerable among our veterans, reduce the quality and accessibility of care, and dismantle critical social equity initiatives. It is imperative that we reject these policies and instead advocate for a VA that fully supports all veterans, regardless of their gender, sexual orientation, or the nature of their healthcare needs. The VA must remain a robust, inclusive, and veteran-focused institution, dedicated to providing comprehensive care that honors the service of all who have worn the uniform.

Summary

This chapter of Mandate for Leadership was written by Brooks D. Tucker. The following summary conveys the content of the document accurately and objectively, without endorsing or critiquing the perspectives of the original authors.

The Department of Veterans Affairs (VA) is committed to being the primary provider of healthcare, benefits, and memorial services for America's veterans and their families. The VA aims to deliver these services with respect, compassion, and competence, ensuring that the veteran is the central focus in every interaction. The department strives to be recognized as a "best in class," "Veteran-centric" system, where decisions are guided by the needs of veterans rather than the preferences of bureaucracy.

At the close of the Obama Administration, the VA faced significant challenges, including low morale among veterans and employees alike. This was largely due to the fallout from a 2014 healthcare access crisis that led to the resignation of Secretary Eric Shinseki. However, by 2020, the VA had regained respect, partly due to the leadership of Secretary Robert Wilkie and his team, who prioritized a "Veteran-centric" approach and fostered a positive work environment. This period saw the VA receiving historic congressional authorizations for healthcare and benefits reform and significant increases in annual appropriations, tripling since the end of the George W. Bush Administration.

The current Biden Administration has adopted some of these governance practices but has not fully maintained the commitment to a "Veteran-centric" philosophy. There is a growing concern that the VA is poorly managing, and sometimes disregarding, provisions of the VA MISSION Act of 2018, which was designed to broaden veterans' access to non-VA healthcare providers. Additionally, efforts to expand disability benefits without adequate planning have led to an erosion of veterans' trust.

The current administration's focus on "social equity and inclusion" within the department, including the controversial introduction of abortion services, has been criticized for diverting attention from the VA's core missions. Critics argue that these initiatives are not only legally questionable but also distract from the essential task of providing care and benefits to veterans.

Departmental History

The history of the Department of Veterans Affairs (VA) is deeply rooted in the post-Civil War era when state veterans' homes were first established to provide medical and hospital treatment for various injuries and diseases. The expansion of veterans' benefits began in 1917, during World War I, when Congress instituted a new system that included disability compensation, insurance for service members and veterans, and vocational rehabilitation for the disabled. These programs were initially managed by three federal entities: the Veterans Bureau, the Department of the Interior's Bureau of Pensions, and the National Home for Disabled Volunteer Soldiers. In 1921, Congress consolidated these programs into the Veterans Bureau.

The establishment of a national VA hospital system followed World War II to accommodate the needs of millions of returning veterans. This system, largely still operational today, was further expanded after the Vietnam War to serve both volunteers and draftees. In recent decades, the VA has shifted its strategy from constructing new, expensive facilities—which are often plagued by budget overruns and delays—to leasing medical properties. This shift reflects the evolution of healthcare, with a growing emphasis on same-day surgical procedures and outpatient care. In 2018, Congress expanded veterans' access to private-sector urgent care outlets as part of the VA's healthcare benefits.

Today, the VA operates 172 inpatient VA Medical Centers (VAMCs), with an average age of 60 years, and 1,113 Community Based Outpatient Clinics (CBOCs), which are newer facilities designed to meet veterans' needs closer to their homes. The VA also oversees a Community Care Network (CCN) through contracts with Optum and TriWest, third-party administrators responsible for ensuring that veterans referred for care outside the VA system receive the services they need. Currently, approximately 6.4 million veterans out of 18 million nationwide use VA healthcare; the remainder rely on other sources like employer-sponsored plans, Tricare, Medicare, and Medicaid.

The VA's disability benefits system has undergone significant changes since the Cold War, especially as it began enrolling large numbers of veterans from World War II, Korea, and Vietnam. The most substantial of these benefits is disability compensation, though there are many others, including the GI Bill and the Home Loan Guaranty, administered through 56 Regional Benefits Offices (RBOs) and numerous satellite sites across the country.

The Agent Orange Act of 1991 dramatically expanded disability benefits for Vietnam veterans, linking various adverse health conditions to their exposure to defoliants like Agent Orange. As these veterans aged, the costs associated with these benefits increased significantly. By 2016-2017, a substantial backlog of disability claims appeals—numbering in the hundreds of thousands—prompted a concerted effort by the VA, Veteran Service Organizations (VSOs), and Congress to streamline the appeals process. This successful initiative, implemented in 2017, greatly reduced the number of pending appeals.

In 2022, the Sergeant First Class Heath Robinson Honoring Our Promise to Address Comprehensive Toxics (PACT) Act addressed health issues presumed to be caused by airborne toxins encountered during the global war on terrorism. The Act further expanded disability benefits for the most recent generation of veterans. However, these ambitious expansions risk overwhelming the VA's ability to process new disability claims and adjudicate appeals efficiently. The VA is currently working to hire additional personnel to manage these claims and is exploring automated processes to accelerate reviews. Nevertheless, delays in hiring and training could lead to significant challenges for the VA and the next administration in 2025.

The VA is expected to face considerable challenges in the coming years, including fiscal pressures, human capital management, and infrastructure concerns. Despite record-high budgets and a workforce exceeding 400,000, the VA is struggling to recruit medical and benefits personnel, especially as the number of new veteran enrollees fails to offset the declining population of older veterans. Additionally, veterans are increasingly migrating from northern states to the South and West, adding complexity to the VA's resource allocation. The department's information technology (IT) systems are also struggling to keep pace with the evolving needs of patient care and record-keeping. As a result, future VA leaders will need to be politically astute, experienced managers capable of innovating and addressing systemic issues.

Mission Statement and Overview

The Department of Veterans Affairs (VA) is dedicated to providing healthcare, benefits, and memorial services to America's veterans and their families, with a focus on respect, compassion, and competence. The VA strives to be a "Veteran-centric" system, prioritizing veterans' needs over bureaucratic preferences.

In 2014, the VA faced a crisis due to a healthcare access scandal, leading to low morale and the resignation of Secretary Eric Shinseki. By 2020, under Secretary Robert Wilkie's leadership, the VA had regained respect, thanks to a renewed focus on "Veteran-centric" governance and improved work environments. This period saw the VA receive historic levels of congressional support for healthcare and benefits reform.

However, the current Biden Administration has not fully maintained this "Veteran-centric" approach. There are concerns about the management of the VA MISSION Act of 2018, which expanded veterans' access to non-VA healthcare providers. Additionally, the administration's focus on social equity and controversial policies, like the introduction of abortion services, has been criticized for distracting from the VA's core mission.

DEPARTMENTAL HISTORY

The VA's roots trace back to the Civil War, with the establishment of state veterans' homes. Over time, especially after World War I, Congress created various veterans' benefits programs, eventually consolidating them into the Veterans Bureau in 1921. Following World War II and the Vietnam War, the VA expanded its hospital network to meet the growing needs of returning veterans.

Today, the VA operates a vast network of medical facilities, including 172 VA Medical Centers and 1,113 Community-Based Outpatient Clinics. The VA also manages a Community Care Network to provide veterans with access to non-VA healthcare providers.

The VA's disability benefits system has evolved significantly, particularly with the Agent Orange Act of 1991 and the PACT Act of 2022, which expanded benefits for veterans exposed to toxins. However, these expansions have strained the VA's ability to process claims, leading to concerns about the system's sustainability.

The VA faces significant challenges, including budgetary pressures, an aging infrastructure, recruitment difficulties, and evolving healthcare needs. Future VA leadership will need to address these issues while maintaining a focus on providing high-quality care and benefits to veterans.

Veterans Health Administration (VHA)

NEEDED REFORMS

The Veterans Health Administration (VHA) requires several key reforms to better align with principles of conservative governance. Among the proposed reforms:

1. **Rescind Controversial Policies**: The VA should eliminate clinical policies, such as those allowing abortion services and gender reassignment surgeries, that do not align with service-connected conditions. These policies are viewed as extensions of a broader ideological agenda rather than essential healthcare services for veterans.
2. **Address Shifting Demographics**: The VA must adapt to the significant generational shift in its patient population. Currently, the veteran population is split between those over and under 65 years of age, with a larger share of healthcare costs going to older veterans. As Vietnam-era veterans age and pass away, new enrollments are not expected to keep pace, necessitating a reassessment of how care is delivered to a declining and more geographically dispersed population.
3. **Strengthen Community Care**: The VHA's budget for Community Care, which allows veterans to seek private-sector healthcare, has grown as demand increases. However, the Biden Administration has reportedly slowed these efforts, sometimes manipulating access standards. A veterans bill of rights and new Secretarial directives are proposed to ensure veterans are fully informed of their Community Care options and to strengthen the implementation of the VA MISSION Act.
4. **Public Accountability**: The VHA should report publicly on its operations, including quality, safety, patient experience, and cost-effectiveness, to ensure continuous improvement and accountability.
5. **Collaboration with Local Entities**: VA Medical Centers are encouraged to collaborate with local academic and private-sector entities to enhance the overall patient experience.

BUDGET

The VHA's aging infrastructure and rising costs necessitate a thorough review:

1. **Independent Audit**: An independent audit of the VA, similar to the 2018 Department of Defense audit, should be conducted to identify deficiencies in IT, management, and contracting.
2. **Facility Realignment**: Many VA facilities are outdated, underutilized, or located in areas with declining veteran populations. The proposed solution includes expanding Community-Based Outpatient Clinics (CBOCs) and exploring partnerships with local healthcare systems to share resources.

PERSONNEL

To improve the efficiency and effectiveness of the VHA:

1. **Extended Term for Under Secretary for Health**: The term should be extended to five years, with the possibility of reappointment to ensure continuity and protect the role from political transitions.
2. **Address Wait Times**: A thorough assessment of clinical appointment loads and the establishment of pilot programs for extended appointment hours are proposed to reduce wait times.
3. **Recruitment and Retention**: The VHA should explore aggressive recruitment strategies, including hiring retired physicians and expanding tuition assistance in exchange for service in underserved areas.
4. **Electronic Health Records (EHR) Implementation**: The VA must prioritize the timely implementation of its new EHR system, as delays have hampered its rollout and raised safety concerns.

Veterans Benefits Administration (VBA)

NEEDED REFORMS

The Veterans Benefits Administration (VBA) faces challenges with the complexity of its benefits system, which often leads to confusion and long-term distrust among veterans. The following reforms are proposed:

1. **Streamlining Disability Claims**: The process for disability claims needs more focused management to improve timeliness and efficiency. The VBA should aim for quicker adjudication and clearer communication with veterans, ensuring that benefits are delivered without frustrating delays.
2. **Performance Targets**: Establishing clear performance targets and publicly reporting on them quarterly would drive consistent improvement in benefit delivery.
3. **"Express 30" Pilot Program**: A new pilot program called "Express 30" is proposed, aiming to process a veteran's first fully developed disability compensation claim within 30 days.
4. **Outsourcing Medical Examinations**: Increasing the use of private companies to perform disability medical examinations could help eliminate delays.
5. **Automation and Technology**: The VBA is encouraged to adopt more advanced technology to automate claims processing. This approach could

reduce costs and improve accuracy but requires significant organizational changes within the VBA to implement effectively.

6. **Reducing Improper Payments and Fraud**: Better tools, training, and management are needed to reduce the substantial amount of money improperly paid out each year.

BUDGET

The VBA's budget and resource allocation need re-examination due to the growing costs associated with expanding benefits:

1. **VASRD Reviews**: The VA Schedule for Rating Disabilities (VASRD) should be reviewed and updated to reflect current needs, potentially leading to significant cost savings.
2. **IT Budget Reassessment**: Given the need for expanded automation, the VBA's Information Technology budget should be reexamined, ensuring it receives sufficient resources to meet modern demands.

PERSONNEL

Reforms in the VBA's workforce and management practices are crucial:

1. **Blended Workforce**: The VBA should employ a more blended workforce, utilizing contractors to process claims, freeing federal employees for other critical tasks.
2. **Improving Acquisition Workforce**: The VBA needs better contractor support and should conduct more outreach to the private sector to enhance its acquisition processes.
3. **Knowledge Exchange Programs**: Establishing programs with top-tier private-sector companies could provide the VBA with insights and methods to improve service delivery.
4. **Leadership and Innovation**: The VBA's leadership should include more innovators and trailblazers with relevant knowledge and technological expertise to drive the department forward.

Human Resources and Administration (HRA)

NEEDED REFORMS

Reforms in Human Resources and Administration are necessary to improve the overall function of the VA:

1. **Rescind Delegations of Authority**: It is recommended that all delegations of authority from the previous administration be rescinded.

2. **Reassign SES Positions**: Career Senior Executive Service (SES) members should be reassigned out of political appointee-designated positions to ensure political control of the VA.
3. **Hybrid and Remote Work Assessment**: A critical review of hybrid and remote work arrangements is needed to determine where in-person collaboration is necessary for maintaining productivity and accountability.

BUDGET

The acquisition of a new Human Resources Information Technology (HRIT) system is critical:

1. **HRIT System Upgrade**: The current system is outdated and inefficient. An upgrade is essential for better personnel management and data-driven decision-making.
2. **Competitive Pay**: Pay and benefits should be expanded in critical skill sets beyond medical care, such as IT and cybersecurity, to compete with the private sector.

PERSONNEL

Improving the culture and management of VA personnel is key to better service delivery:

1. **Mission-Driven Culture**: A culture focused on the VA's mission to serve veterans should be fostered, emphasizing responsiveness and engagement.
2. **Employee Satisfaction**: Increasing employee satisfaction through creative incentives and fostering teamwork is essential for improving recruitment and retention.
3. **Veteran Hiring**: The VA should place greater emphasis on hiring veterans and military spouses, reversing the recent decline in veteran employment at the VA.
4. **Political Appointments**: The VA should work closely with the White House to ensure key positions are filled with fully vetted candidates, recognizing the political significance of the VA.
5. **Labor Relations**: Effective management of relationships with organized labor is crucial, requiring clear direction and strong political will to implement labor reforms.

Analysis: Healthcare under a Second Trump Administration

A potential second Trump presidency could bring significant changes to the American healthcare landscape, building on policies implemented during his first term while potentially pursuing more ambitious reforms. Trump's approach to healthcare has been characterized by efforts to dismantle or weaken the Affordable Care Act (ACA), promote market-based solutions, and reduce federal healthcare spending. However, his policy positions have often been inconsistent, making it challenging to predict exactly how he would approach healthcare in a second term.

One of the most consequential aspects of Trump's healthcare agenda has been his continued opposition to the Affordable Care Act. During his first term, Trump supported legislative efforts to repeal and replace the ACA, though these ultimately failed in Congress. Despite this setback, his administration took executive actions to weaken the law, including expanding access to short-term health plans that do not have to comply with ACA regulations and eliminating the individual mandate penalty. In campaign rhetoric for 2024, Trump has revived promises to repeal and replace the ACA, stating "We're going to fight for much better health care than Obamacare. Obamacare is a catastrophe." However, the political and practical challenges of dismantling a law that has become more popular and widely used since 2017 would be formidable. Over 40 million Americans now receive health coverage through ACA marketplaces or the law's Medicaid expansion. Crafting a replacement plan that maintains similar levels of coverage while satisfying conservative policy goals has proven elusive. Additionally, with Democrats likely to control at least one chamber of Congress, full repeal through legislation would be virtually impossible. As such, a second Trump term may focus more on continued administrative actions to undermine the ACA rather than full repeal.

Trump's approach to government health programs like Medicare and Medicaid could also see significant changes in a second term. While Trump promised not to cut these programs as a candidate in 2016, his administration later supported legislation that would have reduced Medicaid spending and promoted work requirements for beneficiaries. A second Trump term could revive efforts to restructure Medicaid financing, potentially through block grants or per capita caps that would limit federal spending. On Medicare, Trump has sent mixed signals - at times promising to protect the program while also proposing budgets that would reduce Medicare spending. His administration did take some steps to lower prescription drug costs for Medicare beneficiaries, though many of these efforts were blocked by courts. A second term could see renewed attempts to implement drug pricing reforms, potentially including the controversial proposal to tie Medicare drug prices to lower prices paid in other countries.

One area where Trump made lasting policy changes was in promoting price transparency in healthcare. His administration implemented rules requiring hospitals and insurers to publish more information about their negotiated rates and estimated costs of procedures. These transparency initiatives have remained in place under the Biden administration and could be expanded in a second Trump term. Trump has framed these efforts as market-based reforms to empower patients and increase competition. Critics argue the impact on lowering costs has been limited so far, but supporters see potential for these policies to reshape healthcare markets over time if more robustly implemented and enforced.

Immigration and healthcare intersect in several ways that could see policy changes under a second Trump administration. During his first term, Trump implemented the "public charge" rule, which made it more difficult for immigrants to obtain green cards if they had used or were deemed likely to use public benefits like Medicaid. While this rule was reversed by the Biden administration, Trump could seek to reinstate and potentially expand such policies if re-elected. Additionally, Trump has proposed barring undocumented immigrants from accessing public health services beyond emergency care. Such a move would face legal challenges but signals a continued emphasis on restricting healthcare access for immigrant populations.

The COVID-19 pandemic would likely continue to influence healthcare policy in a second Trump term, though perhaps to a lesser degree than during the height of the crisis. Trump's pandemic response was widely criticized, but his administration did oversee the rapid development of vaccines through Operation Warp Speed. In a second term, Trump might emphasize a hands-off approach to pandemic management, deferring more to states and resisting federal mandates or restrictions. However, his stance on vaccines has been inconsistent - taking credit for their development while also at times expressing skepticism about boosters and childhood COVID vaccination. This reflects the complex politics of vaccination among his base.

Abortion and reproductive healthcare could see significant federal policy changes under a second Trump presidency. Trump takes credit for appointing the Supreme Court justices who overturned Roe v. Wade, though he has since tried to stake out a more moderate position on abortion restrictions. Nevertheless, anti-abortion advocates would likely push for federal action to restrict abortion access nationwide. This could potentially include attempts to pass a federal abortion ban after a certain number of weeks of pregnancy, though Trump has been noncommittal on supporting such legislation. His administration could also reinstate and expand policies like the Mexico City Policy restricting federal funding for international organizations that provide abortion services.

DIRECT PRIMARY CARE (DPC)

The proposal advocates for the removal of barriers to Direct Primary Care (DPC), a healthcare delivery model wherein physicians contract directly with patients on a subscription basis, regardless of how or where care is provided. Proponents argue that DPC improves patient access, drives higher quality and lower cost, and strengthens the doctor-patient relationship. The suggestion to clarify that DPC's fixed fee does not constitute insurance in the context of health savings accounts (HSAs) warrants careful examination. While DPC potentially offers benefits such as improved patient access and reduced administrative burden for physicians, it is crucial to critically assess its broader implications for the healthcare system. The model may indeed facilitate clinical focus for physicians by reducing payment-related paperwork and foster continuity of care. However, the promotion of health savings accounts in conjunction with DPC raises significant concerns about equity and efficiency in healthcare resource allocation. HSAs are typically more expensive to administer than centralized systems and can be regressive, potentially shifting scarce health insurance resources to tax-free retirement accounts of healthier and wealthier individuals. This could exacerbate existing healthcare disparities. Furthermore, while DPC might work well within a single-payer system by simplifying implementation, its integration into the current fragmented U.S. healthcare landscape may present challenges. The potential for DPC to create a two-tiered system, where those who can afford subscription fees receive preferential access, must be carefully considered against the principles of equitable healthcare access.

NO SURPRISES ACT

The critique of the No Surprises Act's dispute resolution process highlights legitimate concerns about regulatory ambiguity and inefficiency. The Act, while protecting consumers against balance billing, established a complex system for resolving payment disputes between insurers and providers. This government-mandated dispute resolution process has indeed sown confusion among arbiters and regulators, with judges struggling to ascertain its meaning. The proposal to scrap the dispute resolution process in favor of a "truth-in-advertising" approach warrants critical examination. While the intent to protect consumers and free doctors, insurers, and arbiters from confused and conflicting standards is laudable, the proposed solution may be insufficiently robust to address the underlying issues. The complexity of medical pricing and the urgency of many medical situations significantly limit the efficacy of price disclosures. Patients in emergency and high-stakes medical situations are unlikely to be able to consider or act on complex price information, even if it were readily available. Moreover, such disclosures may often be incorrect or misleading due to the inherent unpredictability of medical care needs. A more comprehensive solution, such as universal coverage under a single-payer system, might more effectively address the root causes of surprise billing and payment disputes. Under such a system, all care would be covered by the same insurance, eliminating the need for complex dispute resolution processes and protecting patients from unexpected bills. However, transitioning to such a system would require significant policy changes and may face substantial political and industry resistance.

SHARED SAVINGS AND REFERENCE PRICING

The proposal to facilitate the development of shared savings and reference pricing plan options merits careful consideration within the context of healthcare economics. The argument posits that under traditional insurance, patients who choose lower-cost care do not benefit financially from that choice, and therefore, barriers to rewarding patients for cost-saving decisions should be removed. The suggestion that the Centers for Medicare & Medicaid Services (CMS) should ensure that shared savings and reference pricing models that reward consumers are permitted aims to introduce market-like incentives into healthcare decision-making. However, this approach may oversimplify the complexities of healthcare markets and consumer behavior. While it's true that insurance often shields patients from the most severe cost consequences of higher prices, studies have shown that even when patients are responsible for price differences, the system doesn't work as intended. Providers frequently can't or won't provide accurate prices in advance, making informed decision-making difficult. Moreover, in healthcare, higher prices are often perceived (albeit incorrectly) as a marker of higher quality, which most consumers demand when it comes to medical care. This perception can undermine the effectiveness of price-based incentives. The concept of "skin in the game" strategies, while intuitively appealing, has not been consistently shown to control healthcare costs effectively. The unique characteristics of healthcare markets, as elucidated by Kenneth Arrow's seminal work, suggest that traditional market mechanisms may not function optimally in this sector. Factors such as information asymmetry, the unpredictability of healthcare needs, and the emotional nature of medical decision-making all contribute to the limitations of consumer-driven approaches in healthcare. Therefore, while shared savings and reference pricing models may have a role in specific contexts, their potential to drive systemic cost control and quality improvement may be limited.

SEPARATION OF ACA EXCHANGE MARKET

The proposal to separate the subsidized Affordable Care Act (ACA) exchange market from the non-subsidized insurance market requires critical examination. The argument posits that the ACA has made insurance more expensive and less competitive, with the subsidy scheme merely masking these impacts. To make health insurance coverage more affordable for those without government subsidies, the proposal suggests that CMS should develop a plan to separate the non-subsidized insurance market from the subsidized market, giving the former regulatory relief from what are termed "costly ACA regulatory mandates." This proposition, however, overlooks the crucial role these mandates play in consumer protection and market stability. The "costly ACA regulatory mandates" include essential protections for patients, such as community rating (where premiums are based on demographics and location, not history of prior illness, which effectively prices the sick out of insurance), standardized insurance coverage categories with transparent disclosure of benefits, and prohibition on "rescission" (the practice of retroactively revoking insurance based on even trivial errors in the application). These provisions are fundamental to ensuring fair access to health insurance, particularly for vulnerable populations. Separating the markets as proposed could lead to a two-tiered system where the non-subsidized market becomes a haven for healthier, wealthier individuals, while those with pre-existing conditions or lower incomes are left in the subsidized market. This could potentially destabilize the risk pools in both markets, leading to higher premiums in the subsidized market and reduced benefits in the non-subsidized market. While the current system built on private insurance has its flaws, maintaining these regulatory protections is crucial for ensuring equitable access to healthcare. A more comprehensive reform approach, potentially moving towards a universal coverage system, might more effectively address the underlying issues of affordability and access without sacrificing essential consumer protections.

HOSPITAL PRICE TRANSPARENCY

The proposal to strengthen hospital price transparency, while well-intentioned, may overestimate its potential impact on healthcare costs and consumer behavior. The 2020 CMS rule requiring hospitals to post prices of common procedures was a step towards increased transparency, but its implementation and effectiveness have been limited. The suggestion to include quality measures in future updates of these rules, combined with shared savings models and other consumer tools, aims to deliver savings for consumers. However, this approach faces several significant challenges. Firstly, compliance with existing price transparency rules has been poor, with many hospitals not fully adhering to the requirements. Secondly, the posted price lists are often so complex and extensive as to be virtually unusable by consumers – encompassing too many procedures, in too many configurations, for too many health plans. The addition of quality measures, while potentially valuable, introduces further complexities. Quality measurement in healthcare is highly contentious, with poor-performing hospitals often legitimately claiming that their statistics are skewed by high-risk cases. Moreover, quality measures are widely subject to manipulation, either by playing to the metric or through misreporting. The assumption that shared savings and consumer tools will lead to significant cost savings is not strongly supported by evidence. Healthcare decisions are often made under conditions of stress, urgency, or limited information, reducing the likelihood that consumers will effectively shop around based on price and quality data. Furthermore, in many medical situations, particularly emergencies or complex treatments, consumer choice is limited or non-existent. A more effective approach to cost containment and quality improvement might involve systemic changes, such as moving towards a single-payer system that covers everyone with the same insurance. This could dramatically reduce administrative costs, which are a significant driver of healthcare expenses in the U.S. Such a system, similar to those in other wealthy nations, could potentially achieve greater efficiency and equity in healthcare delivery and financing.

EXPANSION OF HEALTH PLAN OPTIONS

The proposal to end restrictions on benefits and types of health plans that can participate in the exchanges, building on efforts to expand choices for small businesses and workers, requires careful evaluation. The suggestion includes codifying an expansion of association health plans, short-term health plans, and health reimbursement arrangements (including individual coverage HRAs), as well as giving consumers more flexibility with their healthcare dollars through expanded access to health savings accounts (HSAs). While increased choice may seem beneficial, it's crucial to consider the potential consequences of such expansions. Association health plans and short-term health plans often offer less comprehensive coverage and fewer consumer protections than ACA-compliant plans. They may attract healthier individuals, potentially leading to market segmentation and undermining the risk-pooling mechanisms that are crucial for insurance markets to function effectively. This could result in higher premiums for those remaining in more comprehensive plans, particularly affecting individuals with pre-existing conditions or greater healthcare needs. The promotion of health savings accounts should be considered in the context of their distributional effects and overall system efficiency. While HSAs can provide tax advantages and potentially encourage more conscious healthcare spending, they tend to benefit higher-income individuals disproportionately and may not address the needs of those with chronic conditions or lower incomes who cannot afford to set aside funds for future healthcare expenses. Furthermore, the administrative costs associated with managing numerous individual accounts can be substantial, potentially reducing overall system efficiency. A more equitable and efficient approach might involve focusing on comprehensive coverage that ensures access to necessary care for all individuals, regardless of their ability to save or their employment status. This could involve strengthening and expanding existing public programs, or moving towards a universal coverage system that eliminates the need for complex plan choices and individual savings mechanisms for basic healthcare needs.

In conclusion, while these proposals aim to address genuine challenges in the U.S. healthcare system, they may not fully account for the complexities of healthcare markets and the potential unintended consequences of market-oriented reforms. Many of the suggested changes could exacerbate existing inequalities in healthcare access and potentially increase system-wide costs through fragmentation and increased administrative complexity. A more comprehensive approach, potentially including elements of universal coverage and centralized cost control mechanisms, might more effectively address the underlying issues of access, cost, and quality in healthcare. Such an approach would require significant policy changes and may face substantial political and industry resistance, but it could offer a more sustainable and equitable path forward for the U.S. healthcare system.

Project 2025's approach to abortion is rooted in a fundamentally conservative and religiously-influenced worldview that seeks to dramatically curtail access to abortion services and redefine the legal and social understanding of when life begins. The project proposes a sweeping reorientation of federal policy across multiple agencies and departments to prioritize what it terms "respect for innocent human life from day one (conception)." This framing represents a significant departure from the current legal and medical consensus, which generally does not recognize personhood at the moment of conception. The implications of such a shift would be far-reaching, potentially affecting everything from healthcare policy to criminal law.

One of the most striking proposals in Project 2025 regarding abortion is its recommendation to withdraw the abortion pill mifepristone from the market and enforce existing but little-used laws to prevent its distribution through the mail. This proposal goes beyond even the most restrictive state-level abortion bans implemented in the wake of the Dobbs decision, which overturned Roe v. Wade. By targeting medication abortion, which has become increasingly prevalent and accounts for a majority of abortions in the United States, Project 2025 seeks to limit access to abortion even in states where it remains legal. This approach reflects a recognition of the changing landscape of abortion access in a post-Roe America and represents an attempt to use federal power to restrict abortion nationwide, despite the Dobbs decision's ostensible return of abortion regulation to the states.

The project's recommendations extend beyond direct restrictions on abortion to encompass a broader reshaping of federal policy around conservative Christian values related to family and reproduction. It suggests that the Department of Health and Human Services should maintain a "biblically based, social science-reinforced definition of marriage and family," indicating a desire to infuse federal policy with religious principles. This approach raises significant questions about the separation of church and state and the role of religious beliefs in shaping public policy. Furthermore, the project proposes eliminating coverage for emergency contraception and enforcing the Comstock Act to prosecute those who send and receive contraceptives and abortion pills, potentially rolling back decades of progress in reproductive rights and healthcare access.

Trump's relationship with Project 2025 and its abortion proposals is complex and somewhat ambiguous. Throughout his 2024 campaign, Trump has attempted to strike a more moderate tone on abortion compared to some of his Republican rivals, emphasizing his belief that abortion policy should be left to individual states rather than regulated at the federal level. This stance represents a shift from his first term, during which he appointed three Supreme Court justices who were instrumental in overturning Roe v. Wade and expressed support for federal abortion restrictions. Trump's current position, which includes support for exceptions in cases of rape, incest, and to save the life of the mother, diverges from the more absolutist stance taken by Project 2025.

However, Trump's campaign rhetoric and the reality of his potential governance may not align perfectly. His first term was characterized by a willingness to appoint staunchly anti-abortion officials to key positions and to pursue policies favored by the anti-abortion movement. The involvement of numerous former Trump administration officials in the development of Project 2025 suggests that, despite his public distancing from the project, a second Trump term could see the implementation of many of its proposals, including those related to abortion.

The potential implementation of Project 2025's abortion proposals under a second Trump administration would likely face significant legal and political challenges. Many of the project's recommendations, particularly those that seek to restrict abortion access in states where it remains legal, would almost certainly face court challenges on constitutional grounds. The project's desire to reinterpret the 14th Amendment to guarantee fetal personhood would represent a radical departure from current constitutional interpretation and would likely spark intense legal battles.

Moreover, the political feasibility of implementing such sweeping changes to abortion policy is questionable. Public opinion polls consistently show majority support for legal abortion access, with 61% of adults wanting their state to allow legal abortion for any reason, according to a June 2024 poll by the Associated Press and the University of Chicago's NORC. The backlash against abortion restrictions in the wake of the Dobbs decision, as evidenced by electoral outcomes and ballot initiatives in several states, suggests that aggressive federal action to restrict abortion access could face significant public opposition.

Despite these challenges, the mere existence of Project 2025 and its detailed proposals on abortion policy highlight the ongoing centrality of this issue in American politics and the potential for dramatic policy shifts under a conservative administration. The project's comprehensive approach, which seeks to mobilize multiple federal agencies and reorient policy across various domains to restrict abortion access and promote conservative family values, represents a blueprint for how executive power could be wielded to reshape American society in the absence of new legislation.

Analysis: Childhood and Education in the Conservative Vision

Project 2025 outlines a series of sweeping changes that could profoundly reshape the landscape of children's lives in the United States. This analysis delves deep into the implications of these proposed policies, focusing specifically on how children are perceived and potentially affected across various domains including education, healthcare, nutrition, family structure, and social welfare. Through a critical examination of the project's proposals, we aim to uncover the underlying assumptions about children's roles, rights, and needs that inform these policy recommendations.

EDUCATION: A NARROWING HORIZON?

Project 2025's educational policies reveal a complex and potentially contradictory view of children's educational needs and rights. On one hand, the proposal advocates for increased parental control through a "Parents' Bill of Rights," suggesting a view of children as extensions of their parents rather than as individuals with their own educational interests. This is evident in the recommendation to ban "books and lessons related to critical race theory, systemic racism, and LGBTQIA+ issues" (Heritage Foundation, 2025). Such censorship implies a perception of children as passive recipients of knowledge rather than active, critical learners capable of engaging with diverse and challenging ideas.

The proposed censorship raises significant concerns about the breadth and depth of education available to children. By limiting exposure to certain topics and perspectives, Project 2025 appears to view children's minds as vulnerable to perceived ideological influences rather than as developing intellects capable of critical thinking and nuanced understanding. This approach could potentially leave children ill-equipped to navigate the complexities of a diverse society and global community.

Furthermore, the recommendation to "Transfer Title I, Part A, which provides federal funding for lower-income school districts, to the Department of Health and Human Services, specifically the Administration for Children and Families. It should be administered as a no-strings-attached formula block grant" (Heritage Foundation, 2025, p. 325) suggests a devaluation of targeted educational support for disadvantaged children. This proposal, along with the call to "Eliminate Impact Aid not tied to students" (Heritage Foundation, 2025, p. 326), indicates a shift away from viewing education as a means of addressing systemic inequalities. Instead, it seems to conceptualize education in more individualistic terms, potentially overlooking the broader societal benefits of a well-educated populace and the specific needs of children from diverse socioeconomic backgrounds.

Perhaps most telling is the recommendation to "Eliminate the Head Start program" (Heritage Foundation, 2025, p. 482). Head Start, which provides early childhood education, healthcare, nutrition, and parent involvement services to low-income families, has been shown through longitudinal studies to have positive long-term impacts on children's lives. The proposal to eliminate this program suggests a narrow view of children's developmental needs, focusing primarily on academic outcomes rather than the holistic development that programs like Head Start aim to support. This recommendation appears to overlook the critical importance of early childhood experiences in shaping lifelong outcomes, potentially disadvantaging children from low-income families at a crucial developmental stage.

DISMANTLING FEDERAL EDUCATION INFRASTRUCTURE

At the core of Project 2025's education agenda is a proposal to dismantle the U.S. Department of Education (ED). This recommendation reflects a view of children's education as primarily a local or state concern, with minimal federal oversight or support. However, this perspective overlooks the critical role that federal education policy has played in promoting equity and protecting the rights of marginalized students.

The proposal to eliminate the Head Start program, which provides early childhood education to children in poverty, is particularly concerning. This suggestion implies a devaluation of early childhood education for disadvantaged children, potentially widening achievement gaps before formal schooling even begins. Similarly, the recommendation to discontinue the Title I program, which provides federal funding to schools serving low-income children, suggests a retreat from the federal commitment to educational equity.

These proposals reflect a view of children's education that prioritizes local control and reduced federal spending over ensuring equitable access to quality education for all children, regardless of their socioeconomic background or geographic location.

CIVIL RIGHTS AND PROTECTIONS FOR VULNERABLE STUDENTS

Project 2025's recommendations regarding civil rights in education are particularly alarming from the perspective of children's rights and well-being. The proposals to rescind federal civil rights protections for LGBTQ+ students and undercut federal capacity to enforce civil rights law suggest a narrow view of which children deserve protection and support in educational settings.

Moreover, the suggestion to reduce federal funding for students with disabilities and remove guardrails designed to ensure these children are adequately served by schools indicates a potential retreat from the long-standing federal commitment to inclusive education. This approach risks leaving some of the most vulnerable students without the support they need to access appropriate educational opportunities.

These proposals reflect a perspective that seems to value certain children's rights and needs over others, potentially creating a tiered system of educational access and protection based on factors such as sexual orientation, gender identity, or disability status.

PRIVATIZATION AND SCHOOL CHOICE

Project 2025's emphasis on promoting universal private school choice and privatizing the federal student loan portfolio indicates a shift towards viewing education through a market-based lens. While proponents argue that this approach empowers parents and increases educational options, it raises concerns about the potential for increased segregation and inequality in educational access.

The push for privatization suggests a view of children's education as a consumer good rather than a public right and responsibility. This perspective may overlook the critical role that public education plays in fostering social cohesion, promoting equal opportunity, and preparing all children for civic participation.

IMPLEMENTATION CHALLENGES AND POLITICAL REALITIES

It's important to note that many of Project 2025's most sweeping proposals would require significant congressional cooperation, which may be unlikely given the current political landscape. As pointed out in the Brookings analysis, major changes to existing legislation or the creation of new, controversial programs would require a level of bipartisan support that seems improbable in the current political climate.

Moreover, some proposals, such as the phasing out of Title I funding, might face opposition even from conservative lawmakers, given that many conservative, rural areas benefit significantly from these programs. This highlights the complex interplay between ideology and practical political considerations in shaping education policy.

UNILATERAL EXECUTIVE ACTIONS

While many of Project 2025's proposals would require legislative action, there are several significant changes that a presidential administration could enact unilaterally. These include rolling back civil rights protections for LGBTQ+ students, dismantling federal civil rights enforcement apparatus, and altering student loan repayment plans.

The potential for these unilateral actions underscores the significant impact that executive policy decisions can have on children's educational experiences and rights, even in the absence of legislative changes.

IDEOLOGICAL UNDERPINNINGS

It's crucial to understand that Project 2025's education agenda goes beyond traditional conservative education policy. As noted in the Brookings analysis, many of these proposals align more closely with white Christian nationalist ideology than with traditional conservative principles of limited government.

This ideological foundation is evident in the focus on issues of gender identity, the emphasis on parental rights (narrowly defined), and the proposed removal of protections for certain groups of students. This approach suggests a vision of education that prioritizes the values and beliefs of a specific segment of society, potentially at the expense of diverse student needs and experiences.

CHILDREN'S HEALTH AND NUTRITION

Project 2025's approach to children's health and nutrition reveals a complex and potentially problematic view of children's needs and rights in these areas. The proposal's support for "conscience protections for healthcare providers, allowing them to refuse services based on religious or moral beliefs" (Heritage Foundation, 2025) could potentially limit children's access to comprehensive healthcare. This policy suggests a prioritization of providers' beliefs over children's health needs, potentially leaving some children, particularly those from marginalized communities, without access to necessary medical care.

The promotion of abstinence-only education further underscores a view of children as needing protection from certain types of information rather than as individuals capable of making informed decisions about their health and bodies when provided with comprehensive education. This approach could leave children ill-equipped to navigate the complexities of sexual health and relationships, potentially increasing their vulnerability to health risks.

In terms of nutrition, Project 2025's recommendations paint a concerning picture of how children's basic needs are prioritized. The proposal to "Re-implement work requirements [for SNAP]" (Heritage Foundation, 2025, p. 299) and "Eliminate the heat-and-eat loophole" (Heritage Foundation, 2025, p. 301) could significantly impact children's access to nutritious food, particularly in low-income families. These policies seem to view children's nutrition as secondary to broader ideological goals about work and government assistance, potentially overlooking the critical importance of consistent, adequate nutrition for children's health, development, and academic performance.

The recommendation to reject "Any efforts to expand student eligibility for Federal school meals to include all K-12 students" (Heritage Foundation, 2025, p. 303) is particularly telling. This stance suggests a view that not all children deserve or need access to reliable nutrition through schools, overlooking the potential benefits of universal school meal programs in reducing stigma, improving overall student health, and supporting academic achievement. It implies a perspective that sees children's access to food as contingent on their families' economic status rather than as a basic right or public good.

Moreover, the proposal to "Separate the agricultural provisions of the farm bill from the nutrition provisions" (Heritage Foundation, 2025, p. 298) and to eliminate "The Food and Nutrition Service that administers the food and nutrition programs" (Heritage Foundation, 2025, p. 310) suggest a fundamental restructuring of how children's nutrition is supported at a federal level. These changes could potentially lead to reduced funding and support for programs crucial to many children's food security, indicating a shift away from viewing children's nutrition as a public health concern and towards a more individualized, family-responsibility model.

FAMILY STRUCTURE AND CHILD WELFARE

Project 2025's approach to family structure and child welfare reveals a specific vision of the ideal family environment for children, one that may not align with the diverse realities of many American families. The emphasis on traditional family structures is evident in the recommendation that "Child support in the United States should strengthen marriage as the norm, restore broken homes, and encourage unmarried couples to commit to marriage" (Heritage Foundation, 2025, p. 479). This perspective seems to view children's well-being as inherently tied to a specific family structure, potentially overlooking the quality of relationships and support within diverse family configurations.

The proposal to "Allocate funding to strategy programs promoting father involvement or terminate parental rights quickly" (Heritage Foundation, 2025, p. 482) is particularly striking. While father involvement can indeed be beneficial for many children, this policy suggestion presents a binary view that may not account for the complexities of family dynamics and children's individual needs. The threat of swift termination of parental rights could potentially lead to traumatic separations and disruptions in children's lives, particularly impacting marginalized communities who may face systemic barriers to meeting prescribed standards of involvement.

Furthermore, the recommendation to "Allow child welfare funding to be used for marriage and relationship education" (Heritage Foundation, 2025, p. 480) suggests a redirection of resources from direct interventions for children's welfare to programs promoting a specific family model. This approach implies a view that children's well-being is best served by conforming families to a particular structure, rather than by addressing the diverse and immediate needs of children in various family situations.

[Note: This artifact continues from the previous analysis. The following would be inserted as a new section before the Conclusion.]

THE CHILD AS LABORER: REDEFINING YOUTH EMPLOYMENT

Project 2025's approach to child labor laws represents a significant shift in how children are viewed in the context of work and economic productivity. This perspective is part of a broader trend among conservative policymakers that seeks to redefine the role of youth in the labor force, often in ways that conflict with long-established protections for minor workers.

The proposal put forth in Project 2025 suggests that the Department of Labor should "amend its hazard-order regulations to permit teenage workers access to work in regulated jobs with proper training and parental consent" (Heritage Foundation, 2025). This recommendation reveals a view of children, particularly teenagers, as potential solutions to labor shortages in industries traditionally considered too dangerous for minors. It implies a prioritization of economic needs over the established protections for youth workers, which have been in place for nearly a century.

This perspective on child labor is not isolated to Project 2025. It is part of a larger movement, predominantly among Republican lawmakers and conservative activists, to loosen restrictions on youth employment. For instance, in Iowa, legislation has been passed allowing 14-year-olds to perform assembly work in factories and meatpacking facilities as part of training programs, directly contravening federal child labor laws (Goodman, 2024). In Arkansas, age verification requirements for hiring children have been removed, while Florida has proposed allowing 16 and 17-year-olds to work longer hours on school nights (Goodman, 2024).

These policy shifts suggest a reevaluation of the balance between education and work in children's lives. The traditional view that prioritizes education and limits work hours to protect children's development and academic progress is being challenged. Instead, children are increasingly being viewed as potential workers who can fill gaps in the labor market, even at the cost of their education and safety.

The justification for these changes often cites labor shortages and the need for workforce development. As noted by Goodman (2024), "Some proposals by legislators have even come in direct response to lobbying by industries like restaurants and hospitality, as more employers report difficulties finding workers in a booming economy." This rationale reveals a perspective that sees children primarily through an economic lens, as untapped resources in a tight labor market, rather than as developing individuals whose primary focus should be on education and personal growth.

Moreover, the push to allow minors into more hazardous occupations suggests a concerning shift in how we view children's vulnerability and need for protection. The Fair Labor Standards Act of 1938 was enacted in response to the widespread exploitation of child workers, many of whom suffered serious injuries or health issues due to dangerous working conditions. The current efforts to roll back these protections imply a willingness to expose children once again to these risks, albeit with the caveat of "proper training and parental consent" (Heritage Foundation, 2025).

This shift is not merely theoretical. As Goodman (2024) reports, "Since 2019, there has been an 88% increase in cases in which children were found to be employed in violation of child labor laws." This statistic suggests that even before the proposed policy changes, there is already a trend towards increased child labor, often in violation of existing protections.

The view of children as potential laborers in hazardous industries stands in stark contrast to the developmental perspective that has informed child labor laws for decades. This perspective recognizes that children and adolescents are still developing physically and cognitively, and that exposure to certain work environments can have long-lasting negative impacts on their health, education, and overall well-being.

Furthermore, the emphasis on parental consent in Project 2025's proposal raises questions about how children's autonomy and best interests are balanced against parental rights and economic pressures on families. While parental involvement in decisions about a child's activities is generally seen as positive, in the context of potentially hazardous work, it may not provide sufficient protection for children whose families may be under economic stress.

The approach to child labor evidenced in Project 2025 and related conservative efforts represents a significant shift in how children are viewed in relation to work and economic productivity. It suggests a willingness to prioritize economic needs over established protections for youth, potentially exposing children to physical risks and compromising their educational opportunities. This perspective challenges long-held societal values about the importance of childhood as a time for education, development, and protection from adult responsibilities and dangers.

As we consider these proposed changes, it is crucial to critically examine the long-term implications for children's well-being, education, and future opportunities. The push to relax child labor laws raises fundamental questions about how we, as a society, value and protect childhood, and what responsibilities we believe children should bear in contributing to the economy.

IMMIGRATION AND CHILDREN

The proposal to pursue "the overturning of the Flores Settlement Agreement" (Heritage Foundation, 2025, p. 568) reveals a particularly harsh stance towards immigrant children. The Flores Settlement Agreement sets limits on the length of time and conditions under which children can be incarcerated in immigration detention, with the intent of protecting vulnerable immigrant children from inhumane conditions. Seeking to overturn this agreement suggests a view of immigrant children as fundamentally different from other children, with fewer rights and protections. This approach prioritizes stringent immigration enforcement over the well-being and rights of children, potentially exposing them to extended periods of detention and separation from their families.

Project 2025's proposals reveal a complex and often concerning perspective on children's rights, needs, and roles in society. The project seems to prioritize certain ideological positions – such as promoting traditional family structures, reducing government involvement in social services, and tightening immigration policies – over a comprehensive, evidence-based approach to supporting children's well-being and development.

Throughout the proposals, there's a recurring theme of viewing children primarily as dependents of their parents or as future adults, rather than as individuals with their own rights and needs in the present. This is evident in the emphasis on parental rights in education, the promotion of specific family structures, and the potential reduction of direct services to children in favor of programs aimed at shaping family dynamics.

Moreover, the project's recommendations often seem to overlook the diverse realities of children's lives and the complex factors that contribute to their well-being. By proposing cuts to nutrition programs, advocating for less comprehensive sex education, and suggesting policies that could reduce access to healthcare and educational resources, Project 2025 risks exacerbating existing inequalities and creating new barriers for many children, particularly those from marginalized or low-income backgrounds.

In essence, Project 2025 presents a vision of childhood and children's needs that is at odds with much of the current research on child development, education, and welfare. It suggests a shift away from viewing children's well-being as a public good and towards a more individualized, family-centered approach that may not adequately address the complex needs of all children in a diverse society.

As we consider the potential implementation of these policies, it is crucial to critically examine their underlying assumptions about children and to carefully weigh their potential impacts on the lived experiences of diverse children across the United States. Only through such careful consideration can we ensure that policy decisions truly serve the best interests of all children, supporting their rights, meeting their needs, and fostering their full potential as both present and future members of society.

Analysis: LGBTQ Rights and Protections

In recent years, the political landscape in the United States has witnessed a surge in initiatives aimed at reshaping policies related to LGBTQ+ rights and protections. Project 2025 outlines a series of sweeping policy changes that would profoundly impact LGBTQ+ individuals and communities across the nation.

Project 2025's approach to LGBTQ+ issues is rooted in a conservative ideology that prioritizes what its proponents term as "life and strengthening the family." This framework is predicated on a narrow definition of family structure, explicitly favoring "families comprised of a married mother, father, and their children" as the foundation of a "well-ordered nation and healthy society." This perspective inherently positions LGBTQ+ identities and relationships as oppositional to their ideal societal structure, setting the stage for a wide-ranging rollback of LGBTQ+ rights and protections.

One of the most alarming aspects of Project 2025 is its proposed approach to transgender individuals and issues. The project's documentation reveals a deeply concerning stance, equating the existence of transgender people with pornography and suggesting that their very presence is a form of "sexualization." This rhetoric echoes historical anti-LGBTQ+ campaigns, such as Anita Bryant's "Save Our Children" movement, which sought to frame LGBTQ+ individuals as inherent threats to minors. By positioning transgender identity as something akin to obscenity, Project 2025 lays the groundwork for potential criminalization and systematic discrimination against transgender individuals.

The implications of this ideological stance are far-reaching and multifaceted. In the realm of education, Project 2025 advocates for policies reminiscent of Florida's controversial "Don't Say Gay" legislation, aiming to restrict discussions of LGBTQ+ topics in schools nationwide. This approach not only stifles inclusive education but also potentially criminalizes educators who strive to create safe and supportive environments for all students, including those who identify as LGBTQ+.

In the sphere of civil rights, Project 2025 outlines plans to significantly weaken protections for LGBTQ+ individuals. A key target is the limitation of the Supreme Court's ruling in Bostock v. Clayton County, which extended Title VII's sex discrimination protections to LGBTQ+ individuals. By advocating for a narrow interpretation of this landmark decision and opposing its extension to broader categories of sexual orientation and gender identity, Project 2025 seeks to erode fundamental legal protections for LGBTQ+ Americans in the workplace and beyond.

The initiative's impact would extend to multiple federal agencies and departments. For instance, Project 2025 calls for the Department of Justice to prioritize defending the First Amendment rights of those who would discriminate against LGBTQ+ individuals, effectively sanctioning discrimination under the guise of religious freedom. In the realm of healthcare, the project recommends that the Department of Health and Human Services reverse its focus on LGBTQ+ equity, instead promoting policies that exclusively support traditional nuclear family structures.

Project 2025's vision for reshaping government structures is equally concerning. The plan advocates for the abolition of the Gender Policy Council within the Executive Office of the President, characterizing its work on gender equity and LGBTQ+ issues as promoting a "new woke gender ideology." In its place, Project 2025 proposes new structures aligned with its conservative family values, potentially dismantling years of progress in gender equity and LGBTQ+ rights at the highest levels of government.

The military is another arena where Project 2025 seeks to implement regressive policies. The plan calls for a reversal of policies allowing transgender individuals to serve in the military, echoing the controversial ban implemented during the previous conservative administration. This not only discriminates against capable service members but also sends a broader message about the place of transgender individuals in American society.

On the international stage, Project 2025's recommendations would have far-reaching consequences. The plan advocates for dismantling diversity, equity, and inclusion initiatives within the U.S. Agency for International Development (USAID), including ceasing the promotion of LGBTQ+ rights globally. This shift would not only affect U.S. foreign policy but could also embolden anti-LGBTQ+ movements in countries where LGBTQ+ individuals already face severe discrimination and danger.

The scope and depth of Project 2025's anti-LGBTQ+ agenda are reflected in the individuals involved in its creation. For example, the chapter on State Department policies was authored by Kiron Skinner, a former Trump administration official who was dismissed for unprofessional behavior, including making homophobic remarks. This association underscores the project's alignment with individuals who have demonstrated hostility towards LGBTQ+ rights and inclusion.

It is crucial to note that while Project 2025 focuses heavily on transgender issues, its policies would have broad implications for the entire LGBTQ+ community. The initiative's emphasis on rolling back protections, limiting discussions of LGBTQ+ topics, and promoting a narrow definition of family would affect lesbian, gay, bisexual, and queer individuals as well. This comprehensive approach to reshaping LGBTQ+ policy across multiple sectors of government and society represents a coordinated effort to fundamentally alter the landscape of LGBTQ+ rights in the United States.

Analysis: The End of Environmental and Climate Policies

Project 2025 includes a detailed strategy for completely gutting environmental and climate regulations.

The project calls for a "review of all federal science agencies" and states that "the Biden administration's climate fanaticism will need a whole of government unwinding." This echoes Trump's first term, during which hundreds of scientists were sidelined or pushed out of their government jobs due to policies that diminished the role of science. Project 2025 aims to intensify this approach.

Many sections of Project 2025 addressing climate and environmental policy were authored by oil and gas industry representatives. This aligns with recent revelations by The Washington Post that Trump arranged a private dinner with oil industry executives, asking them to donate a billion dollars to his campaign in exchange for reversing Biden's climate policies and offering other kickbacks.

The Heritage Foundation's approach to climate change is characterized by several key elements:

1. **Climate Change Denial**: The document consistently downplays or outright denies the reality and severity of climate change. It refers to climate change concerns as "climate fanaticism" and a "perceived threat," indicating a fundamental rejection of the scientific consensus on the issue.
2. **Dismantling Climate Action**: The plan aims to systematically dismantle existing climate policies and institutions. This includes proposals to repeal major climate legislation like the Inflation Reduction Act and Infrastructure Investment and Jobs Act, and to eliminate or severely restrict agencies and programs focused on climate research and action.
3. **Promoting Fossil Fuels**: Project 2025 strongly advocates for increased production and use of fossil fuels, framing this as "American energy dominance." It proposes extensive rollbacks of environmental regulations to facilitate oil, gas, and coal extraction.
4. **Limiting Scientific Research**: The plan proposes significant restrictions on climate-related scientific research, particularly within government agencies. It suggests eliminating or defunding key research programs and institutions, and changing how scientific data is collected and used in policymaking.
5. **Reframing Environmental Protection**: The document seeks to redefine environmental protection in a way that prioritizes economic interests over ecological concerns. It proposes to shift focus away from climate change and towards more immediate, localized environmental issues.
6. **State-Level Control**: There's a push to transfer more environmental regulatory power to state governments, except in cases where state regulations (like California's emissions standards) are stricter than federal ones.

This approach represents a fundamental rejection of current climate science and policy, prioritizing short-term economic interests over long-term environmental sustainability. The plan's stance on climate change is deeply intertwined with its broader conservative political agenda, reflecting a worldview that is skeptical of government intervention and prioritizes immediate economic gains over long-term environmental concerns.

DISMANTLING CLIMATE ACTION INFRASTRUCTURE

Project 2025's approach to climate change involves a systematic dismantling of the existing climate action infrastructure in the United States. This is evident in several key proposals:

1. **Eliminating Key Agencies and Programs:**
   * The plan proposes to dissolve the National Oceanic and Atmospheric Administration (NOAA), describing it as "one of the main drivers of the climate change alarm industry." This is a critical blow to climate research, as NOAA is a primary source of climate data and research in the U.S.
   * It suggests eliminating the Office of Energy Efficiency and Renewable Energy (EERE) at the Department of Energy, which is crucial for advancing clean energy technologies.
   * The plan calls for removing climate change from the National Security Council agenda, downplaying its significance as a national security threat.

2. **Defunding and Restricting Research:**
   * Project 2025 proposes significant cuts to climate-related research funding across multiple agencies.
   * It suggests restricting the use of certain scientific models and data, particularly those related to climate change projections.
   * The plan calls for eliminating the use of the social cost of carbon in policymaking, which is a key tool for assessing the economic impacts of climate change.

3. **Regulatory Rollbacks:**
   * The document advocates for rescinding numerous environmental regulations, particularly those aimed at reducing greenhouse gas emissions.
   * It proposes to revoke the EPA's 2009 "endangerment finding" that classified carbon dioxide as a pollutant to be regulated under the Clean Air Act.
   * The plan seeks to limit the EPA's authority to regulate greenhouse gases and to reverse fuel efficiency standards for vehicles.

4. **Restructuring Environmental Agencies:**
   * Project 2025 proposes a major restructuring of the Environmental Protection Agency (EPA), significantly reducing its authority and scope.
   * It suggests shifting environmental regulatory power to state governments, except in cases where state regulations are stricter than federal ones (e.g., California's emissions standards).

5. **International Climate Policy:**
   * The plan calls for withdrawing from international climate agreements, including the Paris Climate Agreement.
   * It proposes to end U.S. participation in global climate finance initiatives, describing them as "climate reparations."

These proposals, if implemented, would effectively dismantle much of the existing U.S. infrastructure for addressing climate change. The plan's approach reflects a fundamental rejection of the need for coordinated, large-scale action on climate change, instead prioritizing short-term economic interests and a reduced role for federal government in environmental regulation.

This dismantling of climate action infrastructure could have far-reaching consequences, potentially setting back U.S. efforts to address climate change by decades and undermining global climate action efforts. It also risks leaving the U.S. unprepared for the increasing impacts of climate change, from extreme weather events to long-term shifts in temperature and precipitation patterns.

A key aspect of Project 2025's plan is using cost-benefit analysis to determine if EPA regulations should stay or go, essentially treating climate science like a series of business transactions. This approach is problematic because it applies a business lens that prioritizes the bottom line over public safety to climate research. Quantifying the long-term effects of environmental pollution is challenging, and Project 2025 aims to make it even more difficult by exempting certain companies from reporting data and banning certain data from being used.

James Goodwin, policy director at the Center for Progressive Reform, compares this strategy to two blades of a scissor: "Those cost-benefit analysis rules are demanding more information, but the other blade is making it harder for EPA to get that information in the first place."
Ironically, while the project frequently cites the need for transparency to justify its sweeping proposals, including replacing scientists in senior ranks with Trump political appointees, it also proposes shielding the public from NOAA's vast data tracking.

A DONOR-DRIVEN POLICY?

Recent revelations show that the Shell USA Company Foundation, associated with oil giant Shell, has been a significant donor to the Heritage Foundation and other conservative organizations involved in Project 2025. Between 2013 and 2022, the Shell foundation donated $544,010 to various conservative groups, including $23,321 specifically to the Heritage Foundation.

The Heritage Foundation's stance on climate change aligns closely with the interests of its fossil fuel donors. In 2023, the Foundation published a commentary stating that "climate change models are poor predictors of warming," directly contradicting the scientific consensus on climate change. This position benefits oil companies like Shell, which reported adjusted earnings of $28.25 billion in 2022.

Project 2025's advisory board includes 14 organizations that have received funding from the Shell USA Company Foundation. Many of these groups share an agenda of building conservative power and often deny or downplay the climate crisis. For instance:

1. **The Heartland Institute,** which received $5,000 from Shell's foundation, published a video in May 2024 incorrectly claiming that "the scientific data continue to show there is no climate crisis."
2. **The American Family Association**, which received $59,264 from Shell's foundation, claims that the "climate change agenda is an attack on God's creation."
3. **Hillsdale College**, which received $105,748, has hosted prominent climate skeptics.

Other Project 2025 advisory board members that received funding from Shell's foundation include the American Center for Law and Justice ($14,321), the Claremont Institute ($1,975), Discovery Institute ($3,300), the Family Research Council ($3,399), First Liberty Institute ($19,100), the Leadership Institute ($7,125), the Media Research Center ($2,528), Students for Life of America ($1,020), and the Texas Public Policy Foundation ($8,275).

The influence of these donors is evident in Project 2025's proposals, which include:

1. A "review of all federal science agencies"
2. Unwinding the Biden administration's climate policies
3. Using cost-benefit analysis to determine if EPA regulations should stay or go
4. Shuttering the law enforcement wing of the EPA's Office of Water
5. Withdrawing from international climate agreements
6. Removing climate policies from foreign aid programs
7. Eliminating federal restrictions on fossil fuel drilling on public lands
8. Blocking wind and solar power from being added to the electrical grid
9. Reconsidering the designation of toxic substances
10. Privatizing the National Weather Service
11. Dissolving the National Oceanic and Atmospheric Administration (NOAA)

These proposals clearly benefit the fossil fuel industry by weakening environmental regulations and climate action.

The Heritage Foundation's influence extends beyond Project 2025. It has a long history of attacking the scientific consensus on climate change, aligning with the interests of its fossil fuel donors. This pattern is part of a broader strategy by conservative organizations to maintain close relationships with groups that wield significant political influence and support the interests of the fossil fuel industry.

As Adrian Bardon, a professor at Wake Forest University who has studied the religious right and climate denialism, notes: "Shell has every reason to want to maintain close relationships with organizations that wield outsize political influence and just happen to reliably support the interests of the fossil fuel industry."
While Shell USA claims that its foundation "does not endorse any organizations" and that "giving is a personal decision not directed by the company," the pattern of donations suggests a clear alignment between the foundation's giving and the interests of the fossil fuel industry.

This network of funding and influence demonstrates how organizations like the Heritage Foundation, driven by the interests of their donors, can shape policy proposals that have far-reaching implications for environmental protection and climate action. Project 2025 serves as a prime example of how donor interests can translate into policy recommendations that prioritize industry profits over environmental concerns and scientific consensus.

Analysis: Project 2025 Labor Strategies and the War on Workers

At the heart of Project 2025's labor proposals are several significant changes to existing laws and regulations:

1. **Amending the National Labor Relations Act (NLRA)**: The plan suggests allowing unions and employers to treat national employment laws as negotiable defaults rather than non-negotiable minimum standards. This could fundamentally challenge the concept of universal minimum labor standards.
2. **Reversing Diversity, Equity, and Inclusion (DEI) Initiatives**: Project 2025 calls for eliminating DEI efforts within labor policy, arguing that they advance race, sex, and other classifications in a discriminatory manner.
3. **Expanding Religious and Moral Exemptions**: Employers would have more leeway to avoid certain labor laws based on their beliefs, potentially affecting anti-discrimination policies and healthcare access.
4. **Reclassifying Home Offices**: The plan seeks to clarify that home offices should not be subject to Occupational Safety and Health Administration (OSHA) regulations.
5. **Permitting states** to prohibit labor unions in private sector industries
6. **Reducing protections for employees** who participate in collective bargaining or unionization efforts
7. **Enabling companies** to dissolve unions despite existing contractual agreements
8. **Mandating secret ballot elections for union formation**, even when employers are willing to recognize unions voluntarily
9. **Removing worker protections** for overtime compensation
10. **Disregarding federal minimum wage standards**
11. **Discontinuing the Public Service Loan Forgiveness Program**, which has eased student debt for many public sector employees
12. **Dismantling merit-based hiring practices in federal agencies**, potentially allowing appointments based on loyalty rather than qualifications
13. **Repealing federal regulations that safeguard minors** from hazardous work environments such as mines and meatpacking facilities

These proposed changes, among others, could significantly alter the landscape of workers' rights and protections in the United States.

WEAKENING OVERTIME PROTECTIONS AND MINIMUM WAGE STANDARDS

One of the most concerning aspects of Project 2025 is its attempt to weaken overtime protections. The plan proposes slashing the overtime threshold, potentially leaving millions of workers in industries such as hospitality and manufacturing working long hours without extra pay. This could result in a de facto pay cut for countless families already struggling to make ends meet. Furthermore, the plan suggests allowing states to opt out of federal overtime and minimum wage laws. This could lead to significant wage disparities across the country and might mean that workers in some regions earn substantially less, exacerbating income inequality. Even without the implementation of these policies, simply reverting to the overtime pay rules under the first Trump administration would slash overtime for 4.3 million workers

UNDERMINING UNIONS AND COLLECTIVE BARGAINING RIGHTS

Project 2025 takes aim at unions, which play a crucial role in ensuring fair wages, benefits, and working conditions for employees. The plan proposes amending the National Labor Relations Act (NLRA) to allow unions and employers to treat national employment laws as negotiable defaults rather than non-negotiable minimum standards. This fundamentally challenges the concept of universal minimum labor standards. The plan also suggests making it easier for workers to decertify unions and banning the "card check" process for union recognition. These changes could significantly weaken labor unions' power and ability to organize workers, potentially leading to reduced worker protections and bargaining power.

ENDANGERING CHILD WORKERS AND WORKPLACE SAFETY

In a move that has drawn sharp criticism, Project 2025 calls for weakening child labor protections. The plan argues that young people should be allowed to work in "inherently dangerous jobs" currently off-limits due to safety concerns. This proposal could see economically vulnerable youth pushed into hazardous work simply because they need the income. The blueprint also seeks to reclassify home offices and clarify that they should not be subject to Occupational Safety and Health Administration (OSHA) regulations. This could jeopardize the health and safety of the growing remote workforce.

ELIMINATING DIVERSITY, EQUITY, AND INCLUSION EFFORTS

Project 2025 calls for eliminating all diversity, equity, and inclusion (DEI) initiatives within labor policy. It proposes banning the collection of demographic data by the Equal Employment Opportunity Commission (EEOC), which could hinder efforts to identify and address systemic workplace discrimination. The plan also advocates for robust protections for religious employers, potentially leading to increased discrimination against LGBTQIA+ individuals and those with different religious beliefs.

ECONOMIC IMPACT AND FISCAL CONCERNS

While supporters argue that Project 2025's proposals would cut red tape and boost economic growth, many economists express doubts about its fiscal impact. The lack of revenue projections in the plan raises questions about its potential to increase the deficit while shifting more of the tax burden onto lower and middle-income Americans.Heidi Shierholz, President of the Economic Policy Institute, cautions that "the plan's tax proposals read like a reverse Robin Hood scheme. It calls for a two-bracket system that would hike taxes on those earning under $150,000 annually by $2,000 to $2,500, while showering the wealthy with massive cuts."

As the 2024 election approaches, Project 2025 presents a distinct vision of what labor policy could look like under a second Trump administration. While many of these proposals would face significant hurdles in Congress, they represent a clear blueprint for a conservative overhaul of workers' rights and protections. For the millions of Americans who depend on hard-won labor laws and regulations, the potential implementation of Project 2025 raises serious concerns about job quality, workplace safety, and economic security. As Celine McNicholas, Director of Policy at the Economic Policy Institute, puts it, "For workers across the country, the stakes couldn't be higher. Defeating this radical agenda will be crucial to preserving a fair and equitable future of work."

SECTION 4: THE ECONOMY

Even more ambitiously, Winfree suggests that the next Administration should think about proposing legislation that would 'effectively abolish' the Federal Reserve and replace it with 'free banking,' whereby 'neither interest rates nor the supply of money' would be 'controlled by government.' – Page 661

The following summary conveys the content of the document accurately and objectively, without endorsing or critiquing the perspectives of the original authors.

Summary

The fourth section begins by emphasizing the importance of prioritizing economic prosperity for ordinary Americans in the next administration. It criticizes "establishment 'elites'" for failing citizens through policies such as unsecured borders, outsourcing manufacturing, reckless spending, and excessive regulation. The author argues that the government's proper role is to secure "God-given, unalienable rights" to enable the pursuit of happiness and free enterprise.

The importance of effective trade policy is highlighted as crucial for the wellbeing of everyday Americans. The text introduces a debate between Kent Lassman and Peter Navarro on conservative trade policy approaches. Lassman advocates for a "humble, limited-government approach" promoting free trade with all nations. He warns that aggressive trade policies could be misused by future leftist administrations to push "climate change" and "equity"-based activism.

Lassman contends that U.S. manufacturing and the economy are not in decline, citing "record-setting real GDP" despite a "long-run decline in manufacturing employment." He argues against the effectiveness of aggressive trade policies in creating manufacturing jobs, referencing Federal Reserve research showing that Trump Administration steel tariffs resulted in a net loss of manufacturing jobs.

Furthermore, Lassman posits that protectionist policies weaken American security. He believes that "trade creates peace" and that China's reliance on trade with the U.S.

makes it less dangerous. He suggests that American cultural influence in China could help transform it "from an authoritarian threat into a freer and less hostile power." Lassman advocates for lowering or repealing tariffs, including the "destructive Trump–Biden tariffs," to make goods more affordable for Americans. He argues that free trade will improve the economy, enhance national security, and prevent future left-leaning administrations from using trade negotiations to benefit labor and environmental interest groups.

In contrast, Peter Navarro strongly disagrees with Lassman's position. He argues that trade policy is essential for an "American manufacturing and defense industrial base renaissance." Navarro identifies two main forces working against this goal: the World Trade Organization's "most favored nation" rules, which he claims encourage high tariffs from trade partners, and China's "economic aggression" through various unfair trade practices.

Navarro emphasizes the importance of trade deficits, arguing that offshoring suppresses American wages and weakens the manufacturing and defense industrial base. He advocates for a trade policy guided by "the principle of reciprocity" to encourage other countries to lower trade barriers or face increased U.S. barriers. Navarro also supports "decoupling" the U.S. economy from China's.

The text highlights Navarro's concerns about China's goals to dominate global manufacturing and supply chains, strengthening its "defense industrial base and associated warfighting capabilities." He points out China's efforts to acquire U.S. intellectual property through various means, including sending students to U.S. universities and partnering with American institutions on research with potential military applications.

Navarro warns of China's "conquest by purchase," using trade surplus revenues to buy American assets. He concludes that current U.S. trade policy benefits allies and adversaries at America's expense, weakening the industrial base while strengthening China's, and ultimately undermining U.S. capabilities and freedom.

CHAPTER 21: DEPARTMENT OF COMMERCE

The National Oceanographic and Atmospheric Administration (NOAA) should be dismantled and many of its functions eliminated, sent to other agencies, privatized, or placed under the control of states and territories – Page 664

Key Policy Proposals

The proposed policies and structural changes in this chapter represent a profound shift towards dismantling and weakening crucial institutions that have long served the American public and protected our economic and national security interests. These changes are not only misguided but also dangerously short-sighted. Let's dissect the key proposals and their likely consequences:

DISMANTLING THE NATIONAL OCEANIC AND ATMOSPHERIC ADMINISTRATION (NOAA)

The recommendation to dismantle NOAA, transferring or privatizing its functions, threatens the very foundation of environmental stewardship and public safety in the United States. NOAA's role in climate monitoring, weather forecasting, and managing marine resources is indispensable. Privatizing these functions could lead to a lack of accountability and transparency, prioritizing profit over public interest.

NOAA's climate research, which the chapter dismisses as "climate change alarmism," is based on rigorous scientific evidence and is critical in guiding global efforts to combat climate change. The suggestion to disband NOAA's climate research undermines the scientific consensus on climate change and could result in the U.S. falling behind in global environmental leadership. This would have catastrophic consequences for future generations, as climate change is already causing unprecedented natural disasters, economic disruptions, and loss of life.

WEAKENING EXPORT CONTROLS AND PROMOTING TECHNOLOGY TRANSFER

The chapter proposes reversing the "Export Control Reform" and imposing stricter regulations to prevent technology transfer to adversaries like China and Russia. While national security is paramount, the approach suggested here is overly aggressive and risks alienating key international partners and allies.

By unilaterally tightening export controls and increasing restrictions on technology transfer, the U.S. risks isolating itself from global innovation networks. Collaboration with allies on technology standards and research is essential for maintaining global competitiveness. Overly stringent controls could stifle American innovation, drive research and development offshore, and harm U.S. businesses that rely on global supply chains. Moreover, the assumption that all technology transfers are inherently dangerous fails to recognize the benefits of international collaboration in advancing technological frontiers.

ABOLISHING THE MINORITY BUSINESS DEVELOPMENT AGENCY (MBDA)

The chapter's critique of the MBDA as perpetuating racial bias is a fundamental misunderstanding of the agency's role. The MBDA is not about perpetuating bias; it is about leveling the playing field in a country where systemic racism has long marginalized minority entrepreneurs. Minority-owned businesses represent one-third of all U.S. businesses and generate $1.7 trillion annually for the economy. Cutting support for these businesses would exacerbate economic inequality and hinder the economic recovery of minority communities disproportionately affected by the COVID-19 pandemic.

The MBDA's programs are essential in providing minority entrepreneurs with the resources, mentorship, and networks they need to succeed. Eliminating or weakening the MBDA would mean abandoning these communities at a time when they need the most support, deepening racial and economic disparities that harm the entire nation.

PRIVATIZING KEY GOVERNMENT FUNCTIONS

The chapter advocates for the privatization of several essential government functions, including the Hollings Manufacturing Extension Partnership (MEP) and the Baldrige Performance Excellence Program. Privatizing these programs would put critical services out of reach for small businesses and manufacturers, particularly those in rural and underserved areas. These programs provide essential support that helps small and medium-sized enterprises (SMEs) innovate and compete globally.

Privatization is not a panacea; it often leads to reduced access, higher costs, and lower quality of services. The government's role in providing these services ensures that they are available to all, regardless of a company's size or location. Removing these supports could cripple small businesses, stifle innovation, and undermine America's industrial base at a time when we need to be investing in our domestic capabilities to compete on the global stage.

CONSOLIDATING STATISTICAL AGENCIES

Merging the Bureau of Economic Analysis (BEA), the Census Bureau, and the Bureau of Labor Statistics (BLS) into a single entity may seem efficient, but it poses significant risks. Each of these agencies plays a unique role in collecting, analyzing, and reporting data that informs public policy, business decisions, and academic research.

Centralizing these functions under one roof could lead to a loss of specialization, reduce the quality and accuracy of data, and introduce biases in data collection and interpretation. Furthermore, such a move could undermine the independence of these agencies, making them more susceptible to political interference. The integrity of economic and demographic data is vital for democracy, and any effort to compromise this should be vigorously opposed.

The proposals laid out in this chapter reflect a dangerous disregard for the institutions and policies that have protected and advanced American interests for decades. The consequences of implementing these changes would be profound, leading to weakened national security, increased economic inequality, diminished scientific capacity, and reduced public access to essential services. Policymakers must reject these shortsighted recommendations and instead focus on strengthening the institutions that uphold our democracy, support economic growth, and ensure justice and equity for all Americans.

Summary

This chapter of Mandate for Leadership was written by Thomas F. Gilman. The following summary conveys the content of the document accurately and objectively, without endorsing or critiquing the perspectives of the original authors.

Gilman opens by discussing the overarching role of the Department of Commerce, which is tasked with promoting economic growth, innovation, and competitiveness, while also providing essential data for American businesses. However, the department has faced significant challenges, including regulatory capture, ideological drift, and a lack of focus, leading to criticism and calls for its abolition in the 1990s.

Despite these challenges, the department remains crucial, particularly in countering the economic decline under the Biden Administration and opposing Communist China. The text argues that while the department has the tools necessary for success, it also requires streamlining and reform to enhance its effectiveness. There is a strong emphasis on the need to consolidate overlapping programs, which could improve accountability and taxpayer return on investment.

PROPOSED POLICIES AND STRUCTURAL CHANGES:

- **Consolidation and Privatization:** Gilman proposes evaluating whether various components of the department, such as the International Trade Administration (ITA) and parts of the Bureau of Industry and Security (BIS), should be merged with other federal entities like the Office of the U.S. Trade Representative (USTR). The potential elimination or privatization of duplicative programs is also suggested.

- **Statistical Agencies Merger:** It is recommended that the Bureau of Economic Analysis (BEA), the Census Bureau, and the Department of Labor's Bureau of Labor Statistics (BLS) be consolidated into a single, more efficient statistical agency.

- **U.S. Patent and Trademark Office (USPTO):** There are two proposals regarding the USPTO: either making it a performance-based organization under the Office of Management and Budget (OMB) or consolidating it with the National Institute of Standards and Technology (NIST) to form a new U.S. Office of Patents, Trademarks, and Standards.

- **National Oceanographic and Atmospheric Administration (NOAA):** Gilman argues for the dismantling of NOAA, with its functions either eliminated, privatized, or transferred to other agencies or state control.

Gilman acknowledges that drastic structural changes are unlikely due to political realities but emphasizes the importance of focusing on policy, strategy, and tactical reforms that can be implemented by an incoming conservative administration.

Let me know when you're ready to move on to the next section.

OFFICE OF THE SECRETARY

The Office of the Secretary (OS) within the Department of Commerce is described as a misnomer, as it encompasses far more than just the Secretary's immediate support staff. Gilman explains that most of OS's budget and personnel are dedicated to administrative, financial, human resources, IT, and other bureaucratic functions, often using outdated and inefficient systems. This leaves the Secretary with minimal direct support, relying

heavily on detailees and indirect funding from the department's bureaus to carry out the President's agenda.

Proposed Reforms:

- **Modernization and Digitization:** The Trump Administration began updating financial management tools, but more must be done to modernize and digitize the department's processes. This would allow resources to be redirected toward the Secretary's and President's priorities.

- **Staffing with Political Appointees:** Gilman stresses the importance of fully staffing OS with political appointees from Day One of a new administration, sending existing detailees back to their home bureaus and replacing them with trusted career staff as needed. Additionally, the department's leadership should fight to restore direct funding and increase the number of political appointee positions within OS to ensure effective implementation of the Secretary's and President's policy objectives.

ADMINISTRATION, BUDGET, AND APPROPRIATIONS

The document highlights that career staff often act as gatekeepers between department leadership and external partners, including the Office of Management and Budget (OMB) and Congress. This can slow down or even halt policy changes, particularly in budget and appropriations matters.

Proposed Reforms:

- **Political Leadership in Key Financial Roles:** The text emphasizes the need for political leadership at the Office of the Chief Financial Officer (CFO) and the Assistant Secretary for Administration (ASA) to ensure alignment with the administration's priorities. Political appointees should be empowered to communicate directly with external partners and monitor internal CFO operations to prevent funds from being diverted to programs that do not align with the administration's goals.

ADVISORY COMMITTEES

Gilman is critical of many advisory committees within the Department of Commerce, suggesting that they are often populated by activists hostile to conservative principles. These committees can impede the implementation of conservative policies.

Proposed Reforms:

- **Review and Abolishment of Committees:** Upon taking office, a conservative administration should review all advisory committees to determine whether they are statutorily required. Those that are not should be abolished, and the membership of remaining committees should be reconstituted to ensure they provide genuine expert advice and contribute productively to the policy-making process. Gilman also advises ensuring compliance with the Federal Advisory Committee Act (FACA) and reviewing how these committees have been integrated into regulations.

INTERNATIONAL TRADE ADMINISTRATION (ITA)

The International Trade Administration (ITA) is presented as a central entity in crafting and implementing U.S. trade policy. Its mission includes expanding trade and investment, fostering job creation, innovation, and economic growth, and providing research and analysis to support trade negotiations led by the U.S. Trade Representative (USTR).

POLICY PRIORITIES FOR ITA:

- **Countering Adversaries:** The ITA should prioritize countering the malign influence of China and other U.S. adversaries.

- **Vigorous Enforcement:** It should enforce trade agreements vigorously and defend against violations to ensure fair competition.

- **Securing Supply Chains:** The ITA should focus on securing access to critical supply chains and technologies, enabling the private sector to drive innovation and remain globally competitive.

Gilman acknowledges that the ITA is managed by a deeply entrenched set of Senior Executive Service officials, many of whom have held their positions for over a decade. While most are non-partisan civil servants, the document warns that some may not fully align with a conservative administration's goals.

Proposed Reforms:

- **Strong Political Leadership:** It is crucial that political appointees fill key policymaking positions in the ITA from the outset to ensure that the bureau fully implements the administration's policy. Assistant Secretary and Deputy Assistant Secretary roles should be prioritized for political appointments.

ENFORCEMENT AND COMPLIANCE

Enforcement & Compliance (E&C) within the ITA plays a critical role in ensuring free and fair trade by enforcing trade agreements and defending against unfair practices like dumping and illegal subsidies.

Controversy on Antidumping and Countervailing Duty Laws (AD/CVD):

- **Protectionism vs. Corrective Action:** The document discusses the debate within conservative circles regarding AD/CVD laws. Some view these laws as protectionist and harmful to economic competitiveness by increasing costs for downstream industries. Others argue that these tariffs are necessary corrective actions against anti-free market activities by other governments, ensuring long-term market health and fairness.

Proposed Reforms:

- **Process Improvements:** Re-establish and expand rigorous in-person verifications, particularly concerning China, and implement advanced analytics and AI to detect circumvention and enforce duties more effectively.

- **Policy Adjustments:** The document advocates for policies that favor U.S. companies in AD/CVD proceedings, ensure senior policymaking positions are held by political appointees, and create a fair process for self-initiating AD/CVD proceedings.

- **Addressing China:** Specific strategies include reviving a China-specific non-market economy unit and developing new methodologies for determining normal values in Chinese anti-dumping cases due to China's unique economic structure and state intervention.

INDUSTRY AND ANALYSIS (I&A)

Industry and Analysis (I&A) serves as a critical component within the Department of Commerce, consisting of a team of economists and industry experts who provide essential analysis to various government partners, including the White House, the U.S. Trade Representative (USTR), and the public. I&A's work is vital in ensuring that national security risk assessments, particularly those conducted by the Committee on Foreign Investment in the United States (CFIUS), include proper economic impact and supply chain analysis. This ensures that adversaries like China cannot exploit the U.S.'s open investment climate.

Core Functions:

- **Impact Assessments:** I&A conducts economic modeling and impact assessments for policy options under consideration by the Administration, playing a crucial role in identifying trade barriers and providing industry-specific expertise during free trade agreement (FTA) negotiations.

- **Data Flow:** The organization also ensures the continuity of cross-border data flows, especially with Europe, helping maintain open and relatively unrestricted channels vital for global trade.

Challenges and Criticisms:

- **Lack of Strategic Focus:** Despite its important functions, I&A's implementation of its mission can sometimes lack focus and energy. For example, the Top Market Reports, which represent a significant portion of I&A's output, are criticized for not serving a specific strategic function and could be better replaced by assessments of industry competitiveness in critical sectors.

Proposed Reforms:

- **Leadership:** Strong and capable leadership is necessary to ensure that Administration priorities permeate I&A's operations. Gilman suggests that political appointees should lead standing teams focused on high-priority issues.

- **Restructuring:** I&A should be permanently restructured to perform ongoing supply-chain analysis, identifying vulnerabilities like those exposed during the COVID-19 pandemic. Permanent teams should be established to focus on strategic decoupling from China, strengthening the defense industrial base, securing critical supply chains, and fostering emerging technologies such as rare earth minerals, semiconductors, artificial intelligence, and quantum computing.

GLOBAL MARKETS AND THE U.S. AND FOREIGN COMMERCIAL SERVICE

The Global Markets (GM) division and the U.S. and Foreign Commercial Service (CS) are tasked with facilitating U.S. export growth and promoting U.S. business interests abroad. However, Gilman notes that strategic planning within these entities has been consistently undermined by rising operational costs, particularly those associated with maintaining overseas staff, against the backdrop of flat or reduced budgets.

Current Structure:

- **Overseas Operations:** CS manages staff across 106 domestic offices and 77 countries globally. Some posts, known as "partner posts," utilize

interagency staff and regionally located CS officials to offer services without a permanent in-country presence.

Challenges:

- **Rising Costs:** The State Department imposes rapidly increasing costs on CS posts overseas, leading to an unsustainable operational model under current resource constraints.

Proposed Reforms:

- **Strategic Resource Allocation:** CS resources should be distributed based on their value in countering adversarial influences (particularly from China), fostering U.S. innovation, maintaining access to critical supply chains, and expanding potential export markets.

- **Operational Restructuring:** Gilman suggests that difficult decisions must be made regarding the value and justification of individual CS posts. If the State Department views a permanent CS presence as vital to national interest, it should bear more of the associated costs.

- **Consolidation:** There is also a recommendation to consolidate the Advocacy Center and SelectUSA, both seen as low-cost tools to drive significant export transactions and foreign direct investment (FDI). Gilman suggests establishing a new Office of Trade and Investment Advocacy, led by a Deputy Assistant Secretary, to manage these efforts and seek congressional authorization to use FDI-promotion tools to encourage reshoring by U.S. businesses.

BUREAU OF INDUSTRY AND SECURITY (BIS)

The Bureau of Industry and Security (BIS) is critical in controlling the export of dual-use technologies that could be used by adversaries to enhance their military capabilities. Gilman highlights the massive scale of technology transfer to adversaries like China and Russia, facilitated by their exploitation of the U.S.'s open economy and education system.

Historical Context:

- **Export Control Reform:** The document criticizes the U.S. government's "Export Control Reform" process between 2008 and 2016, which aimed to loosen the Export Administration Regulations (EAR) to facilitate technology transfer, often to the detriment of national security.

Proposed Reforms:

- **Reversal of Reforms:** Gilman calls for the reversal of these reforms still present in the EAR, arguing that the U.S. needs stronger regulations to protect critical technologies while promoting interoperability with allies.

- **Unilateral Action:** BIS should act unilaterally to implement tighter export controls while coordinating with allies, emphasizing that waiting for international consensus is not an option when national security is at stake.

Emerging and Foundational Technologies:

- **Expanded Controls:** Under the Export Control Reform Act of 2018 (ECRA), BIS was mandated to regulate emerging and foundational technologies. However, Gilman criticizes BIS for controlling only a limited number of technologies and calls for an open, transparent rulemaking process where recommendations for controlling technologies can be submitted and reviewed regularly.

Licensing Procedures and Transparency:

- **Dispute Resolution:** The current process for resolving disputes between various departments over export license decisions should be revised. Gilman suggests giving lead authority in these disputes to the BIS Under Secretary, rather than the Assistant Secretary for Export Administration, to ensure a more balanced consideration of diverging views.

- **Congressional Oversight:** BIS should provide specific congressional committees with detailed data on export licenses to improve oversight and ensure that BIS is adequately protecting national security.

End-Use Checks and EAR Revisions:

- **Strengthening Enforcement:** Gilman stresses the importance of rigorous end-use checks to validate the integrity of the export control system and suggests that BIS should deny export licenses to countries that do not permit adequate checks, such as China and Russia.

- **Modernization of EAR:** Gilman proposes a new export control modernization effort to tighten policies governing licenses to countries of concern, including eliminating loopholes, increasing restrictions on technology transfers, and revising rules on fundamental research to prevent exploitation by authoritarian governments.

Entity List and Sanctions:

- **Expanding the Entity List:** Gilman advocates for adding more Chinese and Russian companies to the Entity List and applying a "policy of denial" for license reviews, prohibiting exports to these entities. It also suggests placing violators of export controls on the BIS Denied Persons List and, in severe cases, subjecting them to sanctions by the Department of Treasury.

Data Transfer and Surveillance Concerns:

- **Executive Order on Data:** The document recommends drafting an executive order to expand export control authority to include the regulation of data exports, particularly to countries of concern. This order would establish a framework for controlling the export of personal data and would be implemented through BIS regulations.
- **Targeting Apps:** BIS should designate app providers known for undermining U.S. national security through data collection and surveillance, such as WeChat and TikTok, to the Entity List. This designation would prevent updates to these apps, rendering them non-operational in the U.S.

NATIONAL OCEANIC AND ATMOSPHERIC ADMINISTRATION (NOAA)

The National Oceanic and Atmospheric Administration (NOAA) is the largest agency within the Department of Commerce, particularly outside decennial census years, accounting for more than half of the department's personnel and operational budget.

Structure and Functions:
- **Main Offices:** NOAA consists of six main offices, including the National Weather Service (NWS) and the National Marine Fisheries Service (NMFS), among others. NOAA positions itself as a provider of environmental information and stewardship services, as well as a leader in applied scientific research.

Criticisms:
- **Climate Change Alarmism:** Gilman argues that NOAA has become a significant driver of climate change alarmism, which the document views as detrimental to U.S. prosperity. It suggests that NOAA's mission is overly focused on predicting and managing unplannable outcomes, corrupting its useful functions.

Proposed Reforms:
- **Breaking Up NOAA:** Gilman advocates for breaking up and downsizing NOAA, transferring its functions to other agencies, privatizing them, or placing them under state control. It argues that the private sector could provide many of NOAA's functions more cost-effectively and with higher quality.
- **Commercialization of NWS Operations:** The National Weather Service should focus on data-gathering operations, leaving the forecasting functions to private companies, which have been shown to provide more reliable forecasts.
- **Review and Streamlining:** Specific functions, such as those of the National Hurricane Center and the National Environmental Satellite Service, should be reviewed for their public safety and business functions, ensuring that data is presented neutrally without bias toward any side of the climate debate.
- **Transfer of NOS Survey Functions:** The document suggests transferring the survey operations of the National Ocean Service to the U.S. Coast Guard and the U.S. Geological Survey to increase efficiency.

STREAMLINING THE NATIONAL MARINE FISHERIES SERVICE (NMFS)

Gilman addresses the overlap between the National Marine Fisheries Service (NMFS) and the U.S. Fish and Wildlife Service. The NMFS is primarily responsible for managing saltwater species, while the Fish and Wildlife Service focuses on freshwater species. This division of responsibilities, however, leads to inefficiencies and duplications.

Proposed Reforms:
- **Streamlining Functions:** Gilman recommends streamlining the goals and operations of these two agencies to reduce overlap and increase efficiency. By harmonizing their efforts, the agencies could better manage aquatic species and conserve resources.

HARMONIZATION OF THE MAGNUSON–STEVENS ACT WITH THE NATIONAL MARINE SANCTUARIES ACT

Gilman points out conflicts between the Magnuson–Stevens Act, which governs fisheries management, and the National Marine Sanctuaries Act, which establishes marine sanctuaries, including no-fishing zones. These conflicts can disrupt effective fisheries management and create regulatory confusion.

Proposed Reforms:
- **Harmonization:** The document suggests harmonizing the Magnuson–Stevens Act with the National Marine Sanctuaries Act to ensure that marine sanctuaries are managed in a way that does not conflict with fisheries management goals. This would involve reviewing the establishment of new marine sanctuaries to ensure they align with the broader goals of fisheries conservation and management.

WITHDRAWAL OF THE 30X30 EXECUTIVE ORDER AND THE AMERICA THE BEAUTIFUL INITIATIVE

Gilman is critical of the 30x30 Executive Order and the America the Beautiful Initiative, which aim to conserve 30% of U.S. lands and waters by 2030. The document argues that these initiatives are being used to advance an agenda that restricts commercial activities, including fishing, and promotes offshore wind energy development at the expense of other industries.

Proposed Reforms:
- **Executive Order Withdrawal:** The document calls for the withdrawal of the 30x30 Executive Order and associated initiatives. It suggests that these programs are detrimental to existing ocean-based industries and should be reevaluated to ensure they do not harm economic activities.

MODIFICATION OF REGULATIONS UNDER THE MARINE MAMMAL PROTECTION ACT AND THE ENDANGERED SPECIES ACT

Gilman addresses the perceived abuse of the Marine Mammal Protection Act and the Endangered Species Act, particularly concerning their impact on fisheries and Native American subsistence activities.

Proposed Reforms:
- **Regulatory Revisions:** The document recommends revising the regulations implementing these acts to prevent their misuse and to reduce the negative impact on fisheries and subsistence activities. This could involve streamlining the regulatory process and ensuring that the acts are applied in a balanced and fair manner.

NEPA EXEMPTION FOR FISHERIES ACTIONS

Gilman highlights the burdensome and redundant nature of the National Environmental Policy Act (NEPA) requirements when applied to fisheries management actions. It notes that the Magnuson–Stevens Act already provides robust analysis of the biological, economic, and social impacts of regulatory actions, making NEPA's additional requirements unnecessary.

Proposed Reforms:
- **NEPA Exemption:** Gilman advocates for granting fisheries management actions an exemption from NEPA requirements. This would streamline the regulatory process, reduce delays, and allow for more timely and effective management of fisheries.

DOWNSIZING THE OFFICE OF OCEANIC AND ATMOSPHERIC RESEARCH (OAR)

The Office of Oceanic and Atmospheric Research (OAR) is identified as a major source of NOAA's climate change research. Gilman criticizes this focus, suggesting that much of OAR's research contributes to climate alarmism rather than practical, applied science.

Proposed Reforms:
- **Disband Climate-Change Research:** The document proposes disbanding the preponderance of OAR's climate-change research activities, which are viewed as unnecessary and alarmist. Gilman also suggests consolidating and reducing OAR's network of research laboratories, undersea research centers, and joint research institutes with universities to eliminate redundancy and bloat.

BREAK UP THE OFFICE OF MARINE AND AVIATION OPERATIONS

The Office of Marine and Aviation Operations (OMAO) provides the ships and planes used by NOAA agencies. Gilman argues that OMAO's assets could be more effectively managed by other agencies or the General Services Administration (GSA).

Proposed Reforms:
- **Reassignment of Assets:** The document recommends breaking up OMAO and reassigning its assets to other federal agencies or the GSA. This would involve transferring responsibility for marine and aviation operations to entities better equipped to manage these resources efficiently.

ENCOURAGING HIGH-QUALITY RESEARCH THROUGH SMALL INNOVATION PRIZES AND COMPETITIONS

Gilman advocates for using small innovation prizes and competitions to encourage high-quality research and development in NOAA's research programs. This approach is seen as a way to stimulate innovation without significantly increasing spending.

Proposed Reforms:
- **Innovation Competitions:** The document suggests that NOAA should lower the barriers to entry for startups and small businesses by offering

innovation prizes and holding competitions in various cities. This would attract a diverse range of innovators and investors, fostering entrepreneurial solutions that align with NOAA's needs.

ENSURING POLITICAL APPOINTEES ALIGN WITH ADMINISTRATION AIMS

Gilman underscores the importance of ensuring that political appointees within scientific agencies like NOAA are fully aligned with the administration's policy goals. The potential for obstructionism is highlighted as a risk if appointees do not share the administration's vision.

Proposed Reforms:

- **Careful Selection of Appointees:** The document calls for particular attention to be paid to the appointment of political leaders in NOAA and other scientific agencies to ensure that they are committed to executing the administration's objectives.

ELEVATING THE OFFICE OF SPACE COMMERCE (OSC)

The Office of Space Commerce (OSC) is identified as the executive branch's advocate for the U.S. commercial space industry. However, its mission has been diminished due to its position within the National Environmental Satellite, Data, and Information Service (NESDIS), which does not prioritize advancing the space economy.

Proposed Reforms:

- **Restoring OSC's Mission:** Gilman suggests moving OSC back to the Office of the Secretary, where it originally existed, to ensure that it can effectively coordinate a whole-of-government commercial space policy. This move would allow OSC to advocate for U.S. leadership in the commercial space sector, which is crucial for future economic competitiveness.

Developing a Unified U.S. Space Policy:

- **Presidential Directive:** The document recommends that the President issue an executive order directing OSC, in collaboration with the National Space Council, to establish a comprehensive government policy for licensing and overseeing commercial space operations. This policy would ensure that the U.S. remains the global leader in commercial space activities, countering the influence of other countries.

BUREAU OF ECONOMIC ANALYSIS (BEA) AND THE OFFICE OF THE UNDER SECRETARY FOR ECONOMIC AFFAIRS

The Office of the Under Secretary for Economic Affairs plays a central role within the Department of Commerce. It is tasked with conducting economic analysis, promoting business and commerce, guiding data-driven decision-making, and increasing access to government data while ensuring privacy and confidentiality. This office oversees two key bureaus: the Bureau of Economic Analysis (BEA) and the Census Bureau.

BEA's Mission and Functions:

- **Economic Indicators:** BEA is responsible for producing critical economic data, including the U.S. gross domestic product (GDP), state and local GDP estimates, foreign trade and investment statistics, industry data, and consumer spending numbers. This data is essential for government and business decision-makers to understand the state of the nation's economy.

Proposed Reforms:

- **Focus on Growth:** A new Administration should ensure that BEA's statistical analysis is conducted consistently and objectively, with a strong emphasis on supporting economic growth and opportunity. The Under Secretary for Economic Affairs should take an active role in guiding BEA's operations to align with Administration priorities.
- **Merging Statistical Agencies:** Gilman suggests studying the feasibility of merging all federal statistical agencies, including the Census Bureau, BEA, and the Department of Labor's Bureau of Labor Statistics (BLS). Such a merger could increase efficiency and improve coordination across departments.

CENSUS BUREAU

The Census Bureau's primary mission is to conduct the decennial census as mandated by the Constitution. However, its activities have expanded significantly to include the economic census, the American Community Survey (ACS), and other functions that extend beyond its core mission.

FOCUS AREAS FOR REFORM:

1. **Day-to-Day Management:**
   - **Leadership and Control:** Strong political leadership is necessary to align the Census Bureau's mission with conservative principles. Gilman stresses the importance of placing appointed staff in key positions early in the Administration to drive priorities, especially in preparation for the 2030 census.
   - **Financial and IT Management:** Gilman calls for a review to control costs and reverse recent failures in upgrading financial management, IT, and human resources systems at the Census Bureau.
   - **Leveraging Technology:** Continuing to integrate technology into the Census Bureau's operations is crucial to reducing costs and delivering accurate and timely data.
   - **Cybersecurity and Confidentiality:** Given the sensitive nature of data collected by the Census Bureau, protecting this information is paramount. Gilman emphasizes the need for robust cybersecurity measures and proper data protocols to ensure compliance with legal requirements under Title 13.

2. **Decennial Census:**
   - **Review and Vetting:** Gilman suggests an immediate audit of the planning and budgeting for the 2030 census, including a new lifecycle cost estimate (LCCE) if necessary, to ensure accuracy and control over the process.
   - **Elimination of Duplicative Functions:** The decennial census operations should be streamlined to eliminate overlaps with ongoing census functions, potentially saving billions of dollars.
   - **Partnership Program Scrutiny:** Gilman advises careful scrutiny of the partnership program, which employs trusted voices in communities to promote census participation. A new Administration should engage with conservative groups to ensure a more accurate count, as underrepresentation in conservative areas affected the 2020 census.
   - **Citizenship Question:** The document advocates for the inclusion of a citizenship question in the 2030 census, arguing that it is a standard practice even endorsed by the United Nations. The Supreme Court's ruling indicates that the Secretary of Commerce has the authority to add this question, making it a priority for the next Administration.
   - **Race and Ethnicity Questions:** Gilman expresses concern over proposed changes to how race and ethnicity data is collected, particularly by combining these questions and expanding available options. A conservative Administration should thoroughly review these changes to prevent potential skewing of data for political purposes.

3. **Other Census Programs:**
   - **American Community Survey (ACS):** Similar to the decennial census, the ACS should be carefully reviewed to ensure that the questions are necessary and not overly intrusive. Collaboration with other departments that use this data is recommended to optimize the survey's utility.
   - **Economic Census:** The economic census, conducted every five years, is a key measure of U.S. business and economic activity. Gilman suggests scrutinizing this survey to ensure it is not intrusive and works effectively with other federal data collection efforts.
   - **Pulse Surveys:** The Census Bureau began experimental pulse surveys during the COVID-19 pandemic to obtain near real-time data. These could be a useful model for improving data collection methods or reducing the Bureau's overall footprint.
   - **Supplemental Poverty Measure (SPM):** The SPM should be reviewed to assess its accuracy and utility in policy-making, particularly in combating issues like homelessness. This measure should be refined to better track poverty trends over time.
   - **Abolition of the National Advisory Committee (NAC):** The NAC, established during the Obama Administration and seen as a platform for left-wing activism, should be abolished. Gilman recommends that the Secretary of Commerce use their authority to terminate this committee, and all other non-

147

statutory standing committees should be reevaluated for potential elimination.

ECONOMIC DEVELOPMENT ADMINISTRATION (EDA)

The Economic Development Administration (EDA) is tasked with investing in local communities to spur private sector growth, especially in distressed or underserved areas. It also serves as a distribution mechanism for emergency relief funds, such as those provided during Hurricane Maria and the COVID-19 pandemic.

Challenges and Criticisms:

- **Technical and Financial Limitations:** Gilman points out that during the COVID-19 pandemic, the EDA struggled to disburse funds efficiently due to a lack of technical and financial capabilities, requiring external contracts to hire the necessary personnel.

Proposed Reforms:

- **Abolition of EDA:** Gilman argues that EDA's functions overlap with other federal grant programs and that it is an impediment to coordinated campaigns advancing Administration priorities. As such, it recommends abolishing the EDA and reallocating its funding to other programs.

- **Consolidation if Abolition Is Not Possible:** If political considerations prevent the EDA's abolition, Gilman suggests consolidating decision-making to the Assistant Secretary's office to better align funding with conservative political purposes. This could involve directing funds to communities affected by policies such as the Biden Administration's energy restrictions.

- **Direct Hiring Authority:** The EDA should continue to leverage the direct hiring authorities established during the Trump Administration to rapidly staff special initiatives or disaster recovery efforts, avoiding the inefficiencies of relying solely on entrenched career employees.

- **Continuation of Disaster Funding:** The EDA should maintain its role in disbursing disaster relief funds but with improved coordination and decision-making to better meet the Administration's goals.

- **Building on Opportunity Zones:** The success of Opportunity Zones, which incentivized over $75 billion in private sector investment in distressed communities by 2020, should be expanded upon. This approach could be a model for further EDA initiatives aimed at promoting private investment in underserved areas.

MINORITY BUSINESS DEVELOPMENT AGENCY (MBDA)

The Minority Business Development Agency (MBDA) is the only federal agency dedicated exclusively to the growth and competitiveness of minority-owned businesses. The Minority Business Development Act of 2021, part of the Bipartisan Infrastructure Investment and Jobs Act, made the MBDA a permanent federal agency, expanding its programs and outreach.

Structure and Mandates:

- **Expansion:** The Act authorized the creation of regional offices and rural business centers, increased the scope of existing grant programs, and mandated grants to minority-serving institutions to cultivate future generations of minority entrepreneurs. It also established a Minority Business Advisory Council to advise the Under Secretary on supporting minority-owned businesses.

Challenges and Criticisms:

- **Philosophical Concerns:** Gilman notes that some conservatives view the MBDA as perpetuating racial bias by focusing on minority advancement rather than economic need. This led the Trump Administration to initially propose eliminating its funding. However, the Administration later shifted its stance, suggesting that the MBDA should focus more on policy rather than offering direct services.

Proposed Reforms:

- **Leveraging MBDA:** Recognizing Congress's recent actions and the agency's role in the economy, Gilman suggests that a conservative Administration should approach MBDA as a tool to promote equal economic opportunity. It should be used to drive a free-market, pro-growth agenda.

- **Focus Areas for MBDA:**
    - **Policy Analysis:** MBDA should focus on analyzing the benefits of free markets, the dangers of socialism and communism, and the negative impacts of taxes and regulations on minority businesses.
    - **Efficiency and Oversight:** MBDA business centers should operate efficiently with strict oversight, clear success metrics, and consequences for poor performance.
    - **Public-Private Partnerships:** The MBDA should prioritize private sector actions over government intervention, using public-private partnerships where necessary.

- **Data and Research:** The MBDA should serve as a clearinghouse for data and research on minority businesses, providing valuable insights for policymakers.
- **Coordination:** The agency should coordinate with other federal agencies, state and local governments, and trade associations to leverage resources and encourage growth and innovation.
- **Trade Practices:** The MBDA should evaluate the impact of unfair trade practices on minority-owned businesses and their employees, advocating for policies that protect these enterprises.

U.S. PATENT AND TRADEMARK OFFICE (USPTO)

The U.S. Patent and Trademark Office (USPTO) is responsible for executing a core constitutional mandate: to "promote the Progress of Science and useful Arts" by securing exclusive rights for authors and inventors. Gilman emphasizes that strong intellectual property (IP) protections are vital for American innovation and economic leadership.

Proposed Reforms:

- **International Leadership:** The document advocates for supporting like-minded countries in leadership roles within the World Intellectual Property Organization (WIPO) and building strong international partnerships to reinforce IP rights globally.

- **Patent Eligibility Reforms:** Gilman suggests re-examining patent eligibility requirements under Section 101 of the Patent Act to better support U.S. leadership in critical and emerging technologies like quantum computing, 5G, and artificial intelligence.

- **Balanced Approach to PTAB:** The Patent Trial and Appeal Board (PTAB) should prioritize rapid and transparent processing of patent applications and appeals, ensuring a balanced approach that protects innovators' rights while preventing abuse of the system.

- **Combatting Trademark Infringement:** The USPTO should work closely with Administration partners and Congress to identify and punish trademark infringers and counterfeiters, protecting American businesses and consumers.

- **Opposition to IP Waivers:** Gilman strongly opposes efforts to provide intellectual property waivers for advanced technologies, including COVID-19 vaccines, through mechanisms like the World Trade Organization's Trade-Related Aspects of Intellectual Property Rights (TRIPS) agreement. Such waivers are seen as detrimental to U.S. innovation and economic interests.

NATIONAL INSTITUTE OF STANDARDS AND TECHNOLOGY (NIST)

The National Institute of Standards and Technology (NIST) is charged with promoting U.S. innovation and competitiveness by advancing measurement science, standards, and technology. NIST is a key player in establishing standards that are essential for industry and commerce, ensuring that U.S. businesses can compete effectively both domestically and globally.

Core Functions and Responsibilities:

- **Measurement and Standards:** NIST is the nation's foremost authority on measurements, including the operation of the atomic clock, which maintains the official time of the United States. It also helps establish standards and best practices across a wide range of industries, which are crucial for maintaining consistency, safety, and quality in manufacturing and other sectors.

Proposed Reforms:

- **Privatizing the Hollings Manufacturing Extension Partnership (MEP):** The Hollings MEP program operates a network of centers that provide advisory services to small and medium-sized manufacturers to improve their processes and strengthen the U.S. industrial base. Originally, MEP centers were intended to transition to self-sustaining private institutions after initial government funding. However, this prohibition on long-term government funding was abolished in 1998. Gilman argues that the business advisory services provided by MEP are more appropriately delivered by the private sector. As such, it proposes legislation to fully privatize existing MEP centers and eliminate this $150 million program.

- **Transfer the Baldrige Performance Excellence Program:** This program helps organizations improve their management and operations, charging fees for its services. Gilman suggests that this function should be fully transferred to the Baldrige Award Foundation, which could operate it as a private entity without government involvement.

- **Increasing Value to Taxpayers:** NIST should reinvigorate the Technology Transfer and Return on Investment (ROI) initiatives started under the Trump Administration. These initiatives aim to speed up the commercialization of science funded by the federal government, ensuring that taxpayer-funded research contributes to economic growth and innovation.
- **Reestablish U.S. Dominance in International Standards:** NIST should find ways to incentivize broader U.S. participation in international standards-setting bodies, while also working to exclude participants from adversarial nations like China. Gilman highlights the importance of standards in facilitating global trade and argues that countries that do not allow open access to their markets should not be setting the standards for those that do. The incoming Administration should consider increased government-sponsored participation in these bodies by private companies and government employees with relevant expertise.

NATIONAL TELECOMMUNICATIONS AND INFORMATION SERVICE (NTIS)

The National Telecommunications and Information Service (NTIS) is an independent agency that ensures federally funded research and data are accessible to the public. However, Gilman argues that NTIS has largely become obsolete due to the widespread availability of the internet and modern digital tools that make federal data and research more easily accessible.

Proposed Reforms:

- **Consolidation with NIST:** The document recommends that the functions of NTIS be moved to NIST and consolidated with its Technology Transfer and ROI initiatives. This consolidation would streamline operations and eliminate redundancy, ensuring that NTIS's mission is carried out more efficiently under NIST's broader mandate.

NATIONAL TELECOMMUNICATIONS AND INFORMATION ADMINISTRATION (NTIA)

The National Telecommunications and Information Administration (NTIA) serves as the executive branch's lead on telecommunications and information policy. The NTIA focuses on issues such as broadband access, spectrum utilization, and other critical aspects of the high-tech economy. Gilman notes that NTIA has suffered from organizational malaise and requires strong, energetic political leadership to implement conservative policies effectively.

Key Challenges:

- **5G Deployment:** One of the primary challenges the next Administration will face is the rapid deployment of 5G technology without compromising other critical priorities. This will require careful management of spectrum allocation, infrastructure development, and international competitiveness.

Proposed Reforms:

- **Support Free Speech and Hold Big Tech Accountable:** Gilman calls for an immediate and thorough review of federal policy regarding free speech online, with the aim of developing policy solutions to address censorship by big tech companies. This includes ensuring that conservative voices are not unfairly silenced on digital platforms.
- **Utilize New Tools to Address National Security Threats:** The NTIA should fully implement the Information and Communications Technology and Services (ICTS) Executive Order authorities established by the Trump Administration. This order is designed to protect U.S. national security by regulating foreign involvement in the U.S. technology sector. Gilman emphasizes the importance of ensuring the long-term success and legal viability of these new tools.
- **Expand Federal Spectrum Utilization:** The NTIA should begin short-term, temporary leasing of government-allocated spectrum to ensure optimal utilization while preserving federal agency use rights. This would allow for more efficient use of valuable spectrum resources, particularly in the context of the growing demand for wireless communications infrastructure.
- **Support the Commercial Space Industry:** The NTIA should advocate for licensing decisions at the Federal Communications Commission (FCC) that enable U.S. dominance in the commercial space industry. This is critical for maintaining U.S. leadership in space-related technologies and industries.
- **Defend U.S. Interests in International Bodies:** Strong U.S. representation at the International Telecommunication Union (ITU) is necessary to protect the interests of both private and government users of the spectrum. Gilman highlights the differing needs of the U.S. compared to other countries, particularly due to the U.S. government's significant investments in satellites and the commercial space industry. NTIA should work closely with the U.S. delegation to ensure maximum adoption of U.S. positions in international telecommunications policy.
- **Set Priorities in Broadband Grant Programs:** The NTIA should reevaluate existing broadband grant programs and establish Administration priorities for future grants. Gilman emphasizes the importance of widespread infrastructure deployment to support 5G adoption in rural and underserved areas, which will be crucial for future economic competitiveness.
- **Review FirstNet:** FirstNet, the national public safety broadband network, should be evaluated for its long-term value in light of modern technologies that may render it obsolete. Gilman suggests that the NTIA conduct this review to determine whether FirstNet remains a viable and necessary investment.

CHAPTER 22: DEPARTMENT OF THE TREASURY

The next conservative Administration should take affirmative steps to expose and eradicate the practice of critical race theory and diversity, equity, and inclusion (DEI) throughout the Treasury Department. – Page 708

Key Policy Proposals

The proposed policies outlined in the chapter reveal a fundamentally flawed approach to governance and economic management. These policies, if implemented, would not only exacerbate existing inequalities but also threaten the stability and sustainability of the U.S. economy. Below is an analysis of the key points and proposed policy changes, dissecting their likely consequences.

FISCAL RESPONSIBILITY AND DEBT MANAGEMENT

The chapter advocates for a reduction in federal spending and the issuance of long-term bonds to manage the national debt. However, this approach is both myopic and dangerous. The insistence on balancing the budget through spending cuts, without considering the need for revenue increases, ignores the reality that many federal programs are crucial to maintaining economic stability and social well-being.

Data shows that deep spending cuts during times of economic recovery can have severe consequences. The austerity measures in Europe during the early 2010s, particularly in Greece and Spain, led to prolonged economic downturns, increased unemployment, and widespread social unrest. In contrast, the American Recovery and Reinvestment Act of 2009, which involved significant government spending, helped the U.S. economy recover more quickly from the Great Recession. Cutting federal spending now, particularly in areas like social safety nets and public investments, would likely slow economic growth and disproportionately harm low-income Americans.

The proposal to issue 50-year bonds to lock in low-interest rates is also fraught with risk. While interest rates are currently low, there is no guarantee they will remain so over the long term. Locking in debt at current rates for such a long duration could leave the U.S. exposed to future financial instability, particularly if inflation or other economic pressures drive interest rates higher. This approach fails to consider the flexibility needed in managing national debt in a dynamic global economy.

TAX POLICY

The proposed tax reforms suggest a dramatic reduction in marginal tax rates, a reduction in corporate tax rates, and the elimination of most deductions and credits. These proposals are fundamentally regressive and would exacerbate economic inequality.

Lowering corporate tax rates, as advocated in the chapter, would primarily benefit the wealthiest individuals and corporations. The 2017 Tax Cuts and Jobs Act, which implemented similar tax cuts, resulted in a massive windfall for corporations, with much of the savings going to stock buybacks rather than job creation or wage increases. According to the Congressional Budget Office, these tax cuts are projected to increase the federal deficit by $1.9 trillion over ten years without delivering the promised economic growth.

Moreover, the elimination of deductions and credits would disproportionately impact middle- and lower-income families. Deductions for mortgage interest, education expenses, and charitable contributions are critical for many families, allowing them to manage the costs of homeownership, education, and community support. Removing these deductions would increase the tax burden on those who can least afford it, while providing further tax relief to the wealthiest Americans.

CLIMATE CHANGE AND ENERGY POLICY

The chapter's rejection of climate change initiatives is not just misguided; it is reckless. The climate crisis is one of the most significant challenges facing the world today, with dire economic, environmental, and social consequences if not addressed. The proposal to withdraw from international climate agreements and to promote fossil fuel investments represents a backward-looking approach that ignores the reality of the global transition towards clean energy.

Investing in renewable energy is not just good for the environment; it's also good for the economy. The renewable energy sector is one of the fastest-growing in the U.S., with the potential to create millions of jobs and drive innovation. A study by the International Renewable Energy Agency (IRENA) found that transitioning to renewable energy could increase global GDP by up to $98 trillion by 2050. By clinging to outdated fossil fuel industries, the U.S. risks falling behind in the global economy, ceding leadership in one of the most critical sectors of the future.

Furthermore, the effects of climate change, including more frequent and severe natural disasters, are already costing the U.S. billions of dollars annually. The National Oceanic and Atmospheric Administration (NOAA) reported that the U.S. experienced 22 separate billion-dollar weather and climate disasters in 2020 alone. Ignoring these realities in favor of short-term economic gains is both irresponsible and dangerous.

DIVERSITY, EQUITY, AND INCLUSION (DEI) INITIATIVES

The chapter's attack on diversity, equity, and inclusion initiatives is not just ideologically driven; it is fundamentally wrong. DEI initiatives are essential for addressing systemic inequalities that have long plagued American society. These programs are not about giving unfair advantages to certain groups; they are about leveling the playing field and ensuring that everyone, regardless of race, gender, or background, has an equal opportunity to succeed.

The argument that DEI initiatives promote "racist policymaking" is a gross mischaracterization. Systemic racism and inequality are deeply embedded in American society, as evidenced by disparities in income, education, and healthcare outcomes across racial and ethnic lines. For example, the median wealth of white households is nearly ten times that of Black households, according to the Federal Reserve's Survey of Consumer Finances. DEI initiatives are a necessary step towards addressing these disparities and building a more just and equitable society.

Moreover, research consistently shows that diverse organizations perform better. A study by McKinsey & Company found that companies in the top quartile for racial and ethnic diversity are 35% more likely to have financial returns above their respective national industry medians. By promoting diversity and inclusion, the Treasury Department can help foster a more innovative and competitive economy.

FINANCIAL REGULATION

The chapter's proposals to weaken financial regulations, including repealing key provisions of the Dodd-Frank Act, are a recipe for disaster. The Dodd-Frank Act was implemented in response to the 2008 financial crisis, which was precipitated by insufficient regulation and excessive risk-taking by financial institutions. The Act's provisions, including the creation of the Consumer Financial Protection Bureau (CFPB) and the Financial Stability Oversight Council (FSOC), are essential for protecting consumers and ensuring the stability of the financial system.

Repealing these protections would pave the way for a return to the conditions that led to the financial crisis. The unchecked power of large financial institutions would increase the risk of another crisis, with potentially devastating consequences for the global economy. Furthermore, the chapter's call for consolidating regulatory agencies could reduce oversight and accountability, making it easier for systemic risks to go undetected.

The policies proposed in the chapter are deeply flawed and represent a dangerous departure from sound governance. They prioritize short-term gains and ideological purity over the long-term health and stability of the economy and society. By cutting taxes for the wealthy, ignoring the realities of climate change, dismantling DEI initiatives, and weakening financial regulations, these policies would exacerbate inequality, undermine economic stability, and leave the U.S. ill-prepared to face the challenges of the 21st century. It is imperative that policymakers reject these proposals and pursue more balanced, evidence-based approaches that promote inclusive growth, sustainability, and resilience.

Summary

This chapter of Mandate for Leadership was written by William L. Walton, Stephen Moore, and David R. Burton. The following summary conveys the content of the document accurately and objectively, without endorsing or critiquing the perspectives of the original authors.

The chapter begins by outlining the broad scope of the U.S. Treasury Department's regulatory and policy influence, emphasizing the need for significant policy changes in the upcoming administration. The primary goals include reducing regulatory barriers to economic growth, cutting compliance costs, promoting fiscal responsibility, enhancing the international competitiveness of U.S. businesses, and safeguarding due process and privacy rights.

The strategies for achieving these objectives involve a combination of executive actions, departmental reorganization, rulemaking, promoting policies in Congress, international actions, and treaties. The key focus areas for the Treasury Department include tax policy and administration, fiscal responsibility, financial regulation, addressing geopolitical threats like China, reforming anti-money laundering systems, and reversing the "equity" and climate agendas of the Biden Administration.

Biden Administration Treasury Department

The chapter criticizes the Biden Administration's Treasury Department for failing to meet its core objectives, citing the significant expansion of the national debt and the undermining of the U.S. dollar's stability due to high inflation. It argues that under Treasury Secretary Janet Yellen, the department has drifted from its core mission, prioritizing issues like equity and climate change, which the authors describe as outside the Treasury's proper mandate.

A notable quote from the chapter captures this sentiment: "No President in modern times—perhaps ever—has been more fiscally reckless than has the Biden Administration." The chapter also highlights the economic impact of these policies on American families, pointing out a decrease in average real annual earnings and a significant drop in the value of 401(k) retirement plans.

Treasury Department Organization

The chapter describes the organizational structure of the Treasury Department, noting its constitutional recognition and its responsibilities in financing the federal government, promoting economic prosperity, and ensuring financial security. It outlines the departmental offices and bureaus within the Treasury, including Domestic Finance, Terrorism and Financial Intelligence, International Affairs, and Tax Policy, among others.

Particular attention is given to the Treasury's role in managing U.S. fiscal operations and overseeing financial institutions, markets, and national security concerns related to financial crimes. The chapter also discusses the extensive reach of the Internal Revenue Service (IRS), which constitutes the majority of Treasury's personnel and budget.

Tax Policy

The chapter emphasizes the critical role of tax policy in influencing the economy and advocates for tax reforms aimed at promoting prosperity. The principles of good tax policy, according to the authors, include raising necessary revenue with minimal economic disruption, protecting families and civil society, and applying taxes consistently without special privileges.

The chapter proposes intermediate tax reforms, such as simplifying the tax code to a two-rate individual tax system and reducing the corporate income tax rate. It also suggests the creation of Universal Savings Accounts to allow for more flexible saving and investing options for Americans, alongside promoting entrepreneurship by reducing taxes on investments and capital.

The authors argue for the repeal of tax increases from the Inflation Reduction Act and push for fundamental tax reform to achieve a consumption tax model, which they believe would minimize government distortion of economic decisions.

Tax Administration

The chapter is highly critical of the IRS, describing it as poorly managed, unresponsive, and increasingly politicized. The authors call for meaningful reforms to improve the efficiency and fairness of tax administration, better protect taxpayer rights, and increase transparency. They argue against the expansion of the IRS workforce, as proposed in the Inflation Reduction Act, and oppose broader information reporting requirements that would increase the administrative burden on taxpayers.

The chapter also proposes increasing the number of presidential appointments within the IRS to improve accountability and management. It highlights the need for better IT systems within the IRS, suggesting that the current deficiencies are more about poor management than a lack of resources.

Taxpayer Rights and Privacy

The authors discuss the importance of protecting taxpayer rights and privacy, noting that while legal protections have improved over the years, they remain inadequate. They propose several reforms, including equalizing the interest rates for overpayments and underpayments, extending the time limit for suing for damages due to improper collection actions, and reforming the tax penalty system.

The chapter also suggests increasing resources for the Office of the Taxpayer Advocate to better assist taxpayers facing wrongful IRS actions and calls for greater transparency and independence for this office.

Fiscal Responsibility

The chapter underscores the importance of making fiscal responsibility a central mission of the Treasury Department. It advocates for balancing the federal budget through reduced federal spending, while maintaining a strong national defense and avoiding tax increases.

- **Debt Management**: The authors suggest that Treasury should take advantage of relatively low interest rates by issuing longer-duration bonds, such as 50-year treasury bills, to reduce interest payments on the debt over time.
- **Transparency**: To promote financial transparency, the chapter recommends that the Treasury should provide Americans with an annual financial statement of the U.S. government, including details on revenues, expenditures, deficits, and debt, as well as each family's pro-rata share of the national debt.

International Competitiveness

The Treasury Department is urged to take a more assertive role in international financial institutions to protect and advance U.S. national interests. The chapter suggests a "carrot-and-stick" approach, where the U.S. increases its involvement in institutions that align with its interests while reducing or eliminating its role in those that do not.

- **Human Capital**: A significant recommendation is to expand the number of U.S. professionals and contractors within these institutions, using this as leverage for future funding and influence.
- **Ownership Levels**: The authors propose adjusting U.S. ownership levels in international financial institutions to maximize leverage and influence.

China and Other Geopolitical Threats

The chapter delves deeper into the geopolitical threats posed by China, particularly in the context of foreign investments and economic strategies. It emphasizes the need for the Committee on Foreign Investment in the United States (CFIUS) to realign its focus to better address these threats, specifically those from China. The Treasury Department, as the chair of CFIUS, is criticized for running an opaque process that tends to prioritize corporate interests over national security.

- **CFIUS Enforcement and Penalty Guidelines**: In October 2022, the Treasury adopted the first-ever CFIUS Enforcement and Penalty Guidelines, which detail the committee's national security risk mitigation requirements. However, the authors argue that there are no clear rules guiding CFIUS on monitoring compliance with these requirements, nor is there a standardized penalty schedule to ensure accountability. This lack of transparency and consistency in enforcement is seen as a significant weakness.
- **Mitigation Monitoring**: The chapter calls for the development of a coherent and transparent mitigation monitoring program to complement the enforcement guidelines. It suggests that CFIUS agencies responsible for national security should have an equal voice in the committee's decision-making process. Moreover, Congress should amend the law to include Chinese greenfield investments, which currently fall outside of CFIUS jurisdiction, as they pose a potential threat to U.S. national and economic security.
- **Department of Defense (DOD) as Co-Chair of CFIUS**: The authors propose making the DOD a co-chair of CFIUS alongside the Treasury Department. This change is intended to balance the committee's process, ensuring that national security concerns are given equal consideration alongside economic and corporate interests. The current imbalance, with the Treasury as the sole chair, is seen as leading to a bias towards permitting transactions that may not align with national security priorities.
- **Greenfield Investments**: The chapter highlights the risk posed by Chinese state-owned enterprises (SOEs) engaging in greenfield investments—where they build new facilities from scratch in the U.S. These investments are often welcomed by state and local governments due to the jobs they create, but they are seen as tools for the Chinese Communist Party to siphon off U.S. assets, technological innovations, and influence. The authors argue for closing the loophole that allows these investments to go unregulated.
- **School of Financial Warfare**: The chapter suggests that the U.S. should develop a specialized school of financial warfare in collaboration with the DOD. This institution would train experts in financial strategies and tools that can be used to defend against and respond to international economic threats, particularly those posed by China. The need for a dedicated group of specialists in this area is highlighted by recent experiences that showed the inadequacy of ad hoc financial actions in dealing with such threats.
- **U.S. Foreign Direct Investment in China**: The authors call for a serious evaluation of U.S. investments in China, particularly those that involve Chinese Communist Party-controlled enterprises, technology transfers, or that enhance China's military capabilities. They recommend the creation of an enhanced reporting system and stronger legal restrictions to safeguard U.S. national security and critical supply chains.

Improved Financial Regulation

The chapter advocates for significant reforms to the U.S. financial regulatory system to promote innovation, efficiency, and reduce the size of government. The current system is described as outdated and cumbersome, with a need for consolidation and clearer statutory authority.

- **Merging Financial Regulatory Functions**: The authors propose legislation to merge several key financial regulatory agencies, including the Office of the Comptroller of the Currency (OCC), the Federal Deposit Insurance Corporation (FDIC), the National Credit Union Administration (NCUA), and the Federal Reserve's non-monetary supervisory and regulatory functions. This consolidation is aimed at streamlining oversight, reducing regulatory costs, and eliminating gaps in regulation.

- **Elimination of Activity Restrictions**: The chapter criticizes the existing restrictions that limit the functions of financial institutions, such as preventing banks from engaging in investment activities. The authors argue that these restrictions make markets less stable and that a more flexible approach should be adopted, allowing financial firms to engage in a broader range of activities while maintaining higher equity or risk-retention standards.

- **Dodd–Frank Act Revisions**: The chapter calls for the repeal of key provisions of the Dodd–Frank Act, specifically Titles I, II, and VIII. Title I established the Financial Stability Oversight Council (FSOC), which the authors argue has effectively created a "too big to fail" problem by singling out certain institutions for stricter regulation. Title VIII similarly gives FSOC broad authority over financial market utilities, while Title II created the Orderly Liquidation Authority (OLA), which provides an alternative to bankruptcy for large financial firms. The authors believe these provisions create moral hazard and should be repealed to prevent future bailouts.

- **Fannie Mae and Freddie Mac**: The chapter discusses the need to end the conservatorships of Fannie Mae and Freddie Mac and to move towards their privatization. The authors argue that these government-sponsored enterprises (GSEs) pose significant risks to the mortgage market and that privatization would lead to a more sustainable housing finance system. They suggest that the Common Securitization Platform should be privatized and made broadly available, and that barriers to private investment should be removed to foster a robust private mortgage market.

Anti-Money Laundering and Beneficial Ownership Reporting Reform

The chapter critiques the current anti-money laundering (AML) and beneficial ownership reporting systems, particularly the role of the Financial Crimes Enforcement Network (FinCEN). The authors argue that FinCEN's regulations impose significant economic costs with little evidence of effectiveness.

- **Cost-Benefit Analysis**: The authors note that FinCEN conducts almost no meaningful cost-benefit analysis or retrospective review of its regulations, which leads to substantial economic harm without clear benefits. They argue that FinCEN's operations are opaque, with insufficient oversight from Congress and the Treasury Department.

- **Transparency and Reporting Requirements**: The chapter calls for increased transparency from FinCEN, including the publication of detailed data on suspicious activity reports (SARs), currency transaction reports (CTRs), AML-CFT prosecutions, convictions, and fines. The authors believe that this data is essential for policymakers to make informed decisions about the effectiveness of the AML-CFT regime.

- **Repeal of the Corporate Transparency Act**: The chapter argues for the repeal of the Corporate Transparency Act, which mandates the reporting of beneficial ownership information. The authors claim that this law targets small businesses disproportionately and imposes excessive costs. They criticize the FinCEN beneficial ownership reporting rule as poorly drafted and overly broad, with cost estimates ranging from $547 million to $8.1 billion annually.

The Equity Agenda

The authors continue their critique of the Biden Administration's focus on "equity" within the Treasury Department. They argue that the promotion of equity initiatives, such as the establishment of the Office for Diversity, Equity, Inclusion, and Accessibility, represents a significant departure from the department's core mission.

- **Reversing Equity Initiatives**: The authors recommend that the next administration should take decisive action to eliminate these initiatives, including disbanding the 25-member Treasury Advisory Committee on Racial Equity. They propose conducting interviews with all officials involved in DEI initiatives to ensure that such activities are completely ended and that any remaining DEI-related operations within the Treasury are exposed and terminated.

Climate-Related Financial Risk

The chapter addresses the Biden Administration's prioritization of climate change within the Treasury Department, specifically through the creation of the "Climate Hub." This office is tasked with coordinating Treasury's efforts to align financial systems with climate mitigation and adaptation goals, including the broader objective of achieving net-zero emissions by mid-century.

- **Criticism of Climate Policies**: The authors argue that this focus on climate change represents a fundamental misalignment of the Treasury Department's core mission. They assert that the historical evidence shows economic growth and technological advancement, driven by human ingenuity, as the best methods to prevent and mitigate the impacts of extreme weather events. The chapter criticizes the Treasury's climate initiatives as having a negligible impact on global weather patterns, particularly given the lack of cooperation from major polluters like China.

- **Withdrawal from International Climate Agreements**: The chapter calls for the next administration to withdraw the United States from international climate agreements, such as the U.N. Framework Convention on Climate Change and the Paris Agreement. The authors view these agreements as detrimental to U.S. economic interests and ineffective in achieving meaningful environmental improvements.

- **Promotion of Domestic Energy Investments**: The authors advocate for using Treasury's tools and authority to promote investment in domestic energy resources, including oil and gas, reversing support for global ESG initiatives and the Principles for Responsible Investment (PRI). They argue that these global initiatives have undermined U.S. energy security and contributed to economic harm.

Other Reforms

The chapter discusses several additional reforms and changes that should be considered by the next administration to streamline the Treasury Department's operations and improve its focus on core responsibilities:

1. **U.S. Coast Guard and Bureau of Alcohol, Tobacco, Firearms, and Explosives (ATF)**: The authors propose that Congress should examine the possibility of returning the U.S. Coast Guard and the ATF to the Treasury Department from their current placements in the Department of Homeland Security and the Department of Justice, respectively. The rationale is that these agencies' original missions align more closely with the Treasury's economic and law enforcement objectives, such as enhancing border security and combating economic crimes.

2. **U.S. Trade and Development Agency (USTDA)**: The chapter recommends eliminating the USTDA, which is responsible for linking U.S. businesses with export opportunities in emerging markets through project planning and reverse-trade missions. The authors argue that these activities are better suited for the private sector and that promoting trade and development would be more effectively achieved through reducing trade barriers and the federal deficit.

CHAPTER 23: EXPORT-IMPORT BANK

Economic fights and national security fights are not won with subsidies. - Page 724

Key Policy Proposals

The Export-Import Bank of the United States (EXIM) is a critical component of American economic strategy. The idea of abolishing EXIM is misguided and overlooks its essential role in leveling the playing field for American businesses, especially in the face of aggressive global competitors like China. The arguments against EXIM, claiming it fosters crony capitalism or disproportionately benefits large corporations, fail to understand the nuanced role it plays in sustaining the U.S. economy, creating jobs, and securing national interests.

ECONOMIC COMPETITIVENESS IN A GLOBAL MARKET

EXIM is crucial for ensuring that American companies can compete internationally. Critics argue that the bank only serves large corporations like Boeing, but this view is short-sighted. EXIM provides financing where private sector banks cannot or will not, particularly in high-risk regions or volatile markets. In 2018, China alone provided over $500 billion in export credits, nearly matching EXIM's entire 90-year history. Without EXIM, American firms would be left at a significant disadvantage, unable to compete with foreign companies backed by their governments. This would result in a direct loss of jobs and economic opportunities in the U.S.

JOB CREATION AND ECONOMIC GROWTH

The assertion that EXIM fails to create jobs is misleading. While it is true that large corporations are primary beneficiaries, these companies are also the largest job creators in the manufacturing sector. EXIM's financing supports these firms in securing international contracts, which in turn sustains and creates high-paying American jobs. The decline in EXIM's financing—from $35.7 billion in 2012 to $5.2 billion in 2022—coincides with increasing competition from foreign ECAs, and any further reduction in EXIM's capacity would likely exacerbate job losses and economic stagnation in sectors crucial to the U.S. economy.

STRATEGIC NATIONAL SECURITY CONCERNS

The suggestion that EXIM should be abolished ignores its vital role in national security. China's Belt and Road Initiative is not just about economic expansion but also about extending its geopolitical influence. EXIM is one of the few tools available to the U.S. to counter this. By providing export credits, the U.S. can ensure that American companies are not edged out of strategically important regions, thereby maintaining U.S. influence and preventing the expansion of Chinese power. The failure to bolster EXIM's capacity could lead to significant geopolitical shifts, with the U.S. ceding ground to China in critical markets.

SUPPORT FOR SMALL BUSINESSES

It is true that small businesses receive a smaller share of EXIM's financing compared to large corporations, but eliminating the bank would not solve this issue. Instead, EXIM's mandate should be expanded to include more targeted support for small and medium-sized enterprises (SMEs). The reduction in support for small businesses—from $2.3 billion in 2019 to $1.6 billion in 2021—is concerning and should be addressed by increasing EXIM's capacity to assist SMEs, thereby fostering innovation and job creation across the broader economy.

WHAT WOULD THIS MEAN?

1. **Expand EXIM's Financing Capabilities**

EXIM's current limitations restrict its ability to fully support American businesses in the global market. By expanding its financing capabilities, the U.S. would enhance its economic competitiveness. This would involve increasing the bank's budget and reducing bureaucratic hurdles, enabling it to respond more effectively to international opportunities. The consequences of this expansion would be a stronger U.S. presence in global markets, more jobs at home, and a robust defense against the economic aggression of rival nations.

2. **Implement Targeted Support for Small Businesses**

To address criticisms of EXIM's focus on large corporations, specific initiatives should be introduced to support small businesses. This could include a dedicated fund within EXIM for SMEs, offering lower interest rates and more accessible financing terms. The result would be a more inclusive approach to export financing, ensuring that smaller firms also have the opportunity to grow internationally, which would contribute to a more diversified and resilient U.S. economy.

3. **Strengthen Oversight and Accountability**

While EXIM's role is indispensable, it is essential to ensure that taxpayer money is used responsibly. Strengthening oversight mechanisms would address concerns about crony capitalism and ensure that EXIM's financing is allocated based on merit and strategic importance rather than political connections. This would enhance public trust in the institution and ensure that its operations align with the broader national interest.

4. **Utilize EXIM as a Strategic Tool Against Chinese Influence**

Rather than abandoning EXIM, the U.S. should use it as a key component of its strategy to counter China's global ambitions. This would involve directing more resources towards projects in regions where China is seeking to expand its influence, such as Africa and Southeast Asia. By doing so, the U.S. can prevent China from gaining a monopoly over critical infrastructure and maintain its own strategic foothold in these regions. The consequence would be a more balanced global power dynamic, with the U.S. retaining its influence and protecting its national security interests.

Abolishing EXIM would be a grave mistake with far-reaching economic and geopolitical consequences. Instead, the U.S. should focus on expanding and reforming the bank to better serve the national interest. This includes increasing its capacity, supporting small businesses, ensuring accountability, and using it as a strategic tool to counter China's growing influence. By doing so, the U.S. can protect its economic future, secure jobs, and maintain its leadership on the global stage.

Summary

This chapter of Mandate for Leadership was written by Veronique de Rugy and Jennifer Hazelton. The following summary conveys the content of the document accurately and objectively, without endorsing or critiquing the perspectives of the original authors.

The Case Against the Export-Import Bank

The chapter opens with a strong stance advocating for the abolition of the Export-Import Bank (EXIM), asserting that it functions as a detrimental entity for both the U.S. economy and its taxpayers. The author argues that EXIM, established in 1934, operates as a federal agency providing export subsidies to private exporting corporations and foreign companies buying U.S. exports. Although the bank's purported mission includes promoting American exports, creating jobs, and supporting small businesses, these goals are, according to the author, misleading and economically harmful.

In 1986, David Stockman, former Director of the Office of Management and Budget under President Ronald Reagan, criticized export subsidies as "a mercantilist illusion" that diminish Gross National Product (GNP) and employment by selling goods for less than their production costs. He pointed out that a significant portion of EXIM's subsidies benefited large corporations like Boeing, General Electric, and Westinghouse, rather than small businesses.

BACKGROUND AND OPERATIONS OF EXIM

EXIM was initially created to finance trade with the Soviet Union but was restructured as an independent government agency in 1945 under President Franklin Roosevelt. Its primary tools include loan guarantees, working capital guarantees, direct loans, and export-credit insurance. Notably, EXIM was largely inactive for four years (2015-2019) due to a lack of a quorum on its board, limiting its ability to finance large projects. Despite this, the U.S. economy and exports thrived without EXIM's involvement, challenging the narrative that the bank is essential for U.S. economic success.

CRITIQUE OF EXIM'S IMPACT ON JOBS AND EXPORTS

The author challenges the claim that EXIM creates or maintains jobs. While supporters cite job creation figures linked to federal spending through EXIM, these figures overlook the jobs lost in other industries due to the redistribution of resources. The assertion is made that most exports financed by EXIM would have occurred without government support, primarily benefiting large corporations with easy access to capital. This, in turn, shifts jobs and opportunities from unsubsidized to subsidized firms, often with no net gain in employment.

Moreover, the author contests the idea that EXIM effectively promotes exports. Instead of increasing the net number of exports, export credit subsidies simply redistribute opportunities among firms. The author highlights that during the period when EXIM was incapacitated, U.S. exports continued to grow, supported by commercial lenders, without any significant negative impact on the economy.

ECONOMIC MISCONCEPTIONS AND THE REAL IMPACT OF SUBSIDIES

The chapter delves into the misconception that increasing exports inherently boosts economic growth. The author argues that exports are, in fact, a cost to the economy because they subtract from GDP. Only when the resources used to produce exports are less than the value of what is received in return do exports contribute positively to economic growth. EXIM, by subsidizing exports, misallocates resources and compels American taxpayers to indirectly support the living standards of foreigners without any substantial benefit to the U.S.

The chapter also criticizes EXIM for failing to level the playing field, as it claims. The bank's focus on competing with foreign export credit agencies (ECAs) is seen as misguided. Instead of fostering genuine competitiveness, EXIM's actions create an illusion of economic strength by engaging in subsidy wars, particularly against countries like China, Germany, and Italy, whose ECAs are often highlighted as examples.

FAILURE TO SUPPORT SMALL BUSINESSES AND RISK TO TAXPAYERS

The notion that EXIM supports small businesses is refuted by data showing that a vast majority of its funding goes to large corporations, particularly Boeing. Over the years, the share of support for small businesses has significantly declined, with less than 0.1% of U.S. small businesses benefiting from EXIM, while the subsidies put them at a disadvantage. Additionally, the chapter raises concerns about EXIM's fiscal responsibility, citing deficiencies in its accounting practices and the Congressional Budget Office's findings that EXIM's programs could cost taxpayers $2 billion, contrary to the bank's claims of saving money.

FAILING TO MEET THE CHINA CHALLENGE

The chapter proceeds to examine the narrative that EXIM is essential for the United States to counter China's growing influence in global markets. This rationale was notably used by both President Trump and President Biden to justify the reauthorization and expansion of EXIM. Proponents argue that EXIM can serve as a strategic tool to combat China's aggressive use of export credit financing to dominate international markets, particularly through initiatives like the Belt and Road Initiative (BRI).

However, the author argues that this perspective is fundamentally flawed. Despite Congress instructing EXIM to focus on China, there has been little to no change in how the bank operates. EXIM continues to direct most of its resources towards large corporations in high-income nations rather than focusing on low-income markets where China is most active. The chapter points out that EXIM's China and Transformation Exports Program (CTEP) managed to authorize only $141.3 million in financing in fiscal year 2022, a minuscule fraction of the $27 billion target set by Congress to be achieved by 2026.

Moreover, the chapter highlights the irony in the U.S. government's approach: while advocating for using EXIM to counter China, the bank itself has subsidized Chinese state-owned companies like China Air in the past. This contradiction undermines the argument that EXIM is an effective tool against Chinese economic influence. The author asserts that the lack of significant changes in EXIM's operations further demonstrates the ineffectiveness of this strategy.

MISPLACED FOCUS ON EMERGING TECHNOLOGIES

EXIM has also attempted to position itself as a supporter of emerging technologies, such as quantum computing and artificial intelligence, as part of its strategy to counter China's influence. However, the author argues that this focus is misplaced. These technologies, the chapter claims, do not require government-backed financing as they already attract substantial commercial investment. Therefore, EXIM's efforts in this area are seen as redundant and ineffective in achieving its stated goals.

CHALLENGES IN THE SEMICONDUCTOR INDUSTRY

The chapter also addresses the semiconductor industry, which has become a focal point in the U.S. government's industrial policy to counter China's ambitions. Despite the strategic importance of this sector, EXIM has been largely inactive in supporting it. This inactivity is contrasted with the Chinese government's heavy-handed subsidies in the semiconductor industry, which, while criticized for inefficiency and corruption, have been part of China's broader strategy to dominate critical technologies. The author suggests that EXIM's failure to adapt to this reality is another indication of its inability to serve as a strategic tool against China.

CONCLUSION: INEFFECTIVENESS OF EXIM AS A STRATEGIC TOOL

The section concludes by reiterating that the idea of using EXIM as a weapon against China is misguided. The author argues that economic and national security challenges posed by China cannot be effectively addressed through subsidies and export credit financing. Instead, the chapter advocates for more substantive and strategic policy changes that do not rely on outdated mechanisms like EXIM.

The Case for the Export-Import Bank

In contrast to the previous argument, this section presents a defense of the Export-Import Bank. The discussion begins with a historical reference to President Ronald Reagan, who, despite initial opposition, ultimately supported the extension of EXIM's charter, recognizing the challenges faced by American businesses in competing internationally. Reagan's famous remark, "Why would I want our businesses competing with two hands tied behind their backs?" is used to underscore the practical need for EXIM in supporting U.S. exports.

EVOLUTION OF THE GLOBAL ECONOMIC ORDER

The section acknowledges that the global economic landscape has shifted dramatically since Reagan's presidency, particularly with the rise of China as a major economic power. China's aggressive use of export credit financing, supported by three dedicated ECAs, is highlighted as a key factor in its ability to outpace other nations in securing international projects. The author notes that in 2018 alone, China provided more than $500 billion in export credit, nearly matching the total financing provided by EXIM throughout its entire history.

China's export credit activity surpasses that of all G7 countries combined, and its Belt and Road Initiative is cited as an example of how China uses export credit financing as a tool of national security and geopolitical influence. This initiative has drawn international criticism for ensnaring developing countries in "debt-trap diplomacy," a strategy that grants China control over critical infrastructure, such as ports and mineral resources, in exchange for financing projects that many of these countries cannot afford.

NEED FOR U.S. RESPONSE

In light of these developments, the section argues that the United States cannot afford to abandon EXIM. Without a functioning export credit agency, American companies would struggle to compete against Chinese firms for international opportunities, and the U.S. would lose influence in key global markets. The author asserts that EXIM is the only tool available to provide the sovereign guarantees often required for large international projects, which private banks are unwilling or unable to offer due to the associated risks.

COMPARATIVE ANALYSIS WITH OTHER NATIONS

The author provides examples of how other countries have adapted their export credit policies in response to China's aggression. Nations like the United Kingdom, Canada, Japan, and Italy have shifted from merely leveling the playing field for their exporters to proactively hunting for international deals and advancing their long-term strategic interests. These countries have also modified their content requirements to attract more business, often to the detriment of U.S. companies. For instance, the UK offered financing to Boeing on the condition that it used Rolls Royce engines instead of those made by General Electric, while Italy offered similar incentives to GE in exchange for moving turbine production to Italy.

IMPACT ON U.S. JOBS AND MANUFACTURING

The section emphasizes that the loss of manufacturing jobs and production capacity in the U.S. is partly due to these aggressive tactics by foreign ECAs. EXIM's role in countering such practices is portrayed as crucial for maintaining U.S. competitiveness and protecting American jobs, particularly in manufacturing.

CRITICISM AND DEFENSE OF EXIM

The author addresses common criticisms of EXIM, such as accusations of "crony capitalism" and being the "Bank of Boeing." These critiques are dismissed as misleading, especially in light of the financial crisis of 2008 when the airline industry heavily relied on EXIM due to the lack of private-sector financing. The cyclical nature of EXIM's portfolio is highlighted, with different industries relying on its support depending on economic conditions.

The section also defends EXIM's practices, such as its principle of additionality, which ensures that the bank only provides financing when the private sector cannot. Additionally, EXIM's stringent risk management practices are praised, noting its low default rate of around 0.5%, which is enviable even by private banking standards.

ECONOMIC JUSTIFICATION AND BENEFITS OF EXIM

The section further elaborates on the economic justification for EXIM, arguing that the bank plays a critical role in supporting macroeconomic growth, particularly in times when private sector financing is unavailable or insufficient. The chapter notes that EXIM operates on the principle of "additionality," meaning it steps in only when private lenders cannot or will not finance certain transactions due to perceived risks. This is crucial in sectors where traditional financing might not be available, especially in high-risk or politically unstable regions.

EXIM'S FINANCIAL PERFORMANCE

The section emphasizes that EXIM does not undercut the private sector but rather complements it by filling gaps in financing. When EXIM provides loans or guarantees, the interest rates are market-driven, ensuring that the agency does not distort the market. Additionally, the chapter highlights EXIM's impressive track record in managing risk, noting its historically low default rate of approximately 0.5%. This prudent management has allowed EXIM to generate profits for the U.S. Treasury, contributing more than $9 billion since 1992 for debt reduction. The chapter underscores that EXIM's operations are a net positive for American taxpayers, contrary to some critics' claims that it is a financial burden.

STRATEGIC IMPORTANCE IN THE GLOBAL ECONOMY

The chapter argues that export credit financing has become an indispensable tool in the global economic competition. Other countries, recognizing the strategic importance of their Export Credit Agencies (ECAs), have increasingly used them to gain economic advantages and secure long-term geopolitical interests. This shift has placed U.S. firms, especially small and medium-sized enterprises (SMEs), at a competitive disadvantage. Without EXIM, the author argues, the U.S. would risk ceding critical economic opportunities and jobs to foreign competitors, particularly from nations that aggressively support their exporters.

ADDRESSING CRITICISMS

The section continues by addressing the criticisms that EXIM is an example of "crony capitalism" or that it primarily serves large corporations like Boeing. The chapter argues that these criticisms are unfounded and often based on a misunderstanding of EXIM's role and operations. For instance, the "Bank of Boeing" label is refuted by explaining that while Boeing has been a significant beneficiary of EXIM financing, this is due to the nature of the aviation industry, where large-scale financing is necessary, and private sector financing is often unavailable. Moreover, EXIM's portfolio is diverse, supporting a wide range of industries over different economic cycles.

NATIONAL SECURITY IMPLICATIONS

The chapter then shifts focus to the national security implications of EXIM. It argues that in the context of global strategic competition, particularly with China, EXIM is not just an economic tool but also a crucial component of the United States' national security strategy. China's aggressive use of export credit financing as part of its broader geopolitical strategy, especially through initiatives like the Belt and Road Initiative (BRI), is highlighted as a key challenge. The chapter asserts that by financing infrastructure and other critical projects in developing countries, China is not only securing economic advantages but also expanding its geopolitical influence, often at the expense of U.S. interests.

EXIM'S ROLE IN COUNTERING CHINESE INFLUENCE

The section argues that EXIM is one of the few tools available to the U.S. government to counteract China's expansive use of export credits. Without EXIM, the U.S. would be at a significant disadvantage in competing for international projects, particularly in regions where Chinese influence is growing. The chapter underscores that maintaining a robust and active EXIM is essential for the U.S. to remain competitive and to safeguard its national security interests in a rapidly shifting global landscape.

STRATEGIC USE OF EXPORT CREDITS

The chapter concludes this section by emphasizing that export credits are no longer just about economic gain but have become a strategic weapon in the global power struggle. EXIM, therefore, should be seen as a critical asset in the United States' economic and national security toolkit. The chapter advocates for continued and even expanded support for EXIM, arguing that the risks of not doing so far outweigh any potential drawbacks.

THE IMPACT OF GLOBAL COMPETITORS

The discussion continues by examining how other countries have adapted their export credit strategies in response to the growing influence of China and the evolving global economic order. The chapter highlights that many U.S. allies, including the United Kingdom, Japan, and Italy, have significantly altered their ECA policies to compete more effectively in the global market. These changes include reducing content requirements and actively seeking to secure international contracts that would otherwise be out of reach for their domestic companies.

CHALLENGES FACED BY U.S. EXPORTERS

The author argues that these shifts in global export credit policies have placed U.S. exporters at a disadvantage, particularly in terms of securing contracts that are critical for maintaining domestic jobs and economic growth. The chapter points out that while other countries have aggressively pursued strategic export deals, the U.S. has been more restrained, often adhering to traditional rules and content requirements that limit its competitiveness. This has led to a situation where U.S. firms are increasingly losing out on international opportunities, which has a direct impact on American jobs and the broader economy.

THE NEED FOR REFORM

The section calls for a reassessment of U.S. export credit policies to better align with the realities of the current global economic environment. The author suggests that the U.S. should consider adopting more flexible and strategic approaches to export financing, similar to those employed by its competitors. This could involve relaxing certain requirements or adopting new strategies that better support U.S. exporters in the face of growing competition from both China and other nations.

CHAPTER 24: FEDERAL RESERVE

In essence, because of its vastly expanded discretionary powers with respect to monetary and regulatory policy, the Fed lacks both operational effectiveness and political independence. - Page 732

Key Policy Proposals

The chapter on the Federal Reserve proposes a series of policy changes that would fundamentally reshape the U.S. monetary system. These recommendations, while presented as necessary reforms, would have significant consequences that must be critically examined.

ELIMINATION OF THE DUAL MANDATE

The chapter advocates for the elimination of the Federal Reserve's dual mandate, which currently requires the Fed to balance price stability with full employment. Removing the employment mandate is a dangerous step backward. The dual mandate has been instrumental in guiding the U.S. economy through periods of both inflation and high unemployment. Abandoning the employment aspect would disproportionately harm working-class Americans, particularly during economic downturns when monetary policy is crucial in stabilizing jobs. Data shows that during the Great Recession, the Fed's dual mandate played a critical role in reducing unemployment from its peak of 10% in 2009 to below 5% by 2016. Stripping away this mandate would remove a vital tool for ensuring broad-based economic recovery.

LIMITING THE LENDER-OF-LAST-RESORT FUNCTION

The chapter also calls for limiting the Federal Reserve's lender-of-last-resort (LOLR) function. This proposal is misguided and ignores the essential role this function plays in preventing systemic collapses. The 2008 financial crisis offers a stark lesson: the LOLR function was crucial in averting a complete meltdown of the global financial system. By providing emergency liquidity, the Fed prevented the failures of major institutions like AIG from cascading through the economy. Limiting this function would increase the likelihood of bank runs and financial panic, leading to more severe recessions. The argument that this function encourages reckless behavior by financial institutions is a simplistic interpretation that overlooks the complex realities of financial markets. Rather than restricting the Fed's capabilities, we should focus on stronger regulatory oversight to mitigate moral hazard without compromising the Fed's ability to act swiftly in crises.

WINDING DOWN THE FEDERAL RESERVE'S BALANCE SHEET

Proposing a dramatic reduction of the Federal Reserve's balance sheet is economically reckless. The Fed's balance sheet expansions have been a crucial tool in stabilizing the economy during periods of crisis. During the COVID-19 pandemic, for instance, the Fed's large-scale asset purchases were essential in maintaining liquidity and preventing a deeper recession. By winding down the balance sheet too quickly, we risk destabilizing financial markets, increasing borrowing costs, and slowing economic recovery. The idea that these purchases distort markets ignores the fact that in times of crisis, such distortions are necessary to prevent broader economic collapse. We should be focused on a gradual, data-driven reduction of the balance sheet, timed carefully to ensure that markets remain stable.

LIMITING FUTURE BALANCE SHEET EXPANSIONS TO U.S. TREASURIES

Restricting the Federal Reserve's asset purchases to U.S. Treasuries is a myopic policy that would handcuff the Fed in times of crisis. During the 2008 financial crisis and the COVID-19 pandemic, the ability to purchase mortgage-backed securities and other assets was critical in stabilizing housing markets and ensuring that credit continued to flow. Limiting the Fed to Treasuries would reduce its flexibility, potentially prolonging recessions and deepening financial crises. The notion that the Fed's involvement in other markets is inherently distortive ignores the benefits these interventions have provided in maintaining economic stability.

ENDING INTEREST PAYMENTS ON EXCESS RESERVES

Finally, the proposal to end interest payments on excess reserves is counterproductive. These payments have been a key tool in managing the money supply and controlling inflation. By paying interest on reserves, the Fed encourages banks to hold onto excess reserves, which helps prevent runaway inflation during periods of economic expansion. Removing this tool would reduce the Fed's ability to manage inflation effectively, potentially leading to higher inflation rates and more volatile economic cycles. This is not just a theoretical concern: in the years following the 2008 financial crisis, interest on excess reserves was a crucial part of the Fed's strategy to gradually normalize monetary policy without triggering inflation.

The proposed policy changes reflect a fundamental misunderstanding of the role the Federal Reserve plays in maintaining economic stability. Far from ensuring greater independence and efficiency, these changes would weaken the Fed's ability to respond to economic crises, exacerbate unemployment, and increase the risk of financial instability. The data is clear: a strong, flexible Federal Reserve, equipped with a dual mandate and the tools necessary to intervene in diverse markets, is essential for maintaining a stable and prosperous economy. These proposals, if implemented, would do far more harm than good, particularly for the most vulnerable Americans.

Summary

This chapter of Mandate for Leadership was written by Paul Winfree. The following summary conveys the content of the document accurately and objectively, without endorsing or critiquing the perspectives of the original authors.

The chapter begins with a historical overview of the Federal Reserve, established in 1913 by Congress to address financial instability caused by irresponsible banking practices and inadequate regulations. Originally, the Fed was designed as a quasi-public clearinghouse and a lender of last resort to prevent financial crises. However, its performance during the Great Depression was criticized for exacerbating economic woes, a pattern of inefficacy that persisted through subsequent decades.

Challenges to the Federal Reserve's Independence

The Federal Reserve's ability to act independently has been compromised over time. Initially decentralized, with regional banks holding significant power, the system evolved into a more centralized structure dominated by the Board of Governors. This shift eroded the intended political independence, exposing the Federal Reserve to political pressures, especially during economic crises. The chapter notes that while the Fed's independence is nominally protected by its mandate to maintain price stability, this independence is undermined during periods of economic instability and by political demands to engage in initiatives like environmental, social, and governance (ESG) objectives.

Legislative Expansions and Consequences

Over the years, Congress expanded the Federal Reserve's powers, particularly during times of economic crisis. The stock market crash of 1929 led to the Fed gaining the authority to set reserve requirements and regulate securities loans. The 1970s saw the introduction of the dual mandate, requiring the Fed to balance price stability with full employment. Following the 2008 financial crisis, the Federal Reserve's role expanded further, incorporating large-scale asset purchases and greater regulatory authority over banks. However, these expansions have not necessarily improved the Fed's efficacy. Instead, they have introduced significant risks, such as the emergence of "too big to fail" financial institutions and an increased likelihood of government debt creation, ultimately compromising the Federal Reserve's neutrality and operational effectiveness.

Broad Recommendations

The chapter presents several broad recommendations aimed at reforming the Federal Reserve to improve its operational effectiveness and independence. These recommendations are divided into specific policy proposals designed to address the key issues identified in the previous section.

1. Eliminate the Dual Mandate

The first recommendation is to eliminate the Federal Reserve's "dual mandate," which was introduced in the 1970s. The dual mandate requires the Federal Reserve to pursue not only stable prices but also maximum employment and moderate long-term interest rates. The text argues that this mandate creates a bias toward inflation, which can lead to economic instability. Instead, the focus should be on protecting the dollar and restraining inflation. By limiting the Federal Reserve's responsibility to maintaining price stability, the economy could avoid the negative effects of monetary policy aimed at stimulating employment.

2. Limit the Lender-of-Last-Resort Function

Another key recommendation is to limit the Federal Reserve's lender-of-last-resort (LOLR) function. This function was originally intended to protect banks during financial crises, but it has evolved into a "standing bailout offer" that encourages reckless lending and speculation. The chapter argues that the LOLR function should be curtailed to reduce moral hazard and ensure that financial institutions behave more prudently, avoiding risky practices that can lead to financial crises.

3. Wind Down the Federal Reserve's Balance Sheet

The chapter also recommends a significant reduction of the Federal Reserve's balance sheet. Since the 2008 financial crisis, the Federal Reserve's assets have ballooned to nearly $9 trillion, consisting mainly of federal debt and mortgage-backed securities. These purchases are criticized for encouraging federal deficits and distorting markets. It is proposed that Congress should limit the types of assets the Federal Reserve can purchase and mandate a gradual reduction of the balance sheet to pre-2008 levels.

4. Limit Future Balance Sheet Expansions to U.S. Treasuries

The Federal Reserve's open market operations should be restricted to U.S. Treasuries, preventing the Fed from intervening in mortgage-backed securities or corporate and municipal debt markets. The chapter argues that such interventions distort the pricing process and resemble credit allocation rather than liquidity provision. By limiting asset purchases to Treasuries, the Federal Reserve would avoid creating economic distortions and focus on providing market liquidity without favoring specific sectors.

5. Stop Paying Interest on Excess Reserves

The final broad recommendation is to end the policy of paying interest on excess reserves, a practice that began during the 2008 financial crisis. This policy effectively incentivizes banks to hold reserves at the Federal Reserve rather than lending money to the public, which has led to a significant increase in excess reserves. The chapter suggests that this practice should be discontinued to encourage banks to lend more actively, thereby supporting economic growth.

Monetary Rule Reform Options

This section delves into various options for reforming the Federal Reserve's approach to monetary policy. The chapter highlights the need for significant changes to curb the inflationary and recessionary cycles caused by the Federal Reserve's current practices. These options are ranked by their effectiveness in restraining the Federal Reserve and the feasibility of their implementation.

1. Free Banking

The most radical option proposed is **Free Banking**, where neither the supply of money nor interest rates are controlled by the government. Under this system, the Federal Reserve would be abolished, and private banks would issue their own currency backed by a valuable commodity, such as gold. Historical examples like the Suffolk System in 19th-century America are cited to demonstrate how free banking can minimize inflation and economic disruptions. The text argues that competition among banks would prevent over-issuance of currency and encourage responsible lending, ultimately leading to stable and sound currencies. However, this option faces substantial political hurdles and would require careful coordination to implement.

2. Commodity-Backed Money

The second option is a **Commodity-Backed Money** system, which involves tying the dollar to a specific amount of a valuable commodity, typically gold. This would limit the government's ability to manipulate money and credit, as new dollars would need to be backed by a hard asset. The process is straightforward: Treasury could set a fixed price for gold, and each Federal Reserve note would be redeemable for a specific amount of gold. This system would act as a self-policing mechanism, forcing the government to maintain fiscal discipline. While less disruptive than free banking, this approach still poses challenges, particularly in ensuring the government adheres to the gold peg.

3. K-Percent Rule

A more politically feasible alternative is the **K-Percent Rule**, originally proposed by Milton Friedman. Under this rule, the Federal Reserve would create money at a fixed rate, such as 3% per year. This rule aims to offer the inflation-control benefits of a gold standard without the economic disruptions associated with a commodity-backed system. However, the chapter notes that the K-Percent Rule could still be vulnerable to political pressures and economic fluctuations, which might undermine its effectiveness.

4. Inflation-Targeting Rules

The Federal Reserve currently operates under an **Inflation-Targeting** framework, where it sets a target inflation rate, often around 2%. The chapter criticizes this approach for potentially causing boom-and-bust cycles by adjusting the money supply to hit the target, often in response to political pressures. This method can lead to instability, as it relies on the Federal Reserve's ability to predict and manage economic conditions, which is inherently challenging.

5. Inflation and Growth-Targeting Rules

Two other prominent reform proposals are **Inflation and Growth-Targeting Rules**: the Taylor Rule and Nominal GDP (NGDP) Targeting. Both aim to stabilize the economy by managing total spending rather than focusing solely on inflation. The **Taylor Rule** adjusts interest rates based on deviations from inflation and real output growth trends, while **NGDP Targeting** keeps total spending growth on a steady path. These rules attempt to mitigate demand shocks but place a significant knowledge burden on central bankers to distinguish between demand-side and supply-side factors.

Minimum Effective Reforms

Given the short-term nature of political cycles, the chapter concludes with a set of **Minimum Effective Reforms** that aim to balance economic benefits with political feasibility. These include:

- **Eliminating the Full Employment Mandate**: Refocusing the Federal Reserve on price stability alone.
- **Specifying Target Inflation Ranges**: Requiring the Fed to declare a clear target inflation range and growth path.
- **Regulating Bank Capital Adequacy**: Focusing the Fed's regulatory activities on ensuring banks have adequate capital.
- **Curbing Last-Resort Lending**: Reducing the Fed's excessive lending practices that contribute to moral hazard.
- **Exploring Alternatives to the Federal Reserve**: Appointing a commission to evaluate the Fed's mission and consider alternatives.
- **Preventing Central Bank Digital Currency (CBDC)**: Avoiding the adoption of CBDCs due to concerns over surveillance and control.

CHAPTER 25: SMALL BUSINESS ADMINISTRATION

Today, initiatives aimed at 'inclusivity' are in fact creating exclusivity and stringent selectivity in deciding what types of small businesses and entities can use SBA programs. – Page 749

Key Policy Proposals

The chapter on the Small Business Administration (SBA) proposes several policy changes that reflect a significant shift in priorities, ostensibly aimed at streamlining the agency. However, these changes raise serious concerns about the potential impact on small businesses, especially those that are already disadvantaged.

One of the core proposals is to narrow the SBA's focus by eliminating what is termed "mission creep"—a critique that the agency has expanded beyond its original mandate. The chapter suggests that inclusivity initiatives have led to "exclusivity and stringent selectivity" in program access. This argument is fundamentally flawed. Programs designed to support underrepresented groups, including minority-owned, women-owned, and veteran-owned businesses, are not about exclusivity but about leveling the playing field. Reducing or eliminating these programs would exacerbate existing inequalities in access to capital, government contracts, and entrepreneurial training, effectively pushing these businesses to the margins.

The chapter's call to cease direct government lending, particularly through programs like the Economic Injury Disaster Loan (EIDL) and Paycheck Protection Program (PPP), underestimates the crucial role these initiatives play in times of crisis. During the COVID-19 pandemic, these programs provided a lifeline to millions of small businesses that lacked the necessary relationships with private lenders. By suggesting that such lending should be left entirely to the private sector, the proposal ignores the reality that private lenders often prioritize larger, more established businesses, leaving small enterprises—especially those in underserved communities—without support. The consequence would be a consolidation of economic power among big businesses, reducing competition and innovation.

The chapter also advocates for a stricter definition of what constitutes a small business, with a push to create a separate category for medium-sized enterprises. While this may seem like a technical adjustment, it risks excluding many businesses from the support they need, particularly in sectors where businesses tend to grow larger by necessity, such as manufacturing. Without access to SBA loans and contracting opportunities, these businesses could struggle to compete, leading to job losses and reduced economic growth in their communities.

Moreover, the suggestion to eliminate project labor agreements (PLAs) in federal contracting, as proposed by the Fair and Open Competition Act, would undermine workers' rights and lead to a race to the bottom in terms of wages and working conditions. PLAs ensure that government projects are completed on time and within budget, while also guaranteeing fair wages and benefits for workers. Removing these agreements would open the door to exploitation and lower standards, hurting workers and the quality of federal projects.

The chapter's approach to the Office of Advocacy within the SBA also warrants scrutiny. While increasing the budget and authority of the Office to challenge regulations that impact small businesses may seem beneficial, the real intent appears to be the weakening of essential regulations that protect public health, safety, and the environment. The argument for "dismantling extreme regulatory policies" is a thinly veiled attack on regulations that prevent corporate abuses. Rolling back these protections would not only harm the environment and public health but would also undermine long-term economic stability by encouraging short-term, profit-driven decision-making at the expense of sustainable growth.

In conclusion, the proposed changes to the SBA outlined in the chapter would lead to a significant rollback of support for small businesses, particularly those in marginalized communities. By narrowing the focus of the SBA and reducing its capacity to directly intervene in the economy, these policies would shift power towards larger businesses and away from the very entrepreneurs the SBA was created to support. The consequence would be a less equitable economy, with reduced opportunities for innovation and growth among small businesses, leading to greater economic disparity and a weaker overall economy.

Summary

This chapter of Mandate for Leadership was written by Karen Kerrigan. The following summary conveys the content of the document accurately and objectively, without endorsing or critiquing the perspectives of the original authors.

The U.S. Small Business Administration (SBA) supports U.S. entrepreneurship by strengthening free enterprise through policy advocacy and offering programs that assist entrepreneurs in launching and growing their businesses in the global marketplace.

Overview

Established in 1953, the SBA was created to aid, counsel, assist, and protect the interests of small businesses, while preserving free competition and strengthening the U.S. economy. Over the years, the SBA has expanded its role, including becoming the primary federal agency for disaster loans, through which it has distributed hundreds of billions of taxpayer dollars. Programs like the Paycheck Protection Program (PPP) during the COVID-19 pandemic have been successful in saving jobs, but others, such as the Economic Injury Disaster Loan (EIDL) Advance, have been riddled with fraud, with the SBA Inspector General identifying $78.1 billion in potentially fraudulent loans and grants.

Origin, History, and Core Functions

The SBA began its core operations in 1954, providing loans, securing a fair share of government contracts for small businesses, and offering business management training. The agency's advocacy role was significantly expanded in the 1970s and 1980s, particularly with the establishment of the Office of Advocacy, which ensures that federal regulations consider the impact on small businesses. Today, the SBA's core functions include:

1. **Access to Capital**: Offering various lending programs, from microlending to debt and equity investment capital.
2. **Entrepreneurial Development**: Providing free or low-cost training through a nationwide network and online platforms.
3. **Government Contracting Support**: Ensuring small businesses secure a significant portion of federal contracts.
4. **Advocacy**: Protecting small businesses from overregulation and conducting small-business research.

Budgetary Fluctuation

The SBA's budget has varied widely depending on political leadership and external events. For instance, President Reagan reduced the agency's budget by over 30%, while the agency's budget soared during the COVID-19 pandemic, reaching over $761.9 billion in FY2020 due to emergency relief efforts. These fluctuations reflect the SBA's evolving role in responding to economic crises and natural disasters.

History of Mismanagement

The SBA has faced persistent issues with mismanagement, fraud, and waste throughout its history. From the mishandling of funds during Hurricane Katrina to widespread fraud in recent COVID-19 relief programs, the agency has often struggled with oversight and accountability. Congress has pressured the SBA to improve transparency and tighten controls, particularly in light of the challenges exposed during the pandemic.

Mission Creep and Enlargement

Over time, the SBA has faced criticism for "mission creep," where its focus has expanded beyond its original mandate. Republicans in the U.S. House of Representatives have raised concerns about the agency becoming too broad, unaccountable, and more selective in the businesses it supports. There is unease that the SBA has shifted from being universally accessible to small businesses to favoring politically prioritized or geographically concentrated entities. This has led to programs that, while aiming for inclusivity, create exclusivity by limiting access to certain small businesses.

Specific issues include the SBA's request to become a "designated voter agency" under President Biden's executive order on "Promoting Access to Voting," the creation of duplicative business training channels, and the push for expanding direct government lending, which duplicates private-sector efforts and risks inefficiency and fraud.

The SBA in a Conservative Administration

A conservative administration would focus on reforming and restructuring the SBA to meet the real needs of small businesses rather than special interests. This involves ensuring that the SBA operates efficiently, with a focus on congressionally authorized programs. Proposed reforms include:

- Appointing a highly qualified SBA Administrator and leadership team who can effectively manage the agency.
- Refocusing the SBA on its core functions, eliminating unnecessary and unauthorized programs.
- Improving accountability by regularly reporting to Congress and responding promptly to recommendations from the Office of Inspector General (OIG) and Government Accountability Office (GAO).
- Ending waste, fraud, and abuse, particularly in COVID-19 relief programs like the PPP and EIDL.

- Ceasing direct government lending and instead supporting small businesses through private-sector channels.
- Modernizing the SBA to better use technology for operations and outreach.

ACCOUNTABILITY AND MANAGERIAL PRACTICE

The SBA has long been criticized for lacking accountability and effective management practices. A future administration would need to instill a culture of accountability by requiring performance metrics and safeguarding taxpayer dollars. Key actions would include:

- Implementing internal procedures to protect program integrity, especially in light of IT and security challenges highlighted in recent OIG reports.
- Ensuring that all outstanding OIG and GAO recommendations are addressed within a specified time frame, such as 90 days, to prevent recurring issues.

STRENGTHENING THE OFFICE OF ADVOCACY

The Office of Advocacy within the SBA plays a crucial role in protecting small businesses from overregulation. However, it has been underfunded and underutilized. Proposed reforms to strengthen the Office of Advocacy include:

- Amending the Regulatory Flexibility Act (RFA) to require agencies to submit proposed rules to the Office of Advocacy for review before they are published, ensuring that small businesses are not adversely affected.
- Expanding the economic analysis required under the RFA to include indirect costs.
- Increasing the budget of the Office of Advocacy by at least 50%, enabling it to hire additional staff and enhance its role in the regulatory process.
- Mandating federal agencies to comply with the RFA and encouraging direct feedback from small businesses through roundtables and online platforms.

COVID-19 LENDING PROGRAM ACCOUNTABILITY AND CLEANUP

The SBA's handling of COVID-19 relief programs, particularly the PPP and EIDL, has been marked by significant challenges, including widespread fraud. A priority for the next administration should be a thorough cleanup and final accounting of these programs. Proposed actions include:

- Bringing in private-sector expertise to help close out these programs efficiently.
- Pursuing legal action against fraudulent recipients and ensuring that ineligible PPP loan recipients repay the funds.
- Cooperating with congressional oversight efforts to review and potentially reverse forgiveness decisions for loans that should not have been approved.

DISASTER LOAN PROGRAM AND DIRECT LENDING

The SBA's disaster loan program, which provides low-interest loans following federally declared disasters, has faced coordination problems with FEMA and has sometimes discouraged individuals from purchasing private disaster insurance. More than 90% of these loans go to individuals rather than small businesses, raising questions about the program's effectiveness. Proposed reforms include:

- Assessing whether disaster loans should be administered by another agency instead of the SBA.
- Clarifying that no new direct lending programs will be developed at the SBA, reducing overlap with private sector lending.

ELIGIBILITY OF RELIGIOUS ENTITIES FOR SBA LOANS

Current SBA regulations exclude certain religious entities from participating in loan programs, a policy that the Trump Administration argued violates the First Amendment. Despite clear Supreme Court precedents against such exclusions, the SBA has not yet acted to remove these unconstitutional provisions. The next administration should:

- Notify Congress that these regulations will no longer be enforced.
- Remove SBA Form 1971, which is used to make religious eligibility determinations.
- Finalize or update the proposed rule to eliminate unconstitutional religious exclusions from SBA programs.

SMALL BUSINESS INNOVATION RESEARCH AND SMALL BUSINESS TECHNOLOGY TRANSFER PROGRAMS

The SBA coordinates and monitors the Small Business Innovation Research (SBIR) and Small Business Technology Transfer (STTR) programs across federal agencies that have substantial research and development (R&D) budgets. These programs are crucial for ensuring that small businesses receive a fair share of federal R&D funding. The SBIR program requires that 3.2% of agency R&D budgets be allocated to small businesses, while the STTR program allocates 0.45% of federal research spending to small firms. These programs have been extended through September 30, 2025.

Research has demonstrated that the SBIR program is particularly effective in funding advanced technologies that transition into the private market. The program also tends to invest more in America's heartland than private venture capital does, thus playing a critical role in balancing the geographic distribution of innovation funding.

The next administration should:

- **Continue the SBIR and STTR programs**: These programs are vital for fostering the next wave of technological innovation that can compete with large technology firms.
- **Urge Congress to expand the SBIR program**: Increasing the required allocation from federal R&D budgets would further support small businesses in developing groundbreaking technologies.
- **Enforce stricter rules on SBIR funding**: Ensuring that funds are invested in U.S.-based capital investments will help maintain domestic technological competitiveness.

DOMESTIC MANUFACTURING AND SMALL BUSINESS

Small businesses in the manufacturing sector face unique challenges, particularly regarding access to capital. Declining domestic business investment and manufacturing employment have exacerbated these issues. Capital-intensive sectors, such as transportation and energy, require substantial up-front investments, making it difficult for small manufacturers to compete. Moreover, when breakthrough technologies funded by U.S. taxpayer money are ready for commercialization, they often lack the necessary domestic manufacturing capacity, leading to their implementation abroad.

To address these challenges, the SBA should:

- **Expand Section 7(a) loans**: Increase the maximum loan principal available to small manufacturers to finance construction and technological upgrades. The proposed SBA Reauthorization and Improvement Act of 2019 suggested raising this cap to $50 million for advanced manufacturing.
- **Reform the Small Business Investment Company (SBIC) program**: Refocus the program to support small businesses in capital-intensive industries, rather than duplicating private venture capital investments in technology startups. Proposed reforms include offering longer-term financing options and making the program more sustainable.

SMALL-BUSINESS SIZE STANDARD MODERNIZATION

The SBA defines what constitutes a "small business" based on industry size standards, but this one-size-fits-all approach can be limiting. In contrast, other major economies consider both small and medium-sized enterprises (SMEs), recognizing the importance of medium-sized businesses in maintaining competition.

The next administration should:

- **Encourage Congress to create a "medium-sized business" classification**: This would allow medium-sized enterprises to access certain SBA programs, particularly those involving capital access for projects where alternative credit is unavailable.

SBA Policy Priorities for 2025 and Beyond

Several legislative initiatives could help reform the SBA and refocus its efforts on core statutory activities:

- **The IMPROVE the SBA Act**: This legislation aims to strengthen the SBA's accountability, transparency, and oversight.
- **The Small Business Regulatory Flexibility Improvements Act**: Requires federal agencies to conduct more thorough economic analysis under the RFA and provide justifications for proposed regulations.
- **The Small Business Regulatory Enforcement Fairness Act (SBREFA)**: Expands the rights of small businesses to participate in agency rulemakings and provides judicial review of agency violations.
- **The Fair and Open Competition Act**: This act seeks to eliminate the use of project labor agreements (PLAs) in federal contracting, which can disadvantage small businesses.
- **The JOBS Act 4.0**: Proposes regulatory improvements and modernization of SEC rules to enhance capital formation and access for small businesses.

Organizational Issues and Budget

The effectiveness of the SBA is closely tied to the qualifications and experience of its leadership. The SBA Administrator should not merely be a symbolic position but rather filled by someone with deep expertise in small-business finance, investment, and administrative law. This expertise is especially crucial during times of crisis, such as the COVID-19 pandemic, where the SBA had to rely heavily on the Department of the Treasury.

The next administration should:

- **Conduct a comprehensive review of SBA programs**: Within six months, evaluate the cost-effectiveness of various loan and grant programs and report to Congress. This could lead to the termination of ineffective programs, consolidation of duplicative functions, and reallocation of resources to more successful initiatives.
- **Hold the SBA budget constant**: Until this review is complete, maintain the agency's budget at its current level, potentially leading to reductions if ineffective programs are terminated.

Personnel Challenges

The SBA continues to expand its programs without ensuring that existing ones are effective or within its expertise. Recent moves to increase the number of licensed Small Business Lending Companies (SBLCs) and create new mission-based SBLCs highlight concerns about the SBA overextending itself.

To address these personnel challenges:

- **Focus on core competencies**: The next administration should rein in idealistic expansions and focus on ensuring that existing programs are well-managed and properly staffed.
- **Outsource where appropriate**: Where private-sector expertise is more efficient, the SBA should outsource certain functions to ensure effective program delivery.

CHAPTER 26: TRADE

The clear lesson learned in both the Obama and Trump Administrations is that Communist China will never bargain in good faith with the U.S. to stop its aggression. - Page 787

Key Policy Proposals

Chapter 26 presents a conservative view of trade and economic policies, particularly concerning the United States' relationship with China and the broader international trade environment. Let's dissect the proposed policies and examine their implications with a focus on economic fairness, international cooperation, and the protection of workers and consumers.

TARIFF RELIEF AND ECONOMIC IMPACT

The document advocates for the repeal of tariffs enacted under Sections 232, 201, and 301, claiming they have failed to achieve their intended goals and have instead harmed American consumers by raising prices. The argument is that these tariffs have burdened ordinary Americans with higher costs, such as an additional $1,200 per household annually, while benefiting a narrow set of special interests, notably within the steel industry.

Analysis: Tariffs, when strategically implemented, can protect vital domestic industries and preserve jobs that might otherwise be outsourced to countries with lower labor and environmental standards. However, the blanket tariffs imposed by the Trump administration have indeed backfired by escalating costs for consumers and businesses alike. The automotive industry, for example, saw significant cost increases due to higher steel prices, which undermined their competitiveness and led to job losses.

The push to repeal these tariffs is prudent, as it would alleviate unnecessary financial burdens on American families and businesses, stimulating economic growth by lowering the cost of goods and services. However, simply removing tariffs without a comprehensive plan risks leaving key industries vulnerable to unfair foreign competition. A balanced approach would involve targeted tariffs where necessary, coupled with strong labor and environmental standards in trade agreements to ensure fair competition.

REJOINING THE TRANS-PACIFIC PARTNERSHIP (TPP)

The text suggests rejoining the TPP, which was abandoned by the Trump administration. The TPP is presented as a critical tool for countering China's influence in the Asia-Pacific region by fostering stronger economic ties with other countries.

Analysis: Rejoining the TPP is a strategic move that would significantly enhance the United States' influence in Asia, a region critical to global economic growth. The TPP would create a vast free-trade zone that could serve as a counterbalance to China's economic power, encouraging member nations to adopt higher labor and environmental standards. This would not only benefit American workers by leveling the playing field but also help to promote global standards that reflect American values.

Furthermore, by re-engaging with the TPP, the U.S. can better ensure that trade agreements include robust protections for workers' rights and environmental sustainability, areas where China has historically been lacking. This would protect American jobs while promoting ethical practices globally.

MUTUAL RECOGNITION AND REGULATORY HARMONIZATION

The document calls for mutual recognition of safety and regulatory standards with key allies, arguing that if a product is deemed safe in Europe or Japan, it should be accepted in the U.S., and vice versa.

Analysis: While harmonizing regulations can facilitate trade and reduce costs, it must be done with caution to ensure that American consumers and workers are not exposed to lower standards that could compromise safety or environmental integrity. The European Union, for instance, has some of the world's highest standards for consumer protection and environmental sustainability, often exceeding those of the United States. Adopting mutual recognition agreements with these countries could potentially raise U.S. standards, benefiting consumers by providing access to safer, higher-quality products.

However, it is essential that any regulatory harmonization does not lead to a race to the bottom. The U.S. must retain the ability to impose stricter standards where necessary to protect public health and the environment. The goal should be to elevate standards globally, not dilute them in the name of trade facilitation.

CLOSING THE EXPORT–IMPORT BANK

The text advocates for closing the Export–Import Bank (EXIM), arguing that it primarily benefits a small number of well-connected companies and that its role in promoting exports can be fulfilled by private banks.

Analysis: The Export–Import Bank plays a crucial role in supporting American jobs and businesses, particularly small and medium-sized enterprises that might struggle to secure financing in the private market. By providing loans, guarantees, and insurance to foreign buyers of American goods, EXIM helps U.S. companies compete in international markets against foreign competitors who often benefit from their governments' financial support.

Closing EXIM would disproportionately harm small businesses and could lead to job losses in industries that rely on export financing to expand their markets. While reforming the bank to ensure transparency and prevent cronyism is necessary, outright closure would be a shortsighted move that undermines American competitiveness on the global stage.

STRENGTHENING DIPLOMATIC AND ECONOMIC ALLIANCES

The document underscores the importance of strengthening alliances through trade agreements and diplomatic engagement, particularly in countering China's growing influence.

Analysis: Strengthening alliances through trade is a cornerstone of effective foreign policy. By working closely with allies to create robust trade agreements, the U.S. can build a united front to address global challenges, including climate change, labor exploitation, and human rights abuses. Such agreements should prioritize the protection of workers, consumers, and the environment, ensuring that trade benefits are broadly shared and do not exacerbate inequalities.

However, trade policy should not be used as a tool to impose unilateral demands on other nations or to isolate countries like China completely. Engagement, rather than confrontation, is a more effective strategy for encouraging positive change. Diplomatic efforts should focus on building consensus and fostering cooperation on issues of mutual concern, such as climate action and fair labor practices.

The conservative proposals prioritize short-term gains for select industries over the broader, long-term interests of the American people and the global community. A more balanced approach would involve targeted tariffs, re-engagement with multilateral trade agreements like the TPP, and strategic use of institutions like the Export–Import Bank to support American workers and businesses. Moreover, the U.S. should lead by example in promoting high standards for labor, environmental protection, and human rights in its trade policies, ensuring that the benefits of trade are widely shared and sustainable for future generations.

Summary

This chapter of Mandate for Leadership was written by Peter Navarro and Kent Lassman. The following summary conveys the content of the document accurately and objectively, without endorsing or critiquing the perspectives of the original authors.

THE CASE FOR FAIR TRADE

Global trade has long been complicated by mechanisms like tariffs, quotas, and export subsidies, which have created significant trade imbalances. Major exporting countries, particularly China, use these tools to amass trade surpluses, often at the expense of others. China's industrial strategy aims for global dominance by replacing foreign companies with domestic firms, posing a significant threat to international trade fairness.

The United States, as a global superpower, must strengthen its manufacturing and defense sectors to maintain its position and protect national security. This requires reshoring production that has been offshored by American companies. However, the World Trade Organization's "most favored nation" (MFN) rule, which mandates equal tariff treatment for all WTO members, has led to the exploitation of American industries and chronic trade deficits, particularly with China.

China's economic aggression, including tariffs, dumping, and forced technology transfers, has further weakened the U.S. industrial base. The COVID-19 pandemic and the Russian invasion of Ukraine have underscored the vulnerabilities of relying on global supply chains, highlighting the need for a more resilient domestic manufacturing base.

The U.S. trade deficit, which soared to $845 billion in 2021, reflects the offshoring of American manufacturing and the challenges facing the U.S. economy. This trade imbalance is a significant economic and national security threat, as reliance on foreign supply chains endangers the U.S.'s ability to produce essential goods, particularly in times of crisis.

To address these issues, the U.S. must adopt trade policies that promote the reshoring of manufacturing and strengthen its defense industrial base, aligning with the principle that "economic security is national security."

CHALLENGE #1: UNFAIR AND NONRECIPROCAL TRADE INSTITUTIONALIZED IN WTO RULES

President Donald Trump, in his 2019 State of the Union Address, called for the United States Reciprocal Trade Act (USRTA). This act would empower the U.S. to impose matching tariffs on countries that place unfair tariffs on American products. The need for such legislation arises from the World Trade Organization's (WTO) "most favored nation" (MFN) rule, which requires WTO members to apply the lowest tariff rates they offer to any one country to all other members. However, this rule does not mandate reciprocal tariff rates, allowing countries to impose significantly higher tariffs on U.S. goods while benefiting from lower U.S. tariffs.

An example of this disparity is seen in the automotive sector: the U.S. applies a 2.5% tariff on imported cars, while the European Union imposes a 10% tariff, China 15%, and Brazil 35%. Similarly, U.S. rice imports from Malaysia face a 40% tariff, while Malaysia faces only a 6.2% tariff when exporting rice to the U.S. The WTO's rules create a situation where high-tariff countries can maintain their protectionist policies while benefiting from lower tariffs in other markets, leaving the U.S. at a disadvantage.

This imbalance is further illustrated by data showing that U.S. exporters face higher tariffs in over 467,000 cases, compared to just over 141,000 cases where the U.S. applies higher tariffs. On average, when foreign countries impose higher tariffs, these are 12.3 percentage points above the U.S. tariffs, while U.S. higher tariffs are only 8.7 percentage points above foreign rates. Notably, China imposes higher tariffs on 10 products for every one Chinese product subject to a higher U.S. tariff, and India has an even higher ratio of 13 to one.

Given these challenges, President Trump advocated for the USRTA, which would enable the U.S. to negotiate with trading partners to lower their tariffs to U.S. levels. If they refuse, the U.S. could raise its tariffs to match the foreign partner's tariffs. A poll conducted shortly after the introduction of the USRTA found that 80% of respondents supported the act. The goal is not to raise tariffs indiscriminately but to use them as leverage to achieve fairer trade agreements.

Simulations conducted by the White House Office of Trade and Manufacturing Policy estimated the impact of the USRTA on the U.S. trade deficit. In one scenario, if trading partners lowered their tariffs to match U.S. levels, the U.S. trade deficit could be reduced by $58.3 billion. In another scenario, if the U.S. raised its tariffs to match higher foreign tariffs, the deficit could be reduced by $63.6 billion. This could potentially create between 350,000 and 380,000 jobs.

For key U.S. trading partners like China, India, and the European Union, implementing the USRTA could lead to significant reductions in bilateral trade deficits. For instance, if China and the EU were pressured to lower their tariffs, the U.S. trade deficit with these regions could decrease by $18.5 billion and $8.0 billion, respectively. If the U.S. instead raised its tariffs to mirror those of China and the EU, the reductions could be much larger: $70.6 billion for China and $25.3 billion for the EU.

In some cases, particularly with countries like India and Taiwan, the impact could be even more pronounced. If India lowered its tariffs to U.S. levels, the bilateral trade deficit with the U.S. could decrease by 24%. If the U.S. raised its tariffs to match India's, the deficit could shrink by 88%.

These findings highlight the extent of unfair and nonreciprocal trade that the U.S. faces under WTO-MFN rules. Implementing the USRTA could significantly reduce the U.S. trade deficit and create hundreds of thousands of jobs. However, the U.S. would still face substantial trade deficits with some partners due to nonreciprocal nontariff barriers, such as Japan's use of these barriers to maintain a significant trade surplus with the U.S.

In response to these challenges, the USRTA would also provide the President with the authority to negotiate the reduction of nontariff barriers. If a foreign country refuses to lower these barriers, the President could impose reciprocal duties to counteract them.

In summary, the USRTA represents a significant step toward leveling the global trading field for American farmers, manufacturers, and workers, addressing the intrinsic unfairness of the current WTO-MFN system. While the USRTA is a powerful tool, other legislative options, like the border adjustment tax proposed by former House Speaker Paul Ryan, could also help address these trade imbalances by shifting U.S. corporate taxes from an origin-based to a destination-based system, leveling the playing field without relying solely on tariffs.

CHALLENGE #2: COMMUNIST CHINA'S ECONOMIC AGGRESSION AND QUEST FOR WORLD DOMINATION

The U.S.-China trade relationship is fraught with challenges, largely due to China's aggressive and protectionist trade policies since its accession to the WTO in 2001.

These policies have led to chronic and massive trade deficits for the U.S. Beyond traditional trade tactics, China employs industrial strategies and technology transfer policies designed to shift global manufacturing and supply chains to China, bolstering its economic and military power.

The Chinese Communist Party (CCP) aims to strengthen China's defense industrial base and global dominance, with the ultimate goal of surpassing the U.S. as the world's leading superpower by 2049. The American president who takes office in 2025 will need to decide whether to continue negotiating with China, despite its history of bad faith, or to pursue economic and financial decoupling as a more effective response to China's aggression.

Institutionalized Aggression: China's economic strategy includes high tariffs, nontariff barriers, currency manipulation, exploitation of sweatshop labor, and dumping of subsidized exports. It also engages in widespread counterfeiting and piracy, with China being the largest source of counterfeit goods globally. China further uses "debt trap" diplomacy, offering substantial loans to developing countries in exchange for natural resources, thus gaining a competitive edge in global markets.

Technology-Forcing Policies: The CCP forces foreign companies to transfer technology to Chinese firms as a condition for market access. This policy is supported by state-sponsored intellectual property theft and espionage, which has targeted key industries like electronics, telecommunications, and pharmaceuticals. The theft of trade secrets alone costs the U.S. between $180 billion and $540 billion annually.

Information Harvesting and Investment: China sends over 300,000 nationals to study and work in U.S. universities and research institutions, where they often acquire technologies critical to military systems, leading to potential violations of U.S. export control laws. Additionally, Chinese state-backed entities invest heavily in U.S. high-tech industries, acquiring cutting-edge technologies that bolster China's strategic goals.

Policy Responses: Given the breadth and depth of China's economic aggression, the U.S. must consider a range of policy responses. These could include expanding tariffs on Chinese goods, incentivizing the onshoring of American production, banning Chinese investment in high-tech industries, and reducing U.S. dependency on Chinese supply chains. Further negotiations with China are seen as fruitless, and a strategy of decoupling is suggested as a more effective means of countering China's ambitions.

YES, TRADE DEFICITS MATTER

The notion that "trade deficits don't matter" has often been used to oppose fair trade policies aimed at reducing the U.S.'s chronic trade deficit. However, Warren Buffett likens America's behavior to a wealthy family selling off parts of their farm and increasing their mortgage to maintain a higher standard of living than their income supports. This metaphor underscores the significant long-term risks associated with persistent trade deficits, which, contrary to the claims of some free trade advocates, do matter greatly for both economic and national security.

Economic Security: Trade deficits directly impact economic growth, which depends on four factors: consumption, government spending, business investment, and net exports. Reducing a trade deficit by increasing exports, as proposed by the U.S. Reciprocal Trade Act (USRTA) or through renegotiating trade deals, would boost GDP growth. For example, if the U.S. successfully pressured India and Japan to lower their tariffs and nontariff barriers, American exports would rise, thereby reducing the trade deficit, increasing GDP, and raising wages across the country. Additionally, when U.S. companies offshore production to countries with cheap labor or lax environmental regulations, it reduces domestic investment and increases the trade deficit, further slowing economic growth.

National Security: Trade deficits also have serious implications for national security. In the short term, trade deficits are balanced by foreign investments in the U.S., such as in government bonds and stocks. While this influx of foreign capital might seem beneficial by lowering mortgage rates and boosting the stock market, it leads to a massive transfer of American wealth offshore. As foreign entities, particularly those from rival nations like China, accumulate U.S. assets, they gain increasing control over key elements of the U.S. economy, including its manufacturing and defense-industrial base. This scenario poses a significant risk: America's freedom and prosperity could be jeopardized not by military conflict but through economic dominance achieved via persistent trade deficits. Moreover, in a broader conflict, the U.S. could find itself vulnerable if its defense industrial base has been outsourced, leaving the country dependent on foreign powers for critical supplies.

In conclusion, trade deficits matter deeply for both economic and national security reasons. It's essential to bring America's trade into balance through policies that promote free, fair, balanced, and reciprocal trade. This approach is vital to safeguarding the country's economic future and national security.

PERSONNEL IS TRADE POLICY

Having clear trade and industrial policies is crucial for achieving economic and national security goals, but it's equally important to have the right personnel in place to implement these policies effectively. The experiences of the Nixon, Reagan, and Trump Administrations highlight the adage that "personnel is policy," meaning that having the wrong people in key positions can lead to ineffective or counterproductive trade policies.

During the Trump Administration, there were significant internal conflicts among key advisers and Cabinet officials regarding international trade and how to handle China's economic aggression. Despite President Trump's bold actions on trade, some of his initiatives were undermined by personnel who did not fully support his vision of fair, balanced, and reciprocal trade.

The most critical position in shaping and executing trade policy is that of the United States Trade Representative (USTR). Historically, Republican USTRs have often been free traders who focused on expanding global trade without challenging the protectionist practices of America's trading partners. However, Trump's appointment of Robert E. Lighthizer marked a departure from this tradition. Lighthizer was not only knowledgeable about the legal mechanisms available to the President but was also committed to advancing Trump's trade agenda. The next Administration should prioritize finding someone with a similar alignment and dedication for this role.

Another essential position is the Under Secretary of Commerce for International Trade, who oversees the International Trade Administration. This agency plays a crucial role in imposing antidumping (AD) and countervailing duties (CVD) to combat trade practices that harm American industries, such as dumping products below cost or unfairly subsidizing exports.

Within the White House, it's also vital that the National Security Adviser, the Chairman of the Council of Economic Advisers (CEA), and the Director of the National Economic Council (NEC) share a unified vision on trade policy. Unfortunately, during much of Trump's tenure, there was a lack of alignment among these key figures, which hindered the effective implementation of trade policies.

The Secretary of Defense also plays a surprisingly significant role in trade policy, particularly in relation to Section 232 of the Trade Expansion Act of 1962. This section gives the President authority to reduce imports that threaten national security. While the Commerce Department leads these cases, they require the Defense Secretary's approval to proceed. Trump's efforts to impose steel and aluminum tariffs were initially resisted by Defense Secretary James Mattis, who did not fully grasp the administration's view that economic security is integral to national security.

Despite the exploitation of American industries and workers by the international trading system and China's economic aggression, entrenched political forces benefit from maintaining the status quo. The lesson of this chapter is clear: America's economic and military strength is continually undermined by a predatory China and an unfair global trading system. Addressing these challenges is essential for restoring American greatness. Ignoring them will only further weaken the U.S. manufacturing and defense industrial base.

THE CASE FOR FREE TRADE

Trade policy is not merely about the exchange of goods and services; it is a reflection of American identity and values. It asks whether America trusts in its tradition of entrepreneurship and innovation or whether it will emulate other nations' strong-arm trade practices. The decisions made in trade policy reflect what Americans believe about themselves and their future.

A Conservative Vision for Trade

This vision is rooted in a belief in the strength of America's founding institutions, its economy, and its people. It acknowledges the progress the U.S. has made over the decades but also recognizes the limitations of trade policy. Trade policy is most effective when it is focused on its primary goals: lowering consumer prices, opening new markets, and helping American workers and businesses specialize in what they do best. It is important to recognize that trade policy alone cannot create jobs or solve every policy problem, as labor force size is more tied to population than to trade.

Recent trends in trade policy have seen an increase in the inclusion of trade-unrelated provisions, such as labor, environmental, and intellectual property regulations, within trade agreements. These provisions, which were initially side agreements in NAFTA, have become central in newer agreements like the United States–Mexico–Canada Agreement (USMCA) and the Indo-Pacific Economic Framework for Prosperity (IPEF). A conservative trade policy should limit these non-trade-related provisions to avoid diluting the core purpose of trade agreements and to prevent them from being hijacked by special interests.

Trade Policy in Foreign Affairs

While trade is not the centerpiece of American foreign policy, it plays a crucial supporting role, particularly in strengthening alliances and countering threats from countries like

China and Russia. Trade can be used strategically to make economic and cultural inroads in adversarial nations. The next American President should leverage trade policy to enhance national security and bolster international alliances.

Lessons from American History

The history of American trade policy offers valuable lessons. In the 19th century, while international tariffs were high, the growth of the internal U.S. market and Western expansion enabled continued economic prosperity. The U.S. Constitution's creation of the world's largest free trade area was a deliberate move that allowed for unprecedented economic growth and specialization. This growth was further fueled by a steady decline in tariffs after World War II, which opened up international markets and allowed for more specialization and innovation.

Fighting Pessimistic Bias

A key challenge for conservative policymakers is combating the pessimistic bias that paints the U.S. economy as being in decline. Despite shifts from agriculture to manufacturing and then to services, the U.S. labor force has remained robust, and the economy has continued to grow. Trade has played a significant role in this growth, making a wide range of goods more affordable and accessible to Americans. In 2022, despite concerns about manufacturing job growth, the U.S. saw a low unemployment rate and record-high real per capita GDP, demonstrating the ongoing strength of the American economy.

In conclusion, a conservative approach to trade policy should focus on maintaining the integrity of trade agreements by keeping them free of unrelated provisions, leveraging trade for strategic foreign policy goals, and fostering a realistic and optimistic view of America's economic future.

IMPLEMENTING THE CONSERVATIVE VISION

To bring the conservative vision for trade to life, the next Administration must take several concrete actions, balancing the needs of economic growth, national security, and conservative principles. These actions include:

- **Tariff Relief**: End tariffs imposed under Sections 232, 201, and 301 to reduce consumer costs, strengthen supply chains, and boost manufacturing. Work with Congress to repeal these provisions to prevent future abuses.

- **Resist Trade Adjustment Assistance**: Avoid increasing trade adjustment assistance, which is often misused for progressive agendas. Support displaced workers without favoring one group over another.

- **Remove Supply Chain Restrictions**: Eliminate unnecessary regulations that limit supply chain flexibility, as seen in the baby formula shortage, to enhance resilience.

- **Enact Mutual Recognition Policies**: Simplify regulations by recognizing safety standards from allied nations like the EU and Japan, reducing costs and opening markets.

- **Close the Export–Import Bank**: End subsidies that primarily benefit a few large corporations and foreign governments, which often run counter to U.S. economic and foreign policy interests.

- **Restore Trade Promotion Authority (TPA)**: Work with Congress to renew TPA, enabling faster negotiation of trade agreements with key allies while keeping trade agreements focused on trade-related issues.

- **Revitalize or Replace the WTO**: Restore the WTO's dispute resolution process or create a new organization for liberal democracies that avoids the pitfalls of the current WTO.

- **Adopt a Strategic China Policy**: Implement a comprehensive strategy to counter China's aggressive economic policies, including targeted tariffs and rejoining the Trans-Pacific Partnership (TPP).

Tariff Relief and Inflation Control

The post-2017 tariffs have raised consumer prices and hurt industries that rely on imported goods, such as automotive and agriculture. By repealing these tariffs, the Administration can lower costs for American families and businesses. Additionally, repealing tariff provisions will prevent future misuse by Presidents and ensure that Congress retains its constitutional authority over trade.

Strengthening American Manufacturing

Despite claims of decline, American manufacturing is at an all-time high in terms of output, largely due to increased productivity. The focus should be on maintaining this momentum through policies that support innovation and efficiency, rather than resorting to protectionism or industrial policy that could stifle growth.

Addressing Retaliatory Tariffs

Tariffs not only raise prices domestically but also invite retaliatory measures from trading partners. These retaliatory tariffs, particularly those imposed by China and the EU, have disproportionately affected American farmers and industries like Harley-Davidson. The next Administration must undo the damage by eliminating these tariffs and fostering more cooperative trade relationships.

Undoing Protectionism
The normalization of protectionist policies under the Trump and Biden Administrations has been detrimental to the U.S. economy. The next conservative Administration must work to reverse these trends and restore a commitment to free trade.

Dealing with Economic Disruption
While trade can cause short-term job displacement, it is a minor factor compared to technological change. Policies should focus on easing this disruption through broader economic reforms rather than imposing trade restrictions.

Trade Adjustment Assistance
While trade adjustment assistance can be useful, it should be approached with caution to avoid misuse by progressive interests. If necessary, direct cash transfers are a more flexible and less politically fraught method of support.

Addressing Supply Chain Vulnerabilities
The baby formula shortage highlighted the risks of protectionist policies. By promoting openness and reducing restrictions, the next Administration can create more resilient supply chains and prevent future crises.

Mutual Recognition of Standards
Implementing mutual recognition of regulatory standards with allies can significantly reduce trade barriers, opening new markets for U.S. products and giving consumers access to more affordable goods.

Repealing the Jones Act
The Jones Act has decimated the U.S. shipbuilding industry and raised costs for domestic shipping. Repealing or significantly reforming this century-old law would bolster U.S. economic and energy security.

Trade and Inflation
While trade liberalization alone cannot solve inflation, it can help by lowering costs and boosting economic growth, making it a valuable tool in managing price stability.

Trade and Foreign Policy
Trade policy should support broader U.S. foreign policy goals, including strengthening alliances and countering threats from authoritarian regimes. This includes negotiating new trade agreements, reforming the WTO, and developing a comprehensive strategy to deal with China.

ANALYSIS: tax cuts for the wealthy

The 2025 Project, a conservative plan for the next Republican president, includes a shockingly regressive tax agenda that would dramatically cut taxes for big business and high-income earners at the expense of everyone else.

In an "intermediate" reform, they propose slashing the corporate tax rate from 21% to 18%, allowing full expensing of capital expenditures, and repealing the recent 15% corporate minimum tax and 1% tax on stock buybacks. The estate tax rate would also be capped at 20% and the temporarily high exemption amount of $12.9 million per person would become permanent. Individual tax rates would decline across the board, with the top rate falling from 37% to 33%.

On international taxes, they want to cut levies on global intangible low-taxed income (GILTI) from the current 10.5% (rising to 13.125% in 2026) to no higher than 12.5%. Credits for foreign taxes on GILTI would increase. But the plan is short on specifics and ignores how reducing expense allocations could allow corporations to completely avoid U.S. tax on foreign income.

The authors demonstrate their ideological bias by smearing the OECD, IMF and World Bank as "left-wing" organizations that the U.S. should defund and abandon merely for daring to suggest that America should make its tax system more equitable.

Their "fundamental reform" opens the door to radical national sales taxes, VATs, flat taxes or cash-flow taxes that would likely eliminate corporate and individual income taxes and payroll taxes that fund Social Security and Medicare. Three of the four options would tax only businesses, not individuals.

A "destination-based cash flow tax" would go even further, subsidizing exports while taxing imports. While the authors claim exchange rates would adjust to offset these distortions, it's clear their true aim is to introduce border-adjusted taxes as tariffs by another name.

The IRS would be hamstrung and politicized under the plan. After rescinding the agency's recent budget increase, its top officials would become political appointees, imperiling its independence and professionalism. The plan calls for restraining information reporting that helps catch tax cheats and for easing penalties on tax avoiders and improper collections.

Belying the plan's lip service about repealing tax breaks, other sections call for new credits and deductions for private school vouchers, non-custodial parents, rural housing, and companies relocating from China.

The overall thrust is unmistakable - to radically tilt the tax code even further in favor of corporations and the rich. By ignoring Social Security, the plan ducks the key driver of long-term deficits. And the lack of any figures on revenue or distributional impacts is telling.

If these ideas become law under a reelected President Trump, especially if Republicans control Congress, inequality will soar, deficits and debt will explode, and critical programs and investments will be starved of funding. The 2025 Project isn't a plan for broadly shared prosperity - it's a shameless giveaway to those who least need it.

HOW COULD THIS IMPACT YOU?

Millions of low- and middle-income families would likely see their taxes rise substantially under Project 2025's tax proposals.

Brendan Duke of the Center for American Progress calculates that a middle-class family earning $100,000 per year with two kids would owe an extra $2,600 in federal income tax under a 15% flat tax due to the elimination of the 10% and 12% brackets, according to an analysis. Scrapping the Child Tax Credit would cost them another $6,600 compared to the current system.

In contrast, a couple with two children making $5 million annually would get a whopping $325,000 tax cut.

"That 15% bracket is a very big deal in terms of raising taxes on middle-class families," the analysis found.

Millions of households making under $168,000 would probably pay more with a 15% rate. Today, the bottom 50% of taxpayers, who earn below $46,000, have an effective 3.3% tax rate after deductions, credits and other benefits.

Other Project 2025 economic proposals include:

- Slashing the corporate tax rate further to 18% from 21%, which was cut from 35% in 2017's Tax Cuts and Jobs Act
- Cutting the capital gains tax on high earners to 15% from 20% currently
- Repealing green energy credits from the Inflation Reduction Act
- Potentially imposing a national consumption tax like a sales tax
- Removing the Fed's full employment mandate

SECTION 5: INDEPENDENT REGULATORY AGENCIES

The FCC needs to change course and bring new urgency to achieving four main goals: Reining in Big Tech; Promoting national security; Unleashing economic prosperity; and Ensuring FCC accountability and good governance. – Page 825

The following summary conveys the content of the document accurately and objectively, without endorsing or critiquing the perspectives of the original authors.

Summary

The text begins by introducing independent commissions loosely affiliated with the executive branch. These commissions are described as "constitutionally problematic" due to the President's inability to remove appointees, despite having the power to appoint them. However, their legitimacy has been generally upheld by courts, and the next Administration has an opportunity to use them "as forces for good" through wise appointments.

The importance of appointing the next chairman of the Federal Communications Commission (FCC) is emphasized. FCC Commissioner Brendan Carr notes that the chairman "is empowered with significant authority that is not shared" with other members. Carr outlines four main goals for the FCC under new leadership: "Reining in Big Tech; Promoting national security; Unleashing economic prosperity; and Ensuring FCC accountability and good governance."

Carr argues that the FCC has a crucial role in addressing "threats to individual liberty posed by corporations that are abusing dominant positions in the market," particularly in relation to Big Tech's influence on political discourse. He advocates for increased transparency from Big Tech companies and suggests reinterpreting Section 230 to eliminate "expansive, non-textual immunities" that courts have granted to these companies.

The text highlights the FCC's actions during the Trump Administration regarding national security threats posed by the Chinese Communist Party, including placing Huawei on its Covered List. Carr expresses concerns about TikTok's risks to U.S. national security and calls for its ban. He also warns about U.S. businesses inadvertently aiding China's artificial intelligence goals and recommends "a comprehensive plan that aims to stop U.S. entities from directly or indirectly contributing to China's malign AI goals."

Regarding the Federal Election Commission (FEC), former Commissioner Hans von Spakovsky emphasizes the need for the Justice Department to "only prosecute clear violations" of the Federal Election Campaign Act. He stresses the importance of maintaining the FEC's bipartisan structure to prevent it from being "weaponized" and opposes efforts to change its composition to an odd number of members.

The summary concludes with brief mentions of the Securities and Exchange Commission (SEC) and the Federal Trade Commission (FTC). David R. Burton argues that the SEC should focus on "reducing impediments to capital formation" rather than pursuing a costly "climate change" agenda. Adam Candeub discusses the FTC's role in using antitrust law to combat the negative effects of dominant firms on democratic principles. He recommends increased cooperation between the FTC and state Attorneys General to enhance enforcement policies in key sectors.

CHAPTER 27: FINANCIAL REGULATORY AGENCIES

The CFPB is a highly politicized, damaging, and utterly unaccountable federal agency. It is unconstitutional. – Page 839

Key Policy Proposals

The proposals outlined in this chapter represent a significant rollback of essential regulations that safeguard the financial system and protect consumers. The recommendations focus primarily on dismantling or weakening the very institutions that were established to prevent the kind of unchecked corporate behavior that led to the 2008 financial crisis.

DISMANTLING OF THE SEC'S REGULATORY FRAMEWORK

The suggestion that the SEC should reduce its regulatory oversight under the guise of "reducing impediments to capital formation" is deeply flawed. The SEC's role in ensuring transparency and accountability in the markets is critical to maintaining investor confidence and preventing fraudulent activities. The proposal to abolish the Public Company Accounting Oversight Board (PCAOB) and fold its functions into the SEC would only dilute the specialized oversight required to monitor corporate accounting practices. This move risks increasing the likelihood of corporate malfeasance, similar to what was seen in the Enron scandal, where inadequate oversight led to massive fraud and economic harm.

Moreover, the proposed elimination of the SEC's climate change reporting rule is shortsighted and dangerous. Climate-related risks are not only real but are also material to investors. By disregarding the importance of these disclosures, the policy fails to acknowledge the long-term financial risks posed by climate change, which could result in significant economic disruptions. Investors deserve transparency regarding these risks, and the costs associated with these disclosures are justified given the potential for future financial instability.

ATTACKS ON DIVERSITY AND INCLUSION

The chapter's stance against diversity, equity, and inclusion (DEI) initiatives within financial regulation is a step backward. By proposing to eliminate DEI offices and regulations that promote equitable representation, the policy ignores the benefits of diversity in decision-making and governance. Diverse boards and leadership teams bring a broader range of perspectives, which has been shown to improve corporate performance and resilience. Disbanding these efforts undercuts progress toward a more inclusive and fair financial system, one that reflects the demographics of the broader society and ensures that all groups have a voice in the economic policies that affect them.

WEAKENING OF THE CFPB

The call to abolish the Consumer Financial Protection Bureau (CFPB) is perhaps the most egregious recommendation. The CFPB was established in the wake of the 2008 financial crisis to protect consumers from predatory financial practices. It has been instrumental in holding financial institutions accountable, recovering billions of dollars for consumers, and ensuring fair practices in the market. Labeling the CFPB as "unaccountable" and "politicized" overlooks the essential role it plays in a balanced regulatory ecosystem. Without the CFPB, consumers would be left vulnerable to the very abuses that contributed to the last financial meltdown—abuses like deceptive lending practices and hidden fees that prey on the most financially vulnerable populations.

CONSEQUENCES OF DEREGULATION

The overarching consequence of these proposed policies is a return to the kind of unregulated, unchecked financial environment that led to severe economic crises in the past. By dismantling critical oversight bodies, weakening consumer protections, and undermining diversity initiatives, these proposals would create a less transparent, less accountable, and more inequitable financial system. The result would likely be greater financial instability, increased corporate malfeasance, and a widening gap between the wealthy and the middle class.

In short, these policies represent a significant step backward. Instead of building on the progress made since the financial crisis to create a more stable, fair, and inclusive financial system, these proposals would dismantle the very safeguards that protect the economy and its participants from the excesses of unbridled capitalism. The need for strong, effective regulation has never been more critical, and rolling back these protections would have dire consequences for the stability and fairness of the U.S. financial system.

Summary

This chapter of Mandate for Leadership was written by David R. Burton. The following summary conveys the content of the document accurately and objectively, without endorsing or critiquing the perspectives of the original authors.

The chapter critiques the current state of U.S. securities laws, emphasizing that nearly nine decades of amendments have resulted in a complex and incoherent regulatory regime. This complexity is exemplified by the SEC's proposed climate change reporting rule, which would significantly increase the costs for public companies and potentially reduce the number of companies available for public investment. The argument is made that the SEC should be reducing barriers to capital formation rather than increasing them.

Key proposals for reform include:

- **Simplified Securities Disclosure System**: Establishing three categories of firms—private, intermediate, and public—each with tailored disclosure requirements and specified secondary markets.

- **SEC and Financial Regulator Reforms**: The chapter argues for significant restructuring of the SEC, including the abolition of the Public Company Accounting Oversight Board (PCAOB) and the Financial Industry Regulatory Authority (FINRA), with their functions to be absorbed into the SEC to improve transparency and efficiency.

- **Opposition to DEI in Financial Regulation**: The text condemns the promotion of diversity, equity, and inclusion (DEI) within financial regulators, advocating for the elimination of DEI offices and regulations, and emphasizing the importance of equal protection under the law and merit-based decisions.

Entrepreneurial Capital Formation

The chapter highlights the barriers entrepreneurs face in raising capital due to current regulations, proposing several key reforms:

- **Streamlining Regulations**: Simplification of Regulation A (small issues exemption) and Regulation CF (crowdfunding) to make it easier for small businesses to raise capital without excessive regulatory burdens.

- **Reform of Accredited Investor Rules**: Either broaden the definition of accredited investor or eliminate the restriction to allow more individuals access to private investments.

- **Exemptions for Small Offerings and Finders**: Provide exemptions from registration requirements for small offerings and intermediaries, reducing regulatory hurdles for entrepreneurs.

- **Permanent EGC Exemptions**: Make Emerging Growth Company (EGC) exemptions permanent to provide ongoing regulatory relief for smaller firms.

Better Capital Markets

The chapter offers several proposals to improve the functioning of capital markets:

- **Preemption of State Regulations**: Advocates for the SEC to preempt state-level securities regulations to create a more uniform national market and reduce compliance costs.

- **Termination of the CAT Program**: Recommends ending the Consolidated Audit Trail (CAT) program due to its high costs and privacy concerns.

- **Abolition of Rule 144**: Calls for the removal of resale restrictions on securities to increase market liquidity and reduce unnecessary regulatory constraints.

- **Prohibition of Non-Material Disclosures**: Strongly opposes the SEC's proposed requirements for non-financial disclosures, such as those related to climate change, arguing they do not benefit investors and impose significant costs.

- **Repeal of Dodd–Frank Disclosures**: Suggests repealing certain Dodd–Frank mandated disclosures that are seen as burdensome and not directly beneficial to investors.

SEC Administration

The chapter discusses various administrative reforms necessary for the SEC to better fulfill its core mission:

- **Improved Data Reporting**: The SEC should publish more detailed and accurate data on securities offerings, markets, and law enforcement activities. An annual data book of time series data is proposed to enhance transparency and decision-making.

- **Resource Allocation**: SEC resources should be focused on core functions, reducing expenditures on ancillary activities that do not fall within the agency's statutory charge.

- **Commissioner Empowerment**: Any three SEC Commissioners should have the power to place items on the agenda and receive adequate staff support, even without the Chairman's approval. This change is aimed at improving the internal governance and responsiveness of the Commission.

- **Elimination of Administrative Proceedings**: The chapter advocates for the elimination of most administrative proceedings (APs) within the SEC, arguing that enforcement cases should be handled in district courts.

Alternatively, respondents in APs should have the option to choose whether their case is adjudicated in an SEC administrative law court or a federal court.

- **Delegation of Authority**: The SEC Chairman, along with possibly the U.S. Government Accountability Office (GAO), should review the delegation of authority within the SEC. The chapter suggests that such delegations be limited and subject to sunset provisions, ensuring accountability and regular review.

Commodities and Derivatives Markets

The chapter addresses the need for modernization and clarification in the regulation of commodities and derivatives markets:

- **Modernization of Commodity Definitions**: Congress should update the definition of "commodity" in the Commodity Exchange Act (CEA) to reflect current market realities, including the treatment of digital assets.

- **Clarification of Digital Asset Regulation**: Both the SEC and the Commodity Futures Trading Commission (CFTC) have failed to provide clear rules for digital assets, opting instead for regulation by enforcement. The chapter calls for joint regulation to define when digital assets should be treated as securities (regulated by the SEC) or as commodities (regulated by the CFTC). If regulatory agencies do not act, Congress should step in to enact legislation that clarifies these issues.

- **Position Limits and Market Liquidity**: The chapter suggests replacing the existing position limits rule with a more flexible system where exchanges set limits based on the specific needs of each market. This would enhance liquidity and reduce market volatility.

Commodity Futures Trading Commission (CFTC) Administration and Improved Commodities and Derivatives Markets

The chapter next addresses the Commodity Futures Trading Commission (CFTC), focusing on the need for administrative improvements and modernization of its regulatory framework for commodities and derivatives markets.

Key proposals include:

- **Modernization of Commodity Definitions**: The chapter emphasizes that the definition of "commodity" in the Commodity Exchange Act (CEA) needs updating to reflect current market realities, particularly with respect to digital assets. The existing definition is described as outdated, primarily listing agricultural commodities, and should be expanded to include digital assets and other modern commodities.

- **Clarification on Foreign Swap Trading Platforms**: The chapter calls for clear guidelines regarding when a foreign swap trading platform must register with the CFTC as a Swap Execution Facility (SEF). The current lack of clarity has led foreign platforms to either exclude U.S. participants or seek exemptions from registration, which hinders market access and liquidity. An express amendment to the CEA is proposed to define the circumstances that require registration.

- **CFTC Chairman's Authority**: There is a recommendation to amend the CEA to authorize the CFTC Chairman to remove the agency's Executive Director without a vote from the full Commission. This change aims to enhance the administrative efficiency and responsiveness of the CFTC.

- **Commissioners' Independence**: The chapter advocates for statutory provisions that establish fixed funding amounts for Commissioners' offices, adjusted for inflation. This would ensure that Commissioners do not need to seek budget or expense approvals from the Chairman or agency staff, thereby strengthening their independence and ability to perform their duties effectively.

- **Resource Allocation and Rulemaking Flexibility**: The CFTC should allocate more resources to its core functions, reducing expenditures on support operations. It also suggests replacing the existing position limits rule, which is seen as too rigid and market-distorting, with greater delegation of authority to exchanges to set appropriate limits for their markets.

- **Streamlining Rules and Definitions**: The chapter calls for a reduction in overly prescriptive rules that implement the CFTC's core principles, advocating for more flexible and principles-based regulation. It also proposes harmonizing the definitions of "U.S. Person" and "Guarantee" across different regulatory requirements, as these definitions currently vary depending on the specific rule or guidance, leading to confusion and compliance difficulties.

- **Removal of Regulatory Categories**: The chapter suggests eliminating certain regulatory categories like "affiliate conduit" and "foreign consolidated subsidiary," which were replaced by the concept of "Significant Risk

Subsidiary" in the 2020 Cross-Border Rule due to their broad and vague scope. This change would simplify compliance and reduce regulatory complexity.

Digital Assets

The text criticizes both the SEC and the CFTC for their inadequate handling of digital asset regulation, arguing that their reliance on enforcement rather than clear rules has been detrimental to the market. The chapter proposes:

- **Joint Regulation for Digital Assets**: A regulation that would clearly define when digital assets are considered securities (under SEC jurisdiction) or commodities (under CFTC jurisdiction), based on whether holders have rights to earnings, profits, or specific payments from the enterprise.
- **Legislative Action if Necessary**: If regulatory bodies do not act, the chapter urges Congress to pass legislation to establish clear guidelines for the treatment of digital assets, thereby providing a stable regulatory environment.

Improved Regulation of the Industry and SROs

The chapter discusses the need for enhanced oversight and reform of self-regulatory organizations (SROs):

- **Transparency and Accountability**: Proposes that FINRA and other SROs should open their board meetings to the public, make agendas available in advance, and publish minutes and rulemakings promptly. This would increase transparency and allow for greater public scrutiny.
- **Public Hearings and SEC Review**: Arbitration and disciplinary hearings conducted by SROs, such as FINRA, should be open to the public, with decisions subject to review by the SEC and limited judicial review.
- **Reform of SRO Fines**: The chapter argues that fines imposed by SROs should not be used to fund the SROs themselves, as this creates a conflict of interest. Instead, fines should go to an investor reimbursement fund or the U.S. Treasury.
- **Cost-Benefit Analysis**: All SRO rulemakings should be subject to meaningful cost-benefit analysis to ensure that regulations are justified and not overly burdensome.
- **Annual Reporting to Congress**: Each SRO should be required to submit a detailed annual report to Congress, covering its budget, fees, enforcement activities, and rulemaking processes.
- **Congressional Oversight**: The text calls for annual congressional oversight hearings on SROs to ensure accountability and proper functioning.

Consumer Financial Protection Bureau (CFPB)

The chapter turns its attention to the Consumer Financial Protection Bureau (CFPB), established by the Dodd–Frank Act in 2010. The CFPB is described as a highly controversial and politicized agency that operates with little accountability due to its independence from congressional oversight and its unique funding mechanism through the Federal Reserve.

Key criticisms and proposed reforms include:

- **Lack of Accountability**: The CFPB's structure, led by a single director who can only be removed for cause, has been challenged in court. The chapter cites the 2020 Supreme Court case *Seila Law LLC v. CFPB*, which ruled that this structure violates the separation of powers. The chapter argues that the CFPB is "utterly unaccountable" and should be abolished, with its functions returned to traditional banking regulators and the Federal Trade Commission (FTC).
- **Funding Mechanism**: The CFPB's funding, which bypasses the traditional congressional appropriations process, is criticized for insulating the agency from political oversight. The chapter points to a 2022 ruling by the Fifth Circuit in *Community Financial Services Association of America v. CFPB*, which found that the CFPB's funding mechanism violates the Appropriations Clause of the Constitution. The chapter supports this decision and advocates for redirecting any unused civil penalty funds collected by the CFPB to the U.S. Treasury, rather than allowing the agency to allocate them at its discretion.
- **Criticism of Enforcement Practices**: The chapter describes the CFPB's enforcement actions as often being politically motivated, with fines and penalties used to fund left-leaning activist groups. This, it argues, creates a "shakedown" mechanism that is detrimental to the rule of law.
- **Proposed Legislative Reforms**: Until the CFPB can be abolished, the chapter suggests several legislative measures to curb its power:
    - **Repeal Section 1071 of Dodd–Frank**: This section requires financial institutions to collect and report data on small business lending, which the chapter argues increases costs and limits access to capital for small businesses.
    - **Limit Enforcement Actions**: The CFPB should be prohibited from taking enforcement actions that are not based on rules developed through a proper rulemaking process, complying with the Administrative Procedure Act (APA).
    - **Choice of Forum for Respondents**: Similar to the earlier discussion on the SEC, the chapter suggests that respondents in CFPB administrative actions should be allowed to choose between having their case heard in an administrative law court or a federal court.
    - **Clarification of "Deceptive, Unfair, and Abusive" Practices**: The chapter calls for a more precise definition of these terms to limit the scope of the CFPB's enforcement actions and reduce the regulatory burden on businesses.

CHAPTER 28: FEDERAL COMMUNICATIONS COMMISSION

It is time for an Administration to put in place a comprehensive plan that aims to stop U.S. entities from directly or indirectly contributing to China's malign AI goals. – Page 853

Key Policy Proposals

The chapter presents a series of policy recommendations that warrant a critical examination for their potential impact on the broader public interest and the principles of fairness, democracy, and economic equity.

REINING IN BIG TECH:

The proposal to reinterpret Section 230 of the Communications Act to eliminate judicially expanded immunities is a dangerous move that could stifle free speech and innovation on the Internet. Section 230 has been a cornerstone of the open Internet, allowing platforms to host a wide range of content without being held liable for third-party postings. The FCC's push to narrow these protections risks empowering the government to dictate what content platforms can or cannot allow, which could lead to over-censorship and a chilling effect on free expression. Moreover, this approach ignores the complexity of online content moderation and the necessity for platforms to have flexibility in managing harmful or illegal content.

The proposal to impose transparency rules on Big Tech, akin to those applied to broadband providers, seems well-intentioned but overlooks the practical challenges. Requiring platforms to disclose detailed information about their algorithms and content moderation decisions could be weaponized by bad actors who seek to exploit the system. While transparency is essential, it must be balanced with the need to protect platforms from constant legal battles and to allow them to operate effectively in a dynamic online environment.

PROMOTING NATIONAL SECURITY

The recommendation to ban TikTok due to its ties to the Chinese government is a stark example of overreach. While national security concerns are valid, an outright ban on a platform used by millions of Americans for free expression sets a dangerous precedent. It suggests a willingness to curtail personal freedoms in the name of security without exploring less extreme measures, such as enhancing data protection regulations or increasing oversight of foreign-owned tech companies.

The expansion of the FCC's Covered List to include more companies with ties to China reflects a broader strategy of economic decoupling, which could have significant consequences for global trade and innovation. By continually adding entities to this list, the U.S. risks isolating itself from the global technology market, driving up costs for American consumers, and stifling innovation by reducing competition. Furthermore, these measures could provoke retaliatory actions from China, escalating tensions and potentially harming American businesses operating abroad.

UNLEASHING ECONOMIC PROSPERITY

The proposal to refill America's spectrum pipeline and streamline infrastructure rules for broadband deployment is fundamentally sound but requires careful implementation. The focus on accelerating 5G deployment and modernizing infrastructure is crucial for maintaining global competitiveness. However, this push should not come at the expense of environmental standards or community input. The rush to deregulate could lead to the unchecked development that harms local communities and ecosystems, reinforcing the need for a balanced approach that integrates public concerns with the need for technological advancement.

ENSURING FCC ACCOUNTABILITY AND GOOD GOVERNANCE

The criticism of current broadband spending policies as wasteful fails to acknowledge the significant strides made in expanding Internet access to underserved communities. The current administration's investment in broadband infrastructure through the American Rescue Plan Act and the Infrastructure Investment and Jobs Act represents a necessary response to decades of underinvestment. Rather than scaling back these efforts, the focus should be on enhancing oversight and ensuring that funds are used effectively to bridge the digital divide, particularly in rural and low-income areas.

The call to rescind outdated FCC regulations and rely more on competition ignores the reality that unchecked market forces often lead to monopolies and reduced consumer choice. The FCC's role in regulating media ownership and ensuring universal service is vital in preserving a competitive, diverse media landscape. Deregulation could lead to further consolidation in the telecommunications industry, reducing the diversity of voices and limiting access to essential services for marginalized communities.

The chapter's recommendations reflect a clear bias toward deregulation and a heavy-handed approach to national security that, if implemented, could have far-reaching consequences for free speech, innovation, and global economic relations. While there

are aspects of the proposals that align with the need for modernization and security, they must be tempered with a commitment to preserving democratic principles, protecting consumer rights, and fostering an inclusive digital economy. The path forward requires not just cutting regulations but also ensuring that the policies in place serve the public good and protect the most vulnerable in society.

Summary

This chapter of Mandate for Leadership was written by Brendan Carr. The following summary conveys the content of the document accurately and objectively, without endorsing or critiquing the perspectives of the original authors.

The **Federal Communications Commission (FCC)** aims to promote freedom of speech, boost economic opportunities, ensure universal access to next-generation connectivity, and enable private sector growth through reforms that support diverse viewpoints and secure communications networks.

OVERVIEW AND BACKGROUND

The FCC, an independent regulatory agency, oversees interstate and international communications via radio, television, wire, satellite, and cable. It is led by five Commissioners, appointed by the President, who serve staggered five-year terms. The Chairperson, chosen by the President, wields significant power, including setting the agency's agenda. The FCC's 2023 budget is approximately $390.2 million, funded primarily through regulatory fees and spectrum auctions, which have generated over $200 billion for the U.S. Treasury.

HIGH-PROFILE FCC MATTERS

Key issues include the regulation of **Section 230** within the Communications Act, the transition to 5G technology, and the administration of the **Universal Service Fund (USF)**, a $9 billion program that subsidizes rural broadband and low-income initiatives, funded through fees on consumer telephone bills.

POLICY PRIORITIES

The FCC needs to focus on four primary goals:

1. Reining in Big Tech:
The FCC should address the significant influence and power of Big Tech, which threatens individual liberties by controlling access to information and suppressing diverse political viewpoints. Proposed actions include:

- **Eliminating judicially created immunities under Section 230** by issuing an order that aligns with a 2020 petition filed during the Trump Administration. This action seeks to narrow the broad immunity currently enjoyed by tech companies.

- **Imposing transparency rules on Big Tech**, similar to those applied to broadband providers, to ensure that platforms like Google and Facebook provide clear and consistent terms of service and accountability through transparent appeals processes.

- **Supporting legislation to reform Section 230** by collaborating with Congress to ensure that Internet companies cannot censor protected speech while still benefiting from Section 230 protections. This includes applying anti-discrimination provisions to Big Tech, akin to the social media law upheld by the Fifth Circuit Court of Appeals in Texas.

- **Empowering consumers** by encouraging Congress to develop rules that give users more control over their online experiences, such as choosing their own content filters and fact-checkers. Additionally, the FCC should work with Congress to strengthen protections against young children accessing social media.

- **Requiring Big Tech to contribute to the Universal Service Fund (USF)**, as these companies benefit from federally supported networks but currently do not pay into the fund. The FCC's funding mechanism, which relies on traditional telephone customers, is unsustainable, and Big Tech should be required to contribute.

2. Promoting National Security:
The FCC should continue to address national security threats, particularly those posed by the Chinese Communist Party (CCP). Key actions include:

- **Banning TikTok** due to its unacceptable risk to U.S. national security and potential for foreign influence campaigns.

- **Expanding the FCC's Covered List** to include more entities with ties to the CCP, ensuring the list is regularly updated to reflect corporate changes.

- **Closing loopholes** that allow banned entities like China Telecom to continue offering services in the U.S. on an unregulated basis.

- **Publishing a foreign adversary transparency list** to identify entities with significant ownership by foreign adversaries, such as China, Russia, and Iran.
- **Fully funding the federal "rip and replace" program** to ensure all insecure network gear is removed and replaced, addressing the current $3 billion shortfall.
- **Launching a Clean Standards Initiative** to counter the CCP's influence in global technology and telecommunications standards.
- **Stopping U.S. companies from aiding the CCP's AI ambitions** by preventing them from providing cloud computing services that enhance Beijing's AI capabilities.

3. Unleashing Economic Prosperity:

To advance economic opportunity, the FCC should:

- **Refill America's spectrum pipeline** by identifying specific airwaves for commercial use and setting aggressive timelines for FCC action.
- **Improve interagency coordination on spectrum issues**, particularly to avoid conflicts like those seen between the FCC and the Federal Aviation Administration (FAA) over 5G spectrum allocation.
- **Modernize infrastructure rules** to streamline the permitting process for broadband builds, especially on federal lands, and reduce costs and delays.
- **Advance America's space leadership** by expediting the approval process for low-earth orbit satellites like StarLink and Kuiper, which can bridge the digital divide and disrupt traditional regulatory frameworks.

4. Ensuring FCC Accountability and Good Governance:

The FCC must enhance oversight and eliminate outdated regulations:

- **End wasteful broadband spending policies** by ensuring that federal funds are directed to unserved communities rather than overbuilding existing networks.
- **Adopt a national broadband strategy** to coordinate federal efforts, avoid duplication, and ensure taxpayer money is used efficiently.
- **Review and rescind outdated FCC regulations**, particularly those that hinder competition and innovation, such as outdated media ownership rules and universal service requirements.

REINING IN BIG TECH

The FCC has a significant role in addressing the influence and power of Big Tech companies, which are seen as a threat to individual liberties by controlling information and suppressing diverse political viewpoints. The text argues that these corporations are not just exercising market power but abusing dominant positions. The FCC is encouraged to act on multiple fronts:

- **Eliminate Court-Added Immunities to Section 230:** The FCC should reinterpret Section 230 to remove broad immunities that courts have added to the statute. Justice Clarence Thomas has pointed out that courts have misconstrued Section 230 to provide sweeping immunity not supported by the statute's text. The FCC should clarify that Section 230(c)(1) only applies when platforms do not remove content provided by others and that Section 230(c)(2) should only protect platforms when they restrict access to certain materials.
- **Impose Transparency Rules on Big Tech:** The FCC should introduce transparency rules similar to those imposed on broadband providers. Big Tech companies like Google and Facebook should be required to disclose their practices, such as how they handle search results or content moderation. These platforms should also provide clear terms of service and establish transparent appeals processes to challenge content removal or account suspensions.
- **Support Legislative Reforms to Section 230:** The FCC should collaborate with Congress to create more comprehensive reforms to Section 230. This includes ensuring that Internet companies cannot censor protected speech while still enjoying Section 230 protections. The text references a social media law in Texas, upheld by the Fifth Circuit Court of Appeals, as a model for anti-discrimination provisions that could be applied to Big Tech.
- **Empower Consumers:** The FCC and Congress should work together to provide users with more control over their online experiences. This could involve allowing consumers to choose their own content filters and fact-checkers. Additionally, the FCC should focus on protecting children from accessing social media platforms despite age restrictions.
- **Require Big Tech to Contribute to the Universal Service Fund (USF):** Big Tech companies benefit from federally supported networks but do not currently contribute to the USF, which funds broadband and rural connectivity programs. The text argues that the FCC's current funding mechanism is unsustainable, and Big Tech should be required to contribute to the program.

PROMOTING NATIONAL SECURITY

The FCC has played a key role in national security, particularly in countering threats from the Chinese Communist Party (CCP). The text proposes several actions to strengthen this role:

- **Ban TikTok:** The text highlights the national security risks posed by TikTok, which could be used by Beijing for foreign influence campaigns. If the Biden Administration does not act, a new administration should ban the app on national security grounds.
- **Expand the FCC's Covered List:** The FCC should regularly update its Covered List, which includes companies like Huawei, to ensure it reflects changes in corporate names and structures. The list should include any company with ties to the CCP's surveillance state.
- **Close Loopholes Allowing Unregulated Operations:** Despite being banned from offering certain services in the U.S., entities like China Telecom continue to operate on an unregulated basis. The FCC should prohibit regulated carriers from interconnecting with insecure providers.
- **Publish a Foreign Adversary Transparency List:** The FCC should compile and publish a list of entities with more than 10% ownership by foreign adversaries, including China, Russia, Iran, Syria, and North Korea. This initiative is supported by a bipartisan bill introduced in the House of Representatives.
- **Fully Fund the "Rip and Replace" Program:** The text calls for full funding of the Secure and Trusted Communications Networks Reimbursement Program, which reimburses providers for removing insecure Huawei and ZTE gear. The program currently faces a $3 billion shortfall.
- **Launch a Clean Standards Initiative:** Building on the Trump Administration's Clean Networks program, a new administration should focus on preventing the CCP from influencing global technology and telecommunications standards.
- **Prevent U.S. Companies from Aiding the CCP's AI Ambitions:** The FCC should develop a comprehensive plan to prevent U.S. companies from indirectly supporting China's AI goals, such as by providing cloud computing services that enhance Beijing's AI capabilities.

UNLEASHING ECONOMIC PROSPERITY

The FCC must advance a pro-growth agenda to ensure that every American has access to next-generation connectivity, which is crucial for economic opportunity and community prosperity. The text outlines several key actions:

- **Refill America's Spectrum Pipeline:** The FCC should continue its efforts to free up airwaves for 5G and other wireless services, which is essential for maintaining U.S. leadership in wireless technology and driving economic growth.
- **Improve Interagency Coordination on Spectrum Issues:** The FCC should work with other federal agencies to resolve disputes over spectrum allocation. Better coordination is needed to ensure that both commercial and federal users have access to the spectrum resources they need.
- **Modernize Infrastructure Rules:** The FCC should streamline the permitting process for broadband infrastructure, particularly on federal lands. Outdated rules have slowed the deployment of necessary infrastructure, leaving many Americans without access to high-speed Internet.
- **Advance America's Space Leadership:** The FCC should expedite its review and approval of low-earth orbit satellite projects like StarLink and Kuiper, which have the potential to close the digital divide and disrupt existing regulatory frameworks.

ENSURING FCC ACCOUNTABILITY AND GOOD GOVERNANCE

The FCC needs to improve oversight and eliminate outdated regulations to ensure that federal technology and telecommunications programs are effective and accountable:

- **End Wasteful Broadband Spending:** The text criticizes current broadband spending policies for potentially wasting taxpayer money and failing to reach unserved communities. The FCC should direct funds to areas without adequate infrastructure rather than overbuilding existing networks.
- **Adopt a National Broadband Strategy:** The FCC should work with Congress to develop a coordinated national strategy for broadband initiatives. The current fragmented approach, with over 100 programs across 15 agencies, risks duplication and inefficiency.
- **Review and Rescind Outdated Regulations:** The FCC should conduct a comprehensive review of its regulations, eliminating those that are no longer necessary or that hinder competition and innovation. The agency should

focus on creating a regulatory environment that supports competition and technological advancements.

HOLDING GOVERNMENT ACCOUNTABLE

The FCC must improve oversight and governance to ensure that federal technology and telecommunications programs operate efficiently and effectively. The text emphasizes the need for a fresh approach to eliminate waste and outdated regulations:

- **End Wasteful Broadband Spending Policies:** The text criticizes current federal broadband spending as prone to waste and misallocation. It argues that recent increases in funding, such as those through the American Rescue Plan Act (ARPA) and the Infrastructure Investment and Jobs Act, have not been paired with proper oversight. The FCC should ensure that these funds are directed to genuinely unserved areas rather than being used to overbuild in regions already serviced by multiple providers. The Treasury Department's 2022 final rules for ARPA spending are singled out as problematic for allowing funds to be spent on upgrading existing high-speed networks rather than expanding access to underserved communities. The text calls for the elimination of government-funded overbuilding.

- **Adopt a National Coordinating Strategy:** The text underscores the need for a national broadband strategy to guide federal efforts and prevent inefficiency. It cites a U.S. Government Accountability Office (GAO) report

that highlights the fragmented nature of U.S. broadband initiatives, with over 100 programs spread across 15 agencies, leading to potential overlap and waste. The text stresses that a lack of guardrails on spending could result in significant waste, fraud, and abuse. A new administration should prioritize oversight, implement a coordinated strategy, and ask the FCC to review existing broadband programs to avoid duplication and improve efficiency.

- **Correct the FCC's Regulatory Trajectory:** The FCC's regulatory approach, rooted in New Deal-era policies, is viewed as outdated in light of rapid technological changes. The text calls for the FCC to embrace competition and innovation by eliminating heavy-handed regulations, particularly those adopted when communication technologies operated in isolated silos. For instance, outdated media ownership rules are seen as restricting investment and competition in a market now characterized by convergence and innovation, where cable providers, wireless companies, and satellite services increasingly overlap. The FCC should engage in a thorough review of its regulations, rescinding those that no longer serve the public interest and focusing on creating a market-friendly environment that fosters competition across a wide range of Internet providers.

CHAPTER 29: FEDERAL ELECTION COMMISSION

When taking any action related to the FEC, the President should keep in mind that, as former FEC Chairman Bradley Smith says, the "greater problem at the FEC has been overenforcement," not underenforcement as some critics falsely allege. – Page 866

Key Policy Proposals

The proposed reforms for the Federal Election Commission (FEC) represent a significant shift towards deregulation and reduced enforcement of campaign finance laws. These changes would have profound implications for the integrity of our electoral system and the influence of money in politics.

NOMINATION AUTHORITY

The proposal to maintain the current structure of three Republican and three Democrat commissioners, while seemingly balanced, perpetuates gridlock and inaction. This structure has led to numerous 3-3 splits on crucial enforcement decisions, effectively paralyzing the FEC's ability to enforce campaign finance laws. The suggestion to "temper" the choice of Democratic commissioners is a thinly veiled attempt to weaken enforcement further. This would exacerbate the already severe problem of the FEC's inability to take action against clear violations of campaign finance law.

DEPARTMENT OF JUSTICE OVERSIGHT

The proposed limitations on the Department of Justice's ability to prosecute campaign finance violations are deeply concerning. Instructing the DOJ to only prosecute "clear violations" and defer to FEC interpretations would severely hamper enforcement efforts. This approach ignores the fact that the DOJ has separate statutory authority and expertise in prosecuting complex financial crimes.The suggestion that the DOJ should not prosecute when there is a 3-3 split at the FEC is particularly problematic. It effectively allows deadlock at the FEC to prevent any enforcement action, even in cases of serious violations. This would create a dangerous loophole for bad actors to exploit.

LITIGATION AUTHORITY

Removing the FEC's independent litigation authority would be a significant blow to the agency's effectiveness. The proposal to have the DOJ handle all FEC litigation ignores the specialized expertise of FEC attorneys in campaign finance law. It would also potentially subject FEC enforcement to political interference from the executive branch.

LEGISLATIVE CHANGES

The proposed legislative changes would dramatically weaken campaign finance regulations:

1. Allowing commissioners to serve only a single six-year term without holdovers could lead to extended periods with a non-functional commission, as we've seen with other agencies like the Federal Election Commission.
2. Opposing efforts to change the FEC's structure to an odd number of commissioners ignores the current dysfunction of the agency. A 3-2 structure with a truly independent chair could break deadlocks and allow for more effective enforcement.
3. Raising contribution limits and indexing reporting requirements to inflation would allow more money to flow into the political system with less transparency. This would exacerbate the already outsized influence of wealthy donors in our elections.

4. Loosening restrictions on party committee coordination with candidates would effectively eliminate one of the few remaining barriers to unlimited spending in elections.

CONSEQUENCES

These proposed changes would collectively gut campaign finance enforcement and flood our political system with even more unaccountable money. The result would be:

1. Increased corruption and quid pro quo arrangements between donors and politicians.
2. A further tilting of the political playing field in favor of wealthy individuals and corporate interests.
3. Decreased transparency in political spending, making it harder for voters to make informed decisions.
4. Erosion of public trust in the integrity of our elections and democratic institutions.

Rather than these regressive changes, we need to strengthen the FEC's ability to enforce existing laws and enact new reforms to reduce the influence of money in politics. This should include stricter contribution limits, enhanced disclosure requirements, and a restructuring of the FEC to break the current deadlock and allow for effective enforcement.

Summary

This chapter of Mandate for Leadership was written by Hans A. von Spakovsky. The following summary conveys the content of the document accurately and objectively, without endorsing or critiquing the perspectives of the original authors.

The Federal Election Commission (FEC) is an independent federal agency established in 1975 to enforce the Federal Election Campaign Act (FECA) of 1971, as amended in 1974. The FEC regulates the raising and spending of funds in federal campaigns for Congress and the presidency, but has no authority over the administration of federal elections, which is handled by state governments. The FEC has exclusive civil enforcement authority over FECA, while the U.S. Justice Department handles criminal enforcement for knowing and willful violations. As an independent agency, the President's authority over the FEC is limited. The FEC's role is particularly sensitive as it regulates political speech and activity, which are protected by the First Amendment. As former FEC Commissioner Bradley Smith noted, the FEC's "regulation of campaign finance deeply implicates First Amendment principles of free speech and association." The chapter emphasizes that the FEC "regulates in one of the most sensitive areas of the Bill of Rights: political speech and political activity by citizens, candidates, political parties, and the voluntary membership organizations that represent Americans who share common views on a huge range of important and vital public policy issues."

NEEDED REFORMS

NOMINATION AUTHORITY

The President's primary power regarding the FEC is the appointment of six commissioners, subject to Senate confirmation. Commissioners serve single six-year terms but often continue serving past their expiration dates until replacements are confirmed. FECA mandates that no more than three commissioners may be from the same party, resulting in a traditional 3-3 split between Democrats and Republicans.A long-standing tradition involves the President consulting with the opposition party's Senate leader when nominating for their party's vacant seat. The chapter notes, "There is a long-held political tradition since the FEC's founding that when a commission slot held by a member of the opposition political party opens up, the President consults with, and nominates, the chosen nominee of the opposition party's leader in the Senate." This bipartisan approach has facilitated easy confirmations, with only one exception in the FEC's history.By 2025, five of the current commissioners' terms will have expired or be nearing expiration. The incoming President must ensure that new Republican nominees share the views of current commissioners who believe in limited regulation and protection of First Amendment rights. The President should also attempt to negotiate with the Democratic Party leader to avoid extreme views on overenforcement.

U.S. DEPARTMENT OF JUSTICE/FEC-RELATED ACTIVITIES

The President has control over the Department of Justice (DOJ) and can influence its approach to criminal enforcement of FECA. Key recommendations include:

1. Directing the DOJ to prosecute only clear FECA violations and avoid infringing on First Amendment activities.
2. Instructing the DOJ not to prosecute individuals under interpretations that the FEC disagrees with.
3. Ensuring the DOJ consults FEC actions, including prior enforcement decisions, regulations, and advisory opinions.
4. Avoiding prosecutions when the FEC commissioners are unable to reach a consensus on the law's requirements.

The chapter states, "It is fundamentally unfair for the DOJ to prosecute an individual for supposedly violating the law when the FEC has previously determined that a similarly situated individual has not violated the law. "The chapter also addresses the contentious relationship between the FEC and DOJ regarding litigation. Unlike most federal agencies, the FEC has independent litigating authority. However, recent issues have arisen where some commissioners have refused to defend the FEC against lawsuits, leading to defaults in litigation. The chapter describes this as "the scandalous spectacle of the Commission—an independent agency of the United States government—defaulting in litigation before federal courts."

To address this, the President should:

- Direct the attorney general to defend the FEC when commissioners fail to authorize the agency's general counsel to do so.
- Consider recommending that Congress amend FECA to remove the FEC's independent litigating authority.

Additionally, the President should request that the FEC or DOJ prepare guidance on FECA provisions and regulations that have been changed or voided by court decisions.

LEGISLATIVE CHANGES

While a President's ability to make changes at an independent agency like the FEC is limited, the President can make legislative recommendations to Congress. The chapter suggests several key changes:

1. **End the practice of commissioners serving long after their term has expired:**
   "The President should prioritize nominations to the FEC once commissioners reach the end of their terms and should be assisted by legislative language either eliminating or limiting overstays to a reasonable period of time to permit the vetting, nomination, and confirmation of successors."

2. **Oppose efforts to change the FEC's structure:**
   The President should "vigorously oppose all efforts, as proposed, for example, in Section 6002 of the 'For the People Act of 2021,' to change the structure of the FEC to reduce the number of commissioners from six to five or another odd number." The current structure ensures bipartisan agreement and protects against partisan weaponization of the FEC.

3. **Reconsider restrictions on party committee coordination:**
   "The overly restrictive limits on the ability of party committees to coordinate with their candidates, for example, violates associational rights and unjustifiably interferes with the very purpose of political parties: to elect their candidates."

4. **Raise contribution limits and index reporting requirements:**
   "Contribution limits should generally be much higher, as they hamstring candidates and parties while serving no practical anticorruption purpose. And a wide range of reporting requirements have not been indexed to inflation, clogging the public record and the FEC's internal processes with small-dollar information of little use to the public."

CONCLUSION

The chapter concludes by emphasizing the importance of balancing enforcement with protection of First Amendment rights. It quotes former FEC Chairman Bradley Smith, who states that the "greater problem at the FEC has been overenforcement," not underenforcement as some critics allege. Smith further argues that the FEC's enforcement efforts "place a substantial burden on small committees and campaigns, and are having a chilling effect on some political speech...squeezing the life out of low level, volunteer political activity." The author stresses that commissioners have a duty to enforce FECA in a fair, nonpartisan, and objective manner while protecting the First Amendment rights of the public, political parties, and candidates. The President has the same duty to ensure that the Department of Justice enforces the law similarly.

CHAPTER 30: FEDERAL TRADE COMMISSION

Unless conservatives take a firm hand to the bureaucracy and marshal its power to defend a freedom-promoting agenda, nothing will stop the bureaucracy's anti-free market, leftist march – Page 873

Key Policy Proposals

The proposed reforms and policy changes represent a concerning shift towards a more interventionist and potentially harmful approach to antitrust and consumer protection. Let's examine the key proposals and their likely consequences:

EXPANDING ANTITRUST ENFORCEMENT BEYOND CONSUMER WELFARE

The suggestion to look beyond price effects and consider broader societal impacts is misguided. This approach would inject subjectivity and political considerations into antitrust enforcement, leading to inconsistent and arbitrary decisions. The consumer welfare standard has provided a clear, objective framework for decades. Abandoning it would create regulatory uncertainty and chill innovation.

INVESTIGATING ESG PRACTICES AS ANTICOMPETITIVE

This proposal is a thinly veiled attempt to undermine corporate social responsibility initiatives. ESG practices often benefit consumers, employees, and society at large. Treating them as potentially anticompetitive would discourage companies from addressing critical issues like climate change and social equity. This would be a significant step backward for corporate governance and sustainability efforts.

SCRUTINIZING "CANCEL CULTURE" AND SERVICE REFUSALS AS UNFAIR TRADE PRACTICES

This approach dangerously infringes on businesses' right to choose their customers and partners. It could force companies to associate with entities or individuals whose values fundamentally conflict with their own. This violates principles of free association and could compel speech, raising serious First Amendment concerns.

EXPANDING FTC AUTHORITY OVER CHILDREN'S ONLINE EXPERIENCES

While protecting children online is important, the proposed measures are overly broad and impractical. Requiring written parental consent for all online contracts would severely restrict access to beneficial online services and educational resources. It fails to account for the realities of how young people use the internet and could impede their digital literacy development.

INCREASING STATE-LEVEL ANTITRUST ENFORCEMENT

Empowering state attorneys general and expanding regional FTC offices would lead to a patchwork of inconsistent enforcement actions. This approach risks creating regulatory chaos, increasing compliance costs for businesses, and potentially harming consumers through overzealous local enforcement.

RECONSIDERING TRADITIONAL ANTITRUST APPROACHES FOR TECH PLATFORMS

The document's skepticism towards established economic theories in antitrust is concerning. While tech platforms present unique challenges, abandoning proven economic principles risks arbitrary enforcement. The suggestion that providing free services might be anticompetitive fundamentally misunderstands the dynamics of multi-sided markets and could harm innovation in the digital economy.

These proposals represent a significant overreach of government authority into the private sector. They would create regulatory uncertainty, stifle innovation, and potentially harm the very consumers they claim to protect. Instead of these misguided reforms, policymakers should focus on targeted, evidence-based approaches to address specific harms while preserving the benefits of our dynamic market economy.

Summary

This chapter of Mandate for Leadership was written by Adam Candeub. The following summary conveys the content of the document accurately and objectively, without endorsing or critiquing the perspectives of the original authors.
The United States' antitrust laws, dating back over a century, form the foundation of America's approach to regulating competition and trade practices. The Sherman Act of 1890, the Clayton Act of 1914, and the Federal Trade Commission Act (FTCA) of 1914 collectively empower the Federal Trade Commission (FTC) to combat anticompetitive, unfair, and deceptive practices in the marketplace. The FTC's regulatory focus primarily revolves around the FTCA and the Clayton Act, with its actions guided by antitrust and market principles. The modern approach to antitrust law emphasizes maximizing consumer welfare through allocative and productive efficiency.

However, a debate has emerged within the conservative movement regarding the scope and intent of antitrust laws.Some conservatives argue for a broader interpretation of antitrust, pointing out that the original authors of these laws did not intend for a purely economic understanding to guide their legislation. They highlight historical statements, such as Senator John Sherman's declaration: "If we will not endure a king as a political power, we should not endure a king over the production, transportation, and sale of any of the necessaries of life."

This perspective emphasizes the potential threats that market concentration poses to democratic institutions and civil society. Former President William Howard Taft expressed concern about the "building of great and powerful corporations" that intervened in politics and threatened the nation with plutocracy. On the other hand, some conservatives maintain that an economic justification is the only coherent approach to antitrust laws. They argue that the first 90 years of U.S. antitrust policy were often unprincipled and resulted in policies that raised prices for consumers while attempting to protect smaller competitors. Judge Robert Bork's influential work, "The Antitrust Paradox," defended various business practices and put consumer welfare at the heart of competition law. Candeub acknowledges the current challenges posed by the use of economic power to undermine democratic institutions and civil society.

Practices such as Environmental, Social, and Governance (ESG) requirements, "de-banking" of industries and individuals, and interference by large internet firms with democratic political discourse are seen as threats to liberal democracy and the rule of law. The text also highlights concerns about monopoly rents and regulatory capture in the U.S. economy, noting that "U.S. corporations are systematically earning far higher profits than they were 25 or 30 years ago." This concentration of economic power is seen as facilitating collusion between government and private actors, potentially undermining the rule of law.

NEEDED REFORMS

SHOULD THE FTC ENFORCE ANTITRUST-OR EVEN CONTINUE TO EXIST?

Some conservatives argue that antitrust enforcement should be solely the responsibility of the Department of Justice (DOJ). They question the constitutionality of the FTC's structure, particularly the fact that its commissioners are not removable at will by the President. This arrangement is seen as potentially violating the Vesting Clause of Article II of the Constitution. The Supreme Court ruling in Humphrey's Executor upholding agency independence is considered ripe for revisiting.There's a broader conservative critique of the post-New Deal expansion of the administrative state, with some hoping for its significant curtailment or elimination. However, a pragmatic view suggests that until there's a return to a constitutional structure more aligned with the Founding Fathers' vision, conservatives should not "unilaterally disarm" but rather use governmental power to further a conservative agenda.Candeub argues that "Unless conservatives take a firm hand to the bureaucracy and marshal its power to defend a freedom-promoting agenda, nothing will stop the bureaucracy's anti-free market, leftist march."

ESG PRACTICES AS A COVER FOR ANTICOMPETITIVE ACTIVITY AND POSSIBLE UNFAIR TRADE PRACTICES

Candeub highlights growing concerns about corporate social advocacy, particularly Environmental, Social, and Governance (ESG) and Diversity, Equity, and Inclusion (DEI) initiatives, potentially being used to launder corporate reputations or obtain favorable treatment from government actors. Recent Senate Judiciary hearings revealed that firms have attempted to use ESG and DEI offerings to avoid antitrust liability. Candeub recommends: "Congress should investigate ESG practices as a cover for anticompetitive activity and possible unfair trade practices." It argues that the business of American business should be business, not ideology. Managers who use corporate resources to advance personal moral beliefs introduce agency problems and appropriate corporate wealth for their own benefit. This is seen as particularly problematic in concentrated industries with market power. Candeub cites Milton Friedman's perspective that socially responsible activities conducted by a corporation distort economic freedom because shareholders do not decide how their money will be spent. This increases the possibility of fraud or management opportunism.

CANCEL CULTURE, COLLUSION, AND COMMERCE

Candeub addresses concerns about businesses refusing service based on political or social views, particularly when these businesses are publicly traded, highly regulated, enjoy legal privileges or market power, and appear to engage in their own political or social agenda unrelated to branding concerns.There's also concern about industry concentration encouraging government collusion that undermines democratic institutions. This collusion can be explicit, such as government working with social media companies to censor politically harmful news, or implicit, such as burdensome regulatory requirements that deter market entrance by smaller entities.

PROTECTING CHILDREN ONLINE

The FTC has a long history of protecting children in various contexts. Internet platforms profit from obtaining information from children without parental knowledge or consent, and the effects of social media on children's well-being are well-documented. Around 2012, American teens experienced a dramatic decline in wellness, with depression, self-harm, suicide attempts, and suicide increasing sharply between 2011 and 2019. The increase coincided with social media use becoming ubiquitous among teens, making it a prime suspect for the sudden rise in mental health issues. Several studies strongly support the notion that social media use is a cause, not just a correlation, of poor mental health and subjective well-being. Social media and other large platforms form millions of contracts with American children annually. Even though minors can void most contracts, most jurisdictions hold them accountable for benefits received under the contract. This potentially makes parents responsible for such contractual relationships, which could be considered an unfair trade practice. Candeub recommends: "The FTC should examine platforms' advertising and contract-making with children as a deceptive or unfair trade practice, perhaps requiring written parental consent. "The current Child Online Privacy Protection Act (COPPA) is deemed insufficient because it only protects children under 13 and prohibits platforms from collecting information using "actual knowledge" rather than "constructive knowledge. "Some conservatives, however, are skeptical about the effects of online experiences on young people, comparing concerns about social media to past concerns about video games, television, and bicycle safety. They argue that calling for regulation undermines conservatives' calls for parental empowerment and personal responsibility. They also worry about unintended consequences, such as increased data collection for age verification purposes.

ANTITRUST ENFORCEMENT

Candeub suggests that state attorneys general (AGs) are more responsive to their constituents than the FTC. It recommends establishing a distinct role in the FTC Chairman's office focused on state AG cooperation and inviting state AGs to discuss enforcement policy in key sectors. The FTC should also consider returning authority to its regional offices, which are more in touch with local issues.

However, some conservatives are less supportive of this idea, viewing it as potentially expanding federal government presence in the states and creating a "Swamp 2.0" scenario.

BIG TECH AND ANTITRUST

Candeub acknowledges the complex nature of regulating large internet platforms. While these platforms have transformed the U.S. economy and generated significant efficiencies, concerns about their market power and impact on society persist. The text notes that traditional economic thinking may not fully capture the effects of technologies that enable increasing returns to scale based on data. It cites the FTC's 2013 decision not to sue Google as an example of how traditional economic theory may be inadequate in predicting Big Tech behavior. According to press accounts, FTC economists made several incorrect predictions, including:

1. Underestimating the growth potential of ads that track users across the web
2. Downplaying the importance of mobile search
3. Predicting that Microsoft, Mozilla, or Amazon would offer viable competition to Google in mobile search

Candeub argues that empirical evidence is difficult to obtain in this rapidly changing market, as most user data is proprietary and markets change quickly. However, a pattern of highly concentrated firms with occasional replacement by successor firms with vast market power seems to be emerging. While the policy implications are not clear, some in the conservative movement believe that a policy response is necessary. Candeub argues that failing to take antitrust enforcement action could result in real injury to important American institutions such as democratic accountability and free speech. The FTC is urged to become more sophisticated in measuring consumer surplus and to be open to behavioral explanations for how platforms create and maintain market power. Candeub suggests considering factors such as habit and small hedonic differences as keys to understanding platform market power.

CONCLUSION

The chapter concludes by reaffirming that conservative approaches to antitrust and consumer protection continue to trust markets over government. However, it acknowledges that conservatives cannot ignore developments in the American economy that appear to:

1. Make government-private sector collusion more likely
2. Threaten vital democratic institutions, such as free speech
3. Threaten the happiness and mental well-being of many Americans, particularly children

ANALYSIS: Deregulation policies

The Heritage Foundation's Project 2025 outlines an ambitious and far-reaching blueprint for deregulation across multiple sectors of the U.S. government. This initiative seeks to significantly reduce federal oversight and regulation, targeting areas such as finance, the environment, housing, transportation, and labor. Advocates argue that this agenda will stimulate economic growth by reducing government intervention, while critics caution that it may empower corporations at the expense of workers, consumers, and environmental protections.

FINANCIAL DEREGULATION

A cornerstone of Project 2025 is its proposal to dismantle key financial regulations established in the aftermath of the 2008 financial crisis. Central to this effort is a reduction in the Federal Reserve's authority to serve as a lender of last resort during economic emergencies—a role that was instrumental in stabilizing markets during both the 2008 crisis and the COVID-19 pandemic. Critics warn that these changes could encourage reckless financial behavior while simultaneously hamstringing regulators' ability to mitigate crises, potentially leading to severe economic disruptions. Estimates suggest that such a scenario could result in the loss of approximately 8.7 million jobs and a substantial decline in GDP.

ENVIRONMENTAL DEREGULATION

Project 2025's environmental agenda is equally comprehensive, proposing substantial cuts to climate change initiatives across federal agencies, including the Environmental Protection Agency (EPA) and the Department of Housing and Urban Development (HUD). The plan advocates for increased production of fossil fuels—oil, coal, and natural gas—while scaling back investments in renewable energy. Additionally, longstanding environmental protections, such as those under the Migratory Bird Treaty Act, would be repealed. Regulations limiting emissions from energy-intensive industries like artificial intelligence and cryptocurrency data centers would also be rolled back, raising concerns about the potential acceleration of climate change. Please refer to the *Analysis* on Project 2025 and climate change for more information.

HOUSING POLICY OVERHAUL

In the realm of housing, Project 2025 envisions a diminished role for HUD, with many of its responsibilities devolved to state and local governments. The plan would eliminate federal efforts to promote affordable housing in suburban areas, restrict non-citizens from accessing federally assisted housing, and terminate the newly established Housing Supply Fund aimed at increasing affordable housing construction. These changes could lead to decreased housing accessibility and affordability, particularly for low-income and marginalized communities.

TRANSPORTATION REFORMS

Transportation policy would undergo significant changes under Project 2025. The initiative advocates for a reduction in federal funding for infrastructure projects, shifting the burden to private financing and public-private partnerships. Funding for public transit expansion would be slashed, and incentives for electric vehicle adoption would be rescinded. This approach could reshape America's transportation system, potentially prioritizing private vehicle use over public transit and slowing the transition to cleaner, more sustainable transportation options.

LABOR RIGHTS AND THE WORKFORCE

Project 2025 poses substantial challenges to labor rights. The plan calls for a dramatic reduction in the influence of the National Labor Relations Board, making it more difficult for workers to unionize, particularly in emerging sectors like technology and the gig economy. This shift could tip the balance of power further in favor of employers, potentially undermining wages, working conditions, and job security for millions of American workers. For more information on the subject, please refer to the *Analysis* on Labor Market in the previous section of this book.

TECHNOLOGY AND DIGITAL POLICY

In the technology sector, Project 2025 offers a mixed approach, combining deregulation with new oversight mechanisms. The plan proposes the abolition of the Federal Trade Commission, which would weaken antitrust enforcement and potentially allow greater consolidation of corporate power in the tech industry. Additionally, it suggests repealing Section 230 protections for social media platforms, a move that could fundamentally alter the landscape of online content moderation. In response to the growing influence of cryptocurrencies, the plan would permit banks to back money with digital currencies, introducing new and untested dynamics into the financial system.

ONWARD!

It is not a mandate to maintain the status quo but just do it a little more efficiently. Rather, it is a mandate to significantly advance conservative principles in practice and demonstrate to the American people that where liberal policies generally fail, conservative solutions succeed in making life better for all of us. – Page 887

The following summary conveys the content of the document accurately and objectively, without endorsing or critiquing the perspectives of the original authors.

Summary

The concept of "Mandate for Leadership" was born out of a realization in 1979 that incoming conservative administrations were often ill-prepared to implement their policy agendas. As noted, former officials like Bill Simon and Jack Eckerd expressed frustration with the lack of concrete plans to move federal bureaucracy in a conservative direction. They found themselves relying on vague directives such as promoting "free markets; smaller, more efficient government; and a stronger national defense," without the practical guidance needed to bring about real change.

In response, the Heritage Foundation took on the challenge of creating a comprehensive guide to conservative governance. This guide, known as the "Mandate for Leadership," was intended to serve as a "guidebook of specific policy recommendations" aimed at reducing the federal government's size and scope, while ensuring it remained within constitutional bounds. The Foundation believed that freeing the private sector from excessive government interference could "result in an explosion of entrepreneurial activity" that would reassert America's economic leadership.

The Mandate's significance was immediately apparent when Ronald Reagan was elected President. The guide's over 2,000 detailed, actionable policy recommendations became the backbone of what came to be known as the Reagan Revolution. These recommendations covered everything from bureaucratic reorganization to "fundamental changes in every imaginable policy area—from tax and regulatory reform to strengthening national defense to reforming social programs." Reagan distributed copies of the Mandate at his first Cabinet meeting, and many of its authors were recruited to implement its proposals.

The chapter emphasizes the tangible outcomes of these policies. Reagan's adoption of Mandate recommendations led to tax cuts and economic reforms that fueled one of the longest periods of peacetime economic growth in U.S. history. The Mandate's influence extended beyond economic policy, playing a crucial role in "rebuilding the United States military," which contributed to the end of the Cold War and the collapse of the Soviet Union. The policies also reinvigorated American patriotism, providing "a collective sense of pride and patriotism that many thought had vanished forever."

The success of the Mandate was not limited to the Reagan administration. The chapter highlights the significant impact of the 2016 edition on the Trump administration. With President Trump implementing 64% of its recommendations within his first year, the Mandate led to "a growing economy and the lowest unemployment rate in five decades—including among minorities and women." The Trump administration also prioritized energy independence, making America a net energy exporter for the first time in half a century.

The chapter underscores the role of the Mandate as a benchmark for conservative administrations. It allowed for the comparison of Reagan's achievements with those of Trump, providing a "yardstick for conservative Presidents to measure their performance relative to one another." More importantly, it enabled the American public to see "concrete evidence of the progress an Administration is making toward reversing the growth of government and implementing conservative solutions."

Reflecting on the challenges faced by previous administrations, the chapter draws parallels between the difficulties of the Carter era and those presented by the Biden administration. The author warns that a conservative administration taking office in 2025 will need to act swiftly to "undo the significant damage" inflicted during the Biden years. A key to this success will be ensuring that the right personnel are in place, as "people are policy." The chapter stresses that these individuals must be "principled" and "aligned with the President's conservative vision" to effectively implement the conservative agenda.

The Mandate's role is clear: it is not merely a guide to maintaining the status quo but a call to "significantly advance conservative principles in practice." The chapter concludes by reiterating the ongoing nature of this struggle, noting that "there are no permanent victories" in Washington, only "permanent battles" in the policy arena. The Heritage Foundation, along with its partners, remains committed to preparing for these battles by continuing the Mandate for Leadership tradition.

Finally, the section closes with a rallying cry, "Onward!"—a call to action, emphasizing that the fight for conservative principles is never over, and that the mission to improve the nation must always continue.

Conclusion

As we conclude our comprehensive analysis of the Heritage Foundation's Project 2025 Mandate for Leadership, it is clear that this document represents a pivotal moment for the future of American democracy. The policy proposals outlined within its pages, if implemented, would fundamentally reshape the relationship between the government and the governed, concentrating power in the hands of a conservative executive while eroding key checks and balances. Throughout this book, we have endeavored to provide an objective, thorough examination of the Mandate's contents, situating its recommendations within the broader context of conservative thought and the contemporary political landscape. By dissecting the document chapter by chapter, we have illuminated both the philosophical underpinnings and the potential real-world implications of its far-reaching proposals. What emerges is a vision of governance that prioritizes ideological purity over institutional integrity, partisan loyalty over public service. From the dramatic expansion of political appointments to the weakening of civil service protections, from the centralization of power in the White House to the sidelining of expert agencies, the Mandate consistently subordinates the machinery of government to the advancement of a conservative agenda.

Yet, as alarming as many of these proposals may be to those committed to liberal democratic norms, it would be a mistake to dismiss them as mere partisan posturing. The Mandate represents the considered judgment of a powerful and influential segment of the American right, one with a proven track record of shaping national policy. Its recommendations, however controversial, cannot be ignored by anyone who cares about the future of our republic.

Ultimately, the choice facing the American people is whether to embrace or reject the vision of conservative nationalism articulated in these pages. It is a choice between a model of governance that views dissent as disloyalty, expertise as elitism, and the separation of powers as an obstacle to be overcome, and one that upholds these core constitutional principles as essential to the preservation of liberty.

As citizens, we have a solemn duty to approach this choice with clear eyes and full information. It is our hope that this book has equipped readers with the knowledge and context necessary to critically evaluate the Mandate's arguments, to see beyond the rhetoric to the underlying realities. But knowledge alone is not enough. The defense of democracy requires constant vigilance and active participation from all who believe in its promise. It demands that we resist the allure of easy answers and simplistic slogans, that we remain ever-watchful for the erosion of our most cherished freedoms and institutions. Above all, it requires a steadfast commitment to the principles of justice, equality, and the rule of law, even - perhaps especially - when they are under assault.

For it is in these moments of challenge and controversy that the true strength of our democratic system is tested and proven. So let us go forward from this analysis not with despair or resignation, but with renewed purpose and resolve. Let us engage in the hard work of citizenship, in the vigorous debate and principled advocacy that are the lifeblood of a free society. And let us never forget that the preservation of our republic is a sacred trust, one that we hold not only for ourselves, but for generations yet to come.

In that spirit, I would humbly ask that if you have found value in this work, if it has deepened your understanding or sharpened your perspective, that you consider sharing your thoughts in a review on Amazon or other platforms.

For it is only through the open exchange of ideas that we can hope to navigate the complex challenges of self-governance.

The struggle for democracy is not a spectator sport. It requires the active engagement of all who would call themselves free. So ,stay informed. Stay involved. And never, ever stop fighting for the ideals that make America not just a country, but a cause - the enduring cause of liberty and justice for all.

Made in the USA
Las Vegas, NV
23 November 2024

12477945R00096